W9-DHK-560

OCEAN

BERING SEA

Kolyma R.

KAMCHATKA PEN.

Lena R.

Okhotsk

Yakutsk

SEA OF OKHOTSK

Yenisei R.

Nikolaevsk

SAKHALIN

S I A N

Krasnoyarsk

P I R E

Amur R.

Blagoveshchensk

Khabarovsk

msk

Lake Baikal

Irkutsk

Vladivostok

SEA OF JAPAN

J A P A N

CHINESE EMPIRE

KOREA

PACIFIC OCEAN

BHUTAN

TAIWAN

INDIA

FRENCH INDO-CHINA

PHILIPPINE ISLANDS (SPAIN)

Lilli Mautner

The Emergence
of Modern Russia

The Emergence of Modern Russia
1801-1917

Sergei Pushkarev

Translated by
Robert H. McNeal
and
Tova Yedlin

Holt, Rinehart and Winston

New York • Chicago • San Francisco • Toronto • London

March, 1966

Library of Congress Catalog Card Number: 63–8819
27278–0113
Printed in the United States of America

To the memory of my wife,
Julia

Author's Preface

THE PRESENT BOOK IS AN EXPANDED AND
revised version of my *Rossiia v XIX veke,* which was published in
Russian in 1956 by the Chekhov Publishing House of the East European Fund in New York. The sections dealing with cultural history
have been enlarged for English-speaking readers, and a new chapter
on events during World War I up to the fall of the monarchy, as
well as an epilogue, have been added. Some illustrative excerpts from
Russian source material had to be omitted because they would lose
their flavor in translation. Portions of the text have been rearranged
in accordance with a revised chapter structure. The bibliography
has been substantially revised to include, in addition to source material
and literature in Russian, the most important items in English.

The book is divided chronologically into several major
periods, and then broken down by subject into four parts: internal
political developments, social and economic conditions, foreign relations, and cultural history. The latter part is the most difficult to
handle in a short survey, and occasionally it comes close to being a
mere enumeration of persons and their major works, which should
nevertheless prove helpful as a reference for further study.

I wish to acknowledge my warm gratitude to the Sterling
Library of Yale University for the opportunity to use its treasures;
to Professor Robert H. McNeal and Mrs. Tova Yedlin for their

difficult and self-sacrificing work of translation; to Professor G. V. Vernadsky, always ready with friendly advice; to my son Boris, who eagerly helped me in preparing the book for publication and who wrote the sections dealing with the natural sciences, painting, and architecture; to Mr. Benjamin Uroff, who was most helpful, particularly in editing those parts of the book which were written by me in English; and, in conclusion, to this country, which has given newcomers from less fortunate parts of the world an opportunity for creative work in freedom and peace of mind.

S.G.P.

New Haven, Connecticut
January 1963

Translators' Preface

WE HAVE UNDERTAKEN THE TRANSLATION
of Mr. Pushkarev's work first of all because it fills a need for a book of moderate length on the period from the beginning of the nineteenth century to the opening of the Soviet era. To be sure, there are sound justifications for treating 1861 as the logical starting point for an investigation of the Russian Empire in the throes of modernization.[1] But there are at least equally cogent reasons for treating the period 1801–1917 as an especially intelligible, cohesive segment of modern Russian history. The opening of the nineteenth century is a more crucial point than the 1860s, the time of the "Great Reforms," with respect to the political institutions of the central government. In the main, the institutions developed by Alexander I lasted until the installation of the short-lived Duma monarchy in 1905. It was around the turn of the eighteenth–nineteenth century, not in the mid-century, that the Russian intelligentsia emerged and began to play the remarkable role that led ultimately to the Revolution of 1917. And the development of the intelligentsia, beginning around 1800, is intimately connected with the rise of modern Russian litera-

---

[1] See C. E. Black (ed.), *The Transformation of Russian Society* (Cambridge, Mass., 1960), 4–7. Professor Hugh Seton-Watson opts for 1861 in his survey *The Decline of Imperial Russia* (New York, 1956).

ture, scholarship, and education. It was at about the turn of the century that the serf order ceased to be an expanding institution and, partly under pressure from the intelligentsia, slowed down to what became a retreat—signalized not only by the emancipation of 1861 but also by the scarcely less important reforms of the state peasants in the 1830s and the further reforms of the era of the Revolution of 1905 and Stolypin. Finally, around 1800, beginning perhaps in the previous decade, Russia assumed her mature role as a great power of Europe, a role she has not since relinquished. It is true in a sense that Russia became a European power with Peter the Great in the early eighteenth century, but it was only with the era of the French Revolution and Napoleon that the Russian Empire attained its full stature as a great power, having intimate and direct contact with European politics beyond the eastern borderlands of Europe. Only after this period, for example, can one speak of Russo-French or Russo-English enmity or alliance as a crucial factor in European diplomacy.

Another quality that recommends Mr. Pushkarev's book to us is the point of view that he brings to his subject. His sympathies are plainly with the liberal tradition and he is no apologist for the autocracy and the old social order, but this does not blind him to the positive and constructive aspects of the old regime. For example, he gives considerable attention to the merits of Kiselev's reform of the state peasantry, a neglected subject in most surveys, and his impression of pre-World War I Russia as a rapidly modernizing society (not without great problems) is an important point of view that has too often been pushed aside in favor of emphasis on the road to revolution or the decline and fall of the imperial order. On the other hand, Pushkarev is acutely aware of the shortcomings of Russian radical and revolutionary movements. Although we do not always concur with his point of view on foreign affairs and some related matters, it seems to us that his accent on the achievements of Russia and Russians of the late imperial era should be enlightening to the numerous public that seems to think that modernization in Russia began with the Bolshevik Revolution.

The present work is not only a translation but a thoroughly revised edition of *Rossiia v XIX veke,* for the substance of the book is considerably amplified and reorganized. In the Russian edition much valuable material, especially quotations from sources, appeared in extensive footnotes. With Mr. Pushkarev's kind consent, we have reorganized this material, integrating most of it into the text of the book, sometimes with added connective expressions, sometimes with condensation or paraphrase. Various other editorial revisions, especially in the latter part of the book, are the responsibility of the translators, although the substantial additions are basically the work of the author. Not wishing to assault the reader with a pervasive system of translators' notes, we have not usually attempted to distinguish between the work of the author and translators. But it should be said here that this book may have shortcomings that are not the author's.

Faced with the annoying necessity of choosing between transliteration and translation ("guberniia" or "province"), we have tried to translate wherever it seems within reason, although words such as "mir," "duma," "zemstvo," and "obrok" seem to be better treated as anglicized expressions than in translation. No two translators agree on a single set of English-Russian equivalents for the many administrative terms that must occur in a work of this sort. We have done our best to find the least inaccurate translations, sometimes departing from any established practice (for example, "superintendent of the peasantry" for *zemskii nachal'nik*). For the reader who may wish to find the Russian of our translations of administrative terms, we have included a glossary of such translations at the end of the book.

In general we have used a somewhat simplified form of the Library of Congress system of transliteration, making exceptions for many proper names that have fairly conventional English spellings that do not conform to this system. Since this book ends before the Old Style or Julian calendar was discarded in Russia, dates are in most cases given according to this style, which means that the corresponding date in the West is twelve days later in the nineteenth century and thirteen days later in the twentieth. When the reader of this book sees a date without any notation he may therefore assume that it is Old Style. For dates involving Russian-Western encounters (battles, treaties, and the like) both the Old Style and the New Style (the latter in parentheses) are given. Finally there are a handful of cases in which dates cited are purely Western, and these are given in New Style, indicated by NS.

We should like to acknowledge the manifold helpfulness of our respective spouses and, especially, the collaboration of Mssrs. Sergei G. and Boris Pushkarev. Not only has Mr. Pushkarev revised and amplified the Russian edition, he has also rendered great assistance to his translators, making suggestions, correcting errors, and regarding with tolerance our various amendments of the original book. The footnotes, selected bibliography, and name index were prepared by Mr. Pushkarev, and their merits are entirely the result of his work.

R.H.M.
T.Y.

January 1963

Contents

page xiii

Maps

Charts

Introduction

Robert H. McNeal

ON THE EVE OF THE NINETEENTH CENTURY
the Russian Empire was officially considered an autocracy, and it was
indeed true that Russia lacked any institutions, even expiring medieval bodies such as the diets of East Europe, that were designed to
limit the power of the sovereign. It was also true that individual
tsars and tsarinas from Peter the Great (1682–1725) to Paul I (1796–
1801) were able to establish justified reputations for capricious self-
indulgence in drink, dress, palaces, and acts of sadistic vengeance or
buffoonery. But it is one thing to be able to force a high nobleman
to spend a mock wedding night in a palace of ice, as did Anna
(1730–1740), and quite a different matter to have a system of central
and regional administration that can function with even a vaguely
satisfactory degree of regularity.

In practice the autocratic Russian empire of the eighteenth
century lacked the institutions and personnel necessary to form such
a system, despite the strenuous efforts of Peter the Great and the lesser
attempts of some of his eighteenth-century successors. Peter successfully demolished the dilapidated administrative institutions of earlier
Muscovy and tried valiantly to replace them with a kind of early
modern bureaucracy that was modeled partly on Sweden. The sovereign was to be advised by a council called the Senate, and the execution of the tsar's policy was to be rationally divided among some

twelve "colleges," which were essentially ministries headed by committees rather than individuals. The administration of the church, a large and crucial institution in early modern Russia, was transferred from the patriarchate to a synod headed by a layman. Peter also attempted to modernize the regional administration of his state, dividing it into new districts called *guberniias,* subject to a governor and bureaucratic staff.

But all of this was a highly qualified success, owing to various defects in the structure itself (for example, the inefficiency of collective responsibility in the colleges), the acute shortage of educated civil servants, and the collapse of national leadership following Peter's death in 1725. By the end of the century the institutions of the central government had become more disorganized than they had been in their early years. Most of the colleges had been abolished and the Senate had been saddled with details and deprived of supreme advisory power, which was for many years exercised by transitory cliques of political potentates. The Petrine scheme for regional government collapsed even more completely after his death, and the establishment by Catherine the Great (1762–1796) of smaller provinces with some new agencies was really only the beginning of effective modernization in this field. Probably the supply of competent civil servants had improved since Peter's day, despite the failure of his answer to this problem: compulsory education and civil or military service for all noblemen. These requirements had been lightened, and by 1762 the service obligation was ended entirely. At the same time, the level of literacy and incidence of higher education advanced, partly due to a steady, though small, stream of Russian students to Western universities and partly due to the establishment of a university in Moscow in 1755. By the eve of the nineteenth century, but not much before it, a class of persons able to operate a modern bureaucacy was appearing in Russia.

Whatever the supply of potential functionaries, the weakness of leadership in eighteenth-century Russia, after Peter the Great, was a severe obstacle to the establishment of a modernized state. It was precisely because the state was officially autocratic that the weakness of individual tsars and tsarinas was so detrimental to effective government. Had the highest authority been more diffused, it would not have mattered so much that between 1725 and 1801 Russia was ruled by four women (whose authority was weakened by the absence of precedent for female sovereigns), two boys, and two unstable men. This peculiar succession was governed by the wishes of a handful of leading politicians, including a number of foreign adventurers, and members of the high nobility who dominated the elite guards regiments of Petersburg. None of these had any real plan for Russia beyond the preservation of their own status. They were content to permit the supreme authority to remain theoretically in the hands of the one autocrat, a situation that was seemingly safe so long as the politicians and guards officers could choose and dominate the ruler, but they were uninterested or suspicious regarding political or social reform. The two adult tsars of the period (Peter III, 1762, and Paul I) were deposed and murdered because they attempted to rule independently of the cliques of tsar-makers; and Catherine the Great, the one ruler of the period who had real political vision and skill, was particularly hampered by the knowledge that she had no claim to the throne except the support of the guards officers, who had murdered her unloved husband and were quite capable of turning against her.

In short, the Russian state in the eighteenth century, although it showed superficial signs of modernization, was competent to collect a modicum of taxes and military recruits but not to undertake any major domestic program. This being the case, it is not surprising that the state was unable effectively to control, much less stop, the rise of the great social problem that was to harass Russia for many years to come: serfdom. Although unfree agricultural labor of various sorts had been widespread in Russia before the eighteenth century, it was only in this era that the greatest single portion of the population fell into outright chattel slavery, susceptible to purchase and sale and virtually unlimited maltreatment. This dismal process involved the extension of the power of the landed nobility over peasants whom they already controlled in large measure and the simultaneous geographical extension of serfdom, especially in the newly colonized south. Except for a few, scarcely enforced, restrictions on the power of the nobility over the serfs, the Russian state did almost nothing to control the practice of serfdom and, indeed, rarely treated it as a problem for public policy. On the contrary, the most notable contributions of the state to the serf problem were the prodigal donation of free peasants to the possession of landlords and the brutal suppression of the rebellions of the desperate serfs. Of these, the most serious occurred in 1773–1774 under the leadership of Emilian Pugachev. Although it left a wide path of terrorized landlords and counterterrorized serfs along the Volga basin, the uprising did not impel the government to acknowledge the severity of the problem. When intellectual critics appeared toward the end of the century, they met only harsh suppression. The first prominent Russian opponent of serfdom, the Western-educated Alexander Radishchev, was sentenced to death (commuted to Siberian exile) by Catherine the Great for having published in 1790 a critique that she considered incendiary.

Radishchev himself, like most of his readers, was a member of the nobility, and the appearance of dissent in this class calls attention to a dilemma of progress that Peter the Great had not anticipated when he set Russians to studying at the school of the West. His main interest in Europe had been technical, but it turned out that his subjects did not limit themselves to Dutch rigging and Swedish musketry. Wealthy nobles who had little interest in ballistics often became eager students of Italian opera or French wine—or even philosophy. Catherine the Great, a German by birth, provided an ideal model for this kind of Westernization. She patronized Diderot, corresponded with Voltaire, and even summoned a decorative, though ineffectual, Legislative Commission (1767–1768), to which she issued a pretentious Instruction that leaned heavily on Montesquieu and Beccaria. As the ruler of Russia, Catherine could not afford to become overly disturbed by the gulf between the ideals of the Enlightenment and the reality of serf-ridden Russia. But some members of the increasingly Gallicized nobility were not inhibited to the same degree, as was indicated by the avid demand in high Petersburg society for Radishchev's suppressed book. No organized or widespread opposition to the existing order developed among educated Russians in the eighteenth century, but the attraction of the emerging intellectual elite to the social ideals of Western Europe promised trouble in the future. If such a group could not find an outlet for its aspirations within the framework of the legal order, its frustration could be as dangerous as that of the serfs.

The internal problems of the Russian state in the eighteenth century did not, however, prevent the territorial expansion of the empire. Peter the Great had at least succeeded in establishing a system of military conscription that was adequate to support the limited warfare of the eighteenth century, and Russia's immediate neighbors, Poland and the Ottoman Empire, were vulnerable at this time. Moreover, Russia did not lack European allies, and her imperial expansion in the eighteenth century did not encounter any serious attempt by frightened Western powers to band together against Russian expansion. Although Russia's gains in the first decades following Peter's death were modest, the Seven Years' War saw Russian forces occupy Berlin (1760), and only the accession to the throne of the erratic Peter III prevented the collapse of Prussia. His successor, Catherine the Great, was not one to let such opportunities slip away. In the twenty-four years of her reign, the three partitions of Poland added a vast western region to the Russian Empire, and two wars with the Turks yielded a large area on the northern shores of the Black Sea. While the territories conquered from Poland were already fairly well populated, the southern reaches of European Russia (sometimes called "New Russia") were still a frontier, and the colonization of this zone, including the establishment of the major city of Odessa, was one of the principal accomplishments of imperial expansion in the later eighteenth century. The potential power of Russia in European politics was demonstrated still more forcefully in the wars of the French Revolution. In this general conflict Russian forces operated, with varying degrees of success, in such far-flung areas as the Greek islands, northern Italy and Switzerland, and Holland. However, the erratic policy of Paul I prevented these actions from having any decisive effect on the course of the struggle.

In sum, it can be said that eighteenth-century Russia was undergoing modernization in various senses of the term, but it should be added that the process was in an early stage of development and that there were many open questions concerning the form that "modern Russia" would assume. Neither the autocratic (or Byzantine or Slavic) tradition, nor any inevitable pattern of modernization (or Westernization or dialectical materialism) could determine the particular answers that men would provide to the open questions of Russian history around 1801. What actually emerged by way of answers, successful or otherwise, is the subject of the following pages.

The Emergence
of Modern Russia

1

The Russian State in the First Half of the Nineteenth Century

Alexander I: Reformer and Reactionary

The autocratic, centralized character of the Russian imperial government at the opening of the nineteenth century inevitably made the personality of the sovereign a matter of great consequence. Alexander I was no exception. His personal background and character were as peculiarly anomalous as the policy of his generation-long reign.

Born in December 1777, the eldest son of the heir-apparent Paul, Alexander was soon taken from his parents by his grandmother, the Empress Catherine, who personally took charge of his upbringing. Hoping to make him the ideal ruler for the future, she sought the best tutors, gave them detailed instructions, and personally composed a primer and various other texts for her pupil. The most influential of the tutors was a French Swiss, La Harpe, a republican and a democrat by conviction, who guided his royal pupil from 1784 to 1794. During his tenure he inspired in Alexander a love for liberty, equality, and fraternity, and if this theoretical liberalism did not endure in Alexander's later years, the monarch's gratitude and friendship for La Harpe did.

Because Catherine and the court spoiled the attractive youth, Alexander did not acquire much specific information, nor did he become accustomed to independent thinking and systematic work. Before he had reached the age of sixteen, his formal education ended with his marriage to the fifteen-year-old Princess Louise of Baden, who adopted the name Elizabeth Alekseevna. Soon afterwards, Catherine embarked on a fruitless plan to make Alexander her successor in place of Paul, who lived in dreary isolation at his "court" at Gatchina, occupied chiefly with the drilling of his small guard. Alexander was also exposed to Gatchina, where he was forced to emulate the life of the professional soldier, and despite strained relations with his father, Alexander developed a sincere love for the "paradomania" of his father's court. After Paul became emperor in 1796, he appointed Alexander military governor of Petersburg, obliging the young prince to enforce the harsh discipline that Paul dictated for the troops and to execute his erratic and often cruel commands.

Between the enlightened court of Catherine and the militaristic court of his father, Alexander passed much of his youth in a state of perpetual moral conflict, and this ambiguous environment evidently obliged Alexander to develop the traits of duplicity, secretiveness, and hypocrisy.

In 1801 some officers who had formed a conspiracy to remove Paul from the throne confided their plan to Alexander, but gave him their oath that they would spare his father's life. This they did not do, and the murder of Paul profoundly disturbed the young Alexander, remaining a heavy weight on his conscience. Quite possibly the feeling of guilt for the murder of his father, whose assassins went unpunished, helped to inspire the mental depression and mystical religious searchings that characterized the last years of Alexander's life.

Alexander's manifesto upon ascending the throne proclaimed that he intended to rule "by the law and in the spirit of our grandmother, the sovereign Empress Catherine the Great, whose memory will be eternally cherished by Us and by all our Fatherland."[1] In 1801 a series of decrees abolished the oppressive, reactionary, and vindictive measures of Paul. All those who had been arrested or exiled by Paul's secret police were released from prison and recalled from exile, and the "secret chancery" itself was abolished, because, as the tsar's decree explained, "in a well-ordered state all crimes must be encompassed, judged, and punished by the universal authority of the

---

[1] All quotations from the tsar's manifestoes, decrees, and rescripts, as well as from the general and special laws, statutes, regulations, and peace treaties with foreign powers are taken from the text of *Polnoe sobranie zakonov Rossiiskoi Imperii* [*Complete Collection of Laws of the Russian Empire*] (St. Petersburg, 1830–1914), where they are all arranged in chronological order and can be found without great difficulty. Specific references are therefore not usually noted in quoting from these documents.

law." "Under pain of certain and harsh punishment" Alexander forbade the application of torture, expressing his intention that "at last, the very name of torture, the shame and reproach of humanity, will be wiped forever from the memory of the nation." Wishing to establish strict legality in the administration of the state, Alexander created a "commission for the codification of the law" to bring system and order to the chaotic legislation of Russia, thus "making one law the foundation and source of the people's welfare."

In the first years of Alexander's reign, his chief advisers and closest collaborators were not the aged magnates of Catherine's day who formally headed the different branches of the state administration, but a circle of young, liberal friends of the new tsar, composing the "secret committee." Its members jokingly called it the "committee of public salvation," and its opponents, the old, conservative bureaucrats, called it the "Jacobin Gang." Its members were Count P. A. Stroganov, who had become a member of the Jacobin Club in Paris in 1790; Count V. P. Kochubei; N. N. Novosiltsev; and the Polish patriot Prince Adam Czartoryski.

In 1804 Alexander's attention turned to questions of foreign policy. The enormous success and the ambitious plans of Napoleon, who proclaimed himself Emperor of the French in 1804, impelled Alexander to enter the coalition of European powers against France. But after the war of 1805–1807 and Russian defeat at Austerlitz and Friedland, the peace of Tilsit in 1807 ushered in a period of alliance and "friendship" with Napoleon (however short-lived it proved to be). Alexander again turned his thoughts to the necessity of basic internal reforms, and selected M. M. Speransky to prepare a plan for basic reform of the political order in Russia. At the same time, Alexander called upon an officer whom he had known at Gatchina, Arakcheev, for the reorganization of the army. Arakcheev held successively the posts of inspector of the artillery (1803), minister of war (1808), and chairman of the war department of the Council of State (1810).

Of Speransky's projected reforms, only the institution of the Council of State was carried out, in 1810, and the following year Alexander's attention was again wholly diverted to foreign policy, especially to the great struggle with Napoleon that was approaching. After the final defeat of Napoleon, Alexander immersed himself in European politics. He played an especially active role at the Congress of Vienna, where he created his strange religio-political brain child, "the Holy Alliance," which he alone sincerely considered "holy."

The events of 1812–1815 produced a profound spiritual

upheaval in Alexander. In 1818 he wrote to the Prussian Bishop Eylert: "The fire of Moscow has enlightened my soul . . . and God's judgment on the icy plains has filled my heart with the warmth of faith, such as I never knew before."[2] Yet Alexander evidently was unable to find peace in any one religion. At different times he associated with the Masons, with the German mystics, with the English Quakers, and at last with the malicious and fanatical Orthodox father, Archimandrite Photius, whom he secretly received in his palace.

For some time after the Napoleonic wars Alexander still did not renounce his constitutional sympathies and plans. He insisted that Louis XVIII, who had been restored to the French throne, give France a constitutional charter. Alexander himself gave the kingdom of Poland, annexed to Russia in 1815 by the treaty of Vienna, a constitution that was quite liberal for this era. In a speech delivered at the opening of the Polish Diet (*seim*) in 1818, the tsar declared his intention to give "liberal institutions" to all the countries in his realm, and he directed Novosiltsev to prepare a draft constitution for Russia. A draft was written but not put into effect because, in 1820, following riots in the Semenovsky Regiment and revolutionary uprisings in Spain and Italy, Alexander abandoned his constitutional plans. He immersed himself completely in European affairs, and at the same time in mysticism and military parades. As a result, the somber figure of the "Gatchina corporal," Arakcheev, finally eclipsed the once bright figure of "Alexander the Blessed," who ended his days in distant Taganrog in complete alienation from Russian society and in an atmosphere of general disillusionment, dissatisfaction, and just plain hostility. Soon after the death of Alexander, November 19, 1825, there arose a legend that he did not in fact die then but went secretly to Siberia, where he completed his life under the assumed name of "Theodore Kuzmich, the hermit."

Plans for Constitutional Reform

In a letter sent La Harpe while still heir to the throne, Alexander wrote that his goal upon becoming tsar was "to give Russia freedom and so save her from the encroachments of despotism and tyranny."[3] It was to implement this goal that, at the conclusion of the first stage of the struggle with Napoleon, Alexander commissioned

[2] N. Schilder, *Imperator Aleksandr I: Ego zhizn' i tsarstvovanie* [*The Emperor Alexander I: His Life and Reign*] (St. Petersburg, 1897), vol. III, pp. 117, 378.
[3] *Ibid.*, vol. I, p. 164.

Speransky to prepare a plan for radical constitutional reform. M. M. Speransky, born in 1772 the son of a rural priest, had first received a clerical education, but then had entered the civil service, soon rising above the mass of bureaucrats. He was distinguished by his great and lucid intellect, his strong yet flexible will, an unusual capacity for work, a great theoretical and practical knowledge, and by his eloquence. He became known to Alexander in 1806, and after the peace of Tilsit the following year, he served as the tsar's secretary and adviser on all administrative and legislative matters. The inner circle of the court and administrative bureaucracy was hostile to Speransky as a "priest's son" and a "climber," but Speransky himself, knowing he was deeply trusted by the tsar, could disregard the intrigue and hostile whispering around him and continue his work on the reform. In 1809 he initiated two reform decrees that only served to strengthen the hostility of the court and bureaucratic circles. The decree of April 3 announced that the court titles of chamberlain and chamberlain-junker did not confer either civil service rank or service rights and privileges, and that to receive these benefits the courtiers "must choose some kind of actual service." (Alexander had made known his own dislike for the courtiers, calling them "floor-polishers.") The second decree, dated August 6, ordered civil servants who did not have university degrees to take specially prepared examinations to qualify for the ranks of "collegiate assessor" and "state councilor."

Speransky worked out his general plan for constitutional reform with the direct and continual participation of Alexander himself, and by the autumn of 1809 the plan was ready.[4] As defined by Speransky, the chief task of the reform was to replace the heretofore autocratic regime with a government that would rest on the basis of "immutable law." His plan divided the entire population of the Russian empire into three basic classes: (1) the nobility; (2) "the middle classes," consisting of the wealthy merchants, the burghers (*meshchane*), and the state peasants, "who possess a set amount of immovable property"; and (3) "the class of the working people," which was to include the landlord's peasants, artisans, urban workers, and domestic servants. The first two classes were to enjoy both civil and political rights (the franchise and the right to hold elective office), while the "working people" were to have only civil rights, in recognition of the principle that "only those who own immovable property or capital may participate in elections."

---

[4] M. M. Speransky, *Plan gosudarstvennogo preobrazovaniia 1809 goda* [*The Plan of State Reform, 1809*] (Moscow, 1905).

Speransky was against the "enslavement" of the landowners' peasants, and he proposed to liberate them gradually from the authority of the landowners. First the obligations and payments that the landowner might demand of his peasants were to be regulated. The peasants would then be liberated from the police and judicial authority of the landlord, and finally they would regain "their ancient right of moving freely from one landowner to another."

The constitution proposed by Speransky provided for three branches of government, legislative, executive, and judicial, each represented by an institution in the central government: the state Duma (legislative assembly), the Governing Senate (cabinet of ministers) and the Judicial Senate (supreme court). A fourth institution, the Council of State, was to coordinate the activities of these three bodies. Only the tsar (in practice, through his ministers) possessed legislative initiative, but all laws had to be approved by both the Council of State and the Duma. The former was to consist of appointees of the tsar, including the ministers, while the Duma was to be indirectly elected by a three-tiered system of popular self-government. In Speransky's proposed constitution this hierarchy was to start with the township *(volost')* duma, to be composed of all owners of immovable property in the township and one elected elder *(starshina)* from every 500 state peasants. Every three years the township duma was to meet to elect a local executive and deputies to the next higher body, the district *(okrug)* duma, which was to exercise comparable powers, including the election of deputies to the next higher body, the province *(guberniia)* duma. This body in turn was to elect deputies to the national or State Duma. The provincial executive was to consist of an appointed governor, assisted by a council of deputies elected by the nobility and middle classes of the province, while a vice governor and council were to administer the district.

Headed by the Judicial Senate, the judiciary in Speransky's plan consisted of four levels, paralleling the hierarchy of the dumas; the courts of the provincial and lower levels were to consist of juries and elected judges who were independent of the central government.

Speransky's constitution, which was distinguished by its sense of proportion and its consistency, was approved in principle by Alexander. But the implementation of the plan under the conditions of serfdom would naturally have encountered major obstacles. For this reason, and because of its general complexity, the reform was initiated at the top with the establishment of the Council of State (1810) and the reorganization of the ministries (1810–1811). Speransky's plans for further reform were then interrupted by internal and external circumstances. His constitution had encountered determined opposition from conservative circles, and at a time when there was already considerable feeling that war with Napoleon was inevitable in the near future, Speransky's French sympathies inspired rumors of "treason." The most articulate literary expression of the opposition was a memorandum "On Ancient and Modern Russia," submitted to Alexander in 1811 by N. M. Karamzin.[5] Without mentioning Speransky by name, this letter sharply criticized the contemporary activities of the government and decisively denounced any plans for the limitation of autocracy, which it considered necessary for the safety and happiness of Russia. In response to persistent pressure, Alexander dismissed Speransky from the civil service in March 1812.

Speransky was recalled to the civil service in 1816 and appointed governor of Penza province. In 1819 he was named governor general of Siberia, whose administration he substantially reformed, and after two years he returned to Petersburg. Under Nicholas I, Speransky became a member of the Council of State, and between 1826 and 1833 he executed the immense task of legal codification, described below. He died in 1839.

Still in hopes of bringing about governmental reform, in 1818 Alexander commissioned Novosiltsev to prepare another draft constitution for Russia. Novosiltsev's draft, entitled "The Charter of the Fundamental Law of the Russian Empire,"[6] was in many respects closely modeled on the Polish constitution of 1815, from which in fact he borrowed the majority of the articles and even many terms. The charter states that "the Sovereign is the sole source of all authority in the Empire," but that "the representative assembly of the state (*seim*) assists the legislative power of the Sovereign."

Novosiltsev's charter envisaged a federative state divided into large regions called "vice regencies," each of which was to have an assembly (*seim*) elected by the landed nobility and persons meet-

---

[5] N. M. Karamzin, "O drevnei i novoi Rossii v ee politicheskom i grazhdanskom otnosheniiakh" [On Ancient and Modern Russia in Its Political and Civil Aspects"], in A. N. Pypin, *Obshchestvennoe dvizhenie v Rossii pri Aleksandr I* [*The Movement of Public Opinion Under Alexander I*] (4th ed.; St. Petersburg, 1908), appendix I, pp. 479–534. [For a translation, see Richard Pipes, *Karamzin's Memoir on Ancient and Modern Russia: A Translation and Analysis* (Cambridge, Mass., 1959).]

[6] "Gosudarstvennaia ustavnaia gramota Rossiiskoi Imperii" ["The Constitutional Charter of the Russian Empire"], Novosiltsev's plan of 1820 in Shilder, *op. cit.*, vol. IV, appendix VI, pp. 479–534. [For a translation into French, see G. Vernadsky, *La Charte Constitutionelle de l'Empire Russe de l'an 1820* (Paris, 1933).]

ing property or educational qualifications. These regional assemblies were to discuss local affairs and select candidates for membership in the national representative assembly of the state. The tsar was to select half of the candidates to serve in this body and to appoint for life all the members of a second national assembly, the Senate. According to the plan, the two national assemblies were to meet only once every five years and were limited to discussion and recommendations on public affairs. The charter also guaranteed basic civil liberties.

But Novosiltsev's charter was not destined to become a fundamental law of the land. After the mutiny in the Semenovsky Regiment in 1820 (discussed below) and the revolutionary disturbances in Europe at this time, Novosiltsev's charter was pigeon-holed, and Alexander once and for all renounced his constitutional endeavors.

Later, at the time of the Polish uprising of 1830–1831, the Polish revolutionary government found the text of Novolsiltsev's charter in Warsaw and printed it. When the Russian General Paskevich took Warsaw in 1831, he found the printed text and reported it to the tsar. Nicholas was deeply upset by the publication of such "revolutionary" experiments of his brother, and he ordered that, if possible, all printed copies of the charter be collected and sent to Russia. There they were consigned to the flames by his order.

The Reform of the Central Government

The collegial system of central government, established by Peter the Great, had become completely disorganized by the end of the eighteenth century. Therefore, regardless of basic constitutional reform, the government was in need of an administrative reorganization. A manifesto of September 8, 1802, announced the establishment of Ministries of War, the Navy, Foreign Affairs, Internal Affairs, Justice, Finance, Commerce, and Public Education. The Ministry of Internal Affairs was obliged to care for not only "the tranquility, peace, and welfare of all the Empire," but also "all aspects of public well-being." That is, it had not only administrative and police functions, but also purely economic responsibilities; in addition, within its scope lay the medical collegium and the postal service. The Ministry of Public Education, the Instruction of the Youth, and the Dissemination of Knowledge was an entirely new institution.

The ministries were organized on the principle of one-man authority and responsibility, unlike the old Petrine collegia in which a committee shared the power and responsibility. To integrate their activities and to consider questions relating to several ministries or to the whole government, a Committee of Ministers was formed. General supervision over the activities of the administration was exercised by the Governing Senate, to which the ministers had to render their accounts together with a report to the tsar.

In 1810–1811, the period of Speransky's influence, a new division of the affairs of state among the ministries was effected. The main sphere of the Ministry of Internal Affairs was now designated as "the supervision, extension, and encouragement of agriculture and industry," and the Ministry of Commerce was abolished. For the "organization of internal security," a special Ministry of Police was established (and then abolished in 1819.) In addition, "Main Administrations" of "the inspection of public accounts," communications, and "the spiritual affairs of alien (nonorthodox) creeds" were established.

On June 25, 1811, "General Regulations for the Ministries" and detailed "Instructions for the Ministries" were issued. The internal organization of the central bureaucratic machine was put in order, and the workings of the system, from the functions of ministers down to heads of departments, subordinate officials, and clerks, were regulated in minute detail. Ministries were divided into departments, departments into sections, and sections into offices *(stoly)*. The heads of departments formed the Minister's Council, although later special officials were added to this council. The Ministry of Spiritual Affairs and Public Education, a peculiar combination, appeared in 1817 during Alexander's mystical religious phase. The ministry lasted until 1824, when it was again divided into its two parts.

At the very beginning of his reign (March 1801) Alexander issued a decree on the establishment of a permanent Council of the Emperor, consisting of twelve members, for the review of all the important affairs of state. The council did not play an important role in state administration, however. Speransky wanted to transform this kind of body into an important and authoritative institution to advise on legislation at the highest level; in his view it would represent the first practical step in the direction of implementing his plan for constitutional reform. Therefore, in 1809 he prepared for the formation of the Council of State, which was then established by manifesto January 1, 1810. This manifesto, written by Speransky of course, explained that the objective of the state reform was "to place the government on a firm, immutable basis of law." It introduced a new order by which all draft laws, statutes, and regulations were to be proposed to and examined by the Council of State, after which they were to be approved by the tsar. The new Council of State consisted of high dignitaries, who were appointed by the tsar, and the ministers, who were members *ex officio*. The tsar or the "presiding member of the council," appointed for one year, presided over the council. The council was divided into four departments: (1) the department of laws; (2) the department of military affairs; (3) the department of civil and spiritual affairs; and (4) the department of the state economy. A general meeting of the council was called whenever necessary, and the administration of the affairs of the council was entrusted to the state secretary, to which post Speransky was appointed.

The Period of Reaction

The war with Napoleon, in which Alexander took so active and fervent a part, ended in 1815. "The whole store of Alexander's will power," writes Schilder, his biographer, "seemed spent in his struggle with Napoleon, which placed the utmost strain on all his physical and spiritual strength, and it is not surprising that the tsar displayed fatigue and mental exhaustion." [7] After returning to Russia, Alexander entrusted the main weight of the administration of this state to Arakcheev, and in the latter years of his reign interested himself chiefly in the realization of the principles of the "Holy Alliance" in Europe and in military affairs. In this period Alexander's insistence on perfection in military drill became an obsession, and drill with the proper "erect bearing" received more attention than marksmanship and readiness for combat. Even Grand Duke Constantine, himself a devoted campaigner of the Gatchina type, wrote General Sipiagin in 1817:

> At present they have started such dancing lessons for the troops of the line that one cannot make any sense of it. . . . I have spent more than twenty years with the troops and can truthfully say that even during the times of the late emperor (Paul) I was one of the leading officers of the troops of the line, but now there is so much spit-and-polish that one is at a loss. . . . [8]

The army was dominated not only by "dancing lessons," but also by stern discipline, enforced by cruel punishments. For a breach of discipline, for carelessness on the line or in uniform, the culprit had to run the gantlet through the ranks—500 or 1000 men—once,

---

[7] Schilder, *op. cit.*, vol. **IV**, p. 4.

[8] *Ibid.*, vol. **IV**, p. 16.

twice, or for a serious infraction as many as six times. This cruel and repulsive form of punishment, which was adopted from the German practice, compelled the men who were drawn up in ranks to play the part of the executioner—to be floggers of their own "guilty" comrades. In some cases these punishments ended with the death of the "criminal."

In October 1820, when Alexander was abroad, the famous mutiny of the Semenovsky Regiment occurred, further strengthening Alexander's reactionary mood. The soldiers of Alexander's favorite regiment had been driven to distraction by the petty persecutions and cruel punishments inflicted by the recently appointed regimental commander, Colonel Schwartz. They displayed disobedience to their officers and demanded Schwartz' dismissal. The ringleaders suffered cruel corporal punishment for their insubordination, and all the personnel of the regiment, including officers and soldiers, were transferred to other army units. The Semenovsky Guards Regiment was then formed anew from personnel of a number of grenadier regiments.

The last years of Alexander's reign have received the label Arakcheevshchina ("the evil reign of Arakcheev"), and both contemporaries and historians of various points of view have drawn the same picture of the almighty Arakcheev. In the period after 1820, Alexander, having renounced all plans for reform, needed not daring reformers but devoted servants and defenders of the existing order. Just such a man was Arakcheev, with his administrative talent, his industriousness, and his personal integrity (he was not an embezzler, as many were), and most of all, his canine loyalty to the tsar. The contemporary Vigel' called him a "bulldog," always ready to administer a fatal bite to the tsar's enemies. In these years all the affairs of state, even the spiritual ones, were considered part of Arakcheev's office, which prepared all reports for the tsar. In the words of Schilder, "he acted as the first, or to put it more precisely, the only minister."[9] The old ministers were merely the submissive executors of his orders. Small wonder that all bowed and scraped before the harsh favorite— "the antechamber of the favorite seemed to be the center to which the governors and potentates of the state streamed from four A.M. on," as one historian has put it. The universities and the academy elected Arakcheev an honorary member. However, the homage paid to Arakcheev in this period fell far short of the limitless servility of the later Stalin era, for on occasion a brave person might even issue a daring challenge to the harsh favorite. Thus, in 1820 the journal

---

[9] *Ibid.*, vol. IV, p. 5.

The Spectator of the Neva (Nevskii Zritel') published a poem dedicated by K. Ryleev "To the Favorite," which began with these lines:

> You, haughty favorite, base and perfidious,
> Ungrateful friend of the tsar whom you flatter,
> Raving oppressor of your fatherland,
> Are a wretch who has squirmed to a lofty position.

According to a contemporary, N. Bestuzhev, the inhabitants of Petersburg awaited the downfall of the impudent poet, but "the accused was ashamed to recognize himself in satire," and the brave poet remained unpunished.[10]

One of the darkest features of Arakcheev's regime was the infamous "military settlements." The idea of these "monstrous institutions," as Vigel' calls them, was evidently Alexander's, and his "true and eternal friend" Arakcheev took the execution of it to heart as commander of the "corps of military settlements." The original idea of military settlements was neither monstrous nor cruel; on the contrary, it was an institution motivated by the humane desire that soldiers should not be torn from their homes and families for twenty-five years. The practical aim of the military settlements was the reduction of expenditures for the upkeep of the army, which was to be placed on a self-sustaining basis.

The military settlers were promised a whole series of privileges and comprehensive economic aid: "they are liberated now and forever from all state exactions and from all the obligations of state peasants"; "the maintenance of their children and their preparation for the service is the responsibility of the state"; "invalids, widows, and orphans will be given rations by the state"; "instead of decrepit structures, new, more comfortable homes will be constructed"; and "agricultural equipment and working and domestic cattle will be allotted to all, for whom such assistance is necessary."

Such were the pleasing prospects that the government placed before the military settlers in the initial decrees. But what happened in practice? For the organization of the military settlements the government transferred certain territories inhabited by state peasants from civil to military administration, and all the able-bodied male inhabitants under age forty-six became soldiers, received uniforms, and were subjected to military discipline. Boys from six to eighteen were also put in uniform and trained in drill. Unmarried soldiers worked

---

[10] Pypin, *op. cit.*, p. 426; Nikolai, Mikhail, and Petr Bestuzhevy, *Vospominaniia* [*Memoirs*] (Moscow, 1931), p. 68.

for their keep as farm hands, living with the families of soldier-farmers. Farm labor was performed by military units in uniform under the directions of officers, and military activity was carried on simultaneously, at the expense of the farm work. The contemporary observer Vigel' writes:

> two conflicting vocations were joined in one yoke; the farmer was made to take up the gun and the soldier the plough; the poor colonists were condemned to perpetual forced labor. . . . Everything was in the Prussian manner, everything was subject to accounting, everything was by weight and measure. Exhausted by labor in the fields, the military colonists were formed into ranks and drilled.[11]

The material condition of the population of Arakcheev's "collective farms" was not so bad. The officers maintained sanitation and order, did not permit anyone to become destitute, and rendered assistance in case of misfortune. But the continual toil, the heavy oppression of severe military discipline, and the minute regulation of the entire life of the colonists was utterly unbearable: riots flared up several times, now in the northern, now in the southern military settlements. The riots were followed by cruel repression, by which "peace and quiet" were restored. The corps of military settlements expanded steadily and included more and more territory. According to Schilder:

> After 1816 the military colonies underwent rapid and extensive development, and by the last years of Alexander's reign they included one third of the Russian Army. At the end of 1825 the special Corps of Military Settlements, under Arakcheev's command, consisted of ninety battalions of Novgorod settlements, thirty-six battalions and 249 squadrons of Kharkov, Ekaterinoslav, and Kherson settlements.[12]

In addition, there were two settlements of artillery brigades in Mogilev province.

The military colonies were an object of hatred among liberal circles in Russian society, strengthening their dissatisfaction with Alexander. This dissatisfaction was intensified by many other aspects of Alexander's foreign and domestic policy (discussed below), such as the campaign of Magnitsky and Runich against the early development of the young Russian universities, the strengthening of

---

[11] F. F. Vigel', *Vospominaniia* (Moscow, 1864–1865), vol. V, p. 120.
[12] Schilder, *op. cit.*, vol. IV, p. 28.

the restrictions of censorship (see chapter 3), and Alexander's policy on the Polish and Greek questions (see chapter 4).

The Question of Succession

On top of all the difficulties of the latter years of Alexander's reign, there was a dynastic problem. Alexander had no children, and the successor to the throne was his brother Constantine Pavlovich, who lived in Warsaw where he was formally only in command of the Polish Army, but in practice was in charge of almost everything. But as early as 1818 Constantine had told the tsar that he did not want to succeed to the throne, in which case it was to pass to the next brother, Nicholas Pavlovich. In 1820 Constantine was officially divorced from his wife, a former German princess, and soon married an aristocratic Polish lady with whom he was in love. In 1822 he wrote his brother a decisive letter renouncing the throne, and Alexander finally decided to settle the question of the succession. However, he approached this question in a very peculiar way. On August 16, 1823, he signed a manifesto on the renunciation of the throne by the Tsarevich Constantine and the designation of Nicholas Pavlovich as his successor. But for some reason he decided to keep the manifesto secret—even from the new heir to the throne. Only three persons knew of the manifesto: Arakcheev, of course; Prince A. N. Golitsyn; and Metropolitan Philaret. Alexander ordered that the original document be preserved in the Uspenskii Sobor (Cathedral of the Assumption) in Moscow until he asked for it or until his death. The only other copies were to be kept in Petersburg, in the Council of State, the Synod, and the Senate, each bearing an inscription in Alexander's own hand: "To be preserved until my request, and in case of my death to be opened, before any other action is taken, in an extraordinary meeting." We shall see (in chapter 3) in what circumstances these packets were opened and how Alexander's strange game of hide-and-seek with his successor resulted in an interregnum in November and December 1825.

Nicholas I: The Crowned Drillmaster

Alexander's youngest brother, Nicholas Pavlovich, was born in 1796 just before his father ascended the throne. After Paul's death in 1801 he was brought up under the direction of the Dowager Empress Marie, who appointed a Baltic German, Count Lamsdorff, as his tutor. Although young Nicholas was exposed to a variety of academic subjects and showed some scholarly ability, especially in foreign languages, his only real interest lay in the army. That his mother and brother only permitted him to join the army in 1814 and even then kept him far from the battlefields was a source of profound anguish to him. He was, however, well pleased with the arrangement of his marriage in 1817 to Charlotte (rechristened Alexandra Fedorovna), the daughter of Tsar Alexander's friends, the king and queen of Prussia.

By this time Nicholas was well settled into the military life he wanted, and in 1818 was named commander of a brigade and inspector general of the military engineers. For seven years before his accession to the throne in 1825, he commanded the Second Brigade of the First Guards Infantry Division, and to the end of his days he remained an enthroned "brigadier general." Since he wanted to command Russia in the same manner that he regulated his guards regiments, the maintenance of the established order, strict discipline, and outward appearance were his constant concerns. By issuing an endless stream of royal statutes, rules and regulations, and also personal decrees, he strove to preserve and regulate every aspect of social, legal, economic, and cultural affairs—from the life of the Kalmyk and Kirghiz peoples and to the activities of the universities, academies, learned societies, insurance firms, and commercial banks.

In the army his exclusive concern was with the soldiers' bearing, drill, and uniforms. A considerable volume of decrees, special orders, and rules dealt with the minutiae of military dress: greatcoats, full-dress coats, frock coats, and trousers with all accessories and decorations—epaulets, shoulder-boards, shoulder loops, collar tabs, cuffs, braid, sleeve-stripes, lace, trouser-stripes, piping, buckles, and buttons. Considerable attention was also paid to the uniform dress of the civil servants in various departments and of students in various institutions of learning. Nicholas tried to "regularize" not only the uniforms of his military and civil subordinates, but even their physiognomies. It was not only permitted but even prescribed that the military wear mustaches, while civil servants had to be clean-shaven. Personal decrees issued in March and April 1838 stated that some officials of the court and the civil service "were permitting themselves to wear mustaches, which are appropriate only to the military." "His Majesty is pleased to find this entirely unseemly," and "commands all heads of civil departments strictly to observe that none of their subordinates wear beards or mustaches, for these go only with military uniforms." Nicholas prized mustaches highly, as a particular adornment of the military appearance, not only for all officers, but for himself. In a special personal decree of 1846, "The Sovereign Emperor is pleased to give his imperial command that henceforth medals of merit shall represent the visage of His Imperial Majesty only with mustaches."

This dashing, sergeant major's "visage in mustaches" subjected Russia to its stern and attentive gaze for thirty years, desiring to see everything, to know everything, to command everything. It is true that Nicholas, unlike another "visage in mustaches" who ruled Russia a century later, truly loved Russia, made an honest effort to serve Russia as its "father-commander," and frequently displayed personal courage in the face of danger. But his understanding of the welfare of Russia was too narrow and one-sided. Alarmed by the revolt of December 1825 (see below) and the revolutionary movement in Europe, he devoted his main attention and concern to the preservation of the social order and of the administrative structure that had long since revealed its instability and required not minor repairs but a basic reconstruction. It is therefore understandable that the all-embracing, energetic, and unceasing activities of Emperor Nicholas did not bring glory or well-being to Russia but, instead, the military and political catastrophe of the Crimean War. On his death bed Nicholas was obliged to acknowledge that he passed on "the command" to his son in a very sad state of affairs.

The revolutionary uprising of December 14, 1825, had a profound effect on Nicholas' policies. First of all, he was alarmed by the very fact that a revolutionary movement was possible as close to the throne as the guards regiments, and that representatives of the most aristocratic Russian families led the uprising. One result was to strengthen his conservative tendencies. Another was to implant in Nicholas a distrust of the Russian aristocratic elite, which resulted in a tendency to depend mainly on the bureaucracy and on Germans from the Baltic provinces of Russia or from Germany. Thus Germans, such as Nesselrode, Kankrin, Benkendorff, Dibich, Kleinmichel, and others surrounded the throne and held quite a few of the leading posts in the upper levels of the administration of the state.

On the other hand, the head clerk of the commission that investigated the uprisings, Borovkov, was instructed to compile from the writings of the Decembrists a systematic collection concerning the internal condition of Russia for the attention of the tsar and high officials. This material and the testimony of the Decembrists disclosed such a mass of abuse and disorder in Russian life and the state administration that Nicholas was obliged to attempt to undertake "all indicated measures" to alleviate the situation. This conviction produced endless sessions of secret committees that considered proposals for the required reforms but achieved almost no real results, apart from a quantity of used paper. It also produced the extraordinary development of the organization and activities of His Imperial Majesty's Own Chancery, through which Nicholas tried to place the different branches of governmental and social life under his personal direction. The former chancery became The First Section of His Imperial Majesty's Own Chancery, which acted as the emperor's private secretariat, preparing papers and reports for the tsar and keeping watch on the execution of imperial orders.

In 1826 a Second Section, dealing with codification, was established, replacing a Commission on the Compilation of Laws. The task of compiling the new "Code of the Laws of Our Fatherland" was entrusted to this newly established section of the imperial chancery. The notorious Third Section, for the supervision of the political police, was established in July of 1826. It was to keep watch on "all suspicious and harmful people," if necessary sending them into exile to keep them "under police surveillance." It was to observe non-Orthodox religious sects, the "schismatic" Orthodox, and foreigners living in Russia, and it was to collect "statistical information of interest to the police" and "lists of all incidents without exception."

After the death of the Dowager Empress Maria Fedorovna in 1828, a Fourth Section of the personal chancery was established for the supervision of educational and philanthropic institutions, including institutes, schools, orphanages, almshouses, and hospitals formerly founded and patronized by the Empress Maria. Later this was called "the department of the Empress Maria's institutions." In 1836 the Fifth Section was established to execute the reform of the administration of state peasants.

Soon after he came to the throne Nicholas brought widespread satisfaction by relieving Count Arakcheev and other unpopular assistants of the late tsar. But two of the leading figures of Alexander's reign, Count Kochubei and Speransky, each played an important role under Nicholas, the former as chairman of the Council of State, the latter in the great work of the codification of the laws during the years 1830–1833. E. F. Kankrin and Count Nesselrode, who served respectively as ministers of finance and foreign affairs during the latter part of Alexander's reign, continued in office for a long time under Nicholas. Kankrin was an efficient and thrifty financial expert, wholly in his element, while Nesselrode was a colorless, bureaucratic mediocrity. Nicholas placed a man of modest intellect and education, General A. Benkendorff, at the head of the political police. The most successful military leaders in the era of Nicholas were Generals I. I. Dibich and I. F. Paskevich. In the 1830s two new figures, characteristic of the reign of Nicholas, appeared on the political scene: Count S. S. Uvarov, who was minister of public education from 1833 to 1849, and Count P. D. Kiselev, who headed the newly established Ministry of State Domains from 1837 until the end of Nicholas' reign in 1855.

Speransky's Codification

The most recent Russian law code before Speransky's time was the *Ulozhenie* of Tsar Alexei Mikhailovich, composed in 1649. All of the abler rulers of the imperial period, Peter the Great, Elizabeth, Catherine the Great, and Alexander I, had staunchly tried to create a new legal code; but all of their efforts failed, and the juridical life of Russia continued to be dominated by chaos, of which everyone complained bitterly and from which everyone, excepting the litigious and the bribetaker, suffered cruelly. When he created the second (codification) section of His Majesty's Own Chancery in 1826, Nicholas appointed as its chief an old, "trusty" bureaucratic official, Balugiansky, but the real organizer and leader of the whole task of codification was Speransky. In 1830 Speransky and his assistants finished the compilation of the forty-five enormous volumes of *The Complete Collection of the Laws of the Russian Empire*. Of these, the last five volumes included annexes (tables, graphs, tables of organization, and tariffs) and indexes (alphabetical and chronological). The first forty volumes brought together over 30,000 laws, beginning with the *ulozhenie* of 1649 (the first number in collection) and finishing with the act of December 1825. A *Second Complete Collection of the Laws*, covering the period from December 1825 until March 1881, and a third, covering almost all the remaining years of the empire, were issued subsequently.

Upon completing this colossal task, Speransky, on order of the tsar, undertook the compilation of the *Code (Svod) of the Laws of the Russian Empire*, and by the end of 1832 he had finished this assignment. The *Code* included only active laws, systematically collected and divided by subject. Only the text of the laws appeared in the *Code*, without any commentary or explanation, and the whole work consisted of short, numbered articles, filling fifteen large volumes.

The *Code* took effect on January 1, 1835. Henceforth, the Russian Empire was formally a state governed "on the precise basis of laws"; the trouble was simply that it was hard to obtain justice against the bureaucratic officials who violated the laws. Of course, the *Code* could not long remain in its original form, for times and laws change. A second edition therefore followed in 1842. In 1845 a criminal code was issued, followed in 1857 by a third edition of the *Code of the Laws of the Russian Empire*. Until the end of the empire individual volumes of the *Code* were reprinted, including amendments and new laws.

The Bureaucratic Apparatus

The bureaucratic apparatus of the Russian Empire assumed its definitive shape under Nicholas I. He hoped that by merely regularizing the form of bureaucratic work he might achieve an improvement of its content. Consequently, innumerable committees drew up endless regulations that governed (or should have governed) the work of all administrative institutions, beginning with the Council of State and ending with the lowest rural police station.

Under Nicholas, the highest organs of the state, the Council of State and the Senate, basically retained their former status and organization, but he did make several changes in the composition of the ministries. In 1826 he established a special Ministry of the Emperor's Court and Estates, and in 1837 a Ministry of State Domains, which was to supervise state-owned land and the peasants who occupied it. Previously this had fallen under the jurisdiction of the Ministry of Finance.

At the head of each province stood a civil governor who was chairman of the provincial administration, consisting of a vice-governor, three councilors, an assessor, and their office staffs. Subordinate to the provincial administration were the treasurer of the province, the architect, and the surveyor. The rural police were responsible to the governor, and in each county of the province they were headed by the district police officer (*zemskii ispravnik*) with his senior or permanent deputy (*zasedatel'*), whom the nobility elected. The county was divided into sections (*uchastki* or *stany*), to which police officials were appointed mainly from among the nobility who owned property in the province. The rural police served as the court of first instance in small cases for people of the lower classes. In the cities the police were headed by the chief of police (*politsmeister* or *gorodnichii*), who was appointed by the central government.

The judicial business of the provinces was conducted by

the chambers of the criminal and civil court. As specified by Catherine's "Regulation on the Administration of the Provinces," issued in 1775, the state appointed the chairmen, but his colleagues on the bench (his "advisers" or "deputies") were elected by the nobility. After 1831 the nobility elected two candidates for the chairmanship of the chambers, whose names were proposed to the senate "to be submitted for the imperial approval." Evidently the government was soon obliged to doubt that the chairmen of the courts elected by the nobility had sufficient juridical knowledge and experience, and in 1837 it established the post of deputy chairman, chosen from among the "councilors" by the minister of justice.

From the time of Catherine until the reforms of the 1860s many positions in the legal and administrative institutions were filled by election by the nobility, and naturally these posts were not always filled by sufficiently able and well-trained candidates. Not only the ordinary man, but Emperor Nicholas himself complained of this. In a decree of January 1, 1832, he stated:

> On the basis of evidence that has come to my attention, I see with regret that elections by the nobility do not always correspond to the expectations of the government. The better nobles either evade service, or do not participate in elections, or agree with equanimity to the election of persons who do not have the qualities required by the duties that are assigned them. As a result, officials of the judiciary not infrequently are insufficiently experienced in the law, and abuses on the part of the police have come to light. . . .

Hoping to improve this situation and to introduce the appropriate order into elections among the nobility, the government issued a "Regulation on the Ordering of Meetings, Elections and Service among the Nobility." Elections were to be conducted at the customary meetings of the nobility of a province, which should be convened "every three years." Only the hereditary nobility holding at least the fourteenth rank (in the table of ranks established by Peter the Great) and owning real estate in the province could vote in the elections, although the other nobles could participate in the meetings without voting. Only nobles who owned at least 100 male serfs who lived on the landowner's property or those who owned at least 8100 acres of uninhabited land could vote in elections for state offices. But nobles who could not fulfill this requirement but did own at least 5 male serfs or 405 acres of uninhabited land, could take part in these elections by pooling their property so that a group of the poorer nobility might qualify as a collective elector having one vote.

With the exception of the office of marshal of the nobility (*predvoditel' dvorianstva*) of a province, all elected offices were open to the poorer members of the nobility. The marshal of the nobility and the chairman of the judicial chambers were confirmed in office by the emperor, and all other officials elected by the nobility were confirmed by the provincial governor.

Officials elected by the nobility were included in the hierarchy of the state bureaucracy, wore the prescribed uniforms and were rewarded for service by advancement in the table of ranks and by decorations. Thus did the government strive, on the one hand, to utilize the landowning nobility as "police chiefs" with respect to their serfs, as Nicholas reportedly said, while, on the other hand, it strove to draw all the passably able nobility into the civil service and array them in the uniforms of the bureaucracy.

For their part, the nobles of Nicholas' era gladly donned bureaucratic uniforms, and some of them evidently were more interested in the uniform and salary than in the service. This is indicated by a decree of the Senate dated February 16, 1844: "The Governing Senate . . . has heard reports of nobility, who are enrolled in the service without any occupation in administrative offices of some province. [The Senate] orders: [that] all provincial administrations . . . are to verify that persons having no duties in the service are not enrolled in it."

The first half of the nineteenth century may be called, in Kliuchevsky's words, "the most bureaucratic era in our history. . . . Now the nobility sinks into the bureaucracy." In local government the nobility was closely intertwined with the bureaucracy and became an instrument of the central authority. Now "the edifice of the Russian bureaucracy is complete," transformed into a complicated and far-flung mechanism, which was especially developed at the center. The central administration developed into the vast machine of bureaucratic offices, which deluged the local institutions in a paper stream of orders, circulars, instructions, "coordinations," questionnaires, and so on. And to the center there poured an opposite stream of reports, memoranda, protocols, and the like. In this paper sea of "incoming" and "outgoing" materials the actual needs of people often drowned, and it was not without reason that it was said in Nicholas' time that the head clerk and not the emperor ruled.

Over the bureaucratized nobility, over the uniformed and red-tape-ridden world of Nicholas' reign, soared the special authority of the sky-blue-uniformed "special corps of gendarmes." The corps was established in 1826 simultaneously with the establishment of the notorious Third Section of his Majesty's Own Chancery, and the head of the Third Section was also the commander of the corps, General Benkendorff. According to the "Regulations of the Corps of Gendarmes," issued in 1836, all of Russia was divided into seven gendarme districts, each with a general of the gendarmery at its head. The commanders of the provincial gendarme administrations were staff officers of the gendarmes (a colonel, lieutenant colonel, or major), and under him there were gendarme commands headed by captains and lieutenants. The corps was intended to assist the Third Section in uncovering subversion and suppressing liberal political ideas. It was also supposed to check on the legality of court decisions and to report on grafting bureaucratic officials, landowners who were cruel to their peasants, or any other disorders. According to the official instructions, officers of the gendarmery should uphold "the peace and welfare" of the population and "perfect justice." However, the real role of the gendarmery was far from the idyl supposed by the tsar, and the net of police in which Nicholas enveloped Russia produced a demoralizing effect.

In sum, the political development of Russia in the first half of the nineteenth century presents a mixed picture of successful modernization and serious restraints upon this evolution. The major institutions of the central government that were established early in the reign of Alexander I (the ministries, the Council of State, the Senate) were by no means perfect, but represented an important degree of rationalization compared to the previous situation; and these institutions proved sufficiently workable to endure for about a century without any major reorganization. In that time the central government of Russia undertook a number of sweeping programs of political and social reform, and it is fair to say that the degree of success that these programs enjoyed is a tribute to the viability of the central institutions. Moreover, the code of law that became the foundation of the government in 1835 was a major improvement over the anarchic legal situation of earlier years and was at least sufficiently operable to last as long as the empire. Even the often-criticized lower bureaucracy, for all its real ineptitude and dishonesty, represented a step toward the regularization of government and provided reformers in the central government with at least some sort of instrument with which to attempt the local implementation of programs for reform.

On the other hand, the insistence of the rulers on maintaining the principle of autocracy and on regulating a needlessly vast number of matters sapped the vitality of the state. The extent of government, especially police, regulation far exceeded the real needs of public security and alienated the intelligentsia, the social group which might have provided the educated personnel and reforming spirit to make the centralized system of government effective. In short, the government took on responsibilities that exceeded its capabilities and ended by suffocating civic spirit—or driving it underground. As both Nicholas I and his heir, Alexander II, recognized, the disaster of the Crimean War of 1853–1856 revealed the shortcomings of the attempt to manage everything through bureaucratic, police, and military command.

2)

The Social and Economic
Situation before the Great Reform

The Nobility

The most privileged social class in imperial Russia was the *dvorianstvo,* which monopolized the right to own serfs and possessed many other legal and social prerogatives. Although "nobility" is probably the most convenient translation of *"dvorianstvo,"* members of this legally defined class (*soslovie*) in most cases did not possess any aristocratic title and should not be considered as "nobility" in the normal English meaning of the term. To be sure, some members of the *dvorianstvo* did bear such hereditary titles as *kniaz'* (prince) or *graf* (count), which had originated in early times or in the reign of Peter the Great, but the great bulk of the Russian nobility consisted of untitled persons, many of whom earned this legal status through the ranks of the civil or military services.

According to the census of 1859, there were about 887,000 members of the nobility in the European Russian population of about 57 million persons, or roughly 1 noble for every 64 persons.*

---

* Population statistics for the Russian Empire are quite rough before the census of 1897, and so vague before 1859 that we shall not attempt to provide data for the earlier years of the century. From the time of Peter the Great until the reforms of the 1860s, most official Russian population statistics enumerate males only, but to give the reader accustomed to think in terms of male and female population a more meaningful impression we shall use approximations of this combined figure. The 1859 figures are approximate at best, and for our purposes the established estimates of male and female population are sufficiently accurate. Although the entire Russian Empire contained about 74 million persons in 1859, the most

In the same year about 104,000 nobles in European Russia were counted as serf-owners, which meant that they and their families had a share in the ownership of some 21,500,000 enserfed peasants. But one should not assume from this that all or most of these families lived on the scale of luxury that could be provided by the labor of several hundred serfs. On the contrary, the distribution of serf-owner- ship was quite uneven, and over 40 percent of the serf-owners had only about 3 percent of all the serfs (or an average of about 16 or 18 serfs per owner), which often meant that these petty nobles lived little better than the serfs they owned. Another 34 percent of the serf-owners possessed about 100 serfs each on the average, which was a more comfortable situation but hardly enough to support the grand style of life that the Westerner often associates with the "serf-owning Russian nobility." Because of their comparative impoverishment, how- ever, the petty nobles valued all the more their fancied status as "old- line nobility" and intensified the exploitation of their few serfs to preserve their gentle status—that is, living without performing manual labor. To supplement the meager income of their estates, members of the petty nobility sometimes entered the service of the state or sought election to the minor offices that were filled by the vote of the societies of the nobility, while some unfortunate ones became hangers-on of their rich and distinguished neighbors.

On the other end of the scale, about 1 percent of all serf- owners in 1859 owned almost 30 percent of the total serf population, averaging about 4500 serfs per owner, while another 2 percent pos- sessed about 15 percent of all serfs, or about 1300 serfs per owner. The loftier strata of the Russian nobility enjoyed its golden age in the second half of the eighteenth century, especially in the reign of Catherine the Great, "the nobles' tsaritsa." The façade of their culture at the end of this period was imposing and not without charm. The wealth and splendor of the imperial court was reflected in the style of the aristocracy. Luxurious palaces with their parks, gardens, orange- ries, theaters, orchestras, choirs, and painters adorned the life of the highest level of the Russian aristocracy, but behind this façade there was the unsightly "rear courtyard" of serfdom, which demoralized and corrupted all levels of society.

Following the stormy era of the Napoleonic wars, in the time of political reaction and obscurantism, the more active and

---

readily available and, for this book, most relevant statistics refer to the 57 million persons in "European Russia"—the fifty provinces west of the Urals and not in- cluding Finland, Poland, or the Caucasus.—R.H.M.

idealistic portion of the aristocracy formed secret societies. These were devoted to the fulfillment, through military uprising, of the ideals of liberty, equality and fraternity, which had been more like intellectual play than genuine convictions for the high aristocracy of Catherine's day. But the failure of the uprising of December 14, 1825, spelled the end of the nobility's political role. As Kliuchevsky wrote, "Now the nobility becomes simply an instrument of the government."

Under Nicholas I the majority of the nobility donned the uniform of the bureaucracy and bedecked themselves with medals, according to their rank and title. But the complete fusion of these groups did not occur. Emperor Nicholas I called himself "the first nobleman" and did not want the hereditary members of that class to sink without a trace into the sea of petty bureaucrats and army officers. Therefore, in the reign of Nicholas I entry into the ranks of the hereditary nobility was significantly restricted, and the preservation of the high aristocracy was encouraged by the creation of the institution of "majorates"—large, indivisible, hereditary estates.

Since the time of Peter the Great, all who attained the lowest officer's rank received a patent of nobility. But a manifesto of June 11, 1845, decreed that only those attaining the first field-grade officer's rank (major) or the fifth civil service rank ("state councilor") would be admitted to the hereditary nobility. Lower ranks received the title of "personal member of the nobility" (that is, life member, not hereditary) or "honorary citizen." Later, in 1856, the opportunities for receiving hereditary membership in the nobility accompanied the civil rank of "actual state councillor" (the fourth rank), the military rank of colonel, and the naval rank of "first captain."

Between the high aristocracy and the petty nobility was a mass of middling landed nobility, living on their obscure estates and occupying themselves with agriculture. In most cases young gentlemen entered the service, mostly military, but they customarily retired after attaining the first or second officer's rank and settled down with their families on their patrimonial estates, where they devoted themselves to agriculture or to a thoughtless and inactive life of aimless freedom. They spent their autumns hunting, their winters in social activities as guests and as hosts. In fact, the marshals of the nobility were obliged to be especially hospitable and lavish if they wanted to be re-elected for the following three-year term.

The educational and moral level of the middling landowners was not, on the whole, very high. "Even in agriculture," wrote the contemporary author Saltykov-Shchedrin, "the attitude of middling landowners was rigid, making no effort at the least improvement of the system. Once established, a custom served as law, but the conception of the limitless peasant labor lay at the base of all calculations,"[1] even though serf labor and the low level of agricultural technique produced poor yields.

In the 1830s and 1840s the more alert nobility entered the business field, established textile mills, tanneries, and distilleries, and attempted to introduce improvements in the yields of their acreage on the English model. In most cases, however, these undertakings ended ruinously, and the expensive machinery that had been imported from England lay about the rear courtyard in broken-down condition, inspiring peasant sneers for the master who had put on foreign airs. Most of these failures were caused by the utter ignorance of the experimenters, insufficient capital, and the poor productivity of serf labor.

The Bureaucracy

The bureaucracy, which attained such large proportions in the reign of Nicholas I, presents sociological problems of its own. Divided by the "Table of Ranks" into fourteen levels, ranging from the lowly "collegial registrar" to the "state chancellor," the bureaucratic class held all the branches of national and local government in its hands. The upper stories of the bureaucratic tower were usually crowded with representatives of the "pillars of nobility," while the lower levels were occupied by a motley mass drawn from all social classes: the nobility, the clergy, the burghers, and others. In addition to the usual bureaucratic vices, the Russian bureaucratic class, which received a very modest salary at this time, was renowned for its money-grubbing and extortionism. This is substantiated by repeated decrees of the tsars against extortion and by the evidence of contemporary witnesses who knew the world of the bureaucracy well from their own experience, men such as Gogol, Vigel', Herzen, and Saltykov-Shchedrin.

Although Nicholas I limited entry to the nobility, he did not want the lower levels of the bureaucracy and other intermediary social groups to merge into the grey mass of the lower classes that were subject not only to the "soul tax" *(podushnaia podat')* and military conscription, but also to corporal punishment. Consequently,

---

[1] M. Saltykov-Shchedrin, "Poshekhonskaia starina" ["Old Times in Poshekhonie"], in *Sobranie sochinenii* [*Collected Works*] (St. Petersburg, 1906 ed.), vol. XII, pp. 376–377.

a manifesto of April 10, 1832, established a new legal class, "honorary citizens," in which membership was either hereditary or personal. Members of this class enjoyed freedom from the "soul tax," military conscription, and corporal punishment and consisted of officials who did not have the right to become members of the nobility, persons with a higher education who were not members of the nobility, the upper crust of the merchants and industrialists, and also the legitimate children of the personal (nonhereditary) nobility.

The Serfs

Although all peasants were not serfs in prereform Russia, the 21,500,000 serfs *(krepostnye krest'iane)* in European Russia constituted the largest single class in the entire population, or about 38 per cent of the total in the European provinces. For comparative purposes, we may note here that there were also in 1859 about 19 million peasants without landlords, settled on state lands *(kazennye krest'iane)* and about 2 million peasants on the lands of the imperial family *(udel'nye krest'iane)*. In other words, the serfs, while constituting the most numerous and certainly most publicized single class, formed scarcely more than half the peasant population.

In both prerevolutionary and Soviet writing the condition of all serfs is portrayed in the gloomiest colors, and all landowners are supposed to have been cruel beasts whose chief pleasure in life lay in tormenting their peasants with all kinds of instruments. Unquestionably there were instances of cruelty, for we find witness of this in the minutes of the courts and in the memoirs of contemporaries, but they are noted there because they were regarded as crimes and not as the prevailing, normal custom, to which no one would have paid attention. While rejecting the saccharine and untrue theory of "patriarchal authority," which depicts the landowners as the solicitous parents of beloved children, we cannot accept the opposite and widespread theory of a uniformly brutal "landowning class." Even if we agree with the view that the landowners saw in their serfs little more than work animals, it is all the more doubtful that the majority of the rural masters found pleasure in the constant torture of their laborers. Saltykov-Shchedrin, whom no one can accuse of sympathy with serfdom, says this of the character of landlord-serf relations in *Old Times in Poshekhonie (Poshekhonskaia starina)* :

> By and large the peasant was provided for because they regarded him as a work animal who performed useful work, as

anyone could see. To exhaust his capacity for work was unprofitable. . . . Therefore, the main secret of good estate management consisted in not exhausting the peasant but at the same time not permitting him to loaf.[2]

It is impossible to give a general picture of the condition of the serfs on 100,000 landowners' estates, because it was exceptionally variegated and subject to change, according to the character of the owner and a multitude of different local circumstances. Pestel, the leader of the Decembrists and a well-known enemy of serfdom, wrote: "The condition of different landlords' peasants is extremely varied. With the best lords they enjoy complete prosperity; with the most evil, they dwell in utter misfortune. Between these two extremes there is a multitude of varying levels of misfortune and prosperity."[3] Since we are unable to give a general, full picture of the living conditions of the serfs, we can only approximately delineate the regions of the worst "misfortune" and comparative "prosperity."

The class of "household serfs" (*dvorovye*), numbering about 1,500,000 of the 21,500,000 serfs in the mid-nineteenth century, were in the worst condition. Deprived of their own home and farm, constantly under the eye of the lord, subject to all the whims and caprices of his arbitrariness, often exhausted by protracted work (especially the young girls of the household), they received only meager food and were slighted as "parasites."

Otherwise the nobility's serfs were divided into two basic groups: the "obrok" peasants, who paid the landowner only a set sum of money, and the "barshchina" peasants, who were obliged to work in the landlords' fields. The numerical relationship of the two groups was subject to change and it varied between the "blacksoil" provinces (*chernozem*—the fertile loam that is common in the southern provinces of Great Russia, such as Voronezh and Kursk) and the "nonblacksoil" provinces (the more northern zone around Moscow, in which less fertile soils predominated).

Statistics for the end of the eighteenth century show that 74 percent of the peasants of the blacksoil provinces were on barshchina, while only 55 percent of the peasants in the nonblacksoil provinces lived under that regime. As the desire for cash income grew among the nobility, the landlords of the comparatively infertile, nonblacksoil provinces increasingly tended to demand obrok rather than barshchina of their peasants. By the late 1850s, the proportion of

---

[2] *Ibid.*, p. 287.

[3] P. I. Pestel, *Russkaia Pravda* [*Russian Law*] (St. Petersburg, 1906), p. 88.

obrok peasants had risen to 68 percent in Moscow province, 70 percent in Vladimir province, and 90 percent in Yaroslavl province.[4] On
the other hand, there was a moderate increase in the proportion of
barshchina peasants in the blacksoil provinces during the first half
of the nineteenth century.

The situation of the obrok peasants was on the whole considerably more favorable than that of the barshchina peasants. They
often had large allotments of land, for the landowners in the nonblacksoil provinces often did not engage directly in agriculture and
allocated all arable land for peasant use. A significant portion of the
population of obrok estates of the central industrial zone went off
in search of a living in the seasonal industries, such as logging. It is
true, however, that the amount of obrok payments in the first half
of the nineteenth century in some places was considerably increased
and frequently became a heavy burden on the peasant.

The condition of the serfs on barshchina estates was worse
in all respects. Here the interference of the lords in the affairs of
the peasant was felt to an immeasurable greater degree. The landowners themselves administered the estates directly if they lived in the
country, or they hired a steward or designated a foreman *(burmistr)*
from among the peasants. The peasants were obliged to work on the
lords' land, normally for three days a week of barshchina, but in
many cases there was also "everybody's day" (sometimes Sunday after
mass), when all the peasants had to work for the landlord. On some
estates four or five days were required of the peasants, in which case
the peasants had to work on their own land on holidays or at night.
Finally, on some exceptional estates, the peasants received a monthly
subsistence payment and worked on the landowners' fields all six days
of the week. Apart from labor obligations (sometimes in addition to
obrok) the peasants customarily paid the lord "table supplies"—
mutton, geese, chickens, eggs, mushrooms—and were obliged to provide cartage for the delivery to market of the produce of the landowners' fields. Among the barshchina peasants the situation of those
belonging to the petty nobility was especially hard, for the exploitation of peasant labor was particularly strong and the interference of
the landowner in the life of the peasant was particularly insistent.[5]

The harsh conditions of serfdom often caused peasant dis-

---

[4] *Velikaia reforma* [*The Great Reform*] (Moscow, 1911), vol. III, p. 124.

[5] For a general description of the condition of the serfs on the eve of the reform
of 1861, see I. I. Ignatovich, *Pomeshchich'i krest'iane nakanune osvobozhdeniia*
[*The Serfs on the Eve of Liberation*] (3d ed.; Leningrad, 1925).

turbances, refusal to perform the obligations to the landowners, and attempts to complain to higher authority. In the reign of Nicholas I historians count 600 cases of peasant disturbances, of which half were suppressed with the help of the army. However, it is necessary to bear in mind that various government officials were zealous beyond the bounds of reason and, desiring to curry favor with the authorities, presented as "mutinies" such peasant actions as refusal to render obligations to a landlord or attempts at collective complaint to the authorities. There were also cases of individual reprisals of peasants against their landlords. In the twenty years between 1835 and 1855 there were about 150 known cases of landlords murdered by serfs and about 75 cases of attempted murder.

Attempts at Serf Reform

The attitude of the Russian public to serfdom was two-sided. The vast majority of landlords and Nicholas' bureaucracy regarded serfdom as one of the primordial bases of Russian life and considered the liberation of the serfs, especially with land, to be impermissible. Emancipation, they believed, would violate the "sacred right of property," and moreover, it would cause a severe political shock, for serfdom was closely linked to autocracy and the landlords served as the main support of the tsarist throne. At the same time, the pick of the nobility intelligentsia—the Decembrists—hated "bound slavery" and demanded its destruction. In the reign of Nicholas the majority of the socially mixed intelligentsia and circles of the nobility intelligentsia ("Westernizers" and "Slavophiles" alike) were inclined against serfdom, but discussion of the question of serfdom in the press was under a strict ban of censorship. Banished from the realm of politics and journalism, the peasant question penetrated the Russian social consciousness through literature. In the 1840s Grigorovich's stories ("The Country" and "Anton Goremyka") and Turgenev's *A Hunter's Sketches* (*Zapiski okhotnika*) were published and a series of other writings (by Herzen, Saltykov-Shchedrin, Pisemsky, and Nekrasov) appeared, attracting the attention of the Russian public to the "bitter fate" of the "younger brother" who languished, deprived of human rights, under the yoke of serfdom.

The first law that contained some limitation of the landowners' power was issued under Paul I. A manifesto of April 7, 1797, ordered: "Let no one under any circumstances oblige a peasant to work on Sunday." The same manifesto stated that three days of barshchina per week per peasant would be enough "to satisfy any economic need," but it did not directly prohibit landlords from demanding more than three days' labor per week. On the other hand, Paul aided the expansion of serfdom by transferring 300,000 male peasants from the authority of the state to the possession of private landowners, and by forbidding "willful movement from place to place" among the peasants in New Russia and the North Caucasus.

Alexander I genuinely wished for the liberation of the serfs, but he encountered opposition among his associates and lacked the decisiveness to realize his intentions. However, he did fulfill his decision against any further transfer of populated state lands into private hands. In his reign, moreover, the serfs of the Baltic provinces were liberated—without land. All in all, the numerical growth of serfdom was virtually ended at the opening of the nineteenth century, and the serf population thereafter remained relatively stable in the neighborhood of twenty-one million.

Although Alexander did not decide to conduct a fundamental and compulsory reform of the condition of the serfs, he issued a law of February 20, 1803, authorizing their liberation with land allotments "upon the arrangement of conditions based on mutual agreement" with the landlord. The peasants who were liberated this way formed a special classification within the state peasantry, "the free agriculturalists." The practical results of the law of 1803 were not great. Under Alexander I about 47,000 male peasants entered the class of "free agriculturalists," and under Nicholas I, 66,000, a total of less than 1 percent of the serfs. It was probably more significant that under Alexander I landlords were forbidden to sentence their serfs to exile in hard labor. Only the court could impose this sentence, "for important criminals."

In the Baltic provinces alone were basic changes in the status of the serfs actually executed in the reign of Alexander I. In 1804 the "Regulation for the Inhabitants of the Lifland Province" was issued, reforming the relations of the peasants to the land and the lord. The peasants became the hereditary tenants of their land allotments, and their obligations to the lord and payment for the land were defined by law or by "revision commissions." The former serfs received personal civil rights and were granted local self-government and peasants' courts. In 1805 similar regulations were applied in the adjacent province of Estland.

The Baltic nobility soon encountered economic disadvantages in the new arrangement, however, and began to seek its revision. While they agreed to the retention of personal freedom by the peasants, they demanded that the land be exclusively the property of the nobility. The government acceded to this pressure and in the "Regulations for the Estland Peasantry," issued in 1816, the first article states that the nobility reserves for itself "only the possession of the land." In 1817 the peasants of Kurland province were "liberated" in the same way, followed in 1819 by the peasantry of Lifland province and the Island of Esel. In all of these cases the peasants gained personal freedom, but in the absence of any land allotments fell into complete economic dependence on the landowners, becoming tenants or hired laborers.

In 1818 Alexander commissioned Arakcheev to prepare a plan for the liberation of the serfs "without hindrance to the landowner." The draft that he prepared proposed the gradual voluntary transfer, by purchase, of the serfs of the nobility to the state peasantry, but the plan was never enacted.

Nicholas I ascended the throne with the intention of improving the condition of the serfs and in the course of his reign established ten bureaucratic secret committees to consider the problem. The "work" of these committees could not and did not yield serious practical results, for all of Nicholas' magnates, Count Kiselev excepted, considered as inadmissible any serious limitations of the landlords' authority or any infringement of the landowners' interest in general.

Nicholas' personal attitude to serfdom was summarized in a speech to the Council of State March 30, 1842: "there is no doubt that serfdom, in its present condition, is a palpable and obvious evil for all. But to touch it now, would be, of course, a still more ruinous evil." However, "it is clear to any reasonable observer that the present situation cannot continue forever. . . . It is necessary to prepare new measures for the gradual transition to another order of things."[6] In 1845 Minister of Internal Affairs Perovsky submitted a note on the gradual limitation of serfdom by a series of measures that would lead the peasant to liberation "by means that would be imperceptible to the peasant." In 1846 the fifth secret committee stated:

> having considered the proposal and explanations of the minister of internal affairs, the committee fully approves of the basic idea: to achieve the liberation of the people of the enserfed class by the gradual restriction of serfdom in a manner imperceptible to

---

[6] A. P. Zablotsky-Desiatovsky, *Graf P. D. Kiselev i ego vremia* [*Count P. D. Kiselev and His Time*] (St. Petersburg, 1882), vol. II, pp. 254–255.

the serfs, not stimulating dangerous rumors among the people and without even uttering the words "freedom" or "liberty."

The committee considered the complete removal of the landowners' authority impossible, for "the authority of the landowner is a tool and a pillar of autocratic power. . . . The authority of the landowner, however, should not be unlimited and the peasantry should be protected against any abuse." [7] Thus did the "all-powerful" government of Nicholas display extreme timidity on the peasant question, setting itself the insoluble task of liberating the serfs in such a way that they would not notice it at all.

On April 2, 1842, a law resulted from the long, secret discussions. It awarded the landlords the option of making agreements with their serfs, by which land could be set aside for the permanent use of the former serfs, henceforth "obligated peasants," in return for a fixed payment. This law caused much unrest and rumor among the landowners, but it had almost no consequences. Only about 25,000 male serfs were transferred to the status of "obligated peasants," and these all belonged to three aristocratic families.

A series of laws introducing (or attempting to introduce) various measures for particular improvements of the lot of the serf or for the limitation of the landowners' arbitrariness were issued in the reign of Nicholas I. In 1827 it was decreed that there must be no less than 12 acres of land per "revision soul" (a male peasant counted in the previous census) for the sale of a landowner's land to be permissible.

A decree of August 30, 1827, regulated and partially limited the right of the landowners to exile their peasants to Siberia (previously only the right of exile *in hard labor* had been restricted). It permitted such exile for persons not over fifty, not decrepit, and not maimed; exiles were not to be counted as a reduction of the landlord's conscription quota. Husbands and wives were not to be separated by exile and young children had to be sent with them (boys up to five years and girls up to ten). An edict of May 2, 1838, forbade the acceptance of serfs without land to secure or pay private debts, and it also forbade the sale (or any alienation) of serfs (with or without land) apart from their families. A decree of January 2, 1841, confirmed the regulation forbidding the sale of peasants apart from their families and established the rule that their residence on a given

---

[7] *Deviatnadtsatyi vek* [*The Nineteenth Century*], pub. by P. Bartenev (Moscow, 1872), vol. II, pp. 189–191.

estate be registered. The law forbade the sale of household serfs and peasants of both sexes to persons who did not own inhabited estates.

The right of landlords to punish their serfs for all kinds of "impudence" had not been regulated by law, and the administration of Nicholas I tried to establish legal norms for this right. The *Code* of 1832 gives the landlords the right to punish their serfs, "but not by mutilation and still less by endangering life." In 1846 the authority of the landlord's domestic court was precisely defined: the landlords or their stewards could submit peasants "to the punishment of forty strokes with the birch or fifteen with the rod, or arrest from one to seven days and in cases of special importance up to two months, providing that the accused is held in a rural jail." For more important felonies and misdemeanors the landlord could send the serf into the work houses for a sentence from two weeks to three months, or to the "corrective" prison from one to six months. The landlords could banish incorrigible or harmful serfs from their estates.

On the other hand, the law made the landlords responsible and punishable by heavy sentence for "maltreatment" of their peasants, meaning mutilation and torture. In 1851 a total of 200 estates of the nobility were in the trusteeship of the government because of the landlord's cruel treatment of his serfs. The trouble with this arrangement was that the serfs, as before, were deprived of the right to complain of their owners, so that proceedings for the prosecution of landlords for maltreatment could be started only on the initiative of the local authorities, and the latter usually did not hurry in this matter. Also, in 1827 it was forbidden to accept the children of bound peasants or household serfs in the gymnasiums (academic secondary schools) or universities, but they were allowed, "as in the past, to study without hindrance in parochial and county schools" and also in agricultural and trade schools.

Under Nicholas I the introduction in the southwestern regions of "inventories" was prepared, and then put into force with the assistance of the energetic governor general of that region, Bibikov. These inventories defined the payments and obligations of the peasants according to the amount of land allotted for their use. In 1847 "Regulations for the Administration of Estates in the Kiev Provinces" came into force, establishing the inventory system in the provinces of Kiev, Volhynia, and Podolia, where the majority of the landowners were Poles. An analogous arrangement was introduced in 1846 in the provinces of the kingdom of Poland, where the peasants had received personal freedom, without any rights to the land, by the decree of Napoleon in 1807. In 1852 it was decided to introduce the inventory system in the provinces of the northwestern region, but this attempt caused dissatisfaction and complaints among the landlords and in 1854 it was decided to reconsider the inventory rules in this area.

The State Peasants

Among the various legally defined classes in prereform Russia, the only one that could rival the serfs in numbers was the class of state peasants *(kazennye krest'iane)*, of whom there were about 19 million in 1859, or about 33 percent of the total population of European Russia. Although these peasants lived on land owned by the government and were not subject to oppression (or sale) by landlords, their juridical and economic situation was quite dismal during the first third of the nineteenth century. The state lands and the peasants living on them were under the control of the Department of State Domains within the Ministry of Finance, which regarded these peasants chiefly as a source of revenue for the treasury. On the local level, financial authority rested in the "economic section of the treasury board" of the Ministry of Finance, and in other matters authority over the state peasants was in the hands of the rural police, particularly the district police officer and his deputies, who were responsible to the Ministry of Internal Affairs. The rural police collected taxes and arrears from the state peasants, and these collections were frequently accompanied by illegal exactions and other abuses that were ruinous for the peasants.

Between the end of the eighteenth century and the time of Kiselev's reform of 1838 (discussed below), the government attempted to regulate self-government among the state peasants, although it never succeeded in providing sufficiently precise definitions of the composition and competence of the various bodies involved. Basically, there were two levels of peasant self-government, the township *(volost')* and the village *(selenie)*, each of which possessed an assembly whose membership was not well defined. In addition, each township, which was to consist of a maximum of 3000 male peasants, had an "administration," consisting of a mayor *(golova)*, who was elected for a two-year term; the elders of the villages comprising the township; and the township clerk. Each village had, in addition to its communal assembly, an elder who was elected for a one-year term and the "tenth-men" *(desiatskie)*—one was elected by each ten families —to assist the work of the police. The village elder was empowered to administer justice in relatively unimportant crimes, and the communal assembly was granted fairly broad powers, including the election of village officers, the release of residents who wished to leave the village, the acceptance of new members, the allotment of land among the residents, the apportionment of all taxes and obligations imposed by the state, the granting of the power of attorney on behalf of the village, and the trial and punishment of minor crimes within the commune (here the jurisdiction of the elder and the assembly overlapped).

In practice the condition of self-government among the state peasants was just as dismal as the bureaucratic administration. Often the elected duties fell to the henchmen of the "mir-eaters," rich peasants who often gained a controlling influence in the commune for the price of a sufficient number of buckets of vodka. Because of the illiteracy and passivity of the peasant masses, the township and village clerks played a major role in rural administration and were distinguished for their extremely low moral level.

On several occasions the higher administration directed the Treasury boards to see that land was allotted to state peasants on the basis of 40.5 acres per "soul" in provinces in which land was plentiful, and 21.6 acres in provinces where it was scarce. But this directive was never fully applied. According to the data of the census of 1836–1840, the allotments of state peasants exceeded 13.5 acres per "soul" only in thirteen of the forty-three provinces of European Russia.

The payments and obligations of the state peasant increased significantly in the first quarter of the nineteenth century. In addition to the "soul" tax on each male and the obrok, the state peasants not only paid various taxes to the local commune, and the "land tax" to the central government, but also "served in kind" in fulfilling such obligations as the corvée (building roads and bridges) and the supply service (the transportation of Treasury and military supplies and personnel, and billeting troops). The hardest of the personal obligations was the conscription of young men into the army for lengthy terms of service.

Crop failure or fire, in the absence of the necessary aid, increased the poverty of the state peasants. In such circumstances, especially following crop failure, it is not surprising that the peasants began to default in the payment of taxes. The government would then adopt forcible measures for the collection of arrears, and this would in turn lead to the further impoverishment of the peasantry. To all of this was added the low level of agricultural practice and dismal cultural conditions on the state-owned countryside: the absence of schools, medical care, and institutions for granting small-scale credit and the abundance of taverns, which extracted the peasants' surplus kopeks and tried their best to make it possible for him to drink as much as possible.

Kiselev's Reform of the State Peasants

Although the government of Nicholas I was impotent to resolve the peasant question as a whole and to eliminate serfdom, it did decide to undertake serious reforms in the matter of the state peasantry. On April 29, 1836, the Fifth Section of His Imperial Majesty's Own Chancery was established for this purpose, headed by General Count Kiselev. He was perhaps the ablest of Nicholas' statesmen and undertook the task with a firm determination that was not typical of the paper-loving bureaucrats of the day. First of all he dispatched to all provinces in which there were state peasants special officials who were to inspect in detail the condition of these peasants, not merely by examing the paper records, but by personally questioning the peasants and studying their complaints and statements. This survey lasted from 1836 until 1840 and gathered substantial data on the condition of the state-owned lands. Not satisfied with the dispatch of inspectors, Kiselev himself toured some provinces to acquaint himself personally with the condition of the peasantry. In his report to the tsar on the results of the investigation, he depicted the sorry plight of the state peasants and insisted on the necessity of serious reform in the administration of state domains. In accord with his proposals a Ministry of State Domains was established at the end of 1837, and was charged with three responsibilities: "the administration of state properties; the trusteeship over the free rural inhabitants; and the supervision of agriculture." A law on the local organs of the new administration was issued the following year.[8] Henceforth, the interests of the state peasants were given first priority in their administration.

The new plan for the administration of the state peasants, which was comparable to Speransky's abortive plan in terms of

---

[8] For the legislative statutes of 1838 on the state peasant administration, see *II Polnoe sobranie zakonov*, vol. XIII, no. 11,189; for a detailed description of Kiselev's reform, see the above-cited works of Zablotsky-Desiatovsky, vols. II and IV, and N. M. Druzhinin, *Gosudarstvennye krest'iane i reforma P. D. Kiseleva* [*State Peasants and the Reform of P. D. Kiselev*] (Moscow, 1946–1958), 2 vols.; see also *Istoriia Rossii v XIX veke* [*History of Russia in the Nineteenth Century*] (pub. by Granat, St. Petersburg, c. 1910) vol. I, chap. VII: M. Bogoslovsky, "Gosudarstvennye krest'iane pri Nikolae I" ["The State Peasants under Nicholas I"] pp. 236–260.

balanced structure, was enacted on April 30, 1838, as the "Regulation for the Administration of the State Domains in the Provinces." It consisted of a four-tiered system, starting on the provincial level, where authority was exercised by a Board of State Domains, headed by a manager. The next lower level consisted of specially designated districts, which in most cases were identical with the counties which formed the basis for the general administration of the state. On this level, a "district superintendent" *(okruzhnoi nachal'nik)* was the authority and guardian for the state peasants. He was to look after the improvement of the morals of peasants in his charge, the establishment of parochial schools, medical care, the procurement of food in years of crop failure, local communications, and the improvement of the peasant economy. Of course, he was also charged with the supervision of the observance of the interests of the state: the collection of taxes, the fulfillment of obligatory labor service, and the provision of army recruits.

Although he was supposed to check on the legality of the actions of the organs of peasant self-government, the district superintendent could not issue orders to the village assembly (unlike the "superintendents of the peasantry," which Alexander III later established). Article 31 of the Regulation on Rural Administration states: "officials of the boards of state properties and district superintendents are not permitted to take part in meetings of the state peasants in the village assembly."

The third level in this hierarchy was the township administration. Townships were enlarged by uniting several rural communes into units of about 6000 male peasants. Each township had an assembly that met every three years and consisted of representatives elected by the village communes on the basis of one representative for every twenty peasant households. The township administration consisted of the township mayor and two deputies. The township assembly elected the mayor, who was confirmed by the Board of State Domains. The township mayor could then continue in office for an indefinite term, but he could be relieved at his own wish, on grounds of incompetence, or because of complains from the peasants. The deputies were elected for three years by the township assembly and were confirmed by the board. The district superintendent appointed the township clerks. In addition to the township administration there were to be the township court *(rasprava)*, consisting of two "honest men," elected by the township assembly and serving under the chairmanship of the township mayor.

The fourth and lowest level in Kiselev's hierarchy was the

village, to which he gave an orderly system of administration, in which the rights and obligations of the peasantry were governed by law. A "rural commune" *(sel'skoe obshchestvo)* was established in each large village, while several small villages were united into a single rural commune. The organs of rural self-government were the assembly of the commune, the rural executive *(nachal'stvo)*, and the rural courts *(raspravy)*.

The rural assembly consisted of members of the rural administration and delegates chosen at the rate of two persons from every ten households. Believing that too many persons in a rural assembly would impede reliable and tranquil consideration of questions before the assembly, Kiselev replaced the participation in the assembly of all members of the commune with elected representation. But for the resolution of a question that had vital significance for every peasant, especially the partition of communal land, all householders were to be invited to the assembly. The subjects under the jurisdiction of the assembly were: the election of rural officers; the release of members of the commune and the acceptance of new ones; the allotment of land among state peasants; the apportionment of the "soul" tax, obligations, and collections among the peasants and means for exacting arrears; the fulfillment of the military conscription quota; the imposition of taxes to pay the expenses of the commune; supervision of the accounts of the tax collector and the inspection of the communal granary; the leasing of forest, meadows, and water rights; regulation of the use of the communal woodland and hayfields; problems concerning the division of land within families; the designation and calling to account of guardians of young orphans; the review of appeals for assistance; and the granting of the power of attorney to carry out the business of the commune.

The assembly elected the executive of the commune, which held office for three years and consisted of a "head elder" *(starshina)* and one to three other elders *(starosty)*. In small communes, numbering up to 200 male peasants, the duties of the head elder and the other elders were merged. The assembly also elected the tax collector and the inspector of the communal granary. Elected "tenth-men" helped to look after the maintenance of law and order on the countryside, and foresters were elected to look after the conservation of the woodland.

The rural courts, chaired by the head elder of the commune and two "honest men" elected by and from the assembly, exercised judicial authority among the state peasants. In 1839 "Rural Court Statutes" and "Rural Police Statutes" were issued to guide the maintenance of law and order on the state-owned countryside. The rural courts could pass final sentence on cases involving no more than five rubles, and it could sentence the guilty to the maximum punishment of fines up to one ruble, arrest or forced labor for six days, and twenty strokes with the birch.

Such was the administrative and judicial order of the state peasants following Kiselev's reforms. When the serfs were emancipated in 1861, Kiselev's system served in considerable measure as the model for the courts and administration in their villages.

In establishing the new organs of peasant administration, Kiselev strove to select able officials and to provide them with an adequate salary, and he constantly impressed upon the officials under him the importance of benevolent relations with the peasants and the strict observance of legality. The spirit of his administration is illustrated by a ministerial circular of 1843 that directed officials

> to promote the development of indigenous communal administration among the peasants, to observe the fulfillment of the rules they have been granted, but not to intervene in the judgment of matters that are within the purview of the rural administration or courts, nor in the decisions of communal assemblies, if these have conducted their affairs according to the rules set forth by law.

Under Kiselev's energetic direction considerable progress was made in surveying the land. Prior to the establishment of the ministry in 1837, there was a total of eighty surveyors in the civil service. In 1856 there were 1419 surveyors and student surveyors, and by that year, 143 million acres of land, or more than half of the arable state lands, had been surveyed. In eighteen provinces the peasant obrok was no longer the same for all individuals, but depended on the peasant's wealth. Of unoccupied state land 6,600,932 acres were transferred to needy state peasants, and 1,350,000 acres were set aside for settlement by 56,000 persons who had formerly possessed no land at all. The allotment of woodland to the rural commune was also undertaken on the ratio of 2.7 acres per "soul." Altogether, 5,961,615 acres of Treasury-owned woodland were transferred to the use of rural communes. Under the program for the peasants with little land, 169,000 souls were resettled, and 6,750,000 acres were given to them in their new settlement on the basis of 21.6 to 40.5 acres per soul.

In its effort to increase agricultural productivity, the government in 1840 issued an order on potato planting in state-owned villages. Peasants who were distinguished for their success in growing potatoes were awarded monetary prizes and gold and silver medals. Unfortunately the peasants were disturbed by the excessive zeal of the local administration for the application of gang labor to the cultivation of potatoes and by the rumors of the transfer of state peasants to the landowners. In 1841–1843 this caused agitation in some towns in the province of Perm, Viatka, Orenburg, Kazan, and Saratov. Here "potato riots," according to Kiselev's report to the tsar, "were suppressed in three provinces without the use of force," but in two the local authorities "acknowledged the necessity of recourse to arms . . . and eighteen rebels were killed."

Regulations concerning the forests, enforced by provincial or district foresters, were introduced to conserve these resources, and steps for the forestation of unwooded localities were undertaken. Kiselev's ministry also carried out the draining of swamps, the clearing of uncultivated land for pasture, and the construction of roads and river wharves. To secure the food supply of the population in years of crop failure, a reserve grain supply was established. To aid individual farmers over 1000 small rural banks and about 100 mutual aid and savings banks were established. In case of fire, a victim who had lost his possessions was granted nonreturnable aid and loans. Mutual fire insurance of peasant buildings was introduced, and it was recommended that homes be constructed with stone or brick foundations. In eighteen years over 7500 of the former and over 90,000 of the latter had been erected, requiring the construction of 600 brick factories.

Kiselev's administration also concerned itself with the spiritual needs of the peasants; 90 new churches were built in state-owned towns and 228 old ones that had fallen into disrepair were restored. Houses were acquired for the parish priests and land allotments were released for their upkeep. The development of public education was at least well started on state-owned lands. In 1838 there were 60 schools and only 1800 pupils among approximately 17 million state peasants, while in 1856 there were 2550 schools and 111,000 pupils, including 18,500 girls. The beginnings of rural medical service were founded with the employment of 79 doctors by the Ministry of State Domains, the establishment of 15 hospitals and the training of midwives and vaccinators.

In short, the eighteen years of Kiselev's administration of the Ministry of State Domains produced substantial progress, enhancing the welfare of the state peasants and simultaneously increasing the revenues of the state.

The Position of the Peasant Commune

Especially in the area inhabited by the Great Russian populace, both serfs and state peasants generally lived in the form of communal, rural society known as the *mir*. In years past there has been much heated debate on the origin of this institution, some writers maintaining that it is very ancient and peculiarly Russian, others denying this contention. The confusion seems to stem from the dual function of the mir: as a social and administrative entity and as a body which allotted land among its member families. In fact, the administrative function has deep historic roots, recorded in the annals of the fifteenth century, while the land-allotment commune was formed only in the eighteenth and nineteenth centuries under the influence of the nobility on their estates and the government on state lands.[9] In discussing the mir in the early nineteenth century it is therefore important to bear in mind this duality of function and the contrasting historical development of the two aspects of the mir.

On the whole the mir was in decline as an institution of peasant self-government in the early nineteenth century. Although A. I. Koshelev claimed that "we have in the peasant mir a vital, strong, and all embracing foundation,"[10] and K. S. Aksakov wrote that the peasants in the mir "understand social questions much better than you, members of the well-born assembly of the nobility,"[11] this seems to have been an idealized picture of the situation. As previously noted, the inspectors dispatched by Kiselev in 1836–1840 described a much less favorable impression of the effectiveness of self-government in the mir at that time. Their reports indicate that in some northern provinces (Volodga, Archangel, and Olonets) where the tradition of peasant self-rule was strong, the situation was not bad, but elsewhere the condition of the mir as a governing body was dismal. Of course, the reform of Kiselev described above entrusted considerable autonomy in the mir, which generally served as the basic level in his administrative system and revived the vitality of the administrative role of the mir on state lands.

---

[9] On the origins of the peasant land commune, see S. G. Pushkarev, "Proiskhozhdenie krest'ianskoi pozemel'no-peredel'noi obshchiny v Rossii" ["The Origins of the Repartitional Peasant Land Commune in Russia"], in *Zapiski russkogo nauchno-issledovatel'skogo ob'edineniia v Prage* (Prague, 1939 and 1941). nos. 67 and 77.

[10] A. I. Koshelev, *Zapiski* [*Memoirs*] (Berlin, 1884), appendix V, p. 122.

[11] K. S. Aksakov, *Zamechaniia na novoe administrativnoe ustroistvo krest'ian v Rossii* [*Notes on the New Peasant Administration in Russia*] (Leipzig, 1861), p. 10.

On the estates of the nobility the decay of peasant self-government seems to have varied considerably. On the large estates the elected bodies of the mir had some chance for survival if the obrok, or cash dues, and not the barshchina, or obligatory labor, was imposed. In such cases the mir often elected the elders and other officers, apportioned the obrok among themselves and held court, all with only the general supervision of the landlord and his agents. On estates which exacted barshchina, however, the obligatory labor was enforced by agents of the landlord whose influence penetrated the entire life of the peasants and stifled the exercise of self-government. On the smaller estates the administrative function of the mir was badly curtailed because of the proximity of the nobility to the peasants. Here the landlord usually held court and imposed penalties himself.

Ever since Peter the Great introduced the "soul" tax, an equal levy on all male peasants regardless of age or wealth, the nobility and the government had encouraged the land-allotment function of the mir as a means of rationalizing the collection of this impost. On many estates, especially where barshchina was practiced, the landlords had attempted to establish a roughly uniform peasant "tax unit" (*tiaglo*), usually including one working peasant couple. From each tax unit, equal obligations to the government and the landlord were exacted, and to equalize the ability of all such units to pay as required an equal portion of land was to be allotted. This required the periodical repartitioning of the land, which was carried out by the mir operating as a land-allotment commune. By the early nineteenth century such a system was very common on the estates of the nobility in Great Russia. The principal features of this system were the partition of the land into strips, obligatory crop rotation (traditionally the three-field system), and a complete or partial repartition of plough-land and hayfields every twelve years, or more often. However, this system of equalization of the land was not practiced exclusively, and especially on estates practicing obrok, one still found both rich and poor peasants.

On state land the government faced somewhat the same problem. The payment of the "soul" tax by the "rich" peasants would not compensate for the arrears of the poor, so the state made a variety of efforts to equalize the land allotments among its peasants. In the eighteenth century a series of decrees attempted to carry out this program through the peasant commune acting as a land-allotment body. The program of enforced periodic land redistribution encountered strong resistance from the state peasants, who were accustomed to buy, sell, exchange, or bequeath their land as if it were personal property. It also intensified the social antagonism between the rich and the poor who stood to gain from any repartition. Nevertheless, by the early nineteenth century equalization had achieved considerable success, despite much difficulty and procrastination.

Kiselev's program for the state lands modified this tendency, for this statesman believed that the equal apportionment of land was "harmful to any radical improvement in agriculture." However, he acknowledged that the land-allotment mir "has its utility in that it eliminates a proletariat, and thus it poses a problem that goes beyond purely economic considerations." He wished to preserve the mir also because, as noted above, he valued it as an administrative and social body, a repository of peasant common law. Kiselev therefore compromised and retained communal land-holding, while attempting to regulate the partitioning of land and to eliminate the excessive division of the land into strips.

By the mid-nineteenth century, then, the mir was very much alive as a land-allotment institution on both nobility and state lands, while it was just beginning its revival as an administrative institution on state lands and was still fairly moribund in this capacity on landlords' estates.

Economic Development: Trade, Industry, and Finance

Without doubt a money economy, industry and trade were developing in Russia in the first half of the nineteenth century, but the tempo of this development was extremely slow in comparison with the economic development of other European countries. In the late eighteenth century Russia was economically on a par with other European countries. In iron smelting, for example, Russia was equal to England and exported about 54,000 tons per year, but by 1859 British iron smelting exceeded Russian production by twelve-fold. Serf labor, forced and unproductive, was retarding Russian industrial development. According to the economic historian Tugan-Baranovsky: "Those branches of production in which serf labor continued to dominate ceased to develop. Europe quickly outstripped us in economic development. The export from Russia of finished goods declined absolutely, and became relatively insignificant."[12]

Serfdom retarded industrial development in two respects.

[12] M. Tugan-Baranovsky, *Russkaia fabrika v proshlom i nastoiashchem* [*The Russian Factory, Past and Present*] (St. Petersburg, 1898), p. 83.

The enserfed peasants, especially those on barshchina, were deprived of all their economic "surplus" by their master and could buy almost no industrial products. In addition, the landowners made an effort to limit themselves to the products of their own farms and craftsmen, from the work of their blacksmiths and carpenters to that of artists. It is true they had to buy fabric for clothing, but even then the garments were usually sewn by domestic tailors and seamstresses. Sugar was considered a luxury item and was served only when guests were present; otherwise the family confined themselves to honey, as in the days of Oleg and Sviatoslav. Thus the internal market for manufactured and luxury goods was exceptionally limited and only the textile industry, especially cottons, found enough demand for its output. Agriculture, with its traditional three-field system, its low crop yields, and its occasional crop failures, remained by far the predominant element in the national economy in the first half of the nineteenth century.

The urban population in Russia in the first half of the century did grow absolutely and relatively. In 1796 the urban population stood at 1,300,000 (about 4 percent of the whole population), and in 1859 it was 4,200,000 (about 6 percent); [13] but compared to the tempo in Western Europe, not to mention America, the increase was quite small. Of course, one must bear in mind that in Russia trade and industry were not exclusively concentrated in the cities, but were dispersed over the whole country, being established in suburbs and even in hamlets in the countryside. In fact, many Russian cities often were not centers of commercial and industrial activity, but were instead stunted and unpopulous administrative centers, in which, except for some churches, only one building stood out—the office building of the bureaucracy. There were a few merchants' shops and homes, but the majority of the city populace, the burghers, lived in small wooden houses and devoted themselves not only to crafts and petty trade but also to agriculture: chickens and geese, pigs and cows, all tranquilly strolled the streets of the "city."

The two capitals of the Russian state, St. Petersburg and Moscow, were the political, economic, and cultural centers of the vast empire. Petersburg, with a population of 425,000 in 1825, the seat of the imperial court and all the central institutions of government, was a city of splendid court life, a city of the military and the bureaucracy. At the same time, it had a growing industry, focused mainly

---

[13] P. Miliukov, *Ocherki po istorii russkoi kul'tury* [*Outlines of Russian Culture*] (5th ed.; St. Petersburg, 1904), vol. I, p. 82.

around shipbuilding and metalworking; there the famed Putilov ordnance works were founded in 1801. Old "Mother Moscow," the former capital, with a population of some 306,000 in 1830, changed its character essentially during the first half of the century. Baron von Haxthausen, a German author who visited Russia in 1843–1844, tells us that in the beginning of the century more than 50 percent of the Muscovite population consisted of gentlefolk and their numerous servants who flocked to the city, particularly during the winter months. In the 1840s, however, "since the rise of the trading and manufacturing activity, the elements of the population of Moscow have been completely changed. . . . The place of the gentlefolk with their innumerable and lazy domestics is now occupied by manufacturers with their equally numerous workmen."[14] Gradually, Moscow became the main center of manufacturing and trade, particularly for the textile industry. The presence of Moscow University also made it the chief center of Russian intellectual life.

Other cities lagged far behind the capitals in size and importance. The largest was Odessa, with a population of 78,000 in 1847, a port city with a multilingual population, the main gateway of Black Sea trade. Other centers of trade and manufacturing in the south were Kiev, Kharkov, and Kishinev, the former two being university seats. In the Baltic provinces, Riga in Latvia and Vilno in Lithuania were most important. Tula near Moscow was known for its highly skilled metalworking industry. In the eastern regions of the country the larger cities, all situated on the banks of the Volga River, were Nizhni Novgorod with its big annual fair and extensive trading connections to most of Russia and to many Asian countries as well; Kazan, the center of Moslem religious life; Saratov, an inland grain port; and Astrakhan, a center of the Caspian fishing industry. The largest city in the Caucasus was Tiflis (Tbilisi) in Georgia. All together, with the exception of the two capitals, there were only sixteen cities in Russia (outside Poland) whose population exceeded 30,000 in 1847.[15]

A numerous, independent, and wealthy bourgeois class such as played such an important role in the political, economic, and cultural life of Europe and North America was absent in Russia. The charter that Catherine gave to the cities in 1785 could not create at

---

[14] Baron von Haxthausen, *The Russian Empire, Its People, Institutions, and Resources* [*trans. from the German*] (London, 1856), vol. I, pp. 47–49.

[15] I. Ditiatin, *Ustroistvo i upravlenie gorodov v Rossii* [*The Organization and Administration of Cities in Russia*] (Iaroslavl, 1877), vol. II, pp. 323–325.

one stroke the "middle estate." Consequently, urban self-government, which this charter introduced, failed to gain the support of either the officials or the populace.

In the first half of the nineteenth century the iron industry stagnated.[16] The Ural Mountains region was the main center of iron smelting, producing about 80 percent of Russian iron, and the mills in the Urals were either government-owned or "possessional." In the latter case, the peasants and craftsman who provided the labor were legally attached to the factory and worked there by way of barshchina; in 1859 there were 158,000 registered "possessional" male peasants in the Urals. Primitive technology (in the absence of free competition), petty bureaucratic regulation of factory life, and forced labor all contributed to the backwardness of metallurgy in the Urals.

Despite the lag in Russian metallurgy in the first half of the nineteenth century, the Russian textile industry, especially cottons, advanced rapidly. Thanks to the introduction of inexpensive and uncomplicated machinery for spinning and weaving cotton, it became the cheapest material for clothing and was in high demand. The average annual import of raw cotton and yarn in Russia in 1816–1820 was about 4320 tons and in 1856–1860 about 50,940 tons—a twelvefold increase in forty years. A peculiarity of the evolution of the Russian textile industy was that the factories gave a strong impetus to the development of cottage industry *(kustarnaia promyshlennost').*[17] This tendency was considerably strengthened by the war of 1812, which destroyed many factories, mainly in Moscow. The workers, a majority of whom were obrok peasants, had taken a liking to textile production and converted their huts into small plants. The subsequent growth of cottage industry in textiles continued throughout the whole first half of the nineteenth century. This activity was especially well developed in the north-central provinces of Great Russia, surrounding Moscow. The workers in the cottages were not independent producers, but depended on manufacturers who distributed yarn to be woven at home and on buyers to whom the

---

[16] For statistical data on the development of industry, trade, and finances during the nineteenth century, see Tugan-Baranovsky, *op. cit.,* 7th ed. (Moscow, 1938), and P. I. Liashchenko, *Istoriia narodnogo khoziaistva SSSR* (Gosizdat, 1947–1948), vol. I. (before 1861) and vol. II (after 1861). [An English translation is *History of the National Economy of Russia* (New York, 1949).] See also P. A. Khromov, *Ekonomicheskoe razvitie Rossii v XIX-XX vekakh, 1800–1917*] [*The Economic Development of Russia in the Nineteenth and Twentieth Centuries, 1800–1917*] (Gosizdat, Moscow, 1950).

[17] Tugan-Baranovsky, *op. cit.,* 1st ed., pp. 208–212.

weavers sold their goods. In addition to the cotton industry, the woolen cloth industry experienced rapid growth in the first half of the nineteenth century, and by 1850 there were about 500 woolen mills. All in all, the number of factories in Russia increased from 4200 in 1815 to 11,000 in 1857, while the number of workers employed in factories rose from 173,000 to 513,000.

In the era of Catherine and the early nineteenth century there were a great number of factories on the estates of the nobility. The peasants who worked in these factories rendered "factory barshchina," which was especially hard and hated. But in the nineteenth century the number of factories on estates continually decreased, and as early as the 1830s these constituted only 15 percent of all Russian factories, while the proportion was only 5 percent in the late 1840s. The factories that remained in the hands of the gentlemen-enterpreneurs were linked directly to agriculture, such as distilleries. The new class of factory owners was formed from the merchants and sometimes from former serfs who had grown rich and purchased their freedom. A striking example of this existed in Vladimir province, where a number of the serfs of Count Sheremetev became successful industrialists, employing over a thousand workers despite their own status as legally unfree people. Among them were the peasant families of Morozov and Zuev, who became the future magnates of the textile industry. Even during the era of serfdom, free, hired labor in factories was replacing serf labor. In 1804 out of 95,000 factory workers, hired laborers numbered 45,000 (48 percent) and in 1825, out of 210,000, hired labor accounted for 115,000 (54 percent). In the 1830s and 1840s the percent of hired factory labor continuously increased.

The development of industry in the Russian Empire proceeded under the invariable patronage of the state. Catherine's industrial legislation liberated industry from the wardship of the state, which Peter the Great had instituted, ended state and private monopolies, and declared freedom of commercial and industrial activity. The College of Manufactures that Peter had established was closed in 1780. In imposing customs duties, however, Catherine II and later Alexander I usually laid duties on imported foreign goods that might compete with the production of Russian industry. In this protectionist motives were mixed with fiscal objectives. The tariffs of 1816 and, especially, 1819 were of a liberal or free-trade character, but the tariff of 1822 returned to protectionism, and was in part prohibitive. This protective-prohibitive tariff remained in effect with some changes until the middle of the nineteenth century, and only the tariffs of 1850 and 1857 ended the protective system enforced by Kankrin, Nicholas' minister of finance.

In the reign of Nicholas the faint beginnings of factory legislation appeared in Russia. The first law "On the Relationships between the Management of Factory Enterprises and Working People, Engaged by Hire" was issued in 1835. In 1845 a code on punishments established the penalty for striking: seven days' to three weeks' arrest, and for the ringleaders three weeks to three months. A factory owner, for "wilfull" reduction in wages previously agreed upon, or for obliging a worker to accept payment in kind instead of money, had to pay a fine ranging from 100 to 300 rubles. In 1845 factory owners were forbidden to order workers under twelve to do night work and the tsar himself ordered factory owners to sign an affidavit to this effect. The local authorities were to see to the observance of the law, but they were obviously poorly prepared for this and the humanitarian law of 1845 soon passed into oblivion.

The development of domestic trade was retarded in the first half of the nineteenth century by inadequate means of communication as well as by the effects of serfdom. Consequently, local markets were isolated from one another and the price of bread varied greatly in different regions in the state, depending on the local harvest and other factors. The paucity of commercial credit and, except in a few cities, the inadequacy of the stores, led to the development of traveling peddlers. The peddlers carried their goods from village to village to sell them to the landowners and peasants, if the latter had hoarded a few kopeks of their own. For the conduct of wholesale trade and for the sale of heavy goods and horses, there were fairs throughout Russia, usually timed to coincide with some major holiday. In the nineteenth century the most important was the renowned "Makarev Fair," which moved from the small town of that name to Nizhni Novgorod in 1817–1818. At Nizhni the trading at the fair greatly expanded and many transactions were concluded there, relating not only to domestic commerce, but also to trade with the countries of the Asian East, from Persia to China. In 1824 sales valued at 40 million rubles were transacted at the Nizhni fair; in 1838 the sum had increased to 130 million.

The foreign trade of Russia grew considerably in the first half of the nineteenth century. The value of Russian exports, which had been about 75 million rubles at the beginning of the century, rose to 230 million on the eve of the serf reform of 1861, and the value of imports to Russia in this period rose from 52 million rubles to 200 million. The main Russian exports were grain, various products of agriculture and animal husbandry, and also timber and various raw materials. Grain, mainly wheat exported through Odessa, constituted 35 percent of Russian exports in the mid-nineteenth century, while all finished goods constituted about 3 percent of the value of Russian exports in 1851–1853. One particularly profitable Russian venture in overseas trade was the "Russian-American Company," which was founded at the end of the eighteenth century and in 1799 received special "privileges" for twenty years, a grant that was then renewed until the middle of the nineteenth century. The company received the exclusive right to the trapping, whaling, and fishing industries of the American mainland and on the Aleutian and Kurile islands. The company could erect trading posts in America ("with the consent of the inhabitants of these regions"), conduct trade "with Russian and foreign enterprises," and was supposed to appoint a "chief governor of the colony" and "elders" "to administer the natives of Alaska and the Aleutian and Kurile islands."

Transportation as a whole was poorly developed in pre-reform Russia. As of old, in summer one traveled on dirt roads and moved freight by water; in winter one traveled by sleigh on the snow or frozen rivers; in the spring and fall one just sat at home because it was possible neither to walk nor to ride through the thick, black mud, not to mention the flooded meadows, swamps, and ravines. The construction of paved roads began only in 1816, and the paved road between Petersburg and Moscow was completed only in 1830. In fact, paved roads did not get much attention in Russia even in the second half of the nineteenth century, for in 1896 there were only about 8000 miles in all. The first railroad, between Petersburg and Tsarskoe Selo, the royal estate not far from Petersburg, was built in 1838. Even so, the minister of finance Kankrin opposed the railroad, which in his opinion could only "instigate private journeys that are needless and thus increase the restless spirit of our age." In 1842, however, the government decided to undertake the construction of the Petersburg–Moscow (Nikolaevskaia) railroad, which was finished in 1851.

State Finance

Catherine's regime had quickly mastered one European invention: making money out of "nothing" or, more precisely, out of paper. The Bank of Assignation was established in 1768 with a circulation fund of 1 million rubles, which it issued as paper money. By 1774 the assignats in circulation had increased to 20 million rubles, and by the end of the Second Turkish War in 1791 it had increased to 150 million. Correspondingly, the value of the paper ruble fell to 50 metal kopeks (half a silver ruble) by the end of Catherine's reign.

At the beginning of Alexander's reign the over-all sum of domestic and foreign debts, together with the assignats in circulation, was about 408 million rubles. With the beginning of a period of prolonged war in 1805, disorganization of the finances of the state went still further. The budgets of 1805–1807 show a significant deficit. A new war in 1808 and 1809 and the imposition of the Napoleonic "continental system" brought continued economic and financial disorder. Renewed issuing of paper money was followed by a new decline in its value. By 1810, 577 million paper rubles had been issued; they fell to 25 percent of the value of a silver ruble.

In 1810–1811 Speransky took up the reform of state finance. His plan envisaged discontinuing the issuance of paper money, reducing expenses and enforcing better control over state expenditures, introducing new taxes and increasing the old ones, and the selling of some state properties. The annual "soul tax," which was 1 ruble per "soul" at the beginning of the century, was raised to 2 and 3 rubles. The obrok payments of state peasants significantly increased. Revenues from artisans and merchants were also increased and a tax was even imposed on the landowners' income, ranging from 1 to 10 percent and applying to estates with an annual income of over 500 rubles It was abolished in 1819, however. Along with the increase of the direct taxes, the price of state-produced salt was raised from 40 kopeks to 1 ruble per pud (36 pounds), a 150-percent increase. Speransky's efforts to put the state finances in order had only an extremely short-lived success. The renewed war with Napoleon in 1812–1815 required new expenditures and further issuing of paper money. The assignats in circulation rose from 581 million rubles in 1811 to 836 million in 1817.

Government finances continued in this sad state down to the 1820s. In 1823 Minister of Finance Kankrin again attempted to apply strict economy in expenditures and to accumulate some metallic reserves. He succeeded in balancing the budget and somewhat improved the value of the assignat, which stood at 26.5 percent of its face value in 1830 and about 33.5 percent in 1839. The government then decided to execute a monetary reform. A manifesto of July 1, 1839, stated that the Russian silver ruble "from this time forward constitutes the main currency of the realm," and the government assignats "remain a subsidiary medium of exchange with a set exchange rate of 1 silver ruble to 3.6 assignats" (that is, the assignat was fixed at 27.7 percent of face value). State bank notes, which were subject to exchange for silver, were issued after 1841 in place of assignats. Previously issued assignats (totalling 595 million rubles, or 170 million at the new exchange rate) bore a constant value in relation to the new banknotes. Kankrin's financial reform seemed successful. The banknotes, which were issued in moderate quantity, kept their value until the Crimean War (1853–1856), when their exchange with silver currency was stopped.

The main expense in the Russian state budget before the reform was the support of the army and navy, which ranged from 50 percent of the budget in 1801 to 42 percent in 1850. Payments on the state debt amounted to 10 to 15 percent of the budget. The "soul" tax and liquor revenues were the most important sources of revenue in pre-reform Russia. After some vacillation between an excise system and the farming out of the liquor monopoly, the latter system (*otkupa*) was established in 1827 and remained in force for more than three decades as one of the pillars of the state budget. Its social effects, however, were pernicious, for it was a permanent source of bribery and all kinds of unsavory profits.

As a whole, the socioeconomic situation of the Russian Empire in the first half of the nineteenth century is not one of unrelieved gloom, even though the institution of serfdom cast its shadow over the entire society. At least the spread of this institution had been halted and the government had associated itself with the principle of peasant reform, and although it was applied quite ineffectually with respect to the serfs, it was quite successful on behalf of the less numerous class of state peasants. This success may be taken as an indication that the bureaucracy, for all its incompetence, was capable of undertaking a major program of social reform when it enjoyed the kind of determined leadership exemplified by Kiselev, who may be considered the precursor of the reformers of the 1860s. Despite these hopeful indications, nevertheless, it is quite obvious that serfdom, which was supported by most of the privileged nobility class, remained the major obstacle to social and economic modernization in Russia at mid-century.

3

Culture and Society
in the First Half of the Nineteenth Century

The sudden end of the gloomy, harsh reign of Paul and the ascent to the throne of a young, humane, and liberal monarch caused a surge of ecstatic joy in Petersburg society. "In homes, in streets people wept for joy, embracing one another as on Easter day," writes the contemporary literateur Karamzin. Poets sang Alexander's praises in odes, and Petersburg ladies referred to him as "our angel."

The first acts of the young tsar, his friendly attitude toward his subjects and his entire conduct (he walked in the streets alone, without any guard) increased his popularity. Literature and journalism awakened from the lethargic state into which Paul had frightened them. These were the years of the birth of Russian journalism, which played such an important role in the course of the whole nineteenth century. In 1802 Karamzin began to edit *The Herald of Europe* (*Vestnik Evropy*), which soon became the most widely read journal. Other journals soon appeared in Petersburg—*The Northern Herald* (*Severnyi Vestnik*), *The Journal of Russian Literature* (*Zhurnal Rossiiskoi Slovestnosti*), *The St. Petersburg Herald* (*S.-Peterburgskii Vestnik*), *The Herald of Zion* (*Sionskii Vestnik,* the Masonic journal), and *The Northern Post* (*Severnaia Pochta,* the official government organ) — and similarly in Moscow — *The Russian Literary News* (*Novosti Russkoi Literatury*), *The Friend of Enlightenment* (*Drug Prosveshcheniia*), *The Moscow Courier* (*Moskovskii Kur'er*), and *The Scholarly Gazette* (*Uchenye Vedomosti,* published by Moscow University).

At the opening of the nineteenth century the government was the chief patron of science and literature. Great numbers of new books—on economical, political, philosophical subjects—were published in the first decade of the nineteenth century, often with government support. The vast majority of these books were expositions or translations of works published in the West in the second half of the eighteenth century, including the works of Montesquieu, Beccaria, Bentham, Kant, and Adam Smith. Karamzin undertook the composition of *The History of the Russian State (Istoriia Gosudarstva Rossiiskogo)*, and in 1803 he was awarded the title of "historiographer" and an annual pension of 2000 rubles. But an especially great advance was made in higher and secondary education in Russia in the first years of the nineteenth century.

Education

When the ministries were created in 1802 they included an entirely new department, the Ministry of Public Education, the Instruction of the Youth and the Dissemination of Knowledge. An old magnate of Catherine's time, Count Zavadovsky, was appointed minister, but the leading work in the organization of schools was really carried out by his deputy, the able M. N. Muraviev. Within the ministry educational affairs were supervised by the "Main Directorate of Schools," which included the six trustees of the educational districts; and the immediate preparation of the reform was conducted by the "Special Commission on Schools." Four kinds of institutions were established by law: (1) parochial schools in rural areas; (2) county schools in the county seats; (3) provincial gymnasiums (academic secondary schools); and (4) universities. Russia was divided into six educational districts with a trustee *(popechitel')* at the head of each. In each district there was to be a university, which was to direct the secondary and primary schools of its district. Accordingly three new universities, in Petersburg, Kharkov, and Kazan, were added to the previously existing ones in Moscow, Vilno (Polish-speaking), and Dorpat (German-speaking). The universities of Kharkov and Kazan were opened in 1804; a pedagogical institute was opened in Petersburg at the same time and converted into a university in 1819.

"University Statutes" were issued in 1804, along with the "Statute of the Educational Institutions Subordinate to the Universities," that is, the gymnasiums and county schools. The universities were divided into four faculties: (1) the moral and political

sciences; (2) the physical and mathematical sciences; (3) the medical sciences; and (4) the philological sciences, which included history.

According to the statutes a university council, composed of professors, made new academic appointments and elected the deans of the faculties, and the rector of the university. The election of the rector (the senior official) was subject to "imperial confirmation" and the election of the deans to confirmation by the minister of public education. The rector, the deans, and the "permanent assessor," who was appointed from among the professors, constituted the administration of the university. The university council and administration jointly exercised autonomous control over not only university affairs but also the activities of the other educational institutions of their district, including the appointment of their directors and teaching staffs. Also, the statutes of 1804 empowered the universities to censor books and other printed matter published in their district. Of course, the life of the newly established universities did not settle down at once. There was a shortage of both students and professors. Only Moscow University, which had been established in 1755, had many students: 215 in 1811; about 500 in 1820; and a little less than 900 in 1825. Initially the provincial universities of Kharkov and Kazan had only a few dozen students, and Kazan began full operations only in 1814. Because of the shortage of Russian professors, there was at first a major contingent of foreign scholars, invited from Germany and France, who lectured in German, French, and Latin.

The subjects to be taught in the gymnasium included: Latin, German, French, geography, history, statistics, "an introductory course in philosophy and esthetics," the elementary foundations of political economy, pure and applied mathematics, experimental physics and natural history, the foundations of commercial science, and technology and drawing. The program of studies in the gymnasium extended over four years. Preparatory to the gymnasium was the county school, with a two-year curriculum that included such subjects as religion, the "duties of man and citizen," Russian grammar (and a second, local language in some places), geography, history, arithmetic, geometry, physics, and drawing.

In 1808 there were 32 provincial gymnasiums and 126 county schools in Russia, and by the 1830s this network had expanded to about 50 gymnasiums and 400 county schools. In Alexander's reign a number of other educational institutions were opened, some on private initiative and with private funds: the Gymnasium of Higher Learning founded by Prince Bezborodko in Nezhin (1805); the Higher School of Jurisprudence (1805); the Demidov Lycee in

Yaroslavl (1805); the Tsarskoe Selo Lycee (1811); and the Rishelevsky Lycee in Odessa (1817). Generally speaking, higher and secondary education expanded significantly in the first half of Alexander's reign.

Higher education in Russia had not yet been firmly established when it encountered grave obstacles, for the reactionary turn in Alexander's foreign and domestic policies and his mystical inclination soon had a direct effect upon the universities. A manifesto of 1817 announced the establishment of the Ministry of Spiritual Affairs and Public Education, which was founded on the premise that "Christian piety has always been the basis of true enlightenment." The idea was not bad, but its execution was extremely unfortunate. One of Alexander's friends, Prince A. N. Golitsyn, was appointed to the new ministry, which was to direct simultaneously public education and "the affairs of all religious denominations." Golitsyn was mild and pious, but soft and weak-willed. His assistants, such as the infamous Magnitsky and Runich, were bigots, hypocrites, and careerists who undertook to propagate "Christian piety" by means of malicious persecution of any appearance of "atheism" or "free-thinking" in the universities. In 1819 Magnitsky was sent to inspect Kazan University and found it to be an abyss of falsehood and free-thinking. He proposed to the tsar that the university be abolished. Alexander did not agree with this severe proposal, but arrived at a rather unhappy solution to the problem. He entrusted Magnitsky himself with the "correction" of the university, naming him trustee of the Kazan educational district. Magnitsky discharged eleven professors, which was nearly half the academic staff, and replaced the elected director with his own appointee. He withdrew all books having "a harmful tendency" from the university library, and instituted a semimonastic, semipenal regime for the students. Runich was appointed trustee of the Petersburg educational district, where he discharged four professors from the university and indicted them in court. Their absurd trial on charges of having committed alleged or imaginary crimes dragged on for a long time, passing through all the necessary legal stages, and the case was dismissed only in the reign of Nicholas I. Kharkov University suffered less from the "new course," and Moscow University did not suffer at all.

In 1824 Prince Golitsyn's "mystical ministry" was dissolved, and the field of religious faith was again separated from general education, but this did not result in any easing of the condition of education or of literature. The aged Admiral Shishkov was appointed minister of public education, and this deeply convinced and stubborn reactionary systematically and persistently conducted a campaign against "free-thinking" in all of its manifestations. The censorship department was now in his hands, and his censors outdid themselves in their conservative zeal.

Soon after his accession to the throne, Nicholas dismissed Runich and Magnitsky, but Shishkov remained a minister until 1828, when he was replaced by Prince Liven; in 1833 Count S. S. Uvarov became minister of public education, a post that he occupied until 1849. Uvarov was the author, or at least the zealous missionary, of the well-known "trinity" of "official nationalism": "Orthodoxy, autocracy, and nationality." In Uvarov's opinion these constituted the primordial foundation of Russian life, "the true guarantee of the strength and greatness of our Fatherland," and they therefore should serve as the guiding principles of the education of Russian youth.

In 1835 a new "General Statute of the Imperial Russian University" was issued, and although it did not entirely abrogate the autonomy of the university councils, it substantially limited it. The regulations of the educational districts, which were issued shortly before the new university statutes, excluded the secondary schools from the competence of the university administration and transferred them to the trustees of the educational district. The universities, too, "are entrusted to the special supervision of the trustees"—and it might be noted that Nicholas sometimes appointed generals as trustees. After 1835, the universities were comprised of three faculties: philosophy, law, and medicine, the philosophical faculty including humanistic and mathematical sections. In 1850 separate "historical-philological" and "physical-mathematical" faculties were established. Courses in theology, church history, and church law were made mandatory for all Orthodox students. The trustee appointed inspectors to supervise the conduct and achievement of the students.

The reign of Nicholas I was also marked by the closing of the Polish University of Vilno in 1832, along with other repressions following the Polish Revolution, and the establishment of the University of St. Vladimir in Kiev in 1833. In 1828 an Institute of Technology was established in Petersburg, and the Institutes of Forestry and Mining were reorganized.

It must be acknowledged that in the 1830s and 1840s (before the European revolutions of 1848) the "guardianship" of Uvarov's administration was not entirely without good intentions and did not suppress the fruitful research and teaching of the professors. Under Uvarov, young scholars who were preparing to become professors were sent to the old German University of Dorpat, in the Russian Empire, or to foreign universities. This practice assisted the development of

Russian scholarship, and from the ranks of the aspiring professors who were sent abroad a whole series of outstanding scholars and university teachers emerged. In Russian universities the '30s and '40s were the time of the fundamental development of the scholarly and social tradition that strove to combine independent scientific research with the propagation of humanistic ideals. In that era the professors in the university lecture halls were, in Herzen's words, "not secular scholars, but missionaries of a humanistic religion." Thus, in the desert of Nicholas' reign the universities were oases of culture that not only advanced scholarship, but also awakened social thought and moral consciousness. Moscow University played a leading part in this development.

Alexander Herzen, who attended Moscow University in the 1830s, testifies:

> The Moscow University grew in importance together with the city itself after 1812. From that time on, a new epoch began for the city. The University became more and more the center of Russian culture [and] . . . grew in influence; the youthful strength of Russia streamed to it from all sides, from all classes of society [except serfs], as into a common reservoir; in its halls they were purified from the superstitions they had picked up at the domestic hearth, reached a common level, became like brothers and dispersed again to all parts of Russia and among all classes of its people.[1]

Among the professors in Moscow, the most popular and influential among the youth was the famous "professor-humanist" T. N. Granovsky, who lectured on universal history. He was the teacher who influenced a whole generation of educated Russian society, including the Westerner Herzen and the Slavophile Constantine Aksakov.

The revolutionary events in Europe in 1848–1849 frightened Nicholas' regime and inspired him to turn special attention to the Russian universities and to adopt special measures to crush their free spirit. Even Count Uvarov seemed too liberal in this era and was replaced as minister of public education by a dark reactionary, Prince Shirinsky-Shikhmatov. In several educational districts the governor general was entrusted with the administration and, consequently, with the control of the university of the district. Elected rectors were replaced with appointed ones. Certain "suspect" subjects, such as the public law of foreign states and philosophy, were excluded from uni-

---

[1] The English translation used here for Herzen, *My Past and Thoughts*, is by Constance Garnett (London, 1924), vol. I, pp. 118–120.

versity instruction. Except in medicine, the number of students whose tuition was not paid by the state was limited to 300 on the theory that students who were financially dependent on the state were more likely to be reliable. Finally, the members of each university administration were directed to keep constant, strict watch over the teaching in their institution. According to a directive of January 23, 1851, the rector and deans were to attend the lectures of the professors every day and compare the actual lecture with the previously approved program, from which no departures were permitted. The restrictions that were introduced into the universities in 1849–1851 were removed only when Alexander II became tsar in 1855.

In 1828 a new statute for the gymnasiums was issued. The gymnasiums were to consist of seven grades, of which the lowest three corresponded to the county schools in curriculum. Religion and church history, Russian literature, and logic were included in the program. In 1831 it was forbidden to send Russian youths under eighteen abroad for their education, to prevent "the harmful consequences" of "alien education."

Secret Societies

The onslaught of Napoleon, reducing "Mother Moscow" to ashes and ending in the flight and destruction of the Grand Army produced a popular patriotic movement. The subsequent war for the liberation of Europe, bringing the Russian army into Paris, aroused "the sense of one's own worth and of heightened love for the Motherland" among the participants in the great struggle, in the words of M. A. Fonvizin, an author of memoirs from the period. On the other hand, the protracted sojourn abroad acquainted intellectual circles among the Russian officers with many of the more liberal ideological trends, social practices, and political institutions of various European countries, giving rise to (or reinforcing) their "free-thinking" and liberal inclinations. In 1816, for example, Colonel Baron Dibich, in a secret report to Field Marshal Barclay de Tolly, wrote: "Officers of the Prussian royal guard are openly saying that no king is needed, that the present situation of world-wide enlightenment requires a republic. It is said that a similar spirit is spreading through our army . . . and that even the officers of your excellency's suite use such expressions."[2]

---

[2] V. I. Semevsky, *Politicheskiia i obshchestvennyia idei dekabristov* [*The Political and Social Ideas of the Decembrists*] (St. Petersburg, 1909), p. 378.

On their return to Russia the officers of the victorious Russian army found the regime of Arakcheev, the slavery of serfdom, the denial of political rights, police oppression, "the universal reign of arbitrariness," Fonvizin called it. After the events of 1820–1821 when the reign of Arakcheev was wholly triumphant in domestic politics and the reign of Metternich was established in international affairs, the sentiments of love and loyalty that liberal officers had formerly felt for Alexander changed at first to disappointment and then to outright hatred or bitterness. After the failure of the uprising of 1825, a participant, P. G. Kakhovsky, wrote to Nicholas I from his prison cell: "The Emperor Alexander brought many of us to this disaster, and he is the real cause of the revolution of December 14. Did he not fan the flame of liberty in our hearts, and did he not afterwards smother it not only in the Fatherland but in all Europe?"[3]

As Kakhovsky indicates, it was not only the domestic policy of Alexander I that caused dissatisfaction among the liberal and patriotic circles of Russian society in the last years of his reign. They accused Alexander of showing partiality to foreigners rather than Russians, whom he scorned and humiliated. Patriotic feelings were outraged that the government granted constitutional institutions to Poland and Finland, which had been annexed to Russia, while the conquering nation itself was considered unworthy of political freedom. In the politics of Europe as a whole, Alexander in 1820–1821 came to complete agreement with the Austrian conservative Metternich, agreeing that all revolutionary or liberalizing movements should be suppressed. In 1821 when the Greek uprising against Ottoman domination began, all of the liberal elements in Europe and Russia sympathized warmly with the heroic struggle of the Greeks for independence. But Alexander, inspired by Metternich, firmly refused any kind of aid to the Greek "rebels," alienated himself from all the liberal groups in Russian society, and strengthened the revolutionary tendencies that Spanish and Italian uprisings in 1820–1821 inspired among Russian officers.

The individuals who headed the secret societies and who later became leaders of the December uprising of 1825 represented the intellectual flower of contemporary Russian society. A considerable portion of them belonged to the high aristocracy and had the

---

[3] *Izbrannye sotsial'no-politicheskie i filosofskie proizvedeniia dekabristov* [Selected Sociopolitical and Philosophical Works of the Decembrists] (Gosizdat, Moscow, 1951), vol. I, p. 511.

prospect of a brilliant career in the service. There were no old men among the participants in the movement, but not all of them were very young. Some were persons of middle age who had already achieved the rank of general or colonel. The Decembrists included writers and poets as well: K. Ryleev, Prince Odoevsky, Alexander Bestuzhev-Marlinsky, and William Kiukhel'beker. Others such as Nicholas Turgenev, Baron V. I. Shteingel', P. I. Pestel, and G. S. Batenkov wrote on these matters as scholars and publicists and later produced a series of valuable "notes" and memoirs.

Liberal attitudes and opposition to the regime of Alexander and Arakcheev was not a monopoly of the future Decembrists, however. In the early 1820s this inclination was characteristic of wide circles of the Russian public, and especially officers, or at least those in Petersburg and Moscow. Batenkov, for example, writes of the mood of the capital when he returned there in 1821 after several years of service in Siberia: "At this time Petersburg was no longer the same city that I had departed from five years before. As soon as a few young people would gather one encountered conversations about the government, indignant towards it, pungent, sarcastic."[4] In society, especially among the youth, the freedom-loving poems of Pushkin— "To Chaadaev," "Folk Tales" *(Skazki),* "Freedom" *(Vol'nost'),* "The Dagger" *(Kinzhal)* , and the epigrams on Arakcheev and Alexander— were well known even though they could not be published under the conditions of censorship but were disseminated in manuscript and learned by heart.

Two types of nationalist organizations devoted to liberation existed in Europe at the beginning of the nineteenth century: one was represented by the German patriotic society the *Tugendbund,* founded in 1808, which set itself the objective of achieving the national, moral, and cultural elevation of the German people as the prerequisite of its future liberation from Napoleon's domination; and the other was the conspiratorial political organization (such as the Italian *Carbonari* or Greek *Heteria)* , which set itself the immediate aim of national revolution and the introduction of a liberal constitution. Both types found their reflection in the circles of the future Russian Decembrists.

The secret political societies of Russia first appeared shortly after the end of the Napoleonic wars. In 1816–1817 a group of guards officers founded a society called "The Union of Salvation," or "The

---

[4] M. V. Dovnar-Zapolsky, ed., *Memuary dekabristov [Memoirs of the Decembrists]* (Kiev, 1906), p. 161; *Izbrannye . . . proizvedeniia dekabristov,* vol. I, p. 175.

True and Faithful Sons of the Fatherland." On the testimony of its members, the basic goals of the Union were the introduction into Russia of representative government and the liberation of the peasants from the bondage of serfdom. Admission to membership in the Union was arrayed with complicated ceremonies, formalities, and vows, in the spirit of the contemporary Masonic bodies. Members of the Union were separated into three grades: "brothers," "men," and "boyars." Only "boyars" and "men" knew all the secret aims and plans of the union. It was decided to adopt the statutes of the German *Tugend-bund,* adapted to Russian conditions, as the basis of the movement. But the life of the first Union was not long, for disagreements and demands for amendment of the statutes soon arose within the membership.

Organized anew in 1818, the Union was named "The Union of Welfare."[5] The activities of the members of this association, according to its statutes, were to be comprised of "the four following, main categories: (1) philanthropy, (2) education, (3) justice, (4) socially useful economic activity." In education, the members of the Union were to combat "absurd devotion to foreign things," and to develop in their pupils an interest in the love of the fatherland. Also, they were "to strive to propagate literacy among the common folk." They were to combat the arbitrary authority of bureaucrats and landlords and "to strive to incline the landlords to good treatment of the peasants, promoting the idea that those in bondage are also human." In ruling their own peasants, members of the Union were to be "good-hearted and philanthropic." The second part of these statutes, which was known only to the founders of the Union and whose wording has not come down to us, established the goal of introducing representative government into Russia.

In 1818–1819 the Union grew rapidly in Petersburg, numbering as many as 200 members there, in Moscow, and in the garrison town of Tul'chin, where the southern "council" was organized by Colonel P. I. Pestel. In the south the Union included, among others, Major General Prince S. G. Volkonsky and the commander of the sixteenth infantry division, Major General M. F. Orlov. Enlightenment and "philanthropic" activities, however, could not satisfy all the members of the Union, and some of the leading members, headed by Pestel, proposed that the question of the political reform of Russia

---

[5] The statutes of the Union of Welfare can be found in Pypin, *op. cit.,* pp. 547–576.

should be placed on the agenda at once and not in the undefined, distant future.

The Union passed through a serious crisis in 1820. Part of the membership resigned, seeing no real results of their activities or real prospects in the future. There was no agreement among the leading members of the Union on political tactics and on the future political order. Moreover, it became known that the government had learned of the existence of the Union and that it was following its activities. The fact of the matter was that the chief of staff of the guards regiments, Dibich, in 1821 submitted a detailed report on the secret society to the high command, including a long list of its participants. Dibich's report was forwarded to Alexander, but the tsar pigeonholed it and took no action on the matter.

In January 1821, a congress of the delegates from the Union in Petersburg, Moscow, and Tul'chin was convened in Moscow and adopted a resolution on the dissolution of the Union. But, according to the historian Semevsky, "the destruction of the society was accomplished only for appearances, to mislead the watchfulness of the government and to dispense with unreliable members." [6] Following this formal closing of the Union of Welfare, secret societies that were from the start directly political and revolutionary were formed. The majority of the members of the Tul'chin council, headed by Pestel, did not recognize the Moscow resolution on the dissolution of the Union, and decided to continue to exist as an independent "Southern Society." A "directory" of two headed the society, Pestel and Iushnevsky, the intendant general of the Second Army. In 1825 a lieutenant colonel of the Chernigov Regiment, Sergei Muraviev-Apostol, was added to the directory. The Tul'chin council was under the direct supervision of the directory. In addition, there were "councils" in Kamenka led by General Prince S. G. Volkonsky and a local landlord, the retired Colonel Vasily Davidov, and in Vasil'kov, led by S. Muraviev-Apostol and M. P. Bestuzhev-Riumin.

In 1822 a secret organization, called the Northern Society, was also formed in Petersburg. The elected "ruler" of the society was a guards captain, Nikita Muraviev, who was more concerned with preparing the future constitution of the Russian state than with any revolutionary activities. In 1823 the Northern Society took on a more definite form of organization. Its founders formed a "supreme duma,"

---

[6] *Obshchestvennye dvizheniia v Rossii v pervuiu polovinu XIX veka* [*The Movement of Public Opinion in Russia in the First Half of the Nineteenth Century*] (St. Petersburg, 1905), vol. I (The Decembrists), p. 33.

which was to elect the leadership, or "directory" of three members: N. Muraviev, Colonel Prince S. Trubetskoi, and Lieutenant Prince E. Obolensky. When Obolensky left in 1824, the romantic poet Ryleev was elected to the directory and soon became the very soul of the Northern Society.

Independent of Pestel's Southern Society, the officers of certain military units stationed in the southern regions formed another secret society in 1823, "The Society of United Slavs." In contrast to the stylish and high-ranking officers who headed the Northern and Southern societies, the Society of United Slavs consisted of young and impecunious officers of undistinguished social background who were assigned to provincial army units. The heads of the organization were three second lieutenants, the brothers Peter and Andrei Borisov, and Ivan Gorbachevsky. In his "notes" Gorbachevsky formulated the program of the society as follows:

> The Society had as its chief objective the liberation from despotism of all of the Slavic tribes, the annihilation of the national hatred that now exists among some of them and the unification of all the lands inhabited by them into a federal union. It proposes to define precisely the boundaries of each state, to introduce a form of democratic representative government for all peoples, and to convene a congress to direct the affairs of the union as a whole and to amend the general, basic laws if need be, letting each state deal with the question of its domestic order, having independence in legislation affecting only itself.[7]

In September 1825, when the troops were stationed in the camp at Leshchinsky (in the Ukraine), an impassioned speech by Bestuzhev-Riumin induced the members of the Society of United Slavs to merge with the Southern Society and to elect representatives to maintain constant ties between the two groups.

As for the plans of the secret societies concerning the future political and social order of Russia, the most specific programs were proposed by Muraviev[8] and Pestel. The opening articles

---

[7] *Izbrannye . . . proizvedeniia dekabristov,* vol. III, p. 22; *Zapiski i pis'ma dekabrista I. I. Gorbachevskogo [The Memoirs and Letters of the Decembrist I. I. Gorbachevsky]* (2d ed.; Moscow, 1925), p. 57.

[8] On Muraviev's constitutional plan, see N. Druzhinin, *Konstitutsiia Nikity Murav'eva* in *Dekabristy i ikh vremia [The Decembrists and Their Era]* (Moscow, 1927), pp. 62–108. For the texts of his constitutional plans, see *Izbrannye . . . proizvedeniia dekabristov,* vol. I, pp. 295–329; Dovnar-Zapolsky, ed., *op. cit.,* pp. 58–71; Semevsky, *op. cit.,* pp. 447–472; Iu. G. Oksman, ed., *Dekabristy [The De-*

of Muraviev's "Constitution" declared that "the people are the source of the supreme authority," and that "the Russian people, free and independent, can belong neither to a person nor a dynasty." The Russian Emperor is only "the supreme civil servant" of the state, whose authority is subject to strict constitutional limitation. Except for the existence of this hereditary executive, Muraviev's plan closely followed the American Constitution, some articles of which he simply translated into Russian. The form of the empire was to be federal, with thirteen states (*derzhavy*) and two regions (*oblasti*). The states were to send three representatives each to the upper house, the "Supreme Duma," of a bicameral legislature called the "Popular Assembly" (*Narodnoe Veche*). The second house was to be the "Chamber of Representatives," consisting of 450 elected deputies. The bicameral principle was also to be found within the states of the federation, along with an elected governor. All citizens were to enjoy equal civil liberties, including personal inviolability, choice of occupation, the right of association, freedom of religion, freedom of the press, the right to petition, and the right of private property, consisting of things but not persons. However, the right to participate in elections was to be restricted; well-to-do property-owners cast direct and equal ballots, while peasants in communes could elect a plenipotentiary to vote on their behalf on the ratio of one plentipotentiary for each 500 male peasants. According to Muraviev's constitution, all judges and civil servants were to be elected.

Although it was never adopted or approved by all of the members, Muraviev's constitution was the political program of the majority in the Northern Society. It encountered objections from various points of view. Pestel, the leader of the Southern Society, expressed especially vigorous criticism of it, with which many members of the Northern Society were inclined to agree. In his testimony Pestel stated: "Many members of the society did not like Muraviev's constitution because of its federal system and the terrible aristocracy of wealth that it creates."[9] A third basic disagreement with Muraviev's constitution, which was maintained by the "southerners" and some "northerners," was with his hereditary monarchy, even though greatly

---

cembrists] (Moscow, 1926), pp. 235–249; and V. E. Iakushkin, *Gosudarstvennaia vlast' i proekty gosudarstvennoi reformy v Rossi* [*The State Power and Plans for Constitutional Reform in Russia*] (St. Petersburg, 1906), pp. 131–161.

[9] *Vosstanie dekabristov: Materialy* [*The Decembrist Uprising: Documents*] (Gosizdat, Moscow, 1927), vol. IV, p. 114; *Izbrannye . . . proizvedeniia dekabristov*, vol. II, p. 181.

limited in authority, for these critics proposed a republican system.

Pestel's political and social program was stated in his famous tract, "The Russian Law"[10] (*Russkaia Pravda,* the name of the code of laws of Kievan *Rus',* to which Pestel alluded to add the sanction of antiquity). This plan for a reformed Russia eschewed federalism and hierarchy in favor of Jacobin centralism and democracy. Pestel visualized the quick overthrow of the old regime and its replacement by a "provisional government" that would exercise dictatorial powers for as much as ten years while the complete reconstruction of the government was in progress. The new state was to be completely uniform in structure and even in national culture, for the Russian language alone was to prevail in the empire. Poland might be excepted from this, providing that an independent Polish state became an ally of Russia, adopting the Russian system of government.

Pestel's radical, egalitarian social program included the rapid abolition of serfdom, for "the possession of other humans as one's property is a shameful matter, contrary to humanity, contrary to natural law, contrary to the Christian faith." Along with the emancipation of the serfs, Pestel proposed an agrarian reform, which attempted to strike a compromise between the egalitarian principle that "the land is the general property of the entire human race," and recognition that private landownership is conducive to agricultural prosperity. Thus, half the land was to belong to private householders and half to village communes.

Although he recognized the right of property as "sacred and inviolable," Pestel opposed the establishment of special political advantages for the rich on the grounds that this would replace a feudal aristocracy with an aristocracy of wealth without improving the condition of the masses. Therefore, "all Russian citizens should exercise equally all individual rights, civil and political," and in particular the franchise. But while he professed that "personal" liberty was the first and most "important right of all citizens," Pestel's Jacobin, centralist principles led him to restrict the substance of individual rights. For example, the education of the youth was to be exclusively in the hands of the state. Moreover, "any private society, established with a permanent [political] aim, must be entirely forbidden, whether the society is overt, which is useless, or secret, which is harmful."

---

[10] The text of Pestel's "Russian Law" can be found in Pestel, *op. cit.* See also *Vosstanie dekabristov: Dokumenty,* vol. VII: *Russkaia Pravda P. I. Pestelia* (Gosizdat, Moscow, 1958); *Izbrannye . . . proizvedeniia dekabristov,* vol. II, pp. 73–162; and Semevsky, *op. cit.,* pp. 500–554.

The political order proposed by Pestel[11] was based on directly elected assemblies on the township, county, and provincial levels, headed by a national "Popular Assembly" (*Narodnoe Veche*) elected by the provincial assemblies. The executive was to be a directorate of five, called the "State Duma" (*Derzhavnaia Duma*), elected for five years by the Popular Assembly from among candidates proposed by the provincial assemblies. The activities of the legislative and executive branches were to be watched by an independent "Supreme Council" (*Verkhovnyi Sobor*) of 120 elected, lifetime "boyars."

In addition to Muraviev's and Pestel's programs, the societies considered many other plans for a future state, but there were no other definite, accepted political programs. Pestel testified to this in his deposition after his arrest: "Very often that which was decided today, would again become the subject of discussion and conflict tomorrow."[12] Generally speaking, one may say that the Southern Society adopted a republican program, while the Northern Society adhered to a constitutional monarchy, but individual members of one or another society often vacillated between a republic and a monarchy. There was still less agreement on the question of tactics. Many members spoke of ways and means of achieving the designated goals, but no society had a definite plan of action.

The question of regicide inspired the greatest controversy. In the Southern Society, Pestel and the majority inclined to the necessity of regicide, while the northerners for the most part disagreed. Concerning the prospects for revolution, Pestel wrote that in the Southern Society "everyone said that the revolution could not begin in the lifetime of the Emperor Alexander Pavlovich, and that it was necessary to await his death or to hasten it." Members of the Southern Society proposed "to hasten" the death of Alexander I during contemplated summer maneuvers in 1826, after which the southern army was to move on Moscow "to proclaim the constitution."

---

[11] Pestel's "Russian Law" remained unfinished and did not include his plan for the political structure of the future Russian republic. He wrote a short outline for a future Russian constitution "Konstitutsiia: Gosudarstvennyi zavet" ["The Constitution: A Testament for the State"], which is quoted in M. V. Dovnar-Zapolsky, *Idealy dekabristov* [*The Ideals of the Decembrists*] (Moscow, 1907), pp. 358–365. See also Semevsky, *op. cit.*, pp. 543–546; *Krasnyi Arkhiv,* 1925, vol. 6 (13), pp. 281–284; and *Izbrannye . . . proizvedeniia dekabristov,* vol. II, pp. 159–162.

[12] *Vosstanie dekabristov: Materialy,* vol. IV, p. 102. This volume includes the complete text of Pestel's testimony before the investigation committee.

According to a substantial majority of the Decembrists, the future revolution was to be strictly military, without any participation of the masses of the people. Most of the officers among the Decembrists opposed revolutionary agitation among the masses of the soldiers. The members of the secret societies hoped that through fairness and humanity they could gain the love and confidence of the soldiers to such a degree that at the vital moment the soldiers would follow their commanders wherever they led them. Only the "Slavs," who were more radical and decisive revolutionaries, believed in the necessity of the participation of the whole populace in the revolution, and they therefore attempted to conduct revolutionary agitation among the soldiers.

The Uprising of December 14, 1825

On November 27, 1825, a courier arrived in Petersburg with the news of the death of Emperor Alexander I in remote Taganrog. The brother of the deceased tsar, Nicholas Pavlovich, did not consider it possible to make use of Alexander's secret manifesto of August 16, 1823, which transferred the throne to him passing over Crown Prince Constantine. He ordered that the troops, governmental institutions, and populace of the capital swear allegiance to the new emperor, Constantine Pavlovich, and he sent a courier to Warsaw, where the new emperor was residing as military commander, to report all the proceedings to him. Constantine affirmed his renunciation of the throne in a letter to his brother, but Nicholas was at first dissatisfied with a personal letter. The correspondence between Petersburg and Warsaw continued, and in the capital a tense and troubled situation of interregnum developed. On the morning of December 12 the government received an urgent report from General Dibich in Taganrog. He had gone through the papers of the late tsar and found the detailed reports of the existence of a widespread revolutionary conspiracy in the army, together with the names of the conspirators. On the same day, Nicholas received from Constantine a reaffirmation of his renunciation; Nicholas finally decided to act. A manifesto of his accession to the throne was prepared and December 14 was designated as the day for a new oath of allegiance—this time to Emperor Nicholas—in Petersburg.

Nicholas passed the twelfth and thirteenth in great fear. He wrote to Prince P. M. Volkonsky, "I must fulfill God's will and my brother's verdict. On the fourteenth I shall be the Sovereign or dead. . . ."[13] He was not sure of the loyalty of the guards regiments and summoned their commanders, trying in every possible way to coax and attract them to his side, thus preparing the Petersburg regiments to accept the new oath.

Alexander's death came as a surprise to the members of the Northern Society, and its Supreme Duma did not have any concrete plan of revolutionary activity. The unexpected interregnum opened unforeseen possibilities for the success of a political *coup*. Following a prolonged conference on the eve of the fourteenth, the conspirators outlined the following plan of action: after inducing the guards regiments not to take the oath to Nicholas, whom the guards regiments disliked because of his cruel, fault-finding attitude toward his subordinates, they would demand that the Senate appoint a "provisional government." According to Fonvizin, "The first action of the provisional government would be to convoke representatives of Russia from all social classes who would settle its [Russia's] future fate and form of government."[14] A draft of the manifesto that was to be issued in the name of the Senate was prepared. It proclaimed the abolition of serfdom and the military settlements; "the equality of all classes before the law"; free choice of one's occupation; freedom of the press; "free exercise of worship for all creeds"; the reduction of the term of service for soldiers to fifteen years; trial by jury; and "the establishment of township, county, provincial, and regional governing bodies with elected members, who should substitute elected members for all previously appointed bureaucrats."[15] To lead the uprising, which was set for December 14, Prince S. P. Trubetskoi, a colonel of the guards, was elected as "dictator."

For his part, Nicholas took all possible measures to insure the legality of his accession to the throne. Along with the manifesto proclaiming his accession he published the manifesto of August 16, 1823, in which Alexander I passed over Crown Prince Constantine in favor of Nicholas, and also the letters in which Constantine affirmed his renunciation of the crown.

The Council of State, the Senate, and the majority of the guards regiments took the oath to Nicholas early on the morning of

---

[13] N. K. Schilder, *Imperator Nikolai I* [*The Emperor Nicholas I*] (St. Petersburg, 1903), vol. I. pp. 251–252.

[14] *Obshchestvennye dvizheniia v Rossii* . . . , vol. I, p. 193.

[15] M. I. Mebel, ed., *Dekabristy: Materialy i dokumenty* [*The Decembrists: Materials and Documents*] ([Kharkov], 1926), pp. 123–125; *Vosstanie dekabristov* . . . , vol. I, pp. 107–108; and *Izbrannye . . . proizvedeniia dekabristov*, vol. I, pp. 363–364.

the fourteenth, despite indecision and delay in some regiments. But in certain units the conspiring officers succeeded in having the oath declined, convincing their soldiers that Constantine had not actually renounced the throne and that the oath to Nicholas was illegal. Some rebellious companies of the Moscow Bodyguards Regiment (about 700 men) arrived on the Senate Square, and in the next few hours they were joined by the Bodyguards Grenadiers (about 1100 men) and then the sailors of the Guards Naval Depot (about 1000 men). The rebels deployed into two squares and soon they were surrounded by a thick crowd of ordinary citizens who expressed their sympathy with the rebels and joined them in awaiting further developments. At the same time the new emperor gathered the troops that had sworn their loyalty to him and surrounded the rebels with his forces, which were many times stronger. Both sides maintained an attitude of passive waiting for some time. The dictator-designate, Trubetskoi, realizing that the great majority of the guards regiments had taken the oath to Nicholas, lost all hope of success and did not appear in the Senate Square. This soon led to confusion and embarrassment in the ranks of the rebels who did not know what they were to do next.

For his part, Nicholas was not sure of the loyalty of his troops and their readiness to fire on their comrades, and for a long time he postponed the decision to take military action against the rebels. One after another, he sent his generals and then Grand Duke Michael Pavlovich and Metropolitan Serafim with the clergy to exhort the rebels to submit. All admonitions failed, and when the military governor of Petersburg, General Miloradovich, one of the heroes of 1812, approached the square of rebels he was shot and killed by one of the conspirators. In view of the failure of the negotiations Nicholas ordered the Horse Guards to attack the rebels. The cavalry mounted the attack sluggishly and unwillingly and were easily repulsed. Twilight approached, and it appeared that there was a danger that the strength of the rebels might be increased by the defection to them of soldiers from the regiments that had taken the oath to Nicholas. At last Nicholas ordered the artillery to advance and open fire with canister shot upon the rebels, who quickly dispersed with great losses.

Toward the end of December the government conducted arrests among the members of the Southern Society, including Muraviev-Apostol, one of the "directors" of the Southern Society. The conspiring officers who remained at liberty released him from arrest, and then under his command, they aroused a revolt in the Chernigov Regiment, about 1000 men and 10 officers joining the uprising. On December 31 the rebels occupied Vasil'kov, and after hearing a public prayer on the square, they moved toward Belaia Tserkov. They proclaimed that "the Russian host is about to establish a peoples' government," hoping that other military units that were scattered in the various cities and towns in the southern area would join them. But on January 3, 1826, Muraviev's force met a government force of hussars with mounted artillery, which dispersed the rebels with canister shot.

Nicholas established a special investigation commission to probe the activities and intentions of "the evil-minded societies." He participated personally in its work, extracting the most revealing and detailed testimony from the arrested members, now by threats and shackles, now by cajolery and promises of mercy. The number of arrested persons, mainly officers, expanded to 600 according to some reports and to considerably more according to other evidence. As the result of almost six months of labor the commission found it necessary to bring 121 members of three secret societies to trial (61 members of the Northern Society, 37 from the Southern, and 23 members of the Union of United Slavs). On June 1 a decree established a "supreme criminal court," which on July 9 reported its verdict to the tsar, based only on the report of the investigating commission without ever seeing the accused. Only a few of them could be charged with "personal activity in the rebellion," while others were charged only with "knowledge of the preparation of a rebellion." An especially large number suffered for "plotting regicide," for "agreeing to participate in the plot" or even merely for "knowledge of the plot."

The court sentenced to death 36 out of the 121 tried. After the emperor had confirmed the verdict, considerably softening the punishment ordered by the court, it took the following form: 5 persons were sentenced to death by hanging; 88 were sentenced to hard labor (from an indefinite term down to only two years); 14 were sentenced to settlement in Siberian exile; and 13 were sentenced to demotion to private. On July 13 the five death sentences were executed (Pestel, Ryleev, Kakhovsky, Muraviev-Apostol, and Bestuzhev-Riumin), and soon after the dispatch of small parties condemned to forced labor or exile in Siberia began. Contemporary witnesses testify to the shocking and depressing impression that the executions made on Russian society, which had grown unaccustomed to capital punishment in the preceding reign. Even Vigel', who was far from sympathizing with the revolution and the revolutionaries, writes: "On that day [July 13] the inhabitants of Petersburg were filled with terror and grief,"[16] and Koshelev writes that "it is impossible to describe the terror and dejection that possessed everyone. It was as if each person had lost his father or brother."[17]

The exiled Decembrists were warmly received by the local population in Siberia. The initial party was put to hard labor in the mines of Nerchinsk, but later all the convicts were brought together in the compound at Chita, under the tolerant and humane commander General Leparsky. Nine of them were joined there voluntarily by their wives, through whom they maintained contact with the outside world, received correspondence, Russian and foreign journals, and books. They built up an excellent library and were able to study and write. By 1839 the last of the convicts had their sentences commuted to settlement in Siberia, and some were permitted to return to Russia.

The Decembrist movement, which aimed at the abolition of serfdom, the equality of civil rights, and the replacement of the autocracy with a free representative government, was too weak, politically and militarily, to attain these goals. It was organized and led by a relatively small group of enlightened liberal aristocrats and young radical army officers, but their plans were alien to the mass of the serf-owning nobility and unknown to the mass of the peasantry, while the groups of the intelligentsia and bourgeoisie in Russia at that time were too small to be significant.

But the Decembrist movement, while failing to achieve its immediate social and political objectives, played a key role in the political and ideological development of the Russian intelligentsia in the decades to come. The radical politicians and thinkers, headed by Herzen, glorified the Decembrists as the apostles and martyrs of Russian freedom and tried, in their own way, to follow in their steps. The government under Alexander II, having granted full amnesty to all Decembrists who survived Siberian exile, partially realized the Decembrist program during the "period of the Great Reforms."

The Intelligentsia

At the end of the eighteenth century the dominant cultural influence in Russia was, of course, French—the French language, French literature, French theater, French styles. In this era Gallomania, "Voltairism," cosmopolitanism, and religious indifferentism reigned among the Russian aristocracy and the intellectuals of mixed social

---

[16] Vigel', *op. cit.*, vol. VII, p. 50.
[17] Koshelev, *op. cit.*, p. 18.

background. Even the future nationalist and conservative Karamzin wrote in his "Letters of a Russian Traveler" (1791–1792) that "the path of enlightenment is the same for all peoples," that "all the nations are as nothing before humanity," and that "the main thing is to become human beings, not Slavs."

The Masonic movement played a major role in the life of the Russian intelligentsia at the end of the eighteenth century. This was not a uniform movement ideologically, socially, or politically, for the title "Mason" often designated widely varying organizations and tendencies. In the latter part of the eighteenth century the ideological center of Russian Masonry was the circle of the litterateurs and publishers Novikov and Schwartz. It was influenced by the German "Rosicrucians" and set moral self-improvement as its basic goal. This tendency opposed the rationalism and materialism of the French Enlightenment, while other Masonic lodges in Russia embraced the ideology of the Enlightenment. In the reign of Alexander I many Masonic lodges were formed in Russia, mainly in Moscow and Petersburg. These lodges included a number of schools and systems, and their membership was both extensive and variegated, including both the highest dignitaries of the empire and the future Decembrists. On the question of religion, one found among the Masons mystics, pietists, and people who were indifferent to any kind of religion. While the characteristic Masonic morality of brotherly love and good works might dominate one lodge, political tendencies of liberalism or even radicalism might manifest themselves in another. In 1822, during the reign of Arakcheev and the beginning of the reactionary movement of the Orthodox Church, the order was issued to close all Masonic lodges and to have all civil servants sign a statement "that they do not belong to such a [Masonic] lodge or secret society and will not belong to one henceforth."

At the beginning of the nineteenth century a nationalist and conservative reaction against the dominant French influence arose in some parts of Russian society. This was reinforced by the political circumstances of the time, the opening of the struggle against Napoleonic France. In 1802 Karamzin wrote a "discourse" "on loving the fatherland and on national pride," in which he appealed to the Russian public for national distinctiveness and national consciousness. Attempting to arouse patriotism among educated Russians, he denounced "slavish imitation" of everything foreign. "It is good and necessary to study," wrote Karamzin, "but woe to the man or nation that must always be the pupil." "We will never be wise with foreign wisdom or renowned for foreign glory." Later, in 1811, in his confidential memoir to the tsar "On Ancient and Modern Russia," Karamzin gave his nationalist and conservative political philosophy a finished formulation. He attacked Peter the Great, who "seeing Europe, wanted to make Russia into Holland," and objected to the borrowing of foreign legal standards and to plans for the limitation of autocracy and the abolition of serfdom.[18]

Other opponents of French influence in literature and life were the old poet Derzhavin and Admiral Shishkov, while I. A. Krylov satirized Gallomania in his comedies *The Stylish Shop* and *The Lesson to the Daughters*. The chorus of anti-French critics was soon joined by the raucous voice of Count Rostopchin, the future commander of Moscow in 1812. In a work of 1807, "Reflections from the Red Staircase" *(Mysli vslukh na krasnom kryl'tse)*, he abused the French and Gallomania in his pseudo-national jargon. (The "Red Staircase" is part of the buildings of the Kremlin, intimately connected with the Russian past.)

The conservative, nationalist, and anti-French tendency was represented in journalism by the periodicals *The Russian Herald (Russkii vestnik)* and *The Son of the Fatherland (Syn otechestva)*. Founded by S. N. Glinka in 1808, the first of these devoted much attention to Russian antiquity, which it idealized, exalted Russian might and Russian originality, and argued against French education and French influence in general.[19] *The Son of the Fatherland*, which N. I. Grech began to publish in 1812 with government financial support, was a militantly patriotic and chauvinistic organ, agitating against Napoleon, France, and French philosophy. The eighteenth century, said this journal, which "was incorrectly named the century of enlightenment, covered the universe with the gloom of a false philosophy."[20] In his opinion Napoleon was "the greatest murderer and incendiary in the history of the world," "a manufacturer of corpses."

Nevertheless, French influence in Russia remained very much alive, and even the Fatherland War of 1812 could not crush it. Returning to Moscow in 1814, Vigel' found all of society speaking French once again. "In a city which the French invaders had recently

---

[18] For Karamzin's memoir, see Pypin, *op. cit.*, appendix I, pp. 479–534 and the Pipes' translation, *op. cit.*

[19] V. N. Bochkarev, "Konservatory i natsionalisty v Rossii v nachale XIX veka" ["Conservatives and Nationalists in Russia at the Beginning of the Nineteenth Century"], in *Otechestvennaia voina i russkoe obshchestvo* [*The Fatherland War and Russian Society*] (Moscow, 1911), vol. II, pp. 194–220.

[20] N. P. Sidorov, "Syn otechestva" ["The Son of the Fatherland"], in *Otechestvennaia voina . . . ,* vol. V, pp. 139–145.

reduced to ashes, everybody [of good breeding] spoke their language."
Chatsky's attacks on Gallomania in Griboedov's celebrated comedy
Woe from Wit (Gore ot uma) show that this proclivity was still alive
in Moscow society in the 1820s.

After the failure of the Decembrist revolt and with it the
collapse of hopes of a political revolution or reformation "on the
French model," the elite of the Russian intelligentsia fell under the
influence of idealist German philosophy. But between Napoleon's invasion of Russia in 1812 and the Decembrist revolt of 1825 lay yet
another phase in the evolution of Russian society, a phase of mystical
religious enthusiasm. The cause of this phase lay partly in the general
atmosphere of religiosity and contrition of the period and partly in
imitation of the spirit that dominated Alexander's court at this time.

In 1812 the "Bible Society" was founded in Petersburg,
modeled after the Bible Society of London. The character of the
society was Christian but interdenominational, and its basic aim was
to print and distribute Bibles to the mass of the populace. Until 1824
the society enjoyed the protection of the government, and it successfully expanded its activities, having eighty-nine branches in provincial
cities at the beginning of 1824.

At that time adherents and propagators of the most varied
religious movement took refuge and flourished in Petersburg: the
mystic Baroness Krüdener and Madam Tatarinova; the head of the
Skoptsy (eunuch) sect, Kondratii Selivanov; and members of the Jesuit
order who founded an academy at Polotsk and opened an institute in
Petersburg for the education of the children of the Russian aristocracy.
This religious pluralism in Petersburg society soon aroused a reaction
on the part of the Orthodox Church, headed by Metropolitan Serafim,
with the notorious Archimandrite Photius as its most active figure.
In 1820 this movement resulted in the issuance of a decree expelling
the Jesuits from Russia and abolishing the schools that they had established for Catholic propaganda and "the perversion" of the Orthodox.
The Masonic lodges were closed in 1822, and in 1824 Metropolitan
Serafim submitted to Alexander a memorandum on the necessity of
closing the Bible Society. Nicholas I finally terminated its activities
in 1826.

The failure of the Decembrists and the harsh punishment
that was inflicted on them produced a stunning impression on intellectual Russian society, the flower of which abruptly found itself in
Siberia. Depressed, terrorized, and subject to the vigilant surveillance
of "the third section," educated society for some time sunk into

intellectual slumber, personal affairs, and the worldly pleasures. In his memoirs, Herzen wrote of this era:

> the first ten years after 1825 were terrible not only because of the outright persecution of any ideas, but also because of the utter emptiness that society manifested. It was degraded, it was disoriented, it was frightened. The better people considered that the former path of development was scarcely possible; a new one they knew not. Grey autumn skies weighed down and cheerlessly beclouded the soul.[21]

The intellectuals, losing hope in the political reformation of Russia and repelled by the prospect of miserable reality, immersed themselves (or tried to) in the depths of abstract philosophy, studying the German idealist philosophers—first Schelling, then Fichte and Kant, and finally Hegel. In fact, interest in the German idealist philosophers arose in Russia even before the Decembrist catastrophe. In 1824 Prince V. F. Odoevsky founded the journal *Mnemozina* in Moscow, which dealt with specialized philosophical questions, and in 1823 a circle of young "lovers of wisdom" was founded, including the Kireevsky brothers, Venevitinov, Prince Odoevsky, Shevyrev, Koshelev, and others. Koshelev recalls in his memoirs: "German philosophy and especially the works of Schelling arrested our attention so that our study of everything else became quite careless, and we devoted all our time to the German philosophers." Professors Vellansky, Galich, Pavlov, Davydov, and Nadezhdin preached Schelling's philosophy from the rostrums of the universities of Petersburg and Moscow. It was the latter university that became the center of intellectual life and moral inspiration during the early 1830s. The students formed circles in which lively discussions dealt with moral and philosophical problems and which propagated devotion to the idealist trinity: truth, goodness, and beauty. N. V. Stankevich's circle enjoyed the greatest success among the idealist university youth, although its influential leader died in 1840 at age twenty-seven. But in the same decade another circle, headed by Herzen and Ogarev, again turned their attention to social and political questions. They studied the writings of the French literary socialists, especially Saint Simon, and developed a positivist and socialist outlook.

The influence of Schelling was replaced by the dominance of Hegel among the philosophical youth in the course of 1830s. According to the literary historian Sakulin, "Hegel was the absolute ruler of their minds and shared his dominance only with the repre-

---

[21] A. I. Herzen, *Byloe i Dumy* [*My Past and Thoughts*] (Leningrad, 1946), p. 291.

sentatives of German poetry and art. . . ." M. A. Bakunin and V. G. Belinsky headed the Moscow Hegelians, and the Aksakovs, Khomiakov, the Kireevskys, V. Botkin, and others joined them. Thus we see that in the 1830s the future "Slavophiles" and "Westerners" both stood under the banner of German idealist philosophy, however sharply their views diverged in the following decade.

In 1836 there was a literary event which made a great impression on society, opening the way for the discussion of the basic issues of Russian history and Russian life and stimulating the crystallization of the two basic trends in Russian social thought in the nineteenth century. This event was the publication in Nadezhdin's journal *The Telescope* of P. I. Chaadaev's "Philosophical Letter,"[22] In Herzen's words the letter was "a black indictment against Russia." The author saw no ray of light in the past, present or future of Russia. "In Western Europe and especially in Catholicism," wrote the historian Kornilov, "Chaadaev saw the true and powerful preserver of the foundations of Christianity and Christian civilization." Meanwhile, Russia, having accepted Christianity from decadent Byzantium and deviating from the truth (that is, Western Christianity), was, in Chaadaev's opinion, "torn away from the world brotherhood" and did not participate in the "sublime procession" of the whole Christian world. "We are entirely without internal development, natural progress. . . . We live without a past or future amidst dead stagnation." Russia has made no contribution to the fund of human civilization and is "some sort of blank in the moral order of the world," said Chaadaev. His letter produced a commotion in official circles, *The Telescope* was closed, and Chaadaev was declared insane.

Chaadaev remained a solitary figure, but his importance lay in the fact that he began the great debate between Westerners and Slavophiles that colored the entire history of the development of Russian social thought in the nineteenth century.

The real "ruler of men's minds" in the younger generation in the second half of the 1830s and in the 1840s was his contemporary, Vissarion Grigor'evich Belinsky, the famous critic and publicist, talented, stormy, impetuous—"the furious Vissarion." Belinsky passed through several stages in his ideological development. In his student years he wrote tragedy, containing sharp protest against serfdom. His real literary debut was the article "Literary Dreams" in 1834, which was followed by a series of other articles by him in the Moscow

---

[22] M. Gershenson, ed., *Sochineniia i pis'ma Chaadaeva* [*The Works and Letters of Chaadaev*] (Moscow, 1914), vol. II, pp. 106–126; E. A. Moskoff, *The Russian Philosopher Chaadaev, His Ideas and His Epoch* (New York, 1937), pp. 29–46.

journals. In these articles Belinsky preached on behalf of the elevation of personal morality, moral self-perfection, self-sacrifice "for the
good of one's fellowmen, one's native land, for the good of mankind."
In 1837 he became acquainted with Hegel (in a one-sided and im-
precise interpretation) and proclaimed a truce with "reasonable reality." In a series of articles, of which "The Anniversary of Borodino,"
written in 1839, is especially characteristic, Belinsky defended and
justified contemporary Russian values and institutions, and especially
the monarchy. In 1839 he left Moscow for Petersburg, where he took
over the literary criticism for Kraevsky's *Notes from the Fatherland (Otechestvennye Zapiski)*. Then in 1840 he broke with Hegel's
"philosophical nightcap," cursed his "vile efforts to make peace with
vile reality," acknowledged that the "idea of liberalism" was "in the
highest level reasonable and Christian"—for its task was the attain-
ment of rights and personal liberty and the restoration of true human
worth—and, finally, he called literature to the service of society. "In
our time, more than ever before," Belinsky wrote in 1847, "art and
literature reflect the social issues. . . . To deny art the right to serve
the interests of society is not to raise it but to lower it, because this
is to deprive it of its vitality, that is, to make it the subject of some
sybarritic pleasure, a toy for idle loafers."[23] At times Belinsky inclined
toward socialism, seeing in it the best means of securing individual
rights.

Belinsky's famous letter to Gogol, written after the appearance of Gogol's book *Selected Passages from Correspondence with
Friends,* was an impassioned act of accusation against the Russia of
Nicholas I. In the conditions of censorship it was impossible to publish Belinsky's letter, but it circulated throughout Russia in handwritten copies and made a strong impression everywhere. As a judge
of contemporary literature, possessing remarkable literary talent, as
a proponent of the ideas of liberty, equality, and humanity, Belinsky
enjoyed great popularity, especially among the youth. Not only in the
capitals but also in the remote backwaters of civilization the young
readers impatiently awaited the next issue of the journals that carried
Belinsky's articles.

Along with the celebrated professor and humanist Granovsky, Belinsky headed the Westerners of the Russian intellectual world.
In the 1840s the left wing of the Westerners moved in the direction

---

[23] V. G. Belinsky, *Polnoe sobranie sochinenii* [*Complete Collection of Works*]
(Moscow, 1953–1956), vol. X, pp. 306, 311; and *Selected Philosophical Works*
(Moscow, 1948), pp. 454, 459.

of socialism and positivism. The political manifestation of this movement was the formation in 1845 of M. V. Butashevich-Petrashevsky's
"circle." A fairly large group of "Petrashevtsians" gathered each Friday
at their leader's home, read and discussed the writings of the French
socialists, predominantly Fourier, and designed plans for the social
and political reconstruction of Russia. Among the participants in the
group were the novelist F. M. Dostoevsky, the poet A. N. Pleshcheev,
and the satirist Saltykov-Shchedrin. The circle was not a political
organization in essence and had no particular plan of action. But
although it was only a "conspiracy of ideas," the government of
Nicholas I, terrified by the European Revolution of 1848, looked on
the members of the Petrashevsky circle as dangerous conspirators.
In 1849 twenty members of the circle were arrested, tried, and sentenced to death, although the sentence was later commuted to exile
in forced labor.

Generally speaking, one may say that the common element
in the teachings of the Westerners was a belief in the unity of human
civilization and in the leadership within this civilization of Western
Europe, which had most fully realized the ideas of humanity, freedom, and progress and which thus showed the true way to all the
rest of mankind. It was therefore considered the task of Russia, a backward, ignorant, semibarbaric country that had entered the general
cause of human cultural development only with Peter the Great, to
throw off its sluggishness and Asiaticness, to draw close to European
West, and to unite with it in a single, cultural family of mankind.

A group of talented and convinced writers and publicists
who were called "Slavophiles" opposed the Westerners' point of view
in the 1840s and 1850s. A. S. Khomiakov, I. V. and P. V. Kireevsky,
C. S. and I. S. Aksakov, Iu. F. Samarin, A. I. Koshelev, Prince
Cherkassky, and others fully or partly adhered to this trend. The first
premise of the Slavophiles was that a single civilization, common to
mankind, did not exist, nor a single path of development for all
nations. Each nation or group of related nations lives its own, independent, peculiar life, based on its "national spirit," which per-
meates all aspects of national life.

Thus, according to Koshelev, the relation (of Russia) to
the Slavs "does not at all constitute the main, essential distinction between our circle and the opposing circle of the Westerners. . . .
Therefore, we should be called not 'Slavophiles,' but, in opposition
to the Westerners, supporters of indigenous civilization or indigenous
peculiarities *(tuzemniki* or *samobytniki)* ."[24]

---

[24] Koshelev, *op. cit.*, pp. 76–78.

In the opinion of the Slavophiles there was a profound difference in principle between Russia and the West. The basic idea on which the Russian nation was founded was the Orthodox Christian creed, which defined the character of the people and permeated its entire way of life. In Constantine Aksakov's words: "The Russian people maintains the Christian faith as the main basis of its entire life. . . . Not in vain is Rus' called Holy Rus'." [25] Or, as Koshelev wrote: ". . . on the teachings of Christianity, preserved in our Orthodox Church, we base our entire way of life, our entire philosophy." [26] According to the Slavophiles, Orthodoxy, as the religion of love and communality *(sobornost')*, was closely linked with the principles of inner truth, spiritual freedom, and the brotherhood of man.

The fulfillment of these principles in Russian life was the commune, the peasant mir, "as a voluntary union for mutual assistance and support." Idealizing historical reality, all the Slavophiles sang rapturous hymns to the peasant mir. According to Aksakov: "The mir is in its essence the sovereign, supreme manifestation of the people, which fully satisfies all the demands of legality, of social justice, of a communal court, and, in sum, of the will of the commune." [27] Or,

> The commune represents a moral choir, and, as in a choir, an individual's voice is not lost, but, subordinated to the general pattern, it is heard in harmony with all the voices. Thus, the individual is not lost in the commune, but, renouncing exclusiveness for harmony with the whole, it finds itself . . . in harmony with equally selfless individuals. [28]

And Khomiakov writes: "The Russian spirit approved for all time the communal society of the mir, the best form of communal life." [29] Koshelev adds: "such a communal *(mirskoi)* order exists in no other land. Luckily, we have it, and in it lies our present strength, and the guarantee of our power and strength in the future." [30]

Having such a high regard for the Russian commune, the Slavophiles, especially Aksakov, held a negative opinion of the state in its European form. Aksakov saw in the West "the worship of the

[25] K. S. Aksakov, *Sochineniia [Works]* (Moscow, 1861), vol. I, p. 20.

[26] Koshelev, *op. cit.*, p. 76.

[27] Aksakov, *Zamechaniia na novoe administrativnoe ustroistvo krest'ian*, p. 52.

[28] Aksakov, *Sochineniia*, vol. I, p. 292.

[29] A. S. Khomiakov, *Polnoe sobranie sochinenii [Complete Works]* (Moscow, 1900), vol. III, p. 198; see also pp. 461–462.

[30] Koshelev, *op. cit.*, appendix V, p. 121.

state," the exaltation of the ideal of external order, of external regularity, of "mechanical organization," guaranteed by state laws with the result of impoverishing man's inner life.

In contrast to the moral and religious basis of Russian life, said the Slavophiles, the Western or "German-Roman" world had built its life on the principles of formal, juridical equity, and external organization. Therefore, neither the Western principles nor Western forms of organization were necessary or suitable for Russia. The only concern of the state was to defend the land from enemies without interfering with its internal life. The people were to possess "full liberty of life and of spirit," freedom of thought and word. According to Aksakov, the correct relation between the state and the "land" (that is, the populace) existed in Muscovite Rus', but Peter the Great destroyed the voluntary union of "the land" and the state. He subordinated "the land" to the authority of the state and "wanted to push Russia onto the Western path, a false and dangerous path." However, only the government personnel, the serving people (of the tsar) followed him, while the people in the true sense, "the common people, remained with their former foundations."

The Slavophiles regarded these "simple folk" with vital interest and deep sympathy, and in this connection interested themselves in Russian folklore, collecting folk epics (*byliny*), songs, and legends. At the same time they disliked the bureaucratic Petersburg monarchy, which was constructed on the European pattern. The Slavophiles' political idea was a patriarchal, popular monarchy, unlimited by a formal constitution but resting on the voluntary support of "the land," with which the tsar would confer on all important issues by calling an "assembly of the land" (*zemskii sobor*), according to the example of the Muscovite tsars.

Despite the ideological differences between the Slavophiles and Westerners, they were in agreement on the practical questions of Russian life. Both movements opposed serfdom and the contemporary bureaucratic political order of the government. Both demanded freedom of speech and the press. In the eyes of Nicholas' government, therefore, both trends were equally unreliable.

The eminent publicist and political figure of the mid-nineteenth century, A. I. Herzen, the founding father of Russian socialism and political radicalism, occupied a special position between the Slavophiles and Westerners. He rejected the religious philosophy of the Slavophiles, their devotion to the "Byzantine church," their monarchism, their nationalism, and their negative attitude toward democratic political forms. Yet he fully shared their sympathy with the common people and the spontaneity of the life of the Russian people, their striving for spiritual freedom, and their high appraisal of the Russian commune. He saw in the commune the germ of a future, just social order that could develop only if it were fertilized by "the Western idea," that is, the Western theory of socialism. Although he was disillusioned concerning the Western bourgeoisie, Herzen continued to believe in Western socialism.

Of the Slavophiles he wrote:

> The importance of their view, its true and essential part, is not at all Orthodoxy nor exclusive nationalism, but in that spontaneous Russian life which they revealed. . . . The producers' cooperative (*artel*) and the rural commune, the sharing of income, the allotment of land, the communal assembly and the uniting of villages in townships that govern themselves, all these are the foundation stones on which to base the temple of our future free, communal way of life. But these foundation stones are only stones and without Western ideas our future temple would remain only a foundation. . . . The rational and free development of the life of the Russian people is compatible with the aspirations of western socialism.[31]

Foreshadowing the hopes of the Russian "populists" (*narodniki*) of the second half of the nineteenth century, Herzen hoped that Russia would pass over from the communal way of life to socialism, avoiding the bourgeois stage of European development.

On the extreme left flank of the Russian and European revolutionary movement stood the aristocrat-revolutionary and romantic-anarchist M. A. Bakunin. More precisely, he did not stand, but continually dashed about Europe, fighting on the barricades, now in Prague, now in Dresden (during the revolution of 1848), delivering addresses at all possible congresses and meetings, composing incendiary articles and appeals, and, in short, exerting superhuman efforts to kindle the flame of world revolution. At first he wanted to foment revolution in order to create a free, Pan-Slav federation, but later his plans expanded and he preached "the destruction of all governments, and on their ruins, the foundation of a world-wide federation of free producers' associations of all countries."

On the extreme right flank of Russian society in the 1830s and 1840s stood the followers and defenders of "official ideology," formulated in 1833 by Count Uvarov in the famous triad "Orthodoxy, autocracy, and nationality." In 1841 the journal *The Muscovite*

---

[31] Herzen, *op cit.*, pp. 284, 293–294.

(*Moskovitianin*) began to appear under the leadership of two conservative professors of Moscow University, M. P. Pogodin and S. P. Shevyrev, accepting in general this official ideology. Among the journalists who tried to write in the spirit desired by the authorities, the well-known trio of O. I. Senkovsky, Grech, and F. V. Bulgarin were especially active. Other journalists and writers of this time were followed by the vigilant eye of Nicholas' censors, trying to give their published works, as the censorship statute of 1826 put it, "a direction that is useful, or at least, unharmful for the welfare of the fatherland." Censorship under Nicholas I was removed from the competence of the universities and given to government bureaucrats, although the censors were often appointed from the ranks of the professors.

Literature

Despite the vigilant censorship and police surveillance, serious journalism, literary criticism, and literature attained a high level of development in the middle of the nineteenth century. We have seen the wealth and variety of journalism and the philosophical movements. The belles-lettres of this period were not less vital, nor did they achieve less success. As Professor Anichkov wrote: "The era of Nicholas, despite the draconic severity of police supervision, was exceptionally rich in its intellectual and literary movements."[32] At the turn of the century G. R. Derzhavin, the old nobleman and poet of Catherine's time, was the generally acknowledged patriarch of Russian poetry, and I. A. Krylov was well known for his comedies and satirical journalism. In 1806 he began to publish his fables (some of them translated from La Fontaine), which were written in exquisite vernacular style and contained the quintessence of simple, artless folk wisdom and common sense. Many of the expressions in these fables became proverbs and sayings and passed into conversational usage.

The two rising Russian literary men at the turn of the nineteenth century were N. M. Karamzin and V. A. Zhukovsky. Karamzin attracted attention with his *Letters of a Russian Traveler* and made his literary debut in belles-lettres in 1792 with the sentimental story "Poor Liza," which enjoyed enormous success. Later he wrote other sentimental stories, and at the beginning of the nineteenth century he occupied himself more with serious journalism. In 1802 he edited the journal *The Herald of Europe,* and in 1803 he started to prepare his famous historical work *The History of the Russian*

---

[32] *Istoriia Rossii v XIX veke,* vol. II, p. 444.

State. Karamzin rendered great service as a reformer of the Russian literary language. Abandoning the heavy "Slavic-Russian" style of Lomonosov and Derzhavin, he brought the literary language closer to the spoken language, and in addition he introduced into Russian many new words, either borrowed directly from foreign languages or formed from Russian roots. The literary Old Believers, headed by Shishkov and protected by Derzhavin, attacked Karamzin's innovations. In Petersburg in 1810 Shishkov and others founded a society called "The Colloquium (*Beseda*) of the Lovers of the Russian Word." As a counterweight to this group, the literary innovators founded a society called "Arzamas," which lasted from 1815 to 1818. It included the literary men Zhukovsky, Batiushkov, Prince Viazemsky, and others, and A. S. Pushkin appeared in it as a lad just out of the lycee at Tsarskoe Selo.

The romantic poet Zhukovsky began his literary work with a translation of Gray's "Elegy Written in a Country Churchyard" in 1801 and soon was celebrated for his ballads, both original and translated. His chief work of translation is the *Odyssey,* which he rendered in Russian with remarkable poetic sense even though he knew no Greek and worked from a German version.

The end of the 1820s and the decade of the '30s witnessed the flowering of Pushkin's poetic talent and his general recognition as "tsar of Russian poetry." After a short-lived and superficial inclination for Byronism, reflected in "The Captive of the Caucasus," "The Fountain of Bakhchisaray," and "The Gypsies," Pushkin became the pioneer of Russian artistic realism. His novel in poetry, *Eugene Onegin,* was completed in 1831 and presented a broad, vivid picture of the life of the high society of the capital and the provincial nobility. His historical drama, *Boris Godunov,* written in 1825 and published in 1830, reflects both Pushkin's interest in the Russian past and the influence of Shakespearean tragedy on his work. In the poems "Poltava" and "The Bronze Horseman" one finds expression of imperial patriotism and high esteem for the work of the mighty founder of the Russian Empire, Peter the Great. In addition, Pushkin's reputation rests on a considerable number of lyric poems, unsurpassed for beauty of poetic form. In his prose works, such as "The Captain's Daughter," "Belkin's Tales," "The Queen of Spades" and others, he created superb models of artistic prose, stylistically simple and lucid, and thus completed the process of creating the Russian literary language, laying the foundation for the brilliant development of Russian literature in the nineteenth century.

Of the many poets of Pushkin's era the greatest were Batiushkov, Iazykov and Baratynsky. K. N. Batiushkov fixed his gaze on the poets of the classical world and the Italian Renaissance, and in his elegant poetry, original and translated, he was the bard of epicureanism. N. M. Iazykov, who was a popular poet of the '20s and '30s, praised his loves, wine, and other joys of life in his resounding poetry, and did not immerse himself in the depths of philosophical meditation. E. A. Baratynsky was of quite another character, a pensive poet whose beautiful, elegiac, and melancholy poetry was permeated with a spirit of pessimism and disillusionment in its appraisal of the character and way of life of contemporary humanity.

Lesser poetic talents, devoted to liberty and social reform, were Ryleev and Prince A. I. Odoevsky, poets of the early 1820s who became Decembrists. In 1823–1825 Ryleev and A. Bestuzhev edited the literary yearbook *The Polar Star* and enjoyed great success.

Outstanding among the many talents of this epoch was A. S. Griboedov, the author of the celebrated comedy *Woe from Wit*. This work was completed in 1824, but in the conditions of censorship it could not be printed and, like Pushkin's freedom-loving poems, it was circulated in manuscript and learnt by heart until its publication in 1833. While its formal structure was that of a classical play, Griboedov's comedy was in essence a remarkable example of literary realism in its portrayal of contemporary Moscow society. A great many of Griboedov's expressions became current proverbs in spoken Russian.

After Pushkin's death in January 1837, from wounds received in a duel, his place in poetry was occupied by the young M. Iu. Lermontov. The unfortunate circumstances of his personal life and the literary influence of Byron made him a pessimist who stood alone and alien in the high society around him, which he regarded with a contempt that found expression in his celebrated poem on the death of Pushkin. Starting his career as an officer in the horse guards, he was twice banished from Petersburg and sent to the Caucasus, where he took part in the fighting against the mountaineers and in 1841 was killed in a duel. The natural beauty of the Caucasus and the heroic struggle of the Caucasian mountaineers made a profound impression on the young Russian officer, and in a series of Caucasian poems, "Izmail Bey," "Hadji Abrek," "Mtsyri," "The Demon," and others, he drew a sublime picture of the natural beauty he had found there and described sympathetically the life and character of its brave and freedom-loving inhabitants. Lermontov's romantic tendency, along with his ability to present magnificent pictures and character studies in the spirit of artistic realism, manifested itself in his famous novel, *A Hero of Our Time* (1839–1840.) The "hero" Pechorin, like the author, was an officer in the Caucasian Army who had abandoned high society, disillusioned, egocentric, and lacking any interest in life or the use of his strength and abilities. In his elegiac and lyrical poems, some of which are permeated with profound religious feeling, Lermontov produced models of poetic perfection on a level with Pushkin.

The third giant of the Russian literature of this period was N. V. Gogol. A collection of his stories of life in the Ukraine, *Evenings on a Farm Near Dikanka,* appeared in 1831, and in 1835 the anthologies *Arabesques* and *Mirgorod* followed. The latter included the well-known historical story "Taras Bulba," portraying the struggle of the sixteenth century Cossacks against their Polish oppressors. Gogol's chief works were the comedy *The Inspector General* (1836) and the "poem" (really a long satirical story) *Dead Souls,* the first volume of which appeared in 1842. These works presented a clear (but highly satirical) picture of the provincial bureaucracy and nobility of the day. A number of fictional personages, depicted in Gogol's characteristic manner, have become symbols and a permanent part of spoken and literary Russian (for example, the impostor Khlestakov, the dreamer Manilov, and the niggard Pliushkin). Gogol's prose was distinguished for its remarkable qualities of clarity, simplicity, and expressiveness. Along with Pushkin, Gogol is considered to be the founder of the Russian realistic literature that developed in the second half of the nineteenth century. At the end of his life Gogol experienced a profound spiritual crisis and thought of himself as called to institute a moral renaissance of the sorry humanity that he had so painfully castigated in his satire. To do so, he prepared a second volume of *Dead Souls,* which was to portray these morally reborn people; but later he burned the manuscript of the sequel. In 1847 he published *Selected Passages from Correspondence with Friends,* in which he undertook the defense of the existing political and social order; it caused indignation in progressive circles and an angry reply from Belinsky.

Among other writers of the 1830s and '40s, A. V. Kol'tsov deserves mention. He emerged from the common people and became a poet of country life, the labor of the peasantry, and the broad Russian steppe. A number of other poets—A. P. Maikov, Ia. P. Polonsky, I. S. Nikitin, A. N. Pleshcheev, and the Ukrainian poet T. G. Shevchenko—began their literary work in this period. Three popular novelists of the 1830s and '40s were M. N. Zagoskin, whose *Iurii Miloslavsky,* or *Russians in 1612,* was the most popular of his historical novels, and I. I. Lazhechnikov, the author of *The House of Ice* and other novels, and A. Bestuzhev-Marlinsky, a former Decembrist and a romantic.

In the second half of the 1840s and the beginning of the '50s the literary work of the majority of the remarkable writers of this epoch began. The golden age of Russian poetry, the era of Pushkin and Lermontov, was replaced by the golden age of Russian realistic literature. The dominant theme of this period was social, sympathy for the "little brother" and a compassion for "the humiliated and insulted," as Dostoevsky put it in the title of a novel. It was Dostoevsky who laid the basis for this "philanthropic" tendency in his story "Poor Folk," which was permeated with profound humanity. It also reflected Dostoevsky's characteristic ability to find features of sublime humanity in the sorriest and, apparently, the most worthless people. D. V. Grigorovich introduced the gray Russian peasant, with his grievous and unmerited suffering, into the "salon" of Russian literature with his stories "The Country" (1846) and "Anton Goremyka" (1847). I. S. Turgenev's stories about rural life began to appear in print in 1847, and in 1852 they came out in a single book, entitled *A Hunter's Sketches* (*Zapiski okhotnika.*) These stories, filled with sincere sympathy for the serfs, caused the reading public to regard the peasants as more humane and attractive persons than the landlords. The work did not make an explicit social declaration, but it was an obvious protest against serfdom and made a great impression on the public, preparing the ground, socially and psychologically, for the abolition of serfdom in 1861.

Other sketches of peasant life that came out in these years were A. F. Pisemsky's *A Bitter Lot, The Carpenters' Artel,* and *Pitershchik.* Later, in 1856 and 1858, S. T. Aksakov's *Family Chronicle* and *Years of Childhood* were published, representing an objective chronicle of rural life around the turn of the century in the eastern regions of Russia.

Saltykov-Shchedrin's sketches began to appear in 1848. They were satirical in form, sometimes acid, sometimes full of good-natured humor, but always permeated with the spirit of humanity, always exposing injustice, arbitrariness, and oppression, always arousing sympathy for the downtrodden and injured.

Scholarship and the Sciences

The first quarter of the nineteenth century was the period of the birth of independent Russian scholarship. With the brilliant but isolated exception of M. V. Lomonosov, Russian scholarship had previously been nourished by the generosity of the European scholarly world. The universities naturally became the centers of scholarly activity, and a series of scholarly and literary societies grew up in and around them at the beginning of the nineteenth century. Under the auspices of Moscow University the Society of Russian History and Antiquity received an imperial charter in 1811, and from the 1840s until the Revolution of 1917 it regularly issued its *Readings* (*Chteniia*), which included valuable historical research and material. The Society of Lovers of Russian Literature (*Slovestnost'*) also was formed in Moscow in 1811. The Moscow Society of Experimental Science was founded in 1805; in 1811 the Mathematical Society received an imperial charter; and in 1817 the Mineralogical Society was founded. In Petersburg the Natural Science Society was established in 1827, the Russian Geographical Society in 1845, and the Archeological-Numismatical Society in 1846. Also of importance was the founding of the Imperial Public Library in Petersburg in 1810 and its opening in 1814. Of course, each university had its library, which grew steadily.

On the threshold of the nineteenth century, not only natural science but even Russian history was in the hands of foreign scholars, mainly Germans. In 1805, for example, Schlözer published, in German, his famous research on the Russian primary chronicle. In 1803, however, the Russian historian Karamzin, with government support, undertook the preparation of a history of Russia. He collected a huge quantity of historical documents, which he later printed as appendixes to his work, and in 1818 eight volumes of his *History of the Russian State* appeared. In all Karamzin wrote twelve volumes of his history, bringing it down to the "Time of Troubles" at the opening of the seventeenth century. Pushkin wrote that Karamzin discovered ancient Russia "as Columbus had discovered America." By 1820 other important scholarly works had been published on law, taxation, and history of philosophy, and philology.

In the 1830s and '40s Moscow University played the most important role in Russian cultural life, not only in education but but also in scholarly research. In this period the indefatigable worker in the field of history was M. P. Pogodin, a professor of Moscow University for many years. Then, following his appointment as professor of history in Moscow in 1846, S. M. Soloviev began his fundamental, new research in Russian history, and in 1851 he began to publish his *History of Russia from the Earliest Times*. Each year a new volume in the work appeared until there were twenty-nine volumes, bringing the history to the year 1775. Other remarkable scholars of Moscow University included the professors of universal history Granovsky and Kudriavtsev, the judicial historians Kavelin, Beliaev, and Kalachov, the professors of literature and philology Buslaev, Tikhonravov, and Bodiansky, and, finally, the talented humanist-surgeon N. I. Pirogov. In this period the gifted linguist A. Kh. Vostokov and the judicial historian K. A. Nevolin worked in Petersburg.

An extremely important institution for the study of Russian history was the Archeographic Commission, which sponsored the Archeographical Expedition of 1829–1834 under the leadership of P. M. Stroev. This project covered the whole of Russia in search of historical sources—chronicles, treaties, laws, and the like—and it succeeded in gathering a great mass of documents, mainly in the archives of monasteries, which were published beginning in 1836.

The physical and mathematical sciences attained an independent footing in Russia only in the second half of the nineteenth century, but there were still significant achievements in the first half of the century. In 1835 the Pulkovo observatory was started not far from Petersburg under the direction of the well-known astronomer V. Ia. Struve. The famous professor of mathematics of Kazan University, N. I. Lobachevsky, created the basis of non-Euclidean geometry. This period also saw the work of the talented biologist K. E. Baer and the chemist who developed anilines, N. N. Zinin.

All in all, the first half of the nineteenth century witnessed the emergence of a Russian culture which was at at once modern, European, and yet distinctively Russian.

The Church

Since the time of Peter the Great, the Russian church had been administered by the Holy Synod, a college (or directorial committee) of bishops, and the Synod itself was supervised by the "overprocurator," appointed by the tsar as "the eye of the sovereign." The authority and influence of the overprocurator in church administration gradually grew. At first merely a supervisor, to see to it "that the Synod may fulfill its mission righteously and honestly," as Peter's instructions prescribed, the overprocurator eventually became virtually a minister of ecclesiastical affairs. However, Alexander I and Nicholas I were not satisfied with the supervision of the overprocurator, and they undertook to supervise the life of the church themselves. The result was constant interference by the administrative authorities in the affairs of the church, for the government tried to regulate and control all sides of ecclesiastical life. For example, a decree of the Synod dated February 14, 1816, the result of a personal decree of the tsar, appeared with the following heading: "On the Cessation of the Use in Singing in Churches of Handwritten Music and on the Printing of Music Books of Famous Composers Approved by the Director of the Choir of the Court, Actual State Councilor Bortniansky." Similarly, early in Nicholas' reign, the Ministry of Internal Affairs issued a book entitled "A Collection of Plans, Façades, and Profiles for the Construction of Stone Churches," which was to serve as an obligatory pattern and guide in the building of new churches.

The tsar was the supreme protector of the church, and the secular government watched over all the congregations. In the case of the Orthodox populace the government even followed their performance of religious obligations. Apostasy from Orthodoxy was forbidden by law, and the fulfillment of the religious sacraments and rites was mandatory. For example, the traditional formula for written evidence began: "Ivan Ivanovich Ivanov [the witness], a member of the Orthodox faith, having been to confession and the Holy Communion annually . . . ." The police were directed to maintain the necessary order, piety, and quiet in churches during the divine service, and the disturbance of these was punishable by fine or arrest from three to seven days.

Local church administration in the nineteenth century was organized on the same bureaucratic basis as secular affairs. Each diocese corresponded to a province. The tsar appointed the bishops upon the nomination of the Synod, and after the late eighteenth century, he awarded them decorations on the same basis as his government ministers, governors, and generals. The bishop appointed the parochial clergy and administered the diocese "entrusted to him" through an ecclesiastical consistory, a bureaucratic church institution that was in charge of the whole "ecclesiastical estate," and in some matters—such as marriage and divorce—laymen as well. The statutes of the ecclesiastical consistory, dated March 27, 1841, regulated their juridical and administrative activities in a most detailed manner. The old traditions of parochial social life and the selection of the parish clergy by the laity was entirely forgotten in this epoch. In fact, during the reign of the Synod the clergy was transformed into the restricted ecclesiastical estate.

At the same time, the government took major steps in the late eighteenth and early nineteenth centuries to raise the educational level of the Orthodox clergy. Four ecclesiastical academies were founded: near Moscow (at the Trinity–St. Sergei monastery) and in

Petersburg, Kiev, and Kazan. Statutes for clerical schools were issued August 30, 1814, organizing a system of schools parallel to the secular educational institutions: the academies corresponded to universities; seminaries in the provincial capitals corresponded to the gymnasiums; and the county seats were to have clerical schools. It was mandatory for the parish clergy to have special clerical education. In 1840 there were about 31,000 Orthodox churches and 53,000 priests and deacons in Russia, although the ecclesiastical estate was, of course, considerably larger, including about 15,000 monks, nuns, and novices in a total of 547 monasteries and convents.

Although the educational level of the parish clergy was undoubtedly improving, its material condition was generally precarious. As a result, the priests raised the fees for religious ministrations, which naturally caused dissatisfaction among the populace, and especially the peasantry. In villages belonging to landowners, the priests were wholly dependent on their landlords, who frequently treated them scornfully and rudely, thus undermining their authority in the eyes of the peasant population.

In its encounters with other religious organizations during the first half of the nineteenth century, the great community of the Russian Orthodox Church experienced success in some areas and losses in others. The number of Orthodox believers in Siberia and the Far East increased, thanks to the efforts of missionaries among the native population. Furthermore, a tendency toward agreement with the synodal (official) Orthodox Church appeared among the Old Believers, the considerable minority that had been formed during the major religious dispute that took place in the seventeenth century. Around 1800 the so-called Coreligionists (*edinovertsy*) emerged among the Old Believers and recognized the hierarchy and dogma of the synodal church, which in return received priests who observed the sacraments according to the old books and rites.

The greatest success for the Orthodox Church was accomplished in 1839 with the unification of the western Russian Uniats and Orthodoxy. A council (*sobor*) of Uniat bishops, headed by Metropolitan Iosif Semashko of Lithuania, was convened in Polotsk in 1839 and determined to request unification with "the Orthodox All-Russian Church of our Forefathers," and the Synod, with the permission of the tsar, accepted the Uniat Church in "full and complete communion" with the Orthodox Church "as an inseparable part of the All-Russian Church."*

---

* The Uniat Church was founded in 1596 by agreement between Orthodox

On the other hand, part of the Orthodox population left the Church for the Old Believers or one of various sects, such as the *Khlysty* (Flagellants), the *Molokane* (Milk-Drinkers), the *Skoptsy* (Eunuchs), the *Dukhobortsy* (Wrestlers of the Spirit), the *Iudeist-vuiushchie* (Judaizers), and the Mennonites. It is impossible to determine the number of the defectors from Orthodoxy with any accuracy, for hundreds and thousands of sectarians, fearing persecution, observed their new faith in secret while appearing to remain members of dominant Orthodox Church. The authorities' attitude toward the sectarians was entirely different under Alexander I and under Nicholas I. In the reign of Alexander the government displayed complete religious tolerance, and no sects suffered persecution. In fact, the head of the *Skoptsy* sect, Kondratii Selivanov, lived for a time in Petersburg in the early nineteenth century, saw the tsar himself, and received some of the magnates of high society. The *Dukhobortsy* and *Molokane* were allotted unoccupied state land north of the Crimea on the basis of 40.5 acres per man with a five-year tax exemption.

Under Nicholas the attitude of the government toward the sectarians underwent an abrupt change, beginning an era of cruel, hardly Christian persecution, not only of the sects, which were designated "especially pernicious," but even of the schismatics, the Old Believers. A decree of October 20, 1830, "On *Dukhobortsy, Ikonobortsy, Molokane,* the *Iudeistvuiushchie,* and other Especially Pernicious Heresies," established enlistment in the army or deportation to Transcaucasia as suitable punishments for the dissemination of their heresies and "for violent behaviour and impudence toward Orthodox clergy." The maintenance of Old Believers' monastic hermitages was punishable by a jail sentence of one to two years. The practices of the police with respect to sectarians and Old Believers and the inquisitorial zeal of some missionaries constitute one of the darkest sides of Nicholas' reign.

Nevertheless, neither the whole church nor all members of the church underwent bureaucratization or spiritual decline. There were many righteous and zealous men among the clergy and monastics and the professors of the ecclesiastical academies published a number

---

ecclesiastical authorities in the White Russian and western Ukrainian regions and the Papacy. The Uniats accepted the authority of the Roman Catholic Church but were permitted the Slavonic language and certain other traditional rites and practices of the Orthodox Church. Bitter feelings and recurrent violence between the Orthodox and Uniat churches have been traditional since then. The success of Metropolitan Semashko's reunion of White Russian Uniats with Orthodoxy was accompanied by charges of coercion and trickery.—R.H.M.

of valuable works, including Russian translations of the works of the Church Fathers. In the spiritual life of the Orthodox Church of this period an outstanding personality was St. Seraphim of Sarov, who died in 1833, the last widely known and venerated saint of the Russian Orthodox Church. In his youth, he entered the Sarov monastery in the province of Tambov, and after almost thirty years of solitude and a rigorous ascetic life, he became a *starets* (elder) in his monastery, that is, a teacher and spiritual leader of the monks and of numerous lay pilgrims—rich and poor, aristocrats and peasants—who visited the monastery by the thousands to receive his counsel, prayer, and consolation. In 1903 Seraphim was canonized in the Sarov monastery, in the presence of the tsar's family and tens of thousands of believers.

The question of the general role of Orthodoxy in the life of the Russian common people and society in the nineteenth century is a complicated one. At the end of the eighteenth century among the Gallicized Russian nobility "unbelief," as Vigel' said, "was regarded as an indispensable condition for enlightenment." The second decade of the century was a time of awakening of interest in religion and religiosity in its varied manifestations. It is difficult, however, to establish what was sincere searching for religion and what was stylish emulation of the imperial court. Even among the Decembrists we see a struggle between two opposing elements: the materialist, positivist world-view and passionate religiosity. Even the Jacobin Pestel hoped to end his life—after a successful revolution—as a monk in the ancient Monastery of the Caves at Kiev.

Of course, the majority of the provincial landowners espoused the formal, external side of Orthodoxy. As Saltykov-Shchedrin wrote, "The religious element was reduced to the level of a simple ritual. They went to mass regularly each Sunday . . . they prostrated themselves, knocked their foreheads on the floor, but their hearts remained dumb." [33]

Positivist and even atheist tendencies appeared among a part of the intelligentsia, especially among the Westerners in the 1840s. But among the Slavophiles a vital consciousness of the sanctity of Orthodoxy and of religious feeling was expressed with intense fervor, and the leader of the Slavophiles, Khomiakov, became an outstanding lay theologian.

And what of the mass of the populace? Constantine Aksakov wrote that "the history of the Russian people is the only history of

---

[33] Saltykov-Shchedrin, *op. cit.*, vol. XII, p. 39.

a Christian people in the whole world"; that "the Orthodox faith is the main basis and foundation of all its life"; and "the history of the Russian people reads like the lives of the saints."[34] But Belinsky and Herzen wrote that the Russian people were essentially atheistic, although not free from superstition.

Where is the truth? Undoubtedly, the majority of the Russian peasantry, like all other peasant classes, perceived religion mainly in its external, formal side, for religious enthusiasm, at least in normal times, is the lot of only a pious minority. But not a few righteous and pious men have emerged from among the Russian people, types that are often met in Russian literature (for example, Nekrasov's "Vlas," Turgenev's "Living Relics," or Shchedrin's "Pakhomovna"). And how many wanderers and pilgrims there were in Russia, completing their distant pilgrimages on foot. Finally, there was one day a year in Russia on which the whole people, from the tsar to the last pauper, were converted in reality into a single, Christian family, fulfilling its high qualities, love, and goodwill. This was the holiday of Easter, the Holy Resurrection of Christ.

---

[34] Aksakov, *Sochineniia,* vol. I, pp. 18–22.

4

Foreign Affairs
from the Napoleonic Era to the Crimean War

The Napoleonic Wars

Alexander began his reign by announcing to the European powers his decision not to interfere in the affairs of other states. On September 26 (October 8), 1801, a peace treaty was concluded in Paris between Russia and France, with which Paul had ceased active hostilities but had not yet concluded a peace treaty. Some three months earlier, on June 5 (17), a treaty of friendship and free trade had been concluded with Great Britain. Early in the summer of 1802, Alexander traveled to Memel for a meeting with the Prussian royal couple; he stayed there seven days and soon became fast friends with King Frederick William III and his fascinating wife, Queen Louise.

However, this circle of friendship did not last long. To Alexander's displeasure, in 1802 Napoleon declared himself Life Consul. That feeling was increased in 1804 by the French seizure of the Duke d'Enghien, which took place on the territory of Baden, and his subsequent execution. The act was especially annoying to Alexander because Baden was the homeland of his wife and because the victim of this aggression was a relative of the French royal house. Alexander protested against France's violation of the security and independence of European states, and France answered in a sharp and insulting note, which contained a reminder of the unpunished murder of Paul I. That same year Napoleon declared himself Emperor of the French and proceeded to seize new territory in Italy and Germany. Alexander thereupon branded Napoleon as a tyrant striving to enslave Europe and agreed to an alliance with Austria and England to stop him. War broke out between Austria and France in 1805, and Alexander sent 50,000 troops, commanded by General M. I. Kutuzov, through Galicia into Moravia to assist Austria. The tsar himself accompanied the army, so that Kutuzov was commander in name only. In the Battle of Austerlitz on November 20 (December 2), fought deep in the Austrian Empire, the combined Russian-Austrian forces were routed by Napoleon, suffering heavy losses. Austria was obliged to conclude the oppressive Treaty of Pressburg with Napoleon, and Prussia concluded a treaty of alliance with France; but Alexander decided to continue the struggle.

After a meeting with the Prussian king at Potsdam, where both rulers swore mutual friendship upon the grave of Frederick the Great, Alexander persuaded Frederick William to conclude a secret treaty of alliance with him in the summer of 1806. In the autumn, his friendship with Alexander drew the Prussian king still closer to the side of Russia. Napoleon then declared war on Prussia; in the Battles of Jena and Auerstadt he routed the Prussian army and, in October 1806, he entered Berlin. Frederick William was forced to withdraw to East Prussia, and Alexander hastened to his aid, mobilizing the entire strength of his state. In Russia a new levy of recruits was conducted, a numerous, temporary "army of the land" (*zemskoe voisko*) or militia being formed to strengthen the regular forces. On order from Alexander, the Holy Synod composed an appeal against Napoleon, characterized by reproaches and abuse, to be read in all the churches of the land. But this renewed effort did not help. After bloody but indecisive battles, at Pultusk in December 1806 and at Eylau in January 1807, Napoleon dealt the Russian army a decisive defeat at Friedland in June 1807, forcing the Russians to withdraw behind the Neman River. Now all of Prussia was in Napoleon's hands, but he was more inclined toward peace after having encountered the fighting spirit of the Russian army. Alexander also wanted peace, for he now had no allies on the continent.

An armistice was concluded June 10 (22), 1807, and three days later the celebrated meeting of Napoleon and Alexander at Tilsit took place on a raft moored in the middle of the Neman River. The two great protagonists of the European political scene played their roles skilfully, first expressing their feelings of mutual esteem. They thereupon concluded not only a peace treaty, but also an alliance. Under the conditions of the peace treaty, signed at Tilsit June 25 (July 7), Napoleon, "because of his esteem for His Majesty, the Emperor of All the Russias," agreed to return to the Prussian monarch the portion of his possessions that lay on the right bank of the river Elbe. Alexander in turn recognized the legitimacy of all of Napoleon's conquests and his appointment of his brothers as kings of various European countries as well. The greater part of what had formerly been Prussian Poland was reconstituted as the Duchy of Warsaw, under the protection of Napoleon and the nominal authority of the king of Saxony, but the Belostok region was ceded to Russia. Upon the demand of his new ally, Alexander agreed to accept the continental system, that is, to discontinue trade with England and to break all relations with her. In a secret agreement, Napoleon in return indicated his willingness to see Russia expand at the expense of the Ottoman Empire and Sweden as a reward for the losses that would be incurred by this policy.

The Treaty of Tilsit and the alliance with Napoleon caused general dissatisfaction in Russian society. Not only was it considered humiliating for Russia, but the continental system, interrupting foreign trade, caused considerable losses for the landowners who exported agricultural products. The decline of foreign trade also brought about the bankruptcy of many business establishments. At the same time, the price of foreign merchandise, for example, sugar, increased enormously. The great expenditures on military needs caused a constant deficit in the national budget; the increased issue of paper money brought about a rapid fall in the value of the notes, and, consequently, a general rise in prices.

Alexander's alliance with Napoleon did not last long. It was still in force in September 1808, however, when Alexander met Napoleon at the Congress of Erfurt. In a secret convention concluded there, Napoleon agreed to the annexation by Russia of the Ottoman provinces of Moldavia and Wallachia, and Russia promised military assistance to Napoleon in case of war between France and Austria. Alexander affirmed his alliance with Napoleon against England as "the general foe of the continent."

When war broke out between Austria and France in 1809, Alexander formally upheld the terms of the treaty by sending his army into Galicia to assist Napoleon against the Austrians. But in fact this move was an empty demonstration, for the Russian army took no part in the military actions. All the same, Napoleon decided to reward his "ally" after the victory over Austria. In 1810 Russia received the eastern part of Galicia, the Tarnopol district, while the greater part of Galicia was annexed to the Duchy of Warsaw.

In 1810 and 1811 the strain in the alliance between the two emperors became more obvious. Alexander demanded of Napoleon a formal commitment that the kingdom of Poland would not be re-established. Napoleon gave the Russian emperor his word, but evaded a written commitment. In addition, Napoleon continued his depredations against German territories, seizing the northern regions and annexing them to French holdings. In this action, Napoleon seized the lands of the Duke of Oldenburg, the husband of Alexander's sister. Alexander formally protested before the courts of Europe against the French violation of existing treaties, and he demanded that Napoleon compensate the Duke of Oldenburg for the loss of his lands. On his side, Napoleon was extremely dissatisfied with Russia's evasion of the continental system. A "Regulation on Neutral Trade for the Year 1811," issued December 19, 1810, permitted entry into Russian ports of "colonial goods"—such as sugar—under a neutral flag (meaning chiefly American ships), which in effect made it possible for English goods to enter Russia. All this time French manufactured goods, mainly luxury items, bore a heavy import duty. Napoleon protested, but in vain, against the Russian tariff policy, and relations between the two allies deteriorated further. Early in 1812 both sides apparently sensed the approach of a great war, and energetically prepared for it. That spring Napoleon wrote to the king of Würtemberg: "War will break out contrary to me [my wishes], contrary to the Emperor Alexander, contrary to the interests of France and Russia. . . . All this is like a scene in an opera, and the English stand behind the stage machinery."[1]

In March 1812, Napoleon concluded treaties of alliance with Prussia and Austria and began to form the Grand Army for his campaign against Russia. In April, Alexander demanded that Napoleon withdraw French troops from Prussia and the Duchy of Warsaw. Napoleon considered this an insulting demand and decided on war. In May, Napoleon organized a brilliant congress of the European monarchs in Dresden, and as the recognized leader of Europe, he moved on the Russian borders at the head of a vast, multinational Grand Army that crossed the Neman River on June 12 (24) into Russian territory.

The basic nucleus of the Grand Army consisted of some 450,000 men, and in the course of the campaign they were re-enforced by a further 150,000 men. A gigantic military supply train, including 10,000 carts, accompanied the army and encumbered its movements. Its extremely varied national composition was an equally serious drain on its strength. No more than half of the soldiers were French, or inhabitants of the regions recently annexed to France, the re-

---

[1] Schilder, *Imperator Aleksandr I*, vol. III, p. 24.

mainder being French "allies," such as Germans, Poles, Italians, Spaniards, Dutch, Portuguese, and Croats. Except for the Poles, who expected Napoleon to re-establish an independent Poland, most of these troops went most unwillingly, for they looked on Napoleon as the alien oppressor of their home countries.

The Russian forces that were deployed in the western border were divided into several armies, and were scarcely one third the numerical size of the Grand Army. The First Army, commanded by Barclay de Tolly, consisted of about 120,000 men and was stationed in the province of Vilno. The Second Army, under General Bagration, consisted of about 45,000 men and was stationed to the south of the First Army; while the Third, or reserve, Army, under General Tormasov, had about 45,000 in Volhynia. A separate corps under General Witgenstein covered the route to the north, that is to Petersburg. To strengthen the regular forces, a manifesto of July 18, 1812, called for a "temporary home militia of landlords' peasants" in some provinces. The state peasantry, which was exempted from this, provided the majority of the recruits in the regular army. The armies of Barclay and Bagration alone had to bear Napoleon's terrible onslaught, and it was obvious that they would have to retreat before their greatly superior opponents. The two armies joined before Smolensk, but after a bloody encounter in the beginning of August, which delayed the French attack, they continued to retreat deep into the country, and the French moved forward behind them, headed toward Moscow.

The advance of the enemy into Russia caused a great upsurge of patriotic feeling among all classes of the Russian people, while the retreat of the Russian forces caused general resentment against the "German" (alien) commander. Barclay was an able commander and an honorable man, and his tactics in 1812 were entirely sensible, but the popular fury fell upon Barclay, and he was pressed from all sides with demands that the Russian army go over to offensive operations. Acceding to public opinion, Alexander appointed as commander in chief the popular, old General Kutuzov, who had just successfully concluded the Turkish War. As the French army penetrated farther into Russia, it was all the more weakened, sustaining large losses from military operations and from illness, moving farther from its base and experiencing grave difficulties in the supply of provisions and forage. These problems were aggravated because the Russian population in the French line of advance retreated along with the army deep into the country, leaving behind only burnt and devastated abandoned areas. Kutuzov saw that further retreat was the wisest tactic, for the French army continually dwindled as it moved deeper into the alien, immense country to meet its doom. But public opinion continued to demand that the attack of the foe be halted and that Moscow not be surrendered to him. Kutuzov therefore felt compelled to stand fast 86 miles west of Moscow in order to give battle to the enemy.

The encounter took place on August 26 before the village of Borodino, and in the stubborn, protracted combat both sides suffered tremendous losses. The Russian army held its positions and was ready to renew the battle on the following morning, but the cautious commander in chief gave the order to retreat. In a military council held September 1 in the village of Fili near Moscow, the question of whether or not to yield Moscow without a battle was heatedly discussed. Kutuzov's decision was to retreat, and the next day the French occupied the city, which by that time had been abandoned by the Russian forces and almost all of its inhabitants. In his report to Alexander, Kutuzov wrote that the army had been so weakened by serious losses suffered in the Battle of Borodino, "I cannot possibly risk a battle." He then declared that "the entry of the enemy into Moscow is not yet the defeat of Russia," for the combat-ready Russian army had been preserved. However, the abandonment of Moscow had a depressing effect on Russia. The commander of Moscow, Count Rostopchin had conducted a propaganda campaign promising an easy victory over Napoleon and now turned indignantly on Kutuzov for giving up the city.

Having occupied Moscow, Napoleon thought he had won the war and approached Alexander with peace proposals, but he received no reply. Meanwhile, fires began to break out in Moscow, engulfing the whole city and accelerating the demoralization and disorganization of the French army. When all the supplies in Moscow had been burned or looted the French army supply situation became serious, for the Russian forces then intercepted or destroyed the French units sent into the countryside for provisions and forage. The brutality of the French foragers and marauders outraged the populace, driving the peasants to take up arms, or even pitchforks, to chase the unwelcome guests away; thus, in addition to the other misfortunes of the French, a "people's war" was raised against them.

On October 7 Napoleon gave the order to retreat and left Moscow. The generally accepted legend that he was "defeated by the cold" in Russia does not correspond to the facts. The winter only finished off the French army, which was already retreating in a state of complete disorganization and low morale. Napoleon acknowledged his defeat as soon as he gave the order to retreat, for nothing ever froze in central Russia at the end of September and the beginning of October. As a contemporary, Vigel', puts the matter:

> Everyone still keeps harping on "General Winter," forgetting that in 1812 the autumn was warmer in our country than in France, that the first defeats of the French at Tarutino and Maloiaroslavets were at the beginning of October and that on the whole distance of almost 265 miles from Moscow to Smolensk, when this "General" still did not appear, whole brigades and divisions of the enemy army began to vanish.[2]

The French attempted to move from Moscow to Kaluga, so as not to retreat by the old, devastated, and deserted route. But in encounters at Tarutino and Maloiaroslavets they were repulsed and forced to return by the old Smolensk road. Followed by the Russian army, surrounded by Cossacks and partisans, the French army melted away in the rapid retreat, which as early as the beginning of November turned into disorderly flight. As early as November 3 the tsar issued a manifesto of thanks to the Russian people for the deliverance of the fatherland from the enemy invasion.

While crossing the River Berezina, to the west of Smolensk in the province of Minsk, November 14–16, the retreating French suffered heavy losses. Under fire of Russian artillery and the weight of great crowds of fugitives, the bridges frequently gave way and thousands of fugitives fell in the river. This is another indication that as late as the middle of November the river still had not frozen, that severe cold had not yet appeared. If there had been really low temperatures only three days earlier, the French could have avoided catastrophe on the Berezina by crossing on the ice. As it was, the majority of the French troops caught at the Berezina perished or were captured.

After this episode, the severe freezing weather really did descend. By the end of the year almost all of the Grand Army had perished. Only a sorry remainder of it—1000 armed men and 20,000 without arms—crossed the Russian border, and Napoleon hastened to France to prepare a new army. On December 25, 1812, a manifesto of the tsar declared the complete liquidation of the invading enemy, for whose defeat "the troops, the nobility, the clergy, the merchants, the common folk, in a word all the ranks and estates of the realm, sparing neither their property nor their lives, were of one spirit."

After the destruction of the Grand Army, Kutuzov advised halting at the borders, but Alexander decided to take upon himself

---

[2] Vigel', *Vospominaniia*, vol. IV, p. 77.

the liberation of Europe from the Napoleonic yoke and ordered his forces westward. Kutuzov died in April 1813 in the Prussian village of Bunzlau, and Alexander himself took command. That autumn the formal command of the allied armies was taken by the Austrian General Schwarzenberg.

In February 1813, the king of Prussia had again concluded an alliance with Alexander. Russian troops soon occupied Berlin and the Prussian monarch called in the Germans to rise for the liberation of the German fatherland from the foreign yoke. At first the war in German territory did not go very well for the allies, but when Austria and England joined the alliance against Napoleon, the balance of power shifted to the allied side. In the three-day "battle of the nations" near Leipzig in October 1813, the Russian, Austrian, and Prussian troops gained a decisive victory over Napoleon; on January 1 (13), 1814, Russian forces crossed the French frontier.

Russia, Austria, Prussia, and England concluded a twenty-year treaty of alliance against Napoleon at Chaumont on February 25 (March 9). Then, following unsuccessful peace negotiations with Napoleon, the allied forces moved on Paris. The French capital capitulated on March 18 (30), and Alexander entered the city at the head of the Russian army.

In an appeal for good conduct on the part of the Russian soldiers, issued before the entry into France, Alexander exhorted: ". . . the enemy, who marched into the heart of our Tsardom, did us much evil, but has suffered a fearful punishment. . . . Do not be like him: inhumanity and cruelty are not pleasing to God Who loves man. Let us forget their deeds. Bring them not vengeance and malice, but friendliness and a hand outstretched in reconciliation."[3] And in fact the conduct of the Russian "barbarians" who entered the capital of civilized Europe, Paris, seemed in contrast much more civilized than that of the civilized French and other Europeans who had previously entered Moscow.

When he received a delegation of Parisians on the day after the triumphal entry, Alexander declared, "I have only one enemy in France, Napoleon." The French Senate formally announced Napoleon to be deposed from the throne and that Louis XVIII, brother of the guillotined Louis XVI, was the monarch of France. On the insistence of Alexander, Louis granted France a constitutional charter, although with a very limited franchise, it is true. In May

---

[3] A. Mikhailovsky-Danilevsky, *Zapiski 1814 i 1815 godov* [*Notes for the Years 1814 and 1815*] (2d ed.; St. Petersburg, 1832), p. 3.

1814, the allies concluded a peace with France by which it renounced its conquests in Europe and returned to the boundaries of 1792. Napoleon signed his abdication from the French throne and received the island of Elba as his possession, retaining the title Emperor. Upon the conclusion of the peace, the allied forces quickly withdrew from France.

The Congress of Vienna and the Holy Alliance

A multitudinous and brilliant congress of European rulers and diplomats that was to negotiate a new order for Europe gathered in Vienna in September 1814. The Napoleonic wars had entirely disrupted the political map of Europe, and now the Congress of Vienna had to decide a multitude of difficult territorial and dynastic questions, of which the Polish-Saxon question was the most difficult. Alexander demanded the annexation of the Duchy of Warsaw to Russia, the Prussian state to be compensated for its loss of Polish land by annexing Saxony. This demand met with opposition from the other powers, and on January 3 (15), 1815, the representatives of Austria, England, and France (Metternich, Castlereagh, and Talleyrand) signed a secret military convention directed against Russia. Diplomatic negotiations in search of a compromise decision were continuing when, in early March, the astounding news arrived that Napoleon had deserted Elba and landed in France. The French troops and populace were going over to his side, and Louis XVIII had fled from Paris.

In fact, he fled so hastily that he forgot the secret treaty of January 3 (15) against Russia, which lay on his desk. When Napoleon again settled down in the palace, he found this treaty and sent it to Alexander in Vienna, in order to show him the duplicity and perfidy of his "allies," to detach him from the coalition. Nevertheless, Napoleon remained Alexander's chief foe. Irked, Alexander called Metternich, showed him the treaty, and before the embarrassed Austrian chancellor could say anything threw the treaty into the fireplace and promised never to mention it again.

The threat of a revival of the Napoleonic Empire inspired the rulers and diplomats in Vienna to settle all questions quickly. On April 21 (May 3) a pact was concluded by Russia, Austria, and Prussia concerning new Polish arrangements, and on May 28 (June 9) the principal act of the Congress of Vienna, establishing a new political order in Europe, was signed. The Duchy of Warsaw was annexed by Russia, and Poznan, as the "Duchy of Poznan," was awarded to Prussia. Galicia, including the Tarnopol region, which had been Russian since 1809, was awarded to Austria, but the city of Cracow, and its environs, was declared "for all time a free, independent, and entirely neutral city under the protection of Russia, Austria and Prussia." A considerable part of the holdings of the king of Saxony, a former ally of Napoleon, was annexed by Prussia, along with the extremely valuable Rhineland provinces. "All the sovereign rulers and free cities of Germany establish among themselves an eternal union, called the general German Bund." Austria received all the possessions of the former republic of Venice, the north and northeastern Adriatic littoral, and Lombardy. The kings and dukes of the various second-rate European powers, who had been deposed by Napoleon, were to be restored wherever possible. As a result of the settlement, Russia, Prussia, and Austria gained territories that added three million, five and a half million, and ten million, respectively, to their populations.

As for Napoleon, the powers at the Congress declared that his return to France "in itself deprives him of the protection of the law," and that "there can be no negotiation or peace with him." The Second Empire of Napoleon lasted only for the famous "hundred days." In June 1815, the English and Prussians defeated him at Waterloo in Belgium, and he had to renounce the throne again. He was captured by the English while attempting to escape to America, and as "a prisoner of all the allied powers," he was exiled to the deserted South Atlantic island of St. Helena, where he died in 1821.

After the exile of Napoleon, the allied powers concluded a second peace treaty with France in November 1815. By its terms France was obliged to pay the allies war reparations of 700 million francs, and seventeen forts were to be occupied by allied forces until the payment of this sum.

In September 1815, during the second allied occupation of Paris, a diplomatic pact unprecedented in history, the Treaty of Fraternal Christian Alliance, was concluded between Alexander and the Austrian and Prussian monarchs. Alexander himself wrote the rough draft of the Holy Alliance, as it is usually called. The treaty consisted of three articles. In the first, the three monarchs promised "to lend aid and assistance to each other on all occasions and in all places" and to treat their subjects "as fathers of families." In the second, the allied monarchs, recognizing Jesus Christ as the true "sovereign of Christian peoples," declared that it was just for the allied governments and their subjects "to consider all of them as members of one Christian nation" and always to act in accordance with the laws of Christianity. The third article expressed readiness to accept in the alliance all powers which recognized its principles. When Alexander proposed this "holy" treaty to the Austrian and Prussian monarchs, they first had some doubts, but they then signed it. The Prussian king did so for the sake of his old friendship with Alexander, which he valued highly, but the Austrian emperor signed only after Metternich had assured him that this "high-sounding and empty document" could bring no harm to Austria. Subsequently, the heads of all the states of Europe, except the pope, the sultan, and the king of England, adhered to the Holy Alliance.

Metternich, the Austrian chancellor, became the leader of international politics on the continent after the Napoleonic wars. In his hands the Alliance became the bulwark of European reaction, an attempt to preserve absolutism and repress all liberal and nationalist movements. The slogan of the Holy Alliance, or more precisely of Metternich and his disciple Alexander, became "the preservation of the thrones and the altars," but just the same some of the thrones of Western and Southern Europe were soon shaken. Revolutions flared up in Spain and Italy (Naples and Piedmont) in 1820–1821, but congresses of the conservative powers meeting in Troppau, Laibach, and Verona determined to suppress the revolutionary movements. This decision was executed, the French army re-establishing "order" in Spain, and the Austrian army acting in Italy.

In 1821 an uprising in Greece against Ottoman domination flared up, and the Ottoman regime answered with a terrible massacre of Christians. The heroic struggle of the Greeks inspired general sympathy, and the Russian public expected Alexander to show support for the Orthodox Greeks, oppressed and slaughtered by the Muslims. But Metternich, the guardian of "order," advised Alexander that the Greek uprising was a manifestation of the revolutionary trend, and by no means should be supported. In a letter of November 18 (30), 1821, Metternich wrote Alexander: "A breach, opened in the alliance of European monarchs by a war with the Turks, would be a breach through which revolution would enter with rapid strides. The fate of civilization is now in the hands of your Imperial Majesty."[4] Alexander accordingly took his stand on the side of civilization in its Austro-Turkish interpretation. The Congress of the Holy Alliance at Verona in 1822 accepted Metternich's viewpoint on legitimacy and declared the Greek uprising to be against a lawful

---

[4] Quoted in Schilder, *Imperator Aleksandr I*, vol. IV, p. 226.

monarch. Thus did the "Holy Alliance" come to the defense of a Muslim throne which was waging war against its Christian subjects.

The Caucasus and Persia

In 1801 the Georgian monarchy, fearing an Iranian invasion, petitioned the Russian emperor to take Georgia under his protection as his vassal. Alexander fulfilled this appeal, affirming a manifesto issued by Paul, January 18, 1801, on the annexation of Georgia. The appearance of the Russians in Georgia disturbed Iran, which declared war on Russia in 1804. Since Russia was occupied with the Napoleonic Wars, she could not divert much military strength against Iran, and the war dragged on until 1813. In that year the Peace Treaty of Gulistan was signed, Iran ceding Russia Georgia, Imeritia, Guria, Mingrelia, Abkhazia, Daghestan, and Azerbaijan, including the cities of Baku and Derbent.

The Russian penetration of the Caucasus was naturally unwelcome to the warlike, free tribes of the region, especially the Muslims. Thus a ceaseless series of Caucasian wars began at the very beginning of the nineteenth century and ended only under Alexander II in the period 1859–1864. Through much of the reign of Alexander I the popular General A. P. Ermolov commanded the active army in the Caucasus, the Separate Caucasian Corps. But he was unable to crush the brave and stubborn resistance of the mountaineers, even though the Russian forces in the Caucasus, regular and Cossack, displayed no little heroism on their own side in the difficult mountain operations. Slowly they penetrated deep into the Caucasus Mountains, building roads and fortresses as they went, including the famous Georgian Military Highway, connecting Tiflis, the capital of Georgia, with the steppeland to the north of the mountains. Step by step new districts were pacified in the mountains. But the Russian position there remained precarious for a long time. New uprisings repeatedly appeared in the pacified districts, requiring new expeditions.

In the mountains of Chechnia and Daghestan a Muslim mystical and nationalist sect called the Miurids arose, uniting the mountain tribes and calling them to a "holy war" against the Russians. In this war the most famous and successful leader of the mountaineers was Imam Shamyl. In the 1840s Russian troops frequently suffered failure against him, and Russian authority almost vanished in the regions where he operated. Only in the reign of Alexander II did the Russian government bring the long, hard struggle with Shamyl and his Miurids to a successful conclusion.

Meanwhile, the Russians had advanced well beyond the Caucasus at the expense of the Iranians, who had attacked in 1826. After the successful offensive of General I. F. Paskevich, which smashed the Iranians at Elisavetpol and took the major fortress of Erivan, the shah was obliged to sign the Treaty of Turkmenchai in 1828. By its terms Iran ceded Russia her lands on the left bank of the River Araks, the predominantly Armenian khanates of Erivan and Nakhichevan, and paid Russia an indemnity.

Russia and Poland

From his youth Alexander had dreamed of re-establishing the Polish state, which his grandmother had dismembered. His close friend, the ardent Polish patriot Prince Adam Czartoryski, encouraged this intention, but Alexander's Russian entourage disapproved of the tsar's Polish sympathies. In any case, Alexander's friendship and alliance with King Frederick William III of Prussia discouraged Polish confidence in Russia, and in the war of 1806–1807 the majority of the Poles favored Napoleon. In the Peace of Tilsit in 1807 Napoleon rewarded them by establishing the Duchy of Warsaw, which was formed from the Polish provinces that he took from Prussia. However, Napoleon did not by this act intend to re-establish an independent Poland, much less restore its former boundaries. He only wanted to have a constant base in East Europe to supply recruits and provisions for his army in case of a possible future war with Austria or Russia. The constitution that Napoleon gave Poland was nominal, like the other Napoleonic constitutions, for the actual power lay only in the hands of the French emperor. A national Polish army of 30,000 men was formed.

Napoleon also established the *personal* freedom of the Polish peasants. The land, however, was declared the property of the nobility and gentry, so the peasants could be only tenant farmers or wage laborers on the estates of the ruling class. In 1807 there were only 2,400,000 inhabitants of the duchy, but it soon received a substantial increase. After the victorious war with Austria in 1809, Napoleon annexed to the duchy the regions of Lublin, Radom, and western Galicia (including Cracow), with a population of 1,500,000, which he took from Austria.

In 1812 the Polish army became part of Napoleon's Grand Army, and in the summer of 1812 the Polish Diet, which had elected Prince Adam Czartoryski as marshal (president), declared the re-establishment of the Polish monarchy and the formation of a general confederation against Russia. In December 1812, the Russian army approached, the supporters of Napoleon in Poland and Lithuania might have expected Russian repressions against them, but Alexander hastened to reassure them. In a manifesto of December 12, he declared his "most kindly forgiveness" to the inhabitants of the "regions formed from Poland," who had participated in the war against Russia, and commanded "all to relegate the past to eternal oblivion and deep silence." In a manifesto to the populace of the Duchy of Warsaw, written in Vilno on December 25, Alexander explained, "You fear vengeance. Do not be afraid. Russia can be victorious but not vengeful." Then in January 1813, the Russian army entered Warsaw. After arriving in Paris in 1814, Alexander gave permission to Polish troops who had fought under Napoleon to return to Poland with their commanders and banners. But he appointed his brother, Grand Duke Constantine Pavlovich, as commander in chief of the Polish army.

The Congress of Vienna then decided that the Polish lands should be "forever annexed to the Russian Empire," excepting Poznan, which was given to Prussia, and Galicia, which was given to Austria. It was further stipulated that the Poles "would have popular representatives and national state institutions."

On November 15 (27), 1815, Alexander signed the constitutional charter of Poland.[5] According to the Constitution of 1815, the king of Poland (the tsar) was crowned in Warsaw and took an oath to observe the constitution. The permanent representative of the crown in Warsaw was his viceroy, under whom the Council of State was formed. Within the council there was a narrower committee, the Administrative Council. Matters of current administration were to be entrusted to five administrative commissions, headed by ministers. The Diet held the legislative power and consisted of two chambers: the Senate, composed mainly of bishops and regional governors appointed for life by the emperor on the nomination of the Senate; the Chamber of Deputies, consisting of 77 deputies elected by the district (*poviat*) diets of the gentry (*szlachta*) and 51 deputies from the cities and townships (*gmin*) elected by citizens meeting a property qualification.

Alexander appointed the elderly General Zaionczek, a former commander of one of the Polish divisions in Napoleon's army, as viceroy of the Kingdom of Poland. However, the main role in ad-

---

[5] The Russian, French, and Polish texts of the constitutional charter of 1815 were published by Professor N. D. Sergeevsky, St. Petersburg, 1907.

ministering the kingdom was played by Grand Duke Constantine and his assistant Senator Novosiltsev, who held the extraconstitutional post of imperial commissioner in the Administrative Council.

According to the Constitution of 1815, the Diet was to be summoned every two years for a session of thirty days. In March 1818, Alexander ceremonially opened the Diet with a speech from the throne in which he called on the representatives of the Kingdom of Poland to prove by their actions that representative institutions "are not in essence a dangerous dream" but, if they are utilized appropriately, "are in complete harmony with the social order and they assure the true well-being of the peoples."[6]

Soon, however, many Poles grew dissatisfied with the administration of Constantine and Novosiltsev, and the government reacted by introducing the censorship of periodicals, and in 1818 by arresting several of the oppositionists. The revolutionary events in Spain and Italy in 1820 encouraged Polish discontent, which was apparent in the second Polish Diet in the autumn of that year, and Polish patriots emulated the revolutionaries of the West in establishing a secret Patriotic Society, which aimed at national independence. However, the third Diet met peacefully in 1825, and Alexander remained satisfied.

In January and February 1826, almost immediately after the Russian uprising of the Decembrists, members of the Patriotic Society were arrested, but the sentences that were meted out to them in 1828 were decidedly lighter than those imposed on the Decembrists. Nicholas I tried to maintain the *status quo* in Poland, but in November 1830, Polish patriots raised an armed revolt against the Russian administration, Tsarevich Constantine and his few Russian guards barely escaping from Poland. In Warsaw the revolutionaries formed a provisional government, which then recognized the commander in chief of the Polish Army, General Chlopicki, as dictator. In January 1831, the Polish Diet declared the end of the reign of Nicholas I and his dynasty in Poland and entrusted power to a national government (*zhond narodovy*) of five members.

At first the Russian troops that were dispatched under General Dibich to suppress the revolt suffered a series of reverses, but in May 1831, they defeated the Poles at Ostrolenka. In June, General Dibich died of cholera, which had already claimed Tsarevich Constantine, and he was replaced by General Paskevich, who took Warsaw by storm and re-established Russian power in Poland.

---

[6] Schilder, *Imperator Aleksandr I*, vol. IV, pp. 86–87.

As the new viceroy of Poland, Paskevich exercised both civil and military authority, and under his regime the supreme criminal court condemned to death 258 leading participants in the uprising. Nicholas commuted these sentences to exile abroad or in Siberia, but he revoked the Polish constitution of 1815 and replaced it with the Organic Statutes of 1832. According to this document, the Kingdom of Poland retained special criminal and civil codes, local self-government, and the use of the Polish language in the courts and civil administration. However, martial law was proclaimed in 1833, and until the death of Nicholas I more than twenty years later, it remained the basis of Paskevich's harsh dictatorship. The Polish army was abolished and the universities of Warsaw and Vilno were closed during this period of military and police rule.

Sweden and Finland

Following the Peace of Tilsit in 1807, antagonism grew between Russia and Sweden, an ally of Britain. Encouraged by the French, the Russians invaded Finland in February 1808, and within a few months they occupied the country, which for centuries had been part of the Swedish kingdom. Without waiting for the conclusion of peace, Alexander proclaimed the conquest of Finland and its annexation by Russia before the end of 1808. At the end of the winter of 1808–1809, the Russian army crossed the frozen Gulf of Bothnia and occupied the Aland Islands. According to the peace treaty signed in Friedrichsham in September 1809, Sweden ceded Finland and the Aland Islands to Russia and also declared her adherence to the Napoleonic continental system.

Having captured Finland, Alexander not only proclaimed to the Finnish people that their laws and rights would be preserved, but he also decided to grant Finland a high degree of political autonomy. This was secured by the Finnish Constitution of 1809, which Speransky helped to draft. Finland, as the Grand Duchy of Finland, was to be a special sort of state. "Finland is not a province but a state," declared Speransky, joined to Russia only by personal union, the emperor of Russia holding the title of "Grand Duke of Finland." The governor general was to be the emperor's representative in Finland, but not the ruler of the country. An Administrative Council was established in 1809 as the head of the civil administration, which in 1816 was renamed the Senate. Legislative power rested with the Diet composed of deputies elected by the different estates of the Finnish people. The first Finnish Diet was opened by Alexander in Borgo in March 1809.[7]

So convinced of the loyalty of his new subjects was Alexander, that in 1811 he added to the Grand Duchy of Finland the province of Vyborg, which had been conquered by Peter the Great and lay in immediate proximity to Petersburg. Soon after the completion of the war with Sweden, Russian troops were withdrawn from Finland and three regiments of light infantry were formed in Finland from the local populace. In 1812 when the Russian garrison, including the guards' regiments, of Petersburg was withdrawn for the struggle with Napoleon, Alexander stationed one of the Finnish regiments in Petersburg on guard duty, including the protection of not only the capital but also the tsar and imperial family. This situation continued for about a year and a half.

Alexander achieved particular diplomatic success in his relations with Sweden, one of the historic foes of Russia. King Charles XIII of Sweden was old, feeble, and did not have an heir. In 1810 the Swedish Riksdag elected the French Marshal Bernadotte as the heir to the throne and regent of the state. Napoleon hoped to find in the future king another obedient vassal, as he had in the rulers in Holland, Italy, and various other European countries. But in 1812 Bernadotte became Alexander's friend and ally and helped him in the struggle with Napoleon.

The Eastern Question

At the very end of the eighteenth century, Napoleon's expedition to Egypt, in 1798, caused alarm in Constantinople over the territorial security and independence of the Ottoman Empire, and this fear impelled the Ottoman government to seek support in Russia. In December 1798, a treaty of alliance was signed in Constantinople between the Ottoman and Russian empires, which in effect made Russia dominant in the Black Sea and established her predominant influence in the Ottoman government. Because this alliance enabled Russian warships to pass the Straits, the Russian fleet, commanded by Admiral Ushakov and later by Admiral Seniavin, played an active role in operations against Napoleon in the eastern Mediterranean. They established Russian control on the islands of the Aegean and

---

[7] On Finland's legal position relative to the Russian Empire, see P. Shilovsky, *Akty otnosiashchiesia k politicheskomu polozheniiu Finliandii* [*Documents Relating to the Political Status of Finland*] (St. Petersburg, 1903).

RUSSIA AND THE
EASTERN QUESTION,
1812-1885

---- Ottoman Empire, 1815 ——— Boundaries, 1885
.... Boundaries proposed in treaty of San Stefano, 1878

Ionian Seas, expelled the French from the Island of Corfu, occupied it, and from the islands of the Ionian Sea formed the Republic of the Seven United Islands, which was in reality a Russian protectorate until 1807.

In 1805 the treaty of 1798 was renewed, but the following year political circumstances in the Balkans altered. Russia went to war with Napoleon and suffered military reverses, while a "French party" was formed within the Turkish government, attempting to replace the Russian alliance with a French one to rid the Balkans of the predominant Russian influence. Napoleon soon offered the Porte a guarantee of the independence and integrity of the Ottoman Empire, and persuaded the sultan to declare war on Russia.

The Russo-Turkish War that began in 1806 dragged on until 1812, neither side achieving a decisive success for a long time. A considerable part of the Russian armed forces in these years was directed to other wars then in progress—with France, Sweden, and Iran. The Ottoman forces also had to fight on two fronts. While meeting the Russians on the Danube, they had to suppress a heroic uprising of the Serbian nation, led by the almost legendary Karageorge.

In 1811 General Kutuzov, the Russian commander in chief on the Danube front, brought the protracted war to a successful conclusion. In that year he completely defeated the Ottoman army at Slobodzeia on the left bank of the Danube, not far from Rushchuk, and in 1812 he concluded peace with the Ottomans at Bucharest. The Treaty of Bucharest, signed May 16, 1812, reaffirmed previous treaties and conventions between Russia and the Ottoman Empire. It assured a "pardon and complete amnesty" for subjects of the sultan who had fought on the Russian side, affirmed the rights and privileges of the Danubian principalities, Moldavia and Wallachia, and formally recognized Serbia as autonomous. The Ottomans retained the right to maintain their garrisons in Serbia, but the internal affairs of the country were to be left to the inhabitants. The River Pruth was recognized as the boundary between Russia and the European provinces of the Ottoman Empire as far as its confluence with the Danube, which formed the boundary down to the Black Sea. Russia thus obtained the province of Bessarabia with cities of Khotin, Benderi, Izmail, and Ackerman and established itself on the mouth of the Danube.

In 1821 the Greeks arose against the centuries-old Ottoman domination. The uprising was prepared by the secret society Heteria, which had its organization earlier in Odessa. In the spring of 1821 Alexander Ypsilanti, a Greek patriot who was a general in the Russian service, led the forces of Heteria from Bessarabia in an invasion of the Danubian principalities, declaring an uprising against the Porte for the freedom and independence of Greece. Revolts against the Ottomans soon broke out in Greece proper and on the islands of the Archipelago. The outbreak in the Danubian principalities was easily suppressed by the Ottoman forces, but in Greece the struggle grew in scope and for some time was the central question of European international politics. The heroic struggle of the Greeks for liberty attracted general sympathy in Russia and the countries of Western Europe. Metternich, however, dissuaded Alexander from intervention, and in an official statement to the Ottoman government the tsar openly condemned the uprising.

Meanwhile, Sultan Mahmud II replied to the Greek revolution with mass slaughter of the Greeks in Constantinople and Asia Minor. Among the victims were Gregory, the seventy-four-year-old patriarch of Constantinople, and three Greek Orthodox metropolitans, who were hanged by the Ottomans on the first day of Easter. Ottoman atrocities caused general indignation in Europe and strengthened sympathy for the Greeks, but Metternich continued to persuade Alexander that assistance to the Greeks would be assistance to European revolution, and Alexander confined himself to diplomatic protests against Muslim atrocities. Meanwhile, sympathy for the Greeks, philhellenism, grew in Europe, especially in France and England, which sent financial donations and volunteer soldiers.

Philhellenism soon found powerful official support in the English government, which hastened to fill the role in the Balkans abandoned by the Russian emperor. In 1823 the new leader of British foreign policy, George Canning, declared that Great Britain could not be indifferent to the struggle of the Greeks for their liberty. Britain recognized the Greeks as having the rights of a belligerent state and observed the blockade of the Ottoman realm that the Greeks had declared.

But the situation of the Greeks remained extremely difficult and dangerous. In 1822 the Greek national assembly in Epidaurus proclaimed a liberal constitution, but this step did not pacify the bitter quarrels of various parties and individual leaders within the movement. The military situation became especially threatening in 1825 when the army and fleet of Muhammad 'Ali, the pasha of Egypt, appeared in support of the Ottomans. The son of the pasha, Ibrahim, commanded the army, which penetrated the Peloponnesus, laying waste the mutinous country.

When Nicholas I came to the throne, he decided to continue the policy of the Holy Alliance and to preserve friendship with Austria and Prussia, but he took an independent position on the Greek question, much to Metternich's annoyance. On April 4, 1826, Nicholas signed a protocol with Britain, by which the two powers agreed to seek the termination of military operations in Greece and the recognition by the sultan of Greek autonomy. France adhered to this agreement the following year in London, July 6, 1827.

The Ottoman government did not fulfill the tripartite demand for the recall of Ottoman and Egyptian military and naval forces from Greece, nor the demand for the establishment of Greek autonomy. In October 1827, the allied naval squadrons—English, Russian, and French—met the Turko-Egyptian fleet at Navarino, on the southern shores of the Peloponnesus, attacked, and destroyed it. The allied ambassadors then left Constantinople, and Ottomans began to prepare for a holy war against the infidels. In this move Russia was considered to be the main Ottoman foe, and it was against Russia that the appeal to holy war was directed. In the spring of 1828, Russian forces were ordered to enter the Danubian principalities, and on

April 14, 1828, Nicholas issued a declaration of war against the Ottoman Empire.

Although the brunt of the fighting fell to the Russians, the French did occupy the Peloponnesus and forced the evacuation of the Egyptian troops, relieving southern Greece of the Turko-Egyptian terror. In the summer of 1828, Ottoman forces withdrew from central and northern Greece as well, retreating into Thessaly and freeing the Greeks from their centuries-old oppression.

Meanwhile, the Russo-Turkish combat continued through 1828 without any decisive results for either side. At the beginning of the summer, Russian troops crossed the Danube and soon took the maritime fortress of Varna. In Asia, General Paskevich took Kars and Akhaltsikh. But the Russian siege of the strong fortress of Silistria on the southern bank of the Danube was unsuccessful, and in autumn 1828, it was lifted, after which Russian forces withdrew to the left bank of the Danube. Military operations were renewed in the spring of 1829, and that summer was marked by major Russian victories. Under its new commander, General Dibich, the Russian army crushed the Ottoman forces in the Battle of Kulevchi, then took Adrianople and threatened Constantinople itself. The fortress of Silistria surrendered, and in Asia Erzurum was taken. The Porte was obliged to sue for peace, which was concluded in Adrianople in September 1829.

According to the terms of the Peace of Adrianople, the western Russo-Turkish boundary was recognized as the River Pruth and the southern (lower) channel of the Danube, leaving the whole delta of the Danube in Russian hands; in the Caucasus, Russia received the eastern Black Sea littoral, including the ports of Anapa and Poti and the regions of the cities Akhaltsikh and Akhalkalaki; and Russia undertook to guarantee the welfare of Moldavia and Wallachia, which were to be established as "independent national governments." A supplementary article to the treaty stated that the princes (*hospodar*) of Moldavia and Wallachia were to be elected for life from among the local nobles (*boyars*), and that the Ottoman authorities were not to interfere in the internal affairs of these Danubian principalities under any pretext whatsoever. The Ottomans agreed to accept the London Treaty of 1827, granting political autonomy to Greece, and were obliged to open the Straits (the Bosporus and Dardanelles to merchantmen of all nations and to pay Russia compensation for her military expenses.

In 1830 Greece, by the agreement of the European powers with the Porte, was recognized as an independent state. As early as 1827 the leader of the pro-Russian party in Greece, Count John Capo d'Istria, formerly Alexander's assistant minister of foreign affairs, had been elected president of Greece. But a cruel struggle between factions in Greece began soon after the conclusion of the Russo-Turkish war. At the same time, the revolution of 1830 in France ruptured the triple alliance of Russia with England and France, causing sharp antagonism between Russia and her former allies. This turn of events intensified the political dissension in Greece. On all sides opposition to Capo d'Istria arose, turning into an armed uprising, and in 1831 he was assassinated. Capo d'Istria's death ended Russian influence in Greece, and in 1832 the London conference of European powers agreed to declare Greece a monarchy and to offer the Greek crown to Prince Otto of Bavaria.

Although Russian influence in Greece was declining, it seemed more durable in the northern Balkans, and for a time even seemed dominant within the Ottoman government itself. For five years after the war of 1828–1829 the principalities of Moldavia and Wallachia were occupied by Russian forces under General Kiselev. As head of the civil government in the principalities, he worked out organic statutes or regulations for them, introducing order into their administrative structure and system of taxation. Kiselev also rendered great service by regulating the relations of the peasant population with the boyar landowners.

In this period events forced the Porte to turn to the Russian emperor for assistance and protection. The governor of Egypt, Muhammad 'Ali, raised a revolt against the sultan and penetrated into Syria in 1832. He defeated the Ottoman forces there, after which he was able to threaten Constantinople. The sultan turned for help to Nicholas, who declared that he "always remained an enemy of mutiny and a true friend of the sultan." In February 1833, Admiral Lazarev's squadron, carrying ten thousand infantry under General Muraviev, sailed into the Bosporus to save the Ottoman Empire from the threatening danger. General Muraviev's troops encamped on the Asian shore of the Bosporus to repulse the possible attack by Egyptian troops. But the Egyptian pasha decided against war with the Russians, and the Ottoman sultan did not have much desire to detain his Russian guests in Constantinople. He therefore hastened to conclude peace with his rebellious Egyptian vassal, yielding Syria to him for temporary occupation. At this time, the summer of 1833, Nicholas sent as his Extraordinary and Plenipotentiary Ambassador General A. F. Orlov to Constantinople, where he concluded a treaty of alliance—valid for eight years—between Russia and the Porte.

This became known as the Treaty of Unkiar-Skelessi after the valley near Constantinople in which the Russian troops were encamped. According to this agreement, the Ottoman Empire was obliged to close the Dardanelles to foreign naval vessels and to fulfill without fail all the provisions of previous peace treaties. Russia was obliged to render the Ottoman military and naval assistance upon request of the sultan. Within two days of the signing of the treaty, the Russian fleet and troop transports withdrew through the Bosporus into the Black Sea.[8]

The Treaty of Unkiar-Skelessi naturally caused dissatisfaction, envy, and mistrust in the West, and Britain and France quickly protested. Their diplomatic representatives in Constantinople went to work with all their might to paralyze, or at least weaken, Russian influence in the Ottoman Empire, and in this they succeeded to a considerable degree.

In 1839, war between the Porte and Egypt was renewed, but this time all the major European powers took the affairs of the Ottomans in hand. In the summer of 1840, a treaty was concluded in London between Britain, Austria, Russia, and Prussia on one side and the Ottoman Empire on the other. According to this convention, the European powers agreed jointly to maintain "the integrity and independence of the Ottoman Empire in the interests of cementing the peace of Europe." If necessary, they were to force Muhammad 'Ali of Egypt to make peace with the sultan. The convention further stated that passage through the Bosporus and Dardanelles should be forbidden to the warships of *all* foreign powers. France at first sided with the Egyptian pasha, but the following year it associated itself with the concert of great powers, and in the summer of 1841, a second convention was signed in London. Its contents were the same as the first, but it was now supported by all five great powers of Europe. Thus Russia lost her predominant influence in the Ottoman Empire, and the integrity and independence of that empire was guaranteed by the European "concert," in which Britain now played first violin.

The revolutionary events in Europe in 1848–1849 and Nicholas' position as the defender of the old order still further deepened the gulf between Russia and the Western powers. Revolutionary disturbances also occurred in 1848–1849 in the Danubian principalities of Moldavia and Wallachia. By agreement between the Russian emperor and Ottoman sultan, Russian and Ottoman troops

---

[8] T. Iuzefovich, ed., *Dogovory Rossii s vostokom* [*Russia's Treaties with the East*] (St. Petersburg, 1869), pp. 89–92.

entered the principalities to restore "order and tranquility" and remained until 1851. Moreover, Nicholas ordered his army into Hungary in 1849 to suppress the revolution there and to re-establish the Hapsburg monarchy, which seemed on the verge of collapse. The result of this excessive legitimism was that four years later Austria "astounded the whole world with its ingratitude" by supporting Britain and France during the period of the Crimean War. Russia gained fame as "the gendarme of Europe" and the hatred not only of revolutionary but also of moderate liberal circles in Europe.

The Crimean War

The Revolution of 1848 produced a new leader in France, Louis Napoleon, the nephew of Napoleon I. In 1848 he was elected president, and in December 1852, was proclaimed Emperor of the French. Nicholas greeted his new imperial colleague with great hostility and would not agree to call him his "brother," as was customary in diplomatic correspondence between monarchs, which greatly offended Napoleon. For his part, the new-fledged emperor of France strove to enhance his imperial glory by military and diplomatic successes as quickly as possible. In particular he chose to remember that previous French kings, "their most Christian majesties," had exercised the right of protecting Roman Catholic believers in the territory of the Ottoman Empire, and he decided that a French ruler should again become the protector of Catholics in the Near East. At his insistence, the Ottoman government took the keys of the temple of Bethlehem from the Orthodox priests in order to give them to the Catholic priests. This victory of the "Latins" caused indignation and protests from the Orthodox populace and clergy, who took their grievances to the Russian emperor as the patron and protector of the Orthodox believers in the Ottoman Empire. This famous quarrel over the keys, for all its seeming insignificance, had serious consequences, for the possession of the keys of the Holy Place of Bethlehem had great symbolic religious significance in the eyes of the Eastern Christians. The loss of the keys was detrimental to the status of Orthodoxy in the Ottoman Empire and diminished the prestige and influence of the supreme protector of Orthodoxy, the Russian emperor.

Nicholas determined to re-establish and strengthen his right as protector of the Orthodox Church in the Ottoman Empire, and for this purpose sent Prince Menshikov to Constantinople as his extraordinary ambassador. But the Ottoman government followed the advice of the Western powers and especially the English ambassador

Stratford de Redcliffe, who was then acting as the sultan's chief adviser in foreign affairs. The Sublime Porte refused to satisfy the Russian demands, and Menshikov left Constantinople, breaking off diplomatic relations with the Ottoman government. In May 1853, Nicholas ordered Russian forces into the Danubian principalities, stating that he did not intend war against the Porte, but only wanted "to have in our hands such a guarantee as will insure the re-establishment of our rights in any case." The Ottomans demanded the withdrawal of Russian forces from the Danubian principalities and turned to the Western powers with an appeal for assistance. In October 1853, British and French squadrons entered the Sea of Marmora, and the Ottoman Empire declared war on Russia. In November the Russian Black Sea fleet, commanded by Admiral Nakhimov, destroyed the weaker Ottoman fleet in the Battle of Sinope, and the army of the Caucasus defeated the Ottoman forces at Bashkadykliar, a small town south of Tiflis province. War between Russia and the Western powers now became inevitable. In February 1854, the British and French fleets entered the Black Sea, and in March these two governments declared war on Russia to protect their ally, the Ottoman sultan, from Russian aggression.

For his part, Nicholas declared, "We neither sought nor seek to gain any preponderant influence in Turkey beyond that which Russia possesses by the existing treaties. . . . Russia fights for the Christian faith and for the defense of her brothers in the faith, who are beset by furious enemies." For Nicholas the greatest disappointment was that Russia's enemies—the Ottoman Empire, Britain, France, and the Kingdom of Sardinia—were joined by Austria, which Nicholas had just saved from internal disintegration. In June 1854, the Austrian government delivered an ultimatum demanding that Russia guarantee the inviolability of the Ottoman possessions and evacuate the Danubian principalities. Nicholas was compelled to accede to this demand, and Moldavia and Wallachia were occupied by Austrians and Ottomans. Moreover, Austria concentrated an "army of observation," one hundred thousand strong, on the Russian borders. Because of the threatening posture adopted by Austria, Nicholas was also forced to station a large army on the Austrian frontier, thereby depriving himself of these forces in the military operations against the Western allies.

No one in Russia knew where the allies would deliver their main blow, and Russia's armed forces were dispersed all around a great expanse from Torneo to Tiflis. England began a naval war, or more precisely, naval demonstrations, everywhere. Her ships bombarded places as distant as Odessa on the Black Sea, the Solovetsky monastery on the White Sea and Petropavlovsk in Kamchatka. Finally, in September 1854, an Anglo-Franco-Ottoman force of 70,000 landed at Eupatoria in the Crimea and soon laid siege to the Russian naval base at Sevastopol. This port was almost unfortified on its land approaches, but military units hastily gathered there. Aided by the civilian populace and led by the military engineer Totleben, improvised fortifications were quickly thrown up. The Russian fleet consisted of sailing vessels that were no match for the steam-driven warships of the powerful allied squadrons, and it was therefore scuttled by the Russian sailors in the entrance to the Bay of Sevastopol to block an invasion by sea. The crews of the ships, commanded by their admirals, then joined the garrison of the fortress. In the course of the next eleven months the officers, soldiers, and sailors of the Sevastopol garrison, aided by the civilian populace, sustained the siege of the fortress with exceptional courage, beating back enemy charges and repairing the damage caused by the ceaseless bombardment. Three illustrious admirals, Nakhimov, Kornilov, and Istomin, were killed in the defense. The efforts of Russian forces, commanded at first by Prince Menshikov and later by Prince Gorchakov, to raise the siege of Sevastopol were unsuccessful, owing to allied victories at Inkerman in October 1854 and on the Chernaia River in August 1855. In late August 1855, the allies succeeded in capturing the bastion of the defenses of Sevastopol, the kurgan (fortified hillock) of Malakhov, and the continued defense of Sevastopol became hopeless. During the night of August 28, Russian troops were withdrawn from the southern part of Sevastopol into the northern section, and allied troops occupied the bloodstained ruins of the fortress.

The Russians found some compensation for the loss of Sevastopol in the capture of the strong fortress of Kars, together with many Ottoman troops, by the Russian army of the Caucasus in November 1855. But heroic feats could not conceal the complete bankruptcy of the governmental system that the Crimean War revealed. Although Nicholas disposed of an army of a million, including the state militia that had been raised to support the regulars, he lacked the strength to defeat a landing of 70,000–100,000 enemy troops. The causes of this military failure, now obvious to everyone, were the chaotic condition of the military supply system, the obsoleteness of Russian weapons, the shortage of ammunition, the absence of adequate means of communication, the want of military leaders who were capable of independent action, the unsatisfactory order of medical-sanitary units, and finally, the terrible cupidity of the supply

chiefs and the abuses in all levels of the military and civil administration.

Nicholas I died in February 1855, in the midst of the
Sevastopol campaign. His son Alexander II, who succeeded him, clearly saw the necessity of radical reform in Russia and therefore wished
to conclude peace. In February 1856, the peace conference opened
in Paris, and on March 18 (30) the treaty was signed. According
to its conditions, the allies returned Sevastopol to Russia, Russia returned Kars to the Ottomans, and the European powers agreed to
"pledge themselves to respect the independence and integrity of the
Ottoman Empire." The sultan notified the powers that he had granted
a *firman* (decree) that ameliorated the lot of all his subjects, without distinction as to religion or ethnic origin, but that the powers
in no case had the right to interfere "in the relations of His High-
ness the Sultan with his subjects or in the internal administration
of his Empire." The Black Sea was declared neutral; the Straits were
opened to the mercantile shipping of all nations, but closed to all
warships; and neither the Russian emperor nor the sultan were to
have the right to maintain armed vessels on the Black Sea or fortifications on its shores (an onerous stipulation that Russia renounced
in 1870 during the turmoil of the Franco-Prussian War). Traffic on
the Danube was recognized as free; new boundaries were drawn in
Bessarabia; and Russia ceded the mouth of the Danube and southern
Bessarabia to Moldavia. The principalities of Moldavia and Wallachia,
subject to the supreme authority of the Porte and guaranteed by the
signatory powers, were to retain their independence, and "none of the
guaranteeing Powers possess the exclusive right to be their protector."
The principality of Serbia, "under the supreme authority of the
Sublime Porte," which had the right to maintain Ottoman garrisons
in Serbia, retained its independence. A supplementary convention
obliged Russia not to fortify the Aland Islands.

Austria and Prussia

The basic principle of Nicholas' foreign policy was the
preservation of the Holy Alliance, inherited from Alexander, and
the fulfillment of all consequent obligations. The difficulty was that
Austria and Prussia regarded this alliance as decidedly not "holy,"
and exploited the political prejudices of the Russian Don Quixote
for their own ends. The cunning and cynical Austrian chancellor,
Metternich, was particularly successful in this. It is true that Nicholas
deviated from the position of the Holy Alliance early in his reign

with respect to the Greek question, but disillusioned with the results of his Greek policy and frightened by the European revolution of 1830, he quickly returned to the embrace of Metternich and the king of Prussia, Nicholas' father-in-law. In 1833 Nicholas saw the Austrian Emperor Francis in Münchengrätz to reach an agreement on all the major questions of European politics. The convention concluded there affirmed the mutual obligation to support the existence of the Ottoman Empire under the existing dynasty, and a secret article stated that Austria and Russia should act in unity to establish a new order in the European possessions of that power in case of an overthrow of the *status quo.* By means of this agreement Metternich, at no cost to Austria, tied his partner's hands and obtained a decisive voice in Balkan affairs. Concerning the Polish question, the two allies mutually guaranteed one another's Polish possessions. In October 1833, a convention between Austria, Prussia, and Russia obliged the three powers to render one another mutual support "to strengthen the conservative system, which constitutes the stable basis of their policies."

In August 1835, Nicholas met with the new Austrian emperor, Ferdinand, and the king of Prussia, Frederick William, in Teplitz. Here the three monarchs again pledged assurance to one another of their loyalty to the alliance. Of course, the alliance was no longer the all-European Holy Alliance, which Alexander had tried to create in 1815, but only a tripartite pact of Austria, Prussia and Russia. But Nicholas continued to consider himself "the defender of the thrones and altars" of Europe, not only by inalienable right but as a sacred duty.

Nesselrode, the dull, bureaucratic diplomat who served as Nicholas' minister of foreign affairs, carried out the policy of friendship for the German states and the preservation of the *status quo,* and did not have the slightest intention of liberating the Slavs under Ottoman or Austrian domination. "Slavism," he maintained in his report to the tsar for the year 1845, "is nothing but the mask which conceals the revolutionary propaganda of the Poles and French, who seek to stir up the Slavic subjects of the Austrian Emperor and the Sultan."[9]

Nicholas wholeheartedly undertook to fulfill this imaginary obligation during the European revolutions of 1848–1849. In March 1848, he issued an emotional, shrill manifesto on the revolutionary events in western Europe. In it he declared that ". . . a mutiny has

---

[9] S. S. Tatishchev, *Vneshniaia politika imperatora Nikolaia I* [*The Foreign Policy of Emperor Nicholas I*] (St. Petersburg, 1887), p. 419.

the impudence to threaten Russia," that "We are ready to meet our foes," and concluded with the exclamation: "God is with us! Understand this, O nations, and submit, for God is with us!" No such enemies appeared in Russia, but an uprising against Hapsburg rule occurred in neighboring Hungary. The revolutionaries, having defeated the Austrian forces, declared the Hapsburg dynasty deprived of rights to the Hungarian crown, proclaimed the independence of Hungary, and elected Louis Kossuth head of the provisional government. The young Austrian emperor, Francis Joseph, who had just ascended the throne, turned to Nicholas with an appeal for help, and Nicholas hastened to restore "order." He sent an army under General Paskevich into Hungary and in a manifesto of April 26, 1849, declared that, in accordance with the appeal of the Austrian emperor for aid "against our common enemies," he had dispatched the Russian army "to advance for the extinction of the mutiny and the destruction of the impudent malefactors who attempted to upset the tranquility of our regions." After a short summer campaign the Russian army forced the Hungarian army to capitulate at Vilagos August 1 (13), 1849, soon after which Paskevich's army returned to Russia, leaving the Austrians to dispose of "the impudent malefactors." And although the leaders of the Hungarian uprising were hanged not by the Russians but by the Austrians, the hatred of liberal Europe was directed mainly at the Russian "gendarme of Europe," and not against the Austrian hangman.

In 1852 Nicholas visited Berlin and Vienna and was received with great honor and expressions of friendly devotion and of loyalty to the alliance, but as Tatishchev writes, "the Holy Alliance was already no more than a spectre." In the course of a year the "ally" Austria appeared in the camp of the enemies of Nicholas' Russia; in fact, Austria mobilized so large an army against Russia and assumed so threatening a posture that the Russian government had to concentrate on its western frontier large military forces that probably would have been sufficient to raise the siege of Sevastopol and hurl the Anglo-French invasion into the sea. It is true that Prussia did not come out against Russia directly, but she did conclude a treaty of coordinated action with Austria in case of Russian aggression.

Thus did Nicholas' foreign policy end in a complete fiasco on all military and diplomatic fronts.

5

The Epoch
of the Great Reforms

The reign of Alexander II (1855–1881) marks a turning point in Russian history. This period saw a series of far-reaching reforms that profoundly altered almost every aspect of national life. The first of these reforms was the most necessary and the most difficult one—the abolition of serfdom. After its enactment had changed social and administrative conditions in rural areas, other reforms became necessary and were enacted in 1864, namely the introduction of local self-government (*zemstvo*) and a reorganization of the judicial system on the basis of modern requirements. Finally a military reform in 1874 established universal military service and brought about a reorganization of the army. The chief architect of these vital changes, the tsar-liberator, was not, however, a reformer by birth, and largely because of his inner conflicts the new state structure was left tragically incomplete when he died.

Alexander II and His Collaborators

Emperor Alexander II was born in Moscow April 17, 1818, the son of Grand Duke (later Emperor) Nicholas Pavlovich and Charlotte, the daughter of King Frederick William III of Prussia and the sister of the future German emperor William I. In 1841 Alexander married a princess of Hesse-Darmstadt, the future empress Maria Alexandrovna, reinforcing the dynastic ties that subsequently influenced his foreign policy.

page 125

Alexander's education was marked by two partly contradictory tendencies—humanitarian and military. The poet Zhukovsky hailed his birth and exhorted the future tsar not to forget, when on the lofty throne, "the most sacred of titles—man." The tsar's family, however, preferred to give the little grand duke more specific rank and titles. Ten days after his birth he was appointed honorary commander of the guards hussar regiment, at seven years he was promoted to coronet and entered on the rolls of the regiment, and at nine years he was appointed commander (*ataman*) of the Cossack troops. Nicholas appointed Lieutenant General Ushakov as head tutor for his son and more than once declared that he "must be a soldier in spirit." Captain Merder, however, a humane and cultured man, was appointed tutor to the boy at the age of six, and two years later the poet Zhukovsky was appointed his "mentor." Their goal in educating the heir to the throne was to develop virtue and humane feelings in him and to offset the predominantly military element in the education of the future tsar.

Eventually Alexander did become a soldier. At eighteen he was promoted to major general "for distinguished service," and to the end of his life he retained his interest in and love for the external side of military affairs: parades, inspections, trooping of colors, drill, and maneuvers. But love of militarism did not destroy Alexander's natural characteristics and those fostered by his education: mildness, kindness, and as his adviser Miliutin said, "good will and gentleness." He was very sensitive and keenly felt his own and others' sorrows.

One must note that Nicholas not only gave his son a military education, but he also tried to prepare him for his future governmental activities. The heir to the throne heard lectures on law from Speransky and on foreign policy from the diplomat Baron Brunnov. And for practical acquaintance with the affairs of state, Nicholas appointed his son, upon attaining his majority, to the Council of State, the Committee of Ministers, the Finance Committee, and even the Holy Synod.

Though not without experience in the affairs of state, Alexander, an admirer of his father, ascended the throne without any definite plan of systematic reform. However, the shock of the military and diplomatic defeat of 1853–1855, which had exposed the backwardness of the country and the bankruptcy of Nicholas' regime, made Alexander recognize the need for basic changes and imbued him with a firm determination to realize whatever reforms were necessary for the good of Russia.

Most difficult was the elimination of serfdom, with which the interests of the landowning class were so tightly bound. Alexander II was not against the landowning nobility as a class. Like his father, he considered himself "the first nobleman (*dvorianin*) of the Empire," and saw the nobility as the "chief bulwark of the throne." Nonetheless, he recognized that the interests of the state required the abolition of serfdom, and he courageously and firmly took this matter in hand, overcoming stubborn resistance from the court and bureaucracy and from the bigoted mass of provincial landowning nobles. The powerful proserfdom party threatened the tsar with both the opposition of the landowning class and inevitable anarchy and chaos, possibly another Pugachev rebellion, which would follow the removal of the landowners' authority over the peasants. But Alexander expressed his feelings clearly in a letter to his friend General Rostovtsev, in October 1859:

> If these gentlemen think to intimidate me with their efforts, they are very mistaken. I am too convinced of the rightness of the sacred enterprise that we have instituted that anyone can stop me short of its completion. . . . In this, as always, I trust in God and in the assistance of such as you, who honestly want this so very sincerely, and, like me, see in it the salvation and the future well-being of Russia. Do not lose heart, as I do not lose heart, however often one is burdened with heavy woes.[1]

In 1861, the serf reform was put into effect. As we shall see, it was a compromise that satisfied no one, even though it was in essence the only possible kind of solution in the circumstances. The aristocracy and provincial nobility bemoaned the destruction of their sacred rights by their tsar, while Herzen in his periodical *The Bell*, published in London, wailed equally loudly that "serfdom is not abolished at all," and that "the tsar betrayed the people."

One can easily understand that such a reaction to the sacred enterprise which Alexander had conducted with such difficulty affected his mild and sensitive spirit. He became disillusioned, weary, and distrustful of people. Just as Alexander I expended too much moral energy in the struggle with Napoleon and seemed to have been broken by it, so Alexander II to some extent overtaxed himself in his struggle with serfdom and the landlords.

Soon personal danger and anxiety were added to the feelings of disillusionment. The emerging revolutionary movement threat-

---

[1] N. P. Semenov, ed., *Osvobozhdenie krest'ian* [*Liberation of the Peasants*] (St. Petersburg, 1889–1892), vol. II, p. 128.

ened the destruction of the "imperial party," and in 1866 Karakozov's
shots opened a series of attempts on the life of the tsar-liberator.
Representatives of the "reactionary gang" (as War Minister Miliutin
called them), in particular Count Shuvalov, the chief of the political
police, exaggerated the revolutionary danger in order to subject the
tsar to their influence. It is not surprising, therefore, that the reform
movement was halted in the 1870s, and that stagnation and even reaction against the liberal course appeared in government. "How striking and regrettable is a comparison with the circumstances in which
I entered the cabinet thirteen years ago," wrote Miliutin. "Then the
tsar sympathized with progress, and moved forward himself. Now he
has lost faith in everything that he has done, in all who surround him,
even in himself." [2]

But it is characteristic of Alexander's indecision that even
in the period when his chief advisers were the reactionaries Shuvalov
and Tolstoy, he did not dismiss his liberal minister of war, D. A.
Miliutin, who in 1874 conducted the last of the great reforms, the
introduction of universal military service.

In the second half of the 1870, the struggle of the Balkan
Slavs against Ottoman domination entirely occupied the attention of
the government and the public, and the tsar again vacillated. With
all his soul Alexander sympathized with the sufferings and struggles
of the Balkan Christians, but for a long time he could not decide
to declare war on the Ottoman Empire, even though he gave Russian
officers permission to join the Serbian army as volunteers. The war,
which eventually did break out, ended with brilliant Russian victories and the peace treaty of San Stefano at the gates of Constantinople. But when England and Austria, fearful of the expansion
of Russian influence, came out against Alexander, he had no allies and
had to give up many fruits of the Russian victory at the Congress of
Berlin.

Again the necessary compromises caused general dissatisfaction, both in Russia and in the Balkans. Especially in Slavophile
circles of Russian society, there were heated protests against the Treaty
of Berlin, and the tsar himself felt bitter and insulted by the concessions he had to make. In 1880 Miliutin wrote in his diary that
"one notices fatigue, boredom in the tsar; he is not much interested
in affairs."

Meanwhile, at home the revolutionary terror increased,
and attempts on Alexander's life became increasingly frequent. At the

---

[2] D. A. Miliutin, *Dnevnik* [Diary] (Moscow, 1947), vol. I, p. 120.

end of his life he became convinced of the inadequacy of security measures that depended on the police. Acting on the advice of his last liberal ministers, Loris-Melikov, Miliutin, and Abaza, he intended to strengthen and complete the great reforms of the first half of his reign. At the very moment when Alexander was about to proclaim a liberal plan drawn up by Loris-Melikov, which called for the participation of elected popular representatives in legislative activity, a bomb hurled by a representative of those who considered themselves to be the "people's will" cut short the life and anxieties of the tsar-liberator and tsar-martyr, changing the course of Russian history.

Concerning Alexander's collaborators, it should be noted that his chief assistants in the course of liberal reforms were military men, despite the widely held opinion that a reactionary spirit is inherent in the military caste. Among Alexander's liberal aides were General Admiral Grand Duke Constantine Nicholaevich and three infantry generals: Rostovtsev, Miliutin, and Loris-Melikov.

The grand duke, younger brother of the tsar, was born in 1824, and in Alexander's reign was in charge of the navy. He had received a good education, was distinguished by his lively, even passionate temperament, and after the Crimean catastrophe he was imbued with a firm belief that radical reforms were necessary. As a member and later as chairman of the Main Committee on Peasant Affairs, he made every possible effort to insure the success of the peasant reform and overcome the opposition. In the navy, Constantine abolished harsh corporal punishment. He ardently supported all the general reforms of Alexander's reign. He was appointed chairman of the Council of State in 1865, and in 1873 he skilfully maneuvered through the council Miliutin's proposed statute establishing universal military service. Upon the accession of Alexander III, Constantine Nicholaevich was relieved of all his high responsibilities and passed from the political scene.

Adjutant General Rostovtsev was appointed to the secret committee on the peasant question, which became the center in which the reform was finally prepared. He devoted himself to the liberation of the serfs with passionate conviction, putting all his strength to the task, not sparing his very life. When the tsar proposed to him that he be chairman of the Editing Commissions, Rostovtsev replied:

> "I accept . . . with a prayer to God . . . with reverence to the tsar who has vouchsafed such a sacred calling to me; with fear before Russia and posterity; with a sense of duty to my conscience. May God and the tsar pardon me, may Russia and posterity pardon me, if I take up a burden that exceeds my

strength, but a sense of duty tells me that I do not have the right to refuse the burden." [3]

In the preparation of regulations on the peasants, Rostovtsev defended the peasants' interests with all his strength, inspiring furious attacks, reproaches, and slander against himself from the opponents of abolition. In the late autumn of 1859, Rostovtsev became seriously ill but did not cease his lively interest in the reform, declaring that "only the shroud can separate me from the peasant question." As he died he whispered to the tsar, who was at his death bed, "Sire, do not fear. . . ."

Dmitrii Alekseevich Miliutin was also a career military officer, a professor of military history in his earlier years, and later, in 1856–1859, the chief of staff of the army of the Caucasus. For his services he was promoted to field marshal and awarded the title of count. In 1861 he became minister of war and remained at this post until the end of Alexander's reign. Overcoming the opposition of court and aristocratic circles, he conducted a series of radical reforms in the armed forces, of which the most important was the introduction of a universal military service. In the Russo-Turkish War of 1877–1878, the new army that he had created successfully passed the test of battle. As a sincere partisan of liberal reform, Miliutin could not remain in the administration of Alexander III. Retiring in 1881, he settled down on his Crimean estate and lived on until ninety-six (he died in 1912), a living monument to the epoch of great reforms.

M. T. Loris-Melikov was a combat general of the army of the Caucasus; he captured the strong Turkish fortress of Kars in 1877 and was made a count for his military service. He was called by the tsar in 1880 to lead the struggle with "the underground" and revolutionary terror, first as chief superintendent of the Supreme Administrative Commission and then as minister of internal affairs. While battling with the terrorists (and exposing himself to personal danger), Count Loris-Melikov advised the tsar that repressive measures, by themselves, were inadequate in the struggle against revolution. He insisted that it was necessary to establish unity between the government and loyal elements of society, satisfying their legitimate needs and attracting representatives of the public into participation in legislative work. After Alexander's death, other advisers replaced the Caucasian general in the guidance of domestic policy.

Of Alexander's civilian collaborators, one must first note the makers of peasant reform. As minister of internal affairs from

---

[3] Semenov, *op. cit.*, vol. I, pp. 48–49.

1855 to 1861 S. S. Lanskoi helped prepare the way for the reform. In his youth he had been a member of the Masons and the Union of Welfare, but in the era of Nicholas he had concealed the liberal convictions of his youth under a bureaucrat's uniform. After Nicholas' death, informed by the new tsar of his intention to liberate the peasants, Lanskoi undertook this assignment gladly, approving the appropriate memoranda, reports, and circulars that had been prepared by his deputy minister, first A. I. Levshin, and later N. A. Miliutin, the brother of the minister of war.

Soon after the emancipation in 1861 Lanskoi was dismissed —with the title of count, to be sure—and his place was taken by P. A. Valuev, a typical bureaucrat with imposing sideburns. He placed great value on his own oratory, which was florid and often vague, loved to write circulars, notes, and memoirs, was a devotee of liberal phrases (even to the point of drawing up plans for popular representation) and very illiberal administrative practices. He wrote that "the Russian mind needs scope," and at the same time tried by all possible means to restrain and control the Russian press.

But the real pillar of the reactionary party in the government at this time was Count D. A. Tolstoy, who in 1866 replaced the liberal A. V. Golovnin as minister of public education. According to Count Tolstoy, the best means of preserving the existing political and social order was the collaboration of three heterogeneous groups: the Orthodox clergy, the corps of gendarmes, and the teachers of Latin and Greek. Tolstoy personified this combination in his personal career, for he served Alexander II from 1866 to 1880 as minister of public education and overprocurator of the Holy Synod, and under Alexander III was minister of internal affairs and the chief of the gendarmes. As a practical matter, however, this strange combination did not harmonize. The Orthodox clergy limited themselves to prayers for the tsar, but had almost no influence on the social and political views of the people, nor did the clergy strive for political influence. The gendarmes arrested political "unreliables" or suspicious persons, sometimes green and essentially harmless youths, but—until too late—they were not able to arrest the terrorists who had persistently prepared for regicide. The teachers of classical languages were intended to divert their students' attention from political activity. Instead, by submitting them to endless sight translations and grammatical cramming, they instilled repulsion against the subjects taught and against the school authorities, forcing the students to seek interesting reading and activity outside school.

Prince A. M. Gorchakov, the state chancellor and minister of foreign affairs, directed Russian foreign policy in the reign of Alexander II, although only nominally in the closing years. The heir to a great title, with an elegant aristocratic manner, he had complete mastery of the French language and traditional diplomatic forms and composed an endless quantity of eloquent diplomatic notes and dispatches.

M. Kh. Reitern, a proponent of economic liberalism and private enterprise, directed state finance from 1862 to 1878. The guiding spirit of the judicial reform under Minister of Justice D. N. Zamiatnin was S. I. Zarudnyi. From 1867 to 1878, however, a conservative, Count Pahlen, held this ministry and attempted to constrain the independence of the new judiciary.

The Coming of Emancipation

On the eve of the reform there were about twenty-one and a half million serfs, male and female, constituting about 30 percent of the population of the Russian Empire. Since the end of the eighteenth century, the best representatives of Russian society had dreamed of lifting, in the words of the Slavophile poet Khomiakov, "the yoke of slavery," from the Russian people. The serfs themselves bore this yoke with increasing discontent, which in the era of the Crimean War manifested itself in disorders among the landlords' peasants who were called into the state militia.

Early in his reign Alexander II recognized the imperative necessity of abolishing serfdom. On March 30, 1856, holding an audience in Moscow for the leaders of the nobility, the tsar delivered a speech that was received with alarm. Stating that "the existing order of the ownership of serfs cannot remain unaltered," he added his famous warning: "it is better to abolish serfdom from above than to await the time when it will begin to abolish itself from below." He then asked the leaders of the Russian nobility "to think over how this would be put into execution," and to pass along his words "for consideration."

The tsar wanted the initiative for reform to come from the landowning nobility, but he soon perceived the necessity of taking the matter into his own hands. In keeping with tradition, the first step in this direction was the formation of a secret committee of dignitaries which was to find some means of solving this infinitely complex task. But Prince A. F. Orlov, the chairman of the Council of State and head of this committee, was a convinced advocate of serfdom, as were the majority of the committee members.

Soon after the tsar's Moscow speech, the advocates of the emancipation, including both Westerners and Slavophiles—Kavelin, Koshelev, Samarin, Prince Cherkassky, and many others—began to formulate their own proposals. Alexander transmitted these for the consideration of the secret committee, but there the only reaction was fruitless discussion. Fortunately, the tsar found support within the royal family from Grand Duke Constantine Nicholaevich and Grand Duchess Helena Pavlovna, around whom a circle of advocates of reform gathered. This group included among others the eminent official of the Ministry of Internal Affairs, N. A. Miliutin, who, along with Rostovtsev, became the main figure in the reform movement.

In the autumn of 1857 the reform received unexpected support from the nobility of Vilno, Kovno, and Grodno provinces, who were dissatisfied with the limitations on their rights imposed by the recently issued "inventories" of peasant obligations. They concluded that it would be in their interest to liberate the peasantry without land, on the pattern of the liberation that Alexander I had carried out in the Baltic provinces (see chapter 2). At the end of October the governor general of Vilno province, Nazimov, came to Petersburg and delivered a petition to this effect from the nobility of these provinces. The tsar and Minister of Internal Affairs Lanskoi took advantage of this opportunity and, November 20, 1857, issued to Nazimov a remarkable rescript that played an immense role in the course of the peasant reform. In this rescript the tsar praised the good intentions of the nobility of Vilno, Kovno, and Grodno provinces authorizing them to form "preparatory provincial committees of the nobility" to draft new statutes for the peasantry. According to the rescript, the basic principles were to be:

> 1. The landowners are to preserve the right of ownership of all the land, but the peasant farmsteads are to be acquired by the peasants as private property through redemption in the course of a fixed period; in addition the peasants are to be allotted the use of a suitable amount of land to maintain themselves and to fulfill their obligations to the landlord and the government; 2. The peasants should be divided into rural communes; the landlords are granted police power on their estates.

Wishing to strike while the iron was hot, Lanskoi ordered that the tsar's rescript and his own supplementary memorandum be printed in large quantity and distributed to the provincial governors and the marshals of the nobility—"for your attention and information in case the nobility of the province entrusted to you should want to direct their thought to the improvement of the way of life of the landlords' peasants." This step had a favorable and immediate effect. Under the influence of the governors who had been aroused by the rescript, the provincial nobility began to bestir themselves, and in one province after another societies of the nobility sent the tsar declarations of their desire "to improve the way of life" of their peasants. These were answered by imperial rescripts establishing committees of the nobility for peasant affairs. But according to Levshin, who played an important role in the Ministry of Internal Affairs at this time, these declarations of the nobility were presented because it was considered "impossible to lag behind the others." "In not one province," wrote Levshin, "was there a sincere desire to liberate the peasants. . . ."[4]

Soviet and even pre-Soviet literature has often stated that the liberation of the peasants was advantageous for the landlords and corresponded to "their class interests," but in actuality the majority of the landlords regarded serf reforms as a violation of their rights and interests. Bogdanov, marshal of the Vladimir province nobility, expressed the prevailing view when he wrote: "The first reaction of the majority of the nobility was necessarily heavy-hearted and sorrowful. . . . Not all were steadfast enough not to mourn the important rights which were, perhaps, outworn, but which constituted the material base of the life of the estate."[5]

The declarations of the government on the impending abolition of serfdom caused amazement, dissatisfaction, grumbling, fright, and panic among the majority of the nobility. The more cowardly of the landlords, expecting a general rebellion of the peasants —a repetition of the time of Pugachev—fled their country estates, the richer going abroad, the poorer to some nearby city. For example, one provincial gentleman foresaw that he would be "hanged from a lamp post, parallel to and simultaneously with," the reformers from Petersburg. Another wrote, " . . . along with the award of freedom to the peasantry, the tsar will sign the death warrant for me and thousands of other landlords." Still another declared, "to destroy this order [serfdom] is to prepare the ruin of the state."[6]

Concurrently with the provincial landlords, who poured forth their woe and their fears in conversation and personal corre-

---

[4] *Russkii Arkhiv* [*The Russian Archives*] (1885), vol. VIII, p. 537.

[5] *Russkaia Starina* [*The Russian Past*] (1881), vol. IV, p. 748.

[6] *Ibid.* (1897), vol. X, pp. 19–21; vol. XI, p. 238.

spondence, the court clique that opposed emancipation tried to intimidate the tsar. In their oral and written reports, they depicted the future reign of a Pugachev or they disclosed plots for "a long-premeditated plan for democratic revolution." According to Soloviev, later a member of the Senate:

> The provincial oppositional movement fed the Petersburg opposition, and the latter supported the provincial opposition. At Petersburg receptions, on military posts, at reviews, in the antechambers of the palace, in the Council of State, in the Senate and in the Council of Ministers . . . one heard more or less energetic protests against the government's intentions.[7]

On the other hand, the intelligentsia responded joyfully to the government's decision to eliminate serfdom. N. G. Chernyshevsky in *The Contemporary* and Herzen in *The Bell* devoted enthusiastic articles to Alexander II. The liberal Westerners and Slavophiles both welcomed "the dawn of day." A lively and comprehensive discussion of the peasant question began in the periodical press, and on December 28, 1857, a public banquet was held in Moscow at which ardent speeches were delivered in honor of the approaching emancipation.

But the growing excitement, along with the newspaper and magazine articles on the impending reform, soon frightened the government, which hastened to dampen public enthusiasm. Banquets like the one in Moscow were forbidden, and the press was permitted to publish only those articles on the peasant question which did not deviate from the government's declared program of reform, which did not inspire enmity between the social classes, and which generally did not "excite the mind."

On February 21, 1858, the secret committee was renamed the Main Committee on Peasant Affairs. On March 4, a "land section," in which the preparatory work on the peasant reform was concentrated, was established within the Ministry of Internal Affairs. A. Ia. Soloviev, a sincere partisan of peasant reform who was director of the "land section," and N. A. Miliutin, who was appointed "temporary acting deputy of the minister of internal affairs," were the chief figures of this stage of the preparation of the reform. On the local level the preparation for the reform was entrusted to provincial committees of the nobility.

Thus, paradoxically, the opponents of the emancipation had to devise a program to this very end, having been "ordered to

---

[7] *Ibid.* (1881), vol. IV, p. 754.

make a voluntary contribution." Understandably, the enthusiasm of the provincial committees was lukewarm to say the least, and work progressed slowly. Each committee was chaired by the marshal of the nobility and included two members from each county, elected from among the nobility who owned settled estates in the county, and two "experienced landlords" appointed by the governor. These appointees included such outstanding supporters of the reform as Prince Cherkassky, Samarin, and Koshelev, and they were usually the most active and progressive element in the ranks of the committees, frequently contending sharply with the proserfdom majority.

The outright defenders of serfdom were fighting a losing battle. Like the Baltic barons in the early nineteenth century, all the committees declared their renunciation of their right to the *person* of the peasant, but the majority steadfastly stressed the inviolability of their right to the *land*. The government's rescripts and supplementary circulars were unclear on this point: on the one hand, they recognized the landlords' *right of ownership* of all the land, but on the other hand, the peasants were to have land allotments set aside for their permanent use. According to the first principle, the landlords had the formal right to dispute the second principle. The landlords of the blacksoil provinces clung to their land with special tenacity and agreed to the emancipation of their serfs either entirely without land or with minimal allotments that would have been insufficient to support a peasant family. The landlords of the central, nonblacksoil provinces valued their land less than the labor of their peasants; these landowners proposed that the peasants purchase their personal freedom to compensate for the loss of obrok payments. The tsar, however, issued a decree in November 1858 forbidding the committees "to admit for discussion" the proposal that the serfs might redeem their personal freedom. A type of compromise was then proposed. In appraising the peasants' land allotments, which were to be purchased, the first desiatina (2.7 acres) of the allotment, which included the peasants' dwellings, were assigned the highest value, and some committees proposed exorbitantly high appraisals of this initial portion.

The government attentively followed the work of the provincial committees and through the governors prodded them forward. At the end of 1858, drafts of the new statutes on the peasantry, composed by the provincial committees, began to arrive in Petersburg. Many committees submitted two drafts, one from the majority and a minority report that frequently was more advantageous for the peasant. Of all proposals from the provincial committees, the most liberal one came from Tver, a major center of Russian liberalism in the following generation, where the committee was headed by A. M. Unkovsky.

A decree was issued March 30, 1859, establishing two Editing Commissions, "for the purpose of compiling a systematic summary of all the proposals on the general regulations concerning the peasants who will cease to be serfs." These Editing Commissions, chaired by General Rostovtsev, were united in a single "joint office" and a series of special sections: (1) the *juridical,* which was to define the rights and obligations of the peasants; (2) the *administrative,* which was to work out a program for the internal organization of peasant communes and the definition of their relations with the landowners and the local authorities; and (3) the *economic,* which was concerned with the size of peasants' farmsteads, allotments, and obligations. A special *financial* commission, also under Rostovtsev, was soon formed to work out the problem of the redemption of peasant allotments.

The joint office of the Editing Commissions consisted of 11 members from the government, appointed by the appropriate ministers, 7 members from the financial commission, and 20 "expert" members, invited by Rostovtsev and confirmed by the tsar from among the experienced landlords. Prince Cherkassky and Samarin played the major role among the invited experts, and of the bureaucrats Soloviev, Zhukovsky, the Semenov brothers, and especially N. A. Miliutin were important. The last-named figure, representing the Ministry of Internal Affairs, was Rostovtsev's right hand and the main figure in the Editing Commission, in fact the leader of its work. The majority of the members of the commission constituted a solid "progressive bloc," which defended as best it could the interests of the emancipated peasants from the assaults of the defenders of the landlords' interests. Very soon, therefore, the commissions came into sharp conflict with the representatives of the committees of the provincial nobility, who appeared in Petersburg at the summons of the government to defend their proposed regulations and to submit their comments on the proposals of the Editing Commissions.

A series of addresses, presented to the tsar by groups of deputies of the nobility and various defenders of their interests, contained vicious attacks on the activities of the Editing Commissions, which, it was alleged, were robbing and destroying the nobility, contrary to the direct intent of the imperial rescripts. While the complaints of the nobility held that it was necessary, as one of them put it, "to restrain the Ministry of Internal Affairs and the Editing Commissions," the heads of these bodies, Lanskoi and Rostovtsev, in their

CHART I. THE EMANCIPATION OF 1861
THE PLANNING MACHINERY

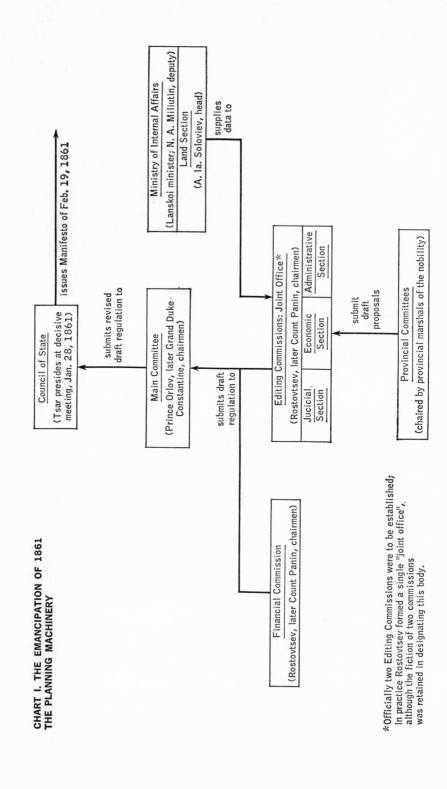

Council of State
(Tsar presides at decisive meeting, Jan. 28, 1861)   issues Manifesto of Feb. 19, 1861

submits revised draft regulation to

Main Committee
(Prince Orlov, later Grand Duke Constantine, chairman)

submits draft regulation to

Editing Commissions: Joint Office*
(Rostovtsev, later Count Panin, chairman)

| Jucicial, Section | Economic Section | Administrative Section |

submit draft proposals

Provincial Committees
(chaired by provincial marshals of the nobility)

Financial Commission
(Rostovtsev, later Count Panin, chairman)

Ministry of Internal Affairs
(Lanskoi minister; N. A. Miliutin, deputy)
Land Section
(A. Ia. Soloviev, head)

supplies data to

*Officially two Editing Commissions were to be established; in practice Rostovtsev formed a single "joint office", although the fiction of two commissions was retained in designating this body.

reports and letters to the tsar energetically defended themselves from these assaults and in turn accused the privileged class of self-interest and opposition to the interests of the state. Lanskoi, for example, stated in a memo to the tsar that the majority of the members of the provincial committees "display little sympathy for the emancipation of the peasants and are motivated only by the private material interests of the landlords. . . . The majority of them, born and raised with the idea of serfdom, cannot comprehend the urgent need for reform and expect only inevitable loss from it."[8]

However, the pressure on the Editing Commissions was too great, and on some points the commissions were obliged to make concessions, especially on the size of peasant land allotments. As a general principle, the commissions held that all land that was being used by the peasants at the moment of emancipation should remain in their hands. Then, over the protests of Rostovtsev, the commissions adopted a decision that made possible the cutting off of land from the peasants' allotment for the benefit of the landlord. This was permitted, first, if the existing peasant allotments exceeded the maximum size established for a given locality and, second, if, after the demarcation of land for peasant allotments, less than one third of all the arable land of a given estate was left to the landlord.

In the autumn of 1859, Rostovtsev's health failed, partly as a result of the nervous strain wrought by the slanders and intrigues of the opponents of serfdom, and on February 6, 1860, he died, mourned by the tsar and all friends of the reform. He was succeeded as chairman of the Editing Commissions by Count V. N. Panin, a hardened bureaucrat of the era of Nicholas and a defender of serfdom. His appointment brought perplexity and apprehension to the progressive camp and elation to the conservatives, but the tsar ordered Panin strictly to continue the work of "Iakob Ivanovich" (Rostovtsev), and the old bureaucrat did not dare disobey. In October 1860, the Editing Commissions finished their work and disbanded, having worked for one year and seven months. There had been over 400 sessions of the joint office, and the special sections had examined some sixty proposals (both majority and minority) from provincial committees and had composed seventeen draft "Regulations," five of which applied to all of Russia and twelve to various regions. In their final form, the "Regulations" of February 19 comprised a weighty volume of 374 pages, containing over 1800 articles.

---

[8] Semenov, *op. cit.,* vol. I, appendix 14.

The draft "Regulations" worked out by the Editing Commissions were submitted to the Main Committee on Peasant Affairs, under the chairmanship of Grand Duke Constantine Nicholaevich, who replaced the original incumbent, the conservative Prince Orlov. Not without difficulty and pressure on individual members did the Grand Duke steer the draft of the Editing Commissions through the Main Committee, after which the draft was submitted to the consideration of the Council of State.

On January 28, 1861, the tsar himself chaired a general session of the Council of State and delivered a major speech reviewing the history of serfdom and the previous attempts to limit it. He then declared his "direct" and "unswerving" determination to abolish serfdom at once, concluding with the following charge to the Council: "I have a right to demand one thing from you: that you set aside all private interests and act not as landlords but as dignitaries of the state, entrusted with my confidence." The Council quickly examined the draft and finished its work in the middle of February. On the suggestion of Prince Gagarin, the Council included a supplementary article by which the peasants were given the option of receiving "gratuitous" allotments, one quarter of the maximum allotment in size, free of charge, if they so desired.

On February 19, the tsar signed the "Regulations" and issued a manifesto on the abolition of serfdom, which ended with these words: "Orthodox people, bless yourselves with the sign of the cross and call God's blessing upon your free labor, which will be the basis of your domestic welfare and the common weal." On March 5, the "will" enunciated by the tsar was proclaimed in the capitals and then the manifesto and the Regulations, printed in vast quantity, were distributed throughout Russia.

What was the first impact of the manifesto? As we might expect, the reaction was diverse and included dissatisfaction from both right and left. The landlords and advocates of serfdom were either indignant or at least disgruntled by the destruction of their "legitimate rights" and the expropriation of their "sacred property." The left, headed by Chernyshevsky at home and Herzen abroad, was disillusioned by the halfway nature of the reform and even denied that serfdom had been abolished. The peasant folk themselves generally received the Regulations of February 19 peacefully and could not but feel the amelioration of their lot in escaping from the landlord's rod. All the same, there was disillusionment and puzzlement in some places and others even experienced agitation and disorders. This reaction was entirely natural in view of the magnitude and complexity of the regulations, which were incomprehensible not only to the illiterate peasants but also to many of the zealous local administrators, who were accustomed to shout and shake their fists but were now entirely unable to understand and interpret the new laws. And yet these men were supposed to untangle the complex, centuries-old web of serf relations.

The peasants were naturally dissatisfied with the terms of the regulations that submitted them to a transitional period of two years of continued bondage and to the future status of "temporary obligation," which could last up to twenty years, pending the conclusion of negotiations between peasant and landlord. It is understandable that the peasants awaited "some other will [edict]," which they thought the tsar had meant to grant them, but which the landlords and bureaucrats had concealed from them. In the first months after the publication of the regulations agitation and disorders occurred in many places, resulting in "pacification" measures, which were especially bloody in the village of Bezdna in Kazan province. In this case, troops fired into an unarmed crowd of peasants, killing several dozen and wounding over one hundred. Responsibility for the use of force lay partly with high-ranking military emissaries whom the tsar sent into each province to assist the local authorities in maintaining order at a supposedly dangerous moment. Moreover, some landlords and bureaucrats saw "mutiny" in every crowd of noisy peasants and each refusal to perform barshchina, and their exaggerated reports sometimes led to "pacification" by the lash, or occasionally by cold steel or firearms. But nowhere were there attacks on troops or police or lynching of landlords. Where there were intelligent and calm administrators, "mutinies" and repressions did not occur; in Yaroslavl province, for example, General M. L. Dubel't "pacified" all mutinies by personally talking with the mutineers.[9]

The Terms of the Serf Reform

According to the first article of the lengthy "General Regulations on Peasants Emerging from Bondage," "The enserfment of peasants settled on landlords' estates and of domestic servants is abolished forever," and the former serfs "are granted by right the status of free rural inhabitants, personally and with respect to property." Beyond this basic guarantee of freedom the regulations contain a multitude of qualifications and complexities.

---

[9] *Russkaia Starina* (1891), vol. II, pp. 469–474.

In the first place, the regulations established a transitional period of at least two years in which the peasants would remain "temporarily obligated," rendering a fixed obrok or barshchina to the landlord. In the first two years the landlord and peasants, with the help of an arbitrator if necessary, were to draw up so-called "statutory charters," which would record precisely the land allotments awarded to the peasant communes. Subsequently, a separate agreement regarding the compensation to be paid for them was to be concluded. Upon the conclusion of these agreements the peasants were to attain the legal status of "peasant property owners" and all obligatory ties to the landlord would cease.

Regulations on the size of peasant land allotments were complex because they attempted to take into consideration the variations in regional agrarian conditions. Three basic zones—blacksoil, nonblacksoil, and steppe—were recognized, and each was subdivided into districts, for which the regulations set maximum and minimum land allotments per soul. These varied widely; for example, in various districts of the blacksoil zone the maximum ranged from 7.4 acres per soul to 16.2 acres; the nonblacksoil zone ranged from 8.1 acres to 18.9 acres; and the steppe ranged from 8.1 to 32.4 acres. Since the minimum allotment in each case was one third of the maximum, it was possible for some peasants to receive as little as 2.5 acres per soul, or even 1.8 acres if they chose to receive a "gratuitous" allotment of one quarter of the maximum—a striking contrast to the possible upper limit in some steppe districts. It has been calculated that in practice the average allotment per soul for the country as a whole turned out to be 8.9 acres, since 10,050,000 souls received 91,800,000 acres of land, including 500,000 who received the inadequate gratuitous allotment.

The question of peasant landownership was complicated by communal possession and redemption payments. Except in certain western provinces, land was transferred from the nobility not to individual peasants or to households but to communes, which equalized the distribution of the land and jointly utilized common pastures and woodlots. Theoretically, individual members of the commune might demand their share of the land, providing they paid for it, and communes might distribute all of their land as the private property of the members if a two-thirds majority so decided. But those options were rarely applied in practice. Compensation of the landlords for the peasant allotments was also a communal affair. Since the peasants lacked the capital to pay for the land outright, the state offered to advance the landlord up to 80 percent of the purchase price in interest-bearing bonds. Once this was done the repayment of the government advance was guaranteed collectively by the peasant commune. Their debt to the state was funded for a forty-nine-year period, and it was the communal responsibility to keep up the annual service to this debt by apportioning each household its share of the payments. Clearly this arrangement gave the commune a powerful motive to retain its redemption-paying members, thus inhibiting the mobility of the individual peasant despite his emancipation from direct obligations to the landowner.

The statutory charters regulating the size of peasant allotments and compensation for the landlord formed an exceedingly complicated and variable system. In the exceptional case that the landowner and the peasants wished to negotiate a voluntary redemption agreement without a financial advance from the state, the price was not fixed by law. And, as previously noted, the peasants might avoid any redemption if they wished to obtain a gratuitous allotment, running the risk of becoming tenant farmers or wage laborers because of the inadequate size of these land allotments. But in most cases the price of the land was officially regulated by a rate-schedue that was supposed to reflect the value of the land, in keeping with the rule that peasants should redeem their land and not their persons. In practice, however, the rate-schedule worked quite favorably for the landowner. In the first place, the rates were calculated on the basis of the obrok payments that were in force at the time, capitalized at 6 percent, and the resulting price exceeded the actual market value of the land. This was markedly the case in the nonblacksoil regions, in which the nobility valued serf *labor* more than the poor *land*. Moreover, the rate per acre set by the schedule often was not directly proportional to the number of acres received by the peasant. In many areas the rate-schedule was higher per acre if the peasants did *not* accept a full allotment; sometimes the price per acre for a minimum allotment was *double* the price per acre for a maximum allotment. Finally, various articles in the regulation permitted the landowning nobility in many districts to keep woodlots and other valuable pieces of property on which the village economy depended. These parcels of land were popularly known as "cutoffs" *(otrezki),* and were galling to the peasants, who often had been accustomed to the use of this land before emancipation. From all of this the peasant often gained the impression that he was really redeeming his person after all, and that the nobility ended up with land that belonged to the peasant by right.

The Administration of the Emancipated Peasants

Because the commune was obliged to shoulder the land-redemption obligation to the state and because the administrative authority of the landlord over the peasant no longer existed, it was necessary to entrust the peasant commune with a considerable degree of authority in local matters. The power of the commune was based on the "village assembly" *(sel'skii skhod),* which elected an elder and other officers. According to article 51 of the regulations, the village assembly was empowered: (1) to elect the local village authorities and the delegates to the township assembly (the next higher administrative level on the countryside); (2) to sentence to banishment from the commune any vicious members; (3) to release members from the commune or to accept new members; (4) to appoint guardians for minors and to check on the fulfilment of their responsibilities; (5) to permit the division of household and property within large families; (6–7) to apportion the arable land and common land of the village among different families; (8–9) to present complaints and appeals concerning communal affairs and to petition the authorities concerning communal needs; (10) to establish taxation to cover communal expenses; (11) to apportion taxes and other obligations; (12) to establish the remuneration of village officials and to check their accounts; (13) to select recruits for compulsory military service; (14) to apportion obrok and barshchina owed to the landlord in the case of the "temporarily obligated" peasants; (15) to exact arrears on various obligations; (16) to make loans and grants; and (17) to grant power of attorney on behalf of the commune. A two-thirds majority was required to decide the more important issues, such as the repartition of arable land and banishment, and the granting of permission to leave the commune was hedged in by formidable legal obstacles. The departing peasant had to renounce his land allotment, show that he was not indebted to the commune or individuals, obtain the consent of his parents, and submit a statement of acceptance from the commune to which he was moving.

Above the level of the village commune the unit of peasant administration was the township, consisting of between 300 and 2000 male peasants. The township administration was composed of its assembly, its executive, and its peasant court. All village and township officials sat in the assembly along with one elected representative from every ten peasant households, while the executive consisted of the elected township elder, the village elders, and the tax collectors.

The court consisted of four to twelve judges elected annually. They could decide disputes between peasants involving 100 rubles or less and could hand down sentences up to six days' labor, fines of three rubles, arrest for a week, or twenty lashes. The township elder was the vital link in the peasant administrative system, for he was "responsible for the preservation of the general order, tranquility and good conduct of the township," and had to fulfill all legitimate demands of a variety of higher officials, including the police. In particular his office was responsible for the management of internal passports in the locality. In fact, the township elder, though elected, soon came to be an agent of the central government, and his office became a typical bureaucratic one with the usual volume of clerical work and correspondence.

Above the township level the affairs of the emancipated peasants were governed by a separate "Regulation on Provincial and County Affairs," which was issued simultaneously with the regulation on emancipation. The main contribution of this law was the creation of the office of "arbitrator" *(mirovoi posrednik),* which played an outstanding role in the practical realization of the February 19 reforms. The arbitrators were selected for a three-year term by the provincial governor from among the local nobility, on the advice of the marshals of the nobility and subject to the confirmation of the Senate. Once appointed, they could be removed only by court order. In each province there were between thirty-five and fifty arbitrators, each bearing varied and important responsibilities. They investigated disputes between peasants and landlords; they approved statutory charters drawn up by the landlords; they supervised the activities of the organs of peasant self-government; and they also supervised the exercise of police and judicial authority on the countryside.

Collectively the arbitrators of a county formed a "county meeting" *(s'ezd),* which was chaired by the county marshal of nobility and included a representative of the central government. On the next higher, provincial, level the general direction of the emancipation process was in the hands of a "provincial office," which was chaired by the governor of the province and included some of the higher bureaucrats and representatives of the nobility.

The arbitrators bore the honorable but difficult task of undoing the centuries-old tangle of serf relationships, and the people who assumed this obligation were the flower of the nobility-intelligentsia. A circular from the minister of internal affairs, dated March 22, 1861, ordered the governors to try by all means to attract to the newly inaugurated office [arbitrator] people who are impartial, educated and sincerely devoted to the sacred affairs that our all-gracious Sovereign has undertaken. . . . For the success of the impending measures it is especially important that the arbitrators enjoy not only authority over the peasants, but also *their full confidence*. . . . In this connection it is necessary that Your Excellency invite as arbitrators only such individuals as are known to *sympathize unquestionably with the reform* and who are well disposed toward the peasants.[10]

The ranks of the "first call" of arbitrators included such outstanding social reformers as Prince Cherkassky, Samarin, the Decembrist Baron Rozen, who had returned from Siberia, the noted surgeon and teacher Pirogov, and Count Leo Nicholaevich Tolstoy.

In 1874 the office of arbitrator was abolished. Their duties were transferred to the county offices of peasant affairs and the general police, judicial, and record offices. The county office for peasant affairs, presided over by the county marshal of the nobility, consisted of a "permanent member," appointed by the government from among the local nobility, the district police officer of the county, the chairman of the county zemstvo council, and one of the "honorary justices of the peace."

Other Categories of Peasant Reform

The peasant reforms of the reign of Alexander II dealt not only with the landlords' peasants but also with the appanage peasants—those living on the estates of the imperial family—and state peasants. As the result of a law of 1866, the two million appanage peasants received land allotments averaging 8 to 12 acres per soul, which was about half again as much as the landlords' peasants received on the average. Still more favorable was the land arrangement for the state peasants, who numbered about nineteen million when their condition was reformed in 1866. The average size per soul of the allotment of the former state peasants was more than 16.2 acres, or almost twice that of the former landlords' serfs. All told, more than 220,900,000 acres or almost all the good, state-owned arable land in European Russia, was allotted to the former state peasants. In return for the land allotted to them, the former state peasants were to pay a state obrok tax, which in 1886 was increased and transformed into

---

[10] *II Polnoe Sobranie Zakonov,* vol. XXXVI, no. 36,770.

redemption payment. The average appraisal per desiatina of the allotments of former state peasants was about 16 rubles, as compared to 27 rubles per desiatina in the case of the landlords' peasants. The duration of the redemption payments was set at forty-four years, beginning with January 1, 1887.

The peasant reforms of 1863–1864 in the northwestern provinces (Vilno, Kovno, Grodno, and Minsk) and in the provinces of the Kingdom of Poland represent a special case. In 1863–1864 the government faced a Polish nationalist revolution in this area and tried to gain the support of the peasants in the struggle against the Polish nobility. A manifesto of March 2, 1864, commended the "sensible thinking" and "steadfast loyalty of the rural populace," who had not joined in the revolution. Thereafter, all the rights of the Polish gentry over the peasants were abolished. All the land which was then used by the peasants, with some additions, was transferred to them as their absolute property, and the redemption payments for the abolition of the old obligations were extremely moderate. In addition, the peasants received communal self-government on the levels of the village and the township *(gmina)*. Of course, the local peasant officials were under the supervision of the Russian bureaucrats.

Rural and Urban Self-Government

Before the era of the great reforms no one had been seriously concerned with the cultural and social needs of the lower strata of the population, especially in rural areas. It is true that in the settlements of state peasants the administration, directed by Kiselev, had laid the foundations of public education, medical care, and insurance, but all this was embryonic and inadequate in comparison with the existing needs. On the estates of the landlords the situation was worse. One rarely saw a school, and hospitals were rarer still. The overwhelming majority of the peasants were illiterate, and in case of illness they had recourse to treatment at home by amateur midwives or quacks. In case of fire they went to the landlord to appeal for aid or, in extreme cases, would turn to beggary. Roads and bridges were in sorry condition, and no one even dreamed of agronomical aid for the peasantry.

After emancipation the government undertook to improve this backward situation, mainly through new institutions of local self-government, the zemstvos, which were designed to enlist the activity of the populace in public affairs up to the provincial level—but not on the national level. On January 1, 1864, the "Regulation on Pro-

CHART II. ZEMSTVO STRUCTURE
(1864-1890)

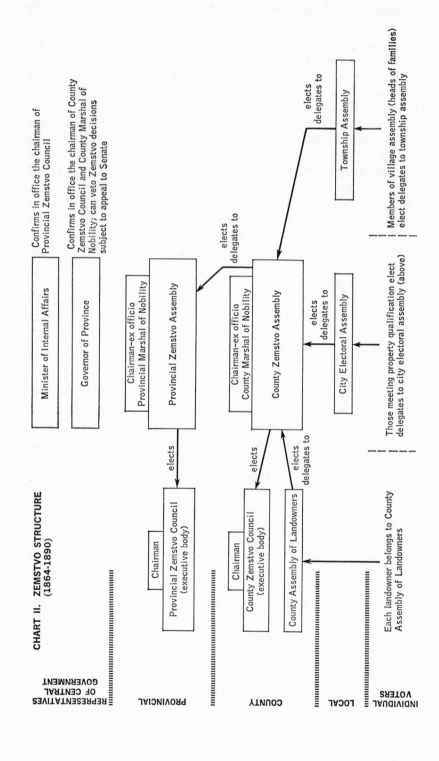

REPRESENTATIVES OF CENTRAL GOVERNMENT

Minister of Internal Affairs — Confirms in office the chairman of Provincial Zemstvo Council

Governor of Province — Confirms in office the chairman of County Zemstvo Council and County Marshal of Nobility; can veto Zemstvo decisions subject to appeal to Senate

PROVINCIAL

Chairman-ex officio Provincial Marshal of Nobility

Provincial Zemstvo Assembly

elects

Chairman

Provincial Zemstvo Council (executive body)

COUNTY

Chairman-ex officio County Marshal of Nobility

County Zemstvo Assembly

elects delegates to

Township Assembly

elects delegates to

City Electoral Assembly

elects delegates to

elects

Chairman

County Zemstvo Council (executive body)

elects delegates to

County Assembly of Landowners

LOCAL

Members of village assembly (heads of families) elect delegates to township assembly

Those meeting property qualification elect delegates to city electoral assembly (above)

INDIVIDUAL VOTERS

Each landowner belongs to County Assembly of Landowners

vincial and County Zemstvo Institutions" introduced the new organs into thirty-four provinces of European Russia, but not in the western provinces with their "unreliable" Polish landowners, nor in the Caucasian or Siberian areas. The new regulation established the authority of the zemstvos over: (1) the management of zemstvo property and funds; (2) the construction and maintenance of local roads; (3) measures to insure food supply in case of emergency; (4) philanthropy and the construction of churches; (5) the insurance of property; (6) "concern for the development of local trade and industry"; (7) public education and public health; (8) the prevention of livestock epidemics and the protection of plants against blights; (9) the fulfillment of the local needs of the military and civil administration, such as transportation and billeting, and participation in the maintenance of postal service in the countryside; (10–11) the apportionment, collection, and allocation of the zemstvo tax; (12) presentation of the government of information and petitions concerning local welfare and needs; and (13) the conduct of elections of the executive organs of the zemstvo.

County zemstvo assemblies were composed of deputies who were elected by three categories of voters: landowners possessing a set amount of property, members of town societies, and members of rural societies. In all the provinces having zemstvo institutions, the county zemstvo deputies numbered about 13,000 persons, of which the noble landowners sent 6200, the peasant societies 5200, and the city societies 1600. The county zemstvo assembly, chaired by the county marshal of nobility, elected the executive organ, the county zemstvo council, consisting of a chairman and two or more members, whose term of office was three years. It also elected deputies to the provincial zemstvo assembly, which was chaired by the provincial marshal of the nobility and elected its council, consisting of a chairman and six members. The chairman of the county and provincial zemstvo councils had to be confirmed in office by the governor of the province and the minister of internal affairs, respectively.

According to article 6 of the regulation establishing them, "The zemstvo institutions act independently within the sphere of matters entrusted to them." However, added article 9, "the head [governor] of the province has the right to suspend the execution of any decision of the zemstvo institutions which is contrary to the laws or the general interest of the state." In this case the zemstvo institutions had the right to appeal the decision of the governor to the Senate, and the Senate would render the final decision in the dispute.

In the zemstvo assemblies the peasants and landlords, the "slaves" and masters of yesterday, met at a common table to deal with a common concern and the atmosphere of the confrontation was surprisingly peaceful and businesslike. The eminent advocate of social reform, Koshelev, commented thus concerning the first meeting of the zemstvo assembly in 1865 in Sapozhok, a small center in Riazan province:

> This first assembly astonished me in many respects: the peasant deputies, our serfs of yesterday, seated themselves among us simply and unceremoniously, as if they had done so for centuries; they listened to us with great attentiveness, they asked for explanations on matters that they did not understand, they agreed with us voluntarily, and not at all in the spirit of the late serf order.

Concerning the assembly of the autumn of 1867, Koshelev wrote: "The assembly sat for eight days and was remarkable for the prevailing spirit of unanimity between individual landowners and the peasants."[11] Another witness, the Englishman D. M. Wallace, who lived in Russia for many years and was an acute observer of Russian life, wrote of the zemstvo assembly of Novgorod province:

> What surprised me most in this assembly was that it was composed partly of nobles and partly of peasants—the latter being decidedly in the majority—and that no trace of antagonism seemed to exist between the two classes. . . . The discussions were carried on chiefly by the nobles, but on more than one occasion peasant members rose to speak, and their remarks, always clear, practical and to the point, were listened to with respectful attention."[12]

Such amicable relations did not exist between the newly created zemstvo institutions and the central government. On the one side, the bureaucracy jealously guarded the prerogatives of its authority, lest zemstvo institutions exceed the limits of their competence. On the other side, zemstvo assemblies, headed originally by the most active and liberal elements of local nobility, found these limits too narrow and wished they could widen them.

We will refer later to the results of the work of the Russian zemstvos and will only note here that concern for public education and the organization of medical care took first priority in their work. Zemstvo teachers, especially women, devoted themselves to the struggle against ignorance, and the zemstvo physician became the typical bearer of tireless and self-sacrificing service to the people.

Until the middle of the nineteenth century, the cities of Russia led a miserable existence and many of them were cities in

---

[11] Koshelev, *Zapiski*, pp. 167–168, 189.

[12] D. M. Wallace, *Russia* (London, 1905 ed.), p. 494.

name only. Of the 595 municipalities of European Russia investigated by government statisticians at the beginning of the 1860s, only one sixth were exclusively commercial and industrial centers. In the rest the populace was partially engaged in agricultural or seasonal work. By 1870, the urban population of the Russian Empire was about eight million, only slightly more than 10 percent of the total population. The number of settlements that were legally considered "cities" reached about 700, but only five of these had a population in excess of 100,000: St. Petersburg, 670,000; Moscow, about 400,000; Warsaw; Odessa; and Kishinev. Only eleven cities had a population between 50,000 and 100,000: Berdichev, Kazan, Kharkov, Kiev, Nikolaev, Riga, Saratov, Tashkent, Tiflis, Tula, and Vilno.[13] Except for the two capitals, most of the larger cities were thus located on the fringes of the empire, and the interior of Great Russia proper was still almost completely rural.

The emancipation of the peasants and the resulting stimulation of the economy intensified the need for urban reform. After long preparatory work, new Municipal Regulations were issued June 16, 1870, establishing a considerable degree of urban self-government in harmony with the zemstvo system in rural areas. The new municipal governments were entrusted with: (1) local administration and finance; (2) public works and building ordinances; (3) municipal services, including emergency food supply, the construction of markets, fire protection, the promotion of commerce and industry, and the establishment of credit institutions; (4) public health, welfare, and cultural institutions; and (5) the submission to the government of reports on local needs.

The chief organ of urban self-government was the municipal duma, composed of at least thirty deputies elected for a four-year term. The duma elected a mayor (*golova*) and the members of the city council. The minister of internal affairs confirmed the election of the mayors of provincial capitals and the provincial governor did the same for county capitals. The franchise in the municipality was granted to persons who owned immovable property, or maintained a commercial or industrial enterprise, or paid the municipality a set tax from commercial or industrial transactions. Working on the principle that the allocation of city finances should be in the hands of those who paid the city taxes, the law of 1870 established the "Prussian" system for the election of representatives in the duma. The

---

[13] A. Suvorin, ed., *Russkii Kalendar' na 1872 god* (St. Petersburg, 1873), pp. 326, 332–347.

electors were divided into three curiae, each of which paid one third of the municipal taxes and elected one third of the total representatives. Thus the voice of a small group of rich taxpayers had the same weight as that of some hundreds of middle-income taxpayers and some thousands of small taxpayers.

According to the regulations, "the municipal administration acts independently within the established bounds of its authority," but in some cases its decisions were subject to the approval of the state authorities. A "provincial office for municipal affairs," was established to supervise the activities of the organs of urban self-government. It was composed of higher provincial officials and representatives of the organs of self-government. The governor could suspend execution of "illegal decisions of the duma" and refer them to the provincial office for consideration. There the decisions of the duma might be revoked. The municipal administration could then submit a complaint against the decision of the provincial office to the first department of the Senate, which passed the final decision.

Judicial Reform

The old courts were one of the darkest blots on prereform Russia. They were characterized by bribe-taking and extortion, arbitrariness, partiality, red tape, endless shunting from department to department, and legal proceedings in the absence of the parties under the cover of "chancery secrets." For each social class there was a different court with elected but ignorant and poorly paid judges. Actually, wrote the scholar Chubinsky, "cases were decided not by the judges but the chancery of the judicial chamber, headed by the all-powerful secretaries," for only they could swim, like fish in water, in the shoreless sea of paper—ambiguous laws, confused instructions, and contradictory decisions of the higher courts. "In criminal cases decisions were awaited for years, the accused often languishing the whole time under guard; in civil cases the parties sometimes succeeded only in growing older and they never reached the conclusion of their case," said Chubinsky.[14] The penal system was extraordinarily cruel. Severe criminal punishments, such as exile at hard labor or in settlement was bound to be accompanied by agonizing corporal punishment; branding, the knout or lash for civilians and the rod, gauntlet, or cat for military personnel. Sometimes these cruel corporal punishments in practice meant a brutal form of death sentence.

---

[14] P. M. Chubinsky, "Sudebnaia reforma," in *Istoriia Rossii v XIX veke,* vol. III, pp. 231–248.

The epoch of the 1860s, permeated with humane and liberal aspirations, destroyed the dark reign of the old court system and re-placed it with just, efficient courts. In 1858–1860 a draft reform of the judicial department of the empire was prepared on the basis of the new "unalterable foundations": the independence of the courts from the authority of the administration, the introduction of jurors, and the elimination of "chancery secrets." On September 29, 1862, the tsar approved the basic foundations of the judicial reform, and a commission was formed to work out the draft of the new judicial institutions and statutes. The official chairman of the commission was State Secretary V. P. Butkov, but in actuality the soul of the com-mission was Zarudnyi, who headed the civil section of the commission. The commission energetically undertook its labors and in eleven months had worked out an excellent draft of the new judicial statutes, which was then examined by the Council of State and confirmed by the tsar November 20, 1864.

Even before the new judicial statutes were put into action, some partial measures for the correction of the old corrupt courts had been adopted. A special "judicial investigator" was created in 1860 to "remove from police execution the conduct of investigation of crimes which are subject to the examination of the courts." And a very important decree of April 17, 1863, "On Some Changes in the System of Punishments," abolished the lash and the branding of prisoners. The birch, up to twenty blows, remained in use only in the township courts, but with a whole series of exemptions. In par-ticular, persons who held an elected public office or who had com-pleted at least three grades of school were exempt. At the same time, running the gauntlet and the "cat" were abolished in the armed forces.

On November 20, 1864, a new judicial system was estab-lished by the simultaneous enactment of "Regulations for Judicial Institutions," statutes for civil legal proceedings, statutes for criminal legal proceedings, and statutes for the punishments which may be imposed by justices of the peace. In 1866 a new code of punishments considerably softened the harsh provisions of the code of 1845.

The competence of the new courts encompassed persons of all estates equally. The new court was, first of all, open and public, with the active participation of both sides. In both civil and criminal cases the so-called "controversial" trial was introduced: in civil cases both sides or their representatives presented their cases, and in criminal cases the state prosecutor and the defense attorney pleaded their cases. The defense was conducted by a lawyer from the newly formed, autonomous "estate of sworn attorneys," which could be entered only by persons with a juridical education. If the accused was financially unable to pay a lawyer, the court appointed a defense attorney for him free of charge.

In serious criminal cases the investigation was conducted by a judicial investigator, who then passed the case on for decision in the district court. The question of the guilt was decided by twelve jurors chosen by lot "from the local inhabitants of all estates" who were registered in appropriate lists.

According to the new regulations, judicial authority pertained to the following institutions. The less important cases were investigated by the justices of the peace *(mirovoi sud'ia)*, who were elected for a three-year term by the county zemstvo assemblies. Their first duty in civil cases and private suits was to try to persuade the parties to a conciliation or to try to end the dispute by amicable agreement. The next higher court of instance was the meeting of the justices of the peace—consisting of the ordinary justices of the peace and special "honorary justices of the peace" in each county. For more important cases, there were district *(okruzhnye)* courts, with civil and criminal departments composed of judges appointed by the government. The appellate courts for the district courts were the "court chambers" *(sudebnye palaty)*, each of which was located in a large city and was the highest court in a "judicial district" *(sudebnyi okrug)*. The highest court in the empire had been the "governing Senate," but after the reform it acted only as a supreme court of appeals. That is, it could only reverse the verdicts of the lower courts if the verdicts violated the judicial procedure established by law.

The senators were appointed "by the immediate discretion of his Imperial Majesty," while members of the district courts and judicial chambers were appointed from candidates nominated by these courts themselves. All who were appointed as members of the courts enjoyed independence and were not subject to removal. "They may not be dismissed without [their own] request," the law stated, and "they are subject to suspension not otherwise than by the verdict of a criminal court."

The leaders of the judicial reform, Minister of Justice Zamiatnin and his collaborators, succeeded in selecting good personnel for the new courts. Partly they were drawn from the best elements of the old courts, for these did not consist only of bribe-takers and swindlers. But the greater portion consisted of young people with a university education, the former student idealists of the 1840s, the pupils of Granovsky and Belinsky. They put the new courts on a high level and won for them great popularity with the public. Interesting cases, especially when eloquent and popular lawyers participated, attracted crowds into the courtrooms and stimulated considerable public interest.

Less important and entirely uncelebrated cases were investigated in the chambers of the justices of the peace, who nonetheless were influential in the inculcation of a popular sense of law. It was in the chamber of a justice of the peace that the ordinary person first felt his equality before the law with the rich and prominent and first had a chance to seek justice before accessible and equitable judges. The justice of the peace addressed everyone in the second person plural, *"vy,"* which had formerly been reserved for the upper classes, attentively heard and impartially judged the important noble, the general, the millionaire, and the peasant in his bast shoes.

However, the democratic and liberal tendencies of the new courts soon caused great dissatisfaction among the conservatives, who regarded the numerous verdicts of "not guilty" as a "shock to the foundations" of society and even a political danger. The government, too, was confused by the liberalism of the new courts, and especially the verdict passed by the Petersburg district court in the case of Vera Zasulich, who in 1878 shot and seriously wounded the police chief of Petersburg, but was acquitted by the jury despite the clear evidence. In 1866 judicial proceedings in cases involving the press were removed from the competence of the district courts and transferred to the judicial chambers. Cases of crimes against the state were also removed from the competence of jury trial. The conduct of investigations in these cases was entrusted to the officers of the separate corps of gendarmes—under the supervision of the prosecutor—and judgment in such cases was rendered in the judicial chamber, or in a special session of the Senate, or in exceptional cases, in the military courts. Another essential limitation on the authority of the judiciary was the rule that to try a civil servant for an offense committed in the course of duty, it was necessary to have the permission of his chief. Finally, it is essential to note that in cases involving the press, political cases, and cases of popular unrest, in which there was insufficient evidence for judicial prosecution, the government had recourse to punishment by administrative order.

Military Reform

The Crimean War exposed the scandalous shortcomings of Nicholas' army and of the whole military organization of Russia. The burden of military service was borne mainly by the lower classes of the population, for the nobility had been free from compulsory military service since 1762 and the wealthy were permitted to purchase exemption from military service. The term of military service was twenty-five years, and it was accompanied not only by military hazards but also by such privations and hardships that the families from which recruits were conscripted in most cases bade them goodbye forever. To become a recruit was regarded as severe punishment. Landlords tried to send as recruits the most depraved or insubordinate elements from their villages, and in the criminal law recruiting was simply enumerated as one of the punishments equal to banishment to Siberia. The recruitment and training of officers was in a most unsatisfactory condition, for there were not nearly enough schools to replenish the army with the necessary officer cadres. And the level of the majority of officers, drawn from the uneducated nobility or from noncommissioned officers of many years of service, was quite low. The mobilization of the army in time of war was difficult because of the lack of trained reserves, commissioned or enlisted.

At the very beginning of Alexander's reign, the most grievous burdens and injustices of the previous period were eliminated. The disciplinary schools for the "cantonists" (soldier's children) were closed and their inmates were discharged from the military class; military settlements were abolished. In 1859 the term of compulsory military service for the newly recruited lower ranks was reduced to 15 years in the army and 14 in the navy. With the entrance of D. A. Miliutin into the administration of the Ministry of War in 1861, energetic and systematic measures were undertaken to execute a fundamental and comprehensive reform of the whole military establishment. In the 1860s Miliutin reorganized the central administration of the military, and in 1864 a regulation on the establishment of military districts introduced a system of local organs of military administration. All of Russia was divided into military districts (in 1871 there were 14—10 in European Russia, 3 in Asiatic Russia, and 1 in the Caucasus), each headed by a commander. This relieved the central military administration in Petersburg of a multitude of small matters and at the same time facilitated faster and more efficient mobilization in the various regions of the state.

In his efforts to train the officer corps, Miliutin completely reorganized the system of military education. The former "cadet corps" were transformed into "military gymnasiums" with a curriculum of general education patterned after the "real gymnasiums" (see below). The higher grades of these schools were set aside for special military training of future officers and constituted special military schools. In view of the insufficient number of existing military schools, military progymnasiums—with a four-year general-education course—and two-year military-cadet schools *(iunkerskie uchilishcha)* were also established. In 1880 there were 9 military schools (including special schools), 16 cadet schools, 23 military gymnasiums, and 8 progymnasiums. For higher military education there were the academies of the general staff, engineering, artillery, and medicine, to which an academy of military law was added.

But the main reform of Miliutin was the introduction of universal military service. The draft as prepared by Miliutin encountered strong opposition in the Council of State and in the special conference on military service. The hardened conservatives and advocates of noble privilege objected to the reform and frightened the tsar with the future "democratization" of the army. But with the support of the tsar and of Grand Duke Constantine Nicholaevich, who was the chairman of the Council of State, Miliutin succeeded in having his draft passed. In December 1873, Alexander said to Miliutin, "There is a strong opposition to the new law . . . , the women are shouting more than anybody else." These of course were not peasant women, but the countesses and princesses surrounding the tsar who could not accept the thought that their Georges would have to serve in the ranks together with the peasant Grishas. In his diary for 1873 Miliutin writes: "the work goes slowly . . . there is much quarrelling . . . a heated meeting. . . . Count D. A. Tolstoy appears again and again there is annoying, bitter and stubborn squabbling. . . ."

On January 1, 1874, a manifesto introduced universal military service, and on the same day a statute concerning military service was published, stating: "the defense of the throne and the fatherland is the sacred duty of every Russian citizen. The male population, without distinction of status, is subject to military service." According to the new law, the call to military service was to take place every November. All young men who were twenty years old by the first of January of the same year had to answer the call, and from those found fit for military service the necessary number of recruits was to be drawn by lot. Those men required in the current year for the reinforcement of the cadres of the army and navy entered the service, while the remainder were enlisted in the militia, which was called up for service only in the case of war. The term of active service in the army was 6 years; and those who served the term were enlisted for a period of 9 years in the reserve—in the navy the corresponding terms were 7 and 3 years. Miliutin's law thus provided Russia for the first time with trained reserves in case of mobilization. Moreover, those serving in the armed forces were granted a number of privileges based on family status and education. Young men who were the sole supporters of their families were excused from service, and the term of service was reduced in various degrees for those who had various levels of education. Young men who had completed a certain level of education and were seventeen years of age entered the army as "volunteers." After completing a short term of service and passing an examination, they were commissioned as officers and entered the reserves.

Under the influence of the spirit of the times and thanks to the efforts of D. A. Miliutin, the character of the life of the Russian army completely changed in the 1860s and '70s. Severe drill and corporal discipline were eliminated, while preparation for combat was improved. Instead of ceremonial parades, soldiers were taught target shooting, fencing, and gymnastics; the military equipment of the army was improved; and at the same time, the soldiers learned to read and write, so that the army of Miliutin compensated to some degree for the lack of schooling in the Russian village.

State Finance and the National Economy

The government of Alexander II inherited from the previous reign a chaotic and disorganized financial system and enormous deficits in the state budget. The government of the new tsar and especially Reitern, the minister of finance from 1862 to 1878, aimed at the establishment of order in state finance and the stimulation of the economic development of Russia, mainly through the construction of railroads. Previously each ministry demanded and spent its budget individually, and all government expenditures were treated as "chancery secrets." In 1862 and 1863 a fundamental reform was executed: a unified treasury was established, that is, all the financial resources of the state were concentrated in the hands of the Ministry of Finance and all funds were distributed through its organs, "the treasuries," central, provincial, and district. The single, general account of income and expenditure ceased to be a state secret, and from 1863 on it was published for general information. A newly reorganized state control looked after the correct implementation of the budget and the expenditure of state funds in general. The local organs of state control were the control chambers, which were established in all the provinces in 1866.

The deficit of the state budget, inherited from the time of the Crimean War, continued to burden the state finance during the 1860s, and to fight the deficit the government often ordered all the government offices to carry out scrupulous economy. In the first half of the 1870s Reitern succeeded in balancing the budget, but the war of 1877–1878 again upset the financial equilibrium. All told, the annual revenues of the government rose from 200 to 630 million rubles in the reign of Alexander II.

One noteworthy reform in financial administration was the abolition of the infamous and outworn system of farming out the sale of alcoholic beverages. Instead, an excise tax was imposed on them, beginning in 1861. With regard to the tariff policy, the tariffs in 1857 and 1867 had a moderate protectionist character, but after January 1, 1877, customs duties were exacted in gold, which increased their real magnitude by one third.

The government clearly recognized the necessity of intensive railroad construction to raise the level of the national economy. But state funds were insufficient for this (and Reitern generally opposed a state-controlled economy), so Russia endeavored to attract private capital, foreign and domestic, for railroad construction by guaranteeing the builders a percentage (usually 5) of profit on invested capital. In 1857 the Main Company of Russian Railroads was established, composed of Russian and foreign capitalists. Later the development of railroads deteriorated and became full of concession rushes and stock-jobbing. There emerged a whole series of railroad companies which conducted their operations chaotically and uneconomically, padding their calculations of construction costs and generally taking advantage of the state. In 1873 the minister of railways, Count Bobrinsky, wrote in his report to the tsar, "The existence of many of our railroad companies is fictitious; their firms are phony; their administration is wrong; their shareholders are figureheads; their shares are not realized."[15]

There is no doubt that the treasury suffered considerable losses from additional payments on guarantees and other payments to the railroad speculators. However, the total growth of the railroad network during that period was quite considerable. At the beginning of the reign of Alexander II, there were some 600 miles of railroads in Russia; in 1880 the figure was about 13,600 miles.

After the abolition of serfdom, the commercial and industrial life of the country began to develop rapidly. The characteristic

---

[15] S. S. Tatishchev, *Imperator Aleksandr II* (St. Petersburg, 1911 ed.), vol. II, p. 189.

evidence of this development was the rapid growth of shareholding companies: in the five years from 1851 to 1855 in all the branches of national economy only 18 shareholding companies were founded with a capital of about 16 million rubles; in the five years from 1866 to 1870, 104 companies with a capital of close to 700 million rubles were founded. It is true that after the crisis of the early 1870s the growth of shareholding enterprises slowed down somewhat, but the magnitude of shareholding was completely beyond comparison with the period before the reforms.

It should be noted that certain branches of industry—such as the Ural mining industry, which depended on serf labor—experienced a temporary halt in their development during the first years after the abolition of serfdom. But in general industry began to develop with incomparably greater speed and success than in the reign of Nicholas. Foreign trade also increased considerably, as the following approximate figures indicate:

	IMPORT	EXPORT	TOTAL TURNOVER
1860	160,000,000 rubles	180,000,000	340,000,000
1880	620,000,000	500,000,000	1,120,000,000

Under Alexander II, banking made great progress, starting with the establishment of the State Bank in 1860 as the government's main financial apparatus. It later opened branch offices in all the important cities, and soon Russia was covered by a network of government, municipal, and private banks such as had been nonexistent in the previous period. To represent the interests of commerce and industry a Council of Commerce and Industry was established by the Ministry of Finance in Petersburg, with a branch in Moscow. In the large cities, stock exchanges came into being, administered by stock-exchange committees.

In conclusion, it should be noted that Reitern, who was preoccupied with the affairs of railroads and banks, took little interest in agriculture at a time when the economic situation of the village was far from excellent. With a low and almost static level of yield from the peasant-owned fields (and with frequent crop failures) and the rapid growth of the village population, which caused a decrease in the area per capita peasant allotments, the economic situation of the peasant population in the 1870s and '80s gradually but steadily deteriorated.

Education and the Press

The reign of Alexander II was the time of rapid, widespread development of periodicals and the considerable growth of their influence upon the public. In 1863, 195 periodicals appeared (or were permitted publication), while in 1880 there were 531. The stern censorship of Nicholas' reign was considerably relaxed at the end of the 1850s, providing the press with wide latitude to discuss cultural, social, and even political problems—such as it never possessed before and now utilized to the utmost. In the 1860s the intelligentsia of mixed social origin grew at an extraordinary rate, intellectually guided by *The Contemporary (Sovremennik)*, led by Chernyshevsky and Dobroliubov, and *The Russian Word (Russkoe Slovo)*, led by Pisarev. The former concentrated its attention on social and political questions and conducted a propaganda of populist and socialist ideas. In *The Russian Word* the nihilists, especially Pisarev, advocated a complete liberation of personality from all authorities, traditions, and prejudices (in the broadest sense of the word). After the closing of *The Contemporary* and *The Russian Word* in 1868, *Notes from the Fatherland (Otechestvennye zapiski)*, edited by Nekrasov and Saltykov-Shchedrin, became the most popular and influential organ of the Russian radical populist intelligentsia, remaining so until the 1880s. In 1866 the liberal organ *The Herald of Europe (Vestnik Evropy)* began to appear. Conservative views were expressed by the *Russian Herald* and the *Moscow Gazette (Moskovskie Vedomosti)*, edited by M. N. Katkov and K. N. Leontiev. The Slavophile organs, *The Russian Colloquium (Russkaia Beseda)*, *The Day (Den')*, *Moscow*, and *The Sail (Parus)*, enjoyed the sympathy of neither the government nor a wide part of the public, and one by one they ceased to appear, voluntarily or under compulsion.

The government, alarmed by the radical and oppositional trends in the periodical press, often applied punitive measures to individual publications, now weakening, now intensifying the censorship. In January 1863, censorship was withdrawn from the jurisdiction of the Ministry of Public Education and transferred to the jurisdiction of the Ministry of Internal Affairs. On April 6, 1865, a law was issued "On the granting of some alleviation and convenience to the Russian press." According to the new, "temporary" regulations, all the issues of periodicals in the capitals were free from precensorship if their publishers requested it, as were all original works of at least 160 pages, translations of at least 320 pages, and academic publications.

Of course, the abolition of precensorship did not mean the abolition of observational and punitive authority. The minister of internal affairs could impose fines on the publishers of newspapers and periodicals; he could forbid the printing of private advertisements, and he could issue warnings. After the third warning, he could stop the publication for the period of six months. To discontinue a publication permanently he needed the consent of the Senate. The "liberal" Minister of Internal Affairs Valuev and his successors made widespread use of the right to restrain the periodical press: from 1865 till 1880, 177 warnings and 52 orders to stop publication were issued.

Following the ascent to the throne of Alexander II, the restraints and limitations on university life, which had been introduced in the reign of Nicholas I, were abolished. The university auditoriums and halls became accessible to all and were filled with motley and tumultuous crowds of the youth of mixed social origin. Meetings of societies, public lectures, parties, and disputes took place one after another and drew crowds of students and outsiders. The students established mutual assistance funds, libraries, reading rooms, and literary enterprises. Under the intellectual influences of Herzen, Chernyshevsky, Dobroliubov, and Pisarev, the political trend of the youth became radical and their state of mind agitated.

Conflicts with university authorities and clashes with police occurred often. In 1861 the minister of public education, Admiral Putiatin, decided "to bring order" into the university by forbidding assemblies and introducing matriculation certificates and identity cards for students. These measures led to serious disorders at the University of Petersburg, which was temporarily closed as a consequence, and the disturbances spread to other universities. At the end of 1861, Admiral Putiatin was relieved from his post as minister of public education and his place was taken by the liberal minister A. V. Golovnin. He prepared and carried through a new university statute, which was approved June 18, 1863. The statute established the autonomy of the universities: the rector, prorector, and the professors were to be elected to the university council, which consisted of all the ordinary and extraordinary professors, and deans were to be elected by meetings of the faculties. The election of deans had to be confirmed by the minister of public education and the rector by the emperor. Committees of professors supervised all the matters concerning teaching; student affairs were to be conducted by a prorector elected by the council; and a university court was established, composed of three judges from among the professors. However, student organizations and student representation were not legalized by the new statute, and the students were regarded simply as individual registrants of the university. The new statutes also permitted persons other than students to audit university lectures.

In 1863 Petersburg University was reopened and university life in all of Russia began to develop normally in spite of the fact that it was interrupted more than once in the 1860s and '70s by outbreaks of student disturbances, which became an established tradition in the life of the Russian university. Other new institutions of higher learning that were opened in the reign of Alexander II were: "The New Russian" university in Odessa (1864); Warsaw University (with Russian as the language of instruction) and the Agriculture and Forestry Institute in New Alexandria near Warsaw (1869); the History and Philosophy Institute in Petersburg (1867); and the Archeological Institute (1877).

Under Alexander the organization of secondary education at first was regulated by the "Statute on Gymnasiums and Progymnasiums," published in 1864. It established two types of secondary schools, the classical gymnasium (with one compulsory classical language) and the "real gymnasium" *(real'noe uchilishche)*, stressing science and technology. The government, frightened by public discontent and student disturbances, decided to reform the school statute of 1864 to secure a peaceful and "reliable" contingent of students for the universities.

Count D. A. Tolstoy, who replaced Golovnin in 1866 as minister of public education, came to the conclusion that it was the study of natural sciences that led to materialism and nihilism, and he therefore decided to ban the natural sciences from the gymnasiums and to make the Latin and Greek languages the main subjects in all classical gymnasiums. During the discussion of Tolstoy's draft in the Council of State, it was rejected by the majority (29 to 19), but the tsar upheld the minority, and Tolstoy's draft became a law July 30, 1871. Henceforth the time and energy of the students at school and at home was loaded with the cramming of vocabulary and grammar and the translations and written exercises that, in the opinion of Tolstoy, must hinder the penetration of free thoughts into the heads of "classicists." And this was to assure that they would become well-behaved and obedient university students, for according to the law of 1871, only persons with gymnasium education could enter the universities. The behavior of the pupils in school and outside of it was regulated in detail by special rules, the fulfillment of which was to be watched by the teachers and their assistants.

In 1872 a statute for the "real gymnasium" appeared, stating that the objective of these schools was to offer "a general education, adapted to practical needs and the acquisition of technical knowledge." The course of studies in the gymnasium lasted for eight years, in the "real gymnasium" for six or seven years.

In 1872 the district schools were renamed city schools, and a number of teacher-training institutes were opened to prepare teachers for them. The organization and the conduct of the affairs of public primary education was governed by the "Regulation on Primary Public Schools," issued July 14, 1864. For the management of the affairs of public education, provincial and district "educational councils" were established, composed of bureaucrats and of representatives of public organizations. The public schools were directed by the Ministry of Public Education or, in the case of parochial church schools, the Holy Synod.

With the entry of Count D. A. Tolstoy into the administration of the Ministry of Public Education, the government applied a dual policy in school affairs: first, to strengthen its own control and supervision and, second, to draw representatives of the nobility into the leadership of public education. In 1869 inspectors were introduced into the public schools. According to the instruction issued to the schools in 1871, the schools were to be "under constant close supervision" of government inspectors who, in reality, watched the "reliability" of the teachers more than their pedagogical work. In 1874 a new "Regulation on Primary Public Schools" was issued. The county and provincial marshals of the nobility were to serve as chairmen of the educational councils at their respective levels, while the directors and the inspectors of public schools were to administer scholastic affairs. "In case of disorder and harmful tendencies," the school was to be closed at the discretion of the district educational council, while the governor held general supervisory authority over the course of primary education in the province.

In the period of Tolstoy and Pobedonostsev, the overprocurator of the Holy Synod, the government showed great sympathy for the parochial schools, and in every way possible encouraged the clergy to manage the schools. However, this project progressed with difficulty, and the activity of the zemstvos in public education proved more successful.

The epoch of Alexander II brought the widespread development of education for women into Russia for the first time. Only a few institutes for young ladies of the nobility had existed in the first part of the nineteenth century, along with a number of half-schools and half-orphanages operated by the Department of the Empress Maria's Institutions. In 1864 and later in 1870, regulations of the Ministry of Public Education on girls' gymnasiums were issued, establishing a course of seven grades, or eight for those preparing to teach. Progymnasiums of three or four grades were also established. At the end of 1880 there were 79 girls' gymnasiums and 164 progymnasiums under the Ministry of Public Education, and 30 gymnasiums and 1 progymnasium among the Empress Maria's Institutions. The number of pupils in the girls' gymnasiums, which in 1864 constituted close to 4000, grew to 27,000 by 1875.

Finally, the 1870s were distinguished in Russia by the beginning of university education for women, a field in which Russia moved ahead of the other European countries. The secondary schools for girls provided a sufficient contingent of students who strove for higher education, and in the 1870s "higher courses for women" emerged with a university curriculum: the courses of Professor Gerié in Moscow, Professor Bestuzhev-Riumin in Petersburg, and the higher medical courses for women in Petersburg, which were later transformed into a medical institute for women.

In evaluating the reforms of Alexander II as a whole, we must recognize that, despite their limitations, they opened for Russia the possibility of peaceful and steady progress. The most important of the reforms, the abolition of serfdom, made Russian citizens out of millions of peasants who had been the private property of their masters. This naturally brought about great changes in social relationships and in the psychology of the people. To be sure, since the peasants were placed under the authority of the peasant commune—and after 1889 under the additional authority of the superintendents of the peasantry—and constituted a separate legal and taxpaying class, they were still limited in their civil rights. Only the reforms of the Stolypin era (beginning in 1906) were to give them full civil equality with other classes.

Moreover, the serf emancipation was not an isolated phenomenon, but was the first and basic development in a comprehensive reform that affected all the major branches of Russian life. The introduction of a considerable measure of self-government in rural areas and in the cities alike represented a major departure from the centralized, bureaucratic tradition of the Russian government and drew some of the most progressive and able persons into active public life—with at least some chance to exert their own initiative, not merely to await bureaucratic orders. This development was buttressed by the introduction of an efficient and equitable legal system that was not inferior in its principles and practices to the judiciary of the most advanced European countries. The military reform not only put an end to the cruelty and injustice that had equated military service with punishment, making it a normal civic obligation, but it also provided Russia with a modern reserve military force such as the other European countries possessed by this time. Although the time of really rapid economic development lay beyond the period of the reform, there were some significant steps forward—notably the beginning of a substantial railroad system. Finally, the educational level of the country continued to improve on the primary, secondary, and higher levels.

Unfortunately, the mistaken policies of the successors of Alexander II and the political immaturity of the intelligentsia and the masses did not permit the country to continue the path of peaceful and progressive development that it had entered upon in the period of the great reforms.

6

The State
and Political Movements in the Second Half
of the Nineteenth Century

Oppositional and Revolutionary
Trends in the 1860s

Following the Crimean War the Russian public, particularly in St. Petersburg and Moscow, was in ferment. The thunder of the cannons of Sevastopol awakened the slumbering Russian empire; the Crimean catastrophe gave rise to general dissatisfaction with the government and to the recognition of the necessity for radical reform of the political and social order. The abolition of serfdom in 1861, however, did not pacify the public agitation. The reform led to dissatisfaction among the conservatives and to complete disillusionment within the radical intelligentsia. Senselessly brutal suppressions of several alleged peasant uprisings, particularly the shooting of peasants in the village of Bezdna, provoked the first series of antigovernment demonstrations in Petersburg.

But the great majority of the peasants, whom the arbitrators conscientiously helped to understand the new order and to regulate their relationship with the former landlords, remained quiet during the reign of Alexander II. All the appeals for an uprising of the peasantry made by revolutionary intellectuals in the 1870s remained unanswered. The common belief that the revolutionary movement in Russia began only as an answer to the reactionary policy of the government does not correspondent to the facts. For the revolutionary movement among the intelligentsia began precisely at the height of the liberal reforms, in the period between the emancipation of peasants and the introduction of zemstvo and judicial reforms in 1864. The first attempt upon the life of Alexander took place as early as 1866 and, in fact, contributed to the reversal of the liberal policies by the government.

Many groups of the Russian intelligentsia and particularly the university youth were not satisfied with the liberal reforms of Alexander II. But their most active, "progressive" elements regarded tsardom and Western parliamentarism with equal distaste and demanded the complete destruction of the existing order in the name of some hypothetical and utterly vague "bright future." Naturally, no government could have fulfilled the demands of extreme anarchism. However, the tsarist regime, frightened by the threat of sedition, began to persecute not only revolutionary anarchists but also liberals, thus enlarging and strengthening the opposition.

At the end of the 1850s and at the beginning of the 1860s, the biweekly *The Bell (Kolokol)*, published in London by Herzen since 1857, was the most influential and popular periodical among progressive circles in Russia. However, Herzen, an old revolutionary romantic and a moderate socialist, soon appeared to be behind the times. He was "overtaken" by radical authors at home, writing in both legally published periodicals and illegal proclamations and leaflets.

The audience for this extremist writing was the new intelligentsia of "mixed social origin" *(raznochintsy)*, which in the 1860s entered upon the political stage. Previously, the Russian intelligentsia had been drawn almost exclusively from the ranks of the nobility. Increasingly the intelligentsia became a group that cut across class lines, including children of the clergy, petty officials, tradesmen, merchants, and a few peasants. Increasingly it was the intelligentsia from the lower social ranks that set the pattern for the intelligentsia as a whole. It was among them that radical views and political opposition flourished.

The most influential publications representing the extremist point of view in the 1860s were the periodicals *The Russian Word (Russkoe Slovo)*, 1859–1866, for which D. I. Pisarev was the leading literary critic, and *The Contemporary (Sovremennik)*, 1836–1866, in which N. G. Chernyshevsky and N. A. Dobroliubov were the most important contributors at that time. The organ of the antinihilist opposition to the radicals was the *Russian Herald (Russkii Vestnik)*, founded in 1856 and published by M. N. Katkov.

Pisarev was the head and the prophet of the Russian nihilists, or as they called themselves, "the thinking realists." Pisarev's slogan was, in the words of A. Kornilov, "the liberation of personality and of human thought from various religious, moral, and family fetters and prejudices." In the opinion of the young "realists," not only the old authorities and former ideals, but all ideals as such were unnecessary and harmful "rubbish." The natural law and the natural necessity for man was to "take pleasure in life" and to enjoy "full freedom of personality." Egoism, wrote Pisarev, is a "system of convictions which leads to the full emancipation of personality," and "when the individual uses his own natural abilities with calculated rationality, then he inevitably increases the total of all human well-being. . . . Fully calculated egoism perfectly coincides with the results of most conscious love of men. . . ." His philosophy of "realism" Pisarev called "contemporary, healthy, fresh materialism,"[1] connected, of course, with atheism, which could not be discussed openly in the legally published press. The subject of Pisarev's constant critical attacks was esthetics and, in particular, the poetry of Pushkin, because he believed art, like science, should serve the practical needs of the majority of people and not merely be the idle pastime of an insignificant minority. In the field of knowledge, said Pisarev, the most useful and necessary subjects were the natural sciences, which alone could revive the people's industry, raise its productivity, and in this way destroy "the poverty and immorality of the masses." "There is in humanity only one evil: ignorance; against this evil there is only one remedy: knowledge."[2]

In order to fight poverty and ignorance, it was necessary first of all "to increase the number of thinking people" among the educated classes of society, and these thinking people would bring society to a state of well-being. Pisarev's admonitions to liberate the personality from all authority were widely accepted by the youth of the day, especially the students. Although Pisarev was not a revolutionary in the political sense, he once wrote a strongly worded anti-government article for an illegal publication. For this, he was arrested in 1862 and sentenced to three years' imprisonment in the fortress of Saints Peter and Paul, where he wrote most of his critical articles for *The Russian Word*. Soon after leaving the fortress in 1866, he accidentally drowned at the age of twenty-eight (June 1868).

If the main content of Pisarev's preaching was "the fight for individuality," his contemporaries Dobroliubov and Chernyshevsky advanced new social ideals, and—together with Herzen—became the ideologists and founders of the Russian populism *(narodnichestvo.)* According to Dobroliubov, literature should be evaluated not accord-

---

[1] D. I. Pisarev, "Realisty," *Sochineniia* [*Works*] (Moscow, 1956 ed.), vol. 3, p. 64.
[2] *Ibid.*, p. 122.

ing to its value as art, but as a factor in social progress or regression, and the analysis of literary works was to serve critics as an occasion for the explanation of social questions. In his articles "The Kingdom of Darkness"—concerning the works of Ostrovsky—and "What is Oblomovism?"—concerning Goncharov's novel *Oblomov*—Dobroliubov severely condemned the mode of life and the morality of contemporary Russian society. In the article "When Will the Day Come?" —in connection with Turgenev's novel *On the Eve*—he asserted that "in our society a desire is awakening to get to the real work: to become aware of the triviality of various nice toys, of the high spiritual deliberations and immutable forms with which we have for so long entertained and filled ourselves."[3] New people, as they became aware of "all the burden and absurdity" of the contemporary social conditions, should lend an attentive ear to "the groan and the cry of the unhappy brethren" and come to their rescue. Dobroliubov accused Russian society of Oblomovlike inertness, apathy, and incapacity for practical action. He contrasted the upper strata of society with ordinary people," who possessed efficiency, seriousness, "the power of goodness," and a capacity for self-sacrifice.

Along with Pisarev, Chernyshevsky conducted a campaign for "the destruction of esthetics"—as Pisarev put it—that is, he argued that the value of literature lay in its utility, which was determined by the degree to which it served the problems and needs for contemporary "reality." As an adherent of European socialism, especially Fourierism, he concentrated upon articles and research in the field of economics. For several years before 1861 he devoted his main attention to the peasant question, ardently defending the necessity of allotting land to the emancipated peasants and of preserving the communal ownership of land. In Chernyshevsky's view, "that form of land ownership which combines the owner, the master, and the worker in one person is best for the success of agriculture. State ownership, with the communal possession, is closest to that ideal."[4] Europe, said Chernyshevsky, had already passed the stage of communal landownership, but Russia could and should use its backwardness to pass over the phase of private landownership and go straight to the "higher stage" of collective ownership. A backward people, said Chernyshevsky, while making use of the knowledge and experience of advanced

---

[3] N. A. Dobroliubov, *Polnoe sobranie sochinenii* [*Complete Collection of Works*] (St. Petersburg, 1911 ed.), vol. 4, p. 51.
[4] N. G. Chernyshevsky, *Polnoe sobranie sochinenii* (St. Petersburg, 1906 ed.), vol. 3, p. 473.

peoples, could "ascend from the lower stage to the higher, bypassing the intermediate logical stages." [5]

In 1862 Chernyshevsky was arrested and, while in prison, wrote his renowned novel *What Is to be Done?* (*Chto delat'?*), which gave the radical intelligentsia a model hero in the person of Rakhmetov, a disciplined, self-sacrificing devotee of fundamental social change. Although the book did not propose a specific political program, it provided moral inspiration for many young radicals in the ensuing decades. In 1864 Chernyshevsky was sentenced by the Senate to hard labor for composing a revolutionary proclamation, "To the Landlords' Peasants," which asserted that true peasant emancipation was impossible under tsarist rule and urged the peasants to be prepared for a future general uprising to win real freedom. The severity of the sentence can be explained by the fact that the government, while lacking direct legal evidence against Chernyshevsky, had reason to suspect him of being the leader of the entire underground revolutionary movement. The writer spent nineteen years in Siberia, including seven at hard labor, and returned to European Russia only in 1883; he died in 1889.

In opposition to the radical leaders of the 1860s stood the talented critic Apollon Grigorev. He maintained that literature and literary criticism should serve not the idea of "abstract humanity, which in reality does not exist," but should grow organically from the national soil and mirror the life of the nation. This movement was half-ironically called the "grass-rooters" (*pochvenniki*), after Grigorev's reference to the national soil (*pochva*). Grigorev worshipped Pushkin and Ostrovsky, whom he regarded as spokesman for the Russian national spirit, but his ideas found few supporters among the intelligentsia.

Along with the open propagation of new ideas on the pages of *The Contemporary* and *The Russian Word,* an illegal, underground Russian press began functioning after 1861. The leaflet entitled "The Great Russian" (*Velikoruss*), which appeared in three issues in 1861, bore a relatively moderate character. It was willing "to begin by trying peaceful means," and called for the submission of a petition to the tsar, demanding that he call the "representatives of the Russian people for the purpose of drawing up a constitution for Russia"; otherwise, "Russia will undergo a dreadful upheaval. . . ." [6]

---

[5] *Ibid.,* vol. 4, p. 331.

[6] V. Bogucharsky, ed., *Materialy dlia istorii revolutsionnogo dvizheniia v Rossii v 60-kh godakh* [*Materials for the History of the Revolutionary Movement in Russia in the 1860s*] (St. Petersburg, 1906), pp. 24–25.

M. L. Mikhailov's proclamation, "To the Young Generation," was of a more radical temper:

> We would not, of course, want the matter to come to a forcible upheaval, but if it cannot be otherwise, we not only will not give up, we will willingly call the revolution to the rescue of the people. . . . If in order to fulfill our striving to redistribute the land among the people it becomes necessary to slaughter a hundred thousand landlords, we will not fear it. . . . We need not a tsar, annointed in the Uspenskii Cathedral, but an elected elder who receives a salary for his services.

Mikhailov's social program was populist: "Our commune is the basic cell, and the collection of such cells is Russia. . . . We want the land to belong not to the individual but to the country; we want each commune to have its allotment with no private landowners; we want it to be impossible to sell the land as they sell potatoes or cabbages. . . ."[7]

But as early as 1862 a proclamation, "Young Russia" *(Molodaia Rossiia)*, published by one of the student circles, used violently revolutionary and even bloodthirsty terms. It divided Russia into two opposing groups: the tsarist party, consisting of landlords, merchants, and civil servants—"in short all the 'have's', all who owned property"—and "the party of the people," the destitute and the oppressed. The proclamation saw the only way out in a

> bloody and inexorable revolution—a revolution which must change radically every single foundation of contemporary society, and do away with all the supporters of the existing order. We are not afraid of the revolution, although we know that a river of blood will be shed, that perhaps there will also be innocent victims; we can foresee all this, and yet we welcome the coming of the revolution; we are ready to sacrifice our own heads in order that it may come sooner, the one [revolution], the long desired one!

The revolution, with the slogan "Long live the social and democratic Russian republic!" was to open with an attack on the Winter Palace, aiming at "the extermination of those living in it," and should the "tsarist party" defend the tsar, the shout was to be, "to axes!" and all possible means to annihilate the conservatives were then to be used. Among the other demands of the "people's party" were: "the

---

[7] *Ibid.*, pp. 2–11.

abolition of marriage as a highly immoral phenomenon and the abolition of the family, an institution which hinders the development of man." [8]

In addition to the proclamations cited here, a dozen or so other revolutionary leaflets were published and circulated in the early 1860s. At the same time the revolutionary group "Land and Liberty" *(Zemlia i Volia)* was organized, but initially, its activities and influence were limited.

To the general discontent, to the revolutionary incitement, were added a spate of fires, which broke out in Petersburg and other cities in the spring and summer of 1862. These were popularly attributed to the nihilists. Though the real arsonists were not found, the government, frightened and confused, began to strike out on all sides. The authors of revolutionary proclamations, or those who were regarded as such, underwent severe punishment. Chernyshevsky, Pisarev, and many other "suspected and unreliable" persons were arrested. Some of them were banished from Petersburg, and thus were given an opportunity to spread their "pernicious ideas" in provincial cities and towns. When Petersburg University was closed, pending a revision of its statute, Herzen wrote in *The Bell:* "Where will you go, Oh youth for whom the gates of learning are closed? *To the people! To the people!* There is your place, you exiles from learning." Thus began the celebrated slogan that was to be repeated in 1869 by Bakunin.

During the repression, adult schools were closed, as well as people's reading rooms, because "harmful trends" were uncovered in some of them. Publication of *The Contemporary* and *The Russian Word* was suspended for a period of eight months, along with Aksakov's Slavophile organ, *The Day (Den'),* which was suspended for four months.

In the years 1863–1864 the attention of the government and the public was deflected from the projected revolution in Russia by a real revolution in Poland and by the diplomatic intervention there of European powers, which gave rise to an upsurge of patriotism. The establishment of the zemstvos and the introduction of judicial reforms in 1864–1865 also attracted much attention, but the revolutionary movement regained public eminence April 4, 1866, when the student Karakozov fired at the tsar. The attempted assassination of the tsar-liberator again gave rise to fear in the court circles and led

---

[8] Ibid., pp. 56-63; see also Vl. Burtsev, ed., *Za sto let (1800–1896)* [*In the Course of a Hundred Years*] (London, 1897), pp. 40–46.

to an intensified reaction. The new head of the Third Section, Count Shuvalov "terrorized" the tsar with his constant reports about revolutionary plots and intrigues; Count Tolstoy took up the task of disciplining the minds of the Russian student youth with his program of classicism. Except for the Ministry of War, the official reform movement subsided, and the government regarded the newly established offices of the zemstvo and the courts with apprehension, fearing that the invisible revolutionary hydra was hiding there. She was, however, elsewhere.

In 1868–1869, a series of "Historical Letters," signed by "Mirtov," appeared in the entirely nonrevolutionary journal *The Week (Nedelia)*. The author of these letters was a retired colonel, P. L. Lavrov, a former professor of the military academy. His letters, which were published in 1870 in a separate edition, made a great impression upon the radical youth, and for many they became a guide for a new period of active struggle.

In his "Letters," Lavrov provided a synthesis of the ideas of Pisarev and of Dobroliubov. He accepted the individualism of Pisarev, but strove to combine it with the social mindedness of Dobroliubov by placing the ideal of social service before the "developed personality." Thus, Lavrov's "formula for progress" advocated: "The development of personality in the physical, intellectual, and moral sense. The embodiment of truth and justice in the social forms." In the past, he argued, only a small minority had benefited from progress, at the expense of the suppressed and suffering majority, and therefore "critically thinking individuals" from among the educated minority were obliged to pay their debt to the masses "through the introduction of scientific understanding and justice in the social structure." It was up to the intellectuals to "inject humanism into the mechanism of life, awaken thought, awaken hatred and repugnance toward the ordinary evil." The moving spirits of progress were necessarily always "lonely, struggling personalities"; and the success of the struggle required, first of all, "energetic and fanatical people who are ready to risk everything and sacrifice everything. . . ." Then, the death and the legend of these martyrs would "inspire thousands with the energy that the struggle requires." Then, the "critically thinking and energetic individuals" would organize a "party of fighters for truth and justice," which would begin the fight against "the decayed social forms." This fight would bestow victory on the "workers for progress." Having outlined this formula for revolution, Lavrov pointed out that in the future "political progress will consist of minimizing the role of government in society; in other words, the elimination of all coercion in the political contract for individuals who disagree with such a contract." [9] The final ideal is the abolition of the state as an institution.

Shortly after the appearance of the "Historical Letters," Lavrov went abroad, and from 1873 until 1878, first in Zurich and later in London, he published a magazine for the Russian revolutionary youth entitled *Forward (Vperëd)*. The keynote article explained that the revolutionary party was carrying on a double struggle: first, it was "a struggle of realist ideology against theological ideology" and, second, it was "the struggle of the worker against the classes of his exploiters, a struggle of free association against the compulsion of the state." For the Russians, the particular foundation for future development was "the peasantry with the communal ownership of land." The peculiarly Russian aims were

> to develop our commune in the sense of communal cultivation of land and the common use of its products, to make the communal assembly the basic political element of the Russian social structure, to absorb private property into communal property, to educate the peasantry to give them an understanding of their social needs, without which it will never be able to make use of its legal rights. . . .

Lavrov called the Russian youth to individual training of mind and will and sought to prepare the nation for social revolution through prolonged and systematic propaganda, because "the reorganization of society must be accomplished not only for the people but by the people." Revolutions "are products not of personal will, not the actions of a small group, but of a whole series of complicated historical processes." [10]

This process seemed painfully slow, however. Another voice from abroad, more influential and decisive, pointed to a shorter way. This was Bakunin, the famous "Apostle of Anarchy." In cooperation with N. I. Zhukovsky, he began in 1868 to publish a newspaper for Russian revolutionaries, *The People's Cause (Narodnoe Delo)*, which declared: "We want full intellectual, social, economic, and political freedom for the people." Intellectual freedom consisted of liberation from "belief in God, in the immortality of soul, and in general of freedom from all kinds of idealism";

---

[9] P. L. Lavrov, *Istoricheskie pis'ma* [*Historical Letters*] (St. Petersburg, 1870), pp. 30, 66, 84, 109, 115–120, 237.

[10] Burtsev., ed., *op. cit.*, pp. 106–112.

from this it clearly follows that we are advocates of atheism and materialism. . . . We hold two basic tenets of economic truth: (1) the land belongs only to those who till it with their hands— to the village communes; (2) capital and the means of production belong to the workers, and workers associations. The true and complete freedom of the people also requires the abolition of the laws of inheritance and the family, including church and civil marriage. . . . In the name of political liberation we first of all want the final annihilation of the state; we want the complete eradication of a state system and its religious, political, military, civilian, bureaucratic educational and economic as well as financial institutions. [In place of the state] a free federation of free workers, of agriculture as well as factory and artisan associations [must emerge].

Bakunin's social and political ideal was "an organization of society through a free federation of workers' associations . . . , at first on the level of the commune, then as a regional federation of communes, followed by the federation of regions into nations and of nations into one brotherly International."[11] According to Bakunin, any state, irrespective of its political form, was simply "systematized coercion, oppression, exploitation, injustice." Therefore Bakunin opposed the Marxist idea of the "dictatorship of the proletariat." He predicted, with acute foresight, that it would amount to "the dictatorship of the leaders of the communist party, of Mr. Marx and his friends," who, after seizing power, would again enslave the masses and submit them to "the direct command of state engineers, who will form a new privileged political and scientific class."[12] For Bakunin, the only means for the complete emancipation of the masses was "the path of combat and rebellion." He believed in the revolutionary instinct of the masses and especially of the Russian peasantry, which he believed to be imbued with the freedom-loving, rebellious, anarchistic spirit of Razin and Pugachev.

While Bakunin remained abroad, S. G. Nechaev undertook to realize the social theories of Bakunin in Russia by attempting to establish a strong revolutionary organization, based on the principle of strict secrecy, centralization, and discipline. In his journal *The People's Vengeance (Narodnaia Rasprava)*, published abroad, Nechaev wrote in 1869:

---

[11] *Ibid.*, pp. 87–89; See also Iu. Steklov, *M.A. Bakunin: ego zhizn' i deiatelnost'* [*M. A. Bakunin's Life and Activity*] (Moscow, 1927), vol. 3, p. 227.

[12] Steklov, *op. cit.*, vol. 3, p. 247.

We want a national peasant revolution. . . . We have only one
negative, invariable plan—general destruction. . . . We frankly
refuse to take any part in the working out of future conditions of
life . . . and therefore we regard as fruitless all solely theoretical
work. . . . We consider destruction to be such an enormous and
difficult task that we devote all our powers to it, and we do not
wish to deceive ourselves with the dream that we will have
enough strength and knowledge for creation.[13]

Nechaev played an important role in the contemporary
revolutionary movement, acting as the mainspring of the student riots
in Petersburg in 1869, and succeeded in building up a fairly broad
revolutionary organization. In 1871 eighty-seven members of his organization were brought to trial, thus giving Dostoevsky the material
for his novel *The Devils (Besy)*. Abroad, Nechaev met Bakunin and
made a very good impression on him. After Herzen's death in 1870,
Nechaev obtained financial help from a fund that Herzen's followers
held to support the publication of revolutionary literature. Nechaev
was arrested in Switzerland in 1872 upon the request of the Russian
government and turned over to the Russian authorities, who imprisoned him for instigating the murder of one of his own followers
some years before. But as a martyr he gained even more prestige
among the revolutionaries, as is indicated by the fact that the "People's
Will" (see below) debated whether their strength would be better
devoted to the assassination of Alexander II or the liberation of
Nechaev from prison.

P. Tkachev, "the Russian Jacobin," a member of Nechaev's
circle, continued the cause of Nechaev. Starting in 1875, he published
the *émigré* journal, *The Alarm (Nabat)*. He renounced the theory of
pure anarchism and advocated the seizure of power by a closely knit,
disciplined revolutionary party and the dictatorship of this party for
the purpose of destroying and rebuilding the structure of society:
"The immediate aim of the revolution must consist in the seizure of
political power and the establishment of a revolutionary state."[14]

Generally speaking, it is possible to summarize the characteristic outlook of the "progressives" of the 1860s, expressed in the
writings of their leaders and prophets: in philosophy and theology—
materialism and atheism; in the social and political sphere—anarchism
and communism; in ethics and esthetics—utilitarianism. It is worth

---

[13] Burtsev, *op. cit.*, pp. 90–96; see also B. Glinsky, *Revolutsionnyi period russkoi
istorii (1861-1881)* (St. Petersburg, 1913), vol. 1, p. 411–412.

[14] Burstsev, *op. cit.*, pp. 133–135.

noting that Herzen, when he met with representatives of the "young *émigrés*" in London, was appalled by their "rudeness, ignorance, recklessness, and self-adoration."

The Polish Uprising of 1863

The rigorous regime of Nicholas I in Poland was considerably softened under Alexander II. The revolutionaries of 1830–1831 were granted an amnesty, and the deported, the banished, and the emigrants were allowed to return to their homeland. But these measures of the Russian government could not reconcile the Poles to the loss of national independence, and by the summer of 1860 feelings of discontent erupted in Warsaw. In the streets, in the squares, and in the churches, patriotic demonstrations began. In February 1861 the army fired into a crowd of demonstrators, killing some of them and wounding others. This action caused indignation among the Poles and intensified the discontent, which then spread from Warsaw to other Polish cities. The policy of the Russian government toward Poland in the early 1860s oscillated: at first there was an intensification of repression, then attempts at reconciliation, and the vice-regents of the tsar in Warsaw were repeatedly replaced within a few months. In 1861–1862 the government made a serious attempt at reconciliation by giving Poland administrative autonomy and local self-government. Finally, in 1862, Alexander II sent his liberal-minded brother Constantine Nicholaevich to be vice-regent of Poland (on the day after his arrival an attempt was made on his life), and appointed the Polish patriot Marquis Wielopolski as head of the civilian government. Native-born Poles were appointed to the offices of local government, and the Polish language was introduced into official correspondence.

None of these measures pacified the revolutionaries. The Polish patriots would not be satisfied with administrative autonomy since their aim was full political independence of Poland "with the boundaries of 1772," that is, with Lithuania and the western Russian provinces included in the Polish state. Naturally these demands were unacceptable to the Russian government, and the agitation in the country continued. The Polish nobility, the Catholic clergy, and a section of the urban population were all adherents of the idea of Polish independence. In January 1863, when the government decreed a levy of conscripts in the cities of Poland for the Russian army, intending to remove the restless urban youth, a rebellion broke out all across the country. The uprising had been prepared beforehand;

groups of armed insurgents attacked units of the Russian army stationed in Poland, and a few hundred sleeping, unarmed Russian soldiers were killed or wounded, naturally causing indignation among the Russian public. The Polish revolutionary government declared the aim of the uprising to be "the complete independence of Poland, Lithuania, and Rus' [Western Russia] as indivisible parts of one Polish state." These demands were unacceptable to the Russian public, whose spokesman at that time became the Slavophile Aksakov and the liberal Westerner Katkov, who appealed to patriotic sentiment and protested against the claims of the Polish revolution. On the other hand, Herzen, in *The Bell,* sided with the Polish rebellion, adopting the slogan "for your freedom and ours," and called upon the Russian officers in Poland not to raise arms against the Poles. This position, however, undermined Herzen's influence in Russia.

At the height of the rebellion the governments of Great Britain, France, and Austria proposed that the Russian government call an international conference on the Polish question, later demanding broad autonomy for Poland, with the introduction of popular representation and an amnesty to all the revolutionaries. Not only the Russian government but also Russian public opinion considered the diplomatic actions of the Western powers intolerable interference into the internal affairs of Russia, and the situation called forth an outburst of patriotism and nationalism. The government was swamped with patriotic addresses from societies of the nobility, the burghers, and the peasants, in which they expressed their readiness to defend the interests and prestige of Russia. This torrent of petitions helped to stiffen the government's resolve to refuse any mediation on the Polish question.

The rebellion spread from Poland to Lithuania and the western Russian provinces, but very soon it displayed a fundamental weakness. The mass of Polish peasantry did not join the rebellion, and the attitude of the peasantry of the provinces of Vitebsk, Kiev, Volhynia, and Podolia was antirevolutionary, supporting the Russian authorities and the army in their fight against the insurgents. Grand Duke Constantine Nicholaevich left Poland, and all power in the country was transferred to the military authority of the governor generals. In 1864 General Muraviev in Lithuania and General Berg in Poland suppressed the rebellion, and the appellation "Kingdom of Poland" was abolished, being replaced by "the Vistula Territory." This territory was divided into ten provinces with a Russian administration and with Russian as the official language. All the autonomous administrative institutions, central and regional, which had been introduced in 1861–1862, were abolished. As was noted earlier, the Polish peasantry was rewarded in 1864 by emancipation from the patrimonial authority of the landowners, and the peasants received land allotments on convenient terms, as well as self-government in the villages.

Revolutionary Movements of the 1870s

Early in the 1870s a movement "to the people" grew up among the radical intelligentsia. Hundreds of young men and women left their families and their occupations and went to the villages as teachers, rural clerks, doctors' assistants, midwives, merchants, pedlars, artisans, and unskilled laborers to live among the masses and to spread their ideas. These men and women were the followers of Bakunin and, to a lesser extent, of Lavrov; the former went to arouse the people to rebellion, while the latter were—or thought that they were—peaceful propagandists of socialist, communist, and anarchist ideals.

In reality, however, the propaganda that they distributed was violently subversive, including books on Razin and Pugachev. Even before the formation of the terroristic "People's Will," witnesses from among the common folk testified before a special commission of the Senate that they had been incited to violence. According to one peasant who testified at the trial of seventy-eight propagandists in 1875: "The accused [student] said that is necessary to destroy the merchants, the nobility and the tsar." And another stated: " . . . he said that these books have to be distributed among the people in order to teach the masses of people to make an uprising during which the government and the landlords must be destroyed." In reply the accused, Diakov, a student of Petersburg University, maintained that he had distributed these works only "to explain certain social and economic problems."[15]

The appearance of the propagandists in the villages naturally aroused the attention of the local authorities, and mass arrests of the propagandists followed. According to the official statistics of the Ministry of Justice, the propaganda effort spread to thirty-seven provinces of European Russia; altogether 770 persons were investi-

---

[15] B. Bazilevsky (V. Bogucharsky), ed., *Gosudarstvennyia prestuplenia v Rossii v XIX veke* [*Political Crimes in Russia in the Nineteenth Century*] (St. Petersburg, 1906), vol. I, pp. 319–334.

gated as suspects (612 men and 158 women), and 265 of them were taken into custody. Mass trials of those accused of revolutionary propaganda soon began, the most important of which was the "trial of the 193" in 1877. As a result of judicial investigation the majority of the accused (including the future assassins of the tsar, Andrei Zheliabov and Sophia Perovskaia) were acquitted for lack of formal evidence, but later many of them were sent by administrative order into the northern provinces and many spent two or three years in prison before the case was taken up in court. These actions of the authorities intensified the revolutionary mood of the youth and the dissatisfaction of the public, which sympathized with the victims of judicial procrastination and police arbitrariness.

The movement "to the people" soon ended as a result of this repression, and also because the people proved to be unreceptive to the socialist, communist, and anarchist propaganda of the populists. The peasantry, of course, did not object to the idea of redistribution of land, but they awaited the order for the redistribution to come from the tsar, and to the horror of their mentors, they showed an inclination toward private ownership of land.

Only in the Chigirinsky county in Kiev province did populists succeed in 1875 in drawing peasants into a radical organization. To achieve this, however, it was necessary to publish in the name of the tsar a "secret royal charter," which called upon the peasants to join a "secret brigade." This body was allegedly under the patronage of the tsar, led by his "secret commissars," and was organized for the sake of fighting the "traitors" to the tsar, the landlords and the officials.

But the revolutionaries who met in Petersburg in 1876 blamed their failures not on the indifference of the peasants but on government repressions and the lack of a party that could undertake the struggle against the regime. Thus in 1878 was born the organization called "Land and Liberty," which published an organ of that name in which the following goals were set forth: the confiscation of the landlords' land: the expulsion and often the complete annihilation of government officials; and the establishment of "cossack circles"—autonomous communes with elected, rotating executives of the people's will. "Such was the invariable program of the popular socialist-revolutionaries Pugachev, Razin, and their followers," said *Land and Liberty*. "No doubt the program remains the same now for the great majority of the Russian people. Therefore we populist-revolutionaries also accept it." The party program also provided for the establishment of a "disorganizing group" to undermine the regime.[16] The new party appeared in the streets of Petersburg December 6, 1876, under its own flag, holding a demonstration near the Kazan Cathedral in which 200 to 300 people took part. G. V. Plekhanov, the future leader of the Russian Social Democratic party, appeared here as the speaker in the name of "Land and Liberty."

The war between Russia and Turkey was still going on in 1877 and 1878 when a strange internal struggle erupted: on one side was the tsar and the government, who had at their disposal a million soldiers and an enormous police force; and on the other side was a small group of revolutionary fanatics who saw Razin and Pugachev as the real national heroes. But the tsar was tired and disillusioned; he had lost faith in people and interest in the affairs of state. Furthermore, the government lacked determination and a clear program. A substantial portion of the public stood aloof in this struggle, assuming the role of observers and very likely sympathizing more with the daring revolutionaries than with the incapable, dull, and frustrated defenders of the existing order.

A girl, Vera Zasulich, opened the combat in January 1878 by shooting and wounding Adjutant General Trepov, the chief of the Petersburg police, whom she selected for assassination because he had ordered the corporal punishment of a political prisoner. To the delight of the Petersburg public and the great indignation of the government, she was acquitted by a jury. The government replied by removing political crimes of the jurisdiction of the regular courts and intensifying security measures. In the summer of the same year, terrorists struck again, killing the head of the gendarmes, Adjutant General Mezentsev, on the streets of the capital in broad daylight, and then safely disappearing. While most of the populace remained passive before this spectacle, the police arrested numerous suspects and the military courts sentenced several terrorists to death. Meanwhile, the revolutionaries established secret printing presses and in several cases put up armed resistance when arrested. They assassinated or attempted the assassination of a number of officials of greater or lesser importance, including Prince Kropotkin, the governor of Kharkov, and General Drenteln, the new chief of the gendarmes. On April 2, 1879, a terrorist named Soloviev attempted to assassinate Alexander II, and the alarmed government undertook desperate efforts to destroy the elusive enemy. In the most important cities temporary governor generals were appointed and granted extraordinary emergency powers.

---

[16] Burtsev, *op. cit.*, pp. 136-140.

In the summer of 1879, "Land and Liberty" held a congress—convening first in Lipetsk and then in Voronezh—during which there were heated discussions on the use of terror and especially the question of assassinating the tsar. The result of this debate was a split in the party and the formation of two new organizations. The smaller group, which opposed political terrorism and considered propaganda their main weapon, formed the "Black Partition" *(Chernyi Peredel,* a reference to peasant redistribution of all land), headed by Plekhanov. The majority formed the "People's Will" *(Narodnaia Volia),* a party that aimed at immediate political revolution and the establishment of democratically elected constituent assembly. The latter's program for the future included: (1) a permanent popular representative body; (2) regional self-government; (3) the autonomy of the mir as an economic body; (4) ownership of the land by the people; (5) the ownership of factories by the workers; (6) freedom of speech, the press, and assembly; (7) universal suffrage; and (8) the replacement of the army with a territorial militia.[17] This party gave up hope of a broad peasant uprising stimulated by propaganda and placed their faith in terrorism, and especially in the assassination of Alexander II.

The Assassination of Alexander II

On February 5, 1880, a bomb exploded in the Winter Palace, killing or wounding soldiers who were on guard. Although the royal family was not hurt, the penetration of the palace by revolutionary dynamiters made a tremendous impression on all concerned. The government again took extraordinary measures to suppress the revolutionary movement, and on February 12, a decree was issued establishing "a supreme administrative commission for the defence of the governmental order and for the preservation of public peace." Count Loris-Melikov was appointed head of the commission and was given extraordinary powers for the struggle against terrorism. The terrorists' answer to the appointment of Loris-Melikov was an immediate attempt on his life, which the government answered with the immediate execution of the would-be assassin.

As virtual dictator, Loris-Melikov brought a fresh approach to the problem of internal security. He envisaged the suppression of the revolutionary-terrorist movement on the one hand by taking strong repressive measures, and on the other by the reconciliation

---

[17] *Ibid.,* pp. 148–152.

of the government with the "well-meaning" elements of the public. In order to make peace between the government and public opinion, Loris-Melikov insisted upon the dismissal of Count Tolstoy, the hated minister of public education.

Repression by administrative fiat was curtailed, the press received greater freedom in discussion of social and political questions, and the government began to pay more attention to the petitions and declarations of the zemstvo meetings. The administration of Loris-Melikov received the quaint name of the "dictatorship of the heart." During the summer months of 1880 there were no major terrorist actions, and it appeared to the government that the country was pacified and that the time had come to return to normal security procedures. By the decree of August 6, 1880, the "supreme administrative commission" was abolished, and Loris-Melikov was appointed minister of internal affairs. The Third Section of the Personal Chancery of His Imperial Majesty, the notorious police organization established by Nicholas I, was abolished as an independent office; and in its place a Department of State Police was established within the Ministry of Internal Affairs. The administration of the corps of gendarmes was also entrusted to the minister of internal affairs, and the governor generals were subordinated to him. In this way all the administrative threads were concentrated in the hands of Loris-Melikov.

The "dictator" intended to reform local administration and institution of self-government, including the peasant village and township institutions, the zemstvos, and the municipal institutions, and wished to enlist representatives of the public, especially from the zemstvos, in the discussion of the proposed reforms. Nor did Loris-Melikov's aspirations fail to elicit a response. The zemstvo assembly of Tver province, which was noted for its liberal tendencies, addressed Loris-Melikov as follows in December 1880: "In a short time your Excellency has been able to justify the trust of the Tsar and many of the hopes of the public. You have introduced straightforwardness and goodwill into the relations between the government and the people, you have wisely acknowledged the lawful needs and desires of the public."[18] In May 1881, immediately after the dismissal of Loris-Melikov from his ministerial post by Alexander III, the Petersburg municipal duma, to demonstrate their appreciation of his efforts, decided to bestow the title of honorary citizen of the city of St. Petersburg on him.

---

[18] A. Kornilov, *Kurs istorii Rossii XIX veka* [*Russian History through the Nineteenth Century*] (Moscow, 1918), vol. 3, p. 233.

To carry on the discussion of proposed reform projects, Loris-Melikov submitted to the tsar a plan by which two preparatory commissions were to be established, one "administrative-economic" and one financial. All the draft laws drawn up by these commissions were to be discussed by a "general commission," consisting of the members of the preparatory commissions and specially elected members of the zemstvo assemblies and the municipal dumas. After having been examined by the general commission, the draft bills were to be considered by the Council of State, to which Loris-Melikov wished to add ten or fifteen representatives from public organizations. This plan, of course, did not constitute a "constitution" in the sense of European parliamentarianism. It envisaged consultation by the government with experienced and educated men from the members of the local governmental bodies. The plan was discussed and approved by a special conference of the Council of State, under the chairmanship of Count Valuev, and on February 17, 1881, it was approved by the tsar.

On Sunday, March 1, 1881, at noon, Alexander approved the announcement enacting Loris-Melikov's plan. Soon afterwards the tsar went to inspect the guards, and on the way back he was fatally wounded by a bomb thrown by one Grinevitsky, a member of the People's Will. The main organizer of the assassination, Zheliabov, had been accidentally arrested on February 27, but a young woman among the conspirators, Sophia Perovskaia, continued his task. On the day of the assassination she stationed four bomb-throwers on the route followed by the tsar, and when the royal carriage passed, she gave the signal to the bombers.

The feelings of Alexander III upon ascending the blood-covered throne of his father can be imagined. Before him was the image of the body of the tsar-liberator, mutilated by the terrorists' bomb. Behind him stood his former tutor, Constantine Pobedonostsev, the "black crow" of Russia reaction, who persistently croaked to the new tsar about impending disasters along the liberal path and the necessity of a "firm hand."

The first few days were spent in consultation to decide what to do and where to go: whether to continue the path of reforms started by Alexander II, or to turn to the right, back to the principles of Nicholas I. Pobedonostsev exerted his influence. On March 6, he wrote the new tsar a long letter about the necessity of "saving Russia" and about the allegedly disastrous path that had been followed by the government of the previous reign. On March 8, the tsar presided over a meeting of the higher government officials to discuss the policy of the government, particularly whether to implement the plan to call upon the members of the zemstvos to participate in the work of the legislature, as approved by Alexander II. The majority of the ministers favored Loris-Melikov's project, but Pobedonostsev delivered a memorable speech in which he not only condemned the various constitutional projects and foretold the ruin of Russia because of the attempt to realize these, but openly criticized and censured all the reforms of the former tsar. However, no decision was taken by Alexander III at this time. The tsar, after having listened to all opinions, decided to review the question once more.

Pobedonostsev eventually was able to persuade his pupil to issue a manifesto, composed by the tutor, announcing the basic principles of the new government. The manifesto was signed by the tsar, without consultation with the other ministers, and published April 29. In it Alexander III declared that the voice of God commanded him to "stand courageously by the task of government . . . with faith in the power and the truth of autocracy, which for the good of the people, we are called upon to reaffirm and to defend from various efforts to weaken it."

As a result of this definite turn in internal policy, all the liberal ministers either resigned voluntarily or were dismissed, including Loris-Melikov (minister of internal affairs), Abaza (finance minister), Miliutin (minister of war), and Saburov (minister of public education). Grand Duke Constantine Nicholaevich was dismissed from his government posts, the most important of which was the chairmanship of the Council of State. In their place came other officials more willing to follow the lead of Pobedonostsev and Katkov, a former liberal journalist, turned conservative.

Nevertheless, the reactionary trend did not prevail exclusively. The new minister of internal affairs, Count N. P. Ignatiev, although appointed upon Pobedonostsev's recommendation, called meetings of "experienced men" from among the zemstvos to discuss some of the current affairs; and he soon submitted a plan to call a *zemskii sobor* (the name of the gathering of persons from various classes in the sixteenth and seventeenth centuries), a plan favored by the Slavophiles. When Pobedonostsev learned of this project, he was panic-stricken and declaimed that this "monstrous" proposal was the "height of absurdity in government," and that its realization would mean "the ruin of the government and the ruin of Russia." The admirer of Slavophile theories immediately lost his ministerial chair, and his place was taken by Count D. A. Tolstoy. The period of reaction was now at hand.

Alexander III and the Period of Reaction

Alexander III became heir to the throne as a result of the death of his elder brother, Crown Prince Nicholas Alexandrovich, who died as a young man in 1865 of tuberculosis. In 1866 Pobedonostsev became the teacher of the new heir-apparent, and after 1881 he was the chief adviser to the tsar. In the summation of his political thought, *A Moscow Symposium (Moskovskii Sbornik)*, published in 1896, Pobedonostsev severely criticized the leading political ideas and institutions prevailing in the West. To him, parliamentary government was "the great lie of our times," because parliaments served not the needs of the people but only interest groups and political manipulators, "who artfully work the strings behind the scenes, moving the marionettes on the stage of democratic elections." He emphasized the need for the close union of church and state, maintaining that separation of the two made the state a representative only of the material interest of society.

Other conservative publicists were Katkov, editor of *The Moscow Gazette (Moskovskie Vedomosti)*, who was succeeded in that post in the 1890s by V. A. Gringmut, and Prince V. P. Meshchersky, publisher of *The Citizen (Grazhdanin)*. N. Ia. Danilevsky and K. N. Leontiev should also be counted among the minority of the intelligentsia that opposed liberal or radical trends. In his book *Russia and Europe (Rossiia i Evropa)*, published in 1869, the biologist Danilevsky advanced the theory that the Russo-Slav and Romano-Germanic cultures could not and should not be merged, a view contrary to that of the liberals and radicals. Leontiev in his two-volume anthology entitled *The East, Russia and the Slavs (Vostok, Rossiia i Slavianstvo)*, published in 1885–1886, attacked the egalitarian, progressive and alleged positivistic-atheistic spirit of the West, and defended the fundamental bases of Russian culture, which he took to be autocracy, Orthodxy, and the peasant mir.

The first problem facing Alexander III was the struggle against the revolutionary movement, and on August 14, 1881, his government published the renowned "Regulation on Measures for the Defense of the Governmental Order and of Public Safety." This "temporary" regulation proved to be quite long-lived, surviving until the end of the tsarist regime. According to this regulation, in places regarded as unsafe because of the activities of the underground, "a state of re-enforced security" (or the higher degree of "a state of extraordinary security") was introduced. In these places the governor

generals or governors could issue "compulsory regulations," violation of which could be punished by arrest for up to three months
or by a fine of up to 500 rubles. They could forbid "various popular,
social, and even private gatherings": they could deport from the region
"unreliable" elements; they could refer cases of attacks on officials and
other criminal activities to the military courts; and they could give
orders to carry out searches and arrests. The "Special Committee of
the Ministry of Internal Affairs," with the participation of members
from the Ministry of Justice, could sentence persons regarded as dangerous to the state and public security to a maximum of five years of
"administrative deportation" to remote areas. Moscow, Petersburg,
and a whole series of other provinces and cities were immediately
declared to be "in a state of re-enforced security," and this irksome
state became permanent.

The next task of the government was to curb the press.
On August 27, 1882, "Temporary Measures concerning the Periodical
Press" were published, containing a whole series of restrictions on the
freedom of the press. "Warnings," bans on retail sale or on placement
of private advertisements, temporary suspension, and, finally, complete
suspension rained on the press, and in January 1884 the *Notes from
the Fatherland,* the most influential radical journal of the 1870s and
early 1880s, was banned.

The next step, as Saltykov-Shchedrin put it, was "bringing
order to the minds." A university reform for this purpose was carried
out in 1884 by Minister of Public Education Delianov, who obediently
fulfilled the wishes of Pobedonostsev, Tolstoy, and Katkov. Published
August 23, 1884, "the General Statute of the Russian Imperial Universities" entirely abolished the autonomy of the university. According
to the text of the statute, the university was "entrusted to the authority
of the trustee of the local educational district." Henceforth, the rector
was to be "elected" by the minister of public education from among
the full professors of the university, and was appointed by imperial
order for four years. The deans were chosen by the trustee of the
educational district from among the professors of the corresponding
faculty, and their appointment to the position was confirmed for
a period of four years by the minister of public education. When a
vacancy for the position of professor occurred, the minister of public
education either filled the vacancy with someone who had the necessary qualifications, according to his own discretion, or allowed the
university to choose the candidate to fill the vacant position, submitting their nominee for the approval of the minister. The minister,
however, could refuse to approve the chosen candidate and appoint

his own. The university curriculum had to be approved by the Ministry of Public Education, while supervision of students' behavior and activities was entrusted to an "inspector of students" and his assistants. The students themselves were again required to wear uniforms, a practice that had been abolished under Alexander II.

In the field of primary education it was considered desirable, in accord with Pobedonostsev's advice, to increase the number of parish-church schools and to strengthen the government control over the schools operated by the zemstvos. As before, Tolstoy's "classicism" flourished in the secondary schools. In 1887 the minister of public education issued a notorious circular that advised limiting the entry of the lower classes to the gymnasiums (contemporaries called it "the circular on cooks' children") and raised tuition fees to forty rubles per year, which was more cash than many peasants saw in a year.

One of the worries of the government of Alexander III was to support the Russian nobility, which, according to the right-wing publicists, was offended by the reforms of the previous reign. In 1885, on the occasion of the centennial of Catherine's Charter of the Nobility, a landmark in the establishment of noble privilege, the tsar issued a rescript stating:

> In the interests of the state we acknowledge that it is good that the Russian nobility, now as in the past, should retain the leading position in the military, in local administration and courts, in the unselfish care for the needs of the populace and in the dissemination, by its example, of the rules for faith and loyalty and a sound basis for public education.

At the same time the state opened a Nobles' Land Bank to support the ownership of land by this class.

A variety of measures sought to increase government control over the local institutions that had been granted considerable authority in the 1860s. The establishment of the office of "superintendent of the peasantry" *(zemskii nachal'nik)* in 1889 placed the peasant commune under the direct surveillance of an agent of the Ministry of Internal Affairs, while the elective office of "justice of the peace," a symbol of local autonomy in justice, was abolished. New regulations on the zemstvos and municipal organs of self-government, in 1890 and 1892, respectively, enlarged the authority of the provincial governors to suspend the decisions of these bodies. The competence and independence of the courts were subjected to various types of curtailment under Alexander III, but the jury remained, despite violent attacks by reactionary journalists on this institution.

In addition to the strengthening of authority of the state, the government of Alexander III undertook a series of measures for the Russification of the borderlands. In the Baltic provinces, the government began a vigorous struggle against Germanization and the social and cultural predominance of the nobility of German origin. In the administration of the Caucasus area, the government strove to "unite it with the other parts of the Empire." In Poland the regime continued the policy of Russification that had been started after the suppression of the uprising of 1863–1864.

A series of restrictive measures was taken against the Jews, who were largely limited to residence in the "pale," that is, the western provinces of the empire. Under Alexander III this zone of Jewish settlement was reduced in size, and even within the limits of the pale, the Jews were forbidden to buy or rent landed property in rural areas. In 1887 a quota for Jewish children in government secondary schools was introduced (in the pale, 10 percent; in the capital cities, 3 percent; and in other places, 5 percent). In 1891 a new decree expelled thousands of Jewish mechanics, masters, and artisans from Moscow, where they had been permitted to settle in 1865, and the municipal regulation of 1892 deprived the Jews of the right to participate in municipal self-government.

The Later Evolution of Political Movements

N. K. Mikhailovsky, critic, publicist, and sociologist, was the most popular and influential spokesman of the radical-populist Russian intelligentsia for almost forty years. Closely affiliated with Lavrov, whose "Historical Letters" formed the background for much of his own thought, Mikhailovsky first of all defended the "subjective" method in sociology. In the social sciences, he said, our aim is not only to know that which exists—as in the study of nature—but also to bring about the realization of certain ideals; we make an appraisal of the knowable phenomena from the point of view of our ideals, the category of value being an inseparable element of the social sciences. This conception was closely related to Mikhailovsky's idea of "twofold truth": our aim should be the combination of "the truth as truth"—objective truth—and the "truth as justice"—subjective truth.

According to Mikhailovsky, the aim of society should be "the struggle for individuality," for the free development of personality. For him the individual human personality is in itself the supreme value in life and therefore should not be subordinated to any social goals. "All social unions," wrote Mikhailovsky, "have only a relative value. They are valuable only to the extent that they help the development of personality. . . . The individual is never to be sacrificed; he is sacred and inviolable. . . ."[19]

He regarded the comprehensive development of personality as incompatible with the division of labor, which allows the worker to become only a cog in the machine. "Only that which diminishes the heterogeneity of the society, while strengthening at the same time the heterogeneity of its individual members, is moral, just, wise, and useful." To realize the possibility of the comprehensive development of personality, constrained and oppressed by the contemporary social order, it was necessary to serve the people, "not in a sense of a nation, but in the totality of the working masses. Labor is the only unifying characteristic of this group . . . ; in labor the individual is expressed most vividly and fully."[20]

One of the essential features of Mikhailovsky's sociological theory was his teaching concerning the forms and degrees of development. He posited the possibility of a "high degree of development of a low form" and also a low degree of development of a higher form.[21] When he applied this conception to the Russian peasant commune he found that degree of development was low, for the agricultural technology of the West was well ahead of Russia. But he maintained that the form of the peasant commune was higher than the agricultural organization of the West, with its landless or proletarianized peasants. In other words, Mikhailovsky joined such Russian writers as Herzen and Chernyshevsky in praising the humane values of communal agriculture, while acknowledging technological superiority of the West. No Slavophile, Mikhailovsky said that "sensible advocates of the commune . . . did not make a fetish of it," but "saw in the commune a secure refuge for the peasant from the approaching miseries of capitalism."[22]

The radical populists of the 1880s and 1890s, while keeping the old banner of "Land and Liberty," had to make considerable changes in their interpretation of history and in their practical program. This re-evaluation became necessary because of the spread of

---

[19] N. K. Mikhailovsky, *Sochineniia* [*Works*] (4th ed.; St. Petersburg, 1906–1907), vol. 4, pp. 451–452.

[20] *Ibid.*, vol. I, p. 166, and vol. V, p. 537.

[21] *Ibid.*, vol. I, p. 494.

[22] *Ibid.*, vol. IV, p. 452.

Marxist ideas among the Russian intelligentsia, the development of capitalism, and the growth of heavy industry in Russia. The populist revolutionaries accepted the main lines of Marx's economic theory. They recognized the necessity of a political struggle for the conquest of power and the important role of the industrial proletariat in this struggle, but they also pointed out some important peculiarities in the social and economic development of Russia. In particular, they maintained that the tradition of communal labor among Russian peasantry and the custom of the communal management of the land of the mir made the peasantry much more receptive to the idea of socialism than the system of private land ownership that existed in Western and Central Europe, transforming the European peasantry into a petty bourgeoisie inaccessible to socialist propaganda.

While accepting the theory of class struggle, the populists modified its content. For them the division did not occur on the lines of the proletariat and the bourgeoisie, but on the lines of "toilers" and people who lived by the labor of others, the "classes of exploiters." The future leader of the Socialist Revolutionary party, V. Chernov, an adherent of Mikhailovsky's "proven formula," wrote in 1900 that the new populists understand "the interests of the *people* as the sum total of the classes of the workers. . . . They are the people as far as they embody and represent the *principle of labor*. We adhere to this formula because it contains more theoretical truth and more living justice—and humanity."[23] "We preached," writes Chernov in his memoirs, "the slogan of the natural solidarity of the city proletariat with the independent, toiling farmer," and we aimed at the creation of "an inseparable union, with the help of the revolutionary-socialist intelligentsia, between the proletariat and the toiling peasantry."[24] The populists rejected the idea that Russia could achieve socialism only by passing through the stage of capitalist development; the peasant did not need "to be boiled in the industrial cauldron" to be able to enter the bright kingdom of socialism.

Beginning in the mid-1880s, the economic, historical, and philosophical ideas of Marxism increasingly attracted the Russian intelligentsia. In 1872 the first volume of Marx's *Das Kapital* was translated into Russian, and the 1890s became, as Chernov put it, the period of a "Marxist craze" among the young generation. During that

---

[23] *Na slavnom postu (1860-1900)* [*On the Glorious Post*] (2d ed.; St. Petersburg, 1906), part 2, p. 197. A symposium dedicated to N. K. Mikailovsky.

[24] V. Chernov, *Zapiski sotsialista-revolutsionera* [*Notes of a Socialist-Revolutionary*] (Berlin, 1922), pp. 164, 277.

period a considerable group of educated economists and talented publicists propagated the ideas of Marxism in legally published books and periodicals. The more outstanding representatives of this activity were: P. B. Struve *(Critical Notes on The Economic Development of Russia,* 1894); M. I. Tugan-Baranovsky *(The Russian Factory, Past and Present,* 1898); "Beltov"—G. V. Plekhanov *(The Monist View of History,* 1895); "Ilin"—V. I. Ulianov, later, Lenin *(The Development of Capitalism in Russia,* 1899); N. A. Berdiaev—who later became a world-famous, non-Marxist philosopher—and S. N. Bulgakov—who later became an outstanding Orthodox theologian. These authors all rejected "the peculiarity" of Russian historical development. They argued that Russia had entered the path of capitalist development to the full extent, and that it consequently must fulfill all the stages of development that constitute the Marxian scheme. Struve, Tugan-Baranovsky, Berdiaev, and others who worked mainly through openly published literature, rather than by clandestine methods—"Legal Marxists"—did not remain orthodox Marxists for long. In the last years of the nineteenth century and at the beginning of the twentieth century almost all of them turned to philosophical idealism and criticized the economic, sociological, or philosophical theories of orthodox Marxism.

The founder of the movement of revolutionary or orthodox Marxism in Russia was Plekhanov. After emigrating in 1880, he—together with a few like-minded persons—founded the first Russian Marxist group, the "Emancipation of Labor," in 1883 and undertook energetic propaganda on behalf of Marxism. That same year he published a booklet on "Socialism and Political Struggle," and in 1884 on "Our Differences," that is, the differences between the Marxists and the populists of the People's Will. In the latter book, Plekhanov severely criticized all the traditional beliefs and ideas of Russian populists, whom he called "Slavophile revolutionaries." He denied the existence of any special path of development for Russia and did not see any reason to think that "our fatherland possesses some kind of a charter of peculiarity, issued to it by history for merits which, however, are unknown to anybody." To the question, "Will Russia pass through the school [epoch] of capitalism?" he replied: "Why should she [Russia] not finish this school which she *has already entered?*"[25]

Concerning the Russian village and the peasantry, Plekhanov remarked that "the sentimental fog of false and affected idealization of the masses of people disappears," that the Russian

---

[25] G. V. Plekhanov, *Nashi raznoglasiia* [*Our Differences*] (St. Petersburg, 1906 ed.; first published in 1884), pp. 204 and 203.

peasants, like their European brothers, were by no means socialists by nature, and they did not in the least aspire to socialism, and that already "the disintegration of our commune is an indisputable and an indubitable fact."[26] If the revolutionaries succeeded in capturing the power and expropriating the big landowners, the peasants would be happy to divide the land among themselves, but no socialism would result.

With regard to the tasks of the revolutionary intelligentsia, Plekhanov demanded the renunciation of the rebellious tendencies of Bakunin and Tkachev. It was necessary that the intelligentsia renounce the idea that they could turn the wheel of history single-handedly, through the use of terror and other activities of "small partisan groups." Instead the vital task of the revolutionary intelligentsia was the creation of a mass socialist workers' party, because "the emancipation of the working class can only be achieved through its own conscious efforts."[27] Plekhanov became one of the most prominent propagandists and theoreticians of Marxism, defending it from the critical attacks of bourgeois scholars and publicists as well as from the "revisionism" of Bernstein and other socialists.

At the beginning of the 1890, Plekhanov was joined by an ally who afterwards caused him much grief. This was a young man with a law degree from St. Petersburg University, V. I. Ulianov, later known by the pseudonym of Lenin. In 1894 he published a booklet entitled *Who Are the "Friends of the People" and How Do They Fight the Social Democrats?*, attacking the populists, notably Mikhailovsky. His important book on the development of capitalism in Russia was published in 1899, and he later wrote a huge number of pamphlets, books, articles, notes, declarations, and letters, which now fill over forty volumes.

The formation of an organized Russian Marxist movement occurred on the threshold of the twentieth century. In 1895, a Marxist "Union for the Struggle for the Emancipation of the Working Class" was formed in Petersburg, and in various other cities with a sizable working population, by groups of intelligentsia and workers who accepted the Marxist program. In 1898, during a clandestine congress in Minsk, the basis was laid for the Russian Social Democratic Workers party (RSDWP or SD). The organ of the new party was *The Spark (Iskra)*, which was published abroad and secretly distributed in Russia. At the opening of the twentieth century the orthodox Marxists of

---

[26] *Ibid.*, p. 299.
[27] *Ibid.*, p. 279.

the SD had to fight against the heresy of "economism" in their ranks. This movement emphasized the necessity of struggle to improve the economic conditions of the working class and was quite indifferent to the political struggle.

The second congress of the representatives of the Social Democratic organizations took place in the summer of 1903—starting in Brussels and finishing in London—adopting a program and statutes for the party. In its program, the new party declared that it considered itself "as one of the detachments of the world army of the proletariat" and set itself the goal of social revolution, which was to realize "the substitution of socialist relations of production for capitalistic." "The necessary condition of this social revolution is the dictatorship of the proletariat, that is, the acquisition of such political power that will enable the proletariat to suppress all sorts of resistance by the exploiters." In Russia, where "capitalism has already become the dominant mode of production . . . , there are still vestiges of the old precapitalist order," of which "the most significant is the tsarist autocracy. Therefore the party "considers the overthrow of the tsarist autocracy and its replacement by a democratic republic," the immediate political task. This "democratic republic" would be established by the Constituent Assembly and would secure "the autocracy of the people," that is, the concentration of authority in the hands of a democratically elected legislative assembly. It would also secure "unlimited freedom of conscience, speech, press, assembly, strikes, and unions," "the right of self-determination for all nations that are members of the state," "the replacement of the standing army by a national militia," "the separation of church and state and of school and church," and the establishment of an eight-hour working day.[28]

During the congress the question of party organization gave rise to serious disagreements and the subsequent division in the party. A slender, rather artificial majority headed by Lenin wanted to establish the party as a small but strong clandestine organization of professional revolutionaries, unquestioningly fulfilling "the instructions of the Central Committee of the party." The minority, headed by Martov, advocated a broad, much freer organization of workers on the pattern of the German Social Democratic party. The names "Bolsheviks" (majority-ites) and "Mensheviks" (minority-ites) originated

---

[28] *Izveshchenie o vtorom s'ezde Rossiiskoi Sotsial-Demokraticheskoi Rabochei Partii* [*Report of the Second Congress of the Russian Social-Democratic Workers Party*] (Geneva, 1903), pp. 7–15.

in this split during the second congress. Soon disagreements on a series of tactical questions were added to the division of the SD on the question of organization. In the subsequent quarrels the Leninists accused the Mensheviks of opportunism and "tailism" *(khvostizm*—the inclination of the Mensheviks to "be at the tail end" of the working masses instead of leading them). The Mensheviks, through P. B. Axelrod, characterized the tactic of the Bolsheviks as "a rebellious, conspiratory, mixture of anarchist and Blanquist* tendencies, cloaked in Marxist or social democratic phraseology."[29]

Simultaneously with the emergence of an organized Marxist movement, the populist movement was also taking form. The Agrarian Socialists League, founded abroad at the end of the nineteenth century, aimed at broadening "the stream of the common revolutionary movement by attracting the toiling masses of the countryside to it." In a pamphlet, *The Immediate Question of the Revolutionary Cause,* published by the League in 1900, Chernov argued for the urgent necessity of revolutionary work in the countryside. "We must revolutionize the village," said Chernov, because the success of revolution in Russia is impossible without support of the "toiling peasantry." "The idea of the nationalization of land and communal, planned socialist organization of production must be presented to the peasantry; the solidarity of interests of the toiling peasantry and of the city proletariat must be explained to the peasantry. . . ."

At the end of the nineteenth century a number of revolutionary-populist groups emerged in various regions of Russia, and in the villages of some provinces "peasant brotherhoods" for revolutionary work in the countryside were established. At the end of 1901, a congress of the representatives of the populist-revolutionary groups established the Party of Socialist Revolutionaries (SR), led by Chernov. The program of the party, which was approved by a party congress in 1905, established as its general goal:

> a planned organization of all labor for the common good. . . . Only by the realization of a free and socialist society will humanity develop unhindered in the physical, spiritual, and moral senses, more and more attaining truth, justice, and solidarity in the forms of life of the people. In this sense the task of revolutionary socialism is the task of all humanity.

The tsarist autocracy in Russia was to be overthrown and replaced

---

* Those following Louis Auguste Blanqui (1805–1881), French revolutionary and advocate of revolutionary conspiracy.—R.H.M.

[29] P. B. Axelrod, *Dve taktiki* [Two Tactics] (St. Petersburg, 1907), p. 4.

by a democratic republic—"in case of need," a temporary revolutionary dictatorship might be established. This state would be based on wide regional and communal autonomy, possibly on "a federative basis for relations between the separate nationalities," which have "the indisputable right to self-determination." The program envisaged a legislative assembly, elected on the basis of universal franchise and proportional representation, with the electorate retaining the referendum and initiative. Concerning civil rights and the rights of labor, the SR program was similar to that of the SD's, but it greatly differed from the latter on the agrarian question, for the SR's planned for the so-called "socialization of land"[30] (see chapter 8). In 1902 the Peasant Union of the SR party was organized especially to conduct propaganda in the countryside. The party organ was the newspaper *Revolutionary Russia (Revolutsionnaia Rossiia)*.

In the field of revolutionary tactics there were important differences between the SD's and SR's. While the SD's advocated only a mass political struggle of the working class and rejected individual terror, the SR's widely practiced terror against all the defenders of "the old order," from highly placed ministers down to the least important police official. Special "combat organizations" were created within the SR party to conduct terrorism, and in 1902–1905 they managed to assassinate two ministers of internal affairs and one grand duke. The central combat organization was headed by Gershuni, and after his arrest in 1903, Azef, who simultaneously directed the revolutionary terrorism and served as a paid informer of the tsarist political police. At the beginning of 1909, Azef was unmasked by the SR expert on police spies, Burtsev, assisted by the former director of the police department, Lopukhin.

The liberal movement in Russia did not establish any active political organization until the beginning of the twentieth century. Previously, the advocates of liberalism consisted mainly of nobles who were active in the zemstvos, and their political activity was expressed either in casual "secret meetings" among themselves or, at the most, in the submission of official petitions for reform.

In the period immediately following the emancipation of the peasants, the nobility of some of the provinces raised the question of a basic reform of the state. In 1862 a sensational petition of the

---

[30] *Programma i organizatzzionnyi ustav Partii Sotsialistov-Revolutsionerov [Program and Organizational Statutes of the Party of the Socialist-Revolutionaries]*, edited by the Central Committee of the Party of the Socialist-Revolutionaries (St. Petersburg, 1906), pp. 18–28.

Tver province nobility not only asked that the tsar abolish all class privileges but also requested "the calling of elected representatives from all the Russian land," which "constitutes the only means for the satisfactory solution of problems that the regulation of February 19 [1861] aroused but did not settle."[31] At the beginning of 1865 the Moscow nobility requested the tsar "to complete" the new state edifice "by the calling of a general assembly of elected persons of the Russian land to discuss the needs common to the whole state." In the years of the Turkish war of 1877–1878 and in the years immediately following the war, there was a revival of the zemstvo liberal movement. In 1877 the liberal organ *The Common Task (Obshchee Delo)* was founded abroad, and then the newspaper *The Free Word (Vol'noe Slovo)*, which advanced and defended a constitutional program.

In 1878–1881 there was a series of secret congresses and meetings of the leaders of the zemstvos, and secret liberal organizations, such as the Liberal League and the Union of the Zemstvos, were established and maintained contact with the press organs abroad. Some provincial assemblies of the zemstvos again turned to the government with constitutional demands. In 1879 a petition of the provincial zemstvo of Tver declared:

> The Sovereign Emperor, in his concern for the good of the Bulgarian people, who had been freed from the Turkish yoke, acknowledged the necessity of granting it [Bulgaria] true self-government, the inviolability of the individual, the independence of the courts, [and] freedom of the press. The zemstvo of the Tver province dares to hope that the Russian people, who carried all the burdens of war with such complete readiness, with such selfless love toward its tsar-liberator, will enjoy the same blessings, which alone may give the people the opportunity to enter, in the words of the Sovereign, the path of gradual, peaceful and legal development.[32]

After the assassination of Alexander II some of the zemstvos (Novgorod, Samara, Taurida, and others) again submitted petitions requesting the completion of the great reforms of the previous reign by the creation of a popular representative body for the discussion of all the needs of the state; but after the policy of Pobedonostsev and Katkov triumphed, all the plans and suggestions of that kind

---

[31] Kornilov, *op. cit.*, vol. 2, pp. 220–221.

[32] *Ibid.*, vol. 3, p. 215.

became "senseless dreams," as Nicholas II characterized them in a famous speech of January 1895.

As a result of the assassination of Alexander II and the reaction that followed, the 1880s became a period of dull stagnation, of public despondency and political indifference. But following an acute famine in the Volga region in 1891–1892, social and political interests revived all over Russia. The declared intention of Nicholas II, who ascended the throne in October 1894, to guard the sanctity of autocracy aroused widespread discontent. In the 1890s there was a considerable increase in zemstvo activities, which was associated with the growth of a so-called "third element," that is, zemstvo employees, teachers, medical doctors and their assistants, statisticians, agronomists, technicians, and clerks. To the extent that they were politically conscious this "third element" tended to stand considerably more to the left than their masters, the elected members of the zemstvo institutions. The politically active element among the employees of the zemstvos adhered mostly to the leftist parties, the SR or the SD, while the most moderate section of the "third element" established the left wing of zemstvo liberalism.

In the cities at the end of the nineteenth century the number of professional people and students grew considerably. The students, long called "the barometer of the public," were the first to start an open struggle against the old regime. Although the first steps of the student movement had an academic character, starting with slogans of protests against the university statute of 1884 and with demands for "academic freedom," the movement soon assumed a more political character under the influence of leftist groups. The occasion for starting a broad student movement was provided in Petersburg February 8, 1899, when the police used their whips to disperse a crowd of students following the annual university celebrations. Immediately "strikes of protest" and "strikes of sympathy" occurred in all the Russian universities. Students excluded from universities for participation in these demonstrations were ordered into military service, a retaliation that aroused public indignation, even though conscription for students now lasted not twenty-five years, as under Nicholas I, but only one or two years.

In 1899 a special commission under the chairmanship of General P. S. Vannovsky was established for the "thorough investigation of the causes and circumstances" of student riots. The commission called for "immediate revision of the statutes of higher and secondary educational institutions and a reform of the students' living conditions." But the commission did not satisfy the student body, and student riots continued. In February 1901, one of the expelled students assassinated the minister of public education, Professor Bogolepov. General Vannovsky, the former minister of war, was appointed in his place and tried to carry out a more liberal policy toward the universities. But he satisfied neither the students nor the higher authorities, and he was soon dismissed. Agitation and disorder in the universities continued until 1905, when the student movement joined the ranks of the general revolutionary agitation.

While the students were engaging in these intermittent protests, various other groups, especially the professions, were organizing all-Russian and regional congresses. The first meeting of the leaders of the zemstvos convened in Moscow in 1902, and such professional groups as doctors, educators, and agronomists met and expressed various demands for the reform, especially for guarantees of individual rights and the extension of self-government.

At the turn of the century the literary organs of Russian liberalism were such monthlies as *Russian Thought (Russkaia Mysl')* and *The Herald of Europe (Vestnik Evropy),* and among newspapers the most solid and influential liberal organ was the Moscow professors' newspaper *The Russian Gazette (Russkie Vedomosti).* In Stuttgart in 1902, P. B. Struve founded a biweekly, *Liberation (Osvobozhdenie),* which was sharply critical of the government. It carried the views of two organizations, a relatively moderate group—the union of the Zemstvo-Constitutionalists—and the more radical Union of Liberation, which was largely composed of members of the intelligentsia. In 1905 the members of these organizations served as the main contingent for the creation of the Constitutional Democratic party (KD or Kadet), which played an important role in the last years of the empire.

In the zemstvos, liberalism was manifest at a congress of zemstvo deputies in Moscow in November 1904. Almost a hundred leaders of the zemstvos, from the thirty-three provinces in which zemstvos were established, participated. The resolution adopted by the congress contained the usual criticism of the bureaucratic system and demanded full civil rights for all citizens, including all nationalities and social classes, and the establishment of a popular representative body to participate in legislation and to control the administration's activities.[33]

---

[33] *Zemskii S'ezd 6-go i sl. noiabria 1904 g.* [*The Zemstvo Congress of November 1904*] (Paris, 1905).

Generally speaking, the Russian bourgeoisie played quite an insignificant role in the political life of the country before the revolution of 1905. Least of all did this class strive to seize power, although according to Marx, it was supposed to be the most intent on this goal. It is true that individual wealthy bourgeois often donated considerable sums of money "to the revolution," but they did it for personal satisfaction and not as an organized and planned political activity of any kind. The majority of the wealthy merchants and industrialists who felt any inclination toward social reform invested their capital in less potentially dangerous undertakings than revolutionary organizations, namely in philanthropic and cultural institutions.

Especially generous in this field were the wealthy merchants of Moscow, who founded or supported museums and galleries (including the famous Tretiakov Gallery), theaters (including the Moscow Art Theater), schools, libraries, hospitals, and asylums. The commercial and industrial class did not create a political party, nor did it strive to seize political power in view of the obvious hopelessness of such an undertaking. But it did create a whole series of large-scale and powerful industrial associations—in mining, oil, metallurgy, and the like—which did "bombard" the government, not with demands for a transfer of power to them, but with petitions on various concrete problems of economic policy. In this way they attained quite considerable and advantageous results—protective tariffs, preferential tariffs on railway transportation, profitable government orders, and also direct subsidies.

Thus did political life on the threshold of the twentieth century show signs of a renewed vigor, following the repressions of the reign of Alexander III. But it is noteworthy that the left was organized earlier and more firmly than the liberal center, while the right—or supporters of the existing order other than civil servants—had practically no political organization.

7

Social
and Economic Affairs on the Threshold
of the Twentieth Century

The Administration of the
Peasantry

The statute of February 19, 1861, promised to give the peasants who were emancipated from the landlord's authority "the personal and property rights of free rural citizens," but this promise was only partly fulfilled. Emancipated from the authority of the landlord, the peasant was now subjected to the authority of the village mir and its administrative organs. He was attached to his rural community by "registration," the land allotment system, and the collective responsibility of the mir. He could obtain release from the commune only with great difficulty. When leaving the commune he had to renounce his land allotment, and if he received either secondary or higher education, entered the civil service, or became a merchant, he ceased to be a member of the peasant class altogether. In this way the most educated and well-to-do elements left the peasant estate as soon as they rose above the gray mass of the rural population.

The guardians of the rural communes were at first the arbitrators, but after the abolition of this office in 1874 there were no organs of state authority left in the village except for the police. After Alexander III ascended the throne, Pobedonostsev and Tolstoy were quick to recognize what they thought was a deplorable absence of authority in the village and saw to it that new organs of authority were created, organs that were to be personal, "firm," and "close to the people."

On July 12, 1889, the statute on "superintendents of the peasantry" *(zemskie nachal'niki)* was issued, establishing new judicial and administrative offices with such extensive authority over peasant affairs that the rural mir and the elective bodies of peasant self-government were essentially deprived of their recently won independence. The superintendents were appointed from among the local hereditary nobility who met fairly modest qualifications in education, property, or service. Very often, they were retired military officers. They were appointed by the provincial governors after consultation with the marshals of the nobility, and the minister of internal affairs confirmed their appointment. In 1898 peasant superintendents *(krestianskie nachal'niki)* with comparable powers were established in Siberia, which had not been subject to the law of 1889.

The duties of the superintendent of the peasantry were to watch over and review all the decisions of the township and village assemblies. If he found that a decision had been passed illegally or that, in his opinion, it was to the disadvantage of the peasants, he did not confirm the decision and made representation to the county assembly of superintendents to have the decision canceled. Moreover, the superintendent took over the judicial authority formerly vested in the justices of the peace, an office that was now abolished.

The statute of 1889 specified that the superintendent was "responsible for the economic well-being and moral standard of the peasants in the area entrusted to him." He exercised disciplinary authority over the elected officials in the village and township administration, whom he could subject, without formal procedure, to reprimand, fines of up to five rubles, or arrest for up to seven days. In case of noncompliance with his "lawful orders or demands," he could also sentence any peasant to arrest for up to three days or a fine of up to six rubles. The township assembly was now allowed merely to nominate two candidates for elder, one of whom the superintendent would select for confirmation in office.

Superior to the superintendent of the peasantry was the county assembly *(uezdnyi s'ezd)*, a new body composed of all (usually five or six) superintendents in a given county and a few other officials of the judicial and administrative departments, under the chairmanship of the marshal of the nobility of the county. Above the county assembly was the "provincial office" *(gubernskoe prisutstvie)*, composed of the vice-governor, the provincial marshal of the nobility, the procurator, and two "permanent members" under the chairmanship of the governor.

The township courts also underwent a thorough transformation. The rural assemblies were now merely to nominate a slate of candidates for the judgeships; from these candidates the superintendent confirmed four as township judges. The county assembly of superintendents appointed one of them chairman of the township court, a position that could also be entrusted to the township elder. On the one hand, the competence of the township court was broadened; it could handle suits between peasants involving up to 300 rubles or cases involving sentences for up to thirty days. Yet, at the same time, its independence was restricted, for the superintendent of the peasantry had the right, if appealed to by the parties involved, to suspend the execution of the verdict of a township court and to report this to the county assembly of superintendents. And, like other township officials, the township judges were subject to the disciplinary authority of the superintendent.

The township courts decided cases not according to the general laws of the state, but according to the peasant "common law," which was uncodified, incomplete, and distinguished by its obscurity and diversity, thus giving wide latitude to the discretion or arbitrariness of the judge. Unqualified judges had difficulty deciding cases; as a result, the clerk of the court was frequently able to play the main part, and many cases were decided by a bribe in money or vodka. No wonder that the township courts were in disrepute among the peasants. Not much better was the exercise of judicial authority by the superintendent of the peasantry, who now replaced the justice of the peace. The superintendents seldom had legal training and often passed judgment according to their mood or "inspiration," rather than law and justice.

In 1890 the "Statute on the Zemstvo Institutions" was revised, changing the electoral procedure for the peasant delegates to the county zemstvo assembly. The peasants in their township assemblies, instead of voting for electors who, in their turn, elected the required number of delegates to the county zemstvo assembly, now merely nominated one or two persons from each township (depending on size) as candidates for the county assembly. From this list of candidates the required number of delegates to the zemstvo assembly was picked by the provincial governor, on the advice of the superintendent of the peasantry. Moreover, the peasants' quota of delegates was reduced from an average of 48 percent to an average of 30 percent of the membership of the zemstvo assemblies; the actual proportion of peasant delegates to each zemstvo assembly, as prescribed by law, varied from county to county.

Thus in the period between 1889 and 1905, more than in the preceding three decades, the peasants were limited in their civil rights, subjected to the control of special judicial and administrative offices, and judged on the basis of special laws. Peasant property rights were similarly subjected to additional limitations under Alexander III. The first to be regulated was the division of property within peasant households. Farm buildings and the immediate adjacent plot of land *(usad'ba)*, as well as livestock and equipment, generally belonged to a peasant household or family as a whole, these families often being considerable in size. If a member of the household, such as an elder son, wanted to form a new household of his own, he could receive his share of the family property by agreement with the other members of the household. A law of 1886, however, made the formation of new households conditional upon the approval of the village assembly, and after 1889 the approval of the superintendent of the peasantry was also required.

The peasant lands outside the household plots in most parts of Russia were held in communal ownership by the peasant mir. Originally, the manner and frequency of redistribution of this commonly held land were fully in the hands of the commune. A law of June 8, 1893, regulated the redistribution of communal lands by prescribing that at least twelve years elapse between repartitions and that each repartition be subject to approval by a two-thirds majority vote in the village assembly and by the superintendent of the peasantry.

The statute of 1861 provided that individual peasants who had paid their redemption dues in full could demand that the commune grant them their land allotments as private property. According to a law of December 14, 1893, the release of land into hereditary tenure was also made subject to the consent of the village assembly. The same law prohibited the selling and mortgaging of the peasant land allotments. In this condition of tutelage and legal separation from the other social groups, the Russian peasantry continued to live until the Revolution of 1905.

There were, however, a number of official acts that sought to improve the legal status of the peasants in the late nineteenth and early twentieth centuries. In 1881 the former serfs of the landlords were called upon to take the oath of allegiance to the new tsar, just like other citizens. In 1885 and 1886, the personal "soul-tax," the burden of which fell primarily on the peasants, was abolished. This eliminated the explicit distinction between the lower, soul-tax paying, classes and the upper classes, which had been exempt from this tax. In 1903, the collective responsibility of the peasant communes was abolished; no longer did they bear the duty of paying arrears of their insolvent or recalcitrant members. A manifesto of August 11,

1904, abolished corporal punishment, which the township courts had previously inflicted on "rural citizens."

But on the whole the general condition of the emancipated peasantry was far from satisfactory, and the living standard of the peasants toward the end of the century had actually declined. The agricultural population of the fifty provinces of European Russia, which in the sixties was 50 million, increased by 1900 to 86 million. As a result, average land allotments declined from 12.9 acres per male peasant in the 1860s to 7.5 acres at the end of the century. This size could have been sufficient for a modest standard of living if the fields had been carefully cultivated and had produced higher yields. But the average yield of the communal peasant lands in the 1860s, 400 pounds of grain per acre, only increased to 520 pounds per acre by the close of the century. Thus output on peasant farms lagged far behind the growth of peasant population. Correspondingly, there was a decline in the average grain harvest per head of rural population, and a deterioration of the general economic condition of the peasants.

In the 1880s the peasant economy improved slightly as a result of the abolition of the soul-tax and the lowering of redemption payments, but at the end of that decade a sharp decline set in again. In 1891 and 1892 complete crop failures occurred in the wide region of the Volga and the central part of the black-soil region, spreading over sixteen provinces and bringing misery and starvation to millions of peasants in these regions. Other crop failures and concomitant famines of limited scope occurred in various parts of the country in 1897, 1898, and 1901.

The Land Question

With surprising unanimity Russian public opinion at the end of the nineteenth and beginning of the twentieth centuries considered two factors to be the cause of peasant poverty: "land shortage" and the burden of the redemption payments that the peasants had to pay for their land. The well-publicized "land shortage" among the Russian peasantry is still discussed by some Russian and foreign historians and publicists. It is a historical myth that is very much alive even though it does not correspond at all to the facts of Russian economic life.

First, the idea of a "land shortage" in Russia conflicts with the indisputable fact that at the turn of the century Russia had one of the lowest population densities in Europe. If one subtracts one third of the European Russian territory, mostly in the north and southeast, as unsuitable for agriculture, it still appears that Russia had more arable land per capita than any other European state. Even if one takes into account that Russia was considerably less urbanized than many European countries, and compares only the amounts of arable land per capita of the agricultural population, Russia comes out far ahead, with 7 acres of arable land per head of rural population as against 4.9 acres in France, 3.4 in Austria, 4.7 in Germany, and 2.7 in Italy.[1] These figures relate only to European Russia— the amount of land in Siberia was much greater—and do not take account of the natural qualities of much of the Russian agricultural land; that of the central black-soil belt and the south was superior to most of Europe, even though the central Volga region often suffered from droughts.

Who owned the arable land in Russia? In the vast majority of cases it was owned by the Russian "toiling peasantry," and only a small part was the property of "landowners and capitalists." According to statistical research on landownership in 1905, the fifty provinces of European Russia (excluding Poland, the Caucasus, and Finland) contained 1,066,500,000 acres of land, of which 418,500,000 acres, mainly the territories of the northern and northeastern forests and the polar tundras, belonged to the state. In the 1860s almost all the state-owned land suitable for agriculture had been granted as allotments to the state peasants. The remaining land, approximately 650,000,000 acres, consisted of two categories:

(1) 375,000,000 acres of "allotment lands" used by peasants (including 335,000,000 acres in the hands of peasants and 40,000,000 acres in the hands of Cossack farmers)

(2) 275,000,000 acres of privately owned land, which in 1905 was distributed among various types of owners as follows:
   (a) nobility—144,000,000 acres (about 50 percent)
   (b) peasants and peasant communes—67,000,000 acres
   (c) merchants and commercial firms—45,000,000 acres
   (d) burghers and other classes—19,000,000 acres.[2]

---

[1] P. Maslov, *Agrarnyi vopros v Rossii* [*The Agrarian Question in Russia*] (3d ed.; St. Petersburg, 1906), vol. I, p. 204.

[2] Very detailed data about the distribution of landed property in Russia in 1905 are given in *Ezhegodnik Rossii 1906 g.* [*Russian Year Book for 1906*], published by the Central Statistical Committee of the Ministry of the Interior (St. Petersburg, 1907), pp. xxv-lvi: "Zemlevladenie v 50 guberniiakh Evropeiskoi Rossii v 1905 g." ["Landownership in Fifty Provinces of European Russia in 1905"]. The figures given there are, of course, in desiatinas, 1 desiatina equaling 2.7 acres.

LAND OWNERSHIP IN 50 PROVINCES OF EUROPEAN RUSSIA, 1905

DESIATINAS

Land owned by the state and by public bodies   154,689,000

(including 89.2 percent held by the treasury;
5.9 percent held by the imperial family;
1.6 per cent held by the church; and
3.3 percent by other public bodies—most
of the area being unsuitable for agriculture)

Privately owned and allotment land   240,503,000

(including 58 percent of allotment land,
predominantly land in crops, and 42 percent
privately owned land, which included forest
areas)

CHART III. THE DISTRIBUTION OF PRIVATE AND ALLOTMENT LAND, 1905

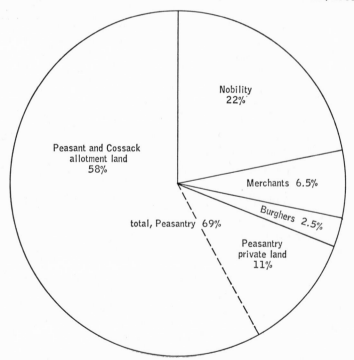

Altogether the peasants in 1905 owned about 442,000,000 acres and the nobility 144,000,000 acres, of which a considerable part was forest. Thus, prerevolutionary Russia was a "peasant kingdom," a country in which peasant landownership was predominant over landlords' land to a much greater extent than in other European countries.

This fact has been acknowledged by unprejudiced students of the agrarian problem, from the monarchist Oldenburg to the Social Democrat Maslov. According to Oldenburg, "A similar predominance of small peasant farms over estates was not to be found either in England or in Germany, nor even in post-revolutionary France. Russia was a country of small peasant holdings. Great estates were islands in the peasant seas."[3] "In France," wrote Maslov at the turn of the century,

> 45% of arable land belongs to the owners of great estates. In England almost all land is in the hands of great landowners. In Prussia 88% of privately owned land belongs to middle and large landowners. Thus, land ownership in Russia is more favorably distributed for a population occupied with agriculture than in other countries. . . .[4]

As to the size of the peasant allotments, one can speak of a "land shortage" only in very limited sense. Half the peasantry, the state peasants, received allotments that were generally quite adequate, averaging 16 to 18 acres per male peasant. The allotments of the landowners' peasants were on the average half the size of these, or 8.9 acres, but here, too, only a minority suffered from an actual land shortage. About 500,000 peasants who had received their land without redemption had inadequate allotments, one quarter of the normal size, and peasants in certain localities in the central and western provinces also lacked adequate land. Of 12,000,000 peasant households in 1905, only 2,857,000 (23.8 percent) had less than 13.5 acres; 5,072,000 households (42.3 per cent) had from 13.5 to 27 acres per household; and 4,070,000 households (33.9 percent) had more than 27 acres. Thus the total number of peasants with inadequate land at the beginning of the twentieth century constituted less than one quarter of the total Russian peasant population. In any case, the poor Russian peasants were provided with more land than their more prosperous European brethren. As George Pavlovsky put it,

---

[3] S. S. Oldenburg, *Tsarstvovanie Imperatora Nikolaia II* [*The Reign of Emperor Nicholas II*] (Belgrade, 1939), vol. I, p. 168.

[4] Maslov, *op. cit.*, vol. I, p. 206.

most writers on the agrarian problem in Russia . . . overlooked the cardinal fact that the peasants were already, as a class, in possession of the greater part of the land in Russia, and of by far the greater part of the agricultural area in particular, and that any possible additions to their holdings at the expense of other classes of proprietors could only have a very limited effect. This was amply proved by the results of the expropriation in 1917–18.[5]

In addition to the alleged land shortage, the second main reason for the impoverishment of the peasants was usually considered to be the supposedly exorbitant and excessive fiscal payments. The soul-tax, abolished in the 1880s, was both burdensome and unjust. As to the land taxes, the redemption payments for the land allotments constituted the main burden. The former landowners' peasants had to pay an average of one and one half rubles annually per desiatina (2.7 acres); the former state peasants paid considerably less. The total sum of the redemption payments, which were abolished in 1905 and 1906, amounted to somewhat over 90,000,000 rubles annually at the opening of the twentieth century, an average of less than one ruble per desiatina. At the rate of 1.5 rubles per desiatina, or 55 kopecks per acre paid by former serfs, the redemption payment per acre was the equivalent of the price of 40 pounds of rye. For a peasant farm yielding on the order of 400 pounds of rye per acre (of which about 100 pounds was needed for seed), this was a fairly heavy tax, but for a well-cultivated farm with a yield on the order of 800 to 1000 pounds per acre this tax would have been quite light. In 1899 the sum of all direct payments to the government, the commune, and the zemstvo from peasant land allotments was 184,000,000 rubles, an average of 56 kopecks per acre,[6] a rate that could be excessive only for poor and primitive peasant farms.

If in comparison with his European counterpart the Russian peasant had a lot of land, and if the fiscal payments were not excessive for a properly managed farm, how can one explain the undeniable poverty of the Russian peasant? The main reason was the extremely low productivity of the peasant farms, a result of technological backwardness rather than lack of land.[7] According to Chuprov,

---

[5] G. Pavlovsky, *Agricultural Russia on the Eve of the Revolution* (London, 1930), p. 96.

[6] *Velikaia reforma* [*The Great Reform*] (Moscow, 1911), vol. VI, p. 218.

[7] D. W. Treadgold, *The Great Siberian Migration* (Princeton, N.J., 1957), chapter 2: "The Peasant in the Homeland." Cf. Pavlovsky, *op. cit.*, p. 86: "the real trouble was

the average yield per acre from peasant fields for the period 1891–1900 in European Russia was only 520 pounds of grain and in some provinces was as low as 280 pounds: nowhere did it exceed 760 pounds, while the application of simple and easily acquired agricultural improvements would be enough to double the harvest in most parts of Russia.[8]

One should note that the productivity of peasant farming was highest in the Baltic provinces, where both the soil and the climate are far less suitable for agriculture than in the interior of Russia, but where more careful methods of cultivation were applied. On the whole, however, the yield of the peasant fields in Russia at the beginning of the twentieth century was 15 to 20 percent lower than the yield on landlords' estates and two, three, or four times lower than the yields in various European countries. For example, the net yield (not counting seed) of wheat at the end of the nineteenth century in Russia was about 380 pounds per acre, as compared with more than 900 pounds in France, some 1000 pounds in Germany, and over 1500 pounds in England.[9]

What kind of an agricultural system was it that permitted the Russian peasant to suffer and sometimes even starve while he possessed a great wealth of land? First of all, the peasants' ways of cultivating the land were primitive and antiquated; they had hardly changed in the forty years since the abolition of serfdom. Most peasants still tilled the soil with the ancient *sokha;* as a result, ploughing was shallow and inefficient. Sowing was done by hand and threshing by flails; harvesting machines were virtually unknown. The quality of seeds was poor, and the use of fertilizer very limited. In allocating land for different crops, the three-field system was used; it meant a regular three-year crop cycle of winter grain, spring grain, and fallow. One third of the arable land was thus lost for grain production.

In many localities hay fields, meadows, and common pastures were ploughed in an effort to raise grain production. Instead, the fallow fields were largely used for the grazing of cattle, but the meager fodder that was to be found there hardly compensated for the withdrawal of one third of the land from grain production, nor for the shrinkage of permanent pasture lands. The decline of cattle

---

that the land was not used to the best advantage, and that the yield of peasant farming was miserably low."

[8] P. D. Dolgorukov and 1. I. Petrunkevich, eds., *Agrarnyi vopros* [*The Agrarian Question*] (St. Petersburg, 1907), vol. II, p. 18: for A. Chuprov.

[9] *Ibid.,* vol. II, p. 226: for V. Levitsky.

raising not only reduced farm income, but resulted in a shortage of manure for the purpose of fertilizing and led to further soil exhaustion.

Closely related to the primitive agricultural technology was the pattern of land ownership. As we have seen, the peasant land was not owned by those who tilled it, for it belonged to the community, which distributed the land according to the number of male "souls" in a family, or according to the number of "mouths" to be fed, or able-bodied "toilers," or in some other way. Of the 375,000,000 acres of peasant allotment lands, the predominant part, 311,000,000 acres (or 83 percent), were communal lands. Only in the western regions of the empire did peasants own farms and, significantly, these regions never experienced widespread famines.

Characteristic of communal land ownership was strip farming and compulsory crop rotation. The allotment lands were usually divided into "near, middle, and far," depending on distance from the village and the convenience of access. Each of these zones in turn was subdivided into several areas according to the quality of the soil, its topographic features, and suitability for different kinds of farming. Within each of these areas every household of a given village received a strip of land. The purpose of this was to achieve an equitable distribution of land, both quantitatively and qualitatively; the result, however, was that a household allotment was often composed of 20 to 30 scattered strips of land, some of them so narrow as to make cultivation difficult. Moreover, the holder of any of the strips located between the fields of others unavoidably had to submit to the pattern followed by his neighbors with respect to crop rotation and work in the fields. Attempts to abandon the three-year-crop cycle, for example, were foredoomed to failure, for a crop sown on a strip surrounded by fallow fields would be destroyed by grazing cattle. Nor was it possible to raise a crop different from that of one's neighbors, for if it were to ripen earlier, it would be impossible to cross the neighboring strips to harvest the field, and if the crop were to ripen after that of the neighboring fields, it would again be trampled down by cattle, since all fields became a common pasture after the harvest.[10]

It is clear that strip farming and compulsory crop rotation alone were formidable roadblocks to agricultural progress, not to speak

---

[10] I. V. Sosnovsky, comp., *Svod trudov mestnykh komitetov o nuzhdakh sel'skokhoziaistvennoi promyshlennosti: Zemlevladenie* [*Summary of the Findings of the Local Committees on the Needs of Agriculture: Landholding*] (St. Petersburg, 1904), pp. 95–100.

of the fact that a peasant had little incentive to improve "his" strips of land if he knew that in a few years many of them would be reallocated and given to somebody else anyway. But, in spite of the enforced conformity and economic inefficiency that the communal pattern of landownership produced, it proved to be extremely "popular" in Russia. It was supported and defended by spokesmen for the most diverse groups, from the Slavophiles and Chernyshevsky to Pobedonostsev and Alexander III. Witte writes in his *Memoirs:*

> The defenders of the commune were loyal, respectable collectors of old rubbish, admirers of old forms because they were old; or police watchdogs who found it more convenient to take care of herds than of individuals; or the partisans of upheaval, who supported all that was easily shaken; and lastly the theoreticians, who saw in the commune a practical implementation of that last word in economic doctrine, the theory of socialism.[11]

The government and rightist circles supported and protected the rural commune not only as an "ancient pillar" of Russian life, but also as a "guarantee" against the emergence of a landless revolutionary proletariat. In fact, however, the elaborate methods to achieve equality among its members did not protect the peasant commune from the interplay of economic forces and from economic differentiation within the commune. Some unfortunate event on the farm —crop failure, a fire, loss of cattle, sickness, or death—might cause the impoverishment of some households in the commune. For example, a family might have an allotment but be unable to till it if they lost their only horse. On the other hand, the well-to-do members of the commune became wealthier either through buying land on the side, with full rights of ownership, or by engaging in trade or usury. The poor members of the commune worked as hired laborers for wealthier neighbors or the neighboring landlord, or took on seasonal jobs while leasing their allotments at a very low rate to the more fortunate members of the commune. Their complete break with the mir was hindered by administrative obstacles as well as by their unwillingness to part with their land allotments completely. Thus, in and around the villages a kind of proletariat did emerge, a group unable to find adequate livelihood in agriculture, and yet one that could not be fully absorbed into the urban labor force, in part because of the insufficient rate of industrialization.

---

[11] S. Iu. Witte, *Vospominaniia* [*Memoirs*] (Berlin, 1922), vol. I, p. 442. See also A. Yarmolinsky, trans., *The Memoirs of Count Witte* (New York, 1921).

At the end of the nineteenth century the worsening economic condition of the peasantry, especially in the "impoverished center" of the country, became an alarming problem. The government appointed committees and held "special conferences" to study the peasant question, particularly after it became clear that the administrative tightening under Alexander III was not producing the expected beneficial results. No tangible accomplishments were made, however, until 1902 when Witte himself, the influential and active minister of finance, undertook the task. A decree of January 22, 1902, appointed a Special Committee on the Needs of the Agricultural Industry with Witte as chairman, and provincial and county committees under the chairmanship of the marshals of the nobility. The committees consisted of persons invited by the chairman: leaders of local administration, the zemstvos, and "experienced persons" from various walks of public life. The committees assembled and published a great wealth of information on the legal and economic conditions in the countryside, but this was the only result of their work.

Still, it would be unjust to say that the government of Alexander III and Nicholas II did nothing to improve the economic condition of the Russian peasantry before 1905. The regime did undertake a number of steps in this direction, even though they were indecisive, limited, and unsystematic.

The settlement of the relationship between the former serfs and their landlords dragged on until the end of the reign of Alexander II. In 1881, there still were more than a million "temporarily obligated" peasants, who paid their landlords obrok. On December 28, 1881 a law ordered the "transfer of these peasants to the status of redemption-paying proprietors as of January 1, 1883." At the same time, a decree reduced the redemption payments by 20 percent on the average. As mentioned above, the soul tax was abolished by 1886, and in 1894, 1896, and 1899, the government further assisted the peasant by wholly or partially canceling arrears on payments due to the state.

In 1882, the Peasant Land Bank was established "to facilitate the purchase of land by peasants." The bank was authorized to issue loans to rural communes, peasant societies, or individual peasants at 5.5 percent interest and 1 percent administrative expenses. In 1898, the interest rate was reduced to 4 percent. The interest on commercial loans at that time was much higher; the legal ceiling was 12 percent.

In 1895, a new statute allowed the bank to buy land for resale to peasants, and the activities of the bank expanded considerably. From the opening of the bank in 1882 to January 1, 1901, a total of 13,775,400 acres was purchased by the peasants through the bank. By January 1, 1907, the total grew to 22,320,000 acres and involved loans totaling 516,000,000 rubles. In all, 1,319,000 peasant families took part in these purchases. The prices on land at the end of the nineteenth century and into the twentieth century appreciated very rapidly. During the first three years of the activity of the bank (1883–1885), the average price of the land bought with the bank's help amounted to 50 rubles per desiatina; in 1900 the price was 83 rubles; and in 1904, 112 rubles. A land market, virtually nonexistent in the period of serfdom, was thus developing rapidly.

In addition to the Peasant Land Bank the government felt the need to provide facilities in the village for small loans, and in 1883 and 1895 steps were taken to encourage the establishment of local peasant banks and savings and loan institutions, which will be discussed in chapter 8 in connection with the development of cooperatives.

In 1886 an important law on landownership by peasants on state lands converted the annual rent paid by them to the state *(obrochnaia podat')* into redemption payments, which were two-thirds higher but were to expire in forty-four years. Effective immediately, the land of the former state peasants, previously regarded as state property, was formally declared to be peasant property. The extent of the lands allotted to the peasantry for gradual redemption was thus greatly increased. Together, the former state and landlords' land formed a huge territory of "allotment" land that could not be bought or mortgaged, and the greater part of which belonged to the repartitional communes.

The relatively high population density in the agricultural areas of central Russia made peasants looking for more land turn their attention across the Ural Mountains, to the boundless virgin plains of Siberia. "Temporary regulations" regarding migration were issued in 1881, but for many years the budget of the offices dealing with the migrants was tiny, and their moves were restricted by cumbersome administrative procedures. After 1891, however, when the construction of the Trans-Siberian Railroad began, the government began actively to encourage migration, first of all trying to populate areas along the railway. In 1896 a special Resettlement Administration was set up within the Ministry of Internal Affairs, and in 1896, 1899, and 1904, regulations granting privileges and subsidies for the migrants were issued. The migrants were authorized to receive loans of 30 to 50 rubles for traveling expenses and 100 to 150 rubles for farm equipment and seeds, repayable after five years in ten annual installments.

Between 1893 and 1903 the government spent 30,000,000 rubles to support migration, and the movement expanded greatly toward the end of the century, even though the period of greatest migration to Siberia came only after 1906 in the era of Stolypin. From 1885 to 1895, 162,000 peasants migrated across the Ural Mountains (14,700 per year), and from 1896 to 1900, 932,000 peasants (186,400 per year).[12]

All land in Siberia was legally owned by the state, with the exception of some territories belonging to Cossack communities or to "His Majesty's Chancellery" *(kabinetskie zemli)*. Thus the government was responsible for providing the settlers with land, and officials of the Resettlement Administration and government surveyors had to locate and stake out suitable and available tracts. They also had to take care of the construction of roads and wells and provide supplies and medical dispensaries for the coming migrants. Groups of newcomers were usually organized into village communities *(sel'skoe obshchestvo)*, and these communities received land for perpetual use of their members according to the norm of 15 desiatinas (about 40 acres) per adult male. For the use of this land the settlers had to pay the government an annual rent; and the land could not be sold, donated, or mortgaged. In such a way communal tenure of land was formally predominant in Siberia, but in contrast to the European Russian peasant commune, "the Siberian commune knew neither periodical redistribution nor any form of "equalization" in which a holder would yield any land to another without payment."[13]

By the beginning of the twentieth century the most fertile and most accessible lands in western Siberia were already occupied by Russian settlers or by the native population, and the accommodation of newcomers became more and more difficult. Meanwhile, the majority of migrants, lured by rumors of abundant land in Siberia, hurried to move there on their own, without asking for permission and entrance certificates from the government. This spontaneous influx of settlers created difficulties and confusion, so that many of the irregular migrants had to return. In the first years of the twentieth century the reverse movement of migrants amounted to 10 to 25 percent. More circumspect peasants therefore first sent "scouts" *(khodoki)* to Siberia to explore possible sites for settlement, and only after the return of the scouts did the peasants wind up their affairs and start on the long journey "toward the sun."

---

[12] For a detailed and competent description of the migration movement see Treadgold, *op. cit.*

[13] *Ibid.,* p. 169.

Recognizing the growing importance of the agrarian problem, the government in 1893-1894 created a new Ministry of Agriculture, which absorbed the former Ministry of State Domains. But the budget of the new ministry was very modest: 30,000,000 rubles or 2 percent of the state budget in 1895. Throughout the latter part of the nineteenth century and up to 1905, the agricultural policy of the government considered the repartitional commune and the special legal status of the peasant to be "inviolable pillars" of the social order; but since it was precisely these "pillars" that were the cause of most of the peasants' difficulties, any measures the government did take could not but be timid and indecisive. It remained for the firm hand of Stolypin to remove these "ancient pillars" and reorient policy after the Revolution of 1905.

As for the nobility, this class occupied the leading position in the local administration and the zemstvos as a result of the policies of Alexander III. But its economic status was far from good, and the basis of its social influence—the land—was rapidly and continuously passing into the hands of the peasants and, to some extent, the merchants and industrialists. Moreover, the holdings of the nobility were shrinking at an accelerating rate: the average annual decrease in their landholdings amounted to some 1,396,000 acres in 1860–1877; 2,025,000 acres in 1877–1896; and 2,640,600 acres in 1897–1900. Of the 270,000,000 acres of land that the nobility owned at the beginning of the 1860s, only 143,740,000 acres remained in their possession by 1905.

The low level of prices on grain in the world market in the last fifteen years of the nineteenth century intensified the agricultural crisis that greatly affected the nobility and speeded up the dissolution of its estates, despite the establishment in 1885 of the Nobles' Bank, a step that helped many of the landlords to retain their estates. The end of the nineteenth century was replete with complaints about the "impoverishment of the center" that affected not only the peasant communities but privately owned estates as well. Many landowners leased their lands, after dividing them into small plots, to the neighboring peasants, who cultivated them in the same primitive manner as their own allotment lands.

However, not all of the landlord estates were declining. Some of them, particularly in the western and southern regions of the country, surmounted the crisis by improving agricultural techniques to increase the yield. On the better estates the traditional three-field system was replaced with crop rotation, fodder was produced, chemical fertilizers applied, and agricultural machinery introduced extensively. In the southwestern region and in some central provinces, the cultivation of sugar beets increased rapidly, from 270,000 acres in the 1860s to more than 1,350,000 acres at the beginning of the twentieth century. The advanced estates were the main suppliers of grain for both home and foreign markets; because of them the export of Russian grain increased steadily at the end of the nineteenth and the beginning of the twentieth centuries, despite the backwardness of Russian agriculture as a whole. The average annual export of grain products from Russia in 1866–1870 was 2,448,000 tons; in 1896–1900 it amounted to 7,992,000 tons, and the substantial increase in productivity these figures reflect was accomplished by a relatively small number of farms. The total number of estates of the nobility in Russia by 1905 was 107,000, but of these only 46,000 had holdings—those in excess of 270 acres—that had real economic significance.

A special group within the agricultural population of Russia were the Cossacks. They were soldier-farmers who performed combat and guard duty on the southern and eastern frontiers of the empire and were incorporated into the regular Russian army as an "irregular cavalry" in wartime. The government needed the services of the Cossacks to the very end of the empire, and when new regions were annexed to Russia, as in the 1860s in the Far East and in Central Asia, new Cossack forces[14] were immediately established on the Amur, the Ussuri, and in the Semirechensk area. By the beginning of the twentieth century there were eleven Cossack forces in all: Don, Kuban, Terek, Orenburg, Ural, Astrakhan, Siberia, Transbaikal, Semirechensk, Amur, and Ussuri. The Cossack community at that time constituted 2.3 percent of the total population, more than 3,000,000 people. According to a law of 1869 concerning "the land settlement of the Cossack forces," each male member of the Cossack community was to receive an allotment of 81 acres of arable land. Thus the Cossack land allotment was four times the average allotment of the state peasants and eight times the allotment of the former landlords' peasants. The minimum size of a Cossack allotment was set at 54 acres. It should be borne in mind, however, that the Cossacks bore the expense of providing their own horses in the army.

The military obligation of the Cossacks, as established in 1874–1875, lasted twenty years, beginning at the age of eighteen. Of these twenty years, three were devoted to training, twelve to active

---

[14] A Cossack *voisko*, that is, host or force, included combat personnel with all their dependents, women and children; therefore, one can properly speak of a Cossack community and of the Cossacks as a social class.

duty, and five to reserve. In peacetime, however a considerable part of those in active duty were on leave, to take care of their families and farms. The administration of the Cossack villages was regulated under Alexander III by a law of 1891, by which the Cossack village *(stanitsa)* assemblies, composed of one representative from each household (or one representative from each five or ten households, depending on the size of the village) elected the commander *(ataman),* the treasurer, and the judges of the village. The higher military commanders and administrative officials were appointed by the government. The largest area of Cossack settlement, the Region of the Don force, stood outside the general structure of provincial administration.

The Political Parties and the Agrarian Question

Such were the problems of Russian rural life and the policies of the government. But what were the solutions proposed by those groups of the Russian public that stood in opposition to the regime? First of all, of course, they advocated the overthrow of the tsarist autocracy and the establishment of a democratic republic. Then the principle "land to the peasant" or "land to the toilers" was to be realized. The agrarian program of the Socialist Revolutionary party, the so-called "socialization of land," was the most popular plan by 1905 and is worth quoting at length from the party program:

> In matters involving the reorganization of agrarian relations, the S.R. Party strives, in the interests of socialism and the struggle against bourgeois property principles, to rely upon the communal labor traditions and forms of life of the Russian peasantry and especially on their widespread conviction that land belongs to no one, that only labor gives one the right to use it. In agreement with its general views on the tasks of the revolution in the countryside, the Party will stand for the socialization of land, i.e. for withdrawing it from circulation as a commodity and transferring it from the private ownership of individuals or groups into the possession of the entire nation on the following principles: all land shall come under the control of central and local organs of popular self-government, starting with democratically organized, classless rural and municipal communes and culminating with regional and central institutions . . . ; the use of land must be equalized on the basis of labor, i.e. the consumer needs must be provided for solely by the application of personal labor, whether singly or in associations; land rent, collected through a special assessment, must be devoted to public purposes; . . . the

land is to become public property without compensation; those who suffer from this change in ownership have merely the right to claim public support for the period necessary to adjust themselves to new conditions of personal existence.

The program appeared clear-cut for both its authors and for much of the audience, even though it posed many insoluble problems in reality. Was it possible to distribute equally "public property" among the toilers, from Minsk to Vladivostok and from Archangel to Ashkhabad?

The Social Democrats ran into great difficulties when developing their agrarian program. At first, they hoped to do without one since, as a purely "workers' party" they did not, seemingly, have to concern themselves with the "peasant bourgeoisie," which, according to the laws of Marxist "scientific socialism," was doomed to inevitable destruction as a result of the class struggle of the proletariat. In agrarian Russia, however, it was politically impossible to ignore 100 million peasants, and therefore the Second Congress of the SD Party accepted the following agrarian program:

> To eliminate the vestiges of serfdom, which are a heavy burden upon the peasants, and in the interests of free development of the class struggle in the countryside, the party demands: (1) the abolition of redemption and obrok payments and special peasant obligations; (2) the abolition of all laws which constrain the peasant in regard to the disposal of his lands; (3) the repayment of the sums of money which were taken from the peasant in the form of redemption and obrok payments; (4) the establishment of peasant committees for the sake of returning to the rural communes . . . lands which were cut off from the peasants' allotments at the time of the abolition of serfdom, and which in the hands of the landlords serve as a means for the oppression of the peasants . . . (5) the authorization of the courts to lower exorbitant rent payments and to declare invalid all contracts of an oppressive character.

The SR's directed violent and sarcastic criticism against the SD proposal to transfer only the landlords' "cutoffs" of 1861 to the peasants. The SR's would give all land to the peasants, while the SD's intended to make only "charitable donations," to give the peasants the "cutoffs" taken from them fifty years ago. The SD's, and especially Lenin, soon realized that in the forthcoming political contest it would be impossible to play "cutoffs" against the ace of trumps represented by the SR program of "socialization." To improve their tactical position the Third Congress of the SD party, a purely

Bolshevik gathering in 1905, without a formal change of the old agrarian program, passed a resolution proclaiming that Social Democrats would "energetically support all revolutionary measures taken by the peasants to improve their situation, including the confiscation of landlord, state, church, monastic, and imperial household lands." A similar resolution was passed by the Mensheviks in the same year.

However, those among the Social Democrats who were not inclined to renounce Marxist theory for the sake of an expedient, demagogic tactic, saw that the confiscation of the great landlord estates and their redistribution among peasants completely contradicted the Marxist theory of social development. They also realized that if this expedient tactic were adopted, the destruction of well-cultivated farms would be a great loss to the national economy and would bring little benefit for the peasants.

Therefore, the chief agrarian theoretician among the Russian Marxists, Maslov, came forward with a program of "municipalization of the land," that is, the transfer of the confiscated estates to regional bodies of local self-government, which were to be organized on democratic principles. This program was accepted by the Fourth Congress of the SD party in 1906, against the objections of Lenin who still wished to promise all the land to the peasants—the "nationalization" of the land, as he put it.

In 1905 liberal and radical circles of the Russian intelligentsia organized the Constitutional Democratic party (the "Party of Popular Freedom") or the KD's (Kadets). The working out of an agrarian program gave rise to heated discussions within the party concerning the possibility and practicality of compulsory expropriation of privately owned land for redistribution among the supposedly land-starved peasants. Some economists, such as Professors A. I. Chuprov and V. F. Levitsky, observed that the Russian peasant "overestimated the geometrical dimensions of the land that he required" and ignored the equally important factor of improved agricultural techniques even when these improvements were within his reach. But the majority of KD's themselves accepted the "geometrical" point of view of the peasants, believing that the main reason for the impoverishment of the peasantry was the "land shortage" and that the compulsory expropriation of privately owned lands was absolutely necessary. The agrarian program of the KD's demanded "an increase of the quantity of land for the people who till it with their own labor," such as landless and land-starved peasants, through the redistribution of state and monastic lands and also through the alienation for this purpose of privately owned lands, "with compensation at a fair price [not the market price] of the present owners."[15]

Thus all the leading opposition parties offered and promised the peasants land that was not there! If the peasants had understood agrarian statistics and had known that the redistribution of the landlords' land could increase their land holdings only by 20 percent, perhaps less, they would not have been lured by the promises and instead would have thought about possible improvements of their own farms. But seeing some huge landlords' estates and not considering how relatively few in number these were, the peasants put absolutely fantastic hopes in the coming "additions" *(prirezki)*, and all the "progressive" political parties supported this illusion.

It is true that in some exceptional cases additional land was indeed necessary to increase inadequate allotments, and that, on the other hand, the great estates that leased land piecemeal to the peasants could have been transferred to the peasants for a very moderate compensation without any harm to the national economy. However, right-wing circles waxed indignant at references to compulsory expropriation of "sacred and inviolable property," forgetting that the founders of the Russian state, the Muscovite princes and Peter the Great, did not treat private property as inviolable or sacred at all when the interest of the state had demanded it. They also forgot that landlord ownership in Russia emerged not from private ownership, but as a result of grants of state lands to state servitors (in return for service) and that only in the eighteenth century did it become private property. Here, as in the political sphere, two blind, stubborn forces collided and fought each other until all power and all property was in the hands of Lenin and his accomplices.

The Growth of Industry and the Labor Question

In 1887, I. A. Vyshnegradsky replaced Bunge as minister of finance, and he was succeeded by Witte, an energetic, capable financier and great statesman, who held this ministry from 1892 until 1903. Under the ministry of Vyshnegradsky and especially under Witte the government undertook energetic and comprehensive measures for the development of domestic industry. The protective customs tariff of 1891 specifically served this purpose. Intensive railway construction

---

[15] See *Polnyi sbornik platform vsekh russkikh politicheskikh partii* [*Complete Collection of the Platforms of All Russian Political Parties*] (4th ed.; St. Petersburg, 1907).

also served to advance the productive capacity of the country. Because of the lack of domestic capital the government encouraged the attraction of foreign capital, especially French and Belgian, which greatly helped the growth of the south Russian metallurgical industry. The sum of foreign capital invested in Russian industry at the beginning of the twentieth century was estimated to be from 700 million to 900 million rubles.

Domestic industrialists received all kinds of privileges from the state, including loans and subsidies. The government paid well for railroad rails, and metallurgical factories boomed as a result of large state orders. The state further protected some branches of industry, such as sugar. The treasury established a production quota for the domestic sugar market, set wholesale prices that were quite favorable to the producer and fixed a minimum to be kept by the manufacturers. Foreign sugar was subject to a high duty, while the treasury paid an export premium to Russian sugar producers, which constituted a return on the excise tax paid by the producers.

As a result of all these measures, the "era of Witte" became a time of a rapid, widespread growth of Russian industry. Witte was often accused of artificially creating heavy industry in Russia, but in his *Memoirs* he replied:

> It has been said that I applied artificial measures in order to develop the industry. What does this stupid phrase mean? By what other measures but artificial is the development of industry possible? All that people do is to a certain extent artificial. Only savages live and govern themselves in an unartificial manner. Everywhere industry was developed by artificial means.[16]

The rate of industrial growth was uneven and was arrested during a general depression in Europe in the middle 1880s, and again at the very beginning of the twentieth century (1901–1903), but the economic progress of Russia in the last decade of the nineteenth century was quite considerable and it was in this period that Russia began to overcome her economic backwardness.

The intensive railway construction begun under Alexander II slowed in the 1880s, but in the '90s it moved forward with extraordinary speed, as the following statistics indicate:

Period	Miles constructed
1861–1870	5833
1871–1880	7225
1881–1890	4970
1891–1900	13,920

---

[16] Witte, *op. cit.*, vol. I, p. 451.

In 1891 construction of the great Trans-Siberian Railroad was started, opening up huge new territories and natural resources. By 1905 the total length of railways was more than 39,000 miles. Government policy towards the railroads changed under Alexander III. Under Alexander II the railroads were built by private companies with a government guarantee of profit; now the government took over railroad construction, and many of the existing lines were bought by the state. Between 1881 and 1894, twenty-four railroads, belonging to fifteen companies and constituting about two thirds of the total trackage in the country were purchased by the government, and their operation was handed over to the Ministry of Transport. True, the state-owned railroads remained in the red for a long time, but for the general economic progress of the country the railroad construction of the "era of Witte" was of basic importance.

Among the most successful developments of the 1890s was the growth of the metallurgical industry in southern Russia. Until 1887 there were only two iron works in the south; by 1899 there were seventeen large iron works, equipped with modern European machinery, and more than a hundred smaller factories. The following table indicates the growth of iron smelting, the basis of the metallurgical industry, and the proportional role of the south in this development:

	Total Production (in tons)	Southern Provinces (in tons)	South as percent of total
1887	648,000	72,000	11
1895	1,566,000	612,000	41
1904	3,240,000	1,998,000	62

In Petersburg and vicinity, the Putilov and Obukhov metallurgical works and the Neva shipyards expanded to giant proportions. Thus the north and south were the main center of the metallurgical industry, while the other major branch of manufacturing activity, textiles, was mainly concentrated in the central provinces around Moscow and Vladimir.

Although Russia lagged behind other industrialized countries in absolute production, her rate of development surpassed the others. In the 1890s iron smelting increased 18 percent in England, 72 percent in Germany, 50 percent in the United States and by 190 percent in Russia. In 1880, Russia occupied seventh place in world iron production; in 1895, fifth place; and in 1900, Russia stood fourth, behind only England, Germany, and the United States. Between 1870 and 1900 Russia's share in the rapidly increasing steel production of the world rose from 2 percent to 8 percent.

Coal mining, another basis of modern industry, also developed rapidly, particularly in the important Donets River basin, or Donbas:

	National Total (in tons)	Donbas Alone
1887	4,976,000	2,250,000
1895	9,990,000	5,364,000
1904	21,546,000	14,382,000

For the 1890s the output of coal increased in England by 22 percent, in Germany by 52 percent, in the United States by 61 percent, and in Russia by 131 percent. Even though these high percentages do reflect a low base, they show that Russia was rapidly ceasing to be a rural society and that her economic development had entered what W. W. Rostow has called the "take-off" stage.[17]

The same rapid progress characterized the Russian petroleum industry. In the last decades of the nineteenth century the output of Russian oil was on par with or exceeded that of the United States, rising from 2 million tons in 1885 to a high of 12.7 million in 1901. In the following decade, however, oil production ceased to expand, partly because of the exhaustion of readily available oil deposits.

The production of consumer goods, such as cotton and sugar also increased. The consumption of cotton in Russia amounted to 102,600 tons in 1880 and in 1890 to 149,000 tons, in 1900 to 288,000 tons and in 1904 to 324,000 tons. With the development of modern, industrial textile production, the domestic or cottage production of cloth in the central provinces declined increasingly in the last decades of the nineteenth century since it was unable to compete with the new factories. Sugar production rose from 225,000 tons in 1880 to 1,143,000 tons in 1904.

The over-all growth of manufacturing industry is characterized by the following figures:

	Number of Factories	Total Sum of Production	Number of Workers
1887	30,900	1,334,500,000 rubles	1,318,000
1890	32,300	1,502,700,000 rubles	1,424,700
1900	38,100	3,005,900,000 rubles	2,373,400

[17] W. W. Rostow, *The Stages of Economic Growth* (Cambridge, Mass., 1960).

Another index of the economic progress of the end of the nineteenth century was the rapid growth of joint-stock companies. In 1899, 1181 companies operated in Russia, with the initial capital of 1,739,000,000 rubles; half of these companies had been established in the 1890s. The turnover of Russian foreign trade in 1881 amounted to 1,024,000,000 rubles (export, 506,000,000 rubles; import, 518,000,000 rubles); and in 1903, 1,683,000,000 rubles (export, 1,001,000,000 rubles; import, 682,000,000 rubles).[18] An expression of Russian industrial progress was the impressive "All-Russian Exhibition of Industry and Arts," held in Nizhni Novgorod in 1896.

It should be noted that the new large-scale industry did not supplant all the widespread peasant handicraft industries *(kustarnye promysly)* in rural areas. Many small producers, either individual peasant families or groups of artisans forming cooperative societies *(arteli)* continued to work their iron, wooden, or textile handicraft wares, chiefly in several central provinces of European Russia: Moscow, Vladimir, Yaroslavl, Nizhni Novgorod, Kaluga, and Tula. The number of peasant artisans to whom this work was a full-time occupation was estimated at the turn of the century to be about 4 million; the number of peasants who practiced handicrafts in addition to their agricultural pursuits surely exceeded this number. The output of the handicrafts industry was never included in industrial production statistics, yet it was substantial in volume and satisfied the needs of a large segment of the population. In comparing the production figures of prerevolutionary Russia with those of other countries and periods, this fact should always be borne in mind.

The total population of the Russian Empire, excepting Finland, was about 146,000,000 in 1905; in the fifty provinces of European Russia, excepting Poland and the Caucasus, the population totalled 110,000,000. According to a study of 1904, there were 679 cities and towns in European Russia, and 949 in the whole empire (outside Finland); yet, 293 of these cities had less than 5000 inhabitants, that is, were in fact villages having only a legal and administrative status of a city. On the other hand, there were 171 settlements with a population over 10,000 which did not have legally an urban status; these were mostly industrial settlements in the newly developing areas of the south, such as Iuzovka, Makeevka, Sinelnikovo,

---

[18] Detailed statistical data concerning the development of Russian trade, industry, and state finances at the end of the nineteenth century and the beginning of the twentieth century are given in P. A. Khromov, *op. cit.*, and P. I. Lyashchenko, *op. cit.*, vol. II.

and some large Cossack stanitsas as well. In cities with a population over 10,000 there were some 19 million inhabitants, and in the large settlements of this category, some 3 million, making for a total of about 22 million. Thus, by 1905, about 16 percent of the Russian population was urbanized. Among the cities, 20 had a population over 100,000, and 175 had a population between 20,000 and 100,000 inhabitants. The four largest cities, with over half a million inhabitants were Petersburg (1,534,000), Moscow (1,092,000), Warsaw (771,000), and Odessa (500,000).[19] Some of the fastest rates of growth were registered by southern industrial cities, including Baku, Rostov on the Don, Ekaterinoslav, Iuzovka, and Krivoi Rog.

Having entered the path of industrialization, Russia did not escape some of its negative effects, characteristic of the nineteenth century. In its initial stages the development of large-scale factory industry was accompanied, as in other European countries by an intensive exploitation of workers, bad working conditions, long hours and poor pay, which, of course, gave rise to resentment and labor protest. In 1884 and 1885, there were strikes and serious labor disturbances in the provinces of Moscow and Vladimir, and in 1896, a large strike took place in the Petersburg textile factories.

To protect the workers the government of Alexander III during the ministry of Bunge promulgated a series of factory laws. Compulsory pay books were issued to regulate relations between factory owners and workers, and the factory owners were compelled to pay for the work in cash, not in kind. Factory labor for children under twelve and night work for minors under seventeen or for women (in textile mills) was forbidden. Youngsters from twelve to fifteen years of age could not work more than eight hours per day and had to have not less than three hours per day free for school. Factory inspection was instituted to supervise compliance with these laws, and owners violating them were subject to fines up to 300 rubles or one month arrest. On the other hand, a law of June 3, 1886, forbade strikes; strikers were subject to up to four months imprisonment and "instigators" from four to eight months.

In provincial capitals "provincial offices for factory affairs," headed by the provincial governor, were established and empowered to issue "compulsory enactments" regulating factories. Partial deviations from the general regulations were permissible for valid reasons.

---

[19] *Ezhegodnik Rossii,* 1906, pp. lviii-lxxii, for St. Petersburg, *Russkii Kalendar',* 1905, p. 138.

On June 2, 1897, a general law was issued, limiting the working hours in factories to eleven and one-half hours for adult males, except for Saturdays, the eve of holidays, and night work, in which cases the limit was ten hours. According to these regulations, "overtime is permissible only on the basis of a special agreement between the director of the industrial plant and the workers. In the employment agreement only overtime that is necessary for technical reasons may be included. . . ." It should be noted that the majority of European countries had no legislative limitation on adult male labor at this time. In 1903 another law recognized the financial responsibility of factory owners for industrial accidents.

State Finance

In the 1880s, we noted the government alleviated the peasants' burden of taxation by reducing redemption payments and abolishing the soul-tax, which had brought in more than 50,000,000 rubles annually. To compensate for this loss of revenue a series of new taxes was introduced in that decade, and taxes that previously existed were raised. The new taxes included an inheritance and gift tax, established in 1882; a 5 percent tax on income from capital, introduced in 1885; a housing tax of 1893; and taxes on income from trade, industry, and transportation. The land tax and the excise taxes on alcohol, sugar, and tobacco were raised along with the customs duties, which were increased considerably by the tariff of 1891. But the principal (and inexhaustible) source of revenue was the monopoly on spirits (mainly vodka), established in 1894–1896. In 1903 the revenue from this source was 542,000,000 rubles, which is a partial explanation for the elimination of deficit budgets after the 1880s. Moreover, under Vyshnegradsky and Witte considerable funds, the so-called "ready cash of the state treasury," which was composed of the surplus from ordinary state revenues and foreign loans, accumulated in the treasury. Under Vyshnegradsky the Russian government was able to carry through a "conversion" of Russian foreign debt, by which payments on the state debt were reduced. In 1890 the gold reserves of the state exceeded 500 million rubles, which enabled Witte to introduce the gold standard in 1896–1897. By this financial reform the ruble was equated to $66\frac{2}{3}$ gold kopecks, and new banknote rubles were declared subject to free and unlimited exchange for gold. The law of 1897 on the gold backing of the banknotes determined that the first 600 million rubles were to be backed by the gold reserve for half that amount and additional issues would be supported on a ruble-for-ruble basis. "Witte's banknotes," as they were called, did in fact freely exchange for gold and enjoyed widespread public confidence.

As we have seen, the state railroads expanded greatly under Witte's financial administration. The operating expenditures of the Ministry of Transport in 1903 came to 456 million rubles, not to mention capital expenditures for the construction of new lines. In the same year, revenues from the state railroads were 453 million rubles. Witte feared neither great financial operations nor great debts, and the state debt grew from 4,905,000,000 rubles in 1892 to 6,679,000,000 rubles in 1903.

The total revenues and disbursements of the state, exclusive of foreign loans, grew as follows:

	Revenues	Expenditures
1881	652,000,000 rubles	732,000,000
1893	1,046,000,000	947,000,000
1903	2,032,000,000	1,883,000,000

Of the revenues in 1903, 89,000,000 rubles came from redemption payments, 542,000,000 from the liquor monopoly, and 242,000,000 from customs duties, while expenditures included 289,000,000 to service the state debt and 466,000,000 for the army and navy.

In general, then, the era of the turn of the century witnessed major progress in the fields of industry, transportation, and finance, for which the leadership of Witte and the activity of the government deserve much credit. But the economic efficiency, administrative autonomy, and social mobility of the Russian peasantry, the majority of the populace, remained on a low level, a backward situation that endured until after the Revolution of 1905 and the era of Stolypin.

8

The Duma Monarchy

The Revolution of 1905

Emperor Nicholas II (1868–1918), who ascended the throne in October 1894 at the age of twenty-six, was deeply religious, patriotic, modest, and kindly in his personal relations. His abilities as a statesman, however, were inadequate to the crises of the stormy era that marked the opening of the twentieth century in Russia. A terrible augury of the tragic events of his reign was the catastrophe on the fields of Khodynka near Moscow. Here more than a thousand persons in the huge crowd that had gathered for the coronation were trampled to death because of the carelessness of the officials in charge of the celebration.

The ultraconservative principles of Alexander III and Pobedonostsev seemed to Nicholas to be the height of political wisdom. In addition to Pobedonostsev, however, he inherited another adviser in the person of the finance minister, Witte. This statesman considered himself a supporter of absolutism in principle, but he strove to remodel Russia's economy on the European pattern and regarded with contempt the reactionary nobility and right-wing parties. The reactionary policies pursued by Pobedonostsev and the industrialization encouraged by Witte could not be easily reconciled, and attempts to do so resulted in constant waverings and hesitations in the policy of Nicholas II. His position was made more difficult by the influence of his domineering wife, Alexandra, a former German princess. Although she was a granddaughter of Queen Victoria and grew up in the English court, she was fanatically devoted to the idea of divinely established, absolute tsarist power, which could not conceivably be limited.

The Russian public expected the new tsar to turn away from the conservative policy of Alexander III toward the liberal principles of the era of great reform, but their hopes were not fulfilled. On January 17, 1895, Nicholas, speaking to the representatives of the nobility, the zemstvos, and the city councils, declared:

> I know that recently in some of the gatherings of the zemstvos voices of persons were heard who were carried away with senseless dreams on the participation of the representatives of the zemstvos in the matters of internal government. Let all know that I, while devoting all my powers to the good of the people, will maintain the basis of autocracy with the same firmness and steadfastness as did my unforgettable late father.

The speech aroused widespread disappointment in liberal circles, and the revolutionaries successfully used it in their propaganda.

Nicholas' regime continued the policy of Russification that had been practiced under Alexander III and attempted to extend it to Finland, which had previously enjoyed complete local self-government. The executor of this unfortunate and unwise policy was General Bobrikov, appointed governor general of Finland in August 1898 with instructions to achieve a "closer union of the Finnish region and the Fatherland which is common to all loyal subjects." The decrees that violated the constitution of Finland and the legally established order in the country caused general opposition, a sense of alienation, and separatism in Finland. The governor general was granted extraordinary prerogatives to suppress the opposition but the dissatisfaction increased; in June 1904, General Bobrikov was assassinated by the son of a Finnish senator. By a manifesto of October 22, 1905, the restrictive decrees of 1900 and 1903 were abolished and the autonomy of Finland was restored.

At the turn of the century opposition to the government, the "Movement of Liberation," was spreading rapidly throughout Russia. As noted previously, disturbances among the university students began in February 1899 and continued without interruption with greater or lesser intensity until 1905, when they merged with the wider revolutionary movement. At the very beginning of the twentieth century the factory workers also entered the political struggle. A massive strike of the textile workers in Petersburg in May 1896 made a great impression on the public, but the demands made were still purely economic in character. However, more intensive propaganda by the socialist circles of the intelligentsia aroused an interest in politics among the workers, and in 1901 in Petersburg and several southern cities there were workers' May Day demonstrations, which reoccurred each year in ever-growing numbers. Seeing the spread of socialist ideas among the workers and fearing the political consequences, the government decided to experiment with "police socialism." Under the direction of Zubatov, the head of the political police in Moscow, workers' societies of mutual assistance were established to improve labor's economic condition through negotiations with factory management, and even through nonpolitical strikes. At first the Zubatov societies had a considerable success, but in 1903 the experiment of "police socialism" was abandoned as too dangerous.

In the spring of 1902 agrarian riots took place in the provinces of Poltava and Kharkov, looting almost eighty estates and burning two. The Party of Socialist Revolutionaries, organized at the end of 1901, resorted to individual terrorism. In April 1902, the "combat organization" of SR party killed Sipiagin, the minister of the interior. His successor, V. K. Plehve, decided to take a "firmer course" in order to suppress the revolutionary and oppositional movement, but his efforts were in vain.

In the spring of 1903 a pogrom, or terrorist riot against the Jews, was carried out in Kishinev by a mob of self-appointed vigilantes called the "Black Hundreds" with the connivance of the police: forty-five Jews were killed and several hundred injured. The pogrom caused great indignation against the government both at home and abroad, and intensified the opposition movement. A second pogrom, which took the lives of twelve victims, took place in Gomel in the fall of the same year.

Also in that year, major strikes, accompanied by political demonstrations and clashes with the army and police, occurred in such southern cities as Baku, Tiflis, Odessa, Kiev, and Ekaterinoslav. In the Urals serious disturbances among the workers occurred in Zlatoust; the riots were crushed and scores of workers shot. Shortly thereafter the governor of Ufa province, Bogdanovich, who had directed the suppression, was assassinated by a terrorist.

Thus a crescendo of unrest and violence—workers' and students' strikes, peasant riots, anti-Jewish pogroms by rightist mobs, terrorist acts against government officials, and repressive countermeasures of the government—were stirring the political life of the country even before the external stress added by the outbreak of war. The war with Japan, which started in January 1904 (see chapter 10), at first diverted the attention of the Russian public from the internal political struggle. But from the beginning, the Japanese war was unpopular and was regarded as an "adventure" or "shady enterprise" of the "court camarilla." The unsuccessful course that the war took aroused, in part, patriotic indignation against the inept government and, in part, malicious joy because the government was more and more discrediting itself. Defeat strengthened revolutionary discontent.

The assassination of Minister of Internal Affairs Plehve in July 1904 aroused almost general joy in the country. At the end of August Prince P. D. Sviatopolk-Mirsky replaced Plehve as minister of internal affairs and announced the willingness of the government to establish a relationship of "confidence" with the public. This declaration was the beginning of a political "springtime," a familiar phenomenon in revolutionary situations. The press was allowed to criticize the regime freely and to discuss openly the necessity for basic reforms. Political speeches were now permitted at banquets, and political resolutions were adopted at public meetings. In October 1904, a conference of the representatives of the liberal and revolutionary-populist movements took place in Paris, and there it was decided to coordinate their actions in the struggle against autocracy. The next month, in Petersburg, representatives of the zemstvos met and decided to put forward demands for a constitution.

The government saw the necessity for concession to public opinion and, on December 12, issued a decree "on the plans for the improvement of the system of government." This measure provided for a fairly comprehensive reform, but spoke of the "preservation of the stability of the fundamental laws," saying not a thing about a popular representation. For this reason it failed to satisfy anyone. Meanwhile, in November and December several unions of professional people were organized in Moscow and Petersburg, and their public meetings and banquets passed resolutions for the introduction of popular representation.

The news of the fall of Port Arthur on December 19, 1904, brought on a new wave of antigovernment demonstrations. By January 1905 the workers entered the political struggle in Petersburg in large numbers. In the autumn of 1903 a legal "Association of Russian Factory Workers" had been established; the head of the association, a priest called Georgii Gapon, had gained great popularity among the workers. At the beginning of January 1905, there was a major strike for the eight-hour day and an increase in wages, and Father Gapon called for a mass procession to the Winter Palace with the intention of presenting a petition to the tsar, requesting not only better working conditions but also the convocation of a constituent assembly. On the morning of January 9, huge crowds of workers moved toward the Winter Palace carrying icons, portraits of the tsar, and petitions. The government had been informed of the demonstration and the streets to the palace were blocked by soldiers and police, who ordered the crowds to disperse. When they did not obey, troops opened fire, killing some one hundred and wounding several hundred more, according to the official figures—which were lower than various private accounts. Father Gapon went into hiding, issued an ineffectual appeal to armed uprising, and in 1906 was assassinated by agents of the SR party, which then believed that he was maintaining secret contact with the police.

The news of Bloody Sunday brought widespread public indignation, and January 9, 1905, became the starting point for the "First Russian Revolution," as it is often called. Strikes of protest, including workers and students, occurred throughout Russia, and on February 4 terrorists retaliated by assassinating Grand Duke Sergei Alexandrovich, the uncle of the tsar and the governor general of Moscow.

Immediately after Bloody Sunday the liberal minister of internal affairs, Prince Sviatopolk-Mirsky, was dismissed and replaced by the conservative bureaucrat A. G. Bulygin. In Petersburg, a decree of January 11 established the office of governor general for that city, and the first incumbent, General D. F. Trepov, was given extraordinary powers to enforce public security. Trepov was hated by the public, who looked upon him as a dictator; the accusation was an exaggeration, but it is true that he later gained great influence over the tsar through the post of "court commander" (administrator of the imperial palaces).

On February 18, 1905, three contradictory enactments were issued. The first was the tsar's manifesto denouncing the disturbances and the raising of opposition in wartime, which were attributed to "the malicious leaders of the revolutionary movement . . . blinded by arrogance," and calling on "loyal citizens of all classes and walks of life" to help the government eradicate sedition. A second decree, addressed to the Senate, granted organizations and private individuals the right to submit to the government "opinions and proposals concerning the improvement of the system of government and the betterment of national well-being." Finally, a rescript addressed to the minister of internal affairs announced that the tsar "henceforth intended to call upon worthy citizens, who are trusted by the people and elected by the populace, to participate in the initial drafting and discussion of legislative proposals. . . ." This was the first time the tsar announced any intention of introducing any form of popular participation in legislation, but the manifesto itself undermined the prospects for representative government by proclaiming the inviolability of the old order. The decrees of February 18 did not pacify the populace, therefore, and when the news of the severe military defeat at Mukden arrived in late February, public unrest was intensified. In addition to demonstrations by workers and students in urban areas in some of the central provinces, there were rural disturbances, accompanied by the destruction of nobles' estates.

In early May a convention of representatives of various national professional organizations—lawyers, doctors, engineers, professors, agronomists, and others—met in Moscow and established the "Union of Unions," which called for a constituent assembly on the basis of universal, direct, equal, and secret suffrage—"four-tail" suffrage, as the political slang of the day called it. The demand for a constituent assembly and the "four tails" became the indispensable slogan of the day, "the mystical basis" of the liberation movement, as the moderate liberal Maklakov later called it.[1]

On April 17, 1905, the government issued a decree granting religious tolerance, ending government repression of the Old Believers and various other sects, but the measure had little influence on the general course of the revolution. During the spring and summer of 1905 the workers' movement continued, and strikes in the cities of the south, Poland, the Caucasus, and the Baltic developed into widespread demonstrations and clashes with the army and police. Now in one city, now in another, martial law was proclaimed and disturbances were suppressed with the help of the army. But the armed forces ceased to be wholly reliable. In June the Black Sea fleet suffered the famous mutiny of the battleship *Potemkin,* which was joined briefly by another battleship, the *Georgii Pobedonosets.*

On June 6, the tsar received a delegation of zemstvo leaders, listened to a fiery speech by Prince S. N. Trubetskoi, a professor of Moscow University, and promised to introduce representative institutions. This intention was realized on August 6 with the publication of a manifesto and two accompanying acts establishing a State Duma with consultative powers, based on an indirect and narrow electoral system. However, the "Bulygin Duma," as the plan was called after the current minister of internal affairs, failed to satisfy anyone because

---

[1] V. A. Maklakov, *Vlast' i obshchestvennost' na zakate staroi Rossii* [*Government and Society in the Last Years of Old Russia*] (Paris, [1932]), part II, p. 365.

of its limitations and the references made in the manifesto to "inviolable autocracy."

On August 27, new "temporary Rules on the Administration of Institutions of Higher Learning" re-established the autonomy to the professors' councils in the universities, granting these bodies authority over the appointment of the rectors and deans and over the policies of university teaching. This act, intended to pacify unrest in the universities, had some undesired political effects, for the universities now became virtually extraterritorial "republics," into which the police were reluctant to enter, while crowds of outsiders came in freely. In September and October the university halls in the capitals were filled with revolutionary-minded citizens, and speeches of all sorts, including even appeals for armed uprising, were freely delivered.

In October a new revolutionary organ, the Soviet (Council) of Workers' Deputies, appeared in Petersburg. With the support of the trade unions, it carried out a general strike that was highly effective in the capital and started publication of its own newspaper, *Izvestiia (The News)*.

Faced with this new threat, the government at last felt obliged to grant major concessions. Witte, who had just received the title of count for his services in negotiating the peace with Japan, submitted a memorandum in which he enumerated the measures that were necessary to appease the public: the establishment of a rule of law, a guarantee of the "blessings of civil liberty," the formation of a State Duma, the elimination of unnecessary repressions, and an attitude of "honesty and sincerity" toward the new system.[2]

At first Witte's memorandum was merely "accepted for guidance," then on October 16 the tsar called an extraordinary meeting of his close advisers, which approved a manifesto such as Witte proposed. The Manifesto of October 17—the October Manifesto—officially marked the end of absolute monarchy in Russia. In it the tsar expressed grief regarding the current disturbances and affirmed that it was his "inflexible will": to grant civil liberty, including freedom of conscience, speech, assembly, and association; to enfranchise the classes not given the vote in the plan of August 6; and to establish the governmental principles that no law was to take force without the approval of the State Duma and that the representatives of the people were to control the actions of appointed authorities. To "unify" the government, the tsar now formed a "council of ministers," a cabinet executive, replacing the former, loosely coordinated ministerial

---

[2] Witte, *op. cit.*, vol. II, pp. 2–5.

apparatus. The chairman of the new council, the first "premier" in Russian history, was Witte.

The October Manifesto brought confusion to local authorities but did not serve to pacify the country any more than had the decrees of February 18. Only the more moderate liberal circles were ready to accept the manifesto as the fulfillment of their constitutional aspirations. The left, especially the SD's and SR's, were not satisfied in the least, while the right refused to accept concessions to the Revolution and demanded the restoration of autocracy.

Although the general strike in Petersburg and the accompanying railroad strike ended soon after the publication of the October Manifesto, disorder continued to spread in the country, including both revolutionary demonstrations and counterrevolutionary pogroms. The number of peasant riots, burnings, and lootings increased in the fall of 1905, and were not subdued by a manifesto of November 3 that appealed for an end to the violence, abolished redemption payments for allotment land, and promised to satisfy "the vital needs of the peasants."

Witte found himself in an exceedingly difficult position as premier, isolated from both left and right. Hoping to find support in liberal circles, he undertook negotiations with representatives of the Kadets concerning the entry of that party into the ministry, but this step failed when the Kadets declared that only a constituent assembly, elected on the "four-tail" principle, would satisfy them.

The threat of open revolution remained severe in November–December 1905. Disturbances in Poland, the Baltic area, the Caucasus, and Siberia increased. Naval mutinies occurred at Kronstadt near Petersburg, at Sevastopol on the Crimea, and on the cruiser *Ochakov*. On November 2, the Petersburg Soviet declared a general strike in protest against the imposition of martial law in Poland. On November 26, the chairman of the Soviet, Khrustalev-Nosar', was arrested, but the next day the Soviet elected the young L. D. Trotsky in his place and stated that it was "continuing to prepare for an armed uprising." On December 2, the Petersburg Soviet issued a Financial Manifesto, calling on the people to refuse to pay taxes, to withdraw their savings from the banks, and to demand that wages be paid only in gold. This attempt to disrupt the financial position of the regime failed, however, and on December 3, the leaders of the Petersburg Soviet were arrested. On December 6, an attempt at another general strike collapsed, except in Moscow; there it turned into an armed uprising by December 9 and was only suppressed nine days later, with the arrival of the Semenovsky Guards to replace less reliable troops of the local garrison. In late December and in January 1906, military expeditions suppressed open revolutionary activity in the borderlands and in Siberia, establishing comparative civil peace following about a year of violence. Nonetheless, individual acts of terrorism continued in considerable number.

Meanwhile, Witte had succeeded in enacting a series of important measures. On October 22, the constitution of Finland was restored. On November 24, new "temporary regulations" for the press abolished all censorship and subjected to legal action the power of the government to impose penalties on periodicals. While enacting these liberal measures, Witte sought to reassert the authority of the government. On December 2, a decree established prison sentences for strikes against "enterprises which are of public or state importance," and regulations of March 4, 1906, required new organizations to register their statutes with the authorities, who could reject the statutes of suspect organizations and could suspend organizations that deviated from their statutes. At the same time public gatherings were required to notify the police in advance.

The main legislative task of Witte, however, was the preparation of the *Code of Fundamental State Laws* which is described below. On the very day of its publication, April 23, Witte was dismissed as premier and replaced by I. L. Goremykin, an old and colorless bureaucrat. Similarly, most of the ministers selected by Witte were replaced, and P. A. Stolypin, the governor of Saratov province, took over the important Ministry of Internal Affairs. Although this ministerial upheaval was unexpected, nobody regretted the departure of Witte. A rather nervous man with an uncontrollable temper, he had been unable to work out a definite program or to reach an agreement with the tsar, with his ministerial colleagues, or with the politicians of the right or left.

Establishment of the
New Legislative System

The machinery of the new legislative system emerged in a series of acts, starting with the Manifesto of August 6, 1905, and culminating in the *Code of Fundamental Laws* of April 23, 1906.

The August plan (the "Bulygin Duma") envisaged merely a "legislative deliberative institution" and established property qualifications that excluded most of the urban populace from the elections. These limitations were revised before the election of the First Duma in March 1906, but most of the provisions of the August plan remained in force. The ministers remained responsible to the tsar only, although the Duma had the right to submit inquiries concerning the ministers' actions and could, by a two-thirds vote, inform the tsar of their dissatisfaction with a ministerial reply. Except for the franchise requirements applied to the large cities, the voting mechanism established in August also lasted through 1906. The essential point was that Duma deputies were elected by an electoral assembly in each province and in twenty-seven large cities (see chart). The provincial assemblies were elected by nonpeasant landowners, peasants (or Cossacks), and townsmen. Nonpeasant landowners who met a substantial property requirement (about 400 acres in central Russia) formed county assemblies, to which lesser landowners sent representatives; these assemblies chose a prescribed number of electors to the provincial assembly. The peasants voted in four stages; delegates elected by the village assembly were sent to the township assembly, which elected a county convention, which in turn sent delegates to the provincial assembly to join the representatives of the other groups in selecting the actual Duma deputies. One Duma deputy from each province was to be a peasant. Women, governors, vice-governors, soldiers, students, men under age twenty-five, and nomads were excluded from the franchise. The maximum term of the Duma was set as five years, but the tsar could dissolve the chamber and call for new elections whenever he wished.

The Manifesto of October 17 declared that the Duma should have more than consultative authority; its assent was to be necessary before any law could come into force. The October Manifesto also promised to enfranchise the classes (mainly urban) that had been excluded in the August plan. This was accomplished in a decree of December 11, 1905, which extended the franchise to virtually all male, adult urban residents. Factory and mining workers were now included in the franchise, but they were treated as a separate class, voting indirectly through three levels (compared to four levels for the peasants, two levels for the urban residents who were not factory workers, and two or three for the richer and poorer landowners). The factory workers met in their places of work and chose delegates to conventions, which in turn chose delegates to the provincial or urban electoral assemblies, which actually elected the Duma deputies. The October Manifesto also promised that the Duma would exercise "supervision" over the legality of the actions of appointed officials, but it turned out that this general provision did not subject the ministers to the Duma.

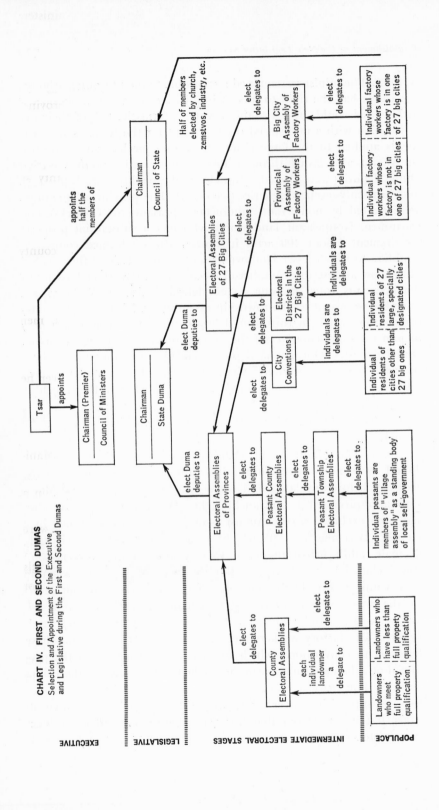

CHART IV. FIRST AND SECOND DUMAS
Selection and Appointment of the Executive
and Legislative during the First and Second Dumas

Tsar

appoints

Chairman (Premier)
Council of Ministers

appoints half the members of

Chairman
Council of State

Half of members elected by church, zemstvos, industry, etc.

elect delegates to

Big City Assembly of Factory Workers

elect delegates to

Individual factory workers whose factory is in one of 27 big cities

Individual factory workers whose factory is not in one of 27 big cities

elect delegates to

Provincial Assembly of Factory Workers

elect delegates to

Chairman
State Duma

elect Duma deputies to

Electoral Assemblies of 27 Big Cities

elect delegates to

Electoral Districts in the 27 Big Cities

individuals are delegates to

Individual residents of 27 large, specially designated cities

elect delegates to

City Conventions

individuals are delegates to

Individual residents of cities other than 27 big ones

elect Duma deputies to

Electoral Assemblies of Provinces

elect delegates to

Peasant County Electoral Assemblies

elect delegates to

Peasant Township Electoral Assemblies

elect delegates to

Individual peasants are members of "village assembly" as a standing body of local self-government

elect delegates to

County Electoral Assemblies

elect delegates to

each individual landowner a delegate to

Landowners who meet full property qualification

Landowners who have less than full property qualification

EXECUTIVE

LEGISLATIVE

INTERMEDIATE ELECTORAL STAGES

POPULACE

On February 20, 1906, a further manifesto and two accompanying decrees elaborated various matters of form and procedure in the new legislative system. The most striking new development in these documents was the unexpected and unpopular creation of a bicameral legislature. The Council of State, which had been a largely bureaucratic, consultative body since the time of Speransky, now became an upper chamber, half to be elected by privileged groups and half to be appointed by the tsar. The elected members were to represent the Church (6), the academic institutions (6), the provincial zemstvo assemblies (34), the provincial societies of the nobility (18), commercial and industrial associations (12), and assemblies of the landlords in provinces without zemstvos (22). This chamber, clearly designed to give weight to the conservative groups in society, was to have the same rights as the Duma, and its assent to all laws was required. The Manifesto of February 20 also attempted to secure the position of the government against legislative opposition by declaring that the Council of Ministers could enact temporary, emergency legislation when the Duma was not in session, a device subsequently embodied in the famous Article 87 of the *Code of Fundamental Laws*.

This Code, published on April 23, 1906, following the elections to the First Duma but preceding its convocation, summarized the preceding enactments regarding the legal position of the Council of State, the State Duma, and the Council of Ministers. But perhaps the most striking feature of the Code was its explicit and repeated emphasis on the power of the tsar and insistence on recognition of "the existence of the supreme autocratic power"—in the words of the heading of the second chapter of the *Code*. Although the tsar "exercises legislative authority in union with the Council of State and the State Duma," the tsar alone had the initiative in legislation affecting the *fundamental laws,* and "without his approval no law may take force." However, the old definition of tsarist power as "unlimited" was excluded from the new laws.

Political Parties

Before the Revolution of 1905 all political parties were illegal in the Russian Empire, but by the end of that year their existence as a natural part of the new legislative system was implicitly accepted by the state, even though they were not specifically sanctioned in the new laws. What was the character of the emergent party politics of Russia and what were the objectives of the various parties?[3]

---

[3] The programs of the various political parties can be found in *Polnyi sbornik*

To the left of all of the parties (and of common sense)
stood the anarchists, who in 1905–1906 enjoyed some measure of popularity in Poland, Moscow, and such southern cities as Odessa and
Ekaterinoslav. They printed leaflets bearing such titles as *The Black
Flag (Chernoe Znamia), The Mutineer (Buntar'),* and *The Stormy
Petrel (Burevestnik);* they preached the complete liberation of the individual from all forms of government authority and advocated either
a loose federation of voluntary workers' association ("the communist
anarchists") or no public organization at all ("the individualist
anarchists").

In practice, the anarchists carried out "expropriations"
(simply robbery) and engaged in terrorism, not only directed against
the police and other state officials, but also "economic" terrorism,
directed against factory owners and officials, and "unmotivated" or
irrational terrorism as well. The plans for political reform that were
so abundant in Russia in 1905 did not interest them in the least, for
the anarchists were as hostile toward representative institutions as
they were toward the tsarist autocracy. In the summer of 1905 when
everyone was talking about the future organization of representative
government, one anarchist proclamation ended with the words,
"Blessed be he who throws a bomb into the *Zemskii sobor* [represent-
ative body] on the first day of its meeting!"

It should be added, however, that these activities of the
Russian anarchists had little in common with the theoretical anarchism of Prince Kropotkin or Count Tolstoy, whose writings the majority
of the anarchists probably never read. Kropotkin was an outstanding
scientist and a tireless prophet of "the idea of mutual assistance" and
high moral values, while Tolstoy preached that evil should not be
resisted by force.

The Russian Social Democratic Workers' party entered the
revolutionary period of 1905–1906 in a state of fragmentation. In addition to the two main factions, the Bolsheviks and Mensheviks,
there were several newly organized national Social Democratic parties,
such as the "Bund" (or All-Jewish Workers' Union) and the Polish,
Lithuanian, Latvian, Ukrainian, and Armenian Social Democratic

---

platform . . . , op. cit. A detailed but somewhat one-sided description of their
political activities in the years 1905–1907 can be found in L. Martov, P. Maslov,
and A. Potresov, *Obshchestvennoe dvizhenie v Rossii v nachale XX veka* [*The Movement of Public Opinion in Russia at the Beginning of the Twentieth Century*],
5 vols. (St. Petersburg, 1909–1914).

parties. The Mensheviks of Georgia were remarkably popular, and such Georgian Menshevik leaders as Zhordania, Ramishvili, Tseretelli, and Chkheidze became leading figures among the Social Democratic Duma deputies.

There was continual factional struggle between the Bolsheviks and the Mensheviks; although the two factions both stood on the theoretical basis of orthodox Marxism and had a common program, they disagreed widely on the question of tactics. At the head of the Bolshevik faction stood Lenin, whose rule was unchallenged there, while the leaders of the Mensheviks were Y. Martov, F. Dan, P. Axelrod, A. Martynov, and A. Potresov. The founder and the chief theoretician of Russian Marxism, Plekhanov, did not belong to any of the factions, but on most questions of tactics he was close to the Mensheviks. The young Marxist leader Trotsky also stood outside party factions; in the realm of theory he proposed the conception of "permanent revolution," by which Russia could pass into the dictatorship of the proletariat without enduring an era of capitalism, while in practice he served briefly as the chairman of the Petersburg Soviet.

In 1905 Plekhanov and the Mensheviks held that the Russian Revolution was "bourgeois" and must end with the transformation of the "regime of feudalism" into a "bourgeois-democratic" system. They therefore recognized both the possibility and acceptability of agreement with the liberal bourgeoisie, to the extent that it struggled against the old regime. Lenin, on the other hand, decisively rejected the idea of cooperation with the liberal bourgeoisie, from which he always expected "betrayal" and "treachery." According to Lenin, the proletariat had to be "the leader of the peoples' revolution" and not "an accomplice of the bourgeoisie," not a "wretched hanger-on of the bourgeois classes." The proletariat, he said, needed an ally, the peasantry, which social democracy would attract by supporting the peasant demand for the confiscation of all landlords' lands. For Lenin the main slogan and the basic aim of the revolution was "the revolutionary and democratic dictatorship of the proletariat and the peasantry." After victory, said Lenin, the proletariat, both the urban and the rural, would immediately have to start a struggle against "the bourgeoisie in general and against the bourgeois peasantry in particular." As early as 1905 Lenin regarded the Russian Revolution as a prologue to a European social revolution.

In accordance with their general views on party tactics the Bolsheviks and the Mensheviks were basically divided on their attitude toward the State Duma. The Mensheviks declared themselves for the participation of the Social Democrats in the Duma and the support of the Duma in its struggle with the government. Lenin's attitude toward the Duma was at first sharply negative, and he preached the tactic of "active boycott" of the Duma. A Bolshevik resolution of September 1905 determined "to call all the truly democratic elements of the public to an active boycott of the Duma, holding in contempt those who would participate in the elections, as traitors of the cause of national freedom." It was decided "to time a general political strike, as well as manifestations and demonstrations on the election day and to use all means to see that the elections should not take place, not hesitating to forcibly disrupt electoral meetings if necessary."[4] In a leaflet issued in January 1906, Lenin shouted: "Down with the Duma, down with the new police fraud! Citizens! Pay homage to the fallen heroes of Moscow by a new preparation for an armed uprising!"

The split in the Social Democratic party and the severe internecine war between the two factions were undoubtedly damaging to its practical success, and therefore at the beginning of 1906 the Central Committee of the Bolsheviks and the Organizational Committee of the Mensheviks agreed to call a "unity congress," which took place in Stockholm in April 1906. The congress succeeded in achieving formal unification of the party, in electing a joint Central Committee and in obtaining the adherence to the Russian SD party of the "Bund" and the Polish and Latvian Social Democratic parties. The majority of delegates to the congress and the majority of the newly elected Central Committee proved to be Menshevik. The congress accepted Maslov's agrarian program—of "municipalization" of land—as well as a decision on the participation of the Social Democrats in the elections to the State Duma. Lenin came to the congress with draft resolutions on "partisan combat action" of SD squads to "destroy the state police and military apparatus" and also "to capture financial means which belong to the enemy [the autocratic government], and to transfer these means for the needs of the uprising."[5] The resolution had no chance of passing and was withdrawn by its authors. This did not prevent Stalin, a faithful Leninist, from directing armed "expropriations" from the State Bank in Tiflis not long after the Stockholm congress.

The SD's did badly in the elections to the short-lived First Duma of 1906, but in the 1907 elections to the Second Duma they

---

[4] V. I. Lenin, *Sochineniia* [*Works*] (2d ed.; Moscow, 1929), vol. VIII, appendices pp. 459, 506.

[5] *Ibid.*, vol. IX, p. 43.

were more successful and elected more than fifty of their representatives, and fifteen "sympathizers." In May 1907, the fifth congress of
the party took place in London. The 180 delegates from the Great
Russian organizations of the party were almost evenly divided—91
Bolsheviks; 89 Mensheviks—and the two factions did not succeed
in reaching agreement on a joint appraisal of the current situation.
Sharp quarrels and factional struggles continued after the Stockholm
and London congresses as before; "unification" proved to be purely
formal. During the years of "reaction," 1908–1910, many SD party
organizations crumbled. Among the Mensheviks there emerged the
so-called "liquidators," who recognized the fact of the collapse of the
illegal party organization and who therefore found it expedient to
transfer the center of gravity of the Social Democrats to the trade
unions and to cultural and educational societies. Among the Bolsheviks
there was a trend toward the boycott of the State Duma and the recall from the Duma of the representatives of the party (the so-called
"recallists"). But Lenin by then had decided to use the Duma for the
purposes of propaganda and from abroad directed the activity of
the Bolshevik faction in the Duma. He prepared speeches for the
Bolshevik representatives and especially for their floor leader, Malinov-
sky, who, it later appeared, was actually a paid police agent. At the
beginning of 1912 the followers of Lenin were formally organized as
a separate party, the Russian Social Democratic Workers' party
(Bolsheviks).

The Party of Socialist Revolutionaries broadened its activity
in the revolutionary years and acquired great popularity among the
intelligentsia of mixed social origin, zemstvo employees, peasants, and
to a considerable degree among the workers. In the elections to the
second State Duma in Petersburg almost half the workers voted for
the SR party.

At the end of 1905 a congress of the party met in Finland;
the congress confirmed the party program, accepted an organizational
statute, chose the central organs of the party, and decided to boycott
the elections to the First Duma. The party continued to combine its
campaign of terrorism against state officials with extensive propaganda
among the peasants. This duality of violent and peaceful tactics was
manifest in disagreements within the party, and in 1906 a Union of
Socialist Revolutionaries Maximalists was established, representing
those who favored increased violence and all-out socialization of
wealth. It was, however, short-lived, and the SR party continued to
include both terrorists and propagandists.

The SR leader and chief theoretician of revolutionary populism was Chernov (alias Gardenin, alias Tuchkin), while G. Gershuni directed the combat organizations until his arrest in 1903. He was replaced by one Azef, a remarkable police agent who for six years organized successful assassinations of government officials and simultaneously delivered his fellow-terrorists into the hands of the police. When he was unmasked in 1909, he disappeared into hiding. Other major figures in the SR party were Ekaterina Breshko-Breshkovskaia ("the grandmother of the Russian Revolution"), M. Natanson, B. Savinkov (a courageous terrorist and gifted novelist), O. Minor, M. and A. Gotz, N. Avksentev, V. Zenzinov, and I. Bunakov-Fundaminsky.

Before the Revolution of 1905 the SR's had established peasant "brotherhoods" and "unions," and when the All-Russian Peasant Union was founded in 1905, they were able to exert a strong ideological influence over it, even though it was not formally affiliated to any party. One hundred peasant delegates representing twenty-two provinces attended the founding congress of this union in Moscow in July–August 1905. The resolutions adopted favored the transfer of all land to the common possession of the people, and its use by those who tilled it, and a democratically elected constituent assembly. During the First Duma of 1906 the Peasant Union conducted an extensive campaign urging peasants to send the Duma petitions demanding "land and freedom," but this came to naught and with the waning of revolutionary spirit the union declined into insignificance.

To the right of the SR's a People's Socialist party was established in 1906. At first it was primarily a group of writers, publicists, and scholars, closely connected with the populist magazine *Russian Wealth (Russkoe Bogatstvo)*, published by V. A. Miakotin, A. V. Peshekhonov, N. F. Anensky, S. P. Melgunov, and others. The new party declared itself to be "the party of all the toilers and not just of one group of them," that its slogan was "All for the people and by the people," that the party set "before itself the ideal of socialism," and that in the field of politics its program was "the rule of the people in its fullest and complete form." Taking into consideration, however, the political changes that were taking place in Russia, the party renounced the tactics of armed uprising and individual political terrorism. The agrarian program of the People's Socialist party demanded the "nationalization of land," with the provision that the land assigned to agriculture should be used only by those who tilled it themselves.

Close to the People's Socialist party in theory stood the *Trudovaia Gruppa* (Labor Group or Trudoviks), which emerged in the State Duma. But this group was only a parliamentary faction and did not have any organizations outside of the State Duma. Its main goal was the satisfaction of the peasants' need for land, as called for by the populist program, and its membership included a number of diversified elements, whose views could not be sharply defined.

Among the nonsocialist parties the most important during the Duma period was the Constitutional Democratic party *(Konstitutsionnodemokraticheskaia* or, in abbreviation, "KD," pronounced and written "Kadet), which was also called the Party of People's Freedom *(Partiia Narodnoi Svobody).* This party was formed by the merger of the Union of Liberation and the Zemstvo Constitutionalist group at a congress held in October 1905 at the height of the general strike. The question of the future form of government—republican or constitutional-monarchical—aroused differences of opinion, and the party program could only make the vague declaration that the constitutional structure of the Russian state should be "determined by fundamental law." Only in January 1906, following the December uprising of 1905, did the second congress of the Kadets accept the principle that "Russia must be a constitutional and parliamentary monarchy." The Kadet program included the usual democratic goal of "four-tail" suffrage, but it did not take a stand on two issues: the immediate introduction of female suffrage and the desirability of a bicameral legislature. The Kadets demanded free cultural self-determination for the non-Russian nationalities of the empire and "autonomy with a representative assembly" for Poland.

Two groups of intellectuals left the founding congress of the Kadets and formed splinter organizations. Supporters of so-called "critical socialism" (contrasted with the "dogmatic socialism" of the SD's and SR's) went to the left, including S. Prokopovich, E. Kuskova, and V. Bogucharsky. Others, including the editor and publisher of the *Herald of Europe,* M. Stasiulevich, and Professors V. Kuzmin-Karavaev and M. Kovalevsky, split off to the right and established the small Party of Democratic Reform.

However, the remaining liberals, led by P. N. Miliukov and including a host of notable intellectuals, such as P. B. Struve, F. I. Rodichev, I. I. Petrunkevich, F. F. Kokoshkin, A. I. Shingarev,

M. M. Vinaver, V. A. Maklakov, the brothers Dolgorukov, V. D. Nabokov and A. A. Kizevetter, were sufficiently strong to form a widespread and influential party in the short time between the congress of
October 1905 and the Duma elections of March 1906. In this first
Duma election the Kadets enjoyed considerable success among the
middle and lower-middle classes in the cities and returned the largest
single delegation of any party in the Duma. This success, however, was
the high point in their popularity; in the Second and Third Dumas
the radicalism of the parties of the left and the tactics of the government both worked to reduce the popular strength of the Kadets.

The Union of the 17th of October or Octobrist party
was established in late October and November 1905, basing its strength
on the moderate nobility and the commercial and industrial leaders,
including the Progressive Economic party and the Commercial-Indus-
trial Union, which had been formed shortly before. The principal
leader of the Octobrists was A. I. Guchkov, a colorful figure whose
grandfather had been a serf and whose father was a successful business-
man. The party included a number of Moscow business leaders, such
as S. M. Chetverikov, G. A. Krestovnikov, P. P. Riabushinsky, as
well as some of the outstanding zemstvo figures, such as D. N. Shipov,
M. A. Stakhovich, and V. D. Rodzianko.

The Octobrist program called for constitutional monarchy,
based on universal suffrage and civil liberty. On the agrarian question
they favored a number of measures for the improvement of the peasants' situation, approving the confiscation of landlords' land only
when other means had failed, and then only with just compensation.
They demanded "the preservation of the Russian state, one and un-
divided" but were willing to make allowances for linguistic and cultural differences among the nationalities.

After the electoral law was revised in 1907 to favor the
wealthier classes, the Octobrists elected almost 150 deputies to the
Third Duma of 1907–1912 and became the leading force in the
chamber. In this period some of the more progressive elements among
the Octobrists departed and formed the Party of Peaceful Reform,
which stood midway between the Octobrists and the Kadets. This
group included some of the most outstanding members of the original
Octobrist party, such as Shipov. Later the Party of Peaceful Reform
distintegrated and its former members, along with the right-wing
splinter group of the Kadets, the Party of Democratic Reform, and
some other deputies to the Third and Fourth Dumas, formed the

"Progressivist" Duma faction, which in 1915 joined the Progressive Bloc with the Kadets and Octobrists.

Immediately to the right of the Octobrists in the Duma were comparatively small factions that lacked formal organization as parties, the Nationalists and the Moderate Rightists. Further to the right came the genuinely reactionary parties, which refused to recognize the legality of the Duma and demanded the restoration of the tsarist autocracy, "as it was in the good old days." One of these was the Russian Monarchist Party, founded in the autumn of 1905 and headed by V. A. Gringmut, the publisher of the *Moscow Gazette*. Still more important was the Union of the Russian People, led by A. I. Dubrovin, V. M. Purishkevich, and N. E. Markov, which soon became a large and active organization that included most of the rightist political groups. The program of the Union of the Russian People held that the welfare of the homeland lay in the preservation of "Orthodoxy, unlimited Russian autocracy, and nationality," the trinity of Nicholas I. The program also asserted that the "Russian nationality is the dominant one . . . the Duma, avoiding any efforts to limit the supreme power of the tsar, must be Russian in nationality. It is obliged to help the law-giver to realize urgent reforms by informing him truthfully of the real needs of the people and of the state." The propaganda of the rightist parties combined ultranationalism and anti-Semitism; the organ of the Union of Russian People, *The Russian Banner (Russkoe Znamia)*, published by Dubrovin, specialized in the hounding of the "Jew-Kadets" and the "Jew-Masons."

From late 1905 through 1906 the Union enjoyed its greatest activity, opening over a hundred sections throughout Russia. It carried on vigorous propaganda by word of mouth and through the press in the cities and the rural districts of the western regions. It organized "tea rooms" for the common folk of the cities, serving them rightist propaganda along with their tea. Finally, it organized "combat teams," which participated in pogroms against Jews and intellectuals or practiced individual terrorism, including the assassination of two Jewish Kadet deputies to the First Duma, Gertsenstein and Iollos, and the Trudovik Karavaev. An attempt on the life of Witte was prepared but failed. During the First and Second Dumas the rightists showered the government with telegrams demanding the dissolution of the "seditious and rebellious gathering," which was "attempting to destroy the Russian Empire."

In 1906 the rightists included only the reactionary elements among the landlords, the state officials, and the clergy, along with a small section of the urban lower classes. But in their pronouncements they spoke in the name of all the Russian people, maintaining that their adversaries were merely a handful of "seditionists" and "aliens." Their constant assurances of the unlimited devotion of all the people toward the "adored monarch" gave the tsar an illusion of popular support, concealing the true situation from him and paving the way for bitter disillusionment in 1917.

The extreme rightists even disliked the antirevolutionary premier of 1906–1911 because he did not wish to return to the autocracy of the nineteenth century. But a section of rightists, led by the hot-tempered Purishkevich, accepted the Duma after its electoral basis had been narrowed in 1907 and was ready to cooperate with Stolypin. Purishkevich withdrew from the Union of the Russian People and established the so-called "Chamber of the Archangel Michael." On the other hand, led by Dubrovin, the hard core of the reactionaries, remaining in opposition to the government, began to dwindle in strength in 1907–1908.

A less noisy but influential form of conservatism, outside of party politics, appeared in May 1906, when representatives of the nobility gathered in Petersburg and formed the Council of the United Nobility, which acted as a kind of lobby, striving to influence the government in the interests of the landowning nobility.

In summary, the emerging system of political parties in Russia was characterized by extreme diversity and, consequently, by a tendency to fragmentation. Including the major parties, splinter parties, and Duma groups that lacked local organizations, there were at least fifteen significant political factions, ranging from the anarchists to the Union of the Russian People. Although Russia was not unique in having a multiparty system in which no one party could hope to gain a majority at the polls, it was inevitable that the disunity in the political life of Russia would handicap the experiment in constitutional monarchy.

The First State Duma

The elections to the State Duma, which were held in March 1906, brought complete victory for the parties of the opposition. Although the designation of the party affiliation of Duma deputies can only be approximate because of continual regrouping, it is roughly true that the First Duma included about 170 Kadets, 100 Trudoviks, 15 Social Democrats, over 50 deputies from the nationalities of the borderlands, 40 members of the Party of Peaceful

Reform or similar groups, 30 moderate rightists, and 100 independents. In other words, of the 513 deputies in the Duma, at least 285, or over 55 percent, were clearly opposed to the government.

On April 27, 1906, the Duma was solemnly opened with a speech of welcome by the emperor in the Winter Palace. The minister of finance of that time, Kokovtsev, recounts in his memoirs that during the first encounter with the people's representatives, the imperial court was bewildered and shocked by the open defiance shown by the members of the Duma.

> A majority of the representatives were dressed in working clothes, many of them as if on purpose, demonstratively occupying the first rows, closer to the throne. . . . In the forefront . . . especially noticeable, was the figure of a tall man in a working shirt and high black boots with an ironic and defiant expression who stared at the throne and at the people around. . . .[6]

A Kadet, Professor S. A. Muromtsev, was elected chairman of the Duma and tried to conduct the meetings of the Duma in a solemn and dignified manner, but he did not always succeed. Immediately after his election, Muromtsev gave the floor, out of turn, to I. I. Petrunkevich, who gave a short but fiery speech demanding an immediate amnesty for those banished and imprisoned on political grounds. In reply to the tsar's speech from the throne, the Duma put forward a series of demands: the appointment of a ministry responsible to the Duma; the abolition of the extraordinary security laws; the abolition of the Council of State (as a "barrier" between the monarch and the people); complete abolition of capital punishment; the satisfaction of the peasants' need for land through the compulsory alienation of privately owned lands; immediate and full amnesty for those convicted for political offenses; and a series of reforms in various fields of government activity.

On May 13, the chairman of the Council of Ministers, Goremykin, read to the Duma a government statement that included a reply to the demands of the Duma. The government promised to "regard with special attention" the development of proposals for needed reforms, but it rejected all the radical demands of the Duma. Specifically, it stressed that "the solution of the agrarian question on the basis proposed by the State Duma is absolutely inadmissable," because "the inalienability and inviolability of property . . . is the fundamental basis of the existence of the state throughout the world."

---

[6] Count V. N. Kokovtsov, *Iz moego proshlago: Vospominaniia* [*Out of My Past: Memoirs*] (Paris, 1933), vol. I, p. 173.

The declaration of the government caused deep disappointment among the members of the Duma, and the more excitable were greatly annoyed and indignant. In a series of vehement speeches the government was sharply criticized and its immediate dismissal demanded. The Kadet Nabokov finished his speech with the famous exclamation: "Let the executive authority submit to the legislative!"

In reply to the declaration of the government the Duma took up its agenda with the resolution: "Recognizing as a necessary condition for the pacification of the state and for the fruitful work of the popular representative assembly the immediate dismissal of the present ministry and its replacement by a ministry which has the confidence of the State Duma, the State Duma turns to its current agenda." [7]

Henceforth, there was uninterrupted conflict between the Duma and the government. Relations grew worse at the beginning of June when a pogrom against the Jews took place in Belostok and the commission dispatched by the Duma to investigate the affair reported the connivance of the local authorities during the pogrom and their direct incitement of it. The Duma showered the government with interpellations regarding the illegal actions of the administration (over 300 inquiries in 70 days), and when the ministers appeared on the rostrum in order to reply, they were usually greeted with loud and prolonged shouts of "Get out!" "Down with him!" "Pogromist!" "Resign!"

The complete divergence of the Duma and the government on the agrarian question became more acute as the discussion on this issue progressed. Two proposals for agrarian reform were introduced in the Duma, one bill by 42 Kadets and another by 104 Trudoviks. Both recommended compulsory expropriation of privately owned lands, but the Trudoviks' bill was much more radical. It contained the usual demands of revolutionary populism that "all the land must belong to the people" and must be granted for use only to those who will till it with their own labor," and that all citizens, including women, should have an equal right to use it. A. S. Stishinsky, the head of the department of agriculture, tried in vain to show with statistical data that the privately owned lands which could be redistributed among the citizens amounted to 94,500,000 acres, or at most 108,000,000 acres with the addition of other categories. Thus, with a general land redistribution the average allotment per each peasant

---

[7] *Stenograficheskie otchety* [*Records of Proceedings*] of the First State Duma, May 13, 1906, p. 353.

male soul would amount to no more than 2.7 acres in addition to the present 8.1 acres, a rather insignificant addition that would cause a considerable loss to the national economy as the result of the breaking up of large-scale farms.

Relations between the government and the Duma became increasingly strained; the speeches of the opposition, which were printed and distributed in the country, became increasingly sharp, and at the same time the revolutionary movement revived again, especially the agrarian unrest, which was accompanied in many places by "illuminations," as one speaker in the Duma called the burning of the landlords' estates.

The government was perplexed and disturbed by the conduct of the Duma and the peasants; only the inert Goremykin preserved undisturbed tranquillity. General Trepov advised the tsar to appoint a Kadet ministry, but after consulting his ministers, the tsar gave up this idea. The minister of internal affairs, Stolypin, negotiated with some of the progressive public leaders concerning their entry into a coalition cabinet, but these negotiations also came to nothing. On June 20, 1906, the government issued a public announcement rejecting the principle of compulsory expropriation of privately owned lands. In turn, the Duma decided to reply with a declaration that it would not withdraw the principle of compulsory alienation and would "reject all suggestions not in accord with this principle." The government regarded this as "a completely illegal action," because, by law, the Duma had no right of direct appeal to the people. On July 8, an imperial manifesto announced the dissolution of the State Duma and the calling of new elections. Close to 180 members adjourned to Vyborg in Finland and issued a manifesto to the people, calling upon them to cease payment of taxes and to evade military service. The left-wing parties appealed to the people to seize full liberty and all the land through revolution. But neither the Vyborg Manifesto, nor the revolutionary proclamations met with wide, popular response.

Stolypin and the Second Duma

After the fiasco of the First Duma, the elderly bureaucrat Goremykin was dismissed as premier; his successor was Stolypin, the minister of internal affairs, who continued to hold that portfolio. Comparatively young—only forty-four—energetic, determined, courageous, patriotic, and eloquent, Stolypin was a newcomer to the upper echelons of Petersburg society and never did become an insider there.

He supported the development of a "renovated order" *(obnovlennyi stroi)* and cooperation with the Duma, but he established as his main task the completion of the peasant reform of 1861: the granting of true personal freedom and the right of private landownership to the peasants. It is true that Stolypin's political practice was not always irreproachable. He understood *raison d'état* too broadly and in the name of the state often violated the law and individual rights, but he sincerely believed that he had to use extraordinary measures to defend the state against revolutionary attack; and it must be remembered that revolutionary terror was still high in 1906–1907.

The formula "pacification first—reforms later" has been erroneously ascribed to Stolypin. In fact, he combined vigorous struggle against revolution with a program of vital reforms. To this end he attempted to include a few progressive public figures in his cabinet, but he was unsuccessful because no "liberal" politicians were ready to participate in a "reactionary" government. Soon after the dissolution of the First Duma, naval mutinies occurred in Sveaborg, Kronstadt, and on the cruiser *Pamiat' Azova,* and there was an attempt to carry out a general strike in Moscow. In Poland, on August 2, there was a massive and prearranged attack on Russian soldiers and police, killing twenty-eight and wounding eighteen in Warsaw alone. On August 12, a tremendous explosion occurred in Stolypin's summer home, killing over thirty persons and wounding an equal number, including Stolypin's three-year-old son and twelve-year-old daughter.

Kokovtsov, the minister of finance, recalls in his memoirs that official circles were amazed by Stolypin's steadiness throughout this crisis, which greatly raised his prestige in official circles. Previously he had been regarded with condescension, as a "novice who had been placed at the top of the ladder by chance," but he now acquired great moral authority, based on his undoubted courage and self-sacrifice in the interest of the country.[8]

On August 13, 1906, General Min, who had led the Semenovsky Regiment in the suppression of the Moscow uprising in December 1905, was killed by an SR woman terrorist. Attempts upon the lives of minor government officials became almost an everyday occurrence, and "expropriations" (in fact, armed robberies) were widely practiced.

The government then took an extraordinary measure in order to fight the revolutionary terror and the violence of the "expropriators." On August 19, under the authority of Article 87 of the

---

[8] Kokovtsov, *op. cit.,* p. 231.

Fundamental Laws, which gave the government the right of emergency legislation, a law was passed establishing field court martials, consisting only of officers, who were to examine cases within a day or two and render verdicts that were to be executed immediately. This law was not submitted to the Second Duma, and in the spring of 1907 it expired, but in the meantime 683 persons had been sentenced to death. On the other hand, the victims of the revolutionary terror in 1906 totalled 768 killed and 820 wounded among the administrative representatives of the state, ranging from the chief military prosecutor and several governors down to ordinary policemen.

On August 25, the government published a program of reforms that it planned to submit to the Duma; and without waiting for the opening of the Second Duma, Stolypin passed several important measures included in this program, under the authority of Article 87 of the Fundamental Laws. Of these measures the most important were concerned with the peasant question (see below), but there was also a regulation of November 15 that forbade commercial and artisan labor on holidays and limited the working day to twelve hours. In December, he also attempted to mitigate the legal restrictions on the Jews, but although the Council of Ministers approved his plan, the tsar, who was personally anti-Jewish, vetoed it. (In 1909, however, Stolypin did succeed in expanding the quotas for Jewish students in secondary schools.)

Of course, the *Code of Fundamental Laws* required that all laws be passed by the Duma if they were to become permanent, and therefore Stolypin's program of reform depended on the new Duma elections, which were scheduled for January 1907. Unfortunately for Stolypin and his program, the voters did not return a large proportion of cooperative deputies. On the contrary, both the right and left wings increased in strength, and the Duma became the scene of severe squabbling, sometimes reaching such scandalous proportions that the Kadet chairman of the Duma, F. A. Golovin, was obliged to adjourn the session. This state of affairs was hardly suited to serious legislative work.

According to the data compiled by the Duma chancery, the composition of the Second Duma was as follows:

Social Democrats (and "sympathizers")	65
Socialist Revolutionaries	37
People's Socialists	16
Trudoviks	104
	Subtotal for the left 222
Kadets	98

Polish "Kolo" (circle)........................ 46
Muslim faction 30
Cossack faction............................. 17
                                    Subtotal for the center.. 191
Octobrists, Moderate-Rightists and Rightists.... 54
Unaffiliated 50

When the Duma opened on February 20, 1907, Stolypin at once set to work to obtain approval for his legislative program. Although one could hardly expect cooperation between tsarist ministers and Social Democrats or Socialist Revolutionaries, there were some signs of compromise. The Kadets and Trudoviks wanted to defend the Duma against an alleged conspiracy of the Black Hundreds and even the SR's declared that terrorism against the government would cease during the term of the Duma, assuring Stolypin that at least he would not be shot by one of the legislators.

On March 6, the premier delivered his major programmatic address, defending the emergency measures enacted between the First and Second Dumas and outlining his new proposals. These included: (1) granting the peasants full legal equality with the other social classes; (2) reforming peasant landownership through the replacement of communal tenure with private ownership; (3) reforming local government; (4) transferring local judicial authority to elected justices of the peace; (5) legalizing trade unions and economic strikes; (6) introducing accident, medical, and old-age insurance; (7) reducing the working day; (8) introducing free (later compulsory) elementary education for all; and (9) redistributing taxation through the introduction of an income tax.

The Second Duma responded to this program with a general discussion of state policy, which was marked by severe criticism from the left. Following these attacks, Stolypin could not restrain himself and replied in a short but impressive address, which concluded with the following words:

> These attacks are designed to engender in the government, in the authorities, a paralysis of will and mind. They can be summarized in two words addressed to the government: 'hands up!' To these two words, gentlemen, the government replies with complete tranquility and awareness of its rightness in these two words: 'not frightened.' [9]

When the debate had concluded, the Duma resolved merely to pass on to its current agenda, "having heard the declaration of the

---

[9] *Stenograficheskie otchety* of the Second State Duma, vol. I, p. 169.

Chairman of the Council of Ministers concerning the draft bills that have been submitted. . . ." This situation of "neither war nor peace" between Duma and government was precarious indeed, and when the government introduced the state budget for the current year, three socialist delegations proposed to reject it without discussion. The Kadets and rightists succeeded in having the budget referred to the finance committee of the Duma for consideration only after four days of debate. When the government introduced a bill authorizing the conscription of recruits for the current year, the left again opposed the government, and the bill passed only because the Polish Kolo agreed to vote for it while many of the Trudoviks abstained.

On May 15, the Duma rejected—215 to 146—a rightist resolution condemning revolutionary terror, a display of hostility which indicated to Stolypin that the Second Duma would reject his central project of peasant reform. Moreover, he had no reason to expect that a Third Duma, if elected on the same basis as the First and Second, would be more cooperative. Although he had no desire to end the Duma as an institution, Stolypin became convinced that it was necessary to change the electoral law if any major reforms were to be achieved. He therefore determined to dissolve the Second Duma and change the electoral system by extralegal means, and the tsar, who was unhappy with the existing Duma, encouraged him to do so.

The pretext for the dissolution of the Duma was alleged revolutionary activity outside the Duma by the Social Democratic deputies. A woman police agent, Shornikova, was planted in the SD organization and drew up incriminating documents that linked Social Democratic Duma deputies to plans for armed uprising. A police search "uncovered" these documents, and the government demanded the arrest of sixteen Duma deputies and the removal of thirty-nine others. The Duma responded by electing a commission of twenty-two to investigate the charges and to report in two days, but on June 3, before their report was ready, an imperial decree dissolved the Second Duma. Later the majority of the SD Duma deputies were arrested, tried, and sentenced to hard labor or settlement in Siberia for four to five years. Although the evidence used in the case was largely fabricated, it remains true that the SD's and SR's were in fact forming clandestine "military organizations" among the soldiers with the objective of armed uprising.

The dissolution of the Second Duma was published simultaneously with new "Regulations on the Elections to the State Duma," which substantially changed the former electoral law without the consent of the Duma. This action was contrary to the *Code of Funda-*

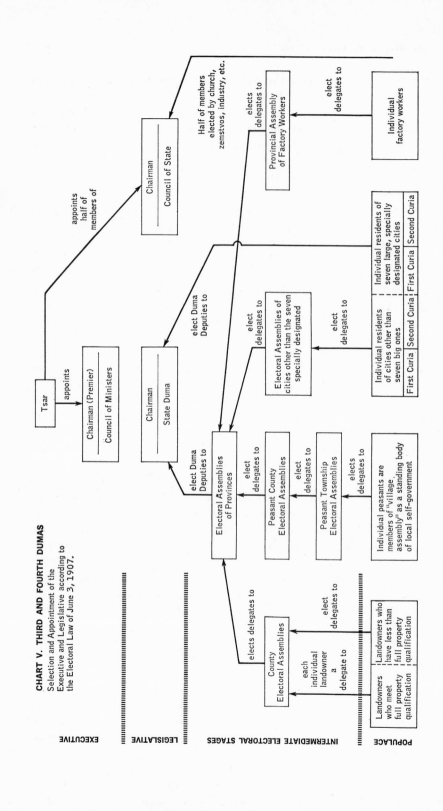

CHART V. THIRD AND FOURTH DUMAS

Selection and Appointment of the
Executive and Legislative according to
the Electoral Law of June 3, 1907.

EXECUTIVE

Tsar

appoints half of members of

appoints

Chairman (Premier)
Council of Ministers

Chairman
Council of State

Half of members
elected by church,
zemstvos, industry, etc.

LEGISLATIVE

Chairman
State Duma

elect Duma
Deputies to

elects delegates to

Provincial Assembly
of Factory Workers

elects
delegates to

Individual
factory workers

elect
delegates to

INTERMEDIATE ELECTORAL STAGES

elect Duma
Deputies to

Electoral Assemblies
of Provinces

elect
delegates to

Electoral Assemblies of
cities other than the seven
specially designated

elect
delegates to

First Curia	Second Curia		First Curia	Second Curia
Individual residents of cities other than seven big ones			Individual residents of seven large, specially designated cities	

elect
delegates to

Peasant County
Electoral Assemblies

elects
delegates to

Peasant Township
Electoral Assemblies

elects
delegates to

Individual peasants are
members of "village
assembly" as a standing body
of local self-government

elects delegates to

County
Electoral Assemblies

elect
delegates to

each
individual
landowner
a
delegate to

POPULACE

Landowners
who meet
full property
qualification

Landowners who
have less than
full property
qualification

mental Laws, and the act of June 3, 1907, was therefore regarded as a *coup d'état*.

According to the new electoral law (see chart) the representation of the borderlands was greatly reduced. In place of 36 deputies, Poland was to send 14, 2 of whom had to be elected by Russian inhabitants of Poland. The Caucasus was reduced from 29 to 10 deputies, and Central Asia was completely deprived of representation in the Duma. Of a total of 442 deputies, European Russia now was to send 403, while Asiatic Russia was to send only 15. In European Russia the proportional weight of the landowners was made predominant in the provincial electoral assemblies, which elected the actual Duma deputies. All told, the landowners elected 51 percent of the provincial electors (instead of the former 32 percent), while the peasants elected 22.5 percent (instead of 42 percent). The urban *curia* (electoral grouping) continued to elect 24.5 percent of the provincial electors, but within this *curia* the new regulations were still more favorable to the wealthy. Previously the city dwellers who met a comparatively modest property qualification voted equally, but under the law of June 1907, they were divided into two *curiae*. The first urban *curia* included only the small minority that could meet a high property qualification, but it elected over half the electors from the cities. The second urban *curia* was also defined by restrictive, but less exclusive, qualifications. The number of electors in the provincial electoral assemblies chosen by the factory workers was reduced in most provinces, declining from 3 percent before June 1907 to 2 percent thereafter. The new regulations provided that each provincial electoral assembly had to choose one Duma deputy from among the landowners, one from among the urban dwellers, and one from among the peasantry (and in the six most industrialized provinces, one from among the factory workers), while the rest of the Duma deputies from the province might be drawn from any *curia*.

Departures from this system were prescribed for certain localities, and eligible urban dwellers in the five largest cities (Petersburg, Moscow, Kiev, Odessa, and Riga) voted directly for Duma deputies, although these voters were also divided into two *curiae* according to wealth. A somewhat similar procedure also applied in Warsaw and Lodz.*

---

* For purposes of comparison, it may be noted that in the earlier electoral system there had been separate assemblies to elect Duma deputies from the provinces *and* from 27 large cities. Under the plan of 1907 there were only provincial electoral assemblies, to which electors from all but seven cities, as well as the countryside,

This attempt to arrange the electoral system in favor of the propertied classes—and dominant ethnic groups—similar to a number of European parliamentary systems in their early years, achieved its objective in the Third and Fourth Dumas, permitting constructive legislative work to proceed at last.

The Third and Fourth Dumas

The decree that dissolved the Second Duma fixed November 1, 1907, as the date for the convocation of the Third, and elections took place during the fall on the basis of the revised electoral law. The gains of the right-wing and moderate parties are reflected in the data on party representation compiled by the Duma chancery:

Rightists	51
Moderate rightists	70
Nationalists (Russian)	26
	Subtotal for the right... 147
Octobrists	154
Polish Kolo	11
Polish-Lithuanian-White Russian Group	7
Muslims	8
Progressivists	28
Kadets	54
Trudoviks	14
Social Democrats	19

This alignment was somewhat changed at the end of the Third Duma when the Nationalists and the Moderate right united and various members left the Octobrists for the right or for the Progressivists, reducing the Octobrists to 121 members in 1912. The Socialist Revolutionaries boycotted the Third and Fourth Dumas entirely. In the course of the Third Duma, three Octobrist leaders held the chair: Khomiakov from 1907 to 1910, Guchkov from 1910 to 1911, and Rodzianko from 1911 to 1912.

In the Third Duma, Stolypin at last found allies in the Octobrists and Nationalists, and his declarations were no longer greeted with shouts and whistling from the majority, but by loud applause. Although the Octobrists virtually played the role of a government party, they did not constitute a majority, while the Kadets and parties of the left stood in uncomprising opposition to Stolypin.

---

went to choose the Duma deputies. But in the seven cities listed above each voter cast a ballot for a Duma deputy, not for a delegate to some intermediate electoral body—R.H.M.

Therefore the premier had to look to the right for support in the Duma, while simultaneously subject to rightist pressure from the court, and it is not surprising that Stolypin's policies acquired a nationalistic hue. For example, a bill introduced in 1909 designated parts of the former Polish provinces of Lublin and Siedlce as the province of Kholm, which was to be strictly Russian in its administration. This "fourth partition of Poland," which Stolypin supported, was the subject of long and heated debate and became law only in 1912.

Another unnecessary display of Russian nationalism was the law of 1910 that subjected the internal affairs of Finland to the legislation of the Duma, while permitting the Finnish Diet to elect two members of the Russian Council of State and four Duma deputies, provided that these representatives knew Russian.

Nationalism again played a major role in the constitutional crisis that was precipitated in March 1911 when Stolypin introduced a bill to establish zemstvos in the provinces of Kiev, Volhynia, Podolia, Minsk, Mogilev, and Vitebsk. According to this bill, the members on the zemstvo councils would be divided into Russian and Polish delegations, with the predominance of the former. The bill was too nationalistic for the opposition and not sufficiently nationalistic for the extreme right. Although the Duma accepted Stolypin's zemstvo bill with some amendments, a combination of extreme rightists and Progressivists rejected it in the Council of State, 92 to 68, not so much because of the bill as from the rightists' personal animosity toward Stolypin. The premier accepted the challenge. He submitted his resignation to the tsar, saying that he would remain in office only if the rejected law was put in force under Article 87 of the Fundamental Law. The tsar, after great hesitation, acceded, and on March 11 he called a three-day recess for the representative bodies, during which the new law was issued as a decree. Such a manipulation of the laws brought down the dissatisfaction of both right and left upon Stolypin. Both houses submitted interpellations concerning the illegal actions of the government and regarded the explanations offered them as unsatisfactory.

Stolypin had difficulties not only in his relations with both legislative bodies but with the court as well. He was never very well liked at the court, where the presence of Grigorii Rasputin complicated his task. This Siberian peasant and self-styled religious seer seemed able to help the heir-apparent Alexis in his sufferings with hemophilia, thus giving Rasputin great influence with the empress, who regarded him as "a man of God." Rasputin made widespread use of his influence in both the affairs of state and Petersburg society, in which he indulged in scandalous adventures. Naturally, the behavior of this strange figure aroused indignation or ironic smiles in all quarters, starting with the grand dukes and ending with the revolutionaries, all tending to undermine the prestige of the tsar. Stolypin tried to remove the *starets* ("spiritual elder"), as Rasputin called himself, but only succeeded in making himself unpopular with the imperial family. When Stolypin's daughter advised him to "open the sovereign's eyes," Stolypin sadly replied, "There is nothing to be done. Every time I have a chance, I warn the sovereign, but recently he told me: 'I agree with you, Peter Arkadievich, but it is better to have ten Rasputins than one of the Empress' hysterical tantrums.' " [10]

Thus Stolypin's position at court grew shaky, while the opposition also whetted their knives for him. At the end of August 1911, the tsar and Stolypin arrived in Kiev to witness the dedication of a monument to Alexander II and military exercises. On the evening of September 1 at a gala performance in the Kiev theater, a terrorist, who was also an agent of the Okhrana, shot and severely wounded Stolypin. The murderer was soon convicted and hanged, but not all the circumstances preceding the assassination were made known to the public, putting the regime in a very bad light. Stolypin died on September 5 in Kiev and was buried in the ancient Monastery of the Caves there. The premiership passed to the former minister of finance, Kokovtsev, and then, in January 1914, to Goremykin, who described himself as "an old fur coat taken out of mothballs."

Under Stolypin's leadership, the government had managed to suppress manifestation of public unrest in 1907–1910, but in the remaining prewar years there were renewed signs of trouble. In 1911 the reactionary minister of education Kasso provoked a virtual strike among the professors of Moscow University by his violations of university autonomy and arbitrary faculty dismissals. Nearly a hundred members of the academic staff submitted their resignations in protest. In 1912 revolutionary newspapers began to reappear, including the new Bolshevik organ *Pravda (The Truth)*, which was repeatedly closed by court order, only to be published again under a revised name. In April 1912, there was a strike in the Lena gold fields of Siberia in which troops fired on strikers, killing 200 and wounding as many, which brought on a strong wave of public indignation. When defending the action of the authorities in the Third Duma, the min-

---

[10] M. Bok, *Vospominaniia o Stolypine* [*Reminiscences about Stolypin*] (New York, 1953), p. 331.

ister of internal affairs, Makarov, uttered the careless words, "Thus has it been, and thus it will be henceforth," which further provoked public wrath and provided the revolutionaries with excellent propaganda. The year 1912 also witnessed a wave of less dramatic strikes, including political as well as economic ones, and the summer of 1914 brought strikes of a more dangerous character.

Matters did not improve with the election of the Fourth Duma in the fall of 1912. The parties of the right and of the opposition both elected about 150 deputies, while the center, including the Octobrists, had about 130.* In the Fourth Duma, however, the Octobrists were inclined to oppose the government far more than they had in the days of Stolypin. This was especially the case following the appointment of Goremykin as premier in 1914.

It would be misleading, however, to leave the impression that the era of the Third Duma was merely one of Russification and legislative quibbling. Not only did basic agrarian reforms take place (as will be described below), not only did a major development of public education occur (see chapter 9), but a variety of measures for public welfare were successfully undertaken by the government and passed by the Duma. Zemstvo institutions were extended to Astrakhan, Orenburg, and Stavropol provinces (the Council of State, however, blocked bills on the extension of the zemstvos to Siberia and on the establishment of a township zemstvo without class distinctions). A law of June 15, 1912, reorganized the local courts, ending the judicial authority of the superintendents of the peasantry and their authority over township courts. Justices of the peace, elected by zemstvo assemblies, were again installed, and appeals against the verdict of township courts were to be heard by a "superior rural court," chaired by the justice of the peace and otherwise composed of the chairmen of the township courts. Thus were peasant courts freed from the interference of the local administrative organs. At first the new rural

---

* The data on party representation is as follows:

Rightists	65
Nationalists (Russian)	88
The "center"	32
Octobrists	98
Progressivists	48
Kadets	59
Poles	15
Muslims	6
Social Democrats	15
Trudoviks	9
Independents	7

judiciary was introduced only in the ten southern provinces, where it began to function in 1913.

On June 23, 1912, a series of laws on workingmen's insurance were issued, obliging factory owners to pay for medical aid to workers and establishing funds for subsidies in case of sickness, injury, and death. These funds were to be based on workers' contributions (one third) and owners (two thirds), and were to be administered by a joint meeting of representatives of the owner and of the workers. In case of total disability the worker was to receive a pension worth two thirds of his wages. Provincial offices on workingmen's insurance were established to supervise this field of activity, and a central organ, the Council of Workers' Insurance, was established in Petersburg under the Ministry of Trade and Industry.

On the eve of the war Russia was thus undergoing a number of administrative and social reforms that were not always spectacular but were of substantial practical value.

Modernization of the Countryside

Of all the legislation of the Duma period the most far-reaching and bold was Stolypin's land reform. Until the Revolution of 1905 the Russian government had considered it necessary to preserve peasant communal landownership as one of the ancient "foundations" of rural life. But Stolypin, who was well acquainted with rural life long before he became premier, came to the conclusion that the peasant commune was a stronghold of stagnation, an obstacle to economic and social progress on the countryside.

During the Revolution of 1905–1906 the necessity of serious measures to improve the legal and economic condition of the peasantry became obvious and urgent. One step in this direction was the decree of November 3, 1905, which abolished the redemption payments for the peasant land allotments and widened the activity of the Peasant Land Bank. This was followed on March 4, 1906, by a law establishing county and provincial "commissions on land organization," which were to improve methods of tenure and utilization.

After the dissolution of the first Duma, Stolypin used the right to promulgate emergency legislation under Article 87 of the Fundamental Laws to introduce a whole series of highly important measures. On August 12 and 27, 1906, decrees were issued transferring arable state lands and land of the imperial family to the authority of the Peasant Land Bank, with the objective of selling these lands on easy terms to the peasants who were in need of land. On September 19, it was decreed that all lands of the tsar in the Altai district that were unpopulated but suitable for settlement should be put at the disposal of the Ministry of Agriculture,[11] which would distribute these to settlers. A decree of October 5 then awarded the peasants equality with other social groups in matters of civil rights, thus rounding out the emancipation of 1861. Henceforth, the peasants could change their place of residence, freely choose their occupation, and enter the civil service or educational institutions without seeking the approval of the mir. The same decree established the equality of the peasants in seeking entry to the civil service, freed the election of peasant deputies to zemstvo assemblies from the confirmation of the provincial governor, abolished the right of superintendents of the peasantry to punish peasants without trial, and ended the arbitrary power of the county assemblies of the superintendents over the verdicts of communal assemblies.

Finally, by the famous decree of November 9, 1906, the peasants were permitted to leave the commune and still retain possession of their land allotments. This decree held that since redemption payments for allotment lands were terminated on November 3, 1905, these lands were from now on free from any legal restrictions that resulted from the redemption debt, and that therefore peasants who so desired could claim their share of the communal arable land as private property without jeopardizing their right to use communal pastures and forests. This measure has often been referred to as Stolypin's "wager on the strong" and has often been distorted to mean a wager on the rural "bourgeoisie" or the "kulaks." Actually, the term "wager on the strong" was used by Stolypin in defending personal landownership against family ownership. In December 1908, some deputies to the Third Duma suggested that if the head of the peasant household were to receive what used to be his family's allotment in full individual ownership, he could squander it on drink, leaving his family destitute. Stolypin, however, pointed out that communal and family ownership hindered initiative and in the past had condemned "ninety million people to bitter bondage. . . . For abnormal and extraordinary phenomena [such as wasteful dissipation] it is necessary to make extraordinary laws. When we make laws for the country as a whole, it is necessary to take into consideration the intelligent and the strong and not the drunkards and weaklings."

---

[11] In 1905, the Ministry of Agriculture was officially renamed Chief Administration of Land Organization and Agriculture (*Glavnoe upravlenie zemleustroistva i zemledeliia*).

In the decree on individual ownership, said Stolypin, the government "placed its wager not on the wretched and the drunkards but on the strong . . . in Russia such strong people are a majority."[12] From the context and the literal meaning of Stolypin's speech it is clear that he considered "the strong" to be the mass of middling, ordinary peasants and not a minority of "rich" kulaks.

Stolypin submitted his agrarian decree to the Second Duma, which failed to take action, and again to the Third Duma. In his speeches to the Dumas he defended the transfer of land to individual, private ownership, and the abolition of compulsory attachment to the commune; and in his great speech on the agrarian question on May 10, 1907, he thoroughly criticized the plans for compulsory expropriation of privately owned lands and their distribution among the peasants, as the left advocated. Armed with statistical data, Stolypin argued that the division of the privately owned lands would fail to increase the total grain production and that the increase in peasant holdings would be unimportant and soon offset by the population increase while the breaking up of large, well-run farms would inflict damage on the whole economy. He acknowledged the possibility of compulsory expropriation only in exceptional cases, if required by modern agrarian practice, to end inefficient strip farming, for example. Stolypin recognized the plight of the peasants, but suggested that the remedy lay not in compulsory expropriation but in the creation of "stable private property." He favored the growth of peasant ownership through government purchase of land for resale to land-hungry peasants, the development of planned migration, the granting of loans on allotment lands, the establishment of easy credit for the improvement of land, and the extensive improvement of cultivation.[13]

After long debate Stolypin's law was passed by the Third Duma and the Council of State. A provision was added that in rural communes in which there had been no general redistribution since the initial allotment of the land to the peasants in the era of the emancipation, the land was to be regarded automatically as private property. On June 14, 1910, the tsar approved Stolypin's agrarian law. In its passage through the Duma the law had encountered strong opposition. The Octobrists, the moderate rightists, the nationalists, the Polish Kolo, and some of the rightists and Progressivists voted

---

[12] *Stenograficheskie otchety* of the Third State Duma, December 5, 1908, pp. 2280–2284.

[13] *Stenograficheskie otchety* of the Second State Duma, vol. II, May 10, 1907, pp. 433–445.

for it, while the Social Democrats, Trudoviks, Kadets, some of the Progressivists, and a considerable part of the rightists voted against it.

Following this success for Stolypin, an extensive "Regulation on Land Organization" was issued on May 29, 1911. Local land commissions *(zemleustroitel'nye komissii)* were now entrusted with the important and complex task of apportioning and delimiting peasant lands for the transfer from communal to private ownership. This process comprised four steps: (1) the submission of an application by individuals or communes to the land commission; if two thirds of a commune requested the establishment of private tenure, then the whole commune was transferred to the new status; (2) the drafting of plans; (3) the delimitation of individual holdings; and (4) the approval of the plans by the parties concerned, or, in case of disagreement, by the decision of the land commission.

Energetic implementation of Stolypin's reform had started in January 1907. At that time there were about 600 surveyors in the civil service; by 1914 this staff had grown until there were 7000 surveyors and assistants working for the land commissions. The work in which they were mainly engaged consisted of documenting the existing holdings of peasants in strips and transferring them to private ownership; then in consolidating the strips into one parcel, the so-called *otrub* holding; or, instead, in the establishment of small peasant farms apart from the villages, the so-called *khutor*.

Stolypin's plan met an urgent need and found a broad response among the peasants. Within five years after 1907 more than 2,500,000 peasant householders submitted applications to leave the commune. The reform was particularly successful in the southern provinces ("New Russia") and in the provinces of the Lower Volga, Samara, and Saratov. By January 1, 1915, 2,719,000 householders had petitioned to have their land consolidated as private allotments, and this process had been completed for 2,000,000 or 22 percent of the total number of householders whose land had been held communally.[14] In addition, almost 500,000 householders received certificates establishing their personal ownership of the land in communes that did not practice periodical repartition. Thus, almost 2,500,000 householders had left the commune and received their land as private property; this represented one quarter of all communal peasants and an area of almost 45,900,000

---

[14] *Statisticheskii ezhegodnik Rossii 1914 goda* [*Statistical Yearbook of Russia for the Year 1914*], pub. by the Central Statistical Bureau of the Ministry of the Interior (Petrograd, 1915), otdel VI: "Zemlevladenie" [section VI: "Landownership"], p. 16.

acres. By this time there were over 3,000,000 householders for whom plans for apportionment of communal land had been drafted. In short, the land reform of the Stolypin period was far-reaching indeed.

According to the data of the economic historian Kosinsky, 6,174,500 households (47 percent of the total) had in the years 1907–1915 submitted applications for various forms of consolidation,[15] which clearly indicates that not only the "kulaks" were interested in the Stolypin reform. It is true, however, that the destruction of the commune with its leveling tendencies intensified the economic stratification of the village. On the one hand, a well-to-do class of peasants emerged, the so-called "Stolypin landlords," while, on the other hand, indigent peasants often sold their allotments and joined the class of hired labor in the village or city. But at least the poor peasants who were unable to keep their farms were able to leave them with the money received for their sale.

As part of the efforts to solve the agrarian question, the government undertook other measures in the interests of the peasants, stimulating the activity of the Peasant Land Bank and the resettlement of land-hungry peasants beyond the Urals. After 1905 thousands of landlords, frightened by the riots in the countryside and the possibility of the forced sale of their land, sold their estates to the Peasant Land Bank, which either resold or rented them or financed their direct purchase by peasants. In the years following 1905 peasants purchased 13,500,000 acres with the help of the bank, raising the total purchases of the bank from its establishment in 1883 to 1915 to 48,800,000 acres.

Resettlement of peasants from the central regions played a certain role in decreasing the land shortage there. In 1905 the management of resettlement was transferred from the Ministry of Internal Affairs to the Ministry of Agriculture, under whose efficient direction the task of allotting and establishing new settlements in Asiatic Russia developed rapidly. Between 1906 and 1913 almost 3,500,000 peasants crossed the Urals, including those without "entrance certificates." Since the local organizations could not always cope with the large numbers of newcomers, almost 500,000 were forced to return. The peak year for resettlement was 1908, in which 759,000 migrants crossed the Urals.[16]

---

[15] V. A. Kosinsky, *Osnovnyia tendentsii v mobilizatsii zemel'noi sobstvennosti* [*The Basic Tendencies in the Transfer of Landownership*] (Prague, 1925), p. 325.

[16] For a detailed description of the resettlement policy and its results, see D. W. Treadgold, *op. cit.*

Stolypin's able and energetic assistant was the head of the Ministry of Agriculture, A. V. Krivoshein. Under his leadership the ministry helped to improve agricultural technology and agronomical education, extended grants and loans for improvements, developed irrigation projects in Central Asia, established model and experimental farms, and supported farmers' cooperatives. Between 1907 and 1914 the expenditures of the ministry rose from 46,600,000 rubles to 146,000,000 rubles. The zemstvos, too, helped the development of agronomy with technicians, demonstration farms, and the sale of equipment on liberal terms.

Thus did Russian agriculture experience an over-all economic and technological advance in the period of Stolypin's reforms, despite the difficulties that arose from breaking up an age-old way of life in the countryside. A good index of progress was the increased demand for farm machinery. In 1900, such machinery was imported to the value of 28,000,000 rubles; in 1908, importation rose to 61,000,000; and in 1913, to 109,000,000. At the same time the domestic production of agricultural machinery rose from a value of 13,000,000 rubles in 1900 to 52,000,000 rubles in 1912. The importation of artificial fertilizer also increased from 108,000 tons in 1900 to 630,000 tons in 1912.

With improved agricultural methods and a larger scale of production, crop yields rose considerably. Instead of the traditional grain harvest of 400–500 pounds per acre, the yield for the period 1908–1913 was 703 pounds per acre for winter rye, 813 for winter wheat, 786 for barley, and 726 for oats. The production and export of wheat increased; the value of grain exports in 1909–1911 reached 750,000,000 rubles annually, although it fell off in the next two years because of the poor harvest of 1911. As a result of improved yields and expanded acreage the annual harvest of all grains rose from about 54,000,000 tons at the turn of the century to 81,000,000 tons on the average for the years 1909–1913, reaching a peak of 97,200,000 tons in 1913. Despite the growth of the population and the increase in exports, the per capita consumption of bread increased and food shortages such as those at the end of the century became a thing of the past.

Corresponding increases occurred in other crops. The annual potato crop had constituted 3,600,000 to 4,500,000 tons in the 1860s and amounted to 25,794,000 tons per year on the average between 1911 and 1915. In the 1860s about 270,000 acres of sugar beets were sown, which increased to 1,890,000 by 1913–1914, while cotton growing in Turkestan reached 612,000 tons per year in 1914. By 1910 the country was supplying 51 percent of the raw cotton it consumed.

Zemstvos, Cooperatives, and Municipal Government

It was not only the work of the central government that brought about the transformation of the Russian countryside. The zemstvo institutions, which were introduced into thirty-four provinces in 1864, also performed a great service. Although the nobility played a predominant role in the zemstvos, the work of these institutions was truly public in character, for the peasants had a far greater interest than the landowners in the construction of hospitals and schools. Changes in the political climate had little influence on the practical work of the zemstvos. Before 1905 the zemstvo leaders were generally inclined to liberalism and constitutionalism. After 1905–1906, when the peasant disturbances frightened the nobility, the majority of the members of zemstvo assemblies shifted to the Octobrists or the rightist groups; but the activity of the zemstvos, with a few exceptions, continued to develop as before.

Aside from education, which is discussed in the following chapter, the principal field of zemstvo activity was public health. Before the zemstvo period, there was no proper medical care in rural areas. At first, the rural populace distrusted doctors and did not follow their prescriptions properly, and doctors were not always sufficiently equipped to give their patients the proper care. But the zemstvo "dokhtor" (an alien word that now penetrated the peasant vocabulary) won his long battle on two fronts: with the zemstvo leaders for fuller financial support and with the peasants to overcome mistrust. At first many zemstvos struggled along with medical assistants and a few visiting doctors, but after the mid-1880s the establishment of permanent and well-equipped medical centers, hospitals, and clinics began. By the end of the century there were 1300 hospitals with 30,000 beds in the thirty-four provinces that had zemstvo institutions, while the zemstvos employed about 2500 doctors and 8000 members of the medical auxiliary staff. By 1913 there were 6773 hospitals with 190,500 beds and 19,000 doctors in fifty-one provinces of European Russia.

Medical assistance was rendered free of charge by the zemstvos, excepting a few that made small charges for medicines. The growth of this form of "socialized medicine" not only increased expenditures but required that an increasing proportion of the budget of the zemstvo institutions be devoted to medicine. In 1877 most

THE PROVINCIAL DIVISIONS
IN EUROPEAN RUSSIA, 1905

———— Boundaries of major administrative regions

The provinces are named after their capital cities except where indicated otherwise. The total number of provincial divisions (variously called *gubernii* and *oblasti*) in the Russian Empire in 1905 was 96, divided as follows: European Russia, 51; Caucasus, 10; Poland, 10; Finland, 8; Siberia, 4; Far East, 4; Steppe Region, 4; and Central Asia, 5.

county zemstvos spent 20 percent of their budget on public health, and by 1901 this had increased to between 25 percent and 33 percent. For some years the government as well as the zemstvos paid little attention to the most important problem of the peasant economy, the low level of agrarian technique. Almost everyone took it for granted that the peasant farmed by the three-field system, tilling the soil with a primitive wooden plough, threshing the grain with a flail, and winnowing it on a shovel in the wind. Only at the turn of the century did the zemstvo and the government conceive that these practices could be changed, and only then did they turn their attention to the improvement of the exploitation of the land. By World War I the honored position acquired by the zemstvo doctor and teacher in the Russian countryside was shared with the zemstvo agronomist. The zemstvo established experimental stations and model farms, fostered improved cattlebreeding, introduced fodder-grass, helped to organize credit for farm improvements, and sponsored the sale of agricultural machinery. By the end of the Stolypin period the iron plough had replaced the antediluvian wooden plough. The increase in zemstvo activity in this field is indicated by the rise in the agronomical share of the zemstvos' budget from 1 percent in 1905 to 6.3 percent in 1912, an absolute increase of from 700,000 rubles to 14,000,000 rubles.

One reason why the zemstvos were able to devote a larger share of their funds to public health, education, and agronomy in the early twentieth century was the reduction of the compulsory contributions of the zemstvos to defray the local expenses of the central government, especially the police, the courts, and the army. In 1895 these expenses had constituted over 20 percent of the zemstvo budget, but by 1912 they accounted for only 4.9 percent. Moreover, government subsidies to the zemstvos, quite insignificant as late as 1908, increased sharply. The total revenues of the zemstvos, derived primarily from real-estate taxes, increased from 65,800,000 rubles in 1895 to 220,000,000 rubles in 1912 in the thirty-four original zemstvo provinces. The aggregate zemstvo revenues for forty-three provinces amounted to 336,373,000 rubles in 1914, not counting revenue from trade and insurance activity. At this time the main items in the expenditures of the zemstvos were as follows:

	Million Rubles	Percent of Expenditures
Education	107.0	30.8
Medical care	82.6	23.8
Public welfare	5.1	1.5

Local administration.........	23.4	6.7
Agronomy and economic measures	28.9	8.2
Veterinary services...........	10.5	3.0
Roads	17.5	5.0
Other, including debt service and contribution to central government expenses.......	72.5	21.0
Total	347.5	100.0

The material progress of the Russian countryside was furthered in this period by the extensive development of cooperatives, especially credit, consumers', and producers' cooperatives. The nineteenth century saw only the faint beginnings of these institutions, but after the turn of the century the cooperative movement, supported by the state and the zemstvos, began to grow rapidly, and it soon encompassed millions of rural citizens. A regulation of 1895 provided for the establishment of several types of cooperatives: credit associations capitalized by the state treasury or zemstvo and other public institutions; savings and loan associations capitalized by the members of the association; and rural or township banks. In 1904 a new regulation entrusted the general direction of these institutions to a special committee of the Ministry of Finance, which was represented by committees in the provinces and sent out auditors to supervise the financial transactions and audit the accounts of the small-scale credit institutions. With the financial support of the government and the zemstvos, the small-scale credit institutions grew at a great rate. Savings and loan associations increased from about 600 with 200,000 members in 1897 to over 3000 with a membership of about 2,000,000 in 1914. Various kinds of credit cooperatives spread over all of Russia; in 1914 they numbered 14,500 with 9,500,000 members and loaned 500,000,000 rubles annually. On January 1, 1913, loans from the State Bank to credit cooperatives stood at 125,000,000 rubles, and the deposits of the members totaled 304,000,000 rubles. This development did the Russian peasant great service by liberating him from the clutches of the local usurer or "kulak" (fist), as the peasants called the moneylenders, who were often local shopkeepers.

On the eve of the war Russia led the world in the development of cooperative credit institutions. In 1912 the Moscow People's Bank was opened, the shareholders of which were mainly cooperative societies and local and district unions of cooperatives, which included one quarter of all credit associations in 1913. Credit cooperatives supplied 70 percent of the capital of this bank—the world's largest cooperative bank—which became the focal point of all Russian cooperatives.

The first consumer cooperatives had emerged in the 1870s, and rapid growth began after "model regulations" for these associations were issued in 1897. By 1905, 948 consumers' cooperatives were in operation, and by 1914, over 10,000 with a membership of 1,530,000. Of these, 8500 cooperatives with 900,000 members were on the countryside. By 1914 the annual turnover of goods handled by consumer cooperatives was 290,000,000 rubles. These bodies also founded local and district unions, and a national union of consumers' cooperatives was established in Moscow in 1898; by 1914 it included 800 local cooperatives. Consumers' cooperatives owned numerous flour mills, tanneries, soap factories, and similar enterprises.

The third important type of cooperative movement in Russia was agricultural producers' associations. Some of these were called "societies" *(obshchestva)*, and in them peasants, zemstvo employees, and other landowners participated. Others, called "associations" *(tovarishchestva)*, were composed almost exclusively of peasants and were found mostly in the western provinces. Although model regulations for agrarian producers' cooperatives were issued in 1897 and 1898, their main growth began after the beginning the agrarian reforms of Stolypin. By 1914 there were 4685 agrarian societies and 1254 associations. Some of these operated experimental stations, provided agricultural machinery and distributed agronomical literature. Others formed unions of producers in specific branches of agriculture, such as poultry raisers, beekeepers, tobacco growers, and flax cultivators. An outstanding example was the Central Association of Flax Cultivators, which included 150,000 farms and had export offices in London, Belfast, and New York. Dairy cooperatives in the rich milk-producing areas of Siberia, especially Tobolsk and Tomsk provinces, developed rapidly after the turn of the century. In 1908 a Union of Siberian butter cooperatives was established and successfully exported Siberian butter, chiefly to England and Germany.

In addition to the three basic types of cooperatives described, there was a multitude of other cooperative societies, including fishermen, loggers, carpenters, masons, longshoremen, and various artisans. The total number of cooperatives of all kinds in 1914 was over 30,000 with a membership of almost 12,000,000, of which a substantial majority were peasants. In 1908 the first All-Russian Congress of Cooperatives met in Moscow, and in 1912 representatives of the credit and agricultural societies met in Petersburg. The scope and vigor of the movement was amply demonstrated in the second All-Russian Congress of Cooperatives, which met in Kiev in 1913 and included over 1500 delegates from various regions and nationalities of the Empire and from all social levels.

In addition to their economic activities the cooperatives were active in cultural affairs. They published books, pamphlets, and periodicals for their members and supported reading rooms, libraries, book stores, social clubs, theaters, exhibitions, and lectures.[17] A school of cooperative work was opened in 1913 at the Shaniavsky People's University in Moscow, and plans were laid to open a special training institute for cooperative work.

The cooperative movement attracted the support of the intelligentsia, and a number of capable theoreticians worked on the problems of cooperative management and economics. All in all it was a remarkable example of the ability of the Russian people to apply creative force and enterprising spirit in the free organization of their economic life, ranging from small, local cooperatives to powerful, central institutions.

Thus did the program of the government, inspired chiefly by Stolypin, and the activities of millions of Russian citizens of all walks of life combine to make the prewar period one of general advance for the Russian countryside.

Urban Development

In the early twentieth century the development of Russian cities was rather uneven. By 1914 there were 1230 cities and towns in the empire, the largest being Petersburg (2,165,000), Moscow (1,806,000), Warsaw (909,000), Odessa (646,000), Kiev (610,000), and Riga (569,000). These cities, and a few other such as Kharkov and Ekaterinoslav, made considerable strides in urban administration and

---

[17] For detailed data on the Russian cooperative movement at the beginning of the twentieth century, see: J. V. Bubnov, *The Cooperative Movement in Russia* (Manchester, 1917); E. T. Blanc, *Cooperative Movement in Russia* (New York, 1924); A. D. Bilimovich, *Kooperatsiia v Rossii* [*Cooperatives in Russia*] (Frankfurt-am-Main, 1955); S. Prokopovich, *Kooperativnoe dvizhenie v Rossii* [*The Cooperative Movement in Russia*] (Moscow, 1913); and E. M. Hayden and A. N. Antsiferov, *The Cooperative Movement in Russia during the War* (James T. Shotwell, ed., *Economic and Social History of the World War* series, New Haven, 1929), which contains a survey of prewar development.

had electricity, electric streetcars, modern water supply and sewerage systems, city slaughterhouses, and a wide variety of institutions devoted to public welfare. However, in the county seats, many of which had less than 10,000 inhabitants, a sleepy, semirural life continued; most of these lacked paved streets, they used kerosene lamps, distributed their water by barrels, and had no idea of a sewerage system.

Municipal self-government made great strides following the Municipal Act *(gorodovoe polozhenie)* of 1870, described earlier in connection with the Great Reforms (chapter 5). In 1892, however, a law on municipal administration considerably restricted the municipal franchise, limiting it to owners of real estate (whose minimum value depended on the size of the municipality) and to owners of industrial and commercial establishments. Small taxpayers were deprived of their votes, and the office of the provincial governor was allowed to interfere freely with municipal affairs. The act of 1892 remained in force to the very end of the empire; plans to repeal it during the Duma period never materialized.

As a result of this legislation, municipal government in the smaller cities was largely in the hands of well-to-do merchants, subject to direct supervision by the Ministry of the Interior. But in a dozen or so larger cities the intelligentsia had an influential voice in the municipal dumas. According to N. I. Astrov:

> The cooperation of bourgeoisie with intellectuals, and the very high standard of the permanent staff of the municipalities, which came to be known by the peculiar name of the "third element," to distinguish it from government officials and from the elected members of the dumas, weakened the unfavorable effects of the limited franchise, and to a certain extent made up for the lack of a truly representative system. A combination of business men and the representatives of the educated and progressive elements became the outstanding characteristic of many municipalities.[18]

Municipal finance in Russia reflected the uneven urban development; in 1913, only 35 municipalities had a budget of more than one million rubles. But the rapid growth of the larger cities in the beginning of the twentieth century was reflected in a sharp increase of their revenues and expenditures; the combined budget of 693 municipalities rose from 153 million rubles in 1904 to 297 million in 1913—nearly one third of these budgets being accounted for by

---

[18] N. I. Astrov, *The Municipal Government and the All-Russian Union of Towns* (James T. Shotwell, ed., *Economic and Social History of the World War* series, New Haven, 1929), pp. 138–139.

Petersburg and Moscow alone. The aggregate budget of all local government—zemstvo and municipal (but not including that of village communes)—amounted to somewhat more than 20 percent of the central government budget in 1913.

Municipal revenues were derived mostly from property taxes, but after the turn of the century they were drawn increasingly from public utilities and other municipal enterprises. In the larger cities, they provided one third to one half of the revenue. The cities made a deliberate effort to buy out private utilities and transportation companies. A notable public enterprise dating back to 1788 were the municipal banks, which numbered 337 in 1915.

Though municipal statistics are unsystematic and not uniform, some impression of the other major items of municipal expense can be gained from the following table, representing the combined budgets of 971 towns in 1912: [19]

	Million Rubles	Percent of Expenditures
Education		12.1
Public health		12.5
Utilities		9.5
Wages, maintenance, operating and administrative expenses		30.2
Debt service		15.2
Contribution to central govt. expense (including police) ..		10.9
Other		9.6
Total	275.6	100.0

In conclusion, one should note that in wartime, the zemstvos and the municipal governments joined in serving the needs of defense. A zemstvo union was active during the Russo-Japanese war of 1904–1905, and in August 1914, there were formed an All-Russian Zemstvo Union and an All-Russian Union of Towns, which became jointly known as *Zemgor*. The Zemgor set up military hospitals, took care of the wounded and of civilian evacuees, distributed food, and collected warm clothing and footwear for the army. These activities were financed by the central government, but their execution was a community effort. Taken together, the work of the zemstvos, the cooperative movement, and the municipal governments was an example

---

[19] *Ibid.*, pp. 141–165 (chapter II: Municipal Budgets and Revenues; chapter III: Municipal Expenditures).

of voluntary and constructive cooperation between the intelligentsia, the nobility, the business community, and the "common man."

Industry and State Finance

As we have seen, the economic growth of Russia in the prewar years was not confined to agriculture but encompassed the entire national economy.[20] The total population of the empire rose from 125,600,000 in 1897 to 178,400,000 in 1914, over 18 percent of whom lived in cities.[21]

Railroad construction proceeded at a slower tempo than in the days of Witte because the basic network in European Russia had been fairly well completed, while the railroads of Asiatic Russia were either under construction or near completion. These included the Tashkent–Orenburg line, which was important for the shipment of cotton from Central Asia; the completion of the Trans-Siberian line around Lake Baikal and the addition of various branch lines in Siberia; and the Amur River line, which was started in 1908. In 1913 the total length of the rail lines in European Russia consisted of 37,783 miles, and the railroads of Asiatic Russia accounted for 7975 miles, in addition to the Chinese Eastern Railway of 1072 miles, which was in Russian hands. At this date the staff of all Russian railroads was 815,000 strong.

Between 1900 and 1913 coal production doubled, rising from 18,054,000 tons to 39,852,000 tons, of which 70 percent was ex-

---

[20] For statistical data on the development of industry, trade, and finance in the beginning of the twentieth century, see *Statisticheskii ezhogodnik* for the years 1904–1916; Lyashchenko, *op. cit.*, vol. II; and Khromov, *op. cit.*

[21] According to the Statistical Yearbook of 1905, in the beginning of the twentieth century the distribution of the population of European Russia by occupation was as follows:

	PERCENT
Agriculture, lumbering, fishing and hunting	74.6
Manufacturing, mining, handicrafts	9.6
Domestic service and day-labor	4.6
Commerce	3.8
Rentiers and pensioners	1.8
Transport and communications	1.6
Civil service and the professions	1.4
Armed forces	1.0
Clergy and employees of religious institutions	.6
Other	1.0

tracted in the Donets Basin, despite the opening just before the war of new mines in rich deposits in the Kuznetsky Basin of western Siberia. There was a temporary hitch in the development of oil production, due in part to the apparent exhaustion of the Baku fields. While Russia had exceeded the United States in oil production in 1900, the latter country was far ahead by 1913, for in this interval Russian production had fallen off from 11,358,000 tons in 1900 to 10,098,000 in 1913. The falling production of the Baku fields was partly offset by the development of the Grozny, Maikop, and Emba fields in the Caucasus. Pig iron production rose from 3,186,000 tons in 1900 to reach 5,094,000 tons in 1913, of which 67 percent came from the southern plants. Consumer goods also increased rapidly. For example, cotton production rose from 288,000 tons in 1900 to 468,000 tons in 1913, while sugar production rose from 882,000 tons to 1,944,000 in the same period.

All told, industry, mining, and communications employed almost 5,000,000 workers. Of these about 2,000,000 were employed in factories that were subject to inspection, and 800,000 (41 percent) of these workers were employed by enterprises that employed more than 1000 workers. This is only one indication of the considerable growth of large-scale corporate organization in Russia in this period. Between 1909 and 1913, 759 new companies were established with an initial capital of 1,005,700,000 rubles, which represented almost one third of the total capitalization of Russian companies in this period. The establishment of large syndicates to set prices and establish marketing agreements was characteristic of this period in Russia as elsewhere. These included "Produgol," which controlled the marketing of Donets Basin coal, "Prodamet," for the metallurgical industry of the South and "Prodvagon," for railroad-car shops of the Ural region. Other syndicates operated in various fields of consumer goods, such as sugar, tobacco, rubber goods, and cotton.

Foreign trade reflected the growth of the Russian economy in this era; the value of exports increased from 762,000,000 rubles to 1,520,000,000 rubles between 1901 and 1913, while imports rose from 593,000,000 rubles to 1,374,000,000 rubles. The balance of commercial banks tripled between 1899 and 1913, rising from 1380 million to 5768 million rubles.

However important the growth of the Russian economy in the early twentieth century, it should not be overestimated, for the productivity of labor, the gross national product per capita, and the standard of living were considerably lower than in the advanced European countries and the United States. The really impressive aspect of Russian economic development in this era is not the absolute level of production achieved, but the rate or tempo of growth. For example, coal production in Russia rose 40 percent in the period 1909–1913, as against a growth rate of 24 percent in the United States, 28 percent in Germany, 7 percent in Britain, and 9 percent in France in the same period. In the case of pig iron, Russian output rose by 61 percent in the period 1909–1913, while the rate of increase in the United States was 20 percent, in Germany 33 percent, in Britain 8 percent, and in France 46 percent. Although the economic backwardness of Russia had not disappeared on the eve of the war, it was clearly disappearing. The standard of living was not high, but it was rising. In the twenty years preceding the war the population of Russia increased by about 40 percent, while the domestic consumption of goods more than doubled. This increase in per capita income is illustrated by the consumption of sugar—from 8 pounds per capita in 1894 to 18 pounds in 1913—or by the deposits in state savings banks—from 680,000,000 rubles at the end of 1899 to 1,704,000,000 rubles at the end of 1913.

The state finances of imperial Russia were maintained on the high level that had been developed by Witte at the end of the nineteenth century. Kokovtsev, who was minister of finance almost continuously from 1904 to 1914, managed to maintain the equilibrium of Russian state finance despite the difficulties posed by the Russo-Japanese War, which cost the government almost 2,500,000,000 rubles. A French loan of about 1,000,000,000 rubles, negotiated by Witte in 1906, helped to meet this expense, and thereafter the sound management of state finances made it unnecessary to resort to further large international loans. The national debt increased, but not alarmingly, from over 7,000,000,000 rubles in 1904 to 8,600,000,000 in 1906 to over 9,000,000,000 in 1909, declining to 8,800,000,000 in 1913.

Ordinary state expenditures (that is, excluding extraordinary expenses for war and capital investment in new railroads) increased rather modestly between 1900 and 1906, due to the impact of the war and revolution; but between 1906 and 1913 there was an increase of about one and one-half times, as the following figures indicate: 1900 — 1,599,000,000 rubles; 1906 — 2,061,000,000 rubles; 1913—3,094,000,000 rubles (the value of the ruble in this period was stable, at about 50 cents, U.S. currency). The distribution of this expenditure between the various departments in the Duma period was as follows (in millions of rubles):

	1906		1913	
	Millions of Rubles	**Percentage of State Expenditure**	**Millions of Rubles**	**Percentage of State Expenditure**
The Senate, State Council, and the Duma	5.7	0.3	9.4	0.3
Ministry of the Imperial Court	16.5	0.8	17.4	0.6
Department of the Holy Synod	29.2	1.4	45.7	1.5
Ministry of Internal Affairs*	136.3	6.6	185.4	6.0
Ministry of Finance	353.2	17.1	482.3	15.6
including state liquor monopoly	*178.3*		*235.0*	
Ministry of Justice	53.5	2.6	92.7	3.0
Ministry of Foreign Affairs	5.9	0.3	11.5	0.4
Ministry of Education ...	44.0	2.1	143.1	4.6
Ministry of Transporation	477.2	23.2	640.6	20.7
including railroad operation	*448.7*		*586.5*	
Ministry of Trade and Industry	31.8	1.5	64.6	2.1
Ministry of Agriculture and State Stud Farm Administration	37.9	1.8	139.1	4.5
Ministry of War	392.5	19.0	581.1	18.8
Ministry of the Navy	111.6	5.4	244.8	7.9
State Auditing Office	9.1	0.4	12.1	0.4
Service of state debt......	356.5	17.3	424.4	13.7

Thus, in 1913 the largest outlay in the budget, 31.1 percent of the total, was for state-owned enterprises, mainly the railroads under the Ministry of Transportation, the liquor monopoly under the Ministry of Finance, and the Post, Telegraph, and Telephone Administration under the Ministry of the Interior. Next followed defense, with 25.8 percent of the budget, and civil administration (including education) with 22.7 percent. Debt service amounted to 13.7 percent, pensions to government employees, 3.9 percent, and church administration, 1.5 percent. The most dramatic changes oc-

---

* Includes the Post, Telegraph, and Telephone Administration with a budget of 76.3 millions rubles in 1913.

curred in education[22] and agriculture: in the seven-year period under review, state expenditures in these two fields tripled and quadrupled, respectively. Expenses for Trade and Industry—including port development—doubled, while the relative weight of expenses for the liquor monopoly, railroad operation, and debt service in the national budget declined.

Although state expenditures nearly doubled between 1900 and 1913, even greater increases in revenues maintained a budgetary surplus. Total revenues rose from 1,704,000,000 rubles in 1900 to 2,271,000,000 in 1906 to 3,417,000,000 in 1913. The largest single source of revenue was the monopoly on alcoholic beverages, which contributed almost 900,000,000 rubles in 1913 (the monopoly yielded over 30 percent of total revenues in 1906 and over 26 percent in 1913). A large source of revenue was the state railroad system, which had run a deficit for many years, but was making money by 1913, despite the considerable expenditures to pay its operating expenses and service its debt. Specifically, the sources of state revenue between 1906 and 1913 were as follows (in millions of rubles):[23]

| | 1906 | | 1913 | |
	Million Rubles	Percent State Revenues	Million Rubles	Percent State Revenues
Direct taxes	163.2	7.2	272.5	8.0
Indirect taxes	494.2	21.8	708.1	20.7
Duties	113.3	5.0	231.2	6.8
State royalties	777.1	34.2	1024.9	30.0
including state liquor monopoly	*697.5*		*899.3*	
Income from state properties	603.3	26.5	1046.6	30.7
including state railroads	*490.9*		*813.6*	
Redemption payments	35.0	1.5	1.2	0.04
Incidental revenues	85.6	3.8	132.9	3.9

The direct taxes included those on real estate, on industry, and on capital; the indirect taxes consisted of customs revenue as well as excise taxes on tobacco, sugar, matches, and petroleum products. The royalties, aside from the liquor monopoly, were the mining,

---

[22] In addition to the Ministry of Education, considerable amounts were spent on education by the Holy Synod (parochial schools), and by the Ministries of War, Trade and Industry, Agriculture, and Transportation.

[23] For detailed data on government finance in 1904–1913, see *Statisticheskii ezhegodnik Rossii,* 1914, section XII.

mint, post, telegraph, and telephone revenues. Income-producing properties other than railroads were mostly forests. The shifts in emphasis in the period under review were from indirect to direct taxes, and from liquor monopoly revenues to revenues from other government enterprises. The peasants' redemption payments went out of existence as a source of state revenue. Though the structural changes in the state budget were less spectacular than its huge absolute increase, both were indicators of progress.

9/

Cultural Development
after the Mid-Nineteenth Century

Education

The educational system of prerevolutionary Russia was, with some exceptions, molded along the lines prevailing in continental Europe, particularly in Germany. The institutions of higher learning included the universities, universities for women, several military academies (general staff, naval, medical, engineering, law), four theological academies, academies and conservatories of art and music, and numerous specialized technological institutes and academies.

At the end of the reign of Alexander II there were eight universities in Russia: in Petersburg, Moscow, Kiev, Kharkov, Kazan, Yurev (Dorpat), Odessa, and Warsaw. During the reign of Alexander III the University of Tomsk was opened in Siberia, and universities were opened in Saratov in 1910, in Perm in 1915, and in Rostov-on-the-Don in 1917. All were state universities, bearing the designation "imperial," but in 1908 they were joined by a "free" institution, the Shaniavsky People's University, which was established by the Moscow municipal government. At the end of the nineteenth century the total number of students in the universities was about 16,000, but in the years before World War I the enrollment increased to about 40,000, with approximately 8000 entrants per year.

The University Statute of 1884 limited the autonomy of the universities by giving the minister of education the power to appoint university rectors (formerly elected by the faculty) and to disregard the faculty vote in the appointment of new professors. This change, however, did not lower academic standards. At the opening of the twentieth century university education in Russia was on a par with Western European standards, and a degree of academic freedom returned in 1905 when the autonomy of the professors' councils was re-established (see chapter 8).

The student bodies of Russian universities were much more diverse in social origin than those in England or Germany, where universities were attended almost exclusively by the children of the aristocracy and the bourgeoisie. Tuition fees were comparatively low, and many students from the peasantry or other poor families studied on scholarships. At the beginning of the 1870s, 72 percent of the students in the Kazan University were supported by scholarships and tuition grants; in Kiev, 70 percent; and in Odessa, 80 percent. In Moscow University in 1876, 59 percent of the students received full tuition grants; in 1900, 1957 out of 4017 students there studied tuition-free, and 877 were supported by scholarships.[1]

Student organizations were illegal, but a considerable number of students did belong to informal *zemliachestva* or "country-men's associations," that is, groups of students from the same town or province headed by councils which, in cases of conflict with authorities, organized student action. After the Revolution of 1905, "countrymen's associations," mutual aid funds, and various student circles—literary, artistic, and scientific—were legalized. Sometimes, they served as a cover for political groups. In Kharkov University in 1907–1910 for example, the student cell of the Socialist Revolutionary party bore the innocuous title "circle for the study of the agrarian problem," and the Social Democratic organization called itself a circle for the study of political economy.

The growth of special educational institutions, which were under the authority of various ministries, exceeded the growth of the universities. In 1884, a Technological Institute was opened in Kharkov, and at the end of the nineteenth century another such institute was founded in Tomsk. In 1898, the Kiev Polytechnic Institute was opened, followed in 1902 by the well-equipped Petersburg Polytechnic Institute, the beloved brain child of Witte, followed by the Don Region Polytechnic Institute in Novocherkassk. In 1891, the Electrotechnical Institute in Petersburg was established, in 1902 a Forestry Institute

---

[1] *Istoriia Rossii v XIX veke*, vol. IX, esp. pp. 145, 155–156. According to the statute of 1884, tuition was set at 10 rubles annually; in 1887, this was increased to 50 rubles. In addition, the student had to pay 40 to 50 rubles annually as an honorarium to his professors; in scientific disciplines, there were additional laboratory fees.

near Petersburg, and soon after an Institute of Mining in Ekaterinoslav. The Petrov Agricultural Academy near Moscow was closed in 1891 because of the political unreliability of its students, but two years later it was replaced by the Moscow Agricultural Institute. Another agricultural institute was established in Voronezh at the opening of the twentieth century, and in 1899 the Oriental Languages Institute was founded in Vladivostok. In the period of the Third Duma the private commercial schools in Moscow and Kiev received the same rights and status as state educational institutions. A private Psychoneurological Institute was opened in Petersburg in 1907.[2]

The state institutions of higher learning were not coeducational until 1915, with the partial exception of a brief period in 1906–1909. Nevertheless, higher education for women was highly developed. In Petersburg, Moscow, Kiev, Kharkov, Kazan, and Odessa there were "higher courses for women" with a university curriculum taught by university professors, and in Petersburg there was also a Women's Medical Institute and a Higher Pedagogical Institute for women. There were in 1915 over 24,000 women enrolled in institutions of higher education, and in this respect Russia surpassed other European countries. All told, prior to the Revolution of 1917, there were some 95 higher educational institutions in Russia, with a 1913–1914 enrollment of over 117,000 students.[3]

Secondary schools preparatory to higher education were the classical gymnasiums, with a stress on the classical languages and humanities, the real gymnasiums, with an emphasis on mathematics and the sciences, and the girls' gymnasiums (without mandatory Greek or Latin). The classical gymnasiums had an eight-year curriculum, and the real gymnasiums one of seven years. In addition, there were the theological seminaries, different types of military boarding schools, and several girls' boarding schools open primarily to the nobility *(instituty)*. Incomplete secondary education was provided by the four-year progymnasiums for boys and girls. Subprofessional training was provided by specialized agricultural, commercial, medical, industrial, and pedagogical secondary schools; vocational training was provided by the trade schools.

---

[2] A list of higher technical schools and their enrollment on the eve of World War I can be found in N. Hans, *History of Russian Educational Policy* (New York, 1931), pp. 239–240; see also W. H. E. Johnson, *Russia's Educational Heritage* (New Brunswick, N.J., 1950), table 33.

[3] A. G. Korol, *Soviet Education for Science and Technology* (New York, 1957), p. 131.

The predominant type of secondary school in Russia following the Tolstoy "reform" in 1871 was the "boys' classical gymnasium," which included mandatory instruction in Latin and Greek. In 1890, the teaching of the classical languages was somewhat reduced and more emphasis placed on Russian. In 1902, as a result of the reforms of General Vannovsky, the oppressive rule of Tolstoy's "classicism" in the gymnasium came to an end. Now Greek became optional in the great majority of gymnasiums and Latin was de-emphasized, while the sciences (practically eliminated from the curriculum in 1871) were reintroduced and history given more emphasis. In 1897, there were close to 58,000 students in the classical gymnasiums, 24,000 in the real gymnasiums and 45,000 in girls' secondary schools.

By 1911 there were 577 secondary schools providing general education for boys, including 316 classical gymnasiums (with an enrollment of 120,000) and 232 real gymnasiums (with some 67,000 students). By 1915 the number of secondary schools increased to 797, including 474 classical gymnasiums (with an enrollment of over 150,000) and 297 real gymnasiums (with over 80,000 students). The number of girls' gymnasiums in 1914 exceeded 800, and their enrollment was over 350,000[4]; the preponderance of girls in gymnasiums reflected the fact that many boys studied in specialized secondary schools.

Most of the secondary schools for boys (354 out of 474 gymnasiums) were supported by the central government, but the girls' secondary schools were maintained chiefly from local sources—by zemstvos, municipalities, and private persons and corporations. The expenditures of the Ministry of Public Education on secondary schools under its administration, which amounted to about 14 million rubles in 1907, rose to 32 million in 1914.

Rapid progress in general secondary education was paralleled by the development of specialized secondary schools. A decree of 1888 provided for the establishment of technical and trade schools, and regulations of 1896, issued on Witte's initiative, set up commercial schools of two kinds: one with a seven-year program, combining general and commercial education; and another with a three-year program for purely commercial education. By 1906, there were 233 commercial schools, which were first administered by the Ministry of Finance and after 1905 were under the authority of the Ministry

---

4 "Memorandum of the Ministry of Education on the Budget of 1916," *Zhurnal Ministerstva Narodnago Prosveshcheniia* [*Journal of the Ministry of Public Education*], July 1916; see also Johnson, *op. cit.*, p. 196.

of Commerce and Industry. Numerous other specialized secondary schools also appeared, including agriculture, surveying, medicine (for training medical assistants and midwives), and art. The growth of public education made the training of primary-school teachers imperative, and special secondary schools were set up for this purpose. By 1915, there were 43 teachers' institutes (normal schools) and 168 teachers' secondary schools and seminaries. Including the long-established military junior or *cadet* and senior or *junker* schools and theological seminaries, Russia possessed in 1915 some 2000 secondary schools with a total enrollment of about 700,000 students.[5]

Between the era of the great reforms and World War I the most fundamental and widespread transformation in Russian education occurred on the primary level. Except for the areas affected by Kiselev's reforms on state-owned lands, the Russian countryside was woefully lacking in primary schools, and peasant illiteracy was almost universal in the 1860s. Progress in this field during the 1870s was very slow, and in 1880 there were only 22,700 rural primary schools in European Russia, with some 1,140,000 pupils. Their expenditures amounted to 6.2 million rubles annually, of which 44 percent was paid for by the zemstvos, 34 percent by rural communes, 12 percent by the central government, and 10 percent by miscellaneous sources, largely private.[6]

By the end of the nineteenth century the need for primary education increasingly attracted the attention of the public and the zemstvos. The government slowly followed their lead, but the influential overprocurator of the Holy Synod, Pobedonostsev, favored the development of parochial schools *(tserkovno-prikhodskie shkoly)*, which stressed religious education. A statute for these schools was issued in June 1884. In educational matters, the parochial schools were under the jurisdiction of the Holy Synod, while the zemstvo schools were subject to the close control of provincial directors and district inspectors appointed by the Ministry of Public Education. In the competition that developed between the parochial and the zemstvo schools, the latter were winning, with public support.

In 1897 regulations for primary schools were issued, containing a model program that became standard for the zemstvo schools. A four-year curriculum included religion, Russian, Church-Slavonic (the language of the Orthodox church service), arithmetic, geography, and Russian history. The parochial schools mostly pro-

---

[5] Johnson, *op. cit.*, p. 196.
[6] *Istoriia Rossii v XIX veke*, vol. VII, p. 165.

vided a lower level of education; some of them were merely "literacy schools" where, in addition to religion, only reading and writing were taught.

According to official statistics quoted by P. Miliukov, the status of primary education in Russia in 1899 was as follows:[7]

	Schools	Pupils
	(Number in Thousands)	
I. RURAL		
1. Primary schools administered by Ministry of Education	29.9	2074.1
2. Parochial schools administered by the Holy Synod	18.3	882.1
3. "Schools of literacy" administered by the Holy Synod	21.5	571.6
Subtotal	69.7	3527.8
II. URBAN		
1. Schools for children administered by the Ministry of Education	5.8	513.1
2. Schools for children under other administration	2.0	103.4
3. Schools for adult education	1.8	89.0
Subtotal	9.6	705.5
Total, rural and urban	79.3	4233.3
III. RELIGIOUS JEWISH AND MUSLIM SCHOOLS (1894)	26.6	489.0

The last category in the above table deserves some elaboration. The language of the primary schools in the Russian Empire (with the partial exception of Poland and the Baltic provinces) was Russian. Jewish and Muslim minorities, however, maintained their own primary schools, confessional in character. In 1912 there were in Russia some 25,000 small schools called *heder*, where religious instruction was given in Yiddish to some 363,000 pupils; there were also several hundred larger, "organized" Jewish primary schools. For secondary and higher education, however, Jewish children had to enter Russian schools, access to which, as long as the schools were government-supported, was limited by the quota system.[8]

---

[7] P. Miliukov, *Ocherki po istorii russkoi kul'tury* [*Outlines of Russian Culture*] (3d ed.; St. Petersburg, 1902), vol. II, p. 382.

[8] F. Gets, "Shkol'noe obuchenie russkikh evreev" ["School Education of Russian Jews"], *Zhurnal M.N.P.*, October 1913, p. 226. According to Gets, in the same journal May 1914 (p. 27), the actual proportion of Jewish students in Russian gymnasiums was 9.8 percent; in the real gymnasiums, 7.3 percent; in the girls' gymnasiums, 13.6 percent; and in the universities, 9.7 percent. The Jewish population in Russia at that time comprised 3.9 percent of the total population.

For Turco-Tatar Muslim children there existed the *mektebe,* a primary school where children were taught by mullahs to read and write in the Tatar language (in Arabic characters) and learned certain prayers and passages from the Koran. For chosen boys there were schools of higher religious learning, called *medresse,* where future mullahs were educated. According to incomplete official statistics for 1912, there were 6728 Muslim schools in European Russia, Siberia, and Transcaucasia with 334,000 pupils, and 7975 more Muslim schools in Russian Central Asia.[9]

In pioneering and financing the development of Russian primary education the zemstvo institutions deserve the major share of credit until the time of the Third Duma, when the central government began to assume an important financial role. At first, teachers' salaries were usually paid by the village communes, with occasional supplementary help from the zemstvos, but the latter soon assumed the full cost of wages as well as school construction and equipment. The zemstvo elementary school attracted well-trained teachers, including many women, and gradually achieved a high educational standard. By 1905 expenditures for primary education amounted to 49.1 million rubles, of which 30.7 percent was paid for by the zemstvos. The share of the central government increased to 20 percent; that of the rural communes declined to 14.7 percent. Municipalities contributed 19.4 percent, private persons 5.4 percent, while 5.3 percent came from fees and 4.5 percent from miscellaneous sources. Over the four decades preceding World War I, zemstvo expenditures for primary education increased as follows:[10]

	Thousands of Rubles	Percent of Total Zemstvo Expenditures
1880	5200	14.3
1890	7266	14.9
1900	15,971	17.9
1905	25,314	20.4
1910	42,882	24.9
1913	90,129	31.0
1914	104,597	31.1

The establishment of popular representation in Russia in 1906 gave very strong impetus to the development of primary educa-

---

[9] N. Bobrovnikov, "Sovremennoe polozhenie uchebnago dela u inorodcheskikh plemen vostochnoi Rossii" ["Contemporary Education of the Native Tribes of Eastern Russia"], *Zhurnal M.N.P.,* May 1917, pp. 64–66.

[10] Hans, *op. cit.,* p. 232, table 4.

tion. Under the pressure of the Duma and the zemstvo leaders, the government began to appropriate more and more funds from the state treasury for this purpose. Much of the credit for increased appropriations for education belonged to E. P. Kovalevsky, vice-chairman and later chairman of the Duma committee on education. In seven years, central government expenditures on primary education more than quadrupled, rising from 23,600,000 rubles in 1907 to 109,800,000 in 1914.

The Duma, the zemstvos and public opinion demanded energetic steps toward the introduction of universal primary education, and as a result the first in a series of laws aiming at this goal was signed by the tsar May 3, 1908; the law provided that all children of both sexes between the ages of eight and eleven were to receive a four-year primary education. The year 1922 was set as the target date for the achievement of universal primary education, and to implement this program huge sums of money were made available by the Duma. Beginning with 1909, Moscow and then scores of other cities started introducing general elementary education. In Petersburg, expenditures on education rose from 11.5 percent of the municipal budget in 1903 to 20.3 percent in 1916. In other cities this share was much less, but small towns which had few other municipal services spent some 20 percent of their budget on schools.

As a result of all these efforts the number of elementary schools in Russia (excluding "schools of literacy" and confessional schools) increased from 55,900 in 1899 to 100,700 in 1911 and 149,500 in 1915. About 60 percent of the elementary schools in 1911 were administered by the Ministry of Education, and about 38 percent by the Holy Synod. The enrollment increased from 3.6 million in 1899 to 6.2 million in 1911 and reached 8.1 million in 1915: this was more than half of the school-age population.[11]

Independent public organizations were also established to raise the level of literacy. In 1861 the Petersburg Committee on Literacy was established by the Free Economic Society and a similar committee was soon founded in Moscow. These organizations did much to develop Sunday classes for adults, public lectures, popular

---

[11] D. M. Odinetz, "Primary and Secondary Schools," in D. M. Odinets and P. J. Novgorodtsev, *Russian Schools and Universities in the World War* (James T. Shotwell, ed., *Economic and Social History of the World War* series, New Haven, 1929), p. 12; Hans, *op. cit.*, p. 233, table 5; and Johnson, *op. cit.*, p. 196. It should be noted that official Russian statistics on school education were not always complete or precise; therefore, some discrepancies in the number of schools and pupils can be found in various surveys of Russian education.

literature, public libraries, and reading rooms. An especially notable example of this sort of activity was the "People's House," a public cultural center established by Countess Panina in Petersburg before 1900.

The zemstvos, on their part, did not limit themselves to the support of schools, but were active in the establishment of public libraries and reading rooms, the establishment of adult education programs, and the publication of inexpensive booklets and brochures designed for the rural population. In 1904 they were operating at least 3000 libraries and reading rooms. Municipal governments also operated libraries, courses for adults, and even popular theaters.

In the last decade before World War I, youth organizations devoted to sports and extracurricular education began to develop. An organization promoted by the military were the *Poteshnye,* named after the regiment of boy-soldiers who were the playmates of Peter the Great. More popular were the *Sokol* (Falcons), patterned after the Czech nationalist organization devoted to physical education and the promotion of Slavic brotherhood. Finally, in 1909, the first Russian Boy Scout troop was founded in Pavlovsk, near Tsarskoe Selo. By 1917 the Scout movement numbered over 50,000 boys and girls.

The cultural backwardness of Russia was thus rapidly disappearing in the last decades before the Revolution of 1917 along with her economic backwardness, but clearly such a radical transformation could not be fully accomplished in a short span of time. The census of 1897 revealed that Russia was only 21 percent literate; by 1914 it is estimated that literacy had risen markedly to approximately 44 percent.[12] This represented a great advance, but still left much to be done.

The Social Sciences and Humanities

The main centers of scholarly activity in the years following the great reforms were the Academy of Sciences, the universities, and a number of scientific societies and organizations. The universities and the various branches of the Academy of Sciences each published its own periodicals, which contained scholarly monographs and articles, while the Ministry of Education for eighty years preceding 1917 issued the monthly *Journal of the Ministry of Public Education,* which in-

---

[12] V. A. Riazanovsky, *Obzor russkoi kul'tury* [*Survey of Russian Culture*] (New York, 1947), vol. II, p. 463.

cluded rich and diverse scholarly works in addition to official items. The Archeographical Commission in Petersburg (founded in 1834) continued its energetic activity, publishing the *Complete Collection of Russian Chronicles, Supplements to the Historical Acts, Acts Pertaining to the History of Southern and Western Russia,* more than thirty volumes of the *Russian Historical Library,* and many other publications. Archeographical commissions were also established in Kiev (1843), Vilno (1863), and Tiflis (1864), and published voluminous collections of documents.

In the 1880s in many provincial capitals archival commissions and provincial historical archives were founded for the study and collection of local antiquities. In 1866, the Russian Historical Society was organized in Petersburg "to collect, examine and disseminate materials on the history of the fatherland." The latter society began immediately to publish collections of historical documents under the title of *Sbornik,* and in its fifty years of activity issued almost 150 valuable volumes and a multivolume biographical dictionary. Every year still another organization, the Society of Russian History and Antiquities at Moscow University, published four volumes of *Readings (Chteniia),* which contained a rich collection of historical and literary materials as well as scholarly monographs. In 1877, the Society of the Lovers of Ancient Literature was established, and by 1916 it had published 188 issues of its *Memorabilia (Pamiatniki drevnei pismennosti),* containing old Russian manuscripts of value for the study of language, church history, and social customs.

In 1888, the Russian Historical Museum was founded in Moscow, and in 1897, the Russian Museum of Emperor Alexander III was opened in Petersburg. The Free Economic Society, founded in 1765, continued its activities; these included current economic research and questionnaire surveys, as well as publishing and educational work. In the 1860s a juridical society was established in Moscow to discuss questions of legal theory and practice, and at the beginning of the twentieth century a religious and philosophical society was formed in Petersburg.

Historical documents, memoirs and articles appeared in a number of historical monthly periodicals: *The Russian Archives (Russkii Arkhiv),* founded by P. I. Bartenev in 1863; *The Russian Past (Russkaia Starina),* founded by M. I. Semevsky in 1870; and *The Historical Herald (Istoricheskii Vestnik),* founded by S. N. Shubinsky in 1880. A rich collection of historical sources was contained in the publication of a number of private archives, such as those of Prince M. S. Vorontsov (forty volumes and index). Substantial collections of government documents, including treaties and the proceedings of the Duma and the Council of State, also appeared. Archeological societies were founded in Petersburg (1846) and Moscow (1864), and in 1850, a state Archeological Commission was organized to direct excavations. In 1869, the first Russian archeological congress took place, and later such congresses were called periodically and published their papers. In 1877, the Archeological Institute was opened in Petersburg, and in 1894, a Russian archeological Institute, directed by the Byzantinist F. I. Uspensky, was established in Constantinople to assist Russian historians and archeologists in the countries of the Near East.

Serious archeological research began with the excavation of Greek settlements in the Kerch area in the 1820s; in the 1860s I. E. Zabelin made Scythian and Greek finds of great value on the lower Dnieper and on the Taman; and in the beginning of the twentieth century B. V. Farmakovsky directed large excavations of the Greek city of Olvia near the mouth of the Bug River. The outstanding student of Hellenic and Iranian civilization on the territory of southern Russia, ancient Scythia, was M. I. Rostovtsev. A great expert on Russian and Byzantine antiquities, N. P. Kondakov, collaborated with Count I. I. Tolstoy in publishing *Russian Antiquities in the Monuments of Art* in six volumes (1889–1898). Excavations of Slavonic burial mounds in central Russia began in 1838; at midcentury, A. S. Uvarov opened a great number of burial mounds in the Vladimir area; and toward the end of the century important excavations were made in the Novgorod and Smolensk areas. The geographic distribution of ancient Russian tribes was traced from the burial mound material by A. A. Spitsyn, who classified and published a wealth of data.

In Russian history one volume of S. M. Soloviev's *History of Russia from Ancient Times* appeared each year from 1851 to 1879; the twenty-nine volumes cover the period up to the beginning of the reign of Catherine the Great and have remained a standard work to this day. Soloviev's successor to the chair of Russian history in Moscow University was V. O. Kliuchevsky, whose lectures and published works concentrated on domestic history, especially the juridical and social relationship between the various classes and estates. Among his works the most outstanding is *The Boyar Duma of Ancient Rus (Boiarskaia duma drevnei Rusi)*, which gives not only the history of this institution but also an analysis of the entire social structure of pre-Petrine Russia. His *Course in Russian History* in five volumes, compiled from his lectures, is distinguished for its literary merits as well as its scholarship. The exceptionally vigorous historical activity at Moscow University around the turn of the century included the works of M. M. Bogoslovsky on the seventeenth century and Peter the Great, M. K. Liubavsky on the Lithuanian-Russian state, A. A. Kizevetter on the eighteenth century, Iu. V. Gotie on the social and economic history of the seventeenth century, and P. N. Miliukov on the cultural history of Russia. N. A. Rozhkov and M. N. Pokrovsky tried to apply the Marxist approach to Russian history, but the latter's writings were more political than historical. In Petersburg University, K. N. Bestuzhev-Riumin held the chair of Russian history for many years (1865 to 1884), followed in 1887 by S. F. Platonov, whose most valuable works dealt with the Time of Troubles; his *Lecture Course in Russian History* was widely used. Platonov's associate at Petersburg University, S. V. Rozhdestvensky, wrote mostly on Russian education in the eighteenth and nineteenth centuries.

Other prominent historians at the turn of the century were A. E. Presniakov (ancient Russia), N. P. Pavlov-Sil'vansky (feudalism), P. G. Liubomirov (Time of Troubles), V. S. Ikonnikov (historiography), N. G. Ustrialov (Peter the Great), N. K. Schilder (Paul I, Alexander I, Nicholas I), Grand Duke Nikolai Mikhailovich (the reign of Alexander I), M. V. Dovnar-Zapol'sky (the Decembrists, as well as the history of western Russia), S. S. Tatishchev (foreign policy under Nicholas I and the reign of Alexander II), and A. A. Kornilov (general history of the nineteenth century). In depth, variety, and originality Russian historical scholarship of this period was equal to that of any other contemporary country. Among the aspects of Russian history that received especially strong emphasis were legal history (Gradovsky, Chicherin, Sergeevich, Diakonov, Vladimirsky-Budanov, Kavelin); the history of the peasantry prior to 1861 (Semevsky, Lappo-Danilevsky, Grekov); the emancipation of the serfs (Semenov, Ignatovich, Ivaniukov, Dzhanshiev); the peasant commune and the agrarian problem (Kachorovsky, Kovalevsky, Kaufman, Maslov, Oganovsky, Rittich); history of cities (Nikitsky, Zabelin, Ditiatin); history of western Russian regions (Antonovich, Kostomarov, Hrushevsky, Lappo, Leontovich, Picheta); and finally the Church and the sects (Metropolitan Makarii, Golubinsky, Shchapov, Prugavin, Bonch-Bruevich).

In the last decade before the 1917 Revolution a series of large collective studies appeared: *The War of 1812 and Russian Society* (7 volumes, 1912); *The Great Reform* (6 volumes, 1911); *History of Russia in the Nineteenth Century* (9 volumes, ca. 1910); and *Social Movements in Russia in the Beginning of the Twentieth Century* (5 volumes, 1909–1914). The scholarly level of these collective works, however, was very uneven; along with factual material they contained a great deal of partisan and polemical journalistic writing. The outside world was by no means ignored by Russian historians. In addition to N. I. Kareev's general, seven-volume *History of Western Europe in the Modern Age,* P. G. Vinogradov did original work on the social order of medieval England, M. M. Kovalevsky wrote on the economic history of Europe, E. V. Tarle and I. V. Luchitsky studied France, and a number of able scholars worked on the Near and Far East. Outstanding authorities on the history of Byzantium were F. I. Uspensky, V. G. Vasilevsky, and A. A. Vasiliev.

In the fields of philology and literary studies there was also much vigorous activity. Talented philologists such as V. I. Dal, I. I. Sreznevsky, and A. A. Shakhmatov published important studies of the modern Russian language and its antecedents. The standard reference works on the history of Russian literature were a general survey in four volumes of A. N. Pypin (first published in the 1890s); *History of Russian Literature in the Ninteenth Century,* in five volumes, edited by D. N. Ovsianiko-Kulikovsky (1908–1911); *Russian Literature in the Twentieth Century,* in three volumes (1914–1916), and the six-volume *Critical and Bibliographical Dictionary of Russian Writers and Scholars,* both edited by S. A. Vengerov. Other notable historians of literature were V. Savodnik, A. N. Veselovsky, P. P. Pekarsky, and A. M. Skabichevsky. In the field of art history one should mention D. V. Ainalov *(Russian Painting from the Sixteenth to the Nineteenth Century);* A. N. Benois *(Russian Nineteenth Century Painting);* and I. E. Grabar' *(History of Russian Art,* in six volumes).

The left wing of the Russian sociological and economic studies was profoundly influenced by the Marxist school, headed by Plekhanov, and the populist school, led by Mikhailovsky until 1904 and by Chernov afterwards. The main lines of their work are treated above along with the social and political movement of the era. But despite the partisan and polemical tendencies of Marxist and populist social scientists, much of their work, particularly the writings of the "legal Marxists," was of real scholarly value. P. B. Struve, S. N. Prokopovich, and M. I. Tugan-Baranovsky made important contributions to the study of Russian economic history; Tugan-Baranovsky also did pioneering theoretical work on the relationship of investment to economic cycles.

Moreover, Marxism, ever since the first Russian translation of *Das Kapital* in 1872, had a considerable influence on nonleftist academic economists in Russia—for example, the labor theory of value, as expounded by Marx, was accepted by many of them. The best-known representatives of this middle-of-the-road academic group were the economist A. I. Chuprov, the economic historian M. M. Kovalevsky, the political economist A. A. Manuilov, and the historians of credit and finance P. P. Migulin and I. Kh. Ozerov. One should also mention E. E. Slutsky, who was among the first to develop a mathematical theory of consumer choice. The outstanding legal theoreticians of the time—decidedly non-Marxist—were P. I. Novgorodtsev, author of *On the Public Ideal (Ob obshchestvennom ideale);* N. M. Korkunov, author of the standard reference work, *Russian Public Law (Russkoe gosudarstvennoe pravo);* L. I. Petrazhitsky *(General Theory of Law);* and A. F. Koni.

One of the outstanding Russian pedagogues was N. I. Pirogov, also known as "the father of Russian surgery." Other prominent theoreticians and practitioners of humanistic methods in teaching were K. D. Ushinsky, V. P. Vakhterov, P. F. Lesgaft, and P. F. Kapterev.

For many years philosophy suffered a sad fate in Russia. The keen interest in the German idealists, characteristic of the 1830s and '40s, soon went out of fashion. In the 1860s, Pisarev's ideas held sway, and philosophy, along with religion, esthetics, and ethics, was thrown overboard as "superfluous rubbish" by much of the "enlightened" public. The religious and philosophical works of A. S. Khomiakov in the mid-nineteenth century are but a minor exception, for they interested only a limited circle of his friends.

But in the last decades of the nineteenth century philosophy emerged from its "exile" and occupied an honored position in the vigorous cultural life of Russia in the decades before World War I. Vladimir Soloviev, who was a popularizer of philosophy as well as a philosopher, played a major role in this development. In his writings he connected the fundamental questions of philosophical knowledge with religious and ethical problems (for example, in his book *The Justification of the Good,* 1895) and established the close tie of abstract philosophy with ethics and religion as a characteristic of the new Russian philosophy. By the beginning of the twentieth century a whole series of talented Russian philosophers appeared, including a number who have attained recognition outside Russia, such as N. O. Lossky, S. L. Frank, S. N. Bulgakov, and N. A. Berdyaev. Interest in philosophy quickly developed in educated circles, and the meetings of the Religious-Philosophical Society were often major events in intellectual life.

The new Russian philosophy was many-sided and diversified. Some philosophers, such as Lossky, worked in the spirit of per-
sonalism and "intuitivism." Some, like Bulgakov, crossed the line
from philosophy into theology; Frank and L. P. Karsavin were concerned with the question of the Absolute, basing themselves on
Nicholas of Cusa. Others, such as A. I. Vvedensky and I. I. Lapshin
and a group of younger philosophers, advocated Neo-Kantianism; Lev
Shestov was an existentialist; and a significant group continued the
positivist tradition, influenced by Ernst Mach and Richard Avenarius.

It is significant that in this development Marxism was
definitely on the wane and some kind of Neo-Orthodox Christianity
was on the rise. This trend first became apparent in 1903, with the
publication of a volume of essays entitled *Problems of Idealism.*
Participants in this controversial anthology included the legal theoretician Novgorodtsev and several idealist philosophers who had been
prominent Marxists (Berdyaev, Bulgakov). The volume contained a
strong critique of prevailing positivist and materialist views. In 1909,
a number of leading scholars, philosophers and journalists, including
the former Marxists Bulgakov, Berdyaev, Struve, and Izgoev, published a second collection of essays, entitled *Landmarks (Vekhi).* The
book caused an uproar in intellectual circles for, in addition to
philosophical discourse, it contained a sweeping indictment of the
radical intelligentsia. The authors of this striking declaration called
on the intelligentsia to "re-examine the very foundations of its traditional world-view, which hitherto has been taken on trust blindly."
The critics found in this traditional world-view "a low level of philosophy, a lack of serious philosophical knowledge and incapacity for
serious philosophical thought." By "fanatically upholding materialism
and atheism," the revolutionary intelligentsia had "distorted her soul
and destroyed her instinct for truth." "The mass of the intelligentsia
was without individuality, with all the features of a herd, its stupid inertness, its radicalism, its fanatical intolerance . . . we may define the
classical Russian intellectual as a militant monk of the nihilist
religion of worldly well-being."[13]

The *Vekhi* group, of course, did not represent the majority
opinion, and several books and many articles defending the intelligentsia and attacking the *Vekhi* group appeared. But the anthology
was widely read, running through several editions in one year, and
its appearance not only reflected the vigorous quality of prewar intellectual life in Russia, but also showed that the intelligentsia was

---

[13] *Vekhi [Landmarks]* (Moscow, 1909), pp. 20, 84, 204.

by no means wedded to Marxist or other materialist modes of thought. In any case, the promising rise of Russian philosophy around the turn of the century was cut short by the Bolshevik Revolution.

The growth of intellectual activity and the increase in literacy in the last decades of the Russian Empire were also reflected in the rapid expansion of the publishing industry. Considerable attention was devoted to the publication of low-cost, high-quality literature for the mass market. The most notable publishing houses were Enlightenment *(Prosveshchenie);* Science and Life *(Nauka i zhizn');* The Intermediary *(Posrednik),* which specialized in low-cost books; A. F. Marx, which supplied cheap editions of Russian writers as supplements to the magazine *Niva;* Brockhaus and Efron, which published an eighty-six volume encyclopedia; the brothers Granat; A. S. Suvorin; F. Pavlenkov; I. D. Sytin in Moscow; and Il'in's Cartographic Institution, which published excellent maps and atlases. The Society for the Dissemination of Technical Knowledge published a great quantity of scientific literature and good novels at lower cost than similar books in the West.

The periodical press, too, grew remarkably. The main literary monthlies in the beginning of the twentieth century were the Marxist *Contemporary World (Sovremennyi Mir);* the populist *Russian Wealth (Russkoe Bogatstvo);* and the liberal *Herald of Europe (Vestnik Evropy)* and *Russian Thought (Russkaia Mysl').* Virtually every field of scientific and artistic activity was represented. The universities and the learned societies and congresses published their papers; each of the central government institutions had its periodical publications; in Moscow, Petersburg, and provincial cities there were newspapers of various trends, from the reactionary Black Hundreds to the anarchists. The newspapers with the greatest circulations in Petersburg were *Speech (Rech')* of the Kadets; the meandering rightist *New Time (Novoe Vremia);* and the *Mercantile Gazette (Birzhevye Vedomosti),* which was not affiliated with any of the parties; and in Moscow, the liberal *Russian Word (Russkoe Slovo)* and the *Russian Gazette (Russkie Vedomosti).* The socialist press was legal, but it had to provide itself with special "stand-by" editors in case an especially abusive issue should lead to the trial of the paper and the sentence of its "responsible editor," usually a worker, to two or three months in prison. His place would then be occupied by his understudy. If the court closed the newspaper, it would simply reappear under a different name, as the Bolshevik *Pravda* did many times in 1912–1914. In 1912 there were 2167 periodical publications in thirty-three languages, including 1585 Russian publications, 234 Polish, 69 German,

47 Lithuanian, 45 Esthonian, 31 Jewish, 21 Armenian, 20 Latvian, 13 Georgian, and 12 Ukrainian ones.[14]

The Natural Sciences

In the fields of science and mathematics, medicine and technology, a series of important organization were established in the latter half of the nineteenth century. In 1859, the Society of Russian Physicians was established (later adding the name "Pirogov" in honor of that physician-social reformer). It carried out extensive medical research as well as professional and social activities. In 1866, the Russian Technological Society, the professional association of engineers, was formed, and in 1890, the Russian Astronomical Society and the Petersburg Mathematical Society appeared.

D. I. Mendeleev, one of the world's great chemists, was the most prominent figure in Russian science in the second half of the nineteenth century. In 1869 he classified chemical elements according to his famous "periodic table," which made it possible to predict a number of elements unknown at that time and to detect errors in atomic weights. Mendeleev also devoted much study to the nature of solutions and the theory of gases. An outstanding teacher, he was vitally interested in problems of Russian industrial development, as well as in social studies.

Mendeleev's contemporaries included N. N. Beketov, who specialized in the field of physical chemistry, and A. N. Butlerov, who developed Lomonosov's brilliant contributions to the molecular and atomic structure of matter, which had been neglected for nearly a century. N. A. Menshutkin studied the velocity of organic reactions, and V. V. Markovnikov the structure of certain organic molecules. The concentration of many distinguished chemists in Petersburg in the 1870s and '80s prepared the ground for a broad development of chemistry in Russia toward the turn of the century. Among the representatives of the next generation were M. I. Konovalov, A. E. Favorsky, N. D. Zelinsky, and S. N. Reformatsky. They contributed to nitration of hydrocarbons, the synthesis of metallo-organic compounds, the study of isomerism, and catalytic reactions. V. N. Ipatiev became particularly known in the West for his work on catalysis under high pressures, and between 1899 and 1916, I. L. Kondakov with S. V. Lebedev, through their work on polymers, developed the

[14] M. Florinsky, *Russia* (New York, 1953), vol. II, p. 1239.

principles of synthesizing rubber. D. P. Konovalov and N. S. Kurnakov worked in inorganic physical chemistry.

The father of nineteenth-century physics in Russia was A. G. Stoletov, known for his investigation of magnetism, photoelectricity, and electric discharges in gases (the "Stoletov effect"). In 1870, he founded the Physics Laboratory at Moscow University. It became the workshop of many notable Russian physicists, among them Stoletov's successor, N. A. Umov (energy flow, magnetism), and P. N. Lebedev, who gained world-wide renown for proving experimentally the pressure of light on solids (1899) and on gases (1907). In 1911, Lebedev established the first privately sponsored physics laboratory in Russia, which contributed to the great expansion of experimental physics before World War I. Extensive research in astronomy, astrophysics, and optics (particularly with regard to the Doppler effect) was carried on at the Pulkovo observatory near Petersburg.

Russia also produced many inventors who worked on the practical applications of physics, but because of the technological backwardness of the country and the language barrier, their importance often went unrecognized in their time. For example, as early as 1802, V. V. Petrov, independently of Sir Humphrey Davy, employed a huge battery with 4200 pairs of plates to produce an electric arc, and used it to melt metal. P. N. Iablochkov in 1875 devised an electric arc lamp with parallel carbon rods, which were manufactured commercially in France and became known as the "Jablochkoff candle." A. N. Lodygin demonstrated an incandescent electric lamp in Petersburg in 1873. About 200 of these were used to light the Admiralty dock, but unreliability of operation prevented commercial production. I. F. Usagin developed a workable electric transformer for the Moscow Industrial Exposition of 1882. In April 1895, A. S. Popov demonstrated before a large audience at the Petersburg University his apparatus for wireless transmission of messages by electromagnetic waves, fifteen months before Marconi applied for his patent.

Greater international impact was achieved by the theoretical work of Russian scientists in various fields of applied physics before and after the turn of the century. Of fundamental importance for the field of metallography and metallurgy was the work of D. K. Chernov, an engineer at the government-owned Obukhov Ordnance Works in Petersburg. Beginning in 1868, he related the changes in the crystalline structure of steel to its cooling process, thus providing a scientific basis for the thermal treatment of metals.

A. N. Krylov developed the theory of hydrodynamics as applied to problems of marine engineering, such as wave motion, ship rolling, and stabilization. N. E. Zhukovsky, who is called the father of Russian aviation, also began his studies in hydraulics and hydrodynamics, but became interested, after 1890, in the theory of flight. In 1904 he published his fundamental equations relating to the theory of uplift. In the same year he founded his Aerodynamic Institute near Moscow, where experimental work was carried out in a wind tunnel. Zhukovsky's close associate and successor in the field of aviation mechanics was S. A. Chaplygin, who between 1902 and 1910 formulated the theory of the pressure of gases on moving obstacles mathematically. Even more forward-looking was the work of K. E. Tsiolkovsky who, starting from a general interest in mathematics and mechanics, developed first the theory of the dirigible and the airplane and then, after 1903, the theory of using rocket propulsion and centrifugal force for interplanetary travel. Though not many people thought seriously about these subjects in his time, he received a prize from the Academy of Sciences in 1899. In the field of structural engineering, basic contributions were made by S. P. Timoshenko, whose concern was with the strength, stability, and vibration of elastic bodies.

All these achievements in the theory of mechanics would have been impossible without a rather sophisticated mathematical tradition, the roots of which date back to Leonard Euler's teaching in Russia in 1727–1741 and 1766–1783. He founded a tradition of mathematical thought in Russia which, unlike the development of physics, was not hampered by technological limitations. As noted earlier, this tradition was carried out in the first half of the nineteenth century by Lobachevsky. In the latter half of the century, P. L. Chebyshev, who died in 1894, was an outstanding thinker in mathematics. Unlike Lobachevsky, whose mind worked in a purely abstract way, Chebyshev sought to tie the problems of mathematics to theoretical and applied problems of natural science. Extremely versatile, he worked in the fields of probability, number theory, integration, theory of functions, and theory of mechanisms. In every one of these fields he outlined several basic methods and problems, which were later further investigated by his numerous followers, including A. M. Liapunov, A. A. Markov (Markov chains), and V. A. Steklov.

Prominent mathematicians independent of the Chebyshev school were N. V. Bugaev, one of the founders of the Moscow Mathematical Society, in which he was active after 1867, and Sofia V.

Kovalevskaia (Korvin-Krukovskaia), who for political reasons was forced to spend much of her time abroad.

In the first decades of the twentieth century, a Moscow school of mathematical thought emerged led by D. F. Egorov and N. N. Luzin. The latter worked mostly in the field of the theory of functions, striving to pursue the axiomatic approach of Lobachevsky, as contrasted with the empirical direction of Chebyshev. Luzin's followers in the Soviet period contributed to fields as diverse as probability, topology, algebra, and mathematical logic.

In the biological sciences, A. O. Kovalevsky and I. I. Mechnikov continued the pioneering work in embryology done by Karl Baer, a Baltic German who spent part of his life in Europe but returned to Russia in 1834. Kovalevsky concentrated on empirical research in comparative embryology, and Mechnikov branched out into general physiology and bacteriology. Mechnikov discovered intracellular digestion in lower animals and the importance of phagocytosis (the ingestion of bacteria and other particles by living cells) in protecting the body against infectious agents. He was also concerned with problems of immunity, contagious diseases, and aging. He spent a considerable part of his life abroad, and joined the Pasteur Institute in Paris in 1890.

The physiology of higher animals was investigated by I. M. Sechenov and I. P. Pavlov. Sechenov succeeded in extracting gases from blood in 1858 and in 1862, through complex experiments, located certain reflex-retarding centers in the brain of the frog. Pavlov's early work was concerned with the nervous activity of the heart and with the physiology of digestion. He devised methods of observing digestion in living animals. His work on the secretion of salivary glands of dogs led him to investigate the physiological activities of the brain and to make his famous discovery of conditioned reflexes. He received the Nobel prize in 1904. Further investigations of nervous activity led him to study hypnosis, sleep, and neurotic disorders, including those experimentally induced. Unlike Sechenov, Pavlov, who was deeply religious, did not interpret his data in a materialistic way. Among other physiologists primarily concerned with the nervous system were N. E. Vvedensky and V. Bekhterev.

The study of microbiology in Russia was initiated by L. S. Tsenkovsky, who was also an outstanding botanist. S. N. Vinogradsky made important discoveries regarding nitrifying bacteria, which build up protein from inorganic molecules, and nitrogen fixating bacteria, which assimilate nitrogen from the air. He headed the microbiology section of the Institute of Experimental Medicine in Petersburg, established in 1891 and made famous by Pavlov. The theoretical and experimental work of Vinogradsky was continued by others who studied soil and water bacteria, fermentation, and the decomposition of cellulose.

Plant physiology was advanced by A. S. Famintsyn in the 1860s. Well known for his work on photosynthesis and chlorophyl was K. A. Timiriazev; plant metabolism in general was a favorite subject of several other Russian botanists. A. N. Beketov and V. L. Komarov studied plant morphology and the geographic distribution of the Russian flora, while N. A. Severtsov and V. M. Shimkevich were notable zoologists and N. I. Vavilov began his major studies in genetics.

On the threshold between biology and geology stood V. O. Kovalevsky, an ardent Darwinist, who did research on evolutionary paleontology in the eighteen seventies. A. P. Karpinsky, the dean of Russian geologists, contributed to paleontology as well as to tectonic analysis and to prospecting of mineral resources. The vastness, geographic variety, and mineral richness of Russia stimulated extensive geological and mineralogical research, best represented by E. S. Fedorov, who studied the symmetry of crystalline structures in minerals, and V. I. Vernadsky, an eminent authority on geochemistry.

Soil science as a separate discipline owes its inception to V. V. Dokuchaev, who was the first to study soils not merely as decomposed rock, but as a distinct natural body interdependent with climate, vegetation, and the animal world. Pedology was further developed by P. A. Kostychev, by V. R. Viliams, who stressed the evolutionary aspect, and by K. D. Glinka, whose book *The Great Soil Groups of the World and Their Development* (1908), revolutionized soil theory when it was translated into foreign languages several years later.

Finally, in the field of geography, fame was achieved by the Russian explorers P. P. Semenov, N. M. Przhevalsky, and N. N. Miklukho-Maklai. Semenov was awarded the surname Semenov-Tian-Shansky for his expeditions to the Tian Shan mountain chain in Central Asia in the 1850s. Przhevalsky explored the highlands of Ussuri, crossed the Gobi desert in 1870–1873, and undertook three expeditions into the areas between Tibet and Turkestan in the '70s and '80s. He discovered the wild camel and the primitive species of horse, now known by his name *(Equus prjevalskii)*. Miklukho-Maklai, whose main interest was in anthropology and ethnography, undertook several trips to New Guinea and Melanesia, where in 1871–1878 he studied the Papuans. Another famed geographer, anthropologist, and archeologist was D. N. Anuchin. A. N. Krasnov developed Dokuchaev's concept of landscape zones. After his journey to the Far East in 1895, he was instrumental in establishing tea plantations in Transcaucasia.

Literature

The years between the Crimean War and the early 1920s form an era of exceptional genius in Russian literature.

Between the time of the Crimean War and the early 1880s three world-renowned novelists, Tolstoy, Dostoevsky, and Turgenev, were at the height of their powers. As a young artillery officer, Tolstoy had participated personally in the defense of Sevastopol, and in his *Sevastopol Tales (Sevastopolskie raskazy)*, he realistically depicted the heroic struggle of the defenders. In the 1860s Tolstoy became interested in pedagogy, wrote articles in this field, and taught in the school at his estate, *Yasnaia Poliana*. In 1867–1869 he published his famous novel *War and Peace (Voina i mir)*, in which he presented a broad and vivid picture of Russian life at the beginning of the nineteenth century, with a detailed description of Russia's struggle against Napoleonic France. In the historical and philosophical part of his novel, Tolstoy developed the idea that in history the main role is played by mass movements, not the wishes and plans of the so-called "great men." Tolstoy's second great novel, *Anna Karenina*, was published in 1873–1876 and depicted the life of contemporary society, predominantly of the upper strata. Tolstoy later wrote a number of tales and short stories, including *The Death of Ivan Ilich (Smert' Ivana Il'icha)* and *The Kreutzer Sonata (Kreitzerova sonata)*, as well as two plays, a tragedy, *The Power of Darkness (Vlast' t'my)*, and a comedy, *The Fruits of Enlightenment (Plody prosveshcheniia)*.

In the 1880s Tolstoy turned from his literary work to moral and religious philosophy and the propagation of his new religion. He developed the teachings of a new Christianity in such works as *A Confession (Ispoved')*; *What I Believe (V chem moia vera)*; *The Kingdom of God is Within You (Tsarstvo Bozhie vnutri vas)*; and *The Critique of Dogmatic Theology (Kritika dogmaticheskogo bogosloviia)*. He rejected the dogmas and sacraments of the Orthodox Church as "pseudo-Christianity" and recognized only the moral teaching of "Christ the man": love of man and abstention from force in combating evil. Tolstoy rejected the state as well as the church, for he regarded both as instruments of violence and oppression. At the same time he opposed forcible revolution and awaited the liberation of humanity through the knowledge of truth and moral regeneration. In Tolstoy's last great novel, *Resurrection (Voskresenie)*, published in 1899, his artistic talent competes with his inclination to moralistic preaching. The antistate and antichurch writings of Tolstoy were published only abroad, but much of this literature penetrated Russia, and in the 1880s and early '90s some members of the intelligentsia were inclined toward Tolstoyism. In 1901 the Holy Synod published its decision that it did not regard Tolstoy as a member of the Orthodox Church, and even though Tolstoy did not deny that he had rejected the Church, the decision of the Synod caused a storm of public indignation in Russia. In November 1910, he determined to leave his estate and wander through the country, a rash enterprise for a man over eighty, and his death in the hamlet of Astapovo aroused a wave of pro-Tolstoy sentiment among the intelligentsia, thousands of whom attended his non-Orthodox funeral at his beloved *Yasnaia Poliana.*

Dostoevsky spent four years at hard labor in Siberia as a result of his participation in the socialist Petrashevsky circle, and after receiving an amnesty from Alexander II in 1856, he returned and described his experience in *Memoirs from the House of the Dead (Zapiski iz mertvogo doma)*, published in 1861. In the next two decades he published the novels that established him as one of the great literary masters of modern times: *The Humiliated and Insulted (Unizhennye i oskorblennye); Crime and Punishment (Prestuplenie i nakazanie); The Idiot; The Possessed (Besy);* and *The Brothers Karamazov (Brat'ia Karamazovy)*. The characteristic features of Dostoevsky's works are the subtlety and depth of psychological analysis by which he penetrates the inner life of his heroes and his deep humanity. In Dostoevsky as in Tolstoy, the artist, thinker, and publicist were combined, but unlike Tolstoy, Dostoevsky did not break with the Orthodox Church. Moreover, he attacked the nihilist ideas of his time; radical and liberal opinion regarded his novel *The Possessed,* based on the trial of the Nechaev group, as a slander of the Russian revolutionary intelligentsia. *The Diary of a Writer (Dnevnik pisatelia)*, written in 1876–1877, was received more sympathetically, despite its Slavophilism. Dostoevsky expressed warm sympathy for the liberation of the Slavs from Turkish oppression and for the future "great All-Slav unification in the name of the Christian truth." But at the same time Dostoevsky expounded the worship of the people and the "people's truth," because the people, according to Dostoevsky, have the image of Christ at heart, for all their sinfulness. His Slavophilism was quite peculiar and opposed to any idea of national superiority. "The Russians," wrote Dostoevsky in his *Diary,* "have two homelands: our *Rus'* and Europe." And in his famous speech on Pushkin in 1880 he repeated that "the destiny of the Russian is undisputably all-European and universal," and that "to become a true Russian" meant "to become a brother of all men, a *universal* man, if you please."

The novels of Turgenev, which appeared in the 1850s, '60s and '70s, provide a vivid picture of the life of the contemporary Russian nobility and intelligentsia. Following his collection of sketches of the nobility and peasantry, *A Hunter's Sketches,* Turgenev published six major novels between 1856 and 1876: *Rudin; A Nest of Gentlefolk (Dvorianskoe gnezdo); On the Eve (Nakanune); Fathers and Sons (Otsy i deti); Smoke (Dym);* and *Virgin Soil (Nov').*

In *Fathers and Sons* he portrays the contemporary nihilist in the person of Bazarov, resulting in a great uproar in the intelligentsia, some of whom regarded Bazarov as a photographic likeness of the nihilist, while others considered it a caricature. The unfolding role of the radical intelligentsia was again Turgenev's theme in *Virgin Soil,* which describes the unsuccessful movement "to the people" in the 1870s. While Turgenev spent much of his life in Western Europe and was a thoroughgoing Westerner in conviction, he nevertheless portrayed Russian life without anger or bias. Only in *Smoke* did Turgenev employ a somewhat satirical style in presenting characters drawn from high society and the revolutionary intelligentsia. Unlike Tolstoy and Dostoevsky, whose intellectual influence, especially as ideologists, remained strong in their later years, Turgenev lost much of his popularity in the later 1870s. The increasingly radical intelligentsia accused him of losing touch with Russian reality, and the pessimistic and mystical character of his later works never achieved any following as ideologies.

Another novelist whose works were intimately involved in contemporary social issues was I. A. Goncharov, the author of *An Ordinary Story (Obyknovennaia istoriia,* 1846); *Oblomov* (1859); and *The Precipice (Obryv,* 1869). Of these *Oblomov* had the greatest social and literary merit, creating the conception of "oblomovism" henceforth the standard Russian expression for the condition of spiritual sluggishness, weak will, laziness, and apathy characteristic of a society based on serfdom. In *The Precipice,* Goncharov portrayed the new intellectual nihilists, whose appearance was partly a response to oblomovism.

From the 1860s through the '80s, M. E. Saltykov, whose pseudonym, Shchedrin, is often hyphenated to his name, defended human freedom, justice, and dignity in writings that established him as one of the greatest Russian satirists. He spent many years in the civil service, and on the basis of his personal experience he lashed out at the cruelty, arbitrariness, selfish hypocrisy, and banality on all levels of Russian society. Not only the bureaucrats, nobility, well-to-do peasants, and ordinary people, but also the liberal talkers, such as the lawyer "Balalaikin," were not spared. His many satirical sketches utilized topical, highly idiomatic "Aesopic language," as Saltykov called it, to evade censorship. Among his outstanding works, ranging from 1856 through 1889, are: *Provincial Sketches (Gubernskie ocherki); The History of a Town (Istoriia odnogo goroda); Gentlemen of Tashkent (Gospoda Tashkentsy); The Golovlov Family (Gospoda Golovlevy);* and *Old Times in Poshekhonie (Poshekhonskaia starina).*

The most outstanding playwright of the period was A. N. Ostrovsky, whose forty plays deal mainly with the civil servants and merchants of the middle class. For example, *The Bankrupt (Svoi liudi—sochtemsia,* 1850) portrays the rascality of some financial manipulators. *Poverty Is No Crime (Bednost' ne porok,* 1854) is a popular comedy of the familiar triangle of the rich merchant's daughter, the old man whom she is supposed to marry, and her impoverished young love. And *The Thunderstorm (Groza,* 1859) is a powerful tragedy concerning the descent to suicide of the wife of a contemptible merchant. Both conservative and radical critics praised Ostrovsky's plays, which attempted objective realism rather than accusation or satire. According to the radical critic Dobroliubov, Ostrovsky's depiction of the "dark kingdom" of the merchant class showed the arbitrariness and stupid wilfulness of the strong and the oppression and suffering of the weak.

Two important but less renowned novelists of this period were A. F. Pisemsky and N. S. Leskov. The former provided a pessimistic and realistic picture of contemporary society in such novels as *A Thousand Souls (Tysiacha dush,* 1858) and *The Burghers (Meshchane,* 1877) in his outstanding tragedy *A Bitter Lot (Gor'kaia sud'bina,* 1859), as well as in his antinihilist novels. Leskov was a talented but controversial writer. Although he was imbued with religiosity, he was not devoted to the traditional Church and in his later years inclined toward Tolstoy's teachings. While his non-Orthodox outlook disturbed the conservative critics, his antinihilist novels, *No Way Out (Nekuda,* 1864) and *At Daggers Drawn (Na nozhakh,* 1870), antagonized the radical public. But both supporters and adversaries respected his talent, especially his entertaining plots— partly legendary and fantastic and sometimes borrowed from folklore—and his colorful, intensely idiomatic language. His most famous work, *Cathedral Folk (Soborianie,* 1872) is the one great Russian novel on the life of the clergy.

A considerable group of Populist novelists were active between 1860 and 1880, idealizing the life of the peasantry, bemoaning the distintegration of the communal and patriarchal way of life, or regretting the failure of the people to attain the ideals of the Populists. Of this group, Gleb Uspensky is the outstanding representative. In *The Manners of Rasteriaeva Street (Nravy Rasteriaevoi ulitsy,* 1866), he described the urban poor and in *Sketches of Rural Life (Ocherki derevenskoi zhizni),* the countryside. By the time of the publication of his novel *The Power of the Soil (Vlast' zemli,* 1882), however, Uspensky had become disillusioned with populism. Other writers of the latter part of the century who dealt with the hard lot of the peasant and the decadence of landlordism were N. N. Zlatovratsky, *The Foundations (Ustoi);* F. M. Reshetnikov *The People of Podlipnoe (Podlipovtsy);* and S. N. Terpigorev *Impoverishment (Oskudenie).*

Although the genius of a Pushkin or a Lermontov was not to be found in the poetry of Russia in the latter half of the nineteenth century, N. A. Nekrasov (the "civic poet"), F. I. Tiutchev (the "philosopher poet"), Count A. K. Tolstoy, and A. A. Fet were poets of considerable merit.

Nekrasov, a member of the radical nobility-intelligentsia, was influential and highly successful as the publisher of *The Contemporary.* He shared the widespread theory of the time that the arts exist to serve society and stated that "you do not have to be a poet, but you are obliged to be a citizen." As the bard of the Russian peasant, his sorrowful lot and his suffering, Nekrasov devoted his art to the people and enjoyed unmatched popularity among the radical intelligentsia, many of whom considered him greater than Pushkin. Partly because of his original development of folkloristic themes, Nekrasov is recognized as one of the great poets of Russia, whether or not one accepts the "civic" theory of poetry that he expounded.

Tiutchev dedicated many of his poems to nature. He regarded nature as a profound mystery, full of primitive chaos, perceived as a harmonious cosmos only because it is seen from without. While acknowledging the tragic duality of creative and destructive powers in the world and in human beings, Tiutchev loved life and his homeland, poor and humble Russia, which he considered unintelligible to the Western world. Most of his poems were written and published in the 1830s, signed only by initials, and he received very little attention until Nekrasov "discovered" his works in 1850 and Turgenev republished a collection of them in 1854. In this sense Tiutchev, who died in 1873, may be considered a poet of the 1860s and '70s.

Count A. K. Tolstoy, a distant cousin of the great novelist, was also a playwright and novelist as well as a poet. His historical trilogy in blank verse, dealing with the death of Ivan the Terrible and the reigns of Fedor Ivanovich and Boris Godunov in the sixteenth and early seventeenth centuries, has been considered the best Russian attempt at the poetic-dramatic chronicle. His interest in the past was also reflected in a number of ballads, partly based on the Russian epic folk songs. While he advised his fellow poets to reject the "civic" theory, "to row against the current in the name of the beautiful," A. K. Tolstoy himself at times descended from his Parnassus to comment on current affairs, dealing satirical blows to both sides.

Fet (or Fet-Shenshin) was one of the most outstanding Russian lyric poets, whose works were mainly dedicated to love or to descriptions of nature. He began his poetic career in the 1840s, but kept silent in the 1860s and '70s when the radical critique declared lyric poetry to be a superfluous amusement of idle aristocrats. In the 1880s, when tastes changed, Fet resumed his activity and in 1883–1891 published four collections of his poems under the general title *Evening Lights (Vechernie ogni)*. The same movement back to lyric poetry in the 1880s is reflected in the works of A. N. Maikov, A. N. Pleshcheev, and Ia. P. Polonsky.

The passing of the golden age of the Russian novel by the mid-1880s did not imply the decline of Russian literature but rather the beginning of a new era, often called the "silver age," which was dominated by scarcely lesser talents of a different character. The first great figure of this period was A. P. Chekhov, whose outstanding short stories and plays established his reputation in the '80s. Between 1887 and 1904 Chekhov's major plays appeared, including *Ivanov, The Sea Gull (Chaika), Uncle Vania (Diadia Vania), Three Sisters (Tri Sestry)*, and the *Cherry Orchard (Vishnevyi sad)*. As presented with a peculiar "Chekhov mood" by the Moscow Art Theater, they founded the international reputation of both the writer and the theater. In the same period Chekhov proved that he was equally the master of the modern, naturalistic short story.

A doctor by profession, Chekhov did not belong to any political movement and remained a free artist despite the implied social criticism in his stories of peasants, ordinary citizens, intelligentsia, or bureaucrats, whose lives are usually drab, filled with triviality and often suffering, and are empty of meaning. Although the majority of Chekhov's stories are imbued with subtle humor or comic episodes, the general mood of his work is pessimistic. Chekhov does not castigate his weak heroes, but regards them with compassion and slight irony, as an experienced doctor might regard sick children. His humanitarian spirit is demonstrated in full measure in his book *Sakhalin,* in which he describes the life of criminals banished to that remote island, which he visited in 1890. His language is simple, concise, and exact, worthy of the greatest literary classics of Russia.

On the eve of the twentieth century Maxim Gorky (A. M. Peshkov) made his stormy appearance on the Russian literary scene and won tremendous public acclaim. In his early stories Gorky wrote in vivid, idiomatic language as a bard of the vagabonds and an advocate of extreme individualism. His early plays, *The Burghers (Meshchanie)* and *The Lower Depths (Na dne,* 1902), also enjoyed tremendous success. Although he was moved more by emotions than by ideology, Gorky hated "bourgeois" society, joined the Social Democrats in 1905, and was close to Lenin and the Bolsheviks, despite repeated disagreements. He thus became the bard of the "conscious proletariat," and some of his later works, such as the plays *The Barbarians (Varvary)* and *Enemies (Vragi),* were essentially propagandistic. In 1906 he visited the United States and declared New York to be "the city of the yellow devil" (the dollar). His major novels, *Foma Gordeev, Mother (Mat'),* A *Confession (Ispoved'), Okurov Town (Gorodok Okurov), Vassa Zheleznova,* and *The Artamonov's Business (Dela Artamonovykh)* are written in the style of an epic narrative but are generally tendentious, portraying righteous, heroic Social Democrats and workers on one side and criminal, vicious representatives of the "exploiters" on the other.

Other writers of a Marxist tendency around the turn of the century were Veresaev (V. V. Smidovich) and E. N. Chirikov. In his *Memoirs of a Doctor (Zapiski vracha,* 1901), Veresaev described the contemporary ideological movements among the intelligentsia, while Chirikov wrote a series of plays and stories on such political topics as the pogroms and agrarian violence of 1905–1906.

The populist point of view in early twentieth century literature is represented by V. G. Korolenko, who was exiled to Siberia in 1879 and later edited the populist journal *Russian Wealth.* Despite his political commitments, Korolenko's stories, essays, and autobiographical work *The Story of My Contemporary (Istoriia moego sovremennika,* 1910) were imbued with tolerance, humanitarianism, and liberty, rather than hate or resentment.

The intellectual background of Russian literature around the turn of the century was remarkably variegated, with older elements such as Marxism, populism, and Tolstoyanism competing with various new ideas. One influential writer was the philosopher V. S. Soloviev, the son of the eminent nineteenth-century historian, who developed an idealistic, mystical Christian conception of a fourth manifestation of God in the person of Sophia, the incarnation of divine wisdom. Soloviev was both theologian and poet, and his image of a mystical Sophia *(Sofia)*, the "Sublime Lady," the "Eternal Feminine," had a profound influence on the emergent symbolist movement in literature. The religious spirit also permeated the writings of Berdiaev and Bulgakov, who began as Marxists but in time turned to a new, idealist philosophy and to Christianity, as has been mentioned above.

Without any "iron curtain" to curtail the intercourse of Russian intellectuals and artists with the West, it is natural that Western styles and conceptions were an integral part of Russian literature in this period. Such writers as Baudelaire, Mallarmé, Rimbaud, Verlaine, Verhaern, Maeterlinck, Poe, Knut Hamsun, and Ibsen, who emphasized "art for art's sake" and individualism, provided the fundamental ideas for numerous literary innovators in Russia.

In the 1890s and the first two twentieth-century decades, two closely related literary schools, "decadence" and "symbolism," emerged. The literary critic Vengerov calls both these movements "neoromanticism" and considers their characteristic feature one of striving to escape from gray, shallow, immediate reality to speed away toward some new horizon. The Russian symbolists, although significantly influenced by the French symbolists, differed from the latter in that the Russians blended poetry with religion and metaphysics in an attempt to penetrate the mystery of the universe, while the French regarded symbolism only as a form of literary expression.

The first advocates of the new movement, who appeared in the 1890s, were A. Volynsky, N. Minsky, and D. S. Merezhkovsky. Volynsky, the leading literary critic of *The Northern Herald (Severnyi Vestnik),* fervently attacked the old criticism, dating back to Belinsky, for its utilitarian approach to art and its "nihilism of life and ethics." He called for the recognition of the metaphysical foundations of moral and spiritual life and looked to Dostoevsky as the main authority on the path of religious regeneration. Somewhat the same point of view was advanced by Minsky in his treatise *In the Light of Conscience (Pri svete sovesti),* and in his poetic, literary, and philosophical works he passed through a complex evolution from the pagan cult of beauty and pleasure to the search for God and attempts to create some kind of "religion of the future." Romance philologist, critic, publicist, novelist, and religious philosopher, Merezhkovsky in his youth had been a devotee of Mikhailovsky's populism and Tolstoy's religious teachings. Later the influence of Nietzsche was added, and finally Merezhkovsky appeared with a new religion, which he called the "Kingdom of the Third Testament." A prolific writer, he published a book of poems, *The Symbols (Simvoly),* several works on Russian literature—including an important study entitled *Tolstoy and Dostoevsky*—a trilogy of historical-philosophical novels on the general theme *Christ and Antichrist,* and a trilogy of historical novels on Russian themes. In his use of historical material Merezhkovsky displayed great erudition, but his artistic achievement is limited, for most of his characters are symbolic figures into whose mouths the writer has put his own philosophical ideas. His main conception was dualism, which must permeate all of history until the reconciliation in the "Third Kingdom of the Holy Ghost and the Holy Flesh." Merezhkovsky's collaborator and cobeliever was his talented and attractive wife, Zinaida Gippius. Although her novels are not highly regarded, she was a talented poetess of the decadent school, full of intense introspection.

Another comparatively important prose writer who may be associated with the symbolist movement is L. N. Andreev, who portrayed the dark and tragic, the reign of blind fate over men, and the futility of the individual who attempts to resist. Among the stories that reflect his attempts to invoke a feeling of horror are *The Red Laugh (Krasnyi smekh), Judas Iscariot,* and *The Seven That were Hanged (Raskaz o semi poveshennykh).* Portraying contemporary life as "madness and horror," Andreev, like some of the decadents, found fundamental reality only in sex and death. In this connection one should note the success of M. P. Artsybashev's semipornographic novel *Sanin* (1907) and the terrorist B. V. Savinkov's macaber novel *The Pale Horse (Kon' blednyi).*

In poetry "the king of the decadents" was K. D. Balmont. His first collection of poems, *Under a Northern Sky (Pod severnym nebom),* appeared in 1894, followed by collections bearing such typically extravagant titles as *Buildings Afire (Goriashchie zdania)* and *Let Us Be Like the Sun (Budem kak solntse).* Balmont was also active as the translator of romantic and symbolist poets, including Shelley, Goethe, Byron, Poe, and Baudelaire. At the turn of the century Balmont was the most popular poet in Russia and some critics have credited him with stimulating the revival of Russian poetry. In 1905 the "bard of the sun," as he called himself, became the bard of revolution and was forced to live abroad from 1906 to 1913.

The acknowledged leader of the symbolist movement soon came to be V. L. Briusov, poet, novelist, translator, critic, journalist, and publisher, expert on the ancient world and on Western literature. He began his poetic work under the influence of the French symbolists, and his first poems were published in 1894 in the anthology *The Russian Symbolists (Russkie simvolisty)*. In 1895 he published a collection of poems under the pretentious title *Chefs d'oeuvre*, followed by numerous other anthologies. Briusov took an active part in the work of the Moscow publishing house *Skorpion* and was the *de facto* editor of the periodical *The Scales (Vesy)*, the organ of the new literary movement, from 1904 to 1909. He translated and published the works of such writers as Poe, Baudelaire, Verlaine, Maeterlinck, and Verhaeren. His historical novels, *The Altar of Victory (Altar' pobedy)* and *The Fiery Angel (Ognennyi angel)*, are, respectively, erudite treatises on the life of Rome in the fourth century and the period of the German Reformation in the sixteenth century.

A famous poet and novelist who undoubtedly belonged to the decadent movement was Fedor Sologub (F. K. Teternikov), a pessimist who saw in life only evil, suffering, cruelty, and madness, and in his novels escaped into a fantastic world of mirages, apparitions, and evil spirits. After his first novel, *Bad Dreams (Tiazhelye sny,* 1896), followed his best-known novel, *A Petty Devil (Melkii bes,* 1907), in which Sologub, himself a teacher, invented a provincial pedagogue called Peredonov, a character full of moral baseness and all kinds of vices who hated people and suffered from a persecution mania.

The most important among the poets of the younger generation of Russian symbolists were Viacheslav Ivanov, Andrei Belyi, and Alexander Blok. Between 1905 and 1911, Ivanov was the acknowledged leader of the Petersburg group of symbolist poets, while Briusov led the Moscow group. A mystic and aesthete, Ivanov drew spiritually and esthetically on Nietzsche, Dostoevsky, and V. S. Soloviev, while his beloved poets were Dante, Goethe, and Tiutchev. In 1905–1906, Ivanov, who was a classical scholar, published *The Hellenic Religion of the Suffering God,* a study of the cult of Dionysus, which he saw as the precursor to Christianity. His first collection of poems, *The Pilot Stars (Kormchiia zvezdy),* was published in 1903 and was followed by numerous others. The poems of Ivanov were not written for the general public and are full of symbols, quotations, mythological names, and erudite allusions. They contain an attempt to create a syncretic religion from the elements of paganism and Christianity, combining the cult of Dionysus with the worship of Christ, to parallel to his poetic combination of elements of classicism and modernism.

Andrei Belyi (B. N. Bugaev) was a poet, romance philologist, literary critic, and theoretician of "symbolism." In his autobiography Belyi writes of his youthful intellectual development: "I understood symbolism not as a literary school at all, but as a new world-outlook, harmoniously combining the religious life, art, and speculative thinking. Three names stood out for me in particular in that period: Nietzsche, Dostoevsky, and Ibsen." Later he added the philosophy of Soloviev. In the first years of the twentieth century Belyi published four of his prose "symphonies" and later a few collections of poems, such as *Gold in Azure (Zoloto v lazuri)*, *The Goblet of Blizzards (Kubok miatelei)*, and *Ashes (Pepel)*. His best known novel, *Petersburg*, was published in 1912.

A. A. Blok is the most outstanding poet of Russian symbolism, and in the opinion of many critics the greatest Russian poet of the twentieth century. The works of Blok showed a constant oscillation between mysticism and realism. In his youth, Blok, like other symbolists, was under the strong influence of the philosophy of Soloviev. Accepting the idea of *Sofia* as the eternal wisdom of God, the symbolists considered her to be at once eternal beauty and eternal love. In 1904 Blok published his famous collection *Poems on the Sublime Lady (Stikhi o prekrasnoi dame)* reflecting these feelings and ideas, which also appear in the collections *The Unexpected Joy (Nechaiannaia radost')* and *Earth in Snow (Zemlia v snegu)*. In these, wrote Briusov, "the struggle of two principles," the divine and the demoniacal, is manifest. Blok, like Belyi and Briusov, welcomed the October Revolution, in which the leading symbolists saw the dawn of new, free life and from which they awaited a new cultural flowering. As Poggioli says, they "mistook the sunset for the sunrise."[15] At the beginning of 1918 Blok wrote his controversial poems *The Twelve (Dvenadtsat')* and *The Scythians (Skify)*.

Around 1910 symbolism began to wane and it was replaced, on the one hand, by two avant-garde literary movements, futurism and cubism, and, on the other hand, by a return to tradition, simplicity, and clarity under the name of "acmeism." The cubists and futurists emerged between 1909 and 1913, intending to deliver "a slap in the face to public taste," to quote the title of one of their manifestoes.

---

[15] R. Poggioli, *The Poets of Russia* (Cambridge, Mass., 1960), p. 126.

They rejected Pushkin, Dostoevsky, Tolstoy, and the symbolists and attempted the most radical experiments in language and style. The principal representatives of this movement were Igor Severianin (I. V. Lotarev), Viktor V. Khlebnikov, and Vladimir Maiakovsky.

The other branch of the reaction against symbolism, acmeism, was a movement led by N. S. Gumilev. In the journal *Appolon* he stated that poets should acknowledge "only the strict search for beauty, only the free, the harmonious, and the clear, only strong and vital art. . . ." "With the acmeists," wrote another member of the movement, Gorodetsky, "the rose again becomes good in itself, with its petals, scent, and color," and not merely a mystical reflection of some exterior values.[16] These principles are embodied in the richly resonant and virile poems of Gumilev and the subtle lyricism of the poetess Anna Akhmatova.

Between 1913 and 1917 another significant school of literature emerged in the field of criticism, "formalism," which accused populist, Marxist, and some idealist critics equally of losing sight of the importance of artistic form in their zeal for content and ideology. Considering technique, form, and style as an end and not merely a means of art, the Russian formalists anticipated the later ideas of the New Criticism in English literature. The principle formalists were V. B. Shklovsky, B. V. Tomashevsky—the author of *The Language of Poetry (Iazyk poezii)*—and B. M. Eichenbaum.

Quite apart from any self-conscious movement, another writer who revived the prestige of traditional realism in the years just before the war was I. A. Bunin, who in 1933, then an emigrant, became the first Russian author to win a Nobel prize. Bunin continued the tradition of Pushkin in poetry and of Chekhov in prose; he loved life but was far from idealizing the world around him. In his major stories from the period 1910–1912, "The Countryside" *(Derevnia)* and "The Dry Valley" *(Sukhodol),* he followed the best Russian realists in his portrayal of rural life.

Music

Although Western operatic and orchestral music was introduced in eighteenth-century Russia under the guidance of Italian musicians, it was only in the nineteenth century that modern Russian music appeared. The most influential Russian composer of the early

---

[16] *Apollon,* January 1913: articles by N. Gumilev (pp. 42–45) and S. Gorodetsky (pp. 46–50).

part of the nineteenth century was D. S. Bortniansky, a composer
of church music, who was educated in Italy and became director
of the choir of the Imperial Chapel in Petersburg. In his numerous
ecclesiastical compositions he tried to preserve old Russian church
melodies, but to harmonize them according to the rules of contemporary Italian music.

But the real founder of modern Russian music of the
"classical" period was M. I. Glinka, of whom the cultural historian
Miliukov writes, "His appearance marks the same stage in the history of music as that of Pushkin in the history of literature." In
his most popular opera *A Life for the Tsar* (or *Ivan Susanin*, 1836),
Glinka combined both national and cosmopolitan elements, which is
not surprising, for Glinka traveled extensively abroad and studied
music in Berlin and Paris, in Italy and in Spain. His second opera
Ruslan and Liudmila (1842)—the libretto for which was one of
Pushkin's folkloristic poems—had a more Russian character and was
a finer musical work than his first; it has been credited with the
establishment of the national style of modern Russian music.

The end of the 1850s and the 1860s was a time as full of
life, movement, and conflict in Russian music as in other fields of
Russian culture, social, and political history. In 1859, the Russian
Musical Society in St. Petersburg was founded under the leadership
of the famous pianist, conductor, and composer Anton Rubinstein;
then a branch of the society was formed in Moscow under the
leadership of Anton's brother, Nicholas. In 1860, a school of music
was founded in St. Petersburg, and in 1862 it became the Petersburg Conservatory. Anton Rubinstein was appointed its director and
remained at the head of the Conservatory until 1891. In 1866, Moscow
followed suit, founding a conservatory headed by Nicholas Rubinstein.
Anton Rubinstein was an internationally famous pianist and a prolific
composer. Of his many operas, the most popular became *The Demon;*
others included *The Maccabees, Nero,* and *Merchant Kalashnikov.*
In his operas, as in his other musical works, A. Rubinstein was a
Westerner, "academic" and conservative.

Violent opposition to the traditional character and academic
style of operatic art came from the so-called "mighty band"
(moguchaia kuchka). M. A. Balakirev, an excellent pianist, was the
initiator and the leader of this group of young idealists and innovators
who rebelled against the traditions in music, just as the "populists" in
literature and the *"peredvizhniki"* in painting were doing at the
same time. The "band" came into being between 1857 and 1862,
and included a young officer of the Engineer Corps, Caesar Cui;

a young military officer, M. P. Musorgsky; a young scientist, A. P. Borodin; and a young naval officer, N. A. Rimsky-Korsakov. Their watchwords were first, individual liberty in musical creation—free of conventional rules and traditions—and second, nationalism and realism in music. Their nationalism, however, did not exclude their alliance with such innovating movements in the West as those led by Berlioz, Schumann, Chopin, Liszt, and Wagner. Immediately after the founding of the Petersburg Conservatory in 1862, Balakirev's group founded the "Free School of Music" there. Under its sponsorship, Balakirev organized and conducted a series of "progressive" concerts with notable success. In 1873, Balakirev retired from the directorship of the Free School, and Rimsky-Korsakov replaced him.

Perhaps the most talented of all the members of Balakirev's circle was Modest Petrovich Musorgsky, the most expressive realist of the group. He produced some eighty songs, some of which were based directly on folk songs and presented vivid and realistic pictures of different episodes in human life, while others displayed considerable romantic beauty. The first version of Musorgsky's great opera *Boris Godunov* was finished in 1870, the second in 1872. The opera was performed in the Mariinsky Theater in Petersburg in 1874 and met a mixed reception from the public and the critics. In 1896 and 1908, it was substantially revised by Rimsky-Korsakov, only later reestablished in its original form. Musorgsky's second opera, *Khovanshchina* (unfinished by Musorgsky and orchestrated after his death by Rimsky-Korsakov), pictured realistically an historical episode from the end of the seventeenth century connected with the great religious schism between the Orthodox and the Old Believers. Both of Musorgsky's great works are not so much operas in the usual meaning of the word as "popular musical dramas," as the composer called them. They contain a broad treatment of popular scenes and a vivid presentation of human passions and human relations; the music here served chiefly as a framework for the realistic content of the drama.

A. P. Borodin, a professor of organic chemistry at the Academy of Medicine in Petersburg, was also a talented musician. He composed many original and colorful works, including three symphonies. His impressive opera *Prince Igor* remained unfinished and was later completed by Rimsky-Korsakov and Glazunov. Its plot involved an unlucky expedition of four Russian princes against the Cumans in the twelfth century, the subject of the greatest Russian folk epic, "The Tale of Igor's Host." This dramatic historical event, including the period of the Russian prince's captivity among the Cumans, gave the composer the idea of combining Russian national motifs with oriental music and oriental dances, as in the famous "Polovtsian Dances."

Caesar Cui was the son of a Frenchman who came to Russia in 1812 with Napoleon's army and stayed on. Cui entered the army and attained the rank of general as a specialist on fortifications. He composed not only technical books on military science but also ten operas, many pieces of orchestral and chamber music, and some 200 songs. As a composer, Cui was considered the weakest among the members of the "mighty band," but his activity as a musical critic and as an ardent propagandist of realistic and nationalist ideas of that group contributed much to their popularity.

The most successful and most influential of all the members of the Balakirev circle was Rimsky-Korsakov. In 1871, at the age of twenty-seven, he was appointed professor of composition and orchestration at the Petersburg Conservatory, where he was a popular and successful teacher for more than forty years. A whole generation of new Russian composers profited by his teaching, including Glazunov, Liadov, Arensky, Ippolitov-Ivanov, Grechaninov, Stravinsky, and Prokofiev. Although a member of the "mighty band," he was not a revolutionary and did not want to rupture the old musical tradition. He studied the works of European masters as well as the Russian folklore, and in 1877–1882 he published valuable collections of Russian songs. He also studied Russian church music and composed several songs for use in church services. In his numerous and diverse works of secular music he tried to combine original Russian elements with the best achievements of Western music. His guiding ideal was the beauty and the intrinsic value of musical works, not their ideological content. Rimsky-Korsakov composed fifteen operas, all but three of them dealing with Russian subjects. The more popular of them are *Pskovitianka, Sadko, The Tsar's Bride,* and *The Golden Cockerel.* His magnificent fantastic opera *The Legend of the Invisible City of Kitezh* (1904) is based on a mystical religious legend dating from the time of the Tatar invasion in the thirteenth century. Historians of music perceive the influence of Richard Wagner in Rimsky-Korsakov's later operas. He also composed three symphonies and many more works for orchestral and chamber music, organized and conducted Russian symphony concerts, and was a prolific composer of "melodies" and "romances." Finally, he wrote an autobiography *My Musical Life,* which is a treasury of music history.

The most outstanding Russian composer at the end of the nineteenth century was Peter Ilich Tchaikovsky, professor of harmony at the Moscow Conservatory. His music is for the most party lyrical and emotional, much influenced by Western music despite his use of Russian folk melodies. Tchaikovsky's outstanding contribution was the creation of Russian symphonic music; he wrote six symphonies, which later became known throughout the world. He also composed many pieces of chamber music and works for the piano, many chorales and lyrical songs; the music for three ballets (Swan Lake, 1876; The Sleeping Beauty, 1889; and the Nutcracker, 1892); and ten operas, the most popular of which were Eugene Onegin and The Queen of Spades.

Russian composers and musicians continued to occupy an important place in the musical world in the twentieth century, both before and after 1917. The new talents that emerged in this century included Glazunov, who became director of the Petersburg Conservatory in 1908 following the death of Rimsky-Korsakov; A. N. Scriabin, whose musical poems were imbued with religious mysticism; and such younger composers as S. V. Rakhmaninov, I. F. Stravinsky, S. S. Prokofiev, and D. D. Shostakovich.

Theater Arts

European theater appeared in Russia in the eighteenth century, sponsored by the Westernizing rulers and aristocrats and leaning heavily on European models. In the reign of Alexander I, the French theater was in vogue as part of the general Gallomania, despite the Napoleonic invasion. Although Russian playwrights, actors, and directors were active in the early nineteenth century, the government still spent considerable sums to support French companies and individual performers, such as the celebrated Mlle. Georges. Although the same models were accepted by the private theaters of a few wealthy landlords of this period, these companies were more "Russian" in that they were composed of serfs, who in time provided the Russian stage with some of its best actors.

A reputable Russian theater appeared in the second quarter of the nineteenth century, parallel with comparable achievements in literature and music. Famous actors such as V. A. Karatygin, P. S. Mochalov, and M. S. Shchepkin (latter two were former serfs) became the object of much admiration, and the major dramatic works of Gogol and Ostrovsky, previously noted in the discussion of literature, were performed. Gogol's comedies, The Wedding and The Inspector General (performed 1836), in which the author's friend Shchepkin acted with great effect, mark the appearance of an indigenous Russian theater of real caliber. In this Gogol's contribution in drama is comparable to Pushkin's in poetry and Glinka's in music. Between 1847 and 1873 Ostrovsky's numerous plays, in which the talented P. M. Sadovsky played many leading roles, greatly enriched the repertoire of the Russian theater.

Prior to the 1830s the Russian theatrical companies were notable for their syncretism, combining operatic, dramatic, and ballet performers in one group. But with the appearance of a more mature theater, the separate arts were represented by special companies. In Petersburg the Alexandrine Theater, established in 1832, was devoted to drama only and the Mariinsky Theater to opera, while in Moscow the Bolshoi Theatre became the great home of opera and the Malyi of drama. In the second half of the century, similar differentiation occurred in the education of the artists of the theater.

In the second half of the nineteenth century, especially at the beginning of the 1880s and again at the beginning of the twentieth century, theatrical life developed in different ways. In Moscow and Petersburg a number of private theaters appeared, besides the imperial—state-supported—ones. In all the provincial capitals and even in some of the cities in the country, permanent theaters emerged and a few were extremely good, such as N. N. Solovtsov's theater in Kiev and that of N. N. Sinelnikov in Kharkov.

The opening of the Moscow Art Theater in Moscow in 1898 had a profound influence in the development of the theater, not only in Russia, but far beyond her borders. The new venture was headed by two distinguished artists, K. S. Alekseev-Stanislavsky—the director of the theater and also a producer, actor, and theoretician of dramatic art—and V. I. Nemirovich-Danchenko—a playwright, critic, and theoretician. The most distinguished actors were V. I. Kachalov, I. M. Moskvin, and O. L. Knipper-Chekhova, who married Chekhov four years before his death in 1904. The theoreticians of the Art Theater protested against all the artificial, conventional, "theatrical," and traditional in the older theater and demanded "art realism," bordering on naturalism, or the representing of "real life." This theater became famous for its performance of Chekhov, in which the actors conveyed the melancholy mood of the author with exceptional fidelity. To achieve this effect the indefatigable producer strove first to achieve the psychological and technical "preparation" of every artist, and then the coordination and harmoniousness of the acting of the whole ensemble. The Stanislavsky "method," one of the most influential forces in the modern theater, is set forth in his books *The Work of the Actor (Rabota aktera nad soboi)* and *My Life in Art (Moia zhizn' v iskustve)*.

In the opera, F. I. Shaliapin came out against the traditional formal conventionality and combined singing and dramatic acting. His realistic portrayal of Boris Godunov in Musorgsky's opera brought him the greatest acclaim. However, not everyone shared the ideas of the realistic and naturalistic theatre. "To recreate life truthfully on the stage is impossible. . . . Where there is art there is convention," wrote the symbolist poet Briusov. This point of view was applied in practice by the producer V. E. Meyerhold, who tried to create a performance in which "the spectator did not forget for a minute that he is looking at an actor, who acts." An exceptionally dynamic, talented dramatic actress, V. F. Komisarzhevskaia, left the stage of the Alexandrine Theater and in 1904 opened her own theater, which at first adhered to the realistic and naturalistic trend. But in 1906, at the invitation of Komisarzhevskaia, the producer Meyerhold began to stage plays in the spirit of "symbolism." This experimental theater, however, did not find an adequate audience and closed in 1908.

The producer and director N. N. Evreinov also experimented in the theater; his credo was "theatricality is a positive idea in art." In 1908 he opened a theater in Petersburg called "The Distorting Mirror" *(Krivoe Zerkalo)*, which was highly successful in staging parodies of both traditional and new plays and lasted until the Bolshevik Revolution. The Moscow Chamber Theater of A. I. Tairov, which opened in 1914, staged futurist and symbolist plays.

Although ballet in Russia goes back to the 1730s, this art remained quite dependent on French and Italian masters until the mid-nineteenth century. At best the ballet in Russia (not yet the Russian ballet) was a technically polished reproduction of Western forms, and in the 1830s after the retirement of the master Carl-Ludwig Didlo, it was not even quite that. But in the second half of the century, under the guidance of the French ballet master Marius Petipa and his colleagues, the Russian ballet emerged, the peer of any in the world by 1900. An especially notable innovation was the combination of the dance and outstanding musical compositions, such as Tchaikovsky's *Sleeping Beauty,* first staged by Petipa in 1890. By this time the style of the Russian ballet had absorbed the technique of the classical European ballet, and in turn influenced the dance of the West.

Around the turn of the century the ballet master M. M. Fokin began to expound his new and striking theories on the role of music and the ballet, not just as accompaniment but as expressive interpretation in itself—on the role of sets and costumes as integral and artistic parts of the ballet and on the composition of the dance, including the corps de ballet and the individual. Fokin's innovations bore the imprint of the American impressionistic dancer Isadora Duncan, who visited Petersburg in 1905, and the new esthetic theories of S. P. Diaghilev and other artists who contributed to the magazine, *The World of Art.*

In 1909 Diaghilev founded a new ballet company, which included such talents as Fokin in choreography, Leon Bakst as designer of scenery and costumes, Nijinsky as the leading male dancer, and the musical scores of Stravinsky. The new company had a sensational success in Paris in 1909, and subsequently continued their triumphs under the name *Ballet russes.* By the time of World War I, Russian companies were among the finest exponents of classical ballet, especially with such ballerinas as the legendary Anna Pavlova.

The Visual Arts

Russia made her greatest contributions to painting in medieval iconography, which reached its climax in the unsurpassed frescoes and panel icons of the fifteenth century at Novgorod and Moscow. Icon painting later lost the purity of its style under alien influences, and by 1800 it had declined into a kind of commercial craft. Secular painting, which did not become important until the time of Peter the Great, struggled for many decades to master unfamiliar Western techniques; but at the turn of the nineteenth century, Russian portraiture by men such as D. G. Levitsky and V. L. Borovikovsky was identical in style with European work of the time.

The end of the Napoleonic Wars ushered in the period of romanticism. Among its exponents were Orest Kiprensky, known mostly for his portraits, such as one of Pushkin (1827); K. P. Briullov, who gained fame in Europe with his enormous canvas "The Last Day of Pompei" (1833); and F. A. Bruni, who concentrated even more on pseudo-classical themes. The major move from romanticism toward realism was made by A. A. Ivanov in "The Appearance of Christ to the People," on which he spent twenty years (1837–1857) trying, through painstaking research, to make it true to the time represented. In the course of this work he also explored bright effects of color and light in bold, refreshing sketches, and even turned to a revival of Byzantine forms to convey a symbolic message.

Meanwhile, genre painting, which concentrated on everyday Russian life, was gaining in importance. The founder of this trend was A. G. Venetsianov, whose dignified and poetic paintings of peasant life date from 1821 to 1847. With the work of P. A. Fedotov in the 1840s, the painting of manners became slightly caricaturistic, and mild satire turned into vehement criticism of church and state in the paintings of V. G. Perov during the 1860s. Perov became the initiator of critical realism, or "committed realism" *(ideinyi realizm)*, as it was also called in Russia, the dominant movement in the nineteenth century. More than two dozen painters, popular in their time, followed in Perov's footsteps. Best known among them was Vladimir Makovsky, who portrayed the lot of the lower classes and the manners of the bourgeoisie.

The movement took shape in a rebellion against the neoclassic "slavery of the academy" in 1863. Imbued with the spirit of protest against tradition and authority that characterized their time, fourteen students resigned from the Petersburg Academy of Art when the theme "The Feast of the Gods at Valhalla" was chosen for the annual competition for the gold medal. Characteristically, the dissidents were not fighting for new forms or techniques of artistic expression but merely for new subject matter. Under the influence of Chernyshevsky, they felt that subject matter was forever more important than form, and that the choice of subject was a question of social responsibility.

To make a living, the dissidents of 1863 formed a cooperative group and arranged joint exhibitions. Their success led, in 1870, to the formation of the Association of Mobile Art Exhibitions. The society of *peredvizhniki* ("the mobile ones"), made a great impact upon the nation by popularizing the art of critical realism throughout the country. It received financial support from P. M. Tretiakov, a wealthy merchant who bought many of their paintings for his private collection. In 1892, he and his brother presented the collection to the city of Moscow, where it formed the core of the famous Tretiakov Art Gallery.

The founder of the society of *peredvizhniki* was I. N. Kramskoy—the ideological leader of the walkout of 1863—who is notable for his almost photographic reproduction (he started as a retoucher in a photography studio) and the psychological intensity of his portraits. More colorful and more powerful were the religious and historic paintings of Nicholas Ge, a friend of Leo Tolstoy. Toward the end of his life he turned away from realism and developed a rather personal technique to convey the horror and agony of his biblical subject matter.

In the 1880s, illustration of historical events emerged as a subtler form of social criticism. In "The Morning of the Execution of the Streltsy" (1881) and "Boyarinia Morozova" (1887), V. I. Surikov displays refined composition and a deep sympathy for the Russian folklore of Muscovite Russia. V. V. Vereshchagin, a lesser artist, was a correspondent in the campaigns of Turkestan and against Turkey and brought back paintings of frightening battle scenes to propagate pacifism.

The movement of the *peredvizhniki* culminated in the long and illustrous career of Ilya Repin. His "Burlaki" (1873), showing the plight of the Volga boat haulers, brought him immediate recognition in Europe. He gained fame in Petersburg as a painter of portraits, popular because of their striking likeness and conventional design. The representation of the human face was undoubtedly Repin's forte. He exploits it in such genre scenes as "The Procession of the Cross in Kursk" (1883) or "Unexpected" (the return of a political prisoner, 1884) and makes an even more overwhelming use of it in his great historical canvases, such as "Ivan the Terrible with the Body of His Son" 1885) and "Zaporozhe Cossacks Drafting a Letter to the Turkish Sultan" (1881). In the "October Demonstration" (1906) and in his later portraits, Repin ventured somewhat outside the strictly realist idiom, but his interest in new techniques remained limited.

The esthetic of the *peredvizhniki* strongly influenced Russian landscape painting. While the seascapes of I. K. Aivazovsky, of which he painted more than 2000, are essentially romantic, the realist viewpoint comes through during the 1860s in the landscapes of A. K. Savrasov and in the botanically accurate views of forests and fields by I. I. Shishkin. Here, portrayal of the Russian countryside was meant to convey a feeling of national character.

The strictly photographic kind of realism in landscape painting was abandoned by A. I. Kuindzhi, who concentrated on exaggerated lighting contrasts. In the 1880s and '90s Isaac Levitan, by far the most sensitive of the Russian landscape painters, gave his canvases colorful brilliance and subtle mood by a restrained use of the impressionist technique. Gradually, the French impressionist influence also penetrated genre painting in the work of other artists, such as F. A. Maliavin (peasant women) and K. A. Korovin (decorative painting).

By the end of the century preoccupation with reality at the expense of artistry had brought critical realism to a dead end. It had made a generation of Russian painters hostile to the idea that the painting itself can be more important than the things it represents, and it had isolated Russia from the mainstream of Western art. Again, time was ripe for a change, but the professorial positions at the Petersburg Academy of Art were by now firmly in the hands of the *peredvizhniki.* A rival artistic movement arose outside the Academy, aiming to liberate Russian art from provincialism, from sentimental and didactic conventions. Associated with it were periodicals such as *The World of Art* (1898–1904), *The Golden Fleece (Zolotoe Runo,* 1906–1909), and *Apollon* (1909–1917). These were reviews of the most advanced artistic opinion, concerned as much with the cultural resources of historic Russia (both ancient and eighteenth-century) as with the latest developments in French art; with painting and literature as much as with theater and music. Among the patrons of the new movement was Savva I. Mamontov, whose country estate at Abramtsevo became a mecca for many artists of the new generation. Others were S. I. Shchukin and I. A. Morozov who, before 1914, collected more than 100 canvases of Picasso and Matisse alone. These collections decisively influenced the development of modern painting in Russia.

Another fundamental influence was the discovery of the medieval Russian icon. Partly hidden under metal settings and covered by numerous layers of varnish and candle soot, their restoration hampered by their liturgical use, medieval icons were effectively concealed from the public eye, despite their public veneration. The cleaning and restoration of icons began around 1903, but it was not until the exhibitions of 1911 and 1913 that the breathtaking beauty of their radiant color and abstract composition was generally revealed.

A forerunner of the new movement in Russian art had been, to some extent, V. M. Vasnetsov, who started as a genre realist but soon became the exponent of Slavic revival with his illustrations of folk tales and ancient legends. His huge religious paintings in the St. Vladimir cathedral in Kiev (1886–1896) were a strained attempt to combine nineteenth-century realism with Byzantine symbolism.

A much more convincing religious style than Vasnetsov's was developed by M. V. Nesterov. Through a cautious substitution of stylized forms for factual detail Nesterov created a profound interpretation of medieval Russian faith, such as in his "Vision of the Young Bartholomeus" (1890), which shocked the social realists. His secular paintings, which often include lonely female figures, radiate intensive, melancholy emotion.

The transition from Nesterov's mystical idealism to symbolist painting was accomplished by M. A. Vrubel, a representative of the turn of the century symbolist movement in Europe. Vrubel did some religious painting and some portrait work, as well as sculpture, but his most important heritage consists of a wealth of semifinished paintings and sketches that reflect his disgust with realism and reveal an agonizing search for new form, in which he closely approached cubism. He was unable to fulfill his aspirations, ending up in a mental institution in 1905.

The subject matter of Slavic revival—folklore scenes, images from fairy tales, or religious paintings—was stylized to different degrees by painters such as I. I. Bilibin, N. K. Roerich, B. M. Kustodiev, and M. V. Dobuzhinsky. Many of these men, associated with the *World of Art* group, also engaged in applied painting, in particular book illustration and stage design.

Among the artists not concerned with Slavic revival, V. A. Serov stands out as the greatest Russian portrait painter next to Repin. With a wide brush stroke and a brilliant play of light, he gave his paintings a simple and immediate appeal. He was also a master of the pencil and did not hesitate to explore impressionist and expressionist technique.

The search for a new style, be it Neo-Rococo (Benois, Lansere), Slavic revival, or impressionist, created a variety of personal expression, but often ended in inconclusive mannerisms characteristic of the period of *Jugendstil*, or Art Nouveau. Dissatisfied young artists after 1905 formed more radical groups, such as the "Jack of Diamonds" *(Bubnovyi valet)* in Moscow or "The Donkey's Tail." Influenced by cubism and futurism, left-wing artists (Burliuk, Grigoriev, Rozanova) were often concerned not only with experimentation, but also with "delivering a slap in the face of public taste"—as were Maiakovsky and the other avant-garde poets. Some of them, however, did succeed in developing a convincing personal style; the visionary painting of Marc Chagall is an outstanding example.

Abreast of the latest developments in Paris and Munich, young Russian artists (many of whom studied in Europe) clearly saw the tendency toward greater and greater abstraction in Western art. In their determined quest for fundamentals, it was inevitable that sooner or later they would carry this tendency to its ultimate end. This happened in 1911 when Michael Larionov, who started by disintegrating landscapes into rays of light, arrived at completely nonrepresentational compositions.

In the same year, Vasily Kandinsky, working in the tradition of Gauguin and Matisse, closely approached nonobjective design in Munich, where in the following year he published his book *On the Spiritual in Art* and became the leader of the famous "Blue Rider" group. After his return to Russia in 1914, recognizable objects completely disappeared from his paintings. With his free, improvised, irregular forms, he became one of the founders of the spontaneous, intuitional, and emotional current in abstract art.

The other direction—intellectual, structural, and geometric —was represented by Kazimir Malevich. Originally a leader of the cubist school in Russia, working in the manner of Picasso and Léger, he made in 1913 what he called his "desperate attempt to free art from the ballast of the objective world" by drawing a black square on a white background. He established simple geometric shapes as the basis of his "suprematism," by which he meant "the supremacy of pure perception." As Alfred H. Barr has pointed out, "As a pioneer, a theorist and an artist," Malevich, "stands at the heart of the movement which swept westward from Russia after the War and, mingling with the eastward movement of the Dutch Stijl group, transformed the architecture, furniture, typography and commercial art of Germany and much of the rest of Europe."[17]

Sculpture, except for wood carving and stone relief, did not exist in Russia from pagan days until the middle of the eighteenth century, for the Orthodox Church did not accept three-dimensional representation of religious images. Only the introduction of the Baroque and neoclassicism into Russia under Catherine II created a demand for secular sculpture, primarily as an element of urban design. The notable neoclassic sculptor was I. P. Martos, known for his monument to the seventeenth-century national heroes Minin and Pozharsky in Red Square (1804–1818) and for numerous funeral figures on tombstones. Martos' practice of dressing Russian historical figures in the togas of Roman emperors was dropped in the second quarter of the century, but the eclectic period that followed produced little work of consequence, particularly as the ties between sculpture and architecture disintegrated.

The second half of the nineteenth century in sculpture, just as in painting, was characterized by "committed realism." The best representative of this movement was Mark Antokolsky, known for his historic sculptures and his sardonic "Mephistopheles" (1882). By 1900, P. P. Trubetskoy became prominent, particularly as a master of the small figurine. His impressionist treatment of light and shade was inspired by Rodin.

A radical break with traditional, representational sculpture occurred in 1913. In that year, Vladimir Tatlin carried the idea

---

[17] Alfred H. Barr, *Cubism and Abstract Art* (New York, 1936), pp. 122–124.

of cubist painting into the three-dimensional world, creating abstract spatial compositions in industrial materials. In 1915 he dispensed with the pedestal and suspended his sculpture in the air from wires. Another important innovator was Alexander Archipenko, whose cubist interest in multiple planes led him to make openings in his figures. Unlike the deliberately "nonbeautiful" compositions of Tatlin, Arkhipenko's figures had elegance and grace. In 1917, Tatlin was joined in Moscow by the brothers Anton Pevsner and Naum Gabo. This meeting led, three years later, to the proclamation of the principles of "constructivism." The "constructivists" did not hesitate to link themselves with the Russian ecclesiastic style, and with the symbolism of Vrubel. Though constructivist sculpture was short-lived in Russia (Gabo and Pevsner emigrated), it had a great impact on stage design in the theaters of Tairov, Vakhtangov, and Meyerhold after the Revolution of 1917. Moreover, the Higher Technical and Art Workshop, a school that Tatlin, Pevsner, and Gabo founded in Moscow in 1918, became the cradle of modern architecture in Russia.

Russian architecture, born under Byzantine influence, reached an early peak in the eleventh and twelfth centuries when a distinct national style emerged in the regions of Kiev, Novgorod-Pskov, and Vladimir-Suzdal. In the next four centuries of relative isolation from Europe, Russian builders, influenced by local wood construction techniques and by oriental ornamentation, developed the exuberant Moscow style. This decayed during the seventeenth century, and interest turned toward the European Baroque, particularly after Peter the Great cut short the indigenous tradition. When toward the end of Catherine's reign, neoclassicism became dominant, the imported Western tradition was thoroughly assimilated by Russian builders in a style known as "Russian Empire."

This style came into full bloom when Alexander I ascended the throne. Large-scale construction, commensurate with the newly won position of Russia as a world power, first centered in Petersburg, then spread to Moscow, as part of the reconstruction after 1812, and to cities such as Odessa, Yaroslavl, and Kazan. Perhaps the greatest contribution of this period was its emphasis on designing architecturally unified urban groupings, not just individual buildings. Monumental sculpture became an intimate part of these urban compositions, and bright colors (mostly yellow and white) were often used in the treatment of building façades. Advanced engineering methods, such as the use of cast iron, were widely employed.

Of the various examples of Russian Empire architecture, the central area of Petersburg, which Henry Russell Hitchcock has called "the finest urban entity of this period," is outstanding.[18] Located here are the Kazan Cathedral (1801–1811) and the Mining Institute (1806–1811) by Voronikhin; the New Admiralty building with its spire—the focal point of the downtown area (1806–1815)—by Zakharov; the Exchange across the Neva (1805–1816) by Thomas de Thomon; and, finally, the majestic space of Palace Square, with its semicircular General Staff buildings and the nearby groupings of the Senate, the Synod, and the Alexandrine Theater, designed by K. I. Rossi (born in Russia of Italian parents), chief architect of St. Petersburg from 1815 to 1832. Though Rossi's architectural detailing was weaker than that of his illustrious predecessors, he is one of the great planners of urban spaces in modern time.

After about 1830 the Empire style declined and Russian architecture with it. Montferrand's St. Isaac's Cathedral in Petersburg (1817–1875) was a vast neoclassical structure rich in materials but lacking in refinement of scale. Most of the barracks, hospitals, and administrative buildings of the reign of Nicholas I were huge, bleak, and monotonous. Moreover, the comprehensive architectural regulations that had guided the growth of Petersburg after 1816 were abandond in 1840 in favor of haphazard speculative construction typical of the early industrial era. Official approval was now given to the eclectic Russian Byzantine style that freely mixed Byzantine, Renaissance, and old Russian details; on commission from Nicholas I, the architect K. A. Ton prepared a set of prototype designs in this style for provincial churches, making architectural confusion mandatory throughout the country.

In the reign of Alexander III a number of architects in Russia—including, ironically, many foreigners—were encouraged by the official nationalism to attempt to revive the Muscovite architecture of the seventeenth century, with its onion-shaped domes and colorful ornamentation. The Church of the Resurrection (1887–1906), commemorating the place in Petersburg where Alexander II was assassinated, is a prime example of this overornamented and heavyhanded design.

Although the architects themselves were generally uncreative in the later nineteenth century in Russia, some bold engineering structures attained architectural significance. For example, the en-

---

[18] Henry Russell Hitchcock, *Architecture: Nineteenth and Twentieth Centuries* (Penguin Books, 1958), p. 14.

gineer V. G. Shukhov devised lightweight steel towers in the form of cylindrical hyperboloids and suspended roof structures with complex curvature, such as those built for the Nizhni Novgorod fair in 1896.

The Russian visual arts of the nineteenth century did not attain the international distinction that was achieved by literature and music. In fact, they did not approach the heights previously attained by Russia in the visual field, excepting the success of Russian Empire architecture, which was really a belated child of the eighteenth century. Only the second decade of the twentieth century radically reversed this situation. Between 1911 and 1922, Moscow established itself in the forefront of esthetic exploration in the visual field, as in the realms of literature, music, and the theater, taking its place alongside the leading artistic capitals of Paris and Munich. This tremendous and promising thrust of creative energy was smothered by the gradual emergence of totalitarian rule between 1922 and 1933.

It is noteworthy, therefore, that the transition from the early nineteenth century to the early twentieth century in the cultural development of Russia was remarkable in both depth and diversity. Despite the previous attempts at Westernization, the country around 1800 was generally backward, or at best quite imitative, in education, scholarship, literature, music, the theater and the visual arts. But the nineteenth century saw the emergence of a highly diversified culture that was at once Russian and cosmopolitan, a national achievement and an integral part of western civilization.

The Church

The close bond between the imperial government and the Orthodox Church continued until the fall of tsardom. The last four tsars were all devoted Orthodox believers and were considered the protectors of the Church, although their appointee, the overprocurator of the Holy Synod, actually headed the ecclesiastical administration. The most renowned holder of this office after the mid-nineteenth century was Pobedonostsev, who took up the post in 1880 under Alexander II and left it only in the Revolution of 1905. In general the overprocurator had a decisive voice in the appointment of bishops and exercised supervisory control over the Synod, which was a committee of the three metropolitans (Petersburg, Moscow, and Kiev) and several bishops. Within each diocese the bishop was supposedly the authority, although administrative affairs were handled in the diocesan "consistory," dominated by a secretary who was appointed by the

Synod but nominated by the overprocurator, to whom he was responsible.

In 1900 there were 49,000 Orthodox churches in the empire, served by 104,500 members of the secular clergy: 2,000 cathedral deans; 44,000 priests; 15,000 deacons; and 43,500 psalmists. The empire was divided into sixty-four Orthodox dioceses and 40,000 parishes and contained about 380 Orthodox monasteries and 170 convents.[19] The regular clergy of these institutions included about 15,000 monks and novices and 48,000 nuns by the opening of the twentieth century. Among the greatest and most respected monasteries, called *lavras,* (Greek for monastery) were: the Kievan Monastery of the Caves, the Trinity - St. Sergius *lavra* near Moscow, and the Alexander Nevsky *lavra* in Petersburg. It was the custom in the Orthodox Church that only the monastic or "black" clergy (as opposed to the secular or "white" clergy) could become bishops or metropolitans. This meant that the monasteries played a major role in the church hierarchy, because the heads of those institutions (archimandrites and abbots—*igumeny*) were the only candidates for episcopal sees. The educational needs of the clerical estate were comparatively well-served by the end of the nineteenth century. There were theological academies (on the university level) near Moscow and in Kiev, Petersburg, and Kazan, 58 seminaries, 183 district schools for the sons of the clergy, and 49 diocesan schools for their daughters.

It is not easy to appraise the role of the Russian Orthodox Church in the life of the country as it emerged in the twentieth century. Among the various difficulties facing the parochial priests, the most obvious was the lack of adequate financial support. In 1900 the 40,000 parish churches (and the mission) received only about ten million rubles from the treasury, which meant that the stipend of most members of the "white" clergy, who usually had families to support, was insufficient, and they depended on payments for various religious ministrations, such as baptisms, marriages, burials. On the more important feast days the parochial clergy visited the houses of their parishioners, brought greetings, sang a short prayer, and received donations in kind or in money. While this way of life kept the Russian priest close to his flock, the financial dependence of the priest, often on very poor peasants, sometimes led to financial negotiations that lowered the moral authority of the clergy. As for the laity, they had little part in the affairs of the Church, apart from attendance at

---

[19] The twelve Roman Catholic dioceses had 3000 parishes (chiefly in the western provinces) and Muslim religious congregations numbered 24,500.

services. Until 1905 they elected only a "church elder," who assisted the priest in parochial financial affairs, and in 1905 a decree provided for elected parochial councils of the laity as optional institutions. But these bodies, over which the priest was to preside, never became important.

But one should not assume that the Church remained somnolent while a modern society evolved in Russia. The clergy made considerable progress in education, and by 1900 the overwhelming majority of parish priests had attended a diocesan seminary (secondary school), which offered a broad curriculum in languages, the humanities, and even the sciences and mathematics. And the intellectual level of the four academies of theology was high indeed. Here, in addition to teaching, professors wrote, translated, and published numerous religious and historical works, including a Russian translation of the Bible in 1876 (Old Slavonic continued to be the language of the services, however). By the turn of the century the academies were also publishing numerous periodicals, some of which expressed liberal views and criticized the Synod. While the members of the Church hierarchy were well educated, the village priests helped to establish primary education on the countryside. As mentioned earlier, Pobedonostsev was afraid of the liberal spirit of the zemstvos, and he supported the establishment of parochial schools for peasant children.

About the turn of the century, when complaints about peasant drunkenness grew loud, the rural clergy founded and supported "temperance societies," and after 1905 they also assisted the social welfare of the peasants by helping the development of cooperatives, sometimes serving as chairmen or directors.

Despite the declining moral authority of the Orthodox clergy in the last decades before the Revolution of 1917, countless priests rendered incalculable spiritual assistance to their flock in time of trouble, often under exceedingly difficult conditions; and some of them, especially the monastic elders *(startsy)*, became famous for their spiritual example and uncommon moral qualities. A particularly revered group of these devoted religious teachers existed at the monastery called *Optina Pustyn'* in Kaluga province. Many intellectual leaders, including Kireevsky, Khomiakov, Dostoevsky, and V. Soloviev, visited the elders of this monastery; and Dostoevsky presented a literary portrait of such a *starets* in Zosima of *The Brothers Karamazov.* One of the most influential of Orthodox clergymen was Father John of Kronstadt (1829–1908), who was widely famed for his ascetic life, his charitable activities, his moving sermons, and his ardent prayers—

which were credited with healing power. He revived the ancient custom of public confession, and his spiritual diary, *My Life in Christ,* became an important work in Russian Christianity.

To some degree the religious spirit of the elders was also manifested by masses of Russian laymen who conducted pilgrimages to such holy places as the Kieven Monastery of the Caves or the Solovetsky Monastery on the White Sea. It is estimated that well over a million pilgrims per year underwent weeks or months of privation, usually traveling on foot, to reach these places. Thousands went to Odessa and traveled by ship to the monastery of Mt. Athos and to the Holy Land, which in the early twentieth century was visited by more pilgrims from Russia than from all other countries combined.

In its relations with the non-Orthodox, the Church in the late nineteenth and early twentieth centuries both gained and lost ground, and its proselytization generally took on more humanitarian form in its dealing with the Eastern peoples than with defectors from Orthodoxy in European Russia. Official policy toward the schismatic branch of the Church (the Old Believers) and the Christian sectarians varied considerably. Under Alexander II the persecutions of the reign of Nicholas I were ended. The largest group of schismatics, the "Priestists" *(Popovtsy),* were allowed to hold their own church council and to establish an independent hierarchy of twelve bishops. The majority of this church agreed to recognize an "encyclical letter" *(okruzhnoe poslanie)* of 1862, displaying a conciliatory attitude toward the secular state. In the reign of Alexander III and the first part of the reign of Nicholas II, however, the influence of Pobedonostsev prevented such a spirit of tolerance. An edict of 1883, while granting normal civil rights to Old Believers, forbade Old Believers and sectarians to manifest their faith in public or to propagandize the Orthodox.

Real religious tolerance was introduced during the Revolution of 1905; an edict of April of that year granted religious freedom and equal rights to all the Christian dissenters except the "perverted" sects such as the "eunuchs." Now the Orthodox were legally free to enter other Christian denominations or return to some non-Christian faith if their ancestors had belonged to it. Between 1905 and 1909 over 300,000 were officially recognized as legal defectors from Orthodoxy. Following the decree of toleration in 1905, Baptist groups, which had been spreading rapidly in the southern provinces, even without toleration, organized the Union of Evangelical Christians in Petersburg and continued to find many new adherents. The total number of Old Believers and sectarians cannot be accurately determined because many were not included in official statistics. On the eve of the twentieth century the number of Christian dissenters from Orthodoxy was officially given as 10 million, while private sources give figures between 20 and 25 million.[20] Orthodox believers were officially numbered at 87 million, or about 70 percent of the total population.

In missionary work among the Eastern peoples the main center was the Kazan theological academy, where oriental languages were taught and the scriptures translated into such languages as Chuvash and Kalmyk. In 1883 the Synod authorized the use of native languages as the equal of Old Slavonic in services conducted among Eastern peoples. Among Orthodox missionaries one outstanding figure was Innocent, bishop of Kamchatka and later metropolitan of Moscow. In the former capacity he implanted Christianity in Kamchatka and Alaska, and as metropolitan he founded the Orthodox Missionary Society in 1870. The Orthodox missionaries even enjoyed modest success in Japan, founding a church there that used the Japanese language and was by 1916 a self-governing, self-supporting congregation of 35,000.

Although the Slavophiles were impressed by the ethical and social importance of Christianity, most of the intelligentsia of the latter half of the nineteenth century were inclined to regard religion as a "medieval survival." Around the turn of the century, however, interest in religion experienced some revival among Russian intellectuals, partly foreshadowed by V. Soloviev and L. Tolstoy. The meetings of the Religious-Philosophical Society in Petersburg between 1901 and 1903 were attended by both Orthodox hierarchs and outstanding secular intellectuals, but this encounter seemed merely to show that they were speaking different languages, one side expounding Orthodoxy, the other some new "home-made" religion. A greater degree of concord was attained in Moscow where the Religious-Philosophical Society was founded in 1907 in memory of V. Soloviev. Two outstanding members of this group, S. Bulgakov and P. Florensky, later became Orthodox priests and renowned theologians. The renewed intellectual interest in religion was paralleled by artistic concern, manifested in some of the poetry of the early twentieth century and in the inspiring rediscovery of the beauty of old Russian icons, long concealed under precious metal and soot.

After the Revolution of 1905 the question of Church reform was raised, and many clergymen and laymen demanded the con-

---

[20] P. Miliukov, *Outlines of Russian Culture*, ed. by M. Karpovich (Philadelphia, 1942), part I: Religion and the Church, pp. 116–117.

vocation of a national Church council *(sobor)*, the re-establishment of the patriarchate, and the limitation of the power of the secular government. In January 1906, the tsar followed the suggestion of the Holy Synod, no longer under Pobedonostsev, and appointed a pre-sobor conference of ten bishops and twenty professors to elaborate a plan for a future sobor. Meetings and discussion followed, but there was no practical result until August 1917, when a sobor consisting of 564 delegates, half laymen, met in Moscow. On October 30 they re-established the patriarchate, but decided that the supreme power in the Church rested with the sobor. Coinciding with the Bolshevik Revolution, this revival of independent spirit in Russian Orthodoxy came at the beginning of a most difficult time in the history of the Church.

10

Foreign Affairs
From the Peace of Paris to the Beginning
of World War 1

Imperial Expansion in Asia

Since Russia's efforts to extend her influence in the Balkans and the Near East had been frustrated by her defeat in the Crimean war, Alexander II concentrated on extending and securing the boundaries of the empire in the Caucasus, in Central Asia, and in the Far East. Russia returned to its activity in the Balkans in the crisis of 1876–1878, but in the meantime considerable territory had been acquired in Asia, and by 1885 the southern boundary of the Russian state between the Black Sea and the Sea of Japan assumed approximately its present shape.

Under Alexander II the half-century-old struggle for the Caucasus was ended. To break the resistance of Muslim mountaineers in the eastern Caucasus, the viceregent of the Caucasus, Prince A. Bariatinsky, launched in 1857 a well-planned advance into the regions of Chechnia and Daghestan. The prolonged and heroic resistance of the mountain tribes headed by Shamyl was finally crushed, and in 1859 Shamyl surrendered to Prince Bariatinsky in the Daghestan village of Gunib. After Prince Bariatinsky left his post because of illness, the Russian forces, commanded by General Evdokimov, completed the conquest of the Cherkess areas in the western Caucasus by 1864.

To prevent the resumption of mountain warfare, the Muslim inhabitants of especially hostile mountain villages (*auls*) were given the choice of resettlement on the plain or emigration to Turkey. Around 200,000 emigrated to Turkey, while the majority submitted to Russian authority. The Caucasus was then divided into administrative districts on the Russian pattern and subjected to the control of Russian officials. The policy of the Russian government was to minimize interference with the ways of life of the native population, so long as they accepted Russian rule, and to win the support of the local aristocracy by giving it opportunities for advancement in the Russian army and civil administration. Shamyl, the celebrated leader of the resistance movement in the eastern Caucasus, was given a pension and resided in "honorable captivity" in Kaluga, and then in Petersburg. He died in 1871 in Mecca during a pilgrimage to Muhammad's grave.

The two Cossack hosts in the northern Caucasus, the Terek and the Kuban, which played an important role in military operations during the Caucasian wars, now turned from active warfare to patrolling, and to the peaceful pursuit of agriculture. The Kuban Cossacks in particular became very prosperous farmers on the fertile steppe land, but their presence remained of considerable strategic value in supporting Russian domination over the Caucasus.

Russia's boundaries in the Far East had been quite stable since the treaty of Nerchinsk in 1689 recognized the Amur River region as Chinese, but in the mid-nineteenth century expansion in this direction was resumed by the energetic governor general of Eastern Siberia, Muraviev. In 1850 a small Russian expedition under Nevel'skoi, a young naval officer, reached the Amur estuary and there established a Russian post, which soon became the city of Nikolaevsk. The Russians also occupied the territory on the left (generally northern and western) bank of the Amur, which they had renounced in 1689, and in 1858 Muraviev, taking advantage of an Anglo-French attack on China the previous year, concluded the Treaty of Aigun, by which China ceded the left bank of the Amur to Russia. By another treaty, signed by General Ignatiev in 1860 in Peking, China also ceded the area between the Ussuri River and the Sea of Japan, the southern arm of Russian territory in the Far East, which became the "Maritime Province." For his role in this expansion Muraviev received the title "Count Muraviev of the Amur." The government attempted to consolidate the Russian position in the East by founding the cities of Blagoveshchensk, Khabarovsk, Nikolaevsk, and Vladivostok; by establishing three new Cossack hosts in the region; and by attempting to attract peasant settlers. However, the immense distance separating the Amur-Maritime area from European Russia prevented significant colonization until the construction of the Trans-Siberian Railroad in the 1890s.

Another Russian territorial acquisition in the Far East was the island of Sakhalin, whose northern half Russia occupied in 1853, taking the rest in 1875, when Japan renounced her claim to the southern half in return for the Kurile Islands. Sakhalin remained very sparsely populated, serving mainly as a penal colony.

In Central Asia between the southern border of Russian Siberia and the northern boundaries of Persia, Afghanistan, and India there was a vast arid and semiarid area inhabited by various Muslim peoples who spoke Turkic languages (the Kirghiz, Kazakhs, Uzbeks, and Turkmens), or Iranian in the case of the Tadzhiks. Many of these people were nomads; they were loosely organized politically and much given to internecine strife. In the first half of the nineteenth century the Russians gradually advanced their military outposts across the vast northern area inhabited largely by the nomadic Kazakhs, the steppe region *(stepnaia oblast')*, which in 1867 was divided into four civil administrative regions *(oblasti).*[1]

To the south of the steppe region lay the three most populous and highly organized states of the whole area: the khanate of Kokand (roughly east of the Aral Sea, lying on the right bank of the Syr River and including the cities of Kokand, Tashkent, and Turkestan); the emirate of Bukhara (roughly southeast of the Aral Sea, lying between the Syr and Amu or Oxus rivers and including the cities of Bukhara and Samarkand); and the khanate of Khiva (roughly south of Aral Sea, lying mainly on the left bank of the Amu River and including the city of Khiva). The conquest of these states occupied about ten years (1864–1873) and required many military campaigns, more as a result of the difficult terrain and climate than of the military efficiency of the natives, who repeatedly suffered heavy losses while inflicting only insignificant casualties upon the Russians. The pretext for these campaigns was usually the depredations of border raids by various tribes which had long been accustomed to plundering and slaving among their neighbors. It must be added, however, that the real need of the Russians to protect territory previously annexed coincided with both commercial interest in Central Asia as a market and supplier of cotton and the zeal of the Russian military commanders for triumphal campaigns. Even after Foreign Minister Gorchakov, while justifying the necessity of the Russian ad-

---

[1] See Richard A. Pierce, *Russian Central Asia, 1867–1917* (Berkeley, 1960), p. 17.

RUSSIAN EXPANSION
IN THE
CAUCASUS AND CENTRAL ASIA,
1801-1895

Russian Empire, 1801

Semidependent Territories, 1801

Acquisitions under Alexander I, 1801-1825

Acquisitions under Nicholas I, 1825-1855

Acquisitions under Alexander II, 1855-1881

Acquisitions under Alexander III, 1881-1894

═══ Georgian Military Highway

╫╫╫╫ Trans-Caspian Railroad

RUSSIAN

Orenburg

Orsk

Aktiubinsk

Ural R.

Don R.

Volga R.

LESSER
ORDA

Kuban R.

Astrakhan

NOGAI

CHERKESS

KABARDA

BLACK
SEA

ABKHAZIA

OSSETIA

Poti
Batum

GEORGIA

Vladikavkaz

CHECHNIA

DAGHESTAN

CASPIAN
SEA

ARA
SEA

Erzurum

Kars

ARMENIA

Erivan

Tiflis

7 KHANATES OF
AZERBAIJAN

Baku

KHANATE OF KHIVA
(Protectorate, 1873-1917)

Khi

Araks R.

Krasnovodsk

KARA-
DESE

OTTOMAN
EMPIRE

Geok-tepe

Askhaba

Teheran

IRAN

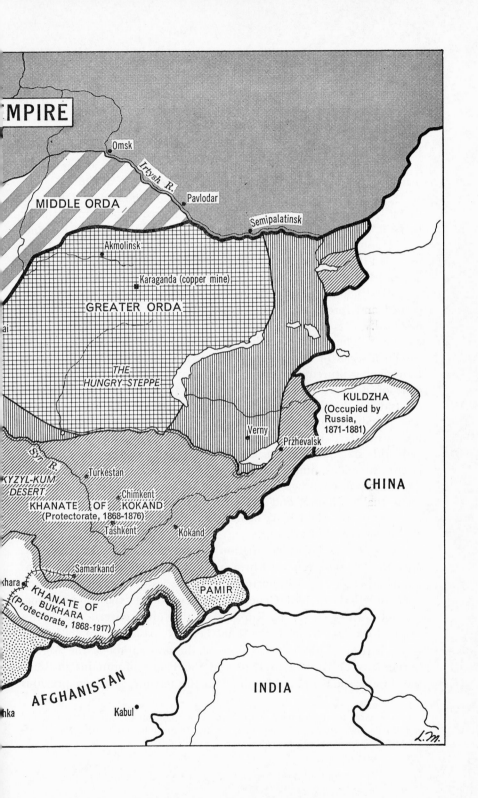

MPIRE

Omsk

Irtysh R.

Pavlodar

MIDDLE ORDA

Semipalatinsk

Akmolinsk

Karaganda (copper mine)

GREATER ORDA

ai

THE HUNGRY STEPPE

KULDZHA
(Occupied by
Russia,
1871-1881)

Verny

Przhevalsk

CHINA

Syr R.

Turkestan

KYZYL-KUM
DESERT

Chimkent

KHANATE OF KOKAND
(Protectorate, 1868-1876)

Tashkent

Kokand

Samarkand

khara

KHANATE OF
BUKHARA
(Protectorate, 1868-1917)

PAMIR

AFGHANISTAN

INDIA

hka

Kabul

L.M.

vance into northern Kokand in his note to the great powers in November 1864, was ready to stop there, the military insisted on pushing onward.[2] War Minister Miliutin insisted that "there is no need to apologize to the English ministry for each forward movement," considering *their* imperial policy,[3] and in the next year General Cherniaev, a major figure in the early Central Asian campaigns, acting on his own initiative, continued his further penetration of Kokand.

Having taken northern Kokand and the city of Turkestan in 1864, Russian forces under Cherniaev proceeded south to Tashkent in 1865. Although this undermined the power of the khan of Kokand, it did not pacify the area, for the emir of Bukhara intervened and occupied the city of Kokand, obliging the khan of Kokand to recognize the overlordship of Bukhara. The following year the Russians were able to dislodge the Bukharans from one of the forts they had occupied and forced the khan of Kokand to recognize the tsar as his overlord.

The next objective was the emirate of Bukhara itself, and in a series of campaigns the Russians, under General K. P. von Kaufman, captured the city of Samarkand and in 1868 forced the emir of Bukhara to cede that city and recognize the suzerainty of the tsar. Of the three main Central Asian states the khanate of Khiva now remained unsubdued, protected by the most forbidding desert so far encountered by the Russians. Only in 1873 did the Russians invade this state, having formed four columns to approach from different directions, under the supreme command of Von Kaufman. Three columns reached the city of Khiva, which fell after typically ineffectual resistance, and the khan was forced to cede outright his territory on the right bank of the Amu River, while also recognizing the overlordship of the tsar.

The Russian occupation of the large, sparsely populated area to the southwest of Khiva and Bukhara, often referred to as Transcaspia, occurred in an intermittent series of campaigns between 1877 and 1884. In 1881 General Skobelev stormed the Tekin stronghold of Geok Tepe; A. N. Kuropatkin, the future governor of Transcaspia, took Askhabad in the Akhal-Tekinsky oasis; and in 1884 Merv was occupied. With the exceptions of the annexation of the Afghan border city of Kushka in 1885 and the Pamir Mountains in 1895, the Transcaspian campaigns filled in the territory between previous

---

[2] An English text of Gorchakov's note may be found in D. C. Boulger, *England and Russia in Central Asia* (London, 1879), vol. I, appendix 3, pp. 318–320.

[3] Miliutin, *Dnevnik*, vol. I, p. 35.

Russian conquests and mountains of northern Persia, the Pamirs and Tien Shan. The latter stages of the advance had been especially disturbing to the British, whose sensitivity for the security of India increased with each new Russian advance. By 1885 there was a real danger of war, for the Russians seemed about to penetrate Afghanistan. Although the acute tension passed after the end of Russian advance in this year, it was only in 1907 that Russia and England really set aside their mutual animosity and came to terms regarding imperial ambitions in the whole region.

The Russian Empire annexed directly the larger part of the vast Central Asian empire that it occupied in 1864–1884, dividing it into a number of new administrative entities. Even the khanate of Kokand, which at first had been allowed nominal independence under its khan, was annexed as the Fergana Region following a revolt in 1876. However, the khanate of Khiva and the emirate of Bukhara retained some measure of autonomy as Russian protectorates.

As a result of these acquisitions in the Caucasus, Central Asia, and the Far East, Russian political control over the vast Eurasian plain was fulfilled. The multinational All-Russian Empire included territories from the Vistula River and the Baltic to the shores of the Pacific, and from the shores of the Arctic Ocean to the spurs of the Himalayan Mountains. The peoples who inhabited these territories were bound together by political and economic ties, and to some extent all nationalities experienced the influence of Russian culture. Much has been said about the persecution or even "forcible Russification" of the ethnic minorities in the Russian Empire. Indeed, the official policy of the Russian government, particularly under the last two tsars, restricted the use of native language in schools and left no room for self-government by ethnic minorities, except in Finland. The restrictive policies of the government, however, found little sympathy among the Russian population. Anti-Semitism persisted among the people in the western provinces, but on the whole the Russians were free from feelings of national superiority and did not regard their neighbors as "inferior races." Ability to establish good neighborly relations with the other peoples who lived under the same roof in particular remained a characteristic of the Russian intelligentsia, which was itself multinational in origin and far from chauvinistic in spirit. In fact, nobody became Russified except those who wanted to become Russian; otherwise each nationality—the Poles, the Jews, the Germans, the Armenians, the Tatars, the Mongols, the Buriats, and more than a hundred others—maintained its own identity, language, religion, and customs.

Russia and the Balkans

The defeat of Russia in the Crimean War and the stipulations of the Treaty of Paris in 1856 did not solve the basic problems that beset the Balkan area throughout the nineteenth and early twentieth centuries. The decline of the Ottoman Empire and awakening of nationalist spirit among its subject peoples continued, while the interests of the European powers were steadily engaged in the shifting situation.

Among the powers Russia had the closest ethnic and religious ties with the Balkan peoples, and as early as the Treaty of Kuchuk Kainarji in 1774 she had claimed the right to intervene in the Ottoman Empire on behalf of its Christian subjects. There was much talk in the West about Russia's intention of using Pan-Slav ideology to achieve political hegemony in the Balkans and part of Central Europe, but in reality Pan-Slavism had originated among the Slavs of the Hapsburg Empire as a protest against Germanization, not as a Russian policy. As Lobanov-Rostovsky states: "It remained the expression of a mood and a dream—that of the liberation of all Slav nations from foreign domination and the formation of some kind of federation between them."[4] Among the Russian Slavophiles there was no consensus concerning the political future of Slavdom, and some even identified Slavdom with Orthodoxy, thus leaving the Western (Roman Catholic) Slavs outside their aspirations. More important, Pan-Slavism was never accepted as an official policy by the Russian government. Neither Nicholas I and his foreign minister Nesselrode, nor Alexander II and his chancellor Gorchakov had any sympathies with Pan-Slav theories. Maintaining very close family ties with German ruling houses, these tsars based their foreign policy on friendship with Germany and Austria: "to speak therefore as the foreign press did of Panslavism as being a Machiavellian policy conceived and officially supported by the government, was sheer nonsense."[5] Only Alexander III was sympathetic to Pan-Slav ideas, but ironically, after the rupture of diplomatic relations with Bulgaria in 1887, he abandoned any active policy in the Balkans, clearing the way for the ascendancy of Austrian influence.

If there was no Pan-Slavism as an officially accepted or clearly defined political doctrine, there were unquestionably deep sympathies in Russia for the Balkan Christians (Rumanians and

---

[4] A. Lobanov-Rostovsky, *Russia and Europe, 1825–1878* (Ann Arbor, 1954), p. 259.
[5] *Ibid.*, p. 263.

Greeks as well as Slavs) who suffered under the yoke of the Ottoman government. This popular sentiment led, in 1858, to the formation of the Slavic Welfare Society in Moscow, headed by the historian M. P. Pogodin. In the following decade similar societies were organized in Petersburg, Kiev, and Odessa. Their purpose was to help the Balkan Slavs develop their national and cultural self-awareness through aid to their educational institutions, as well as to provide facilities for Balkan students in Russian universities and theological schools. Even though the Slavic Welfare societies were primarily concerned with the independence movement in Bulgaria and Serbia, they annoyed the Austrian government in 1867, when a Slavic ethnographic exhibition and congress were held in Moscow. At that time, a large delegation of Slavs from the Austrian empire visited Russia, was honored at dinner parties by Russian Slavophiles, and received by Alexander II at Tsarskoe Selo as "Slavic brothers in a native Slavic country." Platonic as they were, these expressions of kinship were seen by Austria as endangering the loyalty of her Slavic subjects.

While Russia supported the Balkan Christians in their struggle with Turkey, Britain supported the Ottoman Empire, fearing Russian expansion toward the Straits, the Mediterranean, and the trade routes to the Levant and India. Austria, too, opposed Russian policy in the Balkans, partly because she feared the effects of the awakening of the Balkan Slavs upon her own numerous South Slav population and partly because she had her own territorial and commercial ambitions in the Balkans. Despite formal friendship or even alliance with Russia, Austria usually supported Britain against Russia in Balkan politics. Although direct French interest in the Balkans and Near East waned after the fall of Napoleon III in 1870, it retained its place in conferences on the Eastern Question as an accepted prerogative of a great power. In contrast with France, Germany took an increasingly active part in Balkan politics. Bismarck professed disinterest in the Balkans, but after his dismissal in 1890, Kaiser Wilhelm II undertook to expand German interest in the Ottoman Empire: as self-proclaimed protector of Islam; as patron of German commercial development in that region, including the Berlin-Baghdad railroad; and by 1913, as the supporter of the modernization of the Ottoman army. This policy clearly conflicted with the Russian dream of "restoring the cross on the Hagia Sophia" in Constantinople.

Against this background of international politics the Balkan peoples continued their struggles for national independence, an integral part of the general European movement toward national liberation and unification. Following the Peace of Paris in 1856, the Balkan nationalities no longer had any legal basis to appeal to Russia against the Turks, but were instead obliged to turn to the concert of European powers. But by and large the concert, influenced by Britain, would not bring effective pressure to bear upon the Turks, and the frustrated peoples of the Balkans had no recourse but to take up arms against the Ottoman rule, outnumbered though they were.

The principalities of Moldavia, Wallachia, and Serbia, which already enjoyed autonomous status, strove for complete liberation. Napoleon III took an active interest in Moldavia and Wallachia, and urged them to form a united state. With this support the parliaments of these principalities in 1859 elected a common prince, the native boyar Colonel Alexander Cuza, and in December 1861 they proclaimed the merger of Moldavia and Wallachia to form the new state of Rumania. In 1866 Cuza was forced to abdicate because of internal dissension, and the election of Prince Karl of Hohenzollern-Sigmaringen as his successor created a dynastic link between Rumania and Germany. In Serbia the demands of Prince Michael Obrenovich in 1867 for the withdrawal of Ottoman garrisons were supported by the European powers at a time when the Ottoman Empire was embarrassed by a rebellion in Crete. The Turks therefore gave in and withdrew their troops from Belgrade and two other cities.

The next important development was the renunciation by Russia of the clauses of the Treaty of Paris which forbade military activity on and around the Black Sea. The Franco-Prussian War of 1870 provided an opportunity to end this onerous situation, for the other powers were preoccupied and Bismarck was willing to support the Russian renunciation in return for her benevolent neutrality in the war with France. England and Austria waxed indignant at the unilateral Russian action, but could do no more than arrange a conference of the powers in London, in March 1871, which formally abrogated the Black Sea clauses in 1856 and declared against future unilateral changes in international agreements.

The year 1875 saw the beginning of the first major Balkan crisis since the Crimean War. The Slavs in the Ottoman provinces of Bosnia and Herzegovina arose and could not be suppressed by even the most ruthless punitive measures. The severity of Ottoman repressions aroused the sympathy of neighboring Serbia and Montenegro, and the great powers felt obliged to intervene before the crisis spread. In May 1876, the foreign ministers of Russia, Austria, and Germany, whose emperors were at that time signatories of a loose alliance called the Three Emperors' League (*Dreikaiserbund*), met in Berlin and agreed on a memorandum demanding that the Ottoman Empire execute administrative reforms in Bosnia, Herzegovina, and also Bulgaria. France and Italy accepted this plan, but Prime Minister Disraeli of Britain rejected it and collective action was frustrated. Russia and Austria still attempted to meet the impending crisis with a common policy, and in July 1876, the two emperors and their foreign ministers, Gorchakov and Andrassy, met at Reichstadt. Although they agreed that no single, large Slavic state should be established in the Balkans, they failed to define their understanding in greater detail, and in the future years it was the source of quarrels and recriminations.

Meanwhile, the anti-Ottoman revolt spread to the Philippolis district of Bulgaria, and the Turks retaliated by slaughtering 12,000 persons, an atrocity that aroused general indignation in Europe. But Prime Minister Disraeli persisted in his Turcophile policy, despite Gladstone's fiery speeches about "the unspeakable Turk," and the concert of European powers was still unable to act.

But Serbia and Montenegro did act, forming an alliance and declaring war against the Ottoman Empire in June 1876. In this act of indignation they were supported by intense Slavophile and patriotic feelings in Russia. The spokesman of the Slavophiles, I. S. Aksakov, delivered rousing speeches; the Slavic Welfare societies raised substantial donations for the "fighting Slavic brethren"; and thousands of volunteers were permitted to join the Serbian army, including General Cherniaev, a former hero in the conquest of Central Asia and now commander of the Serbian army. Even some revolutionary populists volunteered for service in Serbia.

Despite this assistance, the Serbian army was defeated in October 1876 and began to retreat toward Belgrade. Tsar Alexander demanded that the sultan accept an armistice and negotiation, and to enforce his ultimatum mobilized part of the Russian army, threatening unilateral armed action if negotiations failed.[6] Turkey accepted the ultimatum, and in December 1876 and January 1877, the powers met in Constantinople to draft a plan of autonomous administration for Bosnia, Herzegovina, and Bulgaria, subject to the control of an international commission. But the Ottoman Empire, supported by Britain, declared that it would conduct the reform itself, and in March 1877, the powers convened once more, this time in London, and in a "London Protocol" again insisted that the reforms be supervised by the great powers. Ottoman rejection of this demand as incompatible

---

[6] S. S. Tatishchev, *Imperator Aleksandr II* (2d ed.; St. Petersburg, 1911), vol. II, p. 310.

with her sovereignty was the act that finally decided Alexander II on war.

Previously he had vacillated, influenced by Finance Minister Reitern and War Minister Miliutin, who opposed war, and by public opinion, which relentlessly called for intervention on behalf of the "Slavic brethren." While participating in the attempted solution through negotiation, Alexander simultaneously had prepared for possible war by signing the Budapest convention with Austria in January 1877 and a Russo-Rumanian convention in April. The first of these treaties provided for Austrian neutrality in a Russo-Turkish war, while the second gave the Russian army permission to cross Rumanian soil to fight the Ottoman Empire.

Thus prepared, Alexander responded to the collapse of negotiations by joining the army in Bessarabia and, April 12, 1877, signing a declaration of war, which was greeted with great popular enthusiasm in Russia. The proclaimed objective of the war was "the amelioration and security of the status of the oppressed Christian population of Turkey," and in communicating the Russian decision to the other powers, Gorchakov added that the tsar was convinced that "he is acting in accord with the feelings and interests of Europe." But none of the European powers moved to help Russia, and Britain reproached her for violating the Treaty of Paris, warning that if Russian operations approached Constantinople, Britain would intervene. To this Gorchakov replied that Russia had no such intentions.[7]

The Russian army crossed the Danube in June and a detachment under General Gurko quickly reached Shipka Pass in the Balkan Mountains, the major natural obstacle between the Danube and the Straits. In July and August, however, the Ottoman defenders of the fortified town of Plevna, blocking the Russian route to the mountains, thrice repulsed Russian attacks with heavy losses. The tsar, supported by Miliutin, had to dissuade the commander in chief, Grand Duke Nikolai Nicholaevich, from withdrawing across the Danube, and for some time Russian morale was low. Only in November did the tide turn. On the Caucasian front, where the Russian and Turkish armies were also engaged, the stronghold of Kars fell to the Russians. At the end of the month Osman Pasha, the defender of Plevna, at last surrendered and opened the road to Constantinople. Serbia, which had been forced to sue for peace in February 1877, re-entered the war and occupied Nish, a Serbian town in Ottoman

---

[7] A. W. Ward and G. P. Gooch, eds., *The Cambridge History of British Foreign Policy* (Cambridge, 1923), vol. III, pp. 112–117.

territory. Under Generals Skobelev, Radetzky, and Gurko the Russians steadily advanced to the south, occupying Adrianople in January 1878. The sultan now sued for an armistice, which was signed in Adrianople on January 19, halting the Russian advance a few miles from Constantinople.

This ended one war but threatened to open another. At the sultan's request Disraeli ordered the British Mediterranean squadron to pass the Dardanelles and sail to Constantinople, which it did in February. In answer to Russian protests, the British government replied that the fleet was going to Constantinople to protect British subjects and their property. Alexander indignantly signed an order to occupy Constantinople "for the same purpose" (to protect Russian subjects and property), but changed it to make this advance contingent upon a British landing. However, the Russian commander in chief demonstrably moved his headquarters to San Stefano, a suburb of Constantinople, and the danger of war remained acute until the British warships were withdrawn to the Asian shore of the Sea of Marmora at the request of the sultan.

On February 19, 1878, Russian and Ottoman representatives signed the terms of a preliminary peace. By this settlement Rumania, Serbia, and Montenegro were recognized as independent (no longer merely autonomous) states. Serbia and Montenegro were to receive considerable territorial rewards, while the Muslims living in these countries were guaranteed equal rights.

Bulgaria, including Macedonia and extending on the south to the Aegean Sea, was to be an autonomous principality with a Christian government and a "national militia." The assembly of the notables of Bulgaria was to work out a constitution and to choose a prince "whose appointment was later to be confirmed by the Sublime Porte with the consent of the great Powers." Until then the country was to be administered by a Russian imperial commissioner and the Russian troops were to occupy Bulgaria for a period close to two years, until the creation of the Bulgarian territorial army. The new state had to pay the sultan a contribution, which was to be determined jointly by agreement between Russia, the Ottoman Empire, and the other great powers, and "Ottoman troops were not to be stationed in Bulgaria." In Bosnia and Herzegovina the administrative reforms suggested by the Constantinople conference of the European states were to be introduced immediately. "Organic statutes" were to be introduced in Crete and the European part of the Ottoman Empire to protect the rights of the indigenous population. In Armenia administrative reforms were to be executed to protect the safety of the Armenian population from acts of violence committed by Kurds and Circassians. The Porte was to pay Russia an indemnity of 1,410,000,000 rubles, but after taking Ottoman financial difficulties into consideration Russia agreed to exchange the greater part of the indemnity (1,100,000,000 rubles) for territorial concessions: the Ottomans were to cede Russia the territory around the mouth of the Danube and the region south of it, the Dobruja, which Russia "permitted herself to exchange" with Rumania for the southern part of Bessarabia, which had been alienated from Russia by the provisions of the treaty of 1856; in Asia the Ottomans ceded Russia the districts of Ardahan, Kars, Batum, and Bayazid.

The conditions of the peace of San Stefano aroused strong dissatisfaction in England and Austria. Disraeli again began saber rattling and issued an order to call up the reserves. Austria, referring to the Reichstadt agreement and the Budapest convention, firmly objected to the creation of a Greater Bulgaria and began military preparations. Alexander thus had to face the possibility of a new and difficult war, which he preferred to avoid by settling the issues through diplomatic channels. In May the Russian ambassador to London, Count Shuvalov, succeeded in reaching a secret preliminary agreement with the British as to the final conditions of peace, and in June the meetings of an international congress were opened in Berlin.

Bismarck presided over the Congress of Berlin and attempted to play "the honest broker," although he usually sided against Russia on disputed issues. Russia was represented by the octogenarian Gorchakov and by Shuvalov, who did most of the negotiating. Disraeli represented Britain and Austria, France and Italy also participated. The Balkan countries sent representatives, but these were kept in the background, unable to say much as their fate was decided. The objective of the Anglo-Austrian coalition at the negotiations was to curtail Russian gains in the Treaty of San Stefano as much as possible. At their initiative, the concessions that the congress asked of Russia seemed excessive to Petersburg, and there were moments when the Congress of Berlin appeared likely to break up. In the end, however, Alexander II suppressed his personal humiliation and reluctantly consented to Western demands.

The Treaty of Berlin was signed July 1 (13), 1878, by the great powers of Europe and by Turkey. It confirmed the independence of Rumania, Serbia, and Montenegro but considerably reduced the territorial expansion that the Treaty of San Stefano had awarded to the latter two countries. The greatest change in the Treaty of San Stefano concerned Bulgaria, whose territory was now divided three ways: the south (Macedonia) was returned to the Porte; the north, from the Balkan Mountains to the Danube, including Sofia, became the Autonomous Principality of Bulgaria; and the middle area (south of the Balkan range) became the Province of Eastern Rumelia, to remain under Ottoman rule with administrative autonomy. The governor general of Eastern Rumelia was to be a Christian, appointed by the Turks with the consent of the great powers for a five-year term.

Article 25 of the Berlin settlement departed entirely from the earlier treaty and provided Austria with substantial gains. The provinces of Bosnia and Herzegovina were to be occupied and administered by Austria, and in the sanjak (district) of Novibazar, lying between Serbia and Montenegro, Austria was permitted to maintain garrisons and to build and guard military and commercial lines of communication, even though the area was to remain Ottoman in theory.

Other articles stipulated that Russia might, as in the San Stefano treaty, annex southern Bessarabia in return for ceding the Dobruja to Rumania. Russia was also awarded Ardahan, Kars, and Batum (the latter to be a free port), but she had to return to the Ottomans the valley of Alashkert and the city of Bayazid. Although Britain did not receive any territory under the terms of the Treaty of Berlin, she obliged the sultan to repay her attentions by granting her the right to occupy and administer the island of Cyprus.

Alexander's concessions at Berlin brought great disappointment in Russia and her Balkan clients, weakening the authority of the regime. An angry speech by I. S. Aksakov against Russian diplomacy at Berlin caused his banishment from Moscow, which in turn made an unfavorable impression on the Balkan Slavs. Britain was the unquestioned winner at the congress. She had checked the expansion of Russian influence without a war; she had added Cyprus to her empire; she had preserved a large part of his European possessions for the sultan; and she had contributed to the breakup of the *Dreikaiserbund,* which Russia now blamed for its failure to support her. Austria had also gained by the rebuff to Russian plans and by the acquisition of Bosnia and Herzegovina. The Balkan countries were thoroughly dissatisfied: the Bulgarians by the partition of their country; the Serbians by Austrian expansion; the Rumanians by the loss of southern Bessarabia; and the Greeks for having received no Ottoman territory. The Berlin settlement did not bring lasting peace but only frustration of the national aspirations of the Balkan peoples and the seeds of future war.

The provisions regarding Bulgaria were especially short-lived. Through its commissioner, Prince Dondukov-Korsakov, and a few hundred Russian officers who served as advisers to the new Bulgarian army, Russia played a major role in the formation of the new state. In 1879 the Bulgarian constituent assembly somewhat democratized and then approved a draft constitution prepared by a Russian commission, and the first representative assembly elected as prince of Bulgaria Prince Alexander of Battenberg. The Russians then transferred authority to him and withdrew their troops. At first Russo-Bulgarian relations remained amicable and Russian generals even occupied ministerial posts in Bulgaria, but after a time blunders on both sides and the machinations of Austrian diplomacy weakened this amity.

In the autumn of 1885 an uprising took place in the main city of Eastern Rumelia, Philippopolis. The Bulgarian nationalists expelled the governor general appointed by the sultan and his Ottoman officials, and declared the reunification of the "two Bulgarias." Prince Alexander, after some hesitation, declared himself prince of the united Bulgaria. In the same year a war broke out between Bulgaria and Serbia in which the Bulgarians were the victors. In 1886 Prince Alexander was deposed and a year later an Austrian protégé, Prince Ferdinand of Coburg, was elected prince of Bulgaria. Alexander III refused to recognize Ferdinand as prince of Bulgaria, and in 1887 he broke off diplomatic relations, which were not restored until the end of this reign.

Russian influence in other Balkan countries also declined after the Congress of Berlin. In Turkey British influence remained predominant for some years. Rumania, which became a kingdom in 1881, resented Russia's annexing southern Bessarabia and in 1883 joined the Bismarckian treaty system with Germany, Austria, and Italy. Serbia also proclaimed herself a kingdom in 1882, having concluded a secret alliance with Austria the year before. Greece remained a British client.

As Russian influence faded, Austria gained in the Balkans, partly as the result of her expansion in Bosnia, Herzegovina, and Novi Bazaar and partly through her alliances with Serbia and Rumania. Her economic role in Serbia was especially important, for she acquired the right to build railroads there, and favorable terms of trade as well. In 1889 Alexander III was quite justified in drinking his famous toast "to the sole and faithful friend of Russia, Prince Nicholas of Montenegro."

The Russo-Japanese War

By the end of the nineteenth century Japan had emerged as a great power in the Far East and rapidly assimilated the industrial and military technology of Western Europe. Between the relatively small but thickly populated Japanese islands and the vast but still inert Chinese Empire lay Korea, the natural bridge between Japan and the mainland. In 1894 Chinese troops entered Korea to assist the king, a nominal vassal of China, in suppressing a rebellion. This provided the pretext for Japanese intervention, and in the resulting war the Japanese won easily. By the Treaty of Shimonoseki of April 1895, China recognized the "independence" of Korea (tantamount to recognition of Japanese predominance) and ceded to Japan the Liaotung Peninsula, Formosa, and the Pescadores, not to mention a large indemnity and grant of commercial privileges. Russia, Germany, and France, alarmed by the Japanese success, insisted on the revision of the treaty, and Japan, with considerable resentment, returned the Liaotung Peninsula to China.

Although Russian interest in Korea dated back to 1884, when a Russo-Korean trade agreement had been signed, a new wave of Russian interest in that area, stimulated by the building of the Trans-Siberian Railroad, coincided with the emergence of Japanese imperial power. Moreover, the future Tsar Nicholas II had personally visited the Far East in 1891, and his interest in the area was stimulated by his cousin, Kaiser Wilhelm II, who attempted to distract Russian attention from Europe by turning it toward the "yellow peril" he envisaged in the East.

As minister of finance, Witte advanced Russian economic interest in the East. In 1895 he established a Russo-Chinese Bank, based on French and Russian capital, to develop trade in Manchuria, and in 1896 he negotiated a comprehensive treaty with the Chinese representative Li Hung-Chang, who was in Moscow to attend the coronation of Nicholas II. The new Sino-Russian partnership against Japan included an arrangement for the Russian construction of a railroad across Manchuria, the shortest route from Siberia to Vladivostok. This "Chinese Eastern Railway" was to be financed and owned by the Russo-Chinese Bank, and its profits guaranteed by the Russian government. The company was to receive a substantial right of way across Manchuria, in which it would operate the public administration, including armed police. Since the management of the company, the civil administrators, and the police were Russian, the arrangement was tantamount to the long-term cession of a strategic strip of Manchuria to the Russian government. After thirty-six years, the Chinese government would have the right to buy up the line, or it could wait for eighty years, when it could take over the line without compensation.

During construction of the railroad, Russian influence in Korea was steadily advanced. In 1897 a Russo-Korean Bank was established, Russian military instructors assisted the Korean army and a Russian financial adviser acted virtually as minister of finance. Following an agreement of 1896, both Russia and Japan kept about a thousand troops in Korea to protect their interests.

Additional Russian penetration of East Asia followed an incident in 1897 in which the German government occupied the port of Tsingtao on Kiaochow Bay in retaliation for the death of two German missionaries. When this led to the grant of a ninty-nine-year lease of the port to Germany, Russian naval vessels entered the bays of Port Arthur and Talienwan on the Liaotung Peninsula and the Petersburg government demanded privileges similar to those granted Germany. Consequently, a new Russo-Chinese agreement of March 1898 granted Russia a twenty-five-year lease on Port Arthur and Talienwan.

Having gained this foothold on the tip of the Kwantung Peninsula, Russia linked it to the Chinese Eastern Railway by a treaty of June, 1898, which gave Russia the right to build a railway south from Harbin in Manchuria to Port Arthur and Talienwan. Russia now began the intensive development of the Kwantung Peninsula, changing the name Talienwan to Dalny (called Dairen in English) and constructing modern port facilities. Russian colonists began to settle in the area and Russian public administration was established.

Since Japan had been forced to withdraw from the Liaotung Peninsula only two years earlier, she was indignant over the Russian advance, and to avert war the Russian government recalled its military instructors and financial adviser from Korea, signing a treaty April 13, 1898, which in Witte's opinion "relinquished Korea to the predominant influence of Japan."

The granting of concessions to Germany and Russia did not end the occupation of Chinese ports by European powers. Britain took Weihaiwei on the Yellow Sea, and France took Kwangchow Bay in southern China. These unjustified incursions naturally roused indignation in China and in 1900 the nationalist movement known to Europeans as the "Boxers" arose against the foreigners. The European quarter in Peking was beseiged, various countries sent military expeditions to the rescue and Russian troops occupied Manchuria. When the rebellion had been crushed, the Russians seemed reluctant to with-

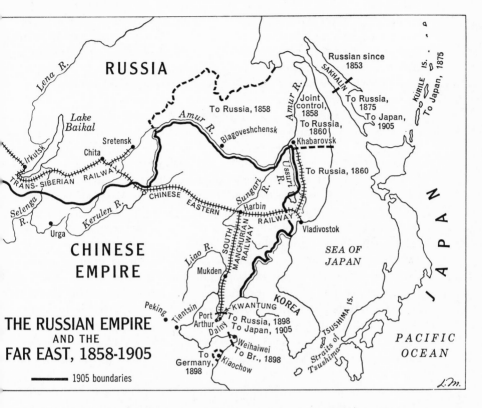

THE RUSSIAN EMPIRE
AND THE
FAR EAST, 1858-1905

─────── 1905 boundaries

draw. Britain, Japan, and the United States brought diplomatic pressure to bear, and in 1902 the Petersburg government promised to return Manchuria to China (except for the Chinese Eastern Railway). However, they were slow to fulfill this promise, and in 1901 Japan attempted to reach an agreement with Russia, recognizing Russian predominance in Manchuria if that country would withdraw its troops, maintain an "open door" for foreign commerce there, and recognize Japanese predominance in Korea. The Petersburg government declined the proposal, and in January 1902, Japan concluded a treaty with Britain, recognizing Japanese predominance in Korea and assuring her of British neutrality should Japan go to war with one other power, or British assistance if Japan were at war with two other countries. Reassured by this alliance, Japan began to prepare for war with Russia, continuing diplomatic negotiations with her in the meantime.

The negotiations were handicapped by the fact that a group of Russian adventurers, especially one Bezobrazov, exerted considerable influence on the tsar. This clique was very militant in its attitude toward Japan and obtained a timber concession on the Yalu River in northern Korea, again implicating Russia in this disputed country. In the summer of 1903 a viceregency was established in the Far East, including the Amur province and the Kwantung region. A "dry-land" admiral, Alekseev, who supported the timber enterprises in Korea and an aggressive policy toward Japan, was appointed viceroy.

Japan protested against the Russian undertakings in northern Korea and demanded the evacuation of Russian troops from Manchuria by the end of 1903, but the unsuccessful diplomatic negotiations dragged until January 1904. On January 24 (February 6), 1904, Japan broke off the negotiations and recalled her ambassador from Petersburg. In Russian government circles and in Admiral Alekseev's command it was not expected that Japan would "dare" to start a war. But during the night of January 27 (February 9) Japanese destroyers attacked Russian ships of the Port Arthur squadron lying on the outer roadstead by the fortress, and inflicted heavy damage upon two Russian battleships and one cruiser. This success immediately assured Japan's superiority on the sea and the possibility of a continuous and almost unhindered supply of troops and military supplies to the mainland. On that same day, January 27, the Russian cruiser *Variag* and gunboat *Koreets* had been destroyed by their crews after a heroic battle with the Japanese squadron at Chemulpo harbor off the shores of Korea.

Aside from the crippling blow to her fleet on the first day of the war, there were other factors that made Russia's prospects for victory in the war fairly bleak. The Japanese ground and naval forces were, in general, superior in weapons, command, and organization; their supply lines were short. Russian military forces, on the other hand, could be concentrated in the Far East only very slowly, because the 3000-odd miles long, single-track Trans-Siberian Railroad had limited capacity, and an important section of the line around Lake Baikal was still under construction. The Russians also had difficulties in their high command. General Kuropatkin, the minister of war, was appointed head of the Manchurian Army. Initially, however, he was under the command of Admiral Alekseev, who had neither military nor administrative talent, but interfered in military decisions. This created an unfortunate dual authority and resulted in the need for constant appeals to Petersburg, where the quarrels between the two commanders had to be settled. The capable and energetic Admiral S. O. Makarov was appointed commander of the Far Eastern fleet, but on March 31, soon after his arrival in Port Arthur, he perished along with his flagship, the *Petropavlovsk*, which exploded when it struck a Japanese mine. Last but not least, the Japanese fought with patriotic conviction, whereas in Russia the war was not popular at all and was considered, not without reason, to have been provoked by a clique of irresponsible Manchurian and Korean adventurers around the Russian throne.

Japanese forces landed in Korea without opposition and in April 1904 crossed the Yalu River, entering Manchuria; in May they landed on the Kwantung Peninsula, cutting off communication between the fortress of Port Arthur and the Russian army in Manchuria. On July 28, the Port Arthur Squadron tried to break through from the besieged port to sail to Vladivostok, but it failed and was destined to be destroyed in the roadstead of the besieged fortress, exposed to the bombardment of the Japanese shore batteries. In August 1904, a prolonged battle was fought in Manchuria at Liaoyang and ended with the retreat of the Russian army.

In October the Second Pacific Squadron sailed from the Baltic to the Far East under the command of Admiral Rozhdestvensky. Its voyage was long and arduous, around Africa, since the British did not allow the main body of the fleet to pass the Suez Canal; most of the coaling had to be done at sea. Moreover, a number of slow, outmoded ships, completely unsuited for long sea voyages, were added to the fleet. Early in the voyage the Russian ships almost provoked war with Britain by firing on British fishing vessels, which were mistaken for Japanese torpedo boats (the Dogger Bank Incident).

At the end of September and beginning of October, General Kuropatkin attempted to assume the offensive but was halted in a bloody battle on the Shaho River. The besieged garrison of Port Arthur put up heroic resistance until December 1904, enduring an almost constant bombardment and repulsing fierce attacks. On December 2, General Kondratenko, the leading spirit of the defense, was killed, and on December 19, General Stessel, first in command of the Russian troops, surrendered the fortress to the Japanese, thus permitting them to transfer their besieging army and its powerful artillery to the Manchurian front.

In February 1905, the Russian army suffered complete defeat in an eighteen-day battle at Mukden and was forced to retreat to the north. Kuropatkin was replaced as commander in chief by General Linevich, who entrenched himself in the new positions at Sipingai, north of Mukden. Here the front was stabilized; the Japanese did not attempt another offensive in Manchuria until the end of the war. In May 1905, Admiral Rozhdestvensky's squadron arrived in the Yellow

Sea, but it was intercepted and annihilated by the Japanese in the Straits of Tsushima between Japan and Korea May 27–29.

Both Russia and Japan wanted peace, for Japan, too, had suffered great losses in manpower and was exhausted to a considerable degree. When President Theodore Roosevelt offered the belligerents his mediation, they accepted. The peace conference assembled in Portsmouth, New Hampshire, at the end of July, with the Russian delegation headed by Witte, and on August 23 the peace treaty was concluded. By its terms the Russian government recognized the "predominant political, military and economic interest of Japan in Korea"; both sides promised to evacuate Manchuria and return it to China; Russia ceded to Japan her lease on Port Arthur, Talienwan (Dairen), and their environs, along with the South Manchurian Railway, which connected these cities with Harbin; Russia also ceded to Japan the southern half of Sakhalin Island and promised not to fortify the rest; Japan received fishing rights along the Pacific coast of the Russian Empire; and Russia was to indemnify Japan for the maintenance of prisoners of war.

Soon after the war the relations between Japan and Russia improved considerably and both sides agreed to divide the spheres of political influence in the Far East. In 1907 Russia concluded a trade and navigation agreement with Japan, a fishing convention, and a (secret) political agreement by which Japan recognized northern Manchuria as a Russian sphere of influence and Russia recognized southern Manchuria and Korea as the Japanese spheres of influence. In 1910 both sides again concluded an agreement on cooperation and maintenance of the *status quo* in China, as well as on the delimitation of spheres of influence. In that year Japan also recognized Outer Mongolia to be in the Russian sphere of influence and then carried out a formal annexation of Korea.

When a revolution occurred in China in 1911, the Russians took advantage of the situation to consolidate their position in Outer Mongolia. An agreement was concluded in Ugra in 1912 with the newly established Mongolian government, by which Russia pledged to help Mongolia to secure its autonomy and Russian subjects were "granted the right to negotiate with the Mongolian government with regard to the exploitation of mining and timber resources, fishing industries," and the like.

In 1913 Russia concluded an agreement with China on the political situation of Outer Mongolia: "China recognizes the autonomy of Outer Mongolia"; "Russia recognizes that Outer Mongolia is under the sovereignty of China"; and both sides committed themselves not to interfere in the internal administration of Mongolia and not to send their troops there. The new status of Outer Mongolia maintained the nominal sovereignty of China but established a Russian protectorate in practice.

During World War I, Japan joined the Triple Entente, took over the German possession of Tsingtao in China, and in December 1916 concluded her last (secret) treaty of friendship and mutual assistance with Imperial Russia.

Russia and the United States

Following Bering's discovery of Alaska in 1741, Russian fur traders and hunters began their penetration of the northwestern part of the Western Hemisphere. In 1799 the Russian-American Company was granted a commercial monopoly and the right to establish local administration in America north of the fifty-fifth parallel, and by 1811 Russian settlers, seeking agricultural land, had established themselves around Fort Ross in the area of San Francisco Bay. An imperial decree of 1821 claimed for Russian subjects the exclusive commercial, fishing, and industrial rights north of the fifty-first parallel, but the Americans and British protested. In 1824 the United States and Russia agreed on 54°40′ as the southern limit of Russian America, and a separate treaty with Britain in the following year defined the Russo-British border in the Yukon.

With the exception of this territorial dispute, the United States and Russia were on good terms throughout the nineteenth century. Alexander I corresponded with President Jefferson and in 1808 welcomed the future president John Quincy Adams as the first American minister to Petersburg. In 1832 the two countries signed a commercial treaty. When the Civil War began in the United States, Alexander II firmly refused to recognize the belligerency of the South and thus discouraged pro-Confederate tendencies in English and French diplomacy. President Lincoln expressed his thanks for the Russian policy, and in 1863 a goodwill visit by a Russian naval squadron was enthusiastically received. An American man-of-war returned the visit in 1866, carrying Assistant Secretary of the Navy Gustavus Fox to convey American congratulations to the tsar on his good fortune in surviving Karakozov's attempt on his life earlier in the year. Fox was most cordially received by the government and the public. In the following year the Russian Empire, preoccupied with the consolidation of its newly acquired territories in the Far East, sold the United States its Alaskan territory for $7,200,000 in gold, a price that seemed excessive to many Americans at the time.

In the first decade of the twentieth century relations between Russia and America took a turn for the worse. In part, this friction resulted from the aggressive imperial policy of Russia in the Far East, especially Manchuria, and her unwillingness to give unqualified assent to Secretary of State Hay's principle of the "open door" to international commerce in China. Another source of ill-feeling was the anti-Jewish tendency in Russia, including both pogroms and legal restrictions. The numerous Russian-Jewish immigrants to America naturally harbored resentment concerning the lot of their people in Russia and helped to arouse public indignation over such outrages as the Kishinev pogrom of 1903. Representatives of Russian revolutionary groups, seeking support abroad, also tended to emphasize the seamy side of Russian life in their appeals to American public opinion. The change in the climate of Russo-American relations was reflected in the abrogation by Congress in 1911–1912 of the early nineteenth-century trade treaty with Russia.

Relations with Western Europe

Following the end of the Crimean War there was a brief tendency toward rapprochement between Russia and France. At the peacemaking conference itself, France opposed English efforts to weaken Russia excessively and Russia was receptive to the possibility of finding a new ally, considering her disappointment in Austria during the Crimean War. But Franco-Russian relations took a turn for the worse in 1863 when Napoleon III offended the Russian government by his demonstrative sympathy with the Polish revolutionaries.

While England, France, and Austria seemed to be unsuitable allies for Russia, Bismarck, who served as Prussian ambassador to Petersburg from 1859 to 1862, impressed the Russian court with the belief that Prussia was Russia's only sincere friend and natural ally. Dynastic ties supplemented this view, for Alexander II was a nephew of the Prussian king (and later kaiser) Wilhelm I and treated his uncle with great respect and confidence. Bismarck relied on Russian friendship during the Franco-Prussian War of 1870–1871. There was a good possibility that Austria, defeated by Bismarck in 1866 and regarded at this time as an ally of France, would intervene against Germany. But Alexander II, while declaring his neutrality in the Franco-Prussian War, made his neutrality conditional on that of Austria. This was not a promise to assist Germany, but it helped deter Austria from intervention, and Germany showed its gratitude by supporting the Russian abrogation of the Treaty of Paris concerning the Black Sea, as noted above.

Russo-German amity in the war of 1870–1871 led to the alignment of these states and Austria in the secret Three Emperors' League of 1873. But this agreement was vague and did not prevent the two Germanic powers from acting in collaboration, without the consent of their Russian ally or even in secrecy from her. The weakness of the agreement was revealed in 1875 when Russia responded to rumors of an impending German attack on France by asking for German assurances that this was not so. When Wilhelm I assured his nephew that he did not have aggressive plans, Foreign Minister Gorchakov annoyed Bismarck greatly by presenting Russia as the savior of the peace. In general Bismarck's attitude toward Russia was ambiguous in the 1870s. As his secret reports to the kaiser indicate, he disliked and feared Russia but chose to maintain ostensible friendship toward her and opposed the aggressive ideas of some members of the German high command. In any case the Balkan crisis of 1875–1878 showed the weakness of the Three Emperors' League as an effective alignment. As we have seen, Austria took an openly hostile line toward her Russian "ally," while Germany remained neutral and Bismarck played the "honest broker" to the disadvantage of Russia.

In 1879 Bismarck conducted a vigorous and rather preposterous anti-Russian campaign in his memoranda to the kaiser and his discussions with the Austrians, for he wished to frighten the pro-Russian kaiser and somewhat reluctant Austrians into accepting a Dual Alliance of the two Germanic empires. Bismarck maintained that the Russians were at once the exponents of Pan-Slavism and nihilism. He considered Miliutin, the renovator of the Russian army, to be the chief villain and Russia to be the main threat to the peace of Europe. This tirade was for a time manifest in inspired newspaper articles and in an absurdly overdone quarantine of the Russian border against the plague. Even so, old Kaiser Wilhelm disliked the terms of the Dual Alliance, which were defensive but obviously treated Russia as the only possible aggressor. Only under the threat of resignation by Bismarck and his entire cabinet did he sign it in 1879; it was thereafter renewed periodically and formed the basis for the alliance of the Central Powers in World War I. In 1882 Bismarck added a Triple Alliance of Germany, Austria, and Italy.

Despite his anti-Russian expressions, it was Bismarck's intention to isolate France, not Russia, and in 1881 he managed to revive the somewhat moribund Three Emperors' League in a revised form.

It was a three-year alliance in which the signatories promised not to go to war against any of their number, should one of them go to war with any outside party, except the Ottoman Empire, in which case prior agreement was necessary among the signatories of the treaty. This assured Russia that her large neighbors would not join Britain against her, but it did not prevent Austria from negotiating a secret treaty with Serbia, nor Rumania from joining the Triple Alliance to the detriment of Russian interests. In 1884 the revived Three Emperors' League was renewed for three years, but in 1887 Russia refused to continue this alliance. In its place Russia and Germany signed the Reinsurance Treaty, a three-year bilateral alliance by which each signatory promised the other benevolent neutrality should either go to war, providing only that Germany should not be the aggressor against France, nor Russia against Austria. A secret additional protocol promised Germany's benevolent neutrality and "moral and diplomatic support" if the Russian emperor found it necessary to assume control of "the key to his Empire" (the Straits) as a defensive measure.[8]

The Russo-German alliances of the 1880s did not prevent a degree of ill will between the two countries, especially in the closing years of the decade. The German press attacked Russian Pan-Slavism and resented the restrictions that the Russophile Tsar Alexander III placed on the Baltic nobility, while the Russian press in turn attacked "Pan-Germanism." When a Russian decree of 1887 forbade foreigners to own land in border provinces, a measure that chiefly affected German subjects in Russian Poland, the German press demanded reprisals. In November 1887, the German government forbade the *Reichsbank* to accept Russian securities as collateral, which produced an abrupt fall in their value as German investors unloaded. French investors helped to buy up the securities, and the Russian government accepted an offer of French bankers to float its state loans in the future. In December 1888, a loan of 500 million francs to the Russian government was floated, and France soon became the chief market for Russian state and industrial securities, paving the way for the political *rapprochement* of these two countries.

This tendency became still more pronounced in 1890 when the young, adventurous Kaiser Wilhelm II dismissed Bismarck and appointed Caprivi, a chancellor who preferred not to renew the Reinsurance Treaty when it expired in the same year. In 1891 the tsar welcomed a visit to Kronstadt by a French naval squadron, a visit the

---

[8] The text (in French) of the Reinsurance treaty is contained in *Die grosse Politik der Europäischen Kabinette, 1871–1914* (Berlin, 1922), vol. 5, no. 1092.

Russians then returned in 1893. By that time detailed negotiations for a defensive military alliance had been in progress for some time, and these were confirmed at the close of 1893 and the beginning of 1894. The existence of the alliance was made public in 1895 and the following year Nicholas II visited Paris and was warmly received.

In the first years of the Franco-Russian alliance the relations of the allies and Britain remained tense, especially in the areas of Franco-British conflict in Africa and Russo-British conflict in Asia. Fear of increasing German naval strength and imperial aspirations helped pave the way for a *rapprochement* of Britain and France, however, and in 1904 they concluded the "Entente Cordiale," resolving their imperial conflicts and leading to military collaboration. Russian relations with Britain remained tense during the war with Japan, Britain's ally in the Pacific, but after 1905 a full *rapprochement* between Petersburg and London became possible. Izvolsky, who became foreign minister in 1906, was eager for such a development, and in August 1907, Britain and Russia resolved their differences in Central Asia by delineating their respective spheres of influence. Concerning Iran (Persia), Britain promised not to solicit commercial or political concessions near the Russian border, while Russia reciprocated concerning the provinces near the Afghan and Indian borders; a central zone was to be left neutral. The Russians acknowledged that Afghanistan lay outside their sphere of influence, while the British promised not to occupy its Afghan territory or use force against it so long as the Afghan emir fulfilled his obligations to Britain. Tibet was recognized as a neutral buffer state under Chinese suzerainty, and both parties agreed not to seek concessions there.[9] Although Britain and Russia made no mutual military commitments or other agreements concerning Europe, the treaty of 1907, buttressed by the Anglo-French and Russo-French agreements, is usually thought of as having established a "Triple Entente," offsetting the Triple Alliance of Germany, Austria, and Italy.

Despite the growing ties between Russia, France, and England, however, Russia and Germany did not become completely estranged. In the beginning of the twentieth century, Germany was still Russia's leading partner in both exports and imports and the active economic relations between the two countries were regulated by the trade agreements of 1894 and 1904. During the Russo-Japanese War Germany gained the gratitude of Russia by maintaining benevolent

---

[9] The text of the Anglo-Russian agreement of August 31, 1907, can be found in *The Cambridge History of British Foreign Policy*, vol. III, pp. 358–361.

neutrality, and in the summer of 1905 Kaiser Wilhelm attempted to capitalize on this by offering the tsar an alliance that would undermine Russo-French relations. At a private meeting on the imperial yacht *Polar Star,* anchored near Björkö, Finland, Nicholas did sign such a treaty, but when Foreign Minister Count Lamsdorf read it, he persuaded the tsar to renounce the agreement unless it could be amended, which the kaiser would not do. Personal relations between the monarchs remained close, however, and in 1910 a meeting of the two at Potsdam resulted in an understanding by which Russia gave up her opposition to the German plan for a Berlin–Baghdad railroad and in turn received assurances that neither Austria nor Germany had any aggressive intentions in the Balkans.

But the Straits remained a perplexing issue between the two powers, and when Germany sent a military mission, headed by General Liman von Sanders, to reorganize the Ottoman army in 1913, a sharp conflict resulted. Von Sanders was appointed commander of the First Turkish Army corps in Constantinople, which the Russian foreign minister Sazonov protested as being tantamount to the establishment of a German garrison on the Bosphorus. The issue was compromised by transferring Von Sanders to the post of inspector general of the Ottoman army and director of its military school. German interest in the Balkans and the Ottoman Empire remained an obstacle to Russo-German relations, especially because Russia's long desire for control of the Straits was somewhat intensified in the years before 1914. As will be noted in connection with the Bosnian crisis of 1908, Russia attempted to arrange Austrian support for her demands on the Porte, and in 1909 Nicholas II visited King Victor Emmanuel of Italy and promised benevolence toward Italian interests in Tripoli and Cyrenaica in return for Italian support of Russia's interests in the Straits.

The general political situation in Europe in the second decade of the twentieth century was growing more and more tense and fraught with dangers. Two mighty groups of powers, the Triple Alliance and the Triple Entente, faced each other with mutual fear and suspicion, ready to defend their "interests" and their "honor." Germany feared encirclement and was building up her military forces, while Germany's adversaries were afraid of German militarism and imperialism. In France, Raymond Poincaré, whom his critics regarded as the embodiment of militarist and revanchist tendencies, became premier and foreign minister in 1912 and president of the republic in 1913. The diplomatic struggle between Russia and Austria-Hungary for influence in the Balkans was becoming increasingly acute after the Austrian annexation of Bosnia and Herzegovina in 1908. In this explosive situation, any spark could easily initiate a European conflagration. This spark was provided in the Balkans.

The Balkan Crisis and the Coming of World War

In the early 1890s Austria rather than Russia exercised the leading political and economic influence in the Balkan states, but under Nicholas II, Russia attempted with some success to regain lost ground. In 1895–1896 the Russian tsar and Bulgarian Prince Ferdinand were reconciled; Ferdinand's son, Boris, was christened in the Greek Orthodox rite and Nicholas II was the godfather. During and after the uprising in Crete and the Greco-Turkish War of 1896–1897 Russia took an active part in the collective action of the European powers which finally forced the Ottoman government to grant administrative autonomy to Crete under the governorship of Prince George of Greece.

In 1897 Russia concluded an agreement with Austria to maintain the *status quo* in the Balkans, but the attempt became ever less effective. In 1903 serious disturbances broke out in Macedonia where two Russian consuls were killed by Muslim fanatics. Nicholas II arrived in Austria in September 1903 to discuss a program of reforms for Macedonia, and after talks between the two emperors in the city of Mürzsteg, an agreement on Macedonia was reached and the earlier agreement supporting the *status quo* was reaffirmed.

In the same year a palace revolt took place in Serbia. King Alexander Obrenovich was assassinated by officer conspirators, and the dynasty of Karageorgevich regained the throne. Under the new government an anti-Austrian course triumphed in Serbia, and nationalist propaganda against the Ottoman Empire and Austria-Hungary was intensified. The Serbs began talking of a Greater Serbia that would include all Yugoslav ethnic groups. Austrian politicians and military leaders, on the other hand, seeing a threat to the integrity of the Danubian Monarchy in the Greater Serbia propaganda, began to contemplate the liquidation of Serbia as an independent state. Formal annexation of Bosnia and Herzegovina, which legally had been under "temporary" Austrian occupation since 1878, was regarded as a step curbing aspirations for a Greater Serbia.

In 1904–1906 the Russian government was preoccupied with the Japanese war and with a revolution at home, but after 1907 it could again turn its attention to the Balkans. In September 1908 a meeting of the Austrian and Russian foreign ministers took place in

Buchlau in Moravia. Here Aehrenthal of Austria and Russia's Izvolsky reached an agreement concerning the possible Austrian annexation of Bosnia and Herzegovina, but Izvolsky presumably gave his consent only on condition that the annexation would be approved by a prior international conference, in which the question of opening the Straits to Russian warships would be settled, with Austria's approval. Aehrenthal, however, understood (or pretended to understand) that the consent of Izvolsky was unconditional, and in October, 1908, Austria proclaimed the official annexation of Bosnia and Herzegovina to Austria-Hungary. At the same time Bulgaria declared its independence from Ottoman rule and Prince Ferdinand proclaimed himself tsar of Bulgaria.

The annexation of Bosnia and Herzegovina created an uproar in Serbia and precipitated an acute political crisis. Serbia protested against the annexation and expected help from Russia, but the latter was still too weak after the disastrous Japanese war and the ensuing revolution, while Austria was supported by her mighty German ally. Thus Russia and Serbia were forced to accept the annexation as a *fait accompli*. But soon after the annexation, Serbian nationalists founded the *Narodna Obrana* (National Defense), a society for the promotion of nationalist interests in the annexed provinces. In Russia the discontent caused by the political setback was combined with a growing interest in Balkan affairs and concern for the fate of the Balkan Slavs. At the same time, there was a growing resurgence of nationalist feelings among the Slavs living under Austro-Hungarian rule.

This Neo-Slav movement found its expression in the two All-Slav congresses, which took place in Prague in 1908 and in Sofia in 1910. The chairman and the principal leader was the able Czech politician Karel Kramář, a great Czech patriot, a sincere friend of Russia, and an advocate of the unity of free Slavic nations. The revival of the idea of Slavic kinship and the renewed determination to complete the struggle for national liberation from Austro-Hungarian and Ottoman oppression coincided, in the Balkans, with a progressive weakening of the Ottoman Empire, which barely survived a Young Turk revolution in 1908 and in 1911–1912 was involved in a war with Italy over Tripoli. This situation presented political and psychological conditions for creating the Balkan League, which was originated in 1912 with the active support of Russian diplomacy.

In March 1912, a treaty of alliance was signed between Serbia and Bulgaria, and in May of the same year a Greco-Bulgarian alliance was concluded. The new alliances were formally pledged to preserve the *status quo,* but secret appendixes and military conventions provided for joint action in a possible war against the Porte. Plans for a future division of the Ottoman European possessions provided that Serbia should gain access to the Adriatic by enlarging her territory to the south, and that Bulgaria should receive the greater part of Macedonia with access to the Aegean Sea. The Russian tsar was to act as arbitrator in case of disagreement among the allies.

At the end of September 1912, Montenegro declared war on Turkey. Within a week Serbia, Bulgaria, and Greece joined Montenegro. Before the end of November the Ottoman armies were completely defeated and had lost all the Porte's European territory except the southeastern part of Thrace. Adrianople was taken by Bulgarian and Serbian troops in March 1913. According to the Treaty of London, concluded in May 1913, nearly all the European territory of the Ottoman Empire (with the exception of Constantinople and the small adjacent part of Thrace) was divided among the Balkan nations. At the insistence of Austria and Italy, however, an independent Albanian state was established, depriving Serbia of the access to the Adriatic she had demanded.

Dissension quickly developed. Serbia decided to look for compensation in Macedonia, which according to the agreement of 1912 was given to Bulgaria. Greece, too, claimed a part of Macedonia. Russia made every effort to settle the controversy that broke out, while Austria-Hungary on the contrary tried to instigate a conflict and urged Bulgaria to war. Since Russia refused to help Bulgaria, Tsar Ferdinand turned again to Austria, and in June 1913, he ordered the Bulgarian army to attack Serbian and Greek troops. Rumania and the Ottomans entered the war against Bulgaria, which was quickly defeated and forced to sue for peace. By the Treaty of Bucharest, concluded in August 1913, Serbia received from Bulgaria the northern and central parts of Macedonia, including the city of Monastyr (Bitoli); Greece obtained southern Macedonia along the Aegean coast, with the two important seaports of Salonika and Kavalla; and Rumania annexed from Bulgaria the southern Dobruja. By the peace treaty of Constantinople, concluded between Bulgaria and Turkey in September 1913, Turkey regained a part of Thrace, including the city of Adrianople.

The two wars of 1912–1913 left the Balkan nations embittered and divided, and the intervention of the great powers added to the confusion. Bulgaria dreamed of revenge; Serbia dreamed of the creation of a Greater Serbia that would include the Croatians, Slovenes, and Bosnians who lived under Hapsburg rule. The Austro-

Hungarian general staff and some politicians demanded a decisive check to Greater Serbian propaganda, and they believed that this required the conversion of the independent Serbian state into a vassal of Austria-Hungary, if not its complete liquidation. A pretext for Austria to implement her designs was provided by the assassination of Archduke Francis Ferdinand, the heir to the Austrian throne, on June 15 (28), 1914, by a young Serbian nationalist in Sarajevo, the capital of Austrian-held Bosnia. The assassin and his accomplices were Austrian subjects, but the Austrian government accused the patriotic Serbian organization *Narodna Odbrana* of masterminding the plot and decided to utilize the shooting in Sarajevo to settle accounts with Serbia.

In fact, it was not *Narodna Odbrana* that inspired and organized the plot, but rather a strictly secret revolutionary organization called *Ujedinjenje ili smrt* (Unification or Death), otherwise called the "Black Hand," founded in 1911 and headed by the Serbian Colonel Dragutin Dimitrijević. Immediately after the incident the Serbian government published an official paper severely condemning the crime, expressed proper condolences, and declared its readiness to hand over to justice any Serbian subjects who might be guilty of complicity. But Austrian military and political leaders, especially Chief of the General Staff Conrad von Hötzendorff and Minister of Foreign Affairs Count Berchtold, decided that time was ripe to crush Austria's bothersome southern neighbor with a military blow. Considering the possibility of Russian intervention on behalf of Serbia, Austria first consulted with the German government and received assurances of unconditional support "to the end." Kaiser Wilhelm, full of indignation against Serbian "bandits" and "regicides," gave Austria a free hand and urged decisive punitive measures against Serbia. In a report of the German ambassador to Vienna concerning the plans of the Austrian government to undertake "a final and fundamental reckoning with the Serbs," the kaiser made the emphatic notation "now or never." [10]

Having received the promise of German support, the Austro-Hungarian government drafted a set of demands that the Serbs could not possibly accept, as even the German ambassador to Vienna, von Tschirschky, acknowledged. The ominous document was approved by the Austro-Hungarian State Council in its meeting on July 6 (19), and on July 10 (23) it was delivered at Belgrade for unconditional

---

[10] Karl Kautsky, comp., *The German Documents relating to the Outbreak of the War* (New York, 1924), no. 7, p. 61.

acceptance within forty-eight hours. The demands of the ultimatum included: suppression of every publication inciting hatred and contempt for the Austro-Hungarian monarchy; dissolution of the *Narodna Odbrana;* elimination without delay of any anti-Austro-Hungarian propaganda in the public instruction of Serbia; removal from military and civil service of all officers and officials guilty of conducting propaganda against Austria-Hungary (the names to be supplied by the Vienna government); cooperation with Austro-Hungarian officials in the suppression of the anti-Austro-Hungarian movement in Serbia; institution of judicial inquiry (with the participation of Austrian officials) against every participant in the conspiracy of June 28 who could be found on Serbian territory:[11]

When published, the Austrian ultimatum to Serbia met with approbation only in Berlin. In London Sir Edward Grey, the British foreign minister, asserted that acceptance of the conditions would signify the end of Serbia as an independent nation. The Italian foreign minister contended that Austria's procedure was aggressive and that the intervention of Russia or France would not make the resulting war defensive, obliging Italy to uphold the Triple Alliance. In Petersburg Foreign Minister Sazonov warned the German ambassador, Count Pourtalès, that the ultimatum, if not mitigated, meant war, and "if Austria-Hungary devours Serbia, we will go to war." [12]

To all of this and to Sir Edward Grey's proposal of a conference of the powers to settle the dispute, the kaiser responded belligerently, insisting on Austria's right to treat Serbia as she wished in settling this question of "honor." Meanwhile the Serbs responded to the ultimatum by appealing to the powers for mediation and by imploring the Russian tsar for his protection. The Russian government advised the Serbs to display maximum compliance to the ultimatum to avoid war, but at the same time promised that Russia would not remain indifferent if Serbia were attacked. Simultaneously, Petersburg appealed to Berlin and Vienna to display moderation and not to insist on unacceptable demands.

Heeding the advice of Petersburg, the Serbian government, led by Prince Regent Alexander and Prime Minister Nikola Pashich, went a long way toward complying with the Austrian demands. It agreed to all of them with the exception of the demand that Austrian officials direct the investigation on Serbian soil, and the reply ex-

---

[11] *Ibid.,* supplement I, pp. 604–605.
[12] *Ibid.,* no. 160, p. 187.

pressed willingness to conduct further negotiations on disputed questions or to submit them to the International Tribunal at The Hague. Even the kaiser agreed that the Serbian reply, which he described as "a capitulation of the most humiliating kind" eliminated "every cause for war," but he still believed that the temporary occupation of Belgrade by the Austro-Hungarian army was necessary to satisfy its honor.[13]

But the Austrian leaders were not satisfied, and on July 15 (28) they declared war on Serbia and began bombarding Belgrade. The German government attempted to restrain its ally, warning that it would not be "drawn wantonly into a world conflagration by Vienna, without having any regard paid to our counsel." [14] But it was too late. The Austrian aggression caused great indignation in Russia, and the government on July 16 (29) ordered the mobilization of four military districts (Kazan, Moscow, Kiev and Odessa) as a deterrent against Austria-Hungary. The Vienna government notified Berlin that they would not be dissuaded from their invasion of Serbia. The greatest concession that the Austro-Hungarian monarchy was willing to offer was publication of a proclamation that it did not intend to annex Serbian territory.

Nicholas II attempted to avert the imminent catastrophe by appealing directly to his cousin in Berlin. In a telegram of July 16 (29), the date of partial Russian mobilization, the tsar referred to Russian indignation over Austrian aggression and the resulting likelihood of war, concluding, "I beg you in the name of our old friendship to do what you can to stop your allies from going too far." [15] This message crossed one from the kaiser, which emphasized the need to punish the assassins, and in the next three days the exchange of telegrams between tsar and kaiser continued, but without reaching agreement. The second telegram from the kaiser seemed conciliatory and led Nicholas to cancel an order for general Russian mobilization, which had been urged on him by Minister of War Sukhomlinov and Chief of Staff Ianushkevich, who considered war inevitable. Foreign Minister Sazonov, too, favored general mobilization. In the absence of agreement with Berlin on measures for conciliation of the Austro-Serbian dispute, the tsar yielded to his advisers July 17 (30), signing the fateful order for general mobilization at 6 P.M. that day, to take effect the next day.

---

[13] *Ibid.*, no. 271, pp. 250–254; and no. 293, p. 273.

[14] *Ibid.*, no. 396, pp. 345–346.

[15] *Ibid.*, no. 332, p. 295.

On July 18 (31), a "state of threatening danger of war" was proclaimed in Germany, and that night the German ambassador to Petersburg, Count Pourtalès, presented Minister of Foreign Affairs Sazonov with an ultimatum demanding that Russia cease mobilization within twelve hours. On the evening of July 19 (August 1) Pourtalès returned to receive his answer. Not receiving a satisfactory reply, he presented Sazonov with a note, prepared in advance, declaring war on Russia. According to Sazonov's memoirs, both men were deeply disturbed by the approaching catastrophe, and the German ambassador could not suppress his tears. Then both diplomats, henceforth transformed into enemies, firmly embraced one another, and the German ambassador, with tottering steps, departed.[16]

---

[16] S. Sazonov, *Fateful Years, 1909–1916* (London, 1928), pp. 212–213.

11

The World War
and the Opening of the Revolution

Wartime Diplomacy, 1914–1917

The fateful week between the Austrian ultimatum to Serbia and the German ultimatum to Russia was filled with feverish diplomatic activity. Heads of states, foreign ministers, and ambassadors exchanged countless telegrams, notes, and reports, endeavoring to avert the imminent catastrophe. Only the Austrian leaders were unshaken in their decision to crush Serbia. On July 30 NS, Count Leopold von Berchtold told the British Ambassador in Vienna, de Bunsen, that "he only [sic] refused to discuss the Austro-Serbian quarrel with Russia, but he is willing to discuss with the latter all questions directly concerning Austria and Russia." To the urgent German proposals for a compromise solution on the basis of a "halt in Belgrade," the Austrian government did not give any reply. Then came the Russian mobilization that frustrated German plans to localize the military conflict. Germany's reaction was swift and far-reaching, and an avalanche of war declarations followed.

Having presented her ultimatum to Russia on July 18 (31), Germany sent to Paris a demand for a declaration of neutrality. The French government, ready to fulfill its obligations as an ally of Russia, answered on July 19 (August 1) that "France will act in accordance with her interests," and two days later Germany declared war on France. England at first remained on the sidelines of the conflict. When Sazonov of Russia turned to the English ambassador in Petersburg with an appeal for support, following the Austrian declaration of war against Serbia, Sir George Buchanan replied that England was not committed to enter the war for the sake of Serbia. However, the German violation of Belgian neutrality in the course of the invasion of France impelled England to join the Franco-Russian alliance. On August 2 NS, Germany presented an ultimatum to Belgium, notifying her that German troops must march to France through Belgium; if Belgium offered no resistance, Germany promised to quit Belgian territory after the end of the war and to make reparation for the damage done; if Belgium resisted, she would be regarded as an enemy; a reply was demanded within twelve hours. On August 3 NS, the imperial chancellor telegraphed to the German ambassador at London: "Please state to Sir Edward Grey that if we should take the step of violating Belgian neutrality, we would do so compelled by the duty of self-preservation. . . . Wedged in between East and West, we had to make use of every means to save ourselves." But neither Belgium nor Britain was willing to yield. Belgium rejected the German ultimatum and appealed for aid to the powers which had guaranteed Belgian neutrality. London immediately sent to Germany an ultimatum demanding that nation respect Belgium's neutrality. At midnight, August 4 NS, Britain declared war on Germany; with the entry of Great Britain, all her dominions and dependencies were involved in the war.

Ironically, the original antagonists among the great powers, the two long-term rivals in the Balkans, Russia and Austria, were not at war until July 24 (August 6), when Austria finally declared war on Russia. But the third member of the Triple Alliance, Italy, refused to follow suit. On July 31 NS, the German ambassador in Rome, Friedrich von Flotow, notified the Foreign Office in Berlin that "the Italian government . . . had again come to the conclusion that Austria's procedure against Serbia must be regarded as an act of aggression and that consequently a *casus foederis*, according to the terms of the Triple Alliance treaty, did not exist." On August 3 NS, the Italian king notified the kaiser of Italy's neutrality, which note provoked an indignant marginal remark by William.*

Later Italy negotiated with both sides involved in the war, but the Central Powers could offer her only Savoy and Tunis at the expense of France. The promises of the Triple Entente were much more enticing, since they included many regions of the Austro-Hungarian Empire which had an Italian-speaking population and which Italian patriots considered *Italia irredenta*. On April 26 NS, 1915, a

---

* All of the above quotations are from documents appearing in Karl Kautsky, comp., *The German Documents Relating to the Outbreak of the War*.

secret treaty was concluded in London between Italy and the Entente, which promised Italy the Trentino, south Tyrol, the region along the northern Adriatic coast including Trieste, Valona in Albania, and several islands. On May 22 NS, 1915, Italy declared war on Austria.

Soon after the beginning of the war the Triple Entente found a new ally in the Far East. On August 15 NS, 1914, Japan demanded that Germany surrender her possessions in the Pacific; the demand rejected, the Japanese declared war on Germany, August 23 NS, and proceeded to occupy German posts in China (on the Shantung peninsula) and on islands in the Pacific.

In September 1914 the Triple Entente became a formal alliance. By the pact concluded in London on August 23 (September 5), England, France, and Russia pledged not to conclude peace separately and agreed that when the terms of peace came to be discussed, none of the allies would demand conditions of peace without the previous consent of each other ally. Japan acceded to the London pact on October 6 (19), 1915.

In the Near East, the powers of the Triple Entente, especially Russia, suffered a serious setback because of the entry of the Ottoman Empire into the war on the side of the Central Powers. Since Germany controlled the Baltic and the Straits were blocked by Ottoman forces, Russia was practically cut off from her Western allies and could obtain badly needed military supplies only through Archangel, a remote port on the White Sea which was ice-blocked a large part of the year, or via the extended route through Vladivostok. On August 2 NS, 1914, the Porte concluded a secret political and military alliance with Germany, binding the Ottoman Empire to intervene and providing for a German "military mission" to take over the supreme command of Ottoman armed forces. On August 10 NS, the Ottoman government declared that the two powerful, new German cruisers *Goeben* and *Breslau*, which were ordered from the Mediterranean to Constantinople—and the internment of which England demanded—had been "purchased" by the Turks and added to their fleet. None of the Russian Black Sea warships could compete with these two cruisers in speed, making them virtually invulnerable in future military operations, while Russia was deprived of her supremacy and her freedom of action on the Black Sea. Nevertheless, the Ottoman Empire initially preserved the perfunctory appearance of neutrality. To overcome Turkish hesitations about openly entering the war, the *Goeben* and the *Breslau* bombarded on October 16 the Russian seaports of Odessa, Sevastopol, and Novorossisk. Russia declared war on the Ottoman Empire on October 20 (November 2), and Great Britain and France followed suit in a few days.

Ottoman involvement in the war gave Russian diplomacy an opportunity to raise the question of the future of Constantinople and the Straits. Soon after the Western Allies undertook a campaign aimed at opening the Dardanelles in February 1915, Foreign Minister Sazonov presented on March 4 ns a memorandum to the French and British ambassadors in Petrograd, declaring that the Russian emperor deemed it necessary to incorporate Constantinople and the Straits, with adjacent territory, into the Russian Empire. The French government agreed immediately, and the British government was also ready to consent if the war should be completed successfully and if British and French demands were fulfilled in the Ottoman Empire and elsewhere.

In April 1916, negotiations between England, France, and Russia led to the conclusion of an agreement regarding the partition of Ottoman possessions in Asia. England was to receive Mesopotamia; France, Syria and Cilicia; and Russia's share was to be the districts of Trebizond and Erzurum in Asia Minor, with a strip along the Black Sea shore west of Trebizond, Turkish Armenia (the provinces Van and Bitlis), and a part of Kurdistan.

In the Balkans the diplomacy of the Central Powers and of the Triple Entente was feverishly set in operation to attract those countries which at first proclaimed their neutrality, namely Bulgaria, Rumania, and Greece. As early as August 6 ns, 1914, Bulgaria concluded a secret treaty with the Ottoman Empire providing for friendship and possible military cooperation. Russian diplomacy tried to secure at least the benevolent neutrality of Bulgaria, while the Central Powers sought its military cooperation in the struggle against Serbia. Both sides promised Macedonia, or parts of it, to Bulgaria. King Ferdinand of Bulgaria was hostile to both Russia and Serbia, and Prime Minister Radoslavov was pro-Austrian; but there were also strong pro-Russian feelings among a number of Bulgarian political and military leaders. The defeats suffered by Russian armies during the summer of 1915, however, helped the Bulgarians make up their minds. In September 1915, the Bulgarian government concluded an alliance with the Central Powers; and in October 1915, while Austro-German forces poured into Serbia from the north, Bulgaria attacked that country from the east and helped to crush the fierce Serbian resistance.

Rumania's international position was peculiar. It was bound to the Central Powers by a formal treaty of alliance, but popular feelings in Rumania were far from friendly toward Austria-Hungary. The chief apple of discord between Rumania and Austria-Hungary was Hungarian Transylvania, inhabited by a Rumanian population of more than three million, who were kept in a state of economic, social, and political subjugation by their Magyar landlords and suffered from the official policy of systematic Magyarization. The Rumanian king, Charles of Hohenzollern, who was friendly toward the Central Powers, was ready to fulfill the treaty obligations, but he failed to persuade the Rumanian government to follow suit. The Crown Council decided that, since Rumania had been neither advised nor taken into consultation concerning the Austro-Hungarian *démarche* in Belgrade, no *casus foederis* existed. After her declaration of neutrality, Rumania was courted by both sides. The Central Powers promised her Russian Bessarabia, while the Allies offered her Hungarian Transylvania. On September 19 (October 2), 1914, Sazonov and the Rumanian ambassador in Petrograd signed an agreement by which Russia recognized the Rumanians' right to annex Transylvania as a reward for Rumanian neutrality. In October 1914, the pro-German King Charles died, and his nephew Ferdinand ascended the throne. After a long period of waiting and negotiations, in which further territorial gains were offered to Rumania, she did enter the hostilities by declaring war on Austria in August 1916.

Greece, like Bulgaria and Rumania, was courted by both sides. King Constantine, brother-in-law of the German emperor, favored the Central Powers, but Premier Eleutherios Venizelos was for Greek intervention on the side of the Allies. The king could not join the Central Powers while his maritime country was entirely at the mercy of the powerful British navy, but Venizelos could not move him to enter the war on the side of the Allies. In the fall of 1915 the Western Allies, with the consent of Venizelos, landed their armed forces at Salonika, but the king remained adamant. Finally, an Allied threat to bombard Athens forced Constantine's abdication, and on June 19 (July 2), 1917, Venizelos formally brought Greece into the war on the Allied side.

The final and decisive factor was the intervention of the United States, which tipped the scales at a time when both sides were severely exhausted by the war. In February 1917, after Germany had begun unrestricted submarine warfare, the United States severed diplomatic relations with her, and on April 6 NS, President Wilson signed a formal declaration of war on Germany. With the entry of the United States the conflict became a world war in the full sense of the term.

Russian war aims, as formulated and proclaimed at the beginning of the war, consisted chiefly of the liberation of Slavic nations from the domination of Germany and Austria-Hungary. In the program for peace, which Sazonov outlined to the French and British ambassadors in Petrograd in September 1914, Russia's own territorial gains were limited to eastern Galicia and a small area along the lower course of the Neman; western Galicia, Poznan, and Silesia were to be included in a future Poland, which was to be united and autonomous "under the scepter of the tsar."

In the very beginning of the war, August 14 NS, the Russian supreme commander, Grand Duke Nicholas Nicholaevich, issued a proclamation to the Polish people, calling for "brotherly" reconciliation between the Russians and the Poles and promising that a new unified Poland, formed from parts of the country now divided among the three neighboring powers, would enjoy self-government, religious freedom, and the use of the native language under the scepter of the Russian tsar. The proclamation, written on Sazonov's initiative and approved by the Council of Ministers, gave only vague promises that did not satisfy the Poles. But the Poles did not like German domination any better, and the population of Russian Poland remained loyal as long as Russian troops occupied the country. In Galicia, however, a Polish legion, formed by Josef Pilsudski, fought with the Austrians against Russia.

In April 1916, when Poland was under German occupation, Sazonov worked out a plan for Polish autonomy, providing for a Polish *seim* (parliament) and local Polish government; in July, the Council of Ministers and the tsar approved Sazonov's plan in principle, but the tsar decided to pigeonhole it, pending the re-entry of Russian troops into Poland. In November 1916, the Central Powers declared the establishment of a "Polish Kingdom," carved out of the former Polish provinces of the Russian Empire; but neither of these hypothetical Polish states was destined to become reality.

Before the Russian army entered Galicia, Grand Duke Nicholas Nicholaevich called upon the Slavic peoples of the Austro-Hungarian monarchy to meet the Russian troops as their friends and promised them liberation from foreign rule. But the first experiment with "liberation" proved to be a failure. After Galicia had been occupied by Russian troops, the civil Russian administration, headed by Governor General Count V. A. Bobrinsky, set out to "Russify" the province and to persecute that part of the local Ukrainian population which showed opposition to "Muscovites." At the same time,

Orthodox clergy, coming from Russia, endeavored to convert the Ukrainians as soon as possible from their Uniat (Greek Catholic) Church to Russian Orthodoxy. These measures naturally caused discontent and dissension among the local population. On the other hand, when Austrian troops and Austrian authorities returned to Galicia, severe persecution of those who had shown any sympathy toward the Russians followed.

The situation was different in Bohemia and Slovakia, where pro-Russian sentiment had traditionally been very strong and where Austrian officials began to persecute Czech nationalists immediately after the beginning of the war. One of the outstanding Czech political leaders, T. G. Masaryk, emigrated to propagate the idea of an independent Czechoslovakia in Western Europe and the United States. Another Czech leader, Karel Kramář, stayed home to head a secret political organization dedicated to the same goal; he was arrested in 1915 and later tried and sentenced to death, but the sentence was subsequently commuted to twenty years' imprisonment. Clearly, neither the Czechoslovaks nor the South Slavs showed any eagerness to fight for the preservation of the Austro-Hungarian monarchy, and occasionally entire Austro-Hungarian regiments, manned by Slavic nationals, voluntarily surrendered to the Russians. In August 1914, a military legion *(druzhina)* of Czech volunteers living in Russia was formed in Kiev; later it was augmented by volunteers from among Czech prisoners of war and expanded to the size of a brigade (two regiments). The tsarist government hesitated to permit the formation of a larger Czechoslovak force in Russia since enlisting prisoners of war to fight against their former country was contrary to international law. Only after the Russian Revolution of 1917 did the Czechoslovak legion in Russia increase to 50,000; it fought against the Germans in the Ukraine and later against the Bolsheviks. In 1920 it was evacuated via the Trans-Siberian Railway to the independent Czechoslovak republic, headed by Masaryk as president and Kramář as prime minister. Shortly before the collapse of the Russian Empire, the formation of a small Yugoslav military force in Russia was begun, following the pattern of the Czech legion.

Meanwhile, toward the end of 1916, the possibility of ending the war presented itself. After German military successes in Rumania, which resulted in the occupation of Wallachia, including Bucharest, the German chancellor announced in the Reichstag his government's willingness to start peace negotiations with the Allies. But the Allies rejected the German offer, deeming it necessary to bring the war to a victorious end. The tsar, December 25, 1916, issued an order to the Russian army and navy, announcing the German peace overture but stating that peace could not be concluded without victory and without the achievement of Russian war aims: the expulsion of the enemy from Russia; the acquisition of Constantinople and the Straits; and the formation of a unified and "independent" Poland from its three separated parts.

The last joint action of tsarist and Allied diplomacy was a conference in Petrograd, held in January and February of 1917 and attended by military and political leaders from Russia, France, Great Britain, and Italy. The conference discussed the over-all military and political position of the Allies, the means of improving the supplies for the Russian armies, and the plans for a joint offensive, which was to start in the spring of 1917.

While the tsar was determined to bring the war to a "victorious end," his extreme opponents, chiefly the Russian Bolsheviks, made every effort to use the difficulties and hardships caused by the war to undermine "tsarism." Early in the war, most European socialists took a patriotic stand and supported their governments. But soon the left-wing socialists began to change their minds. In September 1915 at Zimmerwald (a Swiss village near Bern), an international socialist conference assembled, at which not only the Bolsheviks—headed by Lenin—but also the Socialist Revolutionaries—headed by Chernov— and the Mensheviks—headed by Martov—participated on behalf of Russian socialism. The Zimmerwald conference adopted a resolution condemning the "imperialist" war and proposed a general peace treaty without victors or vanquished, "a peace without annexation or indemnities on the basis of the self-determination of nations." A second international socialist conference in Kienthal (also in Switzerland) in April 1916 adopted similar resolutions. The extremists among the socialists, headed by Lenin, proposed to "change the imperialistic war into a civil war" in the belligerent countries, but the majority of the "internationalist" socialists decided to limit their activity to pacifist propaganda.

The German Foreign Office was quick to realize how profitable to Germany pacifist propaganda in Russia could be and, beginning with the spring of 1915, organized a generous and steady flow of funds in support of antiwar propaganda in Russia. Millions and millions of marks were transferred to Russia for this purpose by way of neutral Copenhagen and Stockholm, where German diplomatic agents worked in contact with Bolshevik "internationalists":

Ganetsky-Fürstenberg, Rakovsky, Radek, and the Social Democrat Helphand, alias "Parvus," who served as the chief intermediary.[1]

Russia's Military Position on the Eve of the War

The war, as the late historian Michael Karpovich put it,

came for Russia at the most inopportune time, when she needed every ounce of her energy for the work of internal reorganization. It interrupted her political, economic and cultural progress; it imposed upon the Empire an overwhelming burden before the latter had an opportunity to establish itself firmly on new and stronger foundations.[2]

It cannot be denied that the Russian government, headed by a weak tsar, proved incapable of organizing the whole strength of the country for struggle against an adversary as powerful as Germany. But a number of objective circumstances placed Russia at a disadvantage. First, Russia's technological and industrial base, decisive in twentieth-century warfare, was much inferior to that of Germany. German industry was quickly placed on a wartime footing, producing an imposing flow of heavy and light ordnance, machine guns and rifles, cartridges and shells. The comparatively weak Russian private industry was unprepared for conversion to military needs, and the output of state-owned plants was insignificant in comparison to wartime needs. For example, the annual output of the state-owned ordnance works in 1914 amounted to only 600,000 shells for the three-inch field gun, while the annual requirements, as estimated by the general staff in 1916, was 42,000,000 rounds, or seventy times as much. Moreover, in the beginning of the war the government made the mistake of calling to the army skilled factory workers, a great number of whom were killed or wounded in the first campaigns. Later, when military production expanded, it had to depend on unskilled labor, and its efficiency suffered accordingly.

The Russian transportation system was similarly inadequate. Germany, with her closely meshed network of railroads and highways, could swiftly transfer and concentrate troops at one or the other sections of the front, as the military situation demanded. Russian troop movements were much slower. The density of the rail net-

---

[1] Z. A. B. Zeman, ed., *Germany and the Revolution in Russia, 1915–1918: Documents from the Archives of the German Foreign Ministry* (London, 1958), *passim.*

[2] M. Karpovich, *Imperial Russia, 1801–1917* (New York, 1932), p. 89.

work in European Russia was about ten times lower than that in Germany; many lines had a very low capacity and inadequate rolling stock. On a crash basis, the Russian government undertook to build some 3600 miles of new railroads during the war, but only half of them were completed in 1917. The most important one of them was the Murmansk Railroad, connecting the rail network of European Russia with the ice-free northern port of Aleksandrovsk and assuring an uninterrupted flow of military supplies. The Russian highway system was much weaker than the railroad system, and motor transportation for the needs of the army was practically nonexistent. The naval blockade of the Baltic and Black seas paralyzed all maritime transport for the duration of the war.

As for the Russian armed forces, the Russian navy had been virtually annihilated in the Russo-Japanese War (only the Black Sea fleet consisting of several outmoded warships remained), and the army had been shaken by the defeats in Manchuria and the revolution that followed. A thorough revamping of the entire military establishment was in progress, but was far from complete, and the German armed forces were superior in almost every respect. To begin with, the German military forces were magnificently organized and skilfully led, while the Russian army lacked talented and energetic senior officers. "Things are moving very slowly at the front, and many generals are making serious blunders. The worst of it is that we have so few good generals," wrote Nicholas II to the tsaritsa in March 1916.[3] While rumors of the "treason" of War Minister V. A. Sukhomlinov must be discounted as wartime hysteria, the facts of his incompetence and complacency—illustrated by his boastful declarations about Russian "readiness" for war—cannot be doubted. With many other top Russian officers, Sukhomlinov shared nineteenth-century notions of combat that relied excessively on manpower and bravery and discounted the importance of military technology.

The western frontier of the Russian Empire was, following old military rules, defended by a line of fortresses, but by 1914 these were hopelessly outdated and could not withstand the fire of heavy artillery. Several of them were, therefore, dismantled, and others were slated for refortification. The strength of the Russian artillery in 1914 was likewise inadequate; each German infantry division had twice as much light artillery as a Russian one, and with regard to heavy artillery the difference was frightening: the Russian army at

---

[3] A. L. Hynes, trans., and C. E. Vulliamy, ed., *Letters of Nicholas II to His Wife* (New York, 1929), p. 157.

the beginning of the war had 60 heavy batteries, while the German army had 381. Russian field artillery was good, but often, especially in 1915, its effectiveness was curtailed by shortages of shells. The Germans were far better supplied with machine guns, while Russia even lacked an adequate supply of rifles. A big disproportion existed with regard to air power. Russian aviation was still in an experimental stage, while German aviation, much more advanced, successfully engaged in air reconnaissance and supplied the German command with valuable data on Russian positions and troop movements.

Of course, the Russian military leadership was not totally unaware of these shortcomings, and following the Balkan wars of 1912–1913, and especially in view of Germany's growing military strength, the Russian government and the Duma approved a Russian major military buildup; the program, scheduled for 1914–1917, provided for a considerable numerical expansion of the Russian army, and for the strengthening of artillery, particularly heavy artillery. Several new battleships were also under construction. But the war broke out too early for any results of this program to be felt.

Military Operations, 1914–1916

The general mobilization which began in July 1914 was carried out with complete success; in its course, 3,115,000 reservists joined the 1,423,000 regular Russian troops. Over the next three years, more than 4 million recruits and more than 6 million territorials (*opolchenie*) were called to the colors, so that the total number of men mobilized in Russia in 1914–1917 exceeded 15 million. Of course, the recruits and the territorials, hastily trained and insufficiently equipped with arms, were second-rate combatants. Comparable numbers of men mobilized in 1914–1918 were more than 13 million in Germany, 9 million in Austria-Hungary, and 8 million in France. The number of Russian troops in combat ranged between 2 and 3 million in 1914.[4] Russia had 70 infantry divisions and 19 brigades at the outbreak of the war; following the mobilization, 35 new infantry divisions were formed; of these 114½ divisions, 94½ were concentrated against Germany and Austria-Hungary; the remainder were deployed in the Caucasus, on the Turkish border.

---

[4] According to German sources, the numbers of troops in the field in 1914 were as follows: Russia—3,341,000; France—2,033,000; England (with dependencies)—204,000; Germany—2,019,500; and Austria-Hungary—1,470,000. See M. Schwarte, ed., *Der Grosse Krieg 1914–1918 in zehn Bänden* (Leipzig, 1921), vol. I, p. 93.

Grand Duke Nicholas Nicholaevich was appointed commander in chief of the Russian armies, and General N. N. Ianushkevich his chief of staff. Historians of the war do not have a high opinion of their strategic abilities, but take into account the fact that they had to change their strategic plans many times in response to the needs of Russia's allies.

Immediately after the declaration of war the principal forces of the German army launched a concentrated attack against the French, and the French government implored Russia to start an offensive against Germany immediately. As early as July 23 (August 5), the French ambassador at Petrograd, M. Paléologue, appealed to the tsar: "I beg Your Majesty to order your troops to take the offensive immediately." The tsar promised to order an advance "the moment mobilization is complete." [5] Responding to French appeals, Grand Duke Nicholas and the commander of the Russian northern front, General Zhilinsky, hastily hurled two Russian armies to attack East Prussia, before their concentration and their transport arrangements had been completed. The First Army, under General P. K. Rennenkampf, advancing from the east, successfully attacked the Germans at Gumbinnen, but after the Germans had retreated, Rennenkampf stopped for rest and lost all contact with the enemy. The newly appointed German commander in the north, General Paul von Hindenburg, and his chief of staff Erich Ludendorff meanwhile quickly concentrated all their forces against the Second Army of General A. V. Samsonov, which advanced from the south. Samsonov's troops, in Winston Churchill's words, "had been marching without rest for 8 or 9 days along sandy tracks in the burning heat of August, weakened from scanty rations, their communications so unorganized that no supplies could reach them from the rear." [6] The German troops, which had a decisive preponderance in artillery, launched a counterattack against Samsonov's army on August 13 (26). While Rennenkampf's Russian troops idly stood by a few dozen miles to the north, the Germans surrounded Samsonov's troops in the region of the Masurian Lakes, near Soldau and Tannenberg, and almost annihilated them. Two out of the five army corps ceased to exist (the Germans took 92,000 prisoners), and the survivors scattered and retreated in disorder. Hindenburg thereupon turned north and

---

[5] Maurice Paléologue, *An Ambassador's Memoirs* (4th ed.; New York, 1925), vol. I, p. 61.

[6] Winston S. Churchill, *The Unknown War: The Eastern Front* (New York, 1931), p. 195.

expelled Rennenkamp's army from East Prussia. But the Russian sacrifice in East Prussia was not in vain; the German command transferred two corps from France to the Eastern front to repulse the Russian attack. This helped the French to halt the German advance and to win a victory on the river Marne.

On the Austrian front, the Austrians began to advance from western Galicia into Russian Poland in the direction of Lublin and Kholm, but soon their advance had to be halted because of a large-scale Russian offensive in eastern Galicia. A great battle in Galicia in August and September of 1914 ended with a decisive victory for Russia. On August 21 (September 3), Russian troops of the southwestern front commanded by General N. Iu. Ivanov, took the capital of eastern Galicia, Lwów. Moving farther to the west, they crossed the river San and pursued the retreating Austrian army, which finally stopped, at the end of September, some 50 miles east of Cracow on the line of the Dunajec between Tarnów and Gorlice. During the great Galician battle in the early fall of 1914, more than 100,000 Austro-Hungarian troops were taken prisoner by the Russians. The strong Austrian fortress of Przemyśl on the river San was besieged by the Russians for several months and surrendered with its garrison of over 100,000 men in March 1915.

In October 1914, the Germans launched an attack on Warsaw that ended in failure and precipitated a German retreat from the Vistula. But a Russian counteroffensive in the direction of Silesia in November 1914 was similarly unsuccessful. A new attempt to invade East Prussia in February 1915 also failed.

In the winter of 1914–1915 the anti-German coalition was active on many fronts. In December 1914 the Austro-Hungarian forces in Serbia were defeated by the Serbs and driven out of the country. In the same month, Ottoman forces tried to attack the Russians in Transcaucasia, but in January the Russian army gained a decisive victory over the Turks at Sarakamysh and began to advance into Ottoman territory. In February, the Allied navy made an attempt to force the Dardanelles, and in April, British and French troops landed on the Gallipoli Peninsula in order to open the road from the Mediterranean to the Black Sea, but their forces proved to be inadequate to this task.

On the Austrian front the Russian high command planned an invasion of the Hungarian plain, and in the early spring of 1915, Russian forces fighting in the snow-covered Carpathian Mountains captured a considerable stretch of the Carpathian range, opening several passes leading into Hungary. But in May 1915 the Russian military situation abruptly changed for the worse, for the German command decided to shift the bulk of military operations from the western to the eastern front.

One factor which weakened the Russian forces considerably by that time was an acute shortage of munitions. As early as August 1914, the chief of staff telegraphed to the minister of war: "The situation in the matter of artillery ammunition is critical. The whole burden of modern warfare falls on the artillery. Continuous fighting for fifteen days and more has upset theoretical estimates." Grand Duke Nicholas Nicholaevich telegraphed the emperor himself: "For more than two weeks there has been a shortage of artillery ammunition. Now General Ivanov reports that he is forced to hold up operations against Przemyśl, as also on the entire front. I find it necessary to request Your Majesty to order that the shipment of shells be hastened." [7] In October 1914 Ivanov telegraphed the Artillery Department: "Supplies of ammunition are entirely exhausted. If not replenished, operations will have to be broken off and the troops retired under most difficult conditions." [8] But the complacent minister of war, Sukhomlinov, found the complaints of the army command exaggerated and failed to take sufficiently energetic steps to alleviate the "ammunition famine."

Another factor was the enormous losses in the officer corps of the Russian army. The Russian officers did not spare themselves when leading their men into attacks. As an observer of Russian military operations, Sir Bernard Pares wrote, "whereas the German and Austrian officers very sensibly took precautions for their safety, Russian officers went into action standing, while commanding their men to crawl forward." [9] It is self-evident that the bravery of the Russian officers cost them dearly. Another observer of the fighting Russian army, General Sir Alfred Knox, testified that by the end of 1914 in many Russian infantry regiments only 10 to 20 officers were left out of 70. [10] Their places were only inadequately filled by noncommissioned officers and by young hastily trained civilians. As a result, the Russian army, while growing in numbers by the constant calling to the colors of millions of new territorials and recruits, was becoming weaker in its leadership. But endurance and patience in the face of

---

[7] Cited in General N. N. Golovine, *The Russian Army in the World War* (New Haven, 1931), pp. 143–144.

[8] Cited in General Sir Alfred Knox, *With the Russian Army, 1914–1917* (New York, 1921), vol. I, p. 220.

[9] Bernard Pares, *The Fall of the Russian Monarchy* (New York, 1939), p. 211.

[10] Knox, *op. cit.*, pp. 189–194.

hardships, which were typical for the rank and file soldiers, continued until the outbreak of the Revolution, as many foreign observers have noted.

The great Austro-German offensive on the Eastern front commenced on April 18 (May 1), 1915, under the command of August von Mackensen, who had amassed formidable forces in western Galicia. "The Germans concentrated upwards of 1500 guns; they fired 700,000 shells in the four hours preceding the attack. The Russians had nothing with which to reply." [11] Austro-German forces broke through the Russian front line between Tarnów and Gorlice, and the painful retreat of the Russian army from Galicia began. In the words of the Russian military historian N. N. Golovine:

> The ordeal endured by the Russian army in the summer months of 1915 was one impossible to describe. The "drum fire" of the enemy's powerful artillery could be answered only by the shots, fired at long intervals, of an artillery which was many times weaker. There were periods during which, in certain regiments, ten rounds a day was made the limit. . . . Against the front of one of the Russian corps of the Third Army, against which the main blow was directed, more than 200 heavy guns, not counting the field artillery, were concentrated by the enemy. At the time this whole Third Army, which consisted of seven corps and was holding a front of about 130 miles, had four heavy guns. [The German heavy artillery,] almost or entirely beyond the range of the Russian field artillery, [showered the Russian trenches with shells] until nothing of the trenches remained, [and then] the German field artillery and machine guns protected the advancing infantry from Russian counter-attacks. [12]

Russian reinforcements, poorly trained and equipped, were constantly moved to the front, but could not stop the German offensive—"only a part of the men at the front were armed, the remainder waited for the death of comrades to take their rifles." Thus, despite frequent defensive stands and counterattacks, the Russian army retreated further, sustaining huge losses. On May 21 (June 3) Przemyśl and on June 9 (22) Lwów were evacuated by the Russians and only a small eastern corner of Galicia remained in their hands.

Neither the Franco-British offensive in Flanders and at Artois in May 1915 nor Italy's entrance into the war brought any appreciable relief for the Russians. On the contrary, in July the Ger-

---

[11] *Ibid.*, p. 282.
[12] Golovine, *op. cit.*, pp. 145, 220–221, 127.

mans expanded their offensive to the entire Eastern front, to Poland and Lithuania. During the rest of the summer all of Russian Poland, Lithuania, and parts of Belorussia and Volhynia were taken by the advancing German and Austro-Hungarian armies. Warsaw was evacuated on July 23 (August 5), and Vilno on September 6 (19). The evacuation of a single city such as Warsaw with its hospitals, factories, railroad shops, schools, and administrative and cultural institutions presented a serious problem. The situation was aggravated by the unwise policy of the Russian military command, which in some areas insisted on the evacuation of the civilian population. Many thousands of local inhabitants left their dwellings voluntarily to escape the horrors of the war, but the majority were ordered to move. The number of officially registered refugees was later put in excess of three million, but amounted to close to six million by private calculations. The roads leading east were jammed by masses of desperate people, with carts carrying their belongings and with domestic animals driven by their owners. The millions of refugees, suffering all kinds of hardships and privations, poured into central Russia, heightening transportation and food supply problems in the rear.

The line of the Russian fortresses along the western border of the empire proved to be entirely useless. Only one of them, Novogeorgievsk (northwest of Warsaw), tried to resist the Germans, but after only three weeks of siege and heavy bombardment it was forced to surrender, August 7 (20), with a garrison of 100,000 men. Other fortresses (Kovno, Grodno, Ivangorod, Brest Litovsk) either did not offer any serious resistance or were evacuated before being attacked.

In the beginning of September 1915, the tsar arrived at the supreme headquarters of the army, located in Mogilev in Belorussia, and assumed the supreme command of the Russian armies. Grand Duke Nicholas Nicholaevich was appointed commander of the Caucasian front. General M. V. Alekseev, hardworking and conscientious, was appointed chief of staff. In October 1915 the great German offensive finally came to an end, and a new frontline was stabilized. It ran from the Baltic Sea, west of Riga, along the Dvina River to Dvinsk, hence south to Pinsk and Kamenets Podolsk, and through the eastern corner of Galicia to the Rumanian border. From May to September, 1915 the Russian armies lost 1,410,000 killed and wounded, and 976,000 prisoners.

The last months of 1915 were relatively quiet on the Russian front. The reinforcements and supplies were flowing continuously; General Alekseev succeeded in bringing order to the army, and the morale of the troops began to improve. Meanwhile, Serbia suffered a tragic fate. In September, Bulgaria joined the Austro-German coalition, and when in October major Austro-German forces invaded Serbia from the north, Bulgarian troops attacked from the east. After heroic resistance through October and November, the Serbian army retreated across the Albanian mountains to the Adriatic coast and was evacuated to Corfu by an Allied fleet. In the autumn of 1915 the Allies gave up their Dardanelles operation and transferred their troops from Gallipoli to Salonika, and later the remainder of the Serbian army, after it had rested and rebuilt, joined the Allied Salonika front.

Naval operations in the Baltic and Black Sea should be briefly mentioned. The construction of three dreadnoughts was started by Russia on the Black Sea on the eve of the war, but they were still not ready by 1916, while the outdated vessels of the Black Sea squadron were unable to catch up with the *Goeben* or to attack Ottoman fortifications on the Bosphorus. But neither was the German-Turkish navy strong enough to attack the Russian base at Sevastopol, and the result was a standoff. The Russian Baltic squadron, also weak in the beginning of the war, was reinforced by 1916 by four newly built dreadnoughts; moreover, five British submarines, which slipped into the Baltic early in the war, joined the Russian fleet and helped to protect the Baltic coast. By mining the gulfs of Riga and Finland and by being constantly on the alert, the Russian navy successfully protected the Baltic coast. On the other hand, the Germans, in view of the British presence in the North Sea, abstained from unnecessary risks and made no major attempts to penetrate the Russian defenses.

By 1916, the "ammunition famine" in Russia was largely overcome as a result of increased production in the government plants, the mobilization of private industry, and increased shipments from the Allies. Sukhomlinov was dismissed in June 1915 and the competent General A. A. Polivanov became war minister. Thus, after the defeats of 1915, the Russian army was able to resume active operations. In February 1916 Russian forces on the Caucasian front took the Turkish city of Erzurum, and in April captured Trebizond, an important port on the Black Sea. In March 1916 the Russians attacked German positions near Lake Naroch in the northern section of the front, near Vilno, but the attack was repulsed with heavy losses, even though it had been prepared by a massive bombardment of German positions.

The spring of 1916 was a difficult time for the Allies in the West. The French army, suffering heavy losses, steadfastly resisted the German onslaught against Verdun, and the Italian army was in a most precarious position in the face of a major Austrian offensive.

The king of Italy telegraphed the tsar asking for help, and once more Russia rendered major assistance to her hard-pressed Allies. In June 1916, the armies of the Russian southwestern front, under General A. A. Brusilov, launched an attack on a wide front and inflicted a series of major defeats on the Austrians, taking about 400,000 prisoners. A wide strip of land in Volhynia (with the city of Lutsk), eastern Galicia, and Bukovina (including its capital, Czernowitz) was gained, and the entire Austrian front was shaken. The Germans again had to hasten to help their Austrian ally. They rushed to the Eastern front 18 divisions from France and 3 German and 2 Ottoman divisions from the Balkans. Brusilov's armies continued their attacks throughout the summer, but after a prolonged and bloody struggle the "Brusilov offensive" was halted with heavy losses on both sides. To quote General Knox: "Brusilov's offensive was the outstanding military event of the year. In the extent of territory regained, in the number of the enemy killed and taken prisoner and in the number of enemy units absorbed, it surpassed all Allied offensives." [13] The strategic results of the Brusilov offensive were most important: the Italian army was saved, inasmuch as the Austro-Hungarians were forced to discontinue their offensive in Italy and to transport fifteen divisions to the Russian front; the pressure on the French army at Verdun and elsewhere was alleviated; and the pressure on the Allies on the Salonika front was also relieved by the weakening of the German-Turkish forces there.

The success of the Brusilov offensive against Austria-Hungary induced Rumania to enter the war on the side of the Allies, but this did not bring the expected advantages. Poorly trained and equipped, the Rumanian troops were soon crushed by the Central Powers; all of Wallachia was taken and on December 6 ns, 1916, Bucharest was occupied. The Rumanian government and the royal court moved to Jassy in Moldavia, and with the help of quickly transferred Russian reinforcements, it was possible to stop the Austro-German advance and to retain a part of Rumanian territory. The Central Powers gained Rumanian oil and wheat, while the strategic position of Russia was only complicated: the Russian command had to create a new, Rumanian front, 250 miles long, in addition to the three fronts previously designated, the northwestern, western, and southwestern. The new front required three Russian armies. Thus the line of Russian defenses now extended from the Baltic to the Black seas.

After the Brusilov offensive was brought to a halt, and after the unsuccessful attempts to break through the German lines on the northern and western fronts in the summer of 1916, there was little military activity on the Russian front, except for an unsuccessful try to break through the German positions near Riga. Nevertheless, the military position of Russia in the beginning of 1917 was not at all bad.

By the beginning of 1917 a formidable number of troops—over six million—were concentrated on the four Russian fronts in Europe. They were adequately supplied with artillery and munitions, even though they remained inferior to the German forces in armaments, especially in the newly developed means of warfare, such as

---

[13] Knox, *op. cit.*, vol. II, p. 551.

aviation and poison gas. Sir Alfred Knox, the British military attaché, was a sharp critic of Russian military shortcomings, but in early 1917 he made the following appraisal of the Eastern front:

> On the eve of the Revolution the prospects for the 1917 campaign were brighter than they had been in March, 1916. . . . The Russian infantry was tired, but less tired than it had been twelve months earlier. The stocks of arms, ammunition and technical equipment were larger than they had been even on mobilization—much larger than they were in the spring of 1915 or of 1916. The leadership was improving every day. The army was sound at heart. The men in the rest of the winter would have forgotten the trials of the past, and would have attacked again with the elan of 1916. There can be no doubt that if the national fabric in rear had held together, the Russian army would have gained fresh laurels in the campaign of 1917, and in all human probability would have exercised a pressure which would have made possible an Allied victory by the end of the year.[14]

But it must be recognized that the losses suffered by the Russian army during the nearly three years of war were tremendous. Accurate statistics do not exist because of the disorganization and loss of military archives during the Revolution, but accepted figures show 1,700,000 dead, 4,950,000 wounded, 2,500,000 taken prisoner, and about 3,000,000 sick. Some 700,000 invalids were released from active service because of wounds or sickness during the war years. The losses of Germany until the end of the war in 1918, for the sake of comparison, are officially given as 1,808,545 killed, 4,247,143 wounded, and 617,922 taken prisoner; those of Austria-Hungary, 1,200,000 killed, 3,620,000 wounded, and 2,200,000 taken prisoner. Of some 2,000,000 enemy prisoners, taken by the Russians, about 160,000 were Germans, 1,737,000 Austro-Hungarians — mostly of Slavic origin — and some 65,000 Turks.

The Economic Consequences of the War

The largest sector of the Russian economy, peasant agriculture, was not seriously damaged by the war in view of the manpower surplus in rural areas. Even though millions of young men were mobilized for the army, their labor could be sufficiently compensated for by the labor of women and of men older than forty-three

---

[14] *Ibid.*, vol. II, pp. 551–552.

and younger than eighteen. An increased demand for cereal crops even led the peasants to expand the area under cultivation, while their cash income also increased because of high prices for agricultural products, government compensation for requisitioned horses and cattle, and government allowances to families of mobilized men. The liquor prohibition also substantially increased peasant savings. Of course, the increase in money income did not raise the peasants' standard of living proportionately, because of the scarcity of manufactured goods and of the growing inflation, which depreciated all savings. And the economy of the large estates was seriously damaged by the war, since the mobilization led to a shortage of hired labor, which was only partially compensated for by the labor of prisoners of war.

Conditions in industry were far less favorable. Mobilization deprived the factories and mines of many thousands of skilled workers and created a shortage of workers in general. The hiring of unskilled help led to a substantial decline in productivity. Moreover, worn out machinery and equipment could not be easily replaced, since many essential items had been imported from abroad and foreign trade came virtually to a standstill.[15] By 1915, the loss of the more industrialized western provinces of the empire and the necessity to convert private industry to military production led to an acute shortage of manufactured goods on the domestic market. But, in spite of these handicaps, the industrial mobilization after the summer of 1915 made it gradually possible to meet the most pressing needs of the military establishment.

The transportation system, barely adequate for peacetime, suffered from the war more than other branches of the Russian economy. Inland waterways could carry only a small portion of the wartime shipments, and the main burden fell upon the railroads. The rail network was taxed far beyond capacity by the need to transfer millions of men and the needed supplies to the front, to evacuate the wounded and millions of refugees, and, in addition, to maintain essential service for the industrial and commercial needs of the cities, whose population expanded greatly—for the urban population of Russia, estimated at 22 million in 1913, had risen to 28 million in 1916. This increase consisted of military reserve units, the workers in war industries, the patients and personnel of military hospitals, the personnel of various auxiliary military services, and the refugees.

---

15 Of 1374 million rubles worth of imports to Russia in 1913, manufactured goods amounted to 450 million rubles, including 190 million rubles in machinery. See *Statisticheskii ezhegodnik Rossii*, 1914, chap. X, pp. 36, 38, 39.

While military traffic on the railroads, which in peacetime amounted to less than one tenth of the tonnage moved, increased about fifteen fold by 1917, the construction and maintenance of rolling stock continually declined. The resulting attrition and increased breakdowns of equipment resulted in an increasingly erratic service for low-priority civilian needs, and the volume of nonmilitary traffic shrank substantially. Hardest hit by the inadequacy of the railroad system were the large cities, where shortages of food, fuel, and raw materials became acute in the winter of 1916–1917.

The war meant, of course, a heavy burden on the state treasury. Government revenues declined because of the general disruption of economic life, and specifically because of the loss of some 700 million rubles annually as a result of the liquor prohibition. Meanwhile, war expenditures soared:

    1914— 1655.4 million rubles
    1915— 8818.4 million rubles
    1916—14,572.8 million rubles
    1917—13,603.0 million rubles (for 8 months)
    total 38,649.6 million rubles

About 62 percent of this war expenditure was covered by loans: 15,837.1 million rubles in domestic loans, and 8070.7 million rubles in foreign loans. Most of the remainder, however, had to be covered by issuing paper money. The normal amount of paper currency in circulation, as of July 16, 1914, was 1633.4 million rubles, which were covered by a 1744.3 million ruble gold reserve. During the war, the sum of paper money in circulation increased to 2946 million rubles by January 1915, 5617 million rubles by January 1916, and 9097 million rubles by January 1917.

The flood of paper money, combined with a scarcity of manufactured goods and of foodstuffs (the latter shortage caused chiefly by the defects of transportation and by the unwillingness of the peasants to sell their products for money that could buy little) caused a general increase in prices and active, sometimes ruthless, speculation. Naturally, the professional classes and the urban workers suffered most from the inflation. Their salaries and wages increased during the war, but this increase lagged behind price increases, and real income dropped as a consequence. According to a generalized estimate, the cost of living increased an average of 53 percent during 1914–1915, while the average rise in wages was only 19 percent. In 1916, conditions worsened considerably. In the summer of that year the price index for foodstuffs climbed to 215 (1913 = 100), and during the winter of 1916–1917 prices increased still more. According to a secret report of the security police *(okhrannoe otdelenie)* in October 1916, the wages of workers in the capital had increased about 100 percent since the beginning of the war, while prices for several key consumer goods items had risen an average of 300 percent. Moreover, some products were impossible to obtain at all, and for many food products the customers had to wait in long queues in front of stores.

The government tried to control prices and to suppress speculation, but its policies were inconsistent and ineffective. Initially, it tried to abstain from interference with the free market, but in November 1915, maximum prices were fixed for government purchases for the army. In February and again in September 1916, additional attempts were made to regulate the food market, fixed prices were established for all grain products, and a law was passed establishing punishments for extraordinary increases in prices on goods, for their concealment, or for refusal to sell. Sugar was rationed and the sale of meat limited to three days a week. Nevertheless, speculation and profiteering became widespread, and food prices were two to four times higher than in 1914.

The economic resources of Russia were far from exhausted at the beginning of 1917, but their use was not rationally organized, and consequently economic conditions in the major centers deteriorated. The refugees, forcibly and often unnecessarily uprooted, were contributing to the housing crisis. Lack of incentive prevented the peasants from selling their stocks of foodstuffs to the cities. Finally, the work of the industrial establishment was seriously disturbed by transportation difficulties. During the winter of 1916–1917 a number of factories, especially in the capitals, were forced to cut production or even to close down because deliveries of fuel and raw material by railroad were disrupted. This led to partial unemployment at a time when the needs of the front and of the large cities demanded increased production. These inefficiencies of organization helped to undermine morale at home at a time when that of the fighting front was still intact.

Social and Political Developments during the War

The magnitude, complexity, and danger of the struggle in which Russia was involved called for a strong leader, with broad and flexible political views and an intimate feeling for the needs and sentiments of his country. Despite his personal integrity and patriotism,

Nicholas II was not such a leader. And, to make things worse, he yielded much of his power to his domineering wife, a person of limited intelligence and a believer in unlimited autocracy. The Duma, as a symbol of representative government, always remained an object of the tsaritsa's animosity. Her mystical religious feeling, heavily flavored with superstition, resulted in the notorious Rasputin becoming her chief adviser and "friend." He then used his position to intervene constantly in government affairs, including the appointment and dismissal of cabinet members. When the tsar left for Mogilev in September 1915 to assume supreme command of the fighting front, he entrusted the tsaritsa informally to be his agent or representative in civil government affairs—"you ought to be my eyes and ears there in the capital while I have to stay here," he wrote her from his headquarters in Mogilev.

And, in fact, the tsaritsa received ministers, heard their reports, and informed the tsar about political and administrative affairs in Petrograd. What was worse, following the advice of the "man of God" (Rasputin), she insisted on the dismissal of those ministers who did not like "our friend" and on the appointment of those persons who were friendly to him. This resulted in frequent changes of ministers ("ministerial leapfrog," as the rightist Duma member Purishkevich called it), which deprived the government of stability and the pursuit of a consistent policy. Partly on his own, partly under the influence of the tsaritsa and her "friend," the tsar changed heads of government departments so often that between July 1914 and February 1917 Russia had 4 premiers, 6 ministers of internal affairs, 3 ministers of foreign affairs, 4 ministers of war, 4 ministers of agriculture, 4 ministers of justice, and even 4 overprocurators of the Holy Synod! Among these there were, of course, some capable and competent individuals, such as Sazonov, Krivoshein or Polivanov; but some of the wartime ministers, in particular Goremykin, Sukhomlinov, N. A. Maklakov, B. V. Stürmer, and A. D. Protopopov were utterly incompetent.

The weakness of the government was aggravated during the war by frequent conflicts between civil and military authorities. The military command enjoyed broad but not clearly defined authority in the areas adjoining the front, and often gave orders there without the consent or even the knowledge of the civilian authorities, which in some cases—such as the refugee movement—led to disorder and disorganization.

Prior to the outbreak of the war, the attitudes of various groups of Russian society toward questions of foreign policy differed substantially. Rightist groups advocated friendly relations with Germany, because they considered that nation a stronghold of conservatism and the monarchical principle. Detailed arguments for this point of view were presented to the tsar in February 1914 in a memorandum by P. N. Durnovo, member of the Council of State, and former minister of internal affairs. Durnovo argued that a fundamental conflict of political and economic interests existed only between Germany and England, but not between Germany and Russia. He believed the latter two countries should be able to coexist in a mutually advantageous friendship, while Russia's alliance with England he considered "fundamentally unnatural." In a war against Germany, Durnovo pointed out, Russia would gain nothing even in the case of victory, and victory was highly unlikely because of Germany's military and industrial superiority; Russia's probable defeat would result in a chaos of anarchy and social revolution.

The liberal elements in Russian society and the liberal press, which dominated public opinion, favored, on the contrary, an alliance with liberal and democratic countries, France and England, in the hope that this alliance would favorably influence the process of liberalization and democratization in Russia.

The Austrian attack on Serbia and the German declaration of war on Russia briefly united different segments of the population with diverse political outlooks in a general upsurge of patriotism, a conviction that it was necessary to repel the German attack. In Petersburg—which was given the Russian name Petrograd soon after the beginning of the war—workers' strikes that had been going on through the summer of 1914 quickly subsided, and a huge patriotic demonstration, including many thousands of workers, was held in front of the Winter Palace.

The peasantry accepted the coming of the war without great enthusiasm, but with a quiet readiness to defend the country. The general mobilization of the army proceeded smoothly, and the number of reservists evading the call to the colors was minimal. To avoid the possibility of drunken excesses during the mobilization, the government forbade the sale of vodka, and this prohibition was maintained for the duration of the war, even though it created an additional hardship for the frontline troops.

The intelligentsia in general accepted the war as a hard necessity and proclaimed the determination to bring it to a "victorious end." The founder and chief theoretician of the Russian Social Democratic party, G. V. Plekhanov, unhesitatingly became a "defensist" and called upon the Russian workers to help repulse the attack of aggressive German militarism. The theoretician of Russian anarchism, Prince P. A. Kropotkin, displayed the same attitude. Among the Mensheviks and the Socialist Revolutionaries there were some "defensists" and some "internationalists," who later stood for the Zimmerwald peace program of the 1915 international socialist conference. Only the Bolsheviks headed by Lenin, who then lived in Switzerland, adopted from the very beginning of the war a "defeatist" attitude, contending that the defeat of tsarist Russia would be in the best interests of the "international proletariat."

To enlist the support of the Duma and to demonstrate national unity, the government summoned both Duma and Council of State for a short session on July 26. The tsar received the members of the legislative chambers in the Winter Palace, stating that "we are not only defending our honor and dignity, but are fighting for our Slavic brothers in blood and in faith." During the course of the Duma session, Foreign Minister Sazonov also stated that Russia "is fighting for her dignity and status as a great power," and that she could not renounce her centuries-old role as the defender of the Slavic nations. In response, the Duma displayed complete unity with the government.

In the words of the Duma president, Rodzianko, "at the meeting of July 26 all the existing party barriers fell. The members of the Duma accepted the necessity of war to a victorious end and decided to give all possible support to the government."[16] Following Rodzianko's speech, as Miliukov relates in his memoirs,

> three ministers, Goremykin, Sazonov and Bark, addressed the Duma, and statements were made by representatives of various nationalities—Poles, Letts, Lithuanians, Jews, Moslems, Baltic Germans and German colonists from the Volga region. All these statements, of course, expressed readiness to defend the homeland and loyalty to the state and the people.

Then Miliukov himself, on behalf of the Constitutional Democratic party, pledged unconditional support for the government in the struggle "for the liberation of our homeland from foreign invasion, for the liberation of Europe and the Slavs from German domination, for the liberation of the entire world from the intolerable burden of ever increasing armament. . . ."[17] The leader of the Trudovik Duma group, A. F. Kerensky, also proclaimed its readiness to cooperate with the

---

[16] M. V. Rodzianko, *Gosudarstvennaia Duma i Fevral'skaia Revoliutsiia 1917 goda* [*The State Duma and the February Revolution of 1917*], in *Arkhiv Russkoi Revoliutsii*, vol. VI, p. 19.

[17] P. N. Miliukov, *Vospominaniia* [*Memoirs*] (New York, 1955), vol. II, p. 190.

government in waging a defensive war. Then the Duma unanimously voted for war credit and approved all legislative measures requested by the government in connection with war needs. Only the small Social Democratic faction abstained from voting. Its five Bolshevik members were arrested for defeatist propaganda in November 1914, tried in February 1915, and sentenced to deportation to Siberia. The government feared workers' protest demonstrations against this sentence, but nothing happened.

In August 1914, two important organizations were created to involve broad segments of the public in the war effort. A conference attended by representatives of thirty-four provincial zemstvos in Moscow decided to establish an All-Russian Union of Zemstvos for the Relief of Sick and Wounded Soldiers, and elected a central committee with Prince G. E. Lvov as president. A network of provincial and district committees was also set up. The organization, receiving broad financial support from the government, helped the military authorities and the Red Cross to establish and maintain military hospitals and hospital trains. Later the committees expanded their activities to include the operation of dining and tea rooms, canteens, baths, storehouses, and workshops and the supply of the army with food, clothing, and footwear. In 1915–1916 the Zemstvo Union also assisted the millions of voluntary and involuntary refugees evacuated from the theater of military operations. In the words of the Union's historian, T. J. Polner,

> in the second half of 1916 the Zemstvo Union had grown to such an extent as to constitute a veritable state within a state. Its annual budget had risen to the huge sum of 600 million rubles. Hundreds of thousands of persons, women as well as men, drawn from all paths of life, were employed directly and indirectly in its service.[18]

The other such organization was the All-Russian Union of Towns, headed by the mayor of Moscow, M. V. Chelnokov, and founded at a conference of mayors of Russian cities in Moscow, also in August 1914. Its goals were similar to that of the Zemstvo Union, even though the scope of its activities was smaller. When in the summer of 1915 a far-reaching mobilization of Russian private industry for the needs of the army became necessary, both unions participated in this drive. They signed contracts with private firms for the

---

[18] T. J. Polner, *Russian Local Government during the War and the Union of Zemstvos* (New Haven, 1930), p. 269.

delivery of military equipment and supplies, and set up production facilities of their own. To coordinate these efforts a Joint Committee of the Unions of Zemstvos and Towns was established, which became known in an abbreviated form as *Zemgor*.

In January 1915, the Duma met for a three-day session and approved the budget and all war credits requested by the government. This time, the small Social Democratic faction (Mensheviks) voted against the budget, while the Trudoviks abstained from voting. The surrender of the Austrian fortresses of Przemyśl in March 1915 provoked patriotic demonstrations in the streets of major cities, but this proved to be the last manifestation of the early war enthusiasm.

In late spring and summer of 1915, the country was shaken and frightened by the series of Russian setbacks in Galicia, and then by the general retreat of the Russian armies, lacking armaments and munitions, in the face of a mighty enemy. Patriotic alarm in Russia was combined with resentment against a government that appeared unable to organize the defense of the country. Rumors of "treason" began to spread, and at the end of May mobs in Moscow reacted by pillaging stores and houses belonging to owners who had German names.

In an attempt to placate the public and to improve conditions, four of the more unpopular ministers were dismissed—Sukhomlinov, the minister of war; N. A. Maklakov, the minister of internal affairs; I. G. Shcheglovitov, the minister of justice; and V. K. Sabler, the overprocurator of the Holy Synod. The new war minister, General Polivanov, took steps to improve military production and supply and to secure the cooperation of the State Duma. Other ministers were also ready to cooperate with the Duma, but Goremykin, the old, passive, narrow-minded bureaucrat, remained at the head of the Council of Ministers. With his negative attitude toward the Duma, he was entirely incapable of directing the government under the trying conditions of the world war.

To alleviate the disastrous shortage of munitions at the front, war-industries committees (*voenno-promyshlennye komitety*) were organized in the summer of 1915, aiming at a voluntary mobilization of private industry for defense work. The initiative in this matter was taken by a congress of representatives of industry and commerce, held in Petrograd at the end of May 1915, which called on industry to unite its efforts in the service of national defense. The Octobrist leader, Guchkov, a well-known Moscow industrialist, headed the Central War Industries Committee, and local committees were organized in twenty-eight cities. They consisted of representatives of industry, commerce, the government, the Unions of Zemstvos and Towns, and labor. The government charter for the committees, signed by the tsar September 9, granted them broad autonomy with regard to their composition, resources, and activities.

To coordinate the defense efforts of the government and of the various public organizations, a Special Council for National Defense was set up in June 1915. Presided over by the war minister, the council included the president and nine members of the Duma, the president and nine members of the State Council, seven ministers, the heads of various departments in the Ministry of War, and representatives of industry, of the All-Russian Unions of Zemstvos and of Towns, and of the newly formed Central War Industry Committee. Shortly thereafter three more special councils were formed: for transportation, presided over by the minister of transportation; for fuel, presided over by the minister of commerce and industry; and for food supply, presided over by the minister of agriculture. Their membership included representatives of the government, the legislative chambers, and public organizations, as above. Government statutes concerning the four special councils were issued August 17, 1915, but the work of these complex and cumbersome organizations hardly justified the hopes put in them. Though the supply of military equipment and munitions did gradually improve, the creeping disorganization of economic life on the home front was not overcome.

Meanwhile in the Duma, during its summer session of 1915, the willingness to carry the war on to a "victorious end" was paralleled by sharp criticism of the government and demands for a "ministry of public confidence." The conflict was aggravated by Nicholas II's decision to take over the supreme command of the front in August 1915. Neither the public nor the Council of Ministers, excepting Goremykin, were sympathetic to this decision. The ministers feared that possible defeats of the army, commanded by the tsar personally, would undermine his prestige; and they feared but could not openly say that in the tsar's absence from the capital the tsaritsa and Rasputin would virtually take over the government. On August 21, 1915 eight ministers signed a letter to the tsar imploring him not to remove Grand Duke Nicholas Nicholaevich from supreme command and sternly warning him: "Your decision threatens Russia, Yourself, and Your dynasty with evil consequences." The ministers further stated that in view of their fundamental disagreements with the chairman of the Council of Ministers, Goremykin, they were "losing faith in the possibility of being of service to You and the country."[19] Minister of War Polivanov and Minister of the Navy Grigorovich did not sign the letter, but informed the tsar that they were in full agreement with their colleagues. This sounded like a collective request to resign, but the tsar remained inflexible: Goremykin continued as chairman of the Council of Ministers, and the tsar took over supreme command.

As could be expected, after the tsar's departure to the supreme headquarters in Mogilev, the empress began to interfere actively in the affairs of state, guided chiefly by the advice of "our friend." Naturally this caused indignation in the Duma and among the public, and undermined the authority of the monarchy. From the correspondence between the tsar and his wife, published after the revolution, it is evident that the unfortunate monarch occasionally tried to resist the interference of Rasputin, usually with little effect.

At the end of the summer of 1915, the majority of the Duma members decided to abandon the attitude of unconditional support for the government which it had maintained during the first year of the war. In August 1915, a coalition of six Duma parties, including about 300 deputies—out of 442 Duma members—formed a so-called Progressive Bloc. The Bloc, which included the "progressive nationalists" on the right and the Constitutional Democrats on the left, but excluded the extreme right and extreme left, adopted a joint program published August 25. It called for "the formation of a united Government, consisting of persons who have the confidence of the country and are in agreement with the legislative institutions as to carrying out, at the earliest time" specific reforms, such as "a strict observance of the principle of legality in administration," amnesty for those convicted of religious or political offenses ("with the exception of spies and traitors"), the autonomy of Poland, a conciliatory policy toward national minorities, freedom for the trade unions and for the labor press, a reform of zemstvo and municipal self-government, and the introduction of a township zemstvo (*volostnoe zemstvo*).[20]

These were moderate and reasonable demands, and many members of the State Council (including former prime minister Count Kokovtsov) sided with the program of the Progressive Bloc. The majority of the ministers, seeing nothing revolutionary in the Bloc's program, were ready to accept it and to work towards its realization jointly with the legislative chambers. But for old Goremykin a parlia-

---

[19] Quoted in F. Golder, ed., *Documents of Russian History* (translated by E. Aronsberg, New York, 1927), pp. 210–211.

[20] Pares, *op. cit.*, pp. 271–273.

mentary combination including members of both the Duma and the Council was in itself "illegal," and its purpose seemed to be the "limitation of the powers of the monarch." Goremykin, together with the tsaritsa, persuaded the tsar to prorogue the session of the Duma; and in the fall of 1915 several ministers who supported the policy of the Progressive Bloc were dismissed: Prince Shcherbatov, the minister of internal affairs (replaced by A. N. Khvostov, backed by Rasputin); Krivoshein, the minister of agriculture; and A. D. Samarin, over-procurator of the Holy Synod, who had come out openly against "our friend."

As a result, the conflict between the government and the Duma intensified. The Progressive Bloc's demand for a cabinet "enjoying the confidence of the country" found quick acceptance among the public, and the War Industries Committees, the Unions of Zemstvos and Towns, provincial zemstvos, and municipal Dumas passed resolutions demanding a "ministry of confidence." Some even went further and demanded a cabinet directly responsible to the Duma.

Meanwhile, among the workers, under the influence of the protracted and unsuccessful war, of growing inflation, and of revolutionary propaganda, the slogan of a war "to a victorious end" came to be regarded with greater and greater sarcasm. The minority of Russian socialists who seriously defended this idea were vehemently abused by the Bolsheviks and the left Socialist Revolutionaries as "social patriots," "lackies of the bourgeoisie," traitors and betrayers of the working class. Those Mensheviks who called themselves "internationalists" adopted the Zimmerwald peace program; and "antimilitarist" (essentially defeatist) propaganda among the workers grew stronger and met with greater and greater response. Deteriorating economic conditions in major cities led to a resumption of strikes, which assumed serious proportions in Moscow in September 1915. A total of 553,000 workers participated in strikes in the course of this year.

At the end of January 1916, the tsar at last dismissed the aged Goremykin from his high post, but the choice of his successor brought only complete bewilderment. The new premier, B. V. Stürmer, a narrow-minded archconservative of very mediocre abilities, handicapped by a German family name and hence suspected of pro-German sympathies or even treason, owed his appointment solely to the patronage of the empress and of "our friend." Later, in the summer of 1916, the same Stürmer added the portfolio of foreign affairs, replacing Sazonov, an experienced and popular diplomat who had tried to establish good relations with the Duma and was held in high esteem both by the Duma and by the public. In March 1916, the capable and popular General Polivanov was replaced by the old, insipid General D. S. Shuvaev as minister of war.

These irrational changes merely increased the estrangement between the government and the public. In an attempt to improve his relations with the Duma, the tsar visited the Tauride Palace on the opening day of the new Duma session, on February 9, 1916, welcomed the Duma members in a speech, and himself listened to an eloquent speech by the Duma president, praising him for appearing among the representatives of the people. But this brief gesture did not produce any practical results, and the atmosphere of mutual misunderstanding persisted.

The growing protests against economic hardship, fanned by antimilitarist propaganda, caused a prolonged strike in the huge Putilov ordnance works in Petrograd in February 1916. During the summer months of 1916, however, when supply difficulties in the major urban centers were not as sharply felt as in winter and when the successful Brusilov offensive attracted the attention of the public, the general mood of the country was relatively quiet. The only exception was a major uprising of the native population in Central Asia, occasioned by the government's attempt to introduce labor conscription in the area (the Asian native population was exempt from military service in the Russian Army). In the fall of 1916, however, when news of military successes ceased and economic difficulties increased, grumbling and resentment against an incompetent government became louder and louder in the cities and among the intelligentsia.

The Road to the Revolution

The Duma which assembled in November 1916 became the forum for an open expression of public discontent. At the session of November 1, Miliukov, the leader of the Kadet party, sharply attacked the government in a famous speech in which he concluded each point of criticism with the caustic question: "What is this: stupidity or treason?" He went so far as to allude to possible treason in or around the imperial court, an accusation that later proved to be without any substance. He declared that the gulf between the government and the Russian public had widened to such an extent that "it had become impassable," and he warned the ministers: "We shall fight you; we shall fight you with all legitimate means until you go!" In vain did the rightist deputy Markov warn Miliukov and other opposition speakers that should the people believe their speeches, they would interpret them as a call to revolt, which in time of war would lead to the destruction of the Russian state. During the session of November 19, Purishkevich, a prominent rightist deputy who now joined the opposition, delivered a highly emotional speech in which he contended that all evil in Russia stemmed from the "dark forces" headed by Grigorii Rasputin, and that economic disorganization was created "with the help of the German party which is at work on our homefront."

The government's answer to the severe attacks of the Duma speakers was rather meek and conciliatory. On November 10, 1916, the generally hated and despised Stürmer was dismissed. To replace him, A. F. Trepov was appointed chairman of the Council of Ministers, and N. N. Pokrovsky became minister of foreign affairs. In the session of November 19, Trepov announced the intent of the government to work together with the legislative institutions in order to bring the war to a victorious end. Hoping to inspire enthusiasm for the war, he made public the agreement concluded in 1915 between Russia, France, and Great Britain that, when victory came, Constantinople and the Straits would belong to Russia. Earlier, in the session of November 4, General Shuvaev, the minister of war, reported on the considerable increase of military production for the Russian army and expressed his conviction "as an old soldier" that "every day we are coming closer to victory." In the period between January 1915 and August 1916, according to Shuvaev's report, the production of three-inch guns increased eight times; the production of rifles, four times; and the production of three-inch shells, 19.7 times. But the optimistic and conciliatory statements of the government failed to impress the opposition majority of the Duma and the public, while the sharp criticism and the charges of treason from the Duma forum spread throughout the country and added fuel to popular discontent.

After Stürmer's dismissal, A. D. Protopopov became a focal point of attacks on the government; a former vice-chairman of the Duma, and an Octobrist, he was appointed minister of internal affairs in September 1916, even though his physical and mental health made him entirely unfit for this key post. Moreover, by accepting the portfolio of internal affairs, he had in the eyes of the Duma "gone over to the enemy," and therefore was looked upon with suspicion and distrust, particularly after it became known that he was favored by the tsaritsa and by Rasputin.

It was not only the Duma which sharply criticized the government and the "dark forces" behind it. The conservative Council of State, by a majority of 94 against 34, adopted a resolution protesting against "irresponsible forces" behind the government and demanding a government that would enjoy "the confidence of the country." The attacks on the government which originated in the legislative chambers spread toward the end of 1916 into the institutions of provincial and local self-government. In December 1916, on Protopopov's orders, police closed the congresses of the All-Russian Zemstvo Union and the All-Russian Union of Towns because of the speakers' sharp attacks on the government, but the congresses nevertheless succeeded in passing political resolutions calling not merely for a "ministry of confidence," but for a government "responsible to the people and to the national representative bodies." The resolution adopted by the All-Russian Union of Towns went so far as to declare "the fatherland in danger" and to assert that there was "only one way out of the present situation, which is leading Russia to certain catastrophe: the reorganization of the government and the establishment of a responsible ministry."[21]

Even the Council of the United Nobility, which spoke for the most conservative elements in Russian society, assembled in December 1916, passed a resolution complaining that "in the administration of the state, irresponsible, dark powers, alien to the legitimate authority, are gaining influence." It demanded the elimination of these "dark powers" and the formation of "a strong government, Russian in thought and feeling, enjoying popular confidence and capable of working in common with the legislative institutions, but responsible to the Monarch alone."[22]

By the end of 1916, the government was thus completely isolated from the populace. The rumors about "dark forces," partly exaggerated, partly absurd (such as the "treason" gossip), spread in the country and rapidly undermined the prestige of the monarchy and the monarch. Since Rasputin was thought of as the embodiment of the "dark forces," a conspiracy was organized among a group of aristocrats and right-wingers to remove him and thereby preserve the prestige, and perhaps the very existence, of the monarchy. The conspirators, Grand Duke Dmitrii Pavlovich, Prince F. F. Iusupov, and the rightist Duma member Purishkevich lured Rasputin to Iusupov's home on the night of December 17, 1916, and murdered him. The tsar was indignant but refrained from legal prosecution. The grand duke and Prince Iusupov were merely sent away from Petrograd.

---

21 Quoted in *Burzhuaziia nakanune Fevral'skoi revoliutsii* [*The Bourgeoisie on the Eve of the February revolution*] (Moscow, 1927), p. 159.

22 Golder, *op. cit.*, pp. 177–178.

During that winter, talk of a palace revolution was heard in certain rightist circles, and plans were discussed for the removal of the tsar and/or the tsaritsa from power, but no action was taken.

Rasputin's murder did not change the political situation and did not reduce the tsaritsa's intervention in government affairs. At the end of December 1916 and in January 1917, the tsar made cabinet changes again: Trepov, whom the tsaritsa did not like, was dismissed and replaced as premier by Prince N. D. Golitsyn, who quite correctly considered himself unfit for the post. Several other ministers—of war, transportation, and justice—were also replaced in January 1917; thus the "ministerial leapfrog" continued unabated until the end of the monarchy.

And what of the two groups of the Petrograd population which actually "made" the February (March) Revolution, the workers and the soldiers? As was pointed out earlier, the workers lost all enthusiasm for a "war to the victorious end" fairly early and became restless because of economic hardships as well as socialist peace propaganda. The dynamics of the labor movement in connection with the war are well illustrated by the number of persons participating in strikes. For Russia as a whole, this amounted to:

January-July 1914—1,450,000 strikers
August-December 1914—   35,000 strikers
1915— 553,000 strikers
1916—1,086,000 strikers

Of the latter figure, 776,000 took part in strikes that had a predominantly economic motivation, while 310,000 took part in strikes that had the character of a political protest against the government and the war. Labor discontent found its sharpest expression in Petrograd, the largest center of the defense industry, which also suffered the most from economic disorganization because of its remoteness from sources of fuel, food, and raw materials, intensified by the naval blockade.

Along with the workers of Petrograd, the military garrison of the capital was another major seedbed of discontent. This garrison consisted of over 160,000 very young or middle-aged people, mostly peasants, who were called soldiers and filled the barracks of the guards regiments. But such "guards reserve regiments" were guards regiments in name only; they had nothing in common with their predecessors, either in training or in *esprit de corps*. They passed most of their time in enforced idleness, almost without any military training because of the lack of officers and weapons. Shut in the army barracks, they ate their rations, longed for the countryside, complained about their lot, and impatiently awaited the time "when this damned war would come to an end." But the end was not in sight. Pacifist and defeatist propaganda and scandalous gossip about "Grishka Rasputin" destroyed what was left of combat spirit and military discipline.

With two such excellent targets of revolutionary propaganda present in the capital, clandestine activities steadily grew. Of course, the majority of Russian socialists were not supported by German agents, but Bolshevik propaganda during the war was heavily subsidized by the German Foreign Office through neutral Sweden.

Fearing an approaching catastrophe, the grand dukes, the members of the Council of State, even ambassadors of Allied countries tried to persuade the tsar to make concessions to the Progressive Bloc, that is, to appoint a cabinet that could enjoy in fact "the confidence of the country," which under the given circumstances meant the confidence of the Duma. The British ambassador, Sir George Buchanan, was especially persuasive in this respect. But all these attempts proved unsuccessful, as did those of the Duma president, Rodzianko. Thus, in February 1917 (March by the Western calendar), the Revolution arrived, predicted by many but prepared for by none.

Evaluated objectively, the military situation of Russia at the beginning of 1917 was not at all catastrophic. During 1916 the Russian army on the Austrian and Ottoman fronts went over to the offensive and achieved a number of major victories, although not on the German-held sections of the front. The shortage of ammunition was a thing of the past, and the army was supplied better than ever before. The morale of the frontline troops was, on the whole, fully satisfactory, as foreign observers such as Alfred Knox or Bernard Pares have testified.[23] But as General Golovine put it, "the further from the firing line, the greater the pessimism."

In the winter of 1916–1917, the political atmosphere, especially in Petrograd, became increasingly tense. On one side stood the tsarist government—isolated, aloof, weak, distrusted, or even despised —on the other side, the intelligentsia, the workers, and the reserve soldiers—weary of the war and of economic difficulties, losing both faith and interest in victory, resentful and grumbling, exaggerating both their own sufferings and the government's mistakes. In such an

---

[23] For understandable reasons that have little to do with history, Soviet writers have attempted to prove that the disintegration of the morale of the army had already started to a considerable degree before February 1917. They exaggerate the proportions of desertion and of cases of insubordination on the front, which in fact were isolated cases and occurred in the armies of all fighting powers.

atmosphere any minor shock could unleash an avalanche of social and political events.

This shock came in Petrograd in February 1917. In the middle of the month severe cold and snowdrifts caused unusually long delays in the delivery of grain and flour by railroad, and a shortage of bread developed, since reserve stocks in the city were seriously depleted. Some bakeries stopped work, long queues appeared at the bakery shops, discontent and irritation grew (people evidently were not as well trained for standing in queues as they later became), and on February 23 industrial strikes and street demonstrations of workers and students began. The police noticed among the demonstrators many junior officers, and the crowds began singing the revolutionary *Marseillaise.* Street demonstrations and clashes with the police occurred, as demonstrations began under the slogan "bread!" but soon became revolutionary in character. Placards appeared with the inscriptions "down with autocracy" and "down with the war." Police could not cope with the demonstrators and the troops were unreliable. In the next few days the workers' disturbances continued, and on February 26 spread to the soldiers of one reserve regiment. When the demonstrations and disorders in the streets of Petrograd became widespread and exposed the inability of the administration to cope with them, Rodzianko, the chairman of the Duma, implored the tsar in two telegrams to replace the existing government with persons who had "the confidence of the country." He did not receive an answer, and the tsar, who considered the Duma a hotbed of opposition, ordered the scheduled session of the Duma prorogued until April 1917. He also ordered troops to be dispatched from the front to suppress the "disturbances." Meanwhile, on February 27 the demonstrators were joined by additional reserve battalions of three guards regiments (the Pavlovsky, Volhynsky, and Litovsky), and the uprising began to turn openly into a revolution. On the same day, following the example of the revolutionary year 1905, a Soviet of Workers' Deputies was organized in Petrograd, with additional delegates from the troops, which made it a Soviet of Workers' and Soldiers' Deputies.

Upon receiving the order to postpone its session, the Duma refused to disperse and created from its members a Provisional Executive Committee, which declared its intention to re-establish order and to create a new "provisional government," "in accordance with the wishes of the population and enjoying its confidence." The committee consisted of the leading members of the Progressive Bloc with the addition of two representatives of leftist groups: A. F. Kerensky, the leader of the Trudoviks; and N. Chkheidze, the leader of the small Menshevik faction in the Duma.

On February 28 the whole city was in the hands of the rebels. Crowds of soldiers and workers came to the Tauride Palace to declare their support for the revolutionary authorities. They listened to speeches of the Duma orators, applauded, shouted "hurrah," and sang revolutionary songs. All the ministers of the tsarist government were arrested, and on March 1 the Executive Committee of the Duma formed a new cabinet, or "provisional government," headed by Prince George Lvov, the president of the All-Russian Zemstvo Union. The new cabinet included Miliukov, the leader of the Kadet party, as minister of foreign affairs; Guchkov, the Octobrist, as minister of defense; and Kerensky, a Trudovik-turned-SR, as minister of justice.

At the outset the new government announced a program that called for: "an immediate general amnesty for all political and religious offenses"; all civil and political liberties "extended to the army in so far as war conditions permit"; the abolition of all social, religious, and national discrimination; immediate preparation for the calling of a Constituent Assembly elected by general and secret vote; a national militia to replace the police; and the democratization of the institutions of local self-government. The seventh point in the program promised "not to dispatch from Petrograd all military units which took part in the revolutionary movement."[24] Thus, the soldiers of the Petrograd reserve units were guaranteed against the hardships and dangers of combat life and were promised a carefree life in the capital, where they were needed "for the defense of the revolution."

The same day, March 1, the newly organized Soviet of Workers' and Soldiers' Deputies published its famous Order No. 1, which in fact abolished the authority of the officers in military units and transferred this power to elected soldiers' committees, thus initiating the disintegration of the Russian army during 1917.

Meanwhile, the tsar proved himself to be entirely helpless amid the swiftly moving revolutionary events. His attempt to order military units from the front to put down the Petrograd uprising failed because of the reluctance of the commanding generals to start a civil war. Only one small detachment commanded by General Ivanov was dispatched to Petrograd from the front, but the military train with this detachment was stopped en route by the supporters of the new government, and the soldiers of the detachment expressed open unwillingness "to fight their own."

---

[24] Golder, *op. cit.*, p. 309.

The train in which the tsar himself tried to reach his palace at Tsarskoe Selo near Petrograd, in an attempt to check the uprising, was also stopped en route at Pskov. There on March 2 Guchkov and V. V. Shulgin, the delegates dispatched by the new government, appeared to obtain the act of abdication. Deserted by all, including the military, the emperor signed a manifesto renouncing the throne on behalf of his brother, Grand Duke Michael Alexandrovich, for he did not want to part with his sick son, the legitimate heir to the throne. Before signing the abdication manifesto, the tsar, on the request of the deputies, signed a decree appointing a new ministry, headed by Prince Lvov, thus giving a semblance of legality to the revolutionary coup. On leaving the army, Nicholas II signed his farewell order to the troops, a document full of sincere patriotism. He called upon the troops to obey the Provisional Government and to bring the war to a victorious end, ranking as treason any thought of an immediate peace.[25] This last order of the tsar was not made public by the provisional government.

After talking with the representatives of the Provisional Government, Grand Duke Michael Alexandrovich, in whose favor Nicholas II had abdicated, did not dare to ascend the throne in the midst of revolution and refused to assume power before the coming Constituent Assembly would decide the future form of government in Russia.

Thus the three-hundred-year-old reign of the Romanov dynasty in Russia was ended. The majority of the urban population greeted the fall of the old regime with loud demonstrations. Many thought at the time that Russia was on the threshold of a "radiant future." But history willed otherwise. It may be fitting to conclude the tragic story with the words of Winston Churchill, even though his interpretation is at variance with many accepted notions:

> Surely to no nation has Fate been more malignant than to Russia. Her ship went down in sight of port. She had actually weathered the storm when all was cast away. Every sacrifice had been made; the toil was achieved. Despair and treachery usurped command at the very moment when the task was done. The long retreats were ended; the munition famine was broken; arms were pouring in; stronger, larger, better equipped armies guarded the immense front. . . . It is the shallow fashion of the time to dismiss the Tsarist regime as a purblind, corrupt, incompetent tyranny. But a survey of its thirty months' war with Germany and

---

[25] *Ibid.,* pp. 53–54.

Austria should correct these loose impressions and expose the dominant facts. We may measure the strength of the Russian Empire by the battering it had endured, by the disasters it had survived, by the inexhaustible forces it had developed, and by the recovery it had made. . . .[26]

In telling the story of the downfall of the Russian monarchy we have not concealed the weaknesses and blunders of the tsarist government, but the facts emphasized by the great British statesman and renowned historian should also be remembered.

---

[26] Winston S. Churchill, *The World Crisis, 1916–1918,* vol. I (New York, 1927), pp. 227–228.

Epilogue

THE READER OF THIS BOOK MAY FIND
that my interpretation of the history of prerevolutionary Russia differs
from many works that have become familiar in the West. There is a
widespread tendency to view Russia under the old regime as poor,
barbaric, "corrupt," "rotten," and "inevitably" doomed. This picture
needs many correctives, to say the least. I am not and never was an
admirer of Russian "tsarism," and as a young radical I experienced
some unpleasant consequences, "normal" in Russia at that time, because of my leftist sympathies and affiliations. But after having overcome my former prejudices and resentment, I have tried to observe
and evaluate the Russian past without either idealizing or vilifying it.

Russian history between 1801 and 1917 was not a monotonous course of a stagnant society governed by "despotic" tsars and an
"insipid" bureaucracy; rather, it was a succession of alternating
periods of substantial progress and of reaction. The periods of progress
were the early reign of Alexander I, characterized by the activities of
Speransky, the "period of great reforms" under Alexander II, assisted
chiefly by Rostovtsev and Miliutin, and the periods of Witte and
Stolypin in the reign of Nicholas II. The three periods of reaction
and stagnation are characterized by the names of Arakcheev, Nicholas I, and Pobedonostsev. To be sure, even in the reigns of Alexander II and Nicholas II there were reactionary currents at work, but
on the other hand the most stagnant period of Russian political life,

page 412

/ ƒ 2ƒ²ƒƒ

the reign of Nicholas I, was characterized by an unprecedented flowering of intellectual life, by the appearance of Pushkin, Lermontov, and
Gogol.

The most rapid and substantial progress in all fields of
Russian life was made during the Duma Monarchy (1906–1914), which
was the closest Russia ever came to constitutional government. To
equate the so-called tsarist despotism with the real totalitarian despotism of the Soviet period is to lose all sense of historical proportion.
One can even read that ideological exclusiveness and the "iron curtain" were not Bolshevik innovations, but have always existed in
Russia—despite the fact that no intelligentsia in Europe was better
acquainted with the outside world, more cosmopolitan, and more
subject to foreign influences through literary and personal contacts
than Russia's (somehow, the eighteenth and nineteenth centuries are
usually confused with the fifteenth and sixteenth centuries). The richness of creative activity in Russian cultural life and the variety of
political currents in prerevolutionary Russia stand in sharp contrast
to the gray monotony of the Communist totalitarian empire. Spectacular technological feats in a few areas of high political priority are
no substitute for the loss of personal and creative freedom.

One can further read much about alleged corruption at
high levels of tsarist government. But, when the Provisional Government and later the Bolsheviks opened confidential archives and conducted the most exhaustive inquiries into the activities of tsarist ministers, they were unable to find any evidence to substantiate these
charges.[1] The lower echelons of the police were not entirely free from
graft, but surely this was not a phenomenon confined to tsarist Russia.

It cannot be denied that by the end of the nineteenth century the political structure of the Russian Empire was obsolete and
the social and economic conditions of the mass of the people left much
to be desired. But the social and political reforms enacted during and

---

[1] In answer to charges of corruption, former Deputy Minister of Internal Affairs
V. I. Gurko has written: "The integrity of the overwhelming majority of the high
officials is beyond question. Only persons who are absolutely unfair can now accuse
our high officials of graft, for all our state archives have been opened and all our
secret documents have been published. The Provisional Government, and later the
Bolsheviks, conducted most exhaustive inquiries into the activities of our ministers
and were unable to detect one compromising fact." *Features and Figures of the Past*
(Stanford, 1939), p. 199.

after the revolution of 1905–1906 essentially changed this situation, opening the road to a better future. Several dispassionate Western observers have noted Russia's rapid progress during that time. As Donald W. Treadgold has put it:

> The years of Nicholas II's reign witnessed a speedy industrial growth; a sweeping transformation of the peasantry into small proprietors; the rapid spread of education; new, diverse, and original cultural developments; the schooling of a generation in political experience through the zemstvos, municipalities, the Duma and the courts; and an amazing growth of Siberia. . . . The old dynastic absolutism left behind it much that was healthy and promising which the new totalitarianism stifled and corrupted.[2]

Or, in the words of Hans Kohn:

> By 1914 Russia was successfully on the way to becoming a full partner of the European community. . . . During the decade preceding the revolution, Russia lived through an era of rapidly growing prosperity; culturally, the fight against illiteracy was started with great vigor, and intellectual and artistic relations with Europe became closer than ever before or since.[3]

But the sociopolitical shortcomings that made the collapse of the Russian Empire possible, though not inevitable, must also be kept in mind. First, there was the weakness of the Russian middle class. A class of peasant proprietors began to emerge only during the Stolypin era, and the city bourgeoisie was neither numerous nor strong enough to offer any organized resistance to the revolutionary storm. Another weakness was the cleavage between the educated groups and the masses. This gap began to close after 1905 because of the spread of education and the expansion of the cooperative movement, but of course the centuries-old gulf could not be eliminated in one decade. The two educated classes—the bureaucracy and the intelligentsia— were hostile to each other and aloof from the peasant masses, who considered them alien groups. The bureaucracy was headed by the Council of Ministers, some members of which were capable and competent state servants. But, during the last reign, the weak tsar, influenced by his hysterical wife and her notorious "friend" Rasputin, made the work of the Council of Ministers very difficult by frequent

---

[2] Donald W. Treadgold, *Twentieth Century Russia* (Chicago, 1959), p. 121.
[3] Hans Kohn, *Basic History of Modern Russia* (Princeton, 1957), p. 73.

changes of personnel and by the appointment of thoroughly incompetent persons to important posts. The tsar's vacillations and errors,
especially during the war, undermined the prestige of the monarchy
and nourished revolutionary agitation.

On the other hand, the politically active part of the intelligentsia was doctrinaire and uncompromising in its political philosophy
and demands. An acute observer of the Russian scene, D. M. Wallace,
relates an interesting conversation with the leader of the Kadet party
(obviously in 1906):

> I ventured to suggest that, instead of maintaining an attitude
> of systematic and uncompromising hostility to the Ministry, the
> party might co-operate with the Government and thereby gradu-
> ally create something like the English parliamentary system, for
> which they possessed such admiration; possibly in eight or ten
> years this desirable result might be obtained. On hearing these
> last words my friend suddenly interrupted me and exclaimed:
> "Eight or ten years? We cannot wait so long as that!"—"Well,"
> I replied, "you must know your affairs better; but in England
> we had to wait for several centuries." [4]

The war caught Russia, as we have seen, militarily unprepared and in the throes of a far-reaching social transformation.
Nevertheless, the Russian armies, poorly equipped and led, fought
bravely for two and a half years against a powerful enemy and greatly
contributed to the final victory of the Allies, a contribution of which,
in Hugh Seton-Watson's words, "both civil and military historians,
both in the West and even in Russia after 1918 showed an astonishing
ignorance." [5] Even though the equipment of the fighting front had
improved substantially by 1917 and the material resources of the
country were still plentiful, wartime hardships and disorganization on
the home front, intensified by the obvious blunders of a weak government clinging to autocratic illusions, created resentment, discontent,
and the loss of faith or even interest in victory among the urban population. The government of Nicholas II, which was blamed by the
people for wartime hardships and failures, lost all prestige and authority, and so the Russian Empire fell under the strain of war, just
as the remaining European empires, the German, the Austro-
Hungarian, and the Ottoman did within the next year and a half. In

---

[4] Wallace, *Russia* (1912 ed.), p. 728.
[5] Hugh Seton-Watson, *The Decline of Imperial Russia* (New York, 1952), p. 361.

the words of M. Karpovich, in view of Russia's progress before the war,

> it would be hardly correct to assert that the revolution was absolutely inevitable. Russia still had to solve many complicated and difficult problems but the possibility of their peaceful solution was by no means excluded. . . . The war made the revolution highly probable, but human folly made it inevitable.[6]

The idea of the inevitability either of the Russian revolution or of any other important historical event is based on a superstitious faith in ironclad laws of historical development, allegedly governing the life of nations. Predictions are frequently quoted to prove the inevitability of the event. This is, in Toynbee's words, only "a facile wisdom after event," for those predictions that do materialize are publicized and praised as prophecies, while perhaps an equal number of those that do not materialize are ignored and forgotten.

History is made not by mythical "laws of historical development" (as Marx believed), but by living human beings with their emotions, passions, beliefs, and prejudices and with their group and individual interests, which they may evaluate either correctly or erroneously. Every great historical personality who has influenced the course of history was an unpredictable historical contingency. On the other hand, the masses of the people, particularly during uneasy and disturbed times, are easily susceptible to the influence of demagogues, who flatter their passions and arouse their frustrated hopes and expectations. In the words of Karl Jaspers,

> human masses as such are not a person . . . they are without content and a tool for anyone who flatters their universal psychological impulses and passions. Human masses are easily able to lose the power of deliberation, rush into the intoxication of change for the sake of change and follow the Pied Piper, who leads them into inferno.[7]

It remains for us to review briefly the road into the inferno which the Russian people took in 1917. The formation of the Provisional Government and of the Petrograd Soviet of Workers' and Soldiers' Deputies created a precarious duality of power: on one side, a legal government with formal responsibility, but without real power; on the other, an institution possessing real power without responsi-

---

[6] Karpovich, *Imperial Russia, 1801–1917*, pp. 94–95.
[7] Karl Jaspers, *The Origin and Goal of History* (New Haven, 1953), p. 130.

bility. A conflict between the Provisional Government and the Petrograd Soviet soon developed with regard to the most difficult decision, that of continuing the war. While the Provisional Government declared its intention to honor Russia's commitments toward her allies and to continue war "to a victorious end," the socialist majority in the Soviet favored the Zimmerwald peace program "without victors and vanquished," even though it recognized the army's duty to defend the country if attacked. But it became extremely difficult to maintain a combat spirit in the army when victory was declared unnecessary, even undesirable.

The Provisional Government tried to realize the promises of its first program: it ordered a re-election of zemstvos and municipal dumas on the basis of a general franchise, set up local committees to prepare a radical agrarian reform, worked on an electoral law for the future Constituent Assembly. But it considered itself, correctly from the legal point of view, as a temporary authority whose main task was to pave the way for the final settlement of all key questions by the future Constituent Assembly. This position gave leftist demagogues a pretext to accuse the Provisional Government of forgetting or "betraying" the needs and demands of the people, which allegedly had to be fulfilled immediately.

The political and administrative structure of the Russian republic was very shaky. The tsarist administrative apparatus and the police were disbanded, but nothing was created to take their place. The Provisional Government appointed its commissioners in provincial cities; they seemed to replace the former governors, but in fact became figureheads without any real authority. Similarly, the competence of the scattered units of the new local militia was vague and undefined. In provincial cities, along with the old institutions of the zemstvos and the dumas, new soviets of workers' and peasants' deputies were formed, with a loud voice but an indefinite sphere of jurisdiction. The peasants and the workers, however, acknowledged more readily the authority of the local soviets than of the Provisional Government in Petrograd.

Economic conditions, especially in the major cities, went from bad to worse because of the growing disorganization in transport and the decline in labor productivity. The parties of "revolutionary democracy"—the Socialist Revolutionaries and the Social Democrats (Mensheviks)—who dominated the soviets spent most of their time in meetings and debates. The Petrograd Soviet declared its readiness to support the Provisional Government, but only in so far as its policy was in agreement with the demands of "revolutionary democracy." Meanwhile, the question of war and peace caused discord not only between the Provisional Government and the soviet, but within the Provisional Government as well. As discipline and order in the army began to vanish, the original decision to continue the war became increasingly unrealistic. Dissension on this question resulted in the retirement of Guchkov and Miliukov from the cabinet in May 1917. The eloquent lawyer Kerensky, who renounced all "imperialist" war aims, became the minister of war and of the navy; and the rich industrialist Tereshchenko became minister of foreign affairs. But political anarchy, economic chaos, and the dissolution of the army continued unabated.

Now the Bolsheviks, led by Lenin, saw their opportunity to fish in troubled waters. In their deceitful but successful game they had two trump cards. One was "land for the peasants" (despite the fact that the peasants already possessed four fifths of the arable land and that the partition which actually took place in 1918 increased their holdings only by 16 percent[8]). The other was "peace." As a means of achieving a "general and democratic" peace, the Bolsheviks proclaimed a policy of "fraternization" with enemy soldiers at the front. Bolshevik peace propaganda, conducted by hundreds of agitators and carried by thousands upon thousands of newspapers and leaflets (generously financed with German money) met with considerable success among the tired and peace-craving soldiers; and so-called fraternization actually began on the Russo-German front. Of course, from the German side, this fraternization was performed by specially trained propaganda and intelligence units, which were sent to the Russian trenches by the German military command to dupe Russian simpletons and to reconnoiter Russian positions.

In May and June 1917, War Minister Kerensky (called ironically by the officers "persuader in chief") made numerous trips to the front in order to explain the political situation to the soldiers and urge them to preserve military discipline and be ready to take the offensive against the enemy, if ordered by the supreme command. Im-

---

[8] A. Bolshakov, *Derevnia posle Oktiabria* [*The Countryside after the October Revolution*] (Leningrad, 1925), p. 28.

pressed by Kerensky's eloquence, the soldiers usually applauded and shouted "hurrah," but the impression was not a long-lasting one, for after Kerensky's departure a Bolshevik agitator would usually take the floor and convince them that it would be utterly stupid to die for the profits of English, American, and French capitalists. The "Kerensky offensive," which started in the beginning of July, ended, after some initial successes, in a crushing defeat and the flight of the Russian Eleventh Army from Galicia.[9]

Meanwhile, events in Petrograd took their fateful course. A Bolshevik uprising in July 1917 was suppressed, but the new government, headed by Kerensky and with moderate socialists participating, was not strong enough to overcome the increasing political and economic chaos. In August, General Kornilov, the supreme commander of the Russian armies, tried to save the situation by creating a military dictatorship. Many facets of the "Kornilov affair" remain unclear and contradictory to this day, but undoubtedly this able and patriotic military commander was not a reactionary and had no personal ambitions for power. But the Kornilov affair frightened the ultraliberal Provisional Government, which was hopelessly addicted to the delusion that counterrevolution and dictatorship could come only from the right, never from the left. Now the Bolsheviks were the recognized allies in the fight against an alleged counterrevolution from the right, and they set out to prepare energetically their real counterrevolution from the left. Lenin, cautiously remaining underground,

---

[9] My patriotic sense was so shocked by this defeat that I decided to interrupt my studies of Russian history at Kharkov University and to take a part, however modest, in the making of history. To defend the Russian Republic, I joined the army as a volunteer—a decision that puzzled both my friends and the local military authorities—and was ordered into the Twenty-fourth Infantry Reserve Regiment located in Mariupol. But my military career soon ended in failure. There was almost no military training in our regiment, but there were endless political discussions. I took, of course, an active part in these discussions, trying to explain to my "comrade soldiers" the necessity to defend the newborn Russian Republic. But after my speeches the Bolsheviks from the ranks of the soldiers would attack vehemently my "bourgeois" attitude, and after listening to our heated debates the bewildered soldiers would frequently say, *"a chert vas razberet kto iz vas govorit pravdu,"* which meant, "the devil only knows which one of you is telling the truth." But the devil inclined the scales more and more to the side of the Bolsheviks, whose slogans —peace and land—seemed to be much simpler and more attractive than my patriotic exhortations. In the fall of 1917 I was assigned to the military school in Poltava, which was disbanded in December.

directed these preparations, which were to lead to the successful putsch of October 25 (November 7), known in Soviet mythology as the "Great October Socialist Revolution."

Was the October *coup d'état* an inevitable sequel of the February revolution? Lenin himself did not think so in October 1917. In his excited and angry letters to the members of the Central Committee of the Bolshevik party (who were inclined to postpone any decisive action until the meeting of the Second Congress of Soviets, scheduled for the beginning of November), Lenin wrote:

> To wait for the Second Congress of the Soviets is either idiocy or treason. Right now it is possible to take power, but if we don't do it immediately, it will be impossible later: Kerensky and the Kornilovists will gather together Cossacks and the revolution will be lost; right now weeks and days decide everything; delay means death! . . . The situation is extremely critical. It is as clear as can be that to delay the uprising now would really mean death. With all my power I wish to persuade the comrades that now everything hangs on a hair . . . we must not wait! We may lose everything! The government is tottering. We must deal it the death blow at any cost." [10]

What did in fact happen in Petrograd on October 25th? According to the later Soviet legend the Petrograd workers and soldiers rose up in order to establish a "socialist republic" in Russia. This was, of course, Lenin's goal, but he did not dare to proclaim it openly at that time. Ostensibly, the two goals of the uprising were to assure the convocation of the Constituent Assembly, delayed by the Provisional Government, and to assure Petrograd's defense against the Germans! In the fall of 1917 the military situation on the northern front caused considerable anxiety in Petrograd: the Germans took Riga, the islands of Oesel and Dago, and rumors arose that an offensive against Petrograd was imminent, and that Kerensky intended to leave Petrograd for Moscow. These rumors were very welcome for Lenin and he instantly proclaimed to his followers that Kerensky's intention was to give Petrograd over to the Germans in order to "strangle the Russian revolution." "This is the slogan for the uprising," he wrote, "the slogan which we must spread among the masses and which will have tremendous effect! It is for defense and to save

---

[10] Lenin, *Sochineniia,* 2d ed., vol. XXI, pp. 362–363.

Petrograd that we must overthrow Kerensky's government and seize power for the Soviets." [11]

Under such high-flown military-patriotic slogans a Bolshevik Military Revolutionary Committee for the Defense of Petrograd was formed in October. On October 25 (November 7) it began its operations, having several hundred armed "red guards" under its command. Without any resistance, they occupied the railroad stations, the telephone and telegraph offices, and the building of the State Bank. The action was successful, but there was no "uprising of workers and soldiers" in Petrograd on that day. The masses remained passive or indifferent: the soldiers remained in their barracks; the workers remained at work in their factories.

The members of the Provisional Government held a long session in the Winter Palace in which they discussed ways to cope with the situation, but because of the garrison's "neutrality" they could call only upon several hundred cadets from the military schools and a women's battalion, formed in the summer of 1917. The defenders found neither food nor munitions prepared for them in the Winter Palace, and by evening the majority of them melted away. On the other hand, the attacking forces were so weak that they could not take the palace by storm (which exists only in Soviet painting and fiction) and began a siege, awaiting reinforcements. In the evening, a thousand or so sailors from Kronstadt arrived; the cruiser *Aurora* entered the Neva River and thundered its six-inch cannons—loaded with blank charges. The defenders, few and confused, were no match for the sailors, who entered the Winter Palace in a midnight attack, all the more easily since the defenders forgot to close and to guard the rear doors of the building. At about two o'clock in the morning the ministers of the Provisional Government were arrested and dispatched to the Peter and Paul Fortress, except for Kerensky, who had left Petrograd in an attempt to summon combat troops from the front. The Bolshevik losses were six killed and several wounded. [12]

---

[11] *Ibid.*, p. 324.

[12] In a speech before the representatives of the Petrograd garrison, October 29, Lenin himself stated: "We seized power almost without bloodshed." *Ibid.*, vol. XXII, p. 31. A detailed and well-documented description of the October Revolution can be found in an excellent book by the late Russian historian S. P. Melgunov, *Kak bol'sheviki zakhvatili vlast'* [*How the Bolsheviks Seized Power*] (Paris, 1953); there is unfortunately no English translation.

On October 26 (November 8), the Second Congress of Soviets, which had convened on the previous night (and had, after the walkout of the Mensheviks and the right-wing Socialist Revolutionaries, a Bolshevik majority of 390 out of 625 delegates, many of whom lacked credentials),[13] approved a new government: the Council of People's Commissars, nominated by Lenin. It also passed Lenin's decrees on peace and on land (the latter borrowed from the Socialist Revolutionary program) and was quickly adjourned. Originally, the new government was also called "Provisional"—to administer state affairs until the convocation of the Constituent Assembly. But the elections to the Constituent Assembly, called by Kerensky's government prior to its deposition, and held in November, showed that the Bolsheviks were in a decided minority. They controlled 168 votes in a body of 703 deputies, or less than 24 percent of the vote. As a result, the Constituent Assembly was disbanded after a one-day session in January 1918, and Lenin's Council of People's Commissars became permanent.

Then, instead of the promised "general and democratic peace without annexations and indemnities," the peace of Brest Litovsk was signed, which ceded to Germany an enormous territory with about a quarter of Russia's population and most of her industrial plant. Neither the emperor nor the republican Russian government could consider such a peace, but Lenin could. In defending the "peace" which he had concluded with the imperial German government Lenin confessed: "It is not a state we stand for . . . It is not national interests we are upholding—we claim that the interests of socialism, the interests of world socialism, rank higher than the interests of the state."[14] In his letter to American workers in August 1918 Lenin contended: "No one can be a socialist who is not ready for the greatest sacrifices from 'his' fatherland in the interests of the World socialist revolution."[15] And: "The Russian revolutionary movement is only one of the detachments of the international socialist army."[16]

---

[13] Soviet writers have acknowledged that "at the Second All-Russian Congress of Soviets there were no accurate lists of delegates, data on the mandates of some delegates were absent from questionnaires, and the lists included a number of comrades with an advisory vote, or guests; the party affiliation of some of them is unknown." Lenin, *op. cit.*, vol. XXIII, appendix 5, note 108, p. 577.

[14] *Ibid.*, vol. XXIII, p. 14.

[15] *Ibid.*, p. 181.

[16] *Ibid.*, p. 146.

The Third International, which Lenin established, proclaimed as its
goal the overthrow of capitalism all over the world and the establishment of the "dictatorship of the proletariat and the international
Soviet republic." [17]

Contrary to some Western notions of Lenin as a "Russian
Bismarck," there was evidently very little of a Russian national idea
in all of this. Even though in his practical politics Lenin was a fol-
lower of the revolutionary methods of Nechaev and Tkachev, his
social and political ideology was decidedly of a Western origin. In his
most mature theoretical work, *The State and the Revolution,* Lenin
repeatedly emphasized that his two fundamental concepts were those
of Marx: that the essence of history is class struggle, and that the
"dictatorship of the proletariat" is the only means for the liberation
of mankind. As Arnold Toynbee has rightly stated:

> Communism . . . is a weapon of Western origin. If it had not
> been invented by a couple of nineteenth-century Westerners, Karl
> Marx and Friedrich Engels, . . . Communism could never have
> become Russia's official ideology. There was nothing in the Rus-
> sian tradition that could have led the Russians to invent Com-
> munism for themselves. [18]

In fact, it was to a large extent the surrender of Russian
national interests by the Bolsheviks which stimulated the gathering of
patriotic forces in Russia to fight Lenin and his party, taking the form
of the White movement and resulting in three years of civil war.
Lenin had to overcome widespread and stubborn resistance from the
South, North, East, and West of the former Russian Empire. In the
summer of 1919, as the White armies converged on Moscow, the situation of the Bolshevik government became extremely precarious—
"comrades, we are in a ring of fire," exclaimed a Communist poet,
admitting the possibility that his revolution would fail, as others had
before.

This is not the place to discuss in detail the causes of the
defeat of the White armies, but these can be mentioned in general
terms. The strong, unified command and centralized administration
of the Reds were opposed by the separate, uncoordinated efforts of
their politically dissident opponents. Systematic terror, ruthlessly

---

[17] Florinsky, *World Revolution and the U.S.S.R.* (New York, 1933), p. 159.
[18] Arnold Toynbee, *The World and the West* (New York, 1953), pp. 11-12.

applied on a large scale, helped the Reds to consolidate power over neutrals and dissidents alike. The greatest disparity between the two sides existed in military equipment and supply: the Red government had at its disposal vast stocks of arms and equipment left over from the demobilized imperial army, while the Whites had to capture their arms from the enemy, and the aid which came from the Allies was usually "too little and too late." The mistakes of the White military command, which had no political experience and, especially, of the civil administration deprived the Whites of the sympathies of the local population, which at first greeted them with great enthusiasm (as I witnessed in Kharkov in June 1919). The ablest military and political leader of the Whites, General P. N. Wrangel, tried to improve this situation in the Crimea in 1920 and to attract the sympathies of the peasants, but it was too late, and the territory under his control was too small. It should be emphasized, however, that neither the Whites nor the Reds were particularly popular among the majority of the peasants, who craved a peaceful life after years of bloody war and many months of civil anarchy and strife.[19] Essentially, the civil war in Russia was a war of two minorities, with the majority of the population remaining neutral. Compared to the World War, the numbers participating in the Civil War were quite small.

The main groups who supported Lenin after he seized power were the factory workers in large cities, who were flattered by the Bolsheviks as a new "ruling class" in Russia; impoverished and disgruntled elements in the countryside (the rural proletariat, or *bednota*); international military units (including Lettish and Chinese ones); and the Kronstadt sailors, who themselves revolted in 1921. The people who took part in the armed struggle against the Bolsheviks belonged to many different political groups: the Committee of Mem-

---

[19] After joining a rifle regiment of the Volunteer Army in Kharkov in June 1919, I entered the Livny district in the province of Orel in September. As a private, in a shabby overcoat and dirty boots, I hoped I could start open conversation with peasants and explain to them the White Army's aims. But the answers to my questions were mostly cautious and evasive. Only one middle-aged man, a demobilized soldier, gave me an angry reply which evidently expressed the peasants' prevailing opinion: "To hell with you all, the Reds, the Whites, the Greens [independent partisans], and all the rest of you! We suffered enough at the front for three years; finally we came back home and expected to find a peaceful life; we have had enough of war. And now you bring the war inside Russia!" The man's anger was quite understandable, but unfortunately he could not foresee Stalin's collectivization.

bers of the Constituent Assembly in Samara and the Directory in Ufa
were composed of Socialist Revolutionaries; the White government in
Archangel was headed by the "popular socialist" N. V. Chaikovsky;
the civilian advisers of General A. I. Denikin, the supreme commander of the southern White army, belonged mostly to the Kadet
Party. The Cossacks, who played an important part in the White
movement, traditionally cherished democratic ideals. In the Urals,
two divisions consisting of workers from the Izhevsk and Votkinsk
factories fought on the side of the Whites. The majority of the former
frontline officers, university students and high-school youths who
formed the initial cadres of the Volunteer Army had no definite political affiliation, but certainly they were not "tsarists" or "reactionaries,"
and neither were their leaders—generals Kornilov, Alekseev, Denikin,
and Wrangel, and Admiral Kolchak.

> We have no regrets for the past,
> the tsar is not our idol

sang Kornilov's men as they went to fight "for freedom and for
Russia." The genuine rightists, who called themselves monarchists and
were headed by the Duma deputy Markov, took no active part in the
White movement.[20]

Lenin himself considered the struggle between the Reds
and the Whites not as a local struggle between Russian Bolsheviks
and Russian tsarists, but as an episode in the world struggle between
the proletariat and the bourgeoisie. In September 1919 he wrote: "He
who cannot understand even now that the war which is going on in
Russia (and beginning throughout the world) is a civil war between
the proletariat and the bourgeoisie is a hopeless idiot."[21]

Actually, the Bolsheviks had to fight not only the bourgeoisie, but to a greater or lesser degree all elements of Russian society, whose resistance was suppressed by a Red army that consisted to
a considerable extent of international units, such as the notorious
Latvian rifles. An uprising in Yaroslavl (carried out chiefly by officers

---

[20] The rightest émigré press subsequently attacked with vehemence the military
commanders of the White armies for leaving the question of Russia's political structure to be decided by the Constituent Assembly instead of raising the banner of
monarchy. The monarchists erroneously considered that the latter would have unified the nation in the struggle against the Bolsheviks.

[21] Lenin, *op. cit.,* vol. XXIV, pp. 459–460.

and intelligentsia) was followed by numerous peasant revolts in the eastern provinces, of which the Antonov rebellion in the province of Tambov became particularly well known. After the bulk of the White armies had been defeated, the Kronstadt sailors who had brought Lenin victory in the October Revolution revolted against the Bolshevik dictatorship, demanding political democracy. The rebellion was suppressed, but the frightened Lenin proclaimed a great retreat from communism and introduced his New Economic Policy.

The White armies' abortive struggle was not in vain. Political and social conditions in Europe in 1919–1920 were extremely unstable, and Lenin was eager to spread the fire of the "world socialist revolution." He waged war on Poland, planned to attack Rumania, and supported "Soviet republics" in Hungary and Bavaria. But his main forces were engaged by the civil war in Russia; in this way Europe received a breathing spell and could restore her exhausted resources. Moreover, the Russian civil war became merely the first and clearest manifestation of resistance to totalitarian dictatorship; in changing forms, these manifestations of opposition have continued in Russia to this day.

The future of Russia—as of any country—is unpredictable. Some writers consider the domination of Marxism-Leninism in Russia as a natural and permanent result of Russia's preceding development. But closer study of Russian history tends to inspire one with the opposite conviction and hope: that the Russian nation is not condemned to live under totalitarian dictatorship forever.

Glossary

The following is a list of some of the recurrent Russian terms that are susceptible to various translations. The English terms in the right-hand column represent the choices used in this book.

Regional and Local Government

golova	mayor
guberniia	province
krai	area or territory
mirovoi posrednik	arbitrator
mirovoi sud'ia	justice of the peace
oblast'	region
okrug	district
predvoditel' dvorianstva	marshal of the nobility
selenie (selo, derevnia)	village
sel'skii skhod	rural assembly
uezd (in Poland, poviat)	county
uezdynyi gorod	county seat
volost' (in Poland, gmina)	township
zemskii ispravnik	district police officer
zemskii nachal'nik	superintendent of the peasantry
zemskaia uprava	zemstvo council
zemskoe sobranie	zemstvo assembly

Social Classes

dvorianstvo (sing., dvorianin)	nobility
dvorovye	household serfs
kazennye krestianie	state peasants
meshchane	burghers

Official Documents

gramota	charter
manifest	manifesto
nakaz	instruction
polozhenie, reglament, uchrezhdenie	regulation
postanovlenie	enactment
rasporiazhenie	order
reskript	rescript
ukaz	decree
ustav	statute (or charter for society)

Selected
Bibliography

FOR EASE OF REFERENCE, THIS BIBLIOG-
RAPHY is divided into twelve sections. Section 1 contains major bibli-
ographic and historiographic works, with those in Russian listed separately for convenience; section 2, primary sources pertaining to the
entire study period; and section 3, observations by foreign visitors to
Russia. Sections 4 and 5 contain textbooks and general surveys for the
entire period and for individual reigns, respectively. From then on the
material is arranged by subject matter: internal political developments (section 6), social and economic conditions, with special emphasis on the history of the peasantry (sections 7 and 8), Russian cultural life (section 10), and foreign policy, with special emphasis on
World War I and its consequences (sections 11 and 12). Section 9,
social and political theory, is separated from the facts of social and
political life only for the sake of convenience, since it is difficult to
draw a clear dividing line between facts and ideologies in sociopolitical
developments, and readers interested in them should consult both
sections 6 and 9.

Several sections are further broken down into subsections,
by subject matter. Within these divisions, a short list of primary
sources comes first, followed by the secondary sources arranged alpha-
betically. The only exception occurs when several items directly relate
to an author or an item in the list, in which case all such works are
grouped together (for example, works *on* Lenin follow the entry
Lenin). Some paperback (pb) editions are indicated for the reader's
convenience.

The titles of primary sources are supplemented with short
explanatory remarks, but space limitations make it impossible to dis-

page 428

cuss the qualities and contents of all the books listed, and brief annotations accompany only some of them. My general observation is that a majority of Western authors have traditionally given a somewhat one-sided picture of prerevolutionary Russia: they have been overly pessimistic in describing its conditions of life, and hypercritical in evaluating the domestic and foreign policy of the Russian government, while positive accomplishments, particularly in the Duma period (1905–1914) have been underrated. Fortunately, there is an increasing number of exceptions to this "rule," and I have pointed out a number of works giving a more balanced picture of the Russian past.

Included in this bibliography are numerous works by prerevolutionary Russian historians that have not lost their value. As for Soviet historical writing, I have found it unnecessary to include the works of M. N. Pokrovsky (to whom history was only "politics projected into the past"), as well as general Soviet surveys, which desperately attempt to compress the wealth and diversity of the Russian past into the Procrustean bed of Marxist-Leninist theory with its obligatory "phases of development": feudalism, capitalism, and imperialism. Included in my list, however, are numerous monographs by Soviet historians which, between an introduction and a conclusion with the usual sociopolitical nonsense, contain useful and factual historical information, sometimes based on a thorough study of sources. (The reader interested in Soviet historiography can consult the following two books: C. E. Black, ed., *Rewriting Russian History: Soviet Interpretation of Russia's Past,* New York, 1956, and K. F. Shteppa, *Russian Historians and the Soviet State,* New Brunswick, N.J., 1962.)

Any selected bibliography will have unavoidable gaps; nevertheless it is hoped that the list that follows will be helpful to student and teacher alike.

1. Bibliography and historiography

The American Bibliography of Slavic and East European Studies, Indiana University Publications (annual). Bloomington, Ind., 1956–1960.

Dutcher, George M., *et al.,* eds., *Guide to Historical Literature.* New York, 1931; 2d ed., publ. by the American Historical Association, G. F. Howe, *et al.,* eds., New York, 1961.

Fisher, Harold, ed., *American Research on Russia.* Bloomington, Ind., 1959.

Gapanovich, Ivan I., *Russian Historiography outside Russia.* Peiping, 1935.

Gregory, Winifred, ed., *List of the Serial Publications of Foreign Governments, 1815–1931* (for the American Council of Learned Societies). New York, 1932. (The section on Russia compiled by V. V. Gsovskii, pp. 577–631; the USSR, pp. 632–716.)

Harvard University, Russian Research Center. *Ten-Year Report and Current Projects, 1948–1958.* Cambridge, Mass., 1958.

Kerner, Robert J., *Slavic Europe: A Selected Bibliography in the West European Languages, Comprising History, Languages and Literature.* Cambridge, Mass., 1918.

Kovalevsky, Pierre, *Manuel d'histoire Russe: Etude critique des sources et exposé historique.* Paris, 1948.

Mazour, Anatole G., *Modern Russian Historiography*, 2d ed. Princeton, 1958; 1st ed., *An Outline of Modern Russian Historiography*, Berkeley, 1939.

Morley, Charles, *Guide to Research in Russian History.* Syracuse, N.Y., 1951.

Strakhovsky, Leonid I., ed., *A Handbook of Slavic Studies.* Cambridge, Mass., 1949.

Yakobson, Sergius, *Five Hundred Russian Works for College Libraries.* Washington, D.C., 1948.

Barashenkov, V. M., *et al.*, eds., *Bibliografiia periodicheskikh izdanii Rossii 1901–1916 gg.*, 3 vols. and Index. Leningrad, 1958–1960. (A bibliography of Russia's periodicals 1901–1916).

Bibliografiia russkoi bibliografii po istorii SSSR. Moscow, 1957. (A list of bibliographical works on Russian history published before 1917, published by Knizhnaia Palata.)

Cherepakhov, M. S., and E. M. Fingerit, eds., *Russkaia periodicheskaia pechat' 1895–Oktiabr' 1917.* Moscow, 1957. (The Russian periodical press from 1895 to October 1917.)

Dement'ev, A. G., *et al.*, eds., *Russkaia periodicheskaia pechat' 1702–1894.* Moscow, 1959. (The Russian periodical press from 1702 to 1894.)

Doronin, I. P., *et al.*, eds. *Istoriia SSSR: Ukazatel' sovetskoi literatury za 1917–1952 gg.*, 2 vols. Moscow, 1956–1958. (Index of Soviet literature on Russian history published between 1917 and 1952.)

Illeritsky, B. E., and I. A. Kudriavtsev, eds., *Istoriografiia istorii SSSR s drevneishikh vremen do Velikoi Oktiabr'skoi sotsialisticheskoi Revoliutsii.* Moscow, 1961 (Historiography of the history of the USSR from ancient times to the Great October Socialist Revolution. A useful factual survey, marred by the usual Marxist-Leninist schematicism and phraseology.)

Lisovsky, N. M., *Russkaia periodicheskaia pechat' 1703–1900.* Petrograd, 1915. (The Russian periodical press, 1703–1900.)

Miliukov, P. N., *Glavnyia techeniia russkoi istoricheskoi mysli,* 3d ed. St. Petersburg, 1913; 1st ed., 1898. (Main currents of Russian historical thought. Covers the eighteenth century and the first half of the nineteenth century.)

Nikitin, S. A., *Istochnikovedenie istorii SSSR XIX veka.* Moscow, 1940. (Studies on sources for the Russian history in the nineteenth century. Covers the period up to the early '90s.)

Rubakin, N. A., *Sredi knig,* vol. 2, 2d ed. Moscow, 1913. (Among books. The second volume includes history and social sciences.)

Rubinshtein, N. L., *Russkaia istoriografiia.* Moscow, 1941.

Tikhomirov, M. N., ed., *Ocherki istorii istoricheskoi nauki v SSSR.* Vol. I, Moscow, 1955; vol. II, 1961. (Essays on historical studies in the USSR.

Special emphasis on the history of national minorities. Vol. I covers the period to the middle of the nineteenth century.)
Volgin, V. P., E. V. Tarle, and A. M. Pankratova, eds., *Dvadtsat' piat' let istoricheskoi nauki v SSSR.* Moscow and Leningrad, 1942. (Twenty-five years of historical studies in the USSR.)

2. General Sources, Collections of Documents, Periodicals Containing Historical Materials, and Memoirs

Russkii Arkhiv, P. Bartenev, ed. Moscow, 1863–1917 (Russian archives. A monthly containing numerous and diverse historical materials.)

Krasnyi Arkhiv. Moscow, 1922–1941. (Red archives, 104 volumes. Materials pertaining chiefly to the history of the nineteenth century and to the first two decades of the twentieth century.)

Arkhiv Russkoi Revoliutssi, I. V. Gessen, ed. Berlin, 1922–1927. (In all, 22 volumes containing a series of interesting memoirs of important public figures of the first two decades of the twentieth century.)

Byloe, Vladimir Burtsev, ed. London, Paris, St. Petersburg, 1900–1926. (The past. Irregular periodical with numerous materials pertaining to the revolutionary movement.)

Statisticheskii Ezhegodnik Rosii. St. Petersburg, 1904–1915. (The Russian statistical yearbook, published by the Central Statistical Bureau of the Ministry of Internal Affairs.)

Golos Minuvshego. Moscow, 1913–1923; continued abroad with subtitle *Na chuzhoi storone.* Berlin, Prague, Paris, 1923–1928. (The voice of the past; since 1923, on foreign soil. Irregular periodical with materials pertaining mainly to the revolutionary movement.)

Gurko, V. I. *Features and Figures of the Past: Government and Opinion in the Reign of Nicholas II.* Stanford, 1939. (A high bureaucrat, assistant minister of internal affairs in 1906, later an elected member of the State Council, Gurko was a keen and competent observer of the contemporary political scene.)

Kokovtsov, V. N., *Iz moego proshlago: Vospominaniia, 1903–1919,* 2 vols. Paris, 1933. *The Memoirs of Count Kokovtsov: Out of My Past,* Fisher, H. H., ed. Berkeley, 1935. (An interesting source, compiled by a level-headed, honest, and competent, if not very outstanding, statesman.)

Lazarevsky, N. I., ed., *Zakonodatel'nye akty perekhodnago vremeni, 1904–1908,* 3d ed. St. Petersburg, 1909. (Legislative acts of the transition period, 1904–1908.)

Miliutin, D. A., *Dnevnik, 1873–1882,* 4 vols. Moscow, 1947–1950. (D. A. Miliutin's diary, 1873–1882, is an outstanding source compiled by Alexander II's liberal war minister who, at the end of the reign, also became the tsar's chief adviser in questions of foreign policy.)

Obzor deiatel'nosti Gosudarstvennoi Dumy tretiago sozyva, 1907–1912. St. Petersburg, 1912. (A survey of the activity of the Third State Duma, compiled by the Duma office.)

Stenograficheskie otchety Gosudarstvennoi Dumy I, II, III, i IV sozyvov.
St. Petersburg, 1906–1917. (Stenographic records of the proceedings of the
1st, 2d, 3d, and 4th State Dumas.)
Stenograficheskie otchety Gosudarstvennogo Soveta. St. Petersburg, 1906–1917.
(Records of proceedings of the Council of State.)
Otchety po Gosudarstvennomu Sovetu. St. Petersburg, 1870–1906. (Annual
reports on the activity of the Council of State.)
Platonov, S. F., ed., *Istoriia Pravitel'stvuiushchago Senata za 200 let, 1711–
1911,* 5 vols. St. Petersburg, 1911. (History of the Governing Senate, 1711–
1911.)
Pobedonostsev, K. P. *Pis'ma k Aleksandru III,* vol. I (1865–1882) and vol. II
(1883–1894). Moscow, 1925–1926. (Pobedonostsev's letters to Alexander III.
Documents that are as important, as they are depressing.)
K. P. Pobedonostsev i ego korrespondenty: Pis'ma i zapiski, 2 vols. Moscow,
1923. (Correspondence of K. P. Pobedonostsev: letters and papers.)
Seredonin, S. M., I. I. Tkhorzhevskii, and N. I. Vuich, *Istoricheskii obzor
deiatel'nosti Komiteta Ministrov.* St. Petersburg, 1902. (A historical survey
of the activity of the Committee of Ministers.)
Russkii biograficheskii slovar', 25 vols. St. Petersburg, 1896–1918. (A Russian
biographical lexicon, published by the Russian Historical Society. Incomplete.)
Polnoe sobranie zakonov Rossiiskoi Imperii, St. Petersburg, 1830–1914. (Complete collection of the laws of the Russian Empire, in chronological order,
consisting of three series: 1st series, containing the laws of 1649–1825, in
45 volumes, was compiled under the guidance of M. M. Speransky and
published in 1830; 2d series, in 55 volumes, contains the laws from December 1825 through March 1881; 3d series, in 33 volumes, the laws of 1881–
1913.)
Svod zakonov Rossiiskoi Imperii. St. Petersburg, 1832. (A systematic Code of
Laws of the Russian Empire, compiled, in 15 volumes, under the guidance
of M. M. Speransky and published in 1832; 2d ed. followed in 1842; 3d
in 1857. The court reform of 1864 required the addition of a 16th volume,
and the constitutional reforms of 1906 required essential additions to the
first volume containing basic state laws: *Osnovnye gosudarstvennye zakony.*)
Russkaia Starina, M. I. Semevsky, ed. St. Petersburg, 1870–1918. (Russian
antiquity. A monthly containing numerous historical materials, including
those of the nineteenth century.)
Deviatnadsatyi Vek, P. Bartenev, ed., 2 vols, Moscow, 1872. (The nineteenth
century. The book contains mostly memoirs and letters from the first half
of the century; the second volume also includes interesting materials concerning the peasant question under Nicholas I.)
Istoricheskii Vestnik, S. N. Shubinsky, ed. St. Petersburg, 1880–1917. (Historical messenger. A popular monthly.)
Vigel', F. F., *Vospominaniia,* 7 vols. Moscow, 1864–1865. A more recent ed.:
Zapiski, 2 vols., Moscow, 1928. (Memoirs of F. F. Vigel'. Vividly written,
colorful, partly caustic, these memoirs from the first half of the nineteenth

century contain many interesting characteristics of contemporary writers and public figures, as well as details concerning the political, social, and cultural life.)

Witte, S. Iu., *Vospominaniia: Tsarstvovanie Nikolaia II*, 2 vols. Berlin, 1922. A more recent ed.: Moscow, 1960: 1st vol. (1849–1894); 2d vol. (1894–October 1905); 3d vol. (October 1905–1911). Count Witte, *The Memoirs*, A. Yarmolinsky, trans. and ed. New York, 1921. (Important and interesting testimonies of the great statesman who, however, after his retirement in 1906 became bitter and resentful against the tsar, the high bureaucracy, and the public, and therefore can not be considered an unbiased witness.)

3. Foreign Observers of the Russian Scene (before 1914)

Babey, Anna M., *Americans in Russia, 1776–1917: A Study of the American Travellers in Russia from the American Revolution to the Russian Revolution*. New York, 1938.

Baring, Maurice, *The Mainsprings of Russia*. New York, 1914 (An interesting and accurate description of the government machine, the oppositional movement, the church, education, and justice, as well as of the character and conditions of life of different social classes.)

Custine, Astolphe L. L., Marquis de, *La Russie en 1839*, 4 vols. Paris, 1843. Trans.: *Russia*, 3 vols., London, 1844; *Journey for Our Time: the Journals of the Marquis de Custine*, New York, 1951. (Contrary to his reputation in the West, the eloquent French marquis, who visited Russia in 1839, was essentially a very ignorant and superficial observer.)

Czartoryski, Prince Adam, *Memoirs and his Correspondence with Alexander I*, 2d ed., 2 vols. London, 1888. (An important testimony from Alexander's close, but later disillusioned, Polish friend.)

De Windt, Harry, *Russia as I know it*. London, 1917 (A friendly English traveler's impressions from his long journeys through European Russia and Siberia at the end of the nineteenth and the beginning of the twentieth centuries.)

————, *Siberia as it is*. London, 1892. (De Windt's impressions of Siberia and the life of the exiles were not as gloomy as Kennan's, see below.)

Graham, Stephen, *Undiscovered Russia*. London, 1912 (A series of essays, sketches, and observations of Russian daily life.)

Haxthausen, August Freiherr von, *Studien über die inneren Zustände, das Volksleben und insbesondere die ländlichen Einrichtungen Russlands*, 3 vols. Hanover, 1847–1852. English abr. trans.: *The Russian Empire, Its People, Institutions, and Resources*, 2 vols., London, 1856. (Haxthausen's work, based on solid studies and personal observations, contained a very detailed description of Russian country life. His "discovery" of the peasant land commune provided the impetus for a long debate on this subject in Russia.)

Kennan, George, *Siberia and the Exile System*, 2 vols. New York, 1891. New abr. ed.: Chicago, 1958. (The horrors of the exile system were exaggerated by Kennan, who believed every word of the exiles and therefore found in Siberia neither revolutionaries nor terrorists, but almost only well-intentioned liberals.)

Loubat, J. F., *Narrative of the Mission to Russia, in 1866, of the Hon. Gustavus Vasa Fox, Assistant Secretary of the Navy*. New York, 1874. (An interesting account of the general enthusiasm which greeted the American good-will mission through Russia.)

Pares, Sir Bernard, *My Russian Memoirs, 1898–1919*. London, 1931. (An eye-witness account of the fateful events during two revolutions and World War I.)

Putnam, Peter, ed., *Seven Britons in Imperial Russia 1698–1812*. Princeton, 1952. (Chap. 6, Robert Ker Porter: Court Painter of Panoramas [1805–1807]; chap. 7, Sir Robert Thomas Wilson: Cavalier of Cataclysm [1812].)

Stead, William T., *Truth about Russia*. New York, 1888. (A survey of Russian life under Alexander III and of Russian foreign policy.)

Wallace, Sir Donald Mackenzie, *Russia*. New York, 1877; rev. ed.: New York, 1905, 1912; Recent ed.: *Russia: On the Eve of War and Revolution*, C. E. Black, ed., New York, pb. ed., 1961. (An important account of Russia's social and political conditions given by a competent and conscientious witness who observed the Russian scene for almost forty years.)

Williams, Harold W. *Russia and the Russians*. New York, 1914. (A fairly detailed and truthful description of Russian political, social, and, in particular, cultural affairs on the eve of World War I.)

Wilson, Sir Robert, General, British Commissioner at the Headquarters of the Russian Army, *Narrative of Events during the Invasion of Russia by Napoleon Bonaparte, and the Retreat of the French Army, 1812*. London, 1860. (Wilson's account is interesting but does injustice to Kutuzov.)

4. Textbooks and General Surveys

Allen, William E. D., *The Ukraine: a History*. New York, 1941. (A balanced and objective study.)

Clarkson, Jesse D., *A History of Russia*. New York, 1961.

Florinsky, Michael T., *Russia: A History and an Interpretation*. New York, 1953, 1955. (Vol. 2 covers the nineteenth and the twentieth centuries. A detailed, factual narrative, based on thorough studies, but too pessimistic in its interpretation.)

———, ed., *Encyclopedia of Russia and the Soviet Union*. New York, 1961.

Harcave, Sidney S., ed., *Readings in Russian History*, vol. 1 (*From Ancient Times to the Abolition of Serfdom*) and vol. 2 (*The Modern Period*). New York, 1962.

———, *Russia, A History*. Philadelphia, 1952; 4th ed., 1959.

Hrushevsky, M. A., *A History of Ukraine*. New Haven, 1941. (Abr. ed. of the study by the leading Ukrainian nationalist historian.)

Istoriia Rossii v XIX veke, 9 vols., St. Petersburg [c. 1910]. (Russian history in the nineteenth century, publ. by the Granat Co. A series of articles and essays, partly scholarly, partly politically partisan.)

Karpovich, Michael M., *Imperial Russia, 1801–1917.* New York, 1932; repr., 1957. (A short but excellent survey.)

Kliuchevsky, V. O., *Kurs russkoi istorii,* vol. 5. Petrograd, 1922; Moscow, 1958. *A History of Russia,* C. J. Hogarth, trans., vol. 5, New York, 1931.

Kohn, Hans, *Basic History of Modern Russia: Political, Cultural and Social Trends.* Princeton, 1957. (A concise but good survey.)

Kornilov, A. A., *Kurs istorii Rossii XIX veka,* 3 vols. Moscow, 1918. Translation: *Modern Russia History from the Age of Catherine the Great to the End of the Nineteenth Century,* New York, 1943; 1952.

Lawrence, John W., *A History of Russia.* New York, 1960.

Leroy-Beaulieu, Anatole, *The Empire of the Tsars and the Russians* (trans. from the French), 3 vols. New York, 1893–1896; 1902–1903.

Mazour, Anatole G., *Russia: Past and Present,* New York, 1951.

———, *Russia: Tsarist and Communist.* Princeton, 1962.

———, *The Rise and Fall of the Romanovs.* Princeton, 1960. (Short, popular.)

Miliukov, P. N., *Ocherki po istorii russkoi kul'tury,* vol. 1 *(Naselenie, ekonomicheskii, gosudarstvennyi i soslovnyi stroi); vol. 2 (Tserkov' i shkola); vol. 3 (Natsionalizm i obshchestvennoe mnenie).* St. Petersburg, 1896–1899; republ. many times in Russia before 1917; rev. ed. vol. 1 (1st part) and vols. 2 and 3, Paris, 1930–1937. (Outlines of Russian culture: vol. 1 [Population, economic, political, and social structure]; vol. 2 [Religion (including dissenters) and education]; vol. 3 [Nationalism and public opinion]. For partial English translation, see section 10, below.)

———, Charles Seignobos, and L. Eisenmann, *Histoire de Russie,* 3 vols. Paris, 1932–1933.

Pares, Sir Bernard, *A History of Russia.* London, 1926; def. ed., New York, 1960.

Platonov, S. F. *Lektsii po russkoi istorii.* Petrograd, 1917. *History of Russia,* E. Aronsberg, trans., New York, 1925.

Pushkarev, S. G., *Obzor russkoi istorii.* New York, 1953. (Survey of Russian history to 1917.)

Riazanovsky, V. A., *Obzor russkoi kul'tury,* 2 vols. New York, 1947.

Sarolea, Charles, *Great Russia: Her Achievement and Promise.* New York, 1916. London ed. entitled: *Europe's Debt to Russia.*

Seton-Watson, Hugh, *The Decline of Imperial Russia, 1855–1914.* New York, 1952; pb. ed., 1961. (A balanced survey with special attention to the history of national minorities.)

Sliozberg, G. B., *Dorevoliutsionnyi stroi Rossii.* Paris, 1933. (Political and social structure of prerevolutionary Russia.)

Spector, Ivar, *An Introduction to Russian History and Culture.* Princeton, 1961; 1st ed., 1949.

Sumner, Benedict H., *A Short History of Russia.* New York, 1943; rev. ed., 1949. (Topically arranged.)

Thomson, Joan, *Russia: The Old and the New*. London, 1948. (A concise popular survey.)

Tompkins, Stuart R., *Russia through the Ages, from the Scythians to the Soviets*. New York, 1940.

Vernadsky, George, *Political and Diplomatic History of Russia*. Boston, 1936. (Chaps. 22–27 present a clear, precise, and reliable narrative of events from the beginning of the nineteenth century to the revolution of 1917–1918.)

——, *A History of Russia*. New Haven, 1929; 5th rev. ed., 1961. (Scholarly, clear, and objective, but the period 1801–1916 is given only some 100 pages.)

Walsh, Warren B., ed., *Readings in Russian History*, 3d ed. Syracuse, N.Y., 1959; 1st ed., 1948.

——, *Russia and the Soviet Union: A Modern History*. Ann Arbor, Mich., 1958.

Weidle, Wladimir, *Russia: Absent and Present*, A. G. Smith, trans. New York, 1952; pb. ed., 1961. (An interesting, if not always convincing, philosophy of Russian history.)

Wren, Melvin C., *The Course of Russian History*. New York, 1958. (A generally balanced survey, but unjust to Stolypin.)

5. Descriptions of Separate Periods by Reigns

Mel'gunov, S. P., *Dela i liudi aleksandrovskogo vremeni*. Berlin, 1923. (Events and persons of the time of Alexander I.)

Nikolai Mikhailovich, Grand Duke, *Imperator Aleksandr I*, 2 vols. St. Petersburg, 1912. (Includes contemporary documents and correspondence.)

Schilder, N. K., *Imperator Aleksandr I: Ego zhizn' i tsarstvovanie*, 4 vols. St. Petersburg, 1897–1898. (Emperor Alexander I: his life and reign. A basic work on the subject, with many important documents in appendices.)

Soloviev, S. M., *Imperator Aleksandr I: Politika—diplomatiia*. St. Petersburg, 1874. (Reprinted in *Sobranie sochinenii*, collected works, publ. by *Obshchestvennaia Pol'za* in the beginning of the twentieth century.)

Strakhovsky, Leonid. I., *Alexander I of Russia: The Man who defeated Napoleon*. New York, 1947.

Gershenzon, M. O., ed. *Epokha Nikolaia I*. Moscow, 1911. (a Collection of articles and documents pertaining to the period of Nicholas I.)

Grunwald, Constantine de, *Tsar Nicholas I*. New York, 1954. (Trans. from the French: *La vie de Nicholas Ier*, Paris, 1946.)

Polievktov, M., *Nikolai I. Biografiia i obzor tsarstvovaniia*. Moscow, 1918. (Nicholas I, a biography and a survey of the reign. A serious, scholarly work.)

Presniakov, A. E. *Apogei samoderzhaviia: Nikolai I*. Leningrad, 1925. (An apogee of autocracy: Nicholas I.)

Schiemann, Theodor, *Geschichte Russlands unter Kaiser Nikolaus I*, 4 vols. Berlin, 1904–1919. (History of Russia under Emperor Nicholas I. A "heavy" scholarly work based on detailed study, with special attention to military and diplomatic history.)

Shilder, N. K., *Imperator Nikolai I*, 2 vols. St. Petersburg, 1903. (A detailed narrative through 1831.)

Almendingen, E. M., *The Emperor Alexander II*. London, 1962. (Vivid popular narrative.)

Graham, Stephen, *Tsar of Freedom: The Life and Reign of Alexander II*. New Haven, 1935.

Mosse, Werner E., *Alexander II and the Modernization of Russia*. New York, 1958.

Tatishchev, S. S., *Imperator Aleksandr II: Ego zhizn' i tsarstvovanie*, 2 vols. St. Petersburg, 1911. (Emperor Alexander II, his life and reign. Indispensable detailed, factual account of the reign of Alexander II.)

Flourens, Emil Leopold, *Alexandre III, sa vie, son oeuvre*. Paris, 1894. (Alexander III, his life and his work.)

Lowe, Charles, *Alexander III of Russia*. New York, 1895.

Charques, Richard, *The Twilight of Imperial Russia*. Fairlawn, N.J., 1958; pb. ed., 1959. (Overly pessimistic in the evaluation of prerevolutionary Russia, but recognizing some essential changes for the better after 1905.)

Oldenburg, S. S., *Tsarstvovanie Imperatora Nikolaia II*. Vol. I, Belgrade, 1939; vol. II., Munich, 1949. (Detailed factual account, written from the monarchist point of view.)

Treadgold, Donald W., *Twentieth Century Russia*. Chicago, 1959. (Part I [New Currents in Old Russia] presents a clear and objective description of Russia's political, social, and cultural conditions before 1917.)

Troyat, Henry, *Daily Life in Russia under the Last Tsar*, M. Barnes, trans. New York, 1962; French ed.: *En Russie au temps du dernier Tsar*, Paris, 1959.

6. Political Developments: the Government and the Opposition

Burtsev, Vladimir, ed., *Za sto let, 1800–1896: Sbornik po istorii politicheskikh i obshchestvennykh dvizhenii v Rossii*. London, 1897. (Collection of materials concerning political and social movements in Russia.)

Iakushkin, V. E., *Gosudarstvennaia vlast' i proekty gosudarstvennoi reformy v Rossii*. St. Petersburg, 1906. (The government and plans for political reform in Russia.)

Venturi, Franco, *Roots of Revolution: A History of the Populist and Socialist Movements in Nineteenth Century Russia*. New York, 1960. (Trans. from the Italian.)

Yarmolinsky, Avrahm, *Road to Revolution: A Century of Russian Radicalism*. New York, 1959.

1801–1855: THE GOVERNMENT; THE DECEMBRISTS; THE PETRASHEVTSY

Speransky, M. M., *Plan gosudarstvennogo preobrazovaniia 1809 goda.* Moscow, 1905. (Speransky's plan of a state reform, 1809.)

——, *Proekty i zapiski,* S. N. Valk, ed. Moscow, 1961. (Speransky's projects and memoranda, including the plan of 1809.)

Korf, M. N., *Zhizn' grafa Speranskago,* 2 vols. St. Petersburg, 1861. (The life of Count Speransky.)

Raeff, Marc, *Michael Speransky, Statesman of Imperial Russia, 1772–1839.* The Hague, 1957.

——, *Siberia and the Reform of 1822.* Seattle, 1956.

Nikolai Mikhailovich, Grand Duke, *Graf P. A. Stroganov,* 3 vols. St. Petersburg, 1903. (Biography and correspondence of a friend and aide to Alexander I.)

Monas, Sidney, *The Third Section: Police and Society in Russia under Nicholas I.* Cambridge, Mass., 1961.

Vosstanie dekabristov: Materialy, 11 vols. Moscow, 1925–1958. (The Decembrist uprising: materials.)

Izbrannye sotsial'no-politicheskie i filosofskie proizvedeniia dekabristov, 3 vols. Moscow, 1951. (Selected sociopolitical and philosophical works of the Decembrists.)

Dekabristy: materialy i dokumenty. Moscow, 1926.

Obshchestvennye dvizheniia v Rossii v pervuiu polovinu XIX veka, vol. 1 *(Zapiski i vospominaniia M. A. Fon-Vizina, kniazia E. P. Obolenskago i barona Shteingelia),* V. I. Semevsky, V. Bogucharsky, and P. E. Shchegolev, eds. St. Petersburg, 1905. (Social movements in Russia during thee first half of the nineteenth century; memoranda and memoirs of M. A. Fon-Vizin, Prince E. P. Obolensky, and Baron Shteingel.)

Memuary dekabristov, M. V. Dovnar-Zapolsky, ed. Kiev, 1906.

Bestuzhevy, Nikolai, Mikhail, and Petr, *Vospominaniia.* Moscow, 1931. (The memoirs of the brothers Bestuzhev.)

Gorbachevsky, I. I., *Zapiski i pis'ma dekabrista.* Moscow, 1925. (Memoirs and letters of the Decembrist Gorbachevsky.)

Iakushkin, I. D., *Zapiski.* St. Petersburg, 1905. (Memoirs.)

Pestel', P. I., *Russkaia Pravda: nakaz Vremennomu Verkhovnomu Pravleniiu.* St. Petersburg, 1906. (The Russian law: an instruction for the supreme provisional government. New ed.: Moscow, 1958, in *Vosstanie dekabristov,* vol. VII.)

Rozen, Baron A. E. *Zapiski dekabrista.* St. Petersburg, 1907.

Trubetskoi, Prince S. P., *Zapiski.* St. Petersburg, 1906.

Mezhdutsarstvie 1825 goda i vosstanie dekabristov v perepiske i memuarakh chlenov tsarskoi sem'i. Moscow, 1926. (The interregnum of 1825 and the Decembrist uprising as reflected in the memoirs and the correspondence of the imperial family.)

Dovnar-Zapolsky, M. V., *Tainoe obshchestvo dekabristov.* Moscow, 1906. (The Decembrist secret society.)

————, *Idealy dekabristov.* Moscow, 1907.

Mazour, Anatole G., *The First Russian Revolution, 1825: the Decembrist Movement.* Berkeley, 1937; 2d print., Stanford, 1961.

Nechkina, M. V., *Vosstanie 14 dekabria 1825 goda.* Moscow, 1951. (The uprising of December, 1825.)

————, *Dvizhenie dekabristov,* 2 vols. Moscow, 1955. (The Decembrist movement.)

Presniakov, A. E., *14 dekabria 1825 goda.* Moscow, 1926.

Pypin, A. N., *Obshchestvennoe dvizhenie v Rossii pri Aleksandre I,* 4th ed. St. Petersburg, 1908. (The social movement in Russia under Alexander I.)

Semevsky, V. I., *Politicheskie i obshchestvennye idei dekabristov.* St. Petersburg, 1909. (The political and social ideas of the Decembrists.)

Zetlin, Mikhail, *The Decembrists,* G. Panin, trans. New York, 1958.

Petrashevtsy: Sbornik materialov, 3 vols., P. E. Shchegolev, ed. Moscow, 1926–1928. (A collection of materials on the Petrashevtsy.)

Delo Petrashevtsev, 3 vols. Moscow, 1937, 1941, 1951. (The trial of the Petrashevtsy.)

Filosofskie i obshchestvenno-politicheskie proizvedeniia Petrashevtsev. Moscow, 1953. (Works.)

Semevsky, V. I., *M. V. Butashevich-Petrashevskii i Petrashevtsy,* in *Sobranie sochinenii,* vol. II. Moscow, 1922. (Collected works.)

1855–1881: THE GREAT REFORMS AND THE POPULIST REVOLUTIONARY MOVEMENT

Davydov, N. I. and N. N. Poliansky, eds., *Sudebnaia reforma,* 2 vols. Moscow, 1915. (The court reform.)

Dzhanshiev, G., *Epokha velikikh reform,* 9th ed. St. Petersburg, 1905; 1st ed., 1892. (The period of the Great Reforms. A series of popular essays and sketches.)

Kucherov, Samuel, *Courts, Lawyers, and Trials under the Last Three Tsars.* New York, 1953.

Zaionchkovsky, P. A., *Voennye reformy 1860–1870 godov v Rossii.* Moscow, 1952. (The military reforms of 1860–1870.)

Bogucharsky, V. (alias B. Bazilevsky, pseuds. of V. Ia. Iakovlev), *Aktivnoe narodnichestvo semidesiatykh godov,* Moscow, 1912. (Active populism of the 1870s.)

————, ed. *Gosudarstvennye prestupleniia v Rossii v XIX veke,* 3 vols. St. Petersburg, 1906. (Political crimes in Russia in the nineteenth century; records of trials.)

————, *Literatura partii Narodnoi Voli.* Paris, 1905. (Literature of the party of the "People's Will.")

————, *Materialy dlia istorii revoliutsionnogo dvizheniia v Rossii v 60-kh godakh.* St. Petersburg, 1906. (Materials for the history of the revolutionary movement of the 1860s.)

———, *Revoliutsionnaia zhurnalistika semidesiatykh godov*. Rostov-on-Don, 1906 (The revolutionary journalism of the 1870s.)

Delo 1-go marta 1881 goda. Odessa, 1906. (The trial of the assassins of Alexander II: official record.)

Footman, David, *Red Prelude: the Life of the Russian Terrorist Zhelyabov*. New Haven, 1945.

Glinsky, B., *Revoliutsionnyi period russkoi istorii (1861–1881)*, 2 vols. St. Petersburg, 1913.

Kluge, Ernfried Eduard, *Die russische revolutionäre Presse in der zweiten Hälfte des neunzehnten Jahrhunderts, 1855–1905*. Zurich, 1948.

Kornilov, A., *Obshchestvennoe dvizhenie pri Alexandre II*. Moscow, 1909. (The social movement during 1855–1881.)

Kropotkin, P. A., *Zapiski revoliutsionera*, N. K. Lebedev, ed. Moscow and Leningrad, 1933; 1st ed., in Russian, London, 1902. Trans.: *Memoirs of a Revolutionist*. Boston, 1930; 1st ed., in English, London, 1899; new ed. by J. A. Rogers, New York, 1962.

Lemke, M., ed., *Politicheskie protsessy v Rossii 60-kh godov*, 2d ed. Moscow, 1923; 1st ed., 1907. (Political trials in Russia in the 1860s.)

Nechaev i Nechaevtsy; sbornik materialov. Moscow, 1931. (A collection of documents concerning Nechaev and his circle, published by Tsentrarkhiv.)

Nomad, Max (pseud.), *Apostles of Revolution*. Boston, 1939. (Includes Bakunin and Nechaev.)

Prawdin, Michael (*pseud.* of M. Charol), *The Unmentionable Nechaev: A Key to Bolshevism*. London, 1961. (Part I, Nechaev; part II, Lenin.)

Stepniak, S. (S. M. Kravchinsky), *Underground Russia: Revolutionary Profiles and Sketches from Life*. New York, 1883. Moscow, 1960.

1881–1914: THE REVOLUTION OF 1905–1906; THE REFORMS OF THE STATE STRUCTURE; AND THE POLITICAL DEVELOPMENTS DURING THE DUMA PERIOD

Revoliutsiia 1905–1907 godov v Rossii: Dokumenty i materialy, 14 vols. (to date). Moscow, 1955–1962. (This important collection, published by the Academy of Sciences of the USSR, presents an enormous, but poorly organized mass of documents, including government reports, revolutionary leaflets and resolutions, newspaper reportages, and the like.)

Lazarevsky, N. I., *Zakonodatel'nye akty perekhodnogo vremeni* (see above, section 2.)

Martov, L., P. Maslov, and A. Potresov, eds. *Obshchestvennoe dvizhenie v Rossii v nachale XX veka*, 5 vols. St. Petersburg, 1909–1914. (The social and political movement in Russia at the beginning of the twentieth century, edited by three Menshevik leaders.)

Axelrod, P. B., *Dve taktiki*. St. Petersburg, 1907. (A pamphlet outlining the tactical differences between the Bolsheviks and the Mensheviks.)

Bock, Mary P., *Vospominaniia o moem otse P. A. Stolypine*. New York, 1953. (Daughter's reminiscences of P. A. Stolypin.)

Chasles, Pierre, *Le Parlament russe: Son organisation, ses rapports avec l'Emperor.* Paris, 1910. (The Russian parliament: its organization and its relations with the emperor.)

Chernov, Viktor, *Zapiski sotsialista-revoliutsionera.* Berlin, 1922. (Memoirs of a Socialist Revolutionary.

————, *Pered burei: Vospominaniia.* New York, 1953. (Before the storm: memoirs.)

Dan, F. I., *Proiskhozhdenie Bol'shevizma.* New York, 1946. (The origins of Bolshevism.)

Gernet, M. N., *Istoriia tsarskoi tiur'my,* 3 vols., 3d ed. Moscow, 1960–1961; 1st ed., 1941. (History of the tsarist prison.)

Harper, Samuel N., *The New Electoral Law for the Russian Duma.* Chicago, 1908.

Korkunov, N. M., *Russkoe gosudarstvennoe pravo,* 2 vols. St. Petersburg, 1913. (Russian state law.)

Lazarevsky, N. I. *Lektsii po russkomu gosudarstvennomu pravu,* vol. I *(Konstitutsionnoe pravo).* St. Petersburg, 1908. (Lectures on Russian state law, vol. I [Constitutional law].)

Lenin, V. I. (Ulianov), *Sochineniia,* 30 vols., 2d ed. Moscow, 1926–1932; 4th ed., 38 vols. and Index, 1941–1958. (Among the prolific writings of Lenin, published either individually or in collections, the second Soviet edition of his collected works, which appeared before the full triumph of "Stalinism," is most useful. It contains extensive explanatory notes with many factual data, a glossary of names with biographical statements, a chronology of events, and numerous documents relating to the period. For English editions, see *Selected Works,* 12 vols., New York, 1935–1938, and *The Essential of Lenin,* 2 vols., London, 1947.)

Meyer, Alfred G., *Leninism.* Cambridge, Mass., 1957. (The author emphasizes the "extreme flexibility" of Leninism.)

Shub, David, *Lenin: A Biography.* Garden City, N.Y., 1948.

Treadgold, Donald W., *Lenin and His Rivals: The Struggle for Russia's Future, 1898–1906.* New York, 1955.

Vernadsky, George, *Lenin, Red Dictator.* New Haven, 1931.

Levin, Alfred, *The Second Duma: A Study of the Social-Democratic Party and the Russian Constitutional Experiment.* New Haven, 1940.

Levitsky, Serge, *The Russian Duma: Studies in Parliamentary Procedure, 1906–1917.* New York, 1958.

Maievsky, B. A., *Borets za blago Rossii.* Madrid, 1962. (A fighter for Russia's weal. Popular account of Stolypin's activities and his tragic death.)

Maklakov, V. A., *Vlast' i obshchestvennost' na zakate staroi Rossii: vospominaniia sovremennika.* Paris, 1932. (Government and society in the twilight of old Russia: memoirs of a contemporary.)

————, *Iz vospominanii.* New York, 1954.

————, *Pervaia Gosudarstvennaia Duma.* Paris, 1939. (The First Duma.)

————, *Vtoraia Gosudarstvennaia Duma.* Paris, n.d. (The Second Duma. All the above quoted works of V. A. Maklakov, a lawyer by profession, present the viewpoint of moderate, balanced liberalism, an outlook rare among the Russian intelligentsia.)

Miliukov, P. N., *God bor'by*. St. Petersburg, 1907. (A year of struggle, 1905–1906.)

————, *Vtoraia Gosudarstvennaia Duma*. St. Petersburg, 1908.

————, *Vospominaniia, 1859–1917*, 2 vols. New York, 1955.

Nikolaevskii, B. *Azeff, the Spy: Russian Terrorist and Police Stool*. Garden City, N.Y., 1934.

Pares, Sir Bernard, *Russia and Reform*. London, 1907.

Plekhanov, G. V. (see below, sect. 9).

Protokoly zasedanii soveshchaniia . . . po peresmotru osnovnykh gosudarstvennykh zakonov. St. Petersburg, 1906. (Minutes of the proceedings of a conference of high government officials, presided at by the tsar, regarding the revision of the fundamental state laws, in April 1906.)

Polnyi sbornik platform vsekh russkikh politicheskikh partii. St. Petersburg, 1907. (A full collection of the programs of Russian political parties.)

Tretii ocherednoi s'ezd Rossiiskoi Sotsial-Demokraticheskoi Rabochei Partii: Polnyi text protokolov. Geneva, 1905. (The third regular congress of the Russian Social Democratic Workers' party: minutes of proceedings. The congress was, in fact, a Bolshevik one.)

Protokoly ob'edinitel'nogo s'ezda Rossiiskoi Sotsial-Demokraticheskoi Rabochei Partii, sostoiavshegosia v Stokholme v 1906 godu. Moscow, 1907. (Minutes of the Unification Congress of the Russian Social Democratic Workers' party in 1906 in Stockholm.)

Londonskii S'ezd Rossiiskoi Sotsial-Demokraticheskoi Rabochei Partii . . . v 1907 godu. Polnyi text protokolov. Paris, 1909. (Minutes of the London Congress of the Russian SD Workers' party in 1907.)

Protokoly pervago s'ezda Partii Sotsialistov-Revoliutsionerov. n.p., 1906. (Minutes of the First Congress of the SR party, which adopted the party program.)

Petergofskoe soveshchanie o proekte Gosudarstvennoi Dumy. Berlin, 1912. (A report on a meeting of cabinet members and other high officials with regard to the establishment of the State Duma in July 1905.)

Spiridovich, A. I. *Istoriia bol'shevizma v Rossii ot vozniknoveniia do zakhvata vlasti, 1883–1903–1917, s prilozheniem dokumentov i portretov*. Paris, 1922. (A history of Bolshevism in Russia, 1883–1917, with documents and portraits, by a general of the tsarist political police.)

Szeftel, Marc, The Political Institutions of the Russian Constitutional Monarchy 1905–1917. (In preparation.)

Trotsky, Leon, *My Life*. New York, 1930.

Walkin, Jacob, *The Rise of Democracy in Pre-Revolutionary Russia: Political and Social Institutions under the Last Three Czars*. New York, 1962.

Wolfe, Bertram D., *Three Who Made a Revolution*. New York, 1948; 3d ed., 1961. (Lenin, Trotsky, and Stalin.)

Zenkovskii, A. V. *Pravda o Stolypine.* New York, 1957. (Truth about Stolypin. Written by one of Stolypin's subordinates.)

7. Social and Economic Conditions (except Agriculture and the Peasantry)

GENERAL SOURCES AND SURVEYS

Statisticheskii ezhegodnik Rossii (see above, sect. 2).
Narodnoe khoziaistvo v 1913 godu. Petrograd, 1914. (The national economy in 1913. A yearbook published by the Ministry of Finance.)
Aziatskaia Rossiia, 3 vols. St. Petersburg, 1914 (Asian Russia, a description of Siberia published by *Pereselencheskoe Upravlenie,* the Resettlement Administration.)

Black, Cyril E., ed., *The Transformation of Russian Society: Aspects of Social Change since 1861.* Cambridge, Mass., 1960.
Khromov, P. A., *Ekonomicheskoe razvitie Rossii v XIX–XX vekakh, 1800–1917.* Moscow, 1950. (Russia's economic development, 1800–1917.)
Liashchenko, P. I., *Istoriia narodnogo khoziaistva SSSR,* 3 vols., 3d ed. Moscow, 1952–1956; 1st ed., 1939, 2 vols. (Vol. 3 of the 3d ed. covers the Soviet period.) Trans.: *History of the National Economy of Russia to the 1917 Revolution,* New York, 1949.
Mavor, James, *An Economic History of Russia,* 2 vols. New York, 1925.
Maynard, John, *Russia in Flux Before October.* London, 1941.
Mendeleev, D. I. *K poznaniiu Rossii,* 7th ed. St. Petersburg, 1912. (Toward an understanding of Russia. The famed scientist's essays commenting on the 1897 census.)
Mirsky, D. S., *Russia, a Social History.* London, 1931.
Sering, Max, ed., *Russlands Kultur und Volkswirtschaft.* Berlin, 1913. (Russia's culture and national economy.)
Wright, G. F., *Asiatic Russia,* 2 vols. New York, 1902.

INDUSTRY, COMMERCE, AND FINANCE

Brandt, V. F., *Inostrannye kapitaly: Ikh vlianie na ekonomicheskoe razvitie strany,* 2 vols. St. Petersburg, 1898–1899. (The influence of foreign capital on the economic development of Russia.)
Finn-Enotaevsky, A., *Kapitalizm v Rossii (1890–1917),* 2d ed. Moscow, 1925.
Gindin, I. F., *Banki i promyshlennost' v Rossii do 1917 goda.* Moscow, 1927. (Banks and industry in Russia before 1917.)
———, *Russkie kommercheskie banki.* Moscow, 1948 (Russian commercial banks.)
———, *Gosudarstvennyi bank i ekonomicheskaia politika tsarskogo pravitel'stva (1861–1892).* Moscow, 1960. (The State Bank and the economic policy of the tsarist government in 1861–1892.)
Migulin, P. P., *Russkii gosudarstvennyi kredit (1769–1903),* 3 vols. Kharkov, 1899–1904. (Russia's state credit in 1769–1903.)

Miller, Margaret S., *The Economic Development of Russia, 1905–1914: With Special Reference to Trade, Industry and Finance.* London, 1937.

Ol', P. V., *Inostrannye kapitaly v Rossii.* Petrograd, 1922. (Foreign capital in Russia.)

Rafalovich, A., *Russia: Its Trade and Commerce.* London, 1918 (Statistics.)

Sobolev, M. N., *Tamozhennaia politika Rossii vo vtoroi polovine XIX veka.* Tomsk, 1911. (Russia's tariff policy in the second half of the nineteenth century.)

Tugan-Baranovsky, M., *Russkaia fabrika v proshlom i nastoiashchem,* 7th ed. Moscow, 1938; 1st ed., 1898. (The Russian factory in the past and the present.)

Ziv, V. S., *Inostrannyi kapital v russkikh aktsionernykh predpriiatiiakh.* Moscow, 1917. (Foreign capital in Russian joint-stock companies.)

INSTITUTIONS OF PUBLIC LIFE: ZEMSTVO, CITIES, COOPERATIVES

Bilimovich, A. D., *Kooperatsiia v Rossii.* Franfurt am Main, 1955.

Blanc, E. T., *Co-operative Movement in Russia.* New York, 1924.

Bubnoff, J. V., *The Co-operative Movement in Russia.* Manchester, 1917.

The Coöperative Movement in Russia during the War. New Haven, 1929. (E. M. Keyden gives a concise survey of cooperative development in Russia in general and of consumers' societies in particular and A. N. Antsiferov describes the development of credit cooperation before the war.)

Ditiatin, I., *Ustroistvo i upravlenie gorodov v Rossii,* vol. 2. Yaroslavl, 1877. (The organization and administration of cities in Russia.)

Ozerov, I., *Bol'shie goroda, ikh zadachi i sredstva upravleniia.* Moscow, 1906. (Large cities, their tasks and means of administration.)

Polner, T. J., *Russian Local Government during the War and the Union of the Zemstvos.* New Haven, 1930. (Chaps. 1 and 2 give an account of Zemstvo activities before the war.)

Prokopovich, S., *Kooperativnoe dvizhenie v Rossii.* Moscow, 1913. (The cooperative movement in Russia.)

Veselovsky, B., *Istoriia zemstva za 40 let,* 4 vols. St. Petersburg, 1909–1911. (A history of the Zemstvos, 1864–1905.)

Vinogradoff, P., *Self-Government in Russia.* London, 1915. (Concise but valuable survey.)

V. V. [Vorontsov], *Artel' v kustarnom promysle,* 2 vols. St. Petersburg, 1895. (The artel-type association in the domestic craft industry.)

DISTINCT SOCIAL GROUPS

Berlin, P. A., *Russkaia burzhuaziia v staroe i novoe vremia.* Moscow, 1922. (The Russian bourgeoisie in old and new times.)

Bill, Valentine T., *The Forgotten Class: The Russian Bourgeoisie from the Earliest Beginnings to 1900.* New York, 1959.

Buryshkin, P. A., *Moskva kupecheskaia.* New York, 1954. (Merchants' Moscow.)

Cresson, William P., *The Cossacks, their History and Country.* New York, 1919.

Dubnow, S. M., *History of the Jews in Russia and Poland from the Earliest Times until the Present,* 3 vols. Philadelphia, 1916–1920. (Trans. from the Russian.)

Greenberg, Louis and M. Wischnitzer, *The Jews in Russia,* vol. I (1801–1881); vol. II (1881–1917). New Haven, 1944, 1951.

Korf, S. A., *Dvorianstvo i ego soslovnoe upravlenie za stoletie 1762–1855.* St. Petersburg, 1906. (The nobility and its organization, 1762–1855.)

Rashin, A. G., *Formirovanie rabochego klassa Rossii.* Moscow, 1940; rev. ed., 1958. (The formation of the working class in Russia.)

Romanovich-Slovatinsky, A. V., *Dvorianstvo v Rossii ot nachala XVIII veka do otmeny krepostnogo prava.* St. Petersburg, 1870; 2d ed., Kiev, 1912. (The Russian nobility from the beginning of the eighteenth century to the abolition of serfdom.)

Sliozberg, G. V., *Dela minuvshikh dnei: zapiski russkago evreia,* 3 vols. Paris, 1933–1934. (Out of the past: memoirs of a Russian Jew.)

Turin, S. P., *From Peter the Great to Lenin: A History of the Russian Labour Movement with special Reference to Trade Unionism.* London, 1935.

Zenkovsky, Serge A., *Pan-Turkism and Islam in Russia.* Cambridge, Mass., 1960.

8. Agriculture and the Agrarian Problem: the Peasantry and the Mir

THE 1801–1861 PERIOD; THE ABOLITION OF SERFDOM

Semenov, N. P., ed., *Osvobozhdenie krest'ian v tsarstvovanie Imperatora Aleksandra II: Khronika deiatel'nosti komissii po krest'ianskomu delu,* 3 vols. St. Petersburg, 1889–1892. (The liberation of the peasants under Alexander II: a chronicle of the activities of the so-called Editing Commissions. Documentary material of primary importance.)

Skrebitsky, A., *Krest'ianskoe delo v tsarstvovanie Imperatora Aleksandra II: Materialy dlia istorii osvobozhdeniia krest'ian,* 4 vols. Bonn, 1862. (Peasant affairs under Alexander II: materials for the history of the liberation of the peasants.)

Zhurnaly Sekretnago i Glavnogo Komitetov po krest'ianskomu delu, 1857–1861, 2 vols. Petrograd, 1915. (The records of the Secret Committee and the Chief Committee on peasant affairs, 1857–1861.)

Zhurnaly i memorii obshchago sobraniia Gosudarstvennogo Soveta po krest'ianskomu delu (v ianvare-marte 1861 goda). Petrograd, 1915. (Records and memoranda of the general session of the State Council concerning peasant affairs, in January–March 1861.)

Blum, Jerome, *Lord and Peasant in Russia from the Ninth to the Nineteenth Century.* Princeton, 1961. (For the period 1801–1861 the book gives an excellent account written with a thorough knowledge of the subject.)

Druzhinin, N. M., *Gosudarstvennye krest'iane i reforma P. D. Kiseleva,* 2 vols. Moscow, 1946–1958. (State peasants and the reform of P. D. Kiselev. An important work based on thorough documentary evidence.)

Ignatovich, I. I., *Pomeshchii krest'iane nakanune osvobozhdeniia,* 3d ed, Leningrad, 1925; 1st ed., 1902. (The serfs on the eve of liberation.)

Ivaniukov, I., *Padenie krepostnogo prava v Rossii.* St. Petersburg, 1903. (The abolition of serfdom in Russia. A good, factual account.)

Kornilov, A. A., *Krest'ianskaia reforma.* St. Petersburg, 1905. (The peasant reform of 1861.)

Pushkarev, S. G., *Proiskhozhdenie krest'ianskoi pozemel'no-peredel'noi obshchiny,* in *Zapiski Russkogo nauchno-issledovatel'skogo ob'edineniia v Prage,* Nos. 67 and 77. Prague, 1939, 1941. (The origins of the peasant repartitional land commune in Russia, in the Proceedings of the Russian Research Society in Prague, Nos. 67 and 77.)

Velikaia reforma, A. K. Dzhivelegov, S. P. Melgunov, and V. I. Picheta, eds., 6 vols. Moscow, 1911. (A series of articles and essays dealing with various aspects of the 1861 peasant reform. Some of the articles are scholarly and objective, others politically partisan.)

Semevsky, V. I., *Krest'ianskii vopros v XVIII i pervoi polovine XIX veka,* 2 vols. St. Petersburg, 1888. (The peasant question in the eighteenth and the first half of the nineteenth century. A detailed account of how the peasant question was discussed in government circles and in the contemporary literature and the press.)

Zablotsky-Desiatovsky, A. P., *Graf P. D. Kiselev i ego vremia,* 4 vols. St. Petersburg, 1882. (Count P. D. Kiselev and his time. Vols. 2 and 4 provide valuable information on the peasant question.)

Zaionchkovsky, P. A., *Otmena krepostnogo prava v Rossii.* Moscow, 1954. (The abolition of serfdom in Russia.)

———, *Provedenie v zhizn' krest'ianskoi reformy 1861 goda.* Moscow, 1958. (The realization of the peasant reform of 1861. Zaionchkovsky's works contain valuable factual details and statistics, but in his Marxist-Leninist interpretation the author sometimes reaches the depths of absurdity.)

THE 1861–1916 PERIOD

Agrarnye programmy. Moscow, 1906. (Agrarian platforms of different political parties, with a preface by P. Maslov, the SD agrarian theoretician.)

Agrarnyi vopros v Sovete Ministrov v 1906 godu. Moscow, 1924. (The agrarian question as discussed by the Council of Ministers in 1906. Documents.)

Chelintsev, A. N., *Sostoianie i razvitie russkogo sel'skogo khoziaistva po dannym perepisi 1916 goda.* Kharkov, 1918. (The status and the development of the Russian rural economy according to the census of 1916.)

———, *Russkoe sel'skoe khoziaistvo pered revoliutsiei.* Moscow, 1928. (The Russian rural economy on the eve of the revolution.)

Dolgorukov, P. D. and S. L. Tolstoy, eds., *Krest'ianskii stroi.* St. Petersburg, 1905. (The social order of the peasants.)

Dolgorukov, P. D. and I. I. Petrunkevich, eds., *Agrarnyi vopros*, 2 vols. Moscow, 1905–1907. (The agrarian question.)

Dubrovsky, S. M., *"Stolypinskaia reforma"; kapitalizatsiia sel'skogo khoziaistva v XX veke.* Leningrad, 1925. (The "Stolypin reform"; development of capitalism in the rural economy in the twentieth century.)

Efimenko, A., *Issledovania narodnoi zhizni.* Moscow, 1884. (Studies of the common people's life.)

Kachorovsky, K. R., *Russkaia obshchina*, 2d ed. Moscow, 1906. (The Russian land commune.)

——, *Narodnoe pravo.* Moscow, 1906. (The people's common law.)

Kaufman, A. A., *Agrarnyi vopros v Rossii.* Moscow, 1908; 2d ed., 1919. (The agrarian question in Russia. Scholarly and objective.)

——, *Russkaia obshchina v protsesse eia zarozhdeniia i rosta.* Moscow, 1908. (The Russian land commune in the process of its origin and growth.)

Khodsky, L. V., *Zemlia i zemledelets*, vol. 2. Moscow, 1899. (The land and the agriculturist.)

Kofod, A. A., *Russkoe zemleustroistvo.* St. Petersburg, 1914. (The land organization in Russia.)

Kosinsky, V. A., *Osnovnye tendentsii v mobilizatsii zemel'noi sobstvennosti.* Prague, 1925. (The basic tendencies in land ownership transactions. Detailed statistics.)

Kovalevsky, M., *Modern Customs and Ancient Laws of Russia.* London, 1912.

Lokhtin, P., *Sostoianie sel'skogo khoziaistva v Rossii sravnitel'no s drugimi stranami.* St. Petersburg, 1901. (The state of agriculture in Russia as compared to other countries.)

Maslov, P., *Agrarnyi vopros v Rossii*, 2 vols. St. Petersburg, 1905–1908; 6th ed., Moscow, 1926. (The agrarian problem in Russia.)

Maynard, John, *The Russian Peasant and Other Studies.* London, 1942; 1st ed., 1912.

Nuzhdy derevni po rabotam komitetov o nuzhdakh sel'skokhoziaistvennoi promyshlennosti. St. Petersburg, 1904. (The needs of the countryside as indicated by studies of local conferences on the needs of the "agricultural industry." A summary of their findings covering different aspects of rural life.)

Oganovsky, N. P., *Sel'skoe khoziaistvo Rossii v XX veke, 1901–1923.* Moscow, 1923. (Russian agriculture, 1901–1923.)

Owen, Launcelot A., *The Russian Peasant Movement 1906–1917.* London, 1937.

Pavlovsky, G. A., *Agricultural Russia on the Eve of the Revolution.* London, 1930. (A good, well-founded account.)

Posnikov, A. S., *Obshchinnoe zemlevladenie v Rossii.* Yaroslavl, 1875. (Communal land ownership in Russia.)

Preyer, W. D., *Die russische Agrarreform.* Jena, 1914.

Prokopovich, S. N., *Krestianskoe khoziaistvo.* Berlin, 1924. (Peasant husbandry.)

Rittich, A. A., *Zavisimost' krest'ian ot obshchiny i mira.* St. Petersburg, 1903. (The dependence of the peasants on the land commune and the mir.)

———, *Krest'ianskoe zemlepol'zovanie.* St. Petersburg, 1903. (The peasant land use.)

———, *Krest'ianskii pravoporiadok.* St. Petersburg, 1904. (The legal status of the peasants.)

Robinson, Geroid T., *Rural Russia under the Old Regime.* New York, 1932; 3d ed., 1957. (An excellent factual account based on exhaustive studies of sources, occasionally overpessimistic in interpretation.)

Shestakov, A. V., *Krest'ianskaia revoliutsiia 1905–1907 godov v Rossii.* Moscow, 1926. (The agrarian riots of 1905–1907 in Russia.)

Stepniak (S. M. Kravchinsky), *The Russian Peasantry: Their Agrarian Condition, Social Life, and Religion.* New York, 1905; 1st ed., 1888.

Treadgold, Donald W., *The Great Siberian Migration.* Princeton, 1957. (An excellent description of the great Siberian migration up to World War I, which also presents a clear and accurate image of the peasant in European Russia.)

Wieth-Knudsen, K. A., *Bauernfrage und Agrarreform in Russland.* Munich, 1913. (The peasant question and the agrarian reform in Russia.)

9. Social and Political Thought and Doctrine; History of the Russian Intelligentsia

Aksakov, Konstantin S., *Sochineniia*, vol. 1. Moscow, 1861. (Collected works.)

Aksakov, Ivan S., *Polnoe sobranie sochinenii*, 7 vols. Moscow, 1886–1887. (Complete collection of works. Vols. 1 and 2, *Slavianskii vopros 1860–1886* and *Slavianofil'stvo i zapadnichestvo*, contain an extensive, if piecemeal, exposition of Slavophile ideas.)

Bakunin, M. A., *Izbrannye sochineniia*, 5 vols. Petrograd and Moscow, 1920–1922. (Selected works published by the anarchist group *Golos Truda*.)

———, *Sobranie sochinenii i pisem*, Iu. M. Steklov, ed., 4 vols. Moscow, 1934–1935. (Collected works and letters, through 1861.)

———, *Oeuvres*, 6 vols. Paris, 1907–1913. (Bakunin's works in French.)

The Political Philosophy of Bakunin: Scientific Anarchism, G. P. Maximoff, comp. and ed. Glencoe, Ill., 1953. (A collection of quotations from Bakunin.)

Carr, Edward H., *Michael Bakunin.* London, 1937; rev. ed., 1961.

Pyziur, Eugene, *The Doctrine of Anarchism of Michael A. Bakunin.* Milwaukee, 1955.

Steklov, Iu., *M. A. Bakunin, ego zhizn' i deiatel'nost'*, 4 vols. Moscow, 1926–1927. (Michael Bakunin's life and activity.)

Belinsky, V. G., *Polnoe sobranie sochinenii*, 13 vols. Moscow, 1953–1956. (Complete collection of works, published by the Academy of Sciences of the USSR.)

———, *Selected Philosophical Works.* Moscow, 1948.

Berdyaev, N. A., *Dukhovnyi krizis intelligentsii*. St. Petersburg, 1910. (The spiritual crisis of the intelligentsia.)

———, *The Origin of Russian Communism*. London, 1937; 2d ed., 1948.

———, *Russkaia ideia; osnovnye problemy russkoi mysli XIX veka i nachala XX veka*. Paris, 1946. (Basic problems of the Russian thought in the nineteenth and the beginning of the twentieth centuries.) Trans.: *The Russian Idea*, London, 1947. (Though Berdyaev's works are quite popular, I agree with the criticism of Prof. N. Poltoratsky, who stated: "The Russian Idea—a book which at first sight looks facile and conclusive—is, in many respects, built on psychological and historical sand. . . . One may detect in this work some of the defects peculiar to Berdyaev as a thinker and writer: subjectivity and shaky conceptual foundations, dialectical duplicity, discrepancies and paradoxicality," *Russian Review*, April 1962, pp. 135 and 122.)

Bulgakov, S. N., *Ot marksizma k idealizmu*. St. Petersburg, 1904. (From Marxism to idealism. A collection of articles written in 1896–1903.)

Chaadaev, P. Ia., *Sochineniia i pis'ma*, M. Gershenzon, ed., 2 vols. Moscow, 1913–1914. (Works and letters. Chaadaev's famous "Philosophical Letters," written in 1829–1831 in French, are to be found in vol. 1; their Russian translation, in vol. 2.

Moskoff, Eugene A., *The Russian Philosopher Chaadayev: His Ideas and His Epoch*. New York, 1937.

Chernov, Viktor, *Konstruktivnyi Sotsializm*. Prague, 1925. (Constructive socialism. A good retrospective summary of the SR ideology.)

Chernyshevsky, N. G., *Polnoe sobranie sochinenii*, 10 vols. St. Petersburg, 1905–1906; 14 vols., Moscow, 1939–1949.

———, *Selected Philosophical Essays*. Moscow, 1953.

Danilevsky, N. Ia., *Rossiia i Evropa*. St. Petersburg, 1871. (Russia and Europe.)

(The Decembrists: see sect. 6 for works concerned with the social and political ideas of the Decembrists.)

Dement'ev, A. G., *Ocherki po istorii russkoi zhurnalistiki 1840–1850 gg.* Moscow, 1951. (Essays on Russian journalism in the 1840s and 1850s.)

Dobroliubov, N. A., *Polnoe sobranie sochinenii*, M. K. Lemke, ed., 4 vols. St. Petersburg, 1911.

———, *Izbrannye sochineniia*. Moscow, 1947. (Selected works.)

Dostoevsky, F. M., *Dnevnik pisatelia*. St. Petersburg, 1877; Paris, 1951 (YMCA Press). Trans.: *The Diary of a Writer*, Boris Brazol, trans., 2 vols., New York, 1949.

Fischer, George, *Russian Liberalism: From Gentry to Intelligentsia*. Cambridge, Mass., 1958.

Hare, Richard, *Pioneers of Russian Social Thought: Studies of Non-Marxian Formation in Nineteenth-Century Russia and of its Partial Revival in the Soviet Union*, New York, 1951.

———, *Portraits of Russian Personalities: Between Reform and Revolution.*

New York, 1959. (A series of essays on Russian thinkers, writers, and statesmen.)

Hecht, David, *Russian Radicals Look to America, 1825–1894.* Cambridge, Mass., 1947.

Hecker, Julius, *Russian Sociology: Contribution to the History of Sociological Thought and Theory.* London, 1934; 1st ed., New York, 1915.

Herzen, A. I., *Polnoe sobranie sochineii i pisem,* ed. by M. K. Lemke, 22 vols. Petrograd, 1917–1925. (Complete collection of works and letters.)

———, *Sochineniia,* 9 vols. Moscow, 1955–1958.

———, *Byloe i dumy.* Moscow, 1946. *My Past and Thoughts,* Constance Garnett, trans., 6 vols. New York, 1924–1928.

———, *The Memoirs,* J. D. Duff, trans., 2 vols. New Haven, 1923.

Malia, Martin E., *Alexander Herzen and the Birth of Russian Socialism, 1812–1885.* Cambridge, Mass., 1961.

Karamzin's Memoir on Ancient and Modern Russia: A Translation and Analysis, Richard E. Pipes. Cambridge, Mass., 1959. (The Russian text was also ed. by R. Pipes, Cambridge, Mass., 1959.)

Katkov, M. N., *Sobranie peredovykh statei "Moskovskikh Vedomostei" s 1863 po 1887 god,* 24 vols. Moscow, 1897–1898. (A collection of Katkov's editorials in the *Moscow Gazette,* 1863–1887.)

Khomiakov, A. S., *Polnoe sobranie sochinenii,* 8 vols., 3d ed. Moscow, 1900. (A complete collection of works.)

Christoff, Peter K., *An Introduction to Nineteenth-Century Russian Slavophilism: A Study in Ideas,* vol. I *(A. S. Xomjakov).* The Hague, 1961.

Kindersley, Richard K., *The First Russian Revisionists: A study of "Legal Marxism" in Russia.* Oxford, 1962.

Kohn, Hans, *Panslavism: Its History and Ideology.* Notre Dame, Ind., 1953; 2d ed., New York, 1960.

———, ed., *The Mind of Modern Russia. Historical and Political Thought of Russia's Great Age (1825–1917).* New Brunswick, N.J., 1955; New York, 1962.

Kropotkin, P. A., *Mutual Aid a Factor of Evolution.* New York, 1902; Boston, 1955.

———, *Modern Science and Anarchism.* London, 1923; 1st ed., 1903.

———, *Fields, Factories, and Workshops, or Industry Combined with Agriculture and Brain Work with Manual Work.* Boston, 1899; rev. ed., New York, 1913.

Woodcock, George and Ivan Avakumovic, *The Anarchist Prince: A Biographical Study of Peter Kropotkin.* New York, 1949.

Lampert, E., *Studies in Rebellion.* New York, 1957. (Belinsky, Bakunin, and Herzen.)

Lavrov, P. L., *Istoricheskie pis'ma.* St. Petersburg, 1870. (Historical letters. A work which became a gospel for the populist movement of the period.)

Lemke, M., *Epokha tsenzurnykh reform, 1859–1865.* St. Petersburg, 1904. (The time of the censorship reforms.)

———, *Ocherki po istorii russkoi tsenzury i zhurnalistiki XIX st.* St. Petersburg, 1904. (Essays on the history of Russian censorship and journalism in the nineteenth century.)

Lenin, V. I. (see sect. 6.)

Leontiev, K. N., *Vostok, Rossiia i Slavianstvo,* 2 vols. Moscow 1885–1886; 2d ed., 1912.

Leontovitsch, Victor, *Geschichte des Liberalismus in Russland.* Frankfurt-am-Main, 1957.

Masaryk, Thomas G., *The Spirit of Russia: Studies in History, Literature and Philosophy.* 2 vols. New York, 1919; 2d ed., 1955.

McLean, Hugh, Martin E. Malia, and George Fischer, eds., *Russian Thought and Politics.* Harvard Slavic Studies, vol. IV, Cambridge, Mass., 1957.

Mendel, Arthur P., *Dilemmas of Progress in Tsarist Russia: Legal Marxism and Legal Populism.* Cambridge, Mass., 1961.

Mikhailovsky, N. K., *Sochineniia,* 6 vols., 4th ed. St. Petersburg, 1906–1907. (Works.)

Billington, James H., *Mikhailovsky and Russian Populism.* Oxford, 1958.

Miliukov, P. N., *Iz istorii russkoi intelligentsii,* 2d ed. St. Petersburg, 1903. (From the history of the Russian intelligentsia. Essays on S. T. Aksakov, Belinsky, Stankevich, Herzen, Granovsky, and the epigonus of Slavophilism, V. S. Soloviev.)

Petrovich, Michael B., *The Emergence of Russian Panslavism, 1856–1870.* New York, 1956.

Pipes, Richard, ed., *The Russian Intelligentsia.* New York, 1961. (A collection of essays, the first four of which deal with the prerevolutionary intelligentsia.)

Pisarev, D. I., *Sochineniia,* 6 vols. St. Petersburg, 1894–1901; 4 vols., Moscow, 1955–1956.

Pisarev, D. I., *Selected Philosophical, Social and Political Essays.* Moscow, 1958.

Plekhanov, G. V., *Sochineniia,* 24 vols. Moscow, 1920–1927. (Works.)

————, *Nashi raznoglasiia.* St. Petersburg, 1906. (Our differences. A caustic polemic against populism, first published in 1884.)

Pobedonostsev, K. P., *Moskovskii Sbornik.* Moscow, 1896. (A collection of essays concerning the church, the state, and different aspects of public life, sharply critical of modern democracy and, especially, of the parliamentary system.)

————, *Reflexions of a Russian Statesman.* London, 1898. (A condensed translation of *Moskovskii Sbornik.*)

Radishchev, A. N., *Puteshestvie iz Peterburga v Moskvu.* Moscow, 1935, repr. from the 1790 ed. (Radishchev's famous book, *Journey from St. Petersburg to Moscow,* though chronologically outside our period, greatly influenced the development of Russian radicalism in the 19th century.)

Materialy k izucheniiu Puteshestvia iz Peterburga v Moskvu. A. N. Radishcheva. Moscow and Leningrad, 1935. (Materials for the study of Radishchev's work.)

Alexander Radishchev's Journey from St. Petersburg to Moscow, Leo Wiener, trans., R. Thaler, ed. Cambridge, Mass., 1958.

Lang, D. M., *The First Russian Radical: Alexander Radishchev, 1749–1802.* London, 1959.

Riabushinsky, V. P., ed. *"Velikaia Rossiia": Sbornik statei po voennym i obshchestvennym voprosam,* 2 vols. Moscow, 1911–1912. ("Great Russia": a collection of essays on military and social themes by a group of statesmanlike liberals.)

Riasanovsky, Nicholas V., *Nicholas I and Official Nationality in Russia, 1825–1855.* Berkeley, 1959.

————, *Russia and the West in the Teaching of the Slavophiles: A Study of Romantic Ideology.* Cambridge, Mass., 1952.

Schelting, Alexander von, *Russland und Europa im russischen Geschichtsdenken.* Bern, 1948.

Simmons, Ernest J., ed., *Continuity and Change in Russian and Soviet Thought.* Cambridge, Mass., 1955.

Soloviev, Vladimir S., *Sobranie sochinenii.* St. Petersburg, 1901. (Collected works, published by Obshchestvennaia Pol'za, vol. 5 [*Natsional'nyi vopros v Rossii*]. The question of nationalities in Russia.)

Struve, P. B., *Patriotica: Politika, kul'tura, religiia, sotsializm; Sbornik statei za piat' let, 1905–1910.* St. Petersburg, 1911. (A collection of articles by an outstanding Russian scholar, politician, and journalist, who turned from Marxism to patriotism and nonchauvinistic nationalism.)

Tolstoy Centenary Edition. Oxford, 1929–1937. (Tolstoy's articles on political and social subjects are included in vols. 20 and 21.)

Tompkins, Stuart R., *The Russian Mind: From Peter the Great Through the Enlightment.* Norman, Okla., 1957. (The period to 1855.)

————, *The Russian Intelligentsia: Makers of the Revolutionary State.* Norman, Okla., 1957. (The period 1855 to 1917.)

Vekhi: Sbornik statei o russkoi intelligentsii. Moscow, 1909. (Landmarks: a collection of articles on the Russian intelligentsia, by N. A. Berdyaev, S. N. Bulgakov, M. O. Gershenzon, A. S. Izgoev, B. A. Kistiakovsky, P. B. Struve, and S. L. Frank. The authors called for a reappraisal of the revolutionary and socialist ideology of the leading members of the intelligentsia, accusing them of atheism, materialism, sectarian intolerance, utopianism, and political nihilism, apparent in their animosity toward the national state. *Vekhi* provoked an indignant reaction among the radical elements of the intelligentsia, reflected in the volumes that follow.)

Intelligentsiia v Rossii: Sbornik statei. St. Petersburg, 1910. (The intelligentsia in Russia: a collection of articles.)

"Vekhi" kak znamenie vremeni. Moscow, 1910. ("Landmarks" as a sign of the times.)

Po "Vekham." Moscow, 1909. (Following the "Landmarks.")

V zashchitu intelligentsii. Moscow, 1909. (In defense of the intelligentsia.)

Venturi, Franco, *Roots of the Revolution: A History of the Populist and*

Socialist Movements in Nineteenth Century Russia. New York, 1960. (Trans. from the Italian: *Il Populismo Russo,* 2 vols. Turin, 1952.)

Volynskii (A. L. Flekser), *Bor'ba za idealizm.* St. Petersburg, 1900. (The struggle for idealism.)

Yarmolinsky, Avrahm, *Road to Revolution: A Century of Russian Radicalism.* New York, 1959. (From Radishchev to "the agony of the People's Will," 1887, with a special emphasis on the period of Alexander II.)

Zhaba, S. P., ed., *Russkie mysliteli o Rossii i chelovechestve: antologiia russkoi obshchestvennoi mysli.* Paris, 1954. (Russian thinkers about Russia and mankind: an anthology of Russian social thought.)

10. Russian Cultural Life

SOME SOURCES AND GENERAL SURVEYS

Arseniev, N. S., *Iz russkoi kul'turnoi i tvorcheskoi traditsii.* Frankfurt-am-Main, 1959. (From the Russian cultural and creative tradition.)

Barsukov, Nikolai, *Zhizn' i trudy M. P. Pogodina,* 22 vols. St. Petersburg, 1888–1910. (The life and the works of the Moscow historian M. P. Pogodin. Contains a wealth of materials on the cultural life of Russia, and particularly of Moscow, in the middle of the nineteenth century.)

Ettlinger, Amrei and J. M. Gladstone, *Russian Literature, Theatre and Art: A Bibliography of Works in English, published 1900–1945.* New York, 1947.

Miliukov, Paul, *Outlines of Russian Culture,* M. Karpovich, ed. Philadelphia, 1942; 1948. (One volume in three parts: I [*Religion and the Church*]; II [*Literature*]; III [*Architecture, Painting, and Music*]. Pb. ed., 1960.)

Riazanovsky, V. A., *Obzor russkoi kul'tury,* 2 vols. New York, 1947. (A survey of Russian culture.)

HISTORY OF LITERATURE

Aikhenvald, Iu. I., *Siluety russkikh pisatelei,* 3 vols. Moscow, 1906–1908; 4th ed., 1913–1914. (Profiles of Russian writers.)

Baring, Maurice, *An Outline of Russian Literature.* New York, 1915; 2d ed., 1928.

———, *Landmarks in Russian Literature.* London, 1916; New York, pb. ed., 1960.

Bowman, Herbert E., *Vissarion Belinsky, 1811–1848: A Study of the Origins of Social Criticism in Russia.* Cambridge, Mass., 1954.

Gorodetskii, B. P., ed., *Istoriia russkoi kritiki,* 2 vols. Leningrad, 1958. (A history of Russian criticism, published by the Institute of Literature of the Academy of Sciences.)

Hare, Richard, *Russian Literature: From Pushkin to the Present Day.* London, 1947; repr., 1955.

Istoriia russkoi literatury, vols. 5–10. Moscow, 1953–1956. (Published by the Academy of Sciences of the USSR, with the standard Marxist-Leninist interpretation.)

Lavrin, Janko, *Russian Writers: Their Lives and Literature.* New York, 1954.
Lemke, Mikhail, *Nikolaevskie zhandarmy i literatura 1826–1855 gg.,* 2d ed.
St. Petersburg, 1909. (The gendarmes of Nicholas I and the literature of
1826–1855.)
Mirsky, D. S., *Contemporary Russian Literature 1881–1925.* New York. 1926.
———, *A History of Russian Literature From its Beginnings to 1900,* F. J.
Whitfield, ed. New York, 1949; pb. ed., 1960.
Muchnic, Helen, *An Introduction to Russian Literature.* New York, 1947.
Ovsianiko-Kulikovsky, D. N., ed., *Istoria russkoi literatury XIX veka,* 5 vols.
Moscow, 1908–1911. (Russian Reprint Series of the ACLS, Ann Arbor,
Mich., 1948.)
———, *Sobranie sochinenii,* 9 vols. St. Petersburg, 1910–1911; Moscow, 1923–
1924.
Poggioli, Renato, *The Poets of Russia, 1890–1930.* Cambridge, Mass., 1960.
Pypin, A. N., *Istoriia russkoi literatury,* vol. 4, 2d ed. St. Petersburg, 1903.
(History of Russian literature.)
———, *Kharakteristika literaturnykh mnenii ot 20-kh do 50-kh godov.* St.
Petersburg, 1890. (Literary opinions from the 1820s to the 1850s.)
Savodnik, V., *Ocherki po istorii russkoi literatury XIX veka,* 2 vols. Moscow,
1918. (An outline of the history of nineteenth century Russian literature.)
Simmons, Ernest J., *An Outline of Modern Russian Literature, 1880–1940.*
Ithaca, N.Y., 1943. (A brief outline.)
———, *English Literature and Culture in Russia (1553–1840).* Cambridge,
Mass., 1935.
Slonim, Marc. L., *The Epic of Russian Literature: From its Origin through
Tolstoy.* New York, 1950.
———, *Modern Russian Literature from Chekhov to the Present.* New York,
1953. (Useful for the study of literature, but not reliable for information
on the social and political background, where the politician prevails over
the scholar.)
———, *An Outline of Russian Literature.* New York, 1958.
Spector, Ivar, *The Golden Age of Russian Literature,* 4th ed. Caldwell, Ida.,
1952; 1st ed., 1939. (Briefly sketched characteristics of writers followed by
excerpts from their works, covering the period from 1782 to 1936.)
Strakhov, N. N., *Bor'ba s zapadom v nashei literature,* 3 vols. St. Petersburg,
1882–1883; 2d ed., 1887–1898. (The struggle against the West in our
literature.)
Tkhorzhevsky, Ivan, *Russkaia literatura,* 2 vols. Paris, 1946.
Vengerov, S. A., *Ocherki po istorii russkoi literatury,* St. Petersburg, 1907.
(An outline of the history of Russian literature.)
———, *Kritiko-biographicheskii slovar' russkikh pisatelei i uchenykh,* 6 vols.
St. Petersburg 1889–1904; 2d ed., 1915–1916, incomplete. (Critico-biograph-
ical lexicon of Russian writers and scholars. An important reference work.)
Vengerov, S. A., ed., *Russkaia literatura XX veka (1890–1910),* 3 vols. Mos-
cow, 1914–1916. (A collection of articles on Russian literature 1890–1910,
by various authors.)

Veselovsky, A., *Zapadnoe vliianie v novoi russkoi literature.* Moscow, 1896; 5th ed., 1916. (The Western influence in modern Russian literature.)

Vladislavlev, I. V., (I. Gul'binsky), *Russkie pisateli XIX–XX st. Opyt biblio-graficheskogo posobia po noveishei russkoi literature.* Moscow, 1908; 4th ed., 1924. (Russian writers of the nineteenth and twentieth centuries. A bibliographical-reference book in modern Russian literature.)

Volynsky (A. L. Flekser), *Russkie kritiki.* St. Petersburg, 1896. (Volynsky vehemently opposed the dominant sociological tendency in literary criticism and advocated a purely aesthetic approach.)

Wiener, Leo, ed., *Anthology of Russian Literature. The Nineteenth Century.* New York, 1903. (The second volume of Wiener's *Anthology of Russian Literature from the Earliest Period to the Present Time.*)

Zavalishin, Vyacheslav, *Early Soviet Writers.* New York, 1958. (Many of the writers became active prior to 1917.)

EDUCATION AND THE SCIENCES

Zhurnal Ministerstva Narodnogo Prosveshchenia, 1834–1917. (A monthly published by the Ministry of Public Education. Contains basic factual material and a chronicle of current events.)

Chekhov, N. V., *Narodnoe obrazovanie v Rossii s 60kh godov XIX veka.* Moscow, 1912. (Public education in Russia since the 1860s.)

Darlington, Thomas, *Education in Russia.* London, 1909. (Board of Education Special Reports on Educational Subjects, vol. 23.)

Demkov, M. I., *Istoria russkoi pedagogii.* Moscow, 1909. (A history of Russian pedagogy.)

Hans, Nicholas A., *History of Russian Educational Policy (1701–1917).* London, 1931.

Johnson, William H. E., *Russia's Educational Heritage.* Pittsburgh, 1950.

Kaidanova, O. V., *Ocherki po istorii narodnogo obrazovaniia v Rossii i v S.S.S.R.,* vol. 1. Brussels, 1938. (Essays on the history of public education in Russia and in the USSR.)

Kapterev, P. F., *Istoria russkoi pedagogii.* St. Petersburg, 1910; 2d ed., 1915.

Leary, Daniel B., *Education and Autocracy in Russia: From the Origins to the Bolsheviki.* Buffalo, 1919.

Medynsky, E. N., *Istoria russkoi pedagogiki do Oktiabr'skoi Revoliutsii.* Moscow, 1938. (History of Russian pedagogy prior to the October Revolution. Heavily Marxist-Leninist.)

Rozhdestvensky, S. V., *Istoricheskii obzor deiatel'nosti Ministerstva Narod-nago Prosveshcheniia 1802–1902.* St. Petersburg, 1902. (A review of the activity of the Ministry of Public Education, 1802–1902).

———, *Ocherki po istorii sistem narodnogo prosveshchenia v Rossii v XVIII–XIX vv.* St. Petersburg, 1912. (Historic essays on the systems of public education in Russia in the eighteenth and nineteenth centuries.)

Bol'shaia Sovetskaia Entsiklopediia (The Great Soviet Encyclopaedia gives ample coverage to the biographies of Russian scientists.)

Kniazev, G. A., *Kratkii ocherk istorii Akademii Nauk SSSR (1725–1945)*. Moscow and Leningrad, 1945. (A short outline of the history of the Academy of Sciences.)

Kuznetsov, B. G., *Ocherki istorii russkoi nauki*. Moscow, 1940. (Essays on the history of Russian science.)

Lazarev, P. P., *Ocherki istorii russkoi nauki*. Moscow, 1950. (Another series of essays on the history of science in Russia.)

Mongait, Alexander, *Arkheologia v S.S.S.R.* Moscow, 1955. Trans.: *Archeology in the U.S.S.R.*, Moscow (Foreign Languages Publishing House), 1959; trans. and adapted by M. W. Thompson, pb. ed., 1961.

Novikov, M. M., *Velikany rossiiskogo estestvoznaniia*. Frankfurt-am-Main, 1960. (The giants of Russian natural science. Essays dealing with the life and the work of eleven Russian scientists.)

Riazanovsky, V. A., *Razvitie russkoi nauchnoi mysli v XVIII–XIX vekakh (nauki o prirode)*. New York, 1949. (The development of the natural sciences in Russia in the eighteenth and nineteenth centuries.)

THE CHURCH AND RELIGION; PHILOSOPHY

Arseniev, N., *Holy Moscow: Chapters in the Religious and Spiritual life of Russia in the 19th Century*. New York, 1940.

Bolshakoff, S., *Russian Nonconformity: The Story of "Unofficial" Religion in Russia*. Philadelphia, 1950.

Bulgakov, S. N., *The Orthodox Church*. New York, 1935.

Conybeare, Frederick C., *Russian Dissenters*. Cambridge, Mass., 1921.

Curtiss, John S., *Church and State in Russia: The Last Years of the Empire, 1900–1917*. New York, 1940.

Fedotov, G. P., ed., *A Treasury of Russian Spirituality*. New York, 1948.

Florovsky, Georgii, *Puti russkogo bogoslovia*. Paris, 1937. (The ways of Russian theology.)

Iswolsky, Helen, *Christ in Russia: The History, Tradition and Life of the Russian Church*. Milwaukee, 1960.

Leroy-Beaulieu, Anatole, *The Empire of the Tsars and the Russians*, vol. 3 *(Religion)*. New York, 1896; 1903.

Lowrie, Donald A., *The Light of Russia: An Introduction to the Russian Church*. Prague, 1923.

Smolitch, Igor, *Russisches Mönchtum: Entstehung, Entwicklung und Wesen, 988–1917*. Würzburg, 1953. (Russian monasticism: its origin, development, and character.)

———, *Leben und Lehre der Starzen*. Vienna, 1936. (Life and teaching of the *Startsy*, or monastic elders.)

Zernov, Nicholas, *The Church of the Eastern Christians*. New York, 1942.

———, *The Russians and Their Church*. New York, 1945.

———, *Eastern Christendom: A Study of the Origin and Development of the Eastern Orthodox Church*. New York, 1961.

Lossky, N. O., *History of Russian Philosophy*. New York, 1951.

Zenkovsky, V. V., *Istoria russkoi filosofii*, 2 vols. Paris, 1948–1950. Trans.: *A History of Russian Philosophy*, G. L. Kline, trans., 2 vols., New York, 1953.

Chizhevsky, Dmitrii, *Hegel v Rossii*. Paris, 1939. (Hegel in Russia.)

Soloviev, Vladimir, *Opravdanie dobra: Nravstvennaia filosofiia*, 2d ed. Moscow, 1899; 1st ed., 1897. Trans.: *The Justification of the Good: An Essay on Moral Philosophy*, London, 1918.

Tolstoy Centenary Edition. London, 1929–1937. (Works concerning religion and ethics are included in vols. 12 and 20.)

Zernov, N., *Three Russian Prophets: Khomiakov, Dostoevsky, Soloviev*. London, 1944.

THE VISUAL ARTS

Barr, Alfred H., *Cubism and Abstract Art*. New York, 1936. (The volume, published by the Museum of Modern Art, contains passages relating to the role of Russian painters in the abstract movement.)

Benois, A. N., *Istoria russkoi zhivopisi v XIX veke*. St. Petersburg, 1901. (History of Russian painting in the 19th century.)

——, *The Russian School of Painting*, New York, 1916.

——, *Vozniknovenie "Mira iskusstva."* Leningrad, 1928. (The origins of the "World of Art.")

Fiala, Vladimir, *Russian Painting of the 18th and 19th Centuries*. Prague, 1953. (Contains 170 color reproductions, with brief biographies of the painters.)

Grabar', Igor, ed., *Istoria russkogo iskusstva*, vols. 3–6. Moscow, 1910–1917. (History of Russian art. The original edition of this fundamental work is incomplete; a new Soviet edition in progress.)

Gray, Camilla, *The Great Experiment: Russian Art, 1863–1922*. New York, 1962.

Hamilton, George H., *The Art and Architecture of Russia*. Baltimore, 1954. (A succinct and well-written account in the Pelican History of Art series, covering the period from Kievan Russia through about 1910.)

Istoria russkoi arkhitektury. Moscow, 1951. (History of Russian architecture. A standard Soviet text, published by the Academy of Architecture of the USSR.)

Kovalenskaia, N., *Istoria russkogo iskusstva pervoi poloviny XIX veka*. Moscow, 1951. (History of Russian art in the first half of the nineteenth century.)

Loukomski, G. K., *History of Modern Russian Painting (1840–1940)*. London, 1945. (Trans. from the Russian.)

Newmarch, Rosa, *The Russian Arts*, New York, 1916.

Nikolsky, V. A., *Istoria russkogo iskusstva: zhivopis', arkhitektura, skul'ptura, dekorativnoe iskusstvo*. Berlin, 1923. (History of Russian art: painting, architecture, sculpture, and decorative art.)

Novitsky, A., *Istoria russkago iskusstva s drevneishikh vremen*, 2 vols. Moscow, 1903. (History of Russian art from ancient times.)

Rice, Tamara T., *Russian Art*. Baltimore, 1949.
Umanskij, Konstantin, *Neue Kunst in Russland, 1914–1919*. Potsdam, 1920.
Voyce, Arthur, *Russian Architecture: Trends in Nationalism and Modernism*. New York, 1948.
Wulff, Oskar, *Die Neurussische Kunst im Rahmen der Kulturentwicklung Russlands von Peter dem Grossen bis zur Revolution*, 2 vols. Augsburg, 1932. (Russian Art in the context of Russian cultural development from Peter the Great to the Revolution.)

RUSSIAN MUSIC

Abraham, Gerald E. H., *Studies in Russian Music: Critical Essays*. London, 1936.
————, *On Russian Music: Critical and Historical Studies*. New York, 1939.
Brook, Donald, *Six Great Russian Composers*. London, 1936. (Glinka, Borodin, Mussorgsky, Tchaikovsky, Rimsky-Korsakov, and Scriabin.)
Calvocoressi, Michel and Gerald Abraham, *Masters of Russian Music*. London, 1936.
Cheshikhin, Vsevolod, *Istoria russkoi opery*, 2d ed. Moscow, 1905. (History of the Russian opera.)
Istoria russkoi muzyki, 3 vols. Moscow, 1957–1960. (A history of Russian music prior to 1917, published by the Moscow Academy of Arts.)
Keldysh, Iu. K., *Istoria russkoi muzyki*, 2 vols. Moscow, 1947–1948.
Lapshin, Ivan I., *Ruská hudba*. Prague, 1947. (Russian music. Trans. from the unpubl. Russian into Czech.)
Leonard, Richard A., *A History of Russian Music*. New York, 1957.
Livanova, T., *Istoria russkoi muzyki*, 2 vols. Moscow, 1940.
Montagu-Nathan, Montagu, *A History of Russian Music*. New York, 1914; 2d ed., London, 1918.
————, *Contemporary Russian Composers*. New York, 1917.
Newmarch, Rosa, *The Russian Opera*. London, 1914.
Rimsky-Korsakov, N. A., *Letopis' moei muzykal'noi zhizni*, 5th ed. Moscow, 1935; 1st ed., St. Petersburg, 1909. (A chronicle of my musical life.) Trans.: *My Musical Life*, New York, 1942.
Sabaneyeff, L., *Modern Russian Composers*. New York, 1927.
Seroff, V. I., *The Mighty Five: The Cradle of Russian National Music*. New York, 1948.

THEATER AND BALLET

Benois, Alexander, *Reminiscences of the Russian Ballet*. London, 1941. (Trans. from the Russian.)
Evreinov, N. N., *The Theatre in Life*. New York, 1923.
————, *Istoria russkogo teatra s drevneishikh vremen do 1917 goda*. New York, 1955. (A history of the Russian theater from ancient times to 1917.)
Gregor, Joseph and Fülop-Miller, René, *The Russian Theatre*. Philadelphia, 1929.

Grigoriev, S. G., *The Diaghilev Ballet, 1909–1929,* Vera Bowen, trans. and ed. London, 1953.

Lifar, Sergei, *Istoria russkogo baleta ot XVII veka do "Russkogo Baleta" Diaghileva.* Paris, 1945. Trans.: *A History of Russian Ballet: From Its Origins to the Present Day,* London, 1954.

Moskovskii Khudozhestvennyi Teatr v illiustratsiiakh i dokumentakh, 1898–1938. Moscow, 1938. (The Moscow Art Theater, illustrations and documents.)

Petipa, M., *The Memoirs of Marius Petipa,* Lillian Moor, ed., Helen Whittaker, trans. New York, 1958.

Pleshcheev, A. A., *Nash balet, 1673–1896.* St. Petersburg, 1896.

Sayler, Oliver M., *The Russian Theatre,* New York, 1923.

Shaliapin, F. I., *Stranitsy moei zhizni, avtobiografia.* Leningrad, 1926; Kiev, 1958. Trans.: *Pages from My Life: An Autobiography,* New York, 1927.

Slonim, Marc, *Russian Theater from the Empire to the Soviets.* Cleveland, 1961.

Stanislavsky, Constantine (K. S. Alekseev), *Moia zhizn' v iskusstve,* 7th ed. Moscow, 1948; 1st ed., 1924. Trans.: *My Life in Art,* Boston, 1924.

———, *An Actor Prepares.* New York, 1959; 1st ed., 1936.

———, *On the Art of the Stage.* New York, 1950; 1961.

Varneke, Boris V., *Istoria russkogo teatra XVII–XIX vekov,* 3d ed. Moscow, 1939; 1st ed., 1908. *History of the Russian Theatre Seventeenth through Nineteenth Century,* trans. by B. Brasol; revised and ed. by B. Martin. New York, 1951.

Vsevolodsky, V. (Gerngross), *Istoria russkogo teatra,* 2 vols. Moscow, 1929. (History of the Russian theater.)

11. Foreign relations prior to 1914

BASIC SOURCES AND GENERAL SURVEYS

Sobranie traktatov i konventsii, zakliuchennykh Rossieiu s inostrannymi derzhavami—Recueil des Trates et Conventions conclus par la Russie avec les puissances etransgeres, F. Martens, ed., 15 vols. St. Petersburg, 1874–1909. (Collection of treaties and conventions concluded by Russia with foreign powers. The documents in French and Russian are supplemented with a substantial historical commentary.)

The Map of Europe by Treaty, since the General Peace of 1814, Sir Edward Hertslet, ed. Vols. I–III (1814–1874), London, 1875; vol. IV (1875–1891), London, 1891.

Mezhdunarodnye otnoshenia v epokhu imperializma: Dokumenty iz arkhivov tsarskogo i Vremennogo pravitel'stv 1878–1917, series II, 1900–1913 (only vols. 18–20 publ., with documents of 1911–1912). Moscow, 1938–1940. (International relations in the period of imperialism: Documents from the archives of the tsarist and Provisional governments.)

Documents diplomatiques français, 1871–1914. Series I (1871–1900), 16 vols.,

Paris, 1929–1959; series II (1901–1911), 14 vols., Paris, 1930–1955; series III, 1911–1914, 11 vols., Paris, 1929–1936. (Publ. by the French Ministry of Foreign Affairs.)

British Documents on the Origins of the War, 1898–1914, G. P. Gooch and Harold Temperley, eds., 11 vols. (in 13 parts). London, 1926–1936.

Die Grosse Politik der Europäischen Kabinette, 1871–1914: Sammlung der diplomatischen Akten des Auswärtigen Amtes, 40 vols. Berlin, 1922–1926. (The foreign policy of the European powers, 1871–1914. A collection of diplomatic acts of the Ministry of Foreign Affairs.)

Pribram, A. F., *The Secret Treaties of Austria-Hungary, 1879–1914,* 2 vols. Cambridge, Mass., 1920–1921. Vol. I (*Texts of Treaties and Agreements,* D. P. Myers and J. G. D'Arcy Paul, trans.) and vol. II (*Negotiations Leading to the Treaties of the Triple Alliance,* with documentary appendices). (Vol. II, Appendix B: The Dual Alliance.)

Russko-germanskie otnoshenia: Krasnyi Arkhiv, vol. I. Moscow, 1922. (Secret diplomatic documents concerning Russo-German relations 1873–1914.)

Adamov, E. A., ed., *Sbornik dogovorov Rossii s drugimi gosudarstvami, 1856–1917.* Moscow, 1952. (A collection of treaties between Russia and other powers, 1856–1917. Texts of treaties in Russian translation.)

Kliuchnikov, Iu. V. and A. Sabanin, eds., *Mezhdunarodnaia politika noveishego vremeni v dogovorakh, notakh i deklaratsiakh, Chast' I: Ot frantsuzskoi revoliutsii do imperialisticheskoi voiny.* Moscow, 1925. (International relations of the modern period, as reflected in treaties, diplomatic notes, and declarations, part I: From the French Revolution to the Imperialistic War.)

Manhart, G. B., *Alliance and Entente, 1871–1914.* New York, 1932. (Excerpts from the most important treaties and agreements of the period.)

Schreiner, G. A., ed., *Entente Diplomacy and the World: Matrix of the History of Europe, 1909–1914.* London, 1921. (Excerpts from diplomatic correspondence.)

The Cambridge History of British Foreign Policy, A. W. Ward and G. P. Gooch, eds., 3 vols. Cambridge, 1923.

Istoria russkoi armii i flota, 15 vols. Moscow, 1911–1913. (A history of the Russian army and navy, publ. by Obrazovanie.)

Iswolsky, A. P., *Recollections of a Foreign Minister.* New York, 1921.

Lamzdorf, V. N., *Dnevnik, 1886–1890.* Moscow, 1926. (Diary. Important records of a Russian assistant minister for foreign affairs.)

———, *Dnevnik, 1891–1892.* Moscow, 1934.

Langer, William L., *European Alliances and Alignments, 1871–1890,* 2d ed. New York, 1950; 1956; 1st ed., 1939. (Contains a detailed annotated bibliography.)

———, *The Diplomacy of Imperialism, 1890–1902,* 2 vols., 2d ed. New York, 1951; 1st ed., 1935.

Lederer, Ivo J., ed., *Russian Foreign Policy: Essays in Historical Perspective.* New Haven, 1962.

Mowat, Robert B., *A History of European Diplomacy, 1815–1914.* London, 1922.

Potemkin, V. P., ed., *Istoria diplomatii,* 3 vols. Moscow, 1941–1945.

Rosen, R. R., Baron, *Forty Years of Diplomacy,* 2 vols. New York, 1922. (Baron Rosen held many different diplomatic posts in Europe, the United States, and Japan; his memoirs end with 1918.)

Rotshtein, F. A., *Mezhdunarodnye otnoshenia v kontse XIX veka.* Moscow, 1960. (International relations toward the end of the nineteenth century.)

Schmitt, Bernadotte E., *Triple Alliance and Triple Entente.* New York, 1934.

Sontag, Raymond J., *European Diplomatic History, 1871–1932.* New York, 1933.

Tarle, E. V., *Evropa v epokhu imperializma, 1871–1919 gg.* Moscow, 1927; 2d ed., 1928. (Europe in the period of imperialism.)

Tatishchev, S. S., *Vneshniaia politika imperatora Nikolaia I.* St. Petersburg, 1887. (The foreign policy of Emperor Nicholas I.)

Taylor, Alan J. P., *The Struggle for Mastery in Europe, 1848–1918.* Oxford, 1954.

RUSSIA'S RELATIONS WITH WESTERN EUROPE

Churchill, Rogers P., *The Anglo-Russian Convention of 1907.* Cedar Rapids, Iowa, 1939.

Daudet, Ernest, *Histoire diplomatique de l'alliance franco-russe, 1873–1893.* Paris, 1898.

Garin, F. A., *Izgnanie Napoleona.* Moscow, 1948. (Napoleon's expulsion from Russia in 1812. A collection of excerpts from contemporary documents, letters, and narratives.)

Gibbs, Peter, *Crimean Blunder: The Story of War with Russia a Hundred Years Ago.* New York, 1960.

Grüning, Irene, *Die russische öffentliche Meinung und ihre Stellung zu den Grossmächten, 1878–1894.* Berlin, 1929. (Russian public opinion and its attitude toward the great powers of Europe, 1878–1894.)

The Kaiser's Letters to the Tsar, N. Y. Grant, ed. London, 1920.

Langer, William L., *The Franco-Russian Alliance, 1890–1894.* Cambridge, Mass., 1929.

Lobanov-Rostovsky, Andrei, *Russia and Europe, 1789–1825.* Durham, N.C., 1947.

———, *Russia and Europe, 1825–1878.* Ann Arbor, Mich., 1954. (A factual, well-balanced survey.)

Marriott, Sir John A. R., *Anglo-Russian Relations, 1689–1943.* London, 1944.

Materialy po istorii franko-russkikh otnoshenii za 1910–1914 gg.: Sbornik sekretnykh diplomaticheskikh dokumentov. Moscow, 1922. (Secret diplomatic documents relating to Franco-Russian relations in 1910–1914.)

Nolde, Boris, Baron, *L'Alliance Franco-Russe.* Paris, 1936.

Otechestvennaia voina i russkoe obshchestvo, A. K. Dzhivelegov, S. P. Melgunov, and V. I. Picheta, eds., 7 vols. Moscow, 1912. (The Fatherland War of 1812 and Russian society.)

Ségur, Count Philip de, *Napoleon's Russian Campaign*, trans. from the French by J. D. Townsend, with an introduction by W. L. Langer. Boston, 1958; 1st English ed., 1825. (Ségur served as quartermaster general of the French army during the Russian campaign of 1812.)

Sergeevsky, N. D., ed., *Konstitutsionnaia khartia 1815 goda i drugie akty byvshego Tsarstva Pol'skogo (1814–1881)*. St. Petersburg, 1907. (The Constitutional Charter of 1815 and other documents of the former Kingdom of Poland, 1814–1881.)

Skazkin, S., *Konets avstro-russko-germanskogo soiuza*, vol. I (1879–1884). Moscow, 1928. (The end of the Austro-Russo-German alliance.)

Tarle, E. V., *Nashestvie Napoleona na Rossiu, 1812 god*. Moscow, 1938; 2d ed., 1943; *1812 god*, M. V. Nechkina, ed., Moscow, 1959. Trans.: *Napoleon's invasion of Russia*, New York, 1942.

——, *Krymskaia voina*, 2 vols., Moscow, 1944–1948; 2d ed., 1950. (The Crimean War.)

Zaionchkovsky, A. M., *Vostochnaia voina 1853–1856 godov v sviazi s sovremennoi politicheskoi obstanovkoi*, 2 vols. St. Petersburg, 1908–1912. (The Eastern war of 1853–1856 and the political situation of the time.)

THE NEAR EAST AND THE CAUCASUS

Rossia na blizhnem Vostoke (Sobranie dokumentov 1801–1915), A. N. Shebunin, ed. Leningrad, 1926. (Russia in the Near East; selected diplomatic documents of 1801–1915.)

Dogovory Rossii s Vostokom politicheskie i torgovye, T. Iuzeforvich, ed. St. Petersburg, 1869. (Russia's political and commercial treaties with the East.)

Allen, William E. D., and Muratoff, Paul, *Caucasian Battlefields: A History of the Wars on the Turco-Caucasian Border, 1828–1921*. New York, 1953.

Baddeley, John F., *The Russian Conquest of the Caucasus*. New York, 1908.

Black, Cyril E., *The Establishment of Constitutional Government in Bulgaria*. Princeton, 1943.

Dranov, B. A., *Chernomorskie prolivy: mezhdunarodno-pravovoi rezhim*. Moscow, 1948. (The Black Sea Straits: their status in international law. Contains a historical survey of the question of the Straits.)

Druzhinin, N. M., ed., *Slavianskii sbornik: slavianskii vopros i russkoe obshchestvo v 1867–1878 gg*. Moscow, 1948. (A Slavic symposium: the Slavic question and the Russian society in 1867–1878.)

Goriainov, S. M., *Bosfor i Dardanelly*. St. Petersburg, 1907.

Gueshoff, I. E., *The Balkan League*, C. Mincoff, trans. London, 1915.

Harris, David, *A Diplomatic History of the Balkan Crisis of 1875–1878: The First Year*. Stanford, 1936.

Helmreich, Ernst C., *The Diplomacy of the Balkan Wars, 1912–1913*. Cambridge, Mass., 1938.

Jelavich, Charles, *Tsarist Russia and Balkan Nationalism: Russian Influence in the Internal Affairs of Bulgaria and Serbia, 1879–1886*. Berkeley, 1958.

Marriott, Sir John A. R., *The Eastern Question: An Historical Study in European Diplomacy*, 4th ed. Oxford, 1940; reprinted 1956; 1st ed., 1917.

Medlicott, William N., *The Congress of Berlin and After: A Diplomatic History of the Near Eastern Settlement, 1878–1880.* London, 1938.

Mosely, Philip E., *Russian Diplomacy and the Opening of the Eastern Question in 1838–1839.* Cambridge, Mass., 1934.

Nikitin, S. A., *Slavianskie komitety v Rossii v 1858–1876 godakh.* Moscow, 1960. (Slavic Committees in Russia in 1858–1876.)

Popov, Nil, *Rossia i Serbia: istoricheskii ocherk russkogo pokrovitel'stva Serbii s 1806 po 1856 god,* 2 vols. Moscow, 1869. (A historical survey of Russian protective influence over Serbia, 1806–1856.)

Puryear, Vernon J., *England, Russia, and the Straits Question 1844–1856.* Berkeley, 1931.

Rodkey, Frederick S., *The Turco-Egyptian Question in the Relations of England, France and Russia, 1832–1841.* Urbana, Ill., 1924.

Seton-Watson, R. W., *Disraeli, Gladstone and the Eastern Question.* London, 1935.

Stavrianos, Leften Stavros, *The Balkans since 1453.* New York, 1958. (A very solid work based on exhaustive studies and including a detailed annotated bibliography.)

Stojanović, Mihailo D., *The Great Powers and the Balkans, 1875–1878.* Cambridge, 1939.

Sumner, Benedict H., *Russia and the Balkans, 1870–1880.* New York, 1937.

Zhigarev, S., *Russkaia politika v Vostochnom Voprose,* 2 vols. Moscow, 1896. (The Russian policy in the Eastern question.)

Zisserman, A. L., *Feldmarshal kniaz' A. I. Bariatinsky, 1815–1879,* 3 vols. Moscow, 1888–1891. (Bariatinsky, appointed in 1857 viceroy in the Caucasus and chief military commander there, played a leading role in the conquest of the area; the appendices contain many documents relating to Bariatinsky's activity.)

CENTRAL ASIA AND THE FAR EAST

Sbornik dogovorov i diplomaticheskikh dokumentov po delam Dal'nago Vostoka 1895–1905. St. Petersburg, 1906. (A Collection of treaties and of diplomatic documents relating to the Far East, 1895–1905. Published by the Russian Ministry of Foreign Affairs.)

Barsukov, I., *Graf N. N. Muraviev-Amurskii,* 2 vols. Moscow, 1891. (Contains many documents of 1844–1861, regarding the administrative, political, and diplomatic activities of Muraviev, the governor general of Eastern Siberia.)

Beveridge, Albert J., *The Russian Advance.* New York, 1903. (Russian expansion in the Far East.)

Boulger, Demetrius Ch., *England and Russia in Central Asia.* London, 1879.

Churchill, Rogers P., *Anglo-Russian Convention of 1907.* Cedar Rapids, Iowa, 1939.

Dallin, David, *The Rise of Russia in Asia.* New Haven, 1949.

Golder, Frank A., *Russian Expansion on the Pacific, 1641–1850.* Gloucester, Mass., 1960; 1st publ., Cleveland, 1914.

Kuropatkin, A. N., General, *The Russian Army and the Japanese War.* 2 vols. New York, 1909.

Lensen, George A., *The Russian Push toward Japan: Russo-Japanese Relations, 1697–1875.* Princeton, 1959.

Lobanov-Rostovsky, Andrei, *Russia and Asia.* New York, 1933; 2d ed., Ann Arbor, Mich., 1951. (A good, scholarly, and readable historical survey.)

Malozemoff, Andrew, *Russian Far Eastern Policy, 1881–1904: With special Emphasis on the Causes of the Russo-Japanese War.* Berkeley, 1958.

McCormick, Frederick, *The Tragedy of Russia in Pacific Asia,* 2 vols. New York, 1907.

Pierce, Richard A., *Russian Central Asia, 1867–1917: A Study in Colonial Rule.* Berkeley, 1960. (An accurate, factual account.)

Price, Ernest B., *The Russo-Japanese Treaties of 1907–1916 concerning Manchuria and Mongolia.* Baltimore, 1933.

Romanov, B. A., *Rossia v Manchzhurii, 1892–1906,* Leningrad, 1928; 1952. Trans.: *Russia in Manchuria, 1892–1906,* Ann Arbor, Mich., 1952.

——, *Ocherki diplomaticheskoi istorii russko-iaponskoi voiny, 1895–1907.* Moscow, 1947. (Outlines of diplomatic history of the Russo-Japanese War; with documents in the appendix.)

Tang, Peter S. H., *Russian and Soviet Policy in Manchuria and Outer Mongolia, 1911–1931.* Durham, N.C., 1959.

Yakhontoff, Victor A., *Russia and the Soviet Union in the Far East.* New York, 1931. (Diplomatic documents, treaties, and declarations of 1689–1928 are found in the appendices.)

RUSSIA AND THE UNITED STATES

Bailey, Thomas A., *America Faces Russia: Russian-American Relations from Early Times to Our Day.* Ithaca, N.Y., 1950. ("Traditionally" overpessimistic in the evaluation of Russian policy.)

Dulles, Foster R., *The Road to Teheran: The Story of Russia and America, 1781–1943.* Princeton, 1944.

Hildt, John C., *Early Diplomatic Negotiations of the United States with Russia.* Baltimore, 1906.

Hulley, Clarence Charles, *Alaska, 1741–1953.* Portland, Ore., 1953.

Laserson, Max M., *The American Impact on Russia: Diplomatic and Ideological, 1784–1917.* New York, 1950. (An accurate, factual study.)

Loubat, J. E., *Narrative of the Mission to Russia in 1866 . . .* (see sect. 3.)

Malkin, M. I., *Grazhdanskaia voina v S. Sh. A. i tsarskaia Rossia.* Moscow, 1939. (The Civil War in the United States and tsarist Russia.)

Okun' S. B., *Rossiisko-Amerikanskaia kompania.* Moscow, 1939. Trans.: *The Russian-American Company,* C. Ginsburg, trans. Cambridge, Mass., 1951.

Sorokin, Pitirim A., *Russia and the United States.* New York, 1944. (An attempt to dispel some well-entrenched prejudices with historical facts.)

Tarsaidze, Alexandre, *Czars and Presidents: The Story of a Forgotten Friendship.* New York, 1958.

Thomas, Benjamin P., *Russo-American Relations, 1815–1867*. Baltimore, 1930.

Tompkins, Pauline, *American-Russian Relations in the Far East (1895–1948)*. New York, 1949.

Williams, William A., *American-Russian Relations, 1781–1947*. New York, 1952.

Woldman, Albert A., *Lincoln and the Russians*. Cleveland, New York, 1952.

Zabriskie, Edward H., *American-Russian Rivalry in the Far East: A Study in Diplomacy and Power Politics, 1895–1914*. Philadelphia, 1946.

12. World War I and the Road to the Revolution

THE OUTBREAK OF THE WAR

Collected Diplomatic Documents Relating to the Outbreak of the European War. London, H. M. Stationary Office, 1915. (Translations of the documents published in the French Yellow Book, the Russian Orange Book, the Belgian Grey Book, the Serbian Blue Book, the German White Book, the Austro-Hungarian Red Book, and the British Blue Book.)

Diplomatic Documents Relating to the Outbreak of the European War, James B. Scott, ed., 2 vols. Carnegie Endowment for International Peace, Division for International Law, New York, 1916. ("Colored" books published by the governments: vol. I, Austria-Hungary, Belgium, and France; vol. II, Germany, Great Britain, Italy, Russia, and Serbia.)

Outbreak of the World War: German Documents, Karl Kautsky, comp., M. Montgelas and W. Schüking, eds. Trans. by Carnegie Endowment for International Peace, Division of International Law, New York, 1924. (A collection of high importance.)

Albertini, Luigi, *The Origins of the War of 1914*, Isabella M. Massey, trans. and ed., 3 vols. New York, 1952–1957.

Fay, Sidney B., *The Origins of the World War*, 2d ed. New York, 1936; 1st ed., 1928.

Gooch, George P., *Before the War: Studies in Diplomacy*, 2 vols. New York, 1936–1938. (Vol. I: *The Grouping of the Powers;* vol. II: *The Coming of the Storm*.)

Remak, Joachim, *Sarajevo: The Story of a Political Murder*. New York, pb. ed., 1959.

Schmitt, Bernadotte E., *The Coming of the War*, 2 vols. New York, 1930.

Seton-Watson, Robert W., *Sarajevo: A Study in the Origins of the Great War*. London, 1926.

Stowell, Ellery C., *The Diplomacy of the War of 1914: The Beginnings of the War*. Boston, 1915.

Tuchman, Barbara W., *The Guns of August*. New York, 1962.

SOURCES AND GENERAL SURVEYS

Buchanan, Sir George, *My Mission to Russia and Other Diplomatic Memoirs*, 2 vols. Boston, 1923.

Churchill, Winston S., *The World Crisis*, vol. I (1911–1914); vol. II (1915); vols. III–IV (1916–1918); vol. V (*The Aftermath*). New York, 1923–1929.
———, *The World Crisis*, abr. and rev. ed. New York, 1931.
Documents of Russian History, 1914–1917, F. A. Golder, ed.; E. Aronsberg, trans. New York, 1927.
Durnovo, P. N., "Zapiska," in *Krasnaia Nov*, 1922, no. 6, pp. 178–199. (Memorandum presented to the tsar in February 1914 by Member of the State Council P. N. Durnovo, warning against the dangers of an imminent war with Germany.)
Graham, Stephen, *Russia and the World: A Study of the War and a Statement of the World Problems that Now Confront Russia and Great Britain*. New York, 1915; rev. ed., London, 1917.
Grey, Sir Edward, *Twenty-five Years, 1892–1916*, 2 vols. New York, 1925.
The Letters of the Tsar to the Tsaritsa, 1914–1917. New York, 1929.
Letters of the Tsaritsa to the Tsar, 1914–1916, with an Introduction by Sir Bernard Pares. London, 1923.
Marye, George T., *Nearing the End in Imperial Russia*. Philadelphia, 1929. (By the American ambassador to Russia, 1914–1916.)
Monarkhia pered krusheniem, 1914–1917: Bumagi Nikolaia II i drugie dokumenty. Moscow, 1927. (The monarchy before its downfall: papers of Nicholas II and other documents.)
Paleologue, Maurice, *An Ambassador's Memoirs*, 3 vols. New York, 1923–1925.
Perepiska Nikolaia i Aleksandry Romanovykh, vols. 3–5. Moscow, Tsentrarkhiv, 1923–1927. (The Correspondence between Nicholas and Alexandra Romanov, 1914–1917.)
Sazonov, Serge, *Fateful Years, 1909–1916*. London, 1928. (Memoirs of the Russian foreign minister.)

DIPLOMACY DURING THE WAR

Adamov, E. A., ed., *Konstantinopol' i prolivy*, 2 vols. Moscow, 1925–1926. (Constantinople and the Straits. A collection of diplomatic documents for 1914–1917, preceded by a survey by Adamov.
Gottlieb, Wolfram W., *Studies in Secret Diplomacy during the First World War*. London, 1957.
Mowat, Robert B., *A History of European Diplomacy, 1914–1925*. London, 1927.
Nekliudov, A. V., *Diplomatic Reminiscences before and during the World War, 1911–1917*, 2d ed. London, 1920. (Nekliudov was the Russian minister to Sofia and Stockholm, successively.)
Mezhdunarodnye otnoshenia v epokhu imperializma: Dokumenty iz arkhivov tsarskogo i vremennogo pravitel'stv, series III (1914–1917), 10 vols. Moscow, 1931–1938. (International relations in the period of imperialism: documents from the archives of the tsarist and the Provisional governments.)

Price, Morgan Ph., ed., *The Diplomatic History of the War*. New York, 1914. (Includes various documents and speeches of 1914.)

Smith, Jay C., *The Russian Struggle for Power, 1914–1917: A Study in Russian Foreign Policy during the First World War*. New York, 1956.

RUSSIA'S WAR EFFORT AND MILITARY OPERATIONS

Churchill, Winston S., *The Unknown War: The Eastern Front*. New York, 1931.

Danilov, Iu. N., General, *Rossia v mirovoi voine 1914–1915 gg*. Berlin, 1924. (Russia in World War I, 1914–1915.)

Golovin, N. N., General, *Voennye usilia Rossii v mirovoi voine*. Paris, 1939. (Russia's military efforts in World War I.)

———, *The Russian Army in the World War*, New Haven, 1931.

Gurko, V. I., General, *Memoirs and Impressions of War and Revolution in Russia, 1914–1917*. New York, 1918.

Knox, Sir Alfred, General, *With the Russian Army, 1914–1917*, 2 vols. New York, 1921. (Extracts from the diary of a military attaché.)

Ludendorf, Erich von, General, *Ludendorf's Own Story, August 1914– November 1918*, 2 vols. New York, 1919. (Trans. from the German.)

Pares, Sir Bernard, *Day by Day with the Russian Army, 1914–1915*, London, 1915.

Washburn, Stanley, *Field Notes from the Russian Front*, 2 vols. London, 1915.

Zaionchkovsky, A. M., *Mirovaia voina 1914–1918*, 2d ed. Moscow, 1931. (The World War of 1914–1918.)

THE IMPACT OF THE WAR ON INTERNAL DEVELOPMENTS IN RUSSIA AND THE ROAD TOWARD THE REVOLUTION

The Carnegie Endowment for International Peace, Division of Economics and History, *Economic and Social History of the World War: Russian Series*, New Haven, 1928–1932. The socioeconomic conditions created by the War are described in the following ten volumes of this series:

S. O. Zagorsky, *State Control of Industry in Russia during the War*, 1928.

Russian Public Finance During the War: A. M. Michelson, "Revenue and Expenditure"; P. A. Apostol, "Credit Operations"; M. W. Bernatzky, "Monetary Policy," 1928.

Nolde, Baron Boris E., *Russia in the Economic War*, 1928.

The War and the Russian Government: P. P. Gronsky, "The Central Government"; N. I. Astrov, "The Municipal Government and the All-Russian Union of Towns," 1929.

Russian Schools and Universities in the World War: D. M. Odinetz, "Primary and Secondary Schools"; P. I. Novgorodtsev, "Universities and Higher Technical Schools," 1929.

The Cooperative Movement in Russia During the War: E. M. Kayden, "Consumers' Cooperation"; A. N. Antsiferov, "Credit and Agricultural Cooperation," 1929.

Food Supply in Russia During the World War: K. J. Zaitsev and N. V. Dolinsky, "Organization and Policy"; S. S. Demosthenov, "Food and the Market in Foodstuffs," 1930.

Russian Agriculture During the War: A. N. Antsiferov, "Rural Economy"; A. D. Bilimovich, "The Land Settlement," 1930.

T. J. Polner, Russian Local Government during the War and the Union of Zemstvos, 1930.

The Cost of the War to Russia: S. Kohn, "The Vital Statistics of European Russia during the World War, 1914-1917"; Baron A. F. Meyendorff: "Social Cost of the War," 1932.

Burzhuazia nakanune fevral'skoi revoliutsii. Moscow, 1927. (The bourgeoisie on the eve of the February Revolution; documents of 1914-1917.)

Chamberlin, William H., The Russian Revolution, 1917-1921, 2 vols. New York, 1935; 1952. (The first volume.)

Chernov, V. M., The Great Russian Revolution, P. E. Mosely, trans. New Haven, 1936.

Fisher, Harold H., and Olga H. Gankin, The Bolsheviks and the World War: The Origins of the Third International. Stanford, 1940.

Florinsky, M. T., The End of the Russian Empire. New Haven, 1931; pb. ed., 1962.

Lukomsky, A. S., General, Vospominaniia, Berlin, 1922. Trans.: Memoirs of the Russian Revolution, London, 1922.

Melgunov, S. P., "Zolotoi nemetskii kliuch" k bol'shevitskoi revoliutsii. Paris, 1940. (The German "golden key" to the Bolshevik revolution.)

Naumov, A. N., Iz utselevshikh vospominanii, 1863-1916, 2 vols. New York, 1954-1955. (The memoirs of Naumov, who was minister of agriculture, 1915-1916.)

Padenie tsarskogo rezhima po materialam Chrezvychainoi Komissii Vremennogo Pravitel'stva, 7 vols. Leningrad, 1925-1927. (The collapse of the tsarist government, according to the materials collected by a Special Commission of the Provisional Government.)

Pares, Sir Bernard, The Fall of the Russian Monarchy: A Study of the Evidence, New York, 1939; 1946; pb. ed., 1961.

Prokopovich, S. N., Voina i narodnoe khoziaistvo, 2d ed. Moscow, 1918. (The war and the national economy.)

Rodzianko, M. V., Krushenie imperii, in Arkhiv Russkoi Revoliutsii, vol. XVII. Berlin, 1926. Rearranged English version: The Reign of Rasputin: An Empire's Collapse, New York, London, 1927. (The collapse of the empire. Emotional memoirs of the last Duma president.)

Shavelsky, Georgii, Vospominania poslednego protopresvitera russkoi armii i flota, 2 vols. New York, 1954. (Memoirs of the last chief presbyter of the Russian army and navy.)

Trotsky, Leon, The History of the Russian Revolution, Max Eastman, trans., 3 vols. New York, 1932.

Vernadsky, George, The Russian Revolution, 1917-1931, New York, 1932.

Zeman, Z. A. B., ed., *Germany and the Revolution in Russia, 1915–1918; Documents from the Archives of the German Foreign Ministry.* New York, 1958. (Documentary evidence of the imperial German government's considerable financial support of the Bolsheviks in 1915–1918.)

ADDENDUM: After this book had gone to press, a valuable general survey of Russian history was published—Nicholas V. Riasanovsky, *A History of Russia,* New York, 1963.

Name and
Subject Indexes

Name Index

The index contains, whenever possible, the full names, dates, and positions of historical figures mentioned in the text. Modern authors quoted in the text are not included, but may be found in the bibliography. Not all dates given are completely reliable, and in some cases dates or full names had to be omitted for lack of information. The names of persons known under pseudonyms are listed under the assumed name, with the real name added in brackets. Most of the Russian given names that follow have not been anglicized, but the reader will not find it difficult to match names that have been anglicized in the text.

Subject Index

Academy of Sciences, 292
Adrianople, Armistice of (1878), 349
Adrianople, Peace of (1829), 116
Agriculture, 41, 42, 46, 211–212, 217–
218
improvements in (1900–1913),
269–270
Afghanistan, 343
and Russo-British Treaty (1907),
363
Aigun, Treaty of (1858), 338
Aland Islands, 112, 122
Alarm, The, 177
Alaska, 359
All-Russian Peasant Union, 246
All-Russian Union of Towns, 277,
398, 405
All-Russian Union of Zemstvos, 277,
398, 405
Anarchism, 175, 176, 177
Anarchists, 83, 242
Appanage peasants, 28
and law of 1866, 147
Arbitrators, 145, 147
Architecture, 329–331
Armenia, 349
Armenian Social Democratic party,
242–243

Army, 10, 15, 53
military settlements of, 12, 13
and military youth organizations,
292
and Order No. 1, 409
and outbreak of February Revolution, 406
prereform conditions in, 155–156
and Reform of 1860–1873, 156–
157
Semenovsky Regiment of, 4, 8, 11
and universal military service
(1874), 157–158
and World War I, 381–382, 387
Auerstadt, Battle of, 97
Austerlitz, Battle of, 3, 97
Austria
Alliance of Chaumont (1814), 103
alliance with Germany (1879), 361
alliance with Russia, 96
annexes Bosnia and Herzegovina,
366
attitude during Crimean War,
120, 124
and Balkan crisis (1875–1878), 361
and Congress of Vienna, 104
convention of 1877, 348